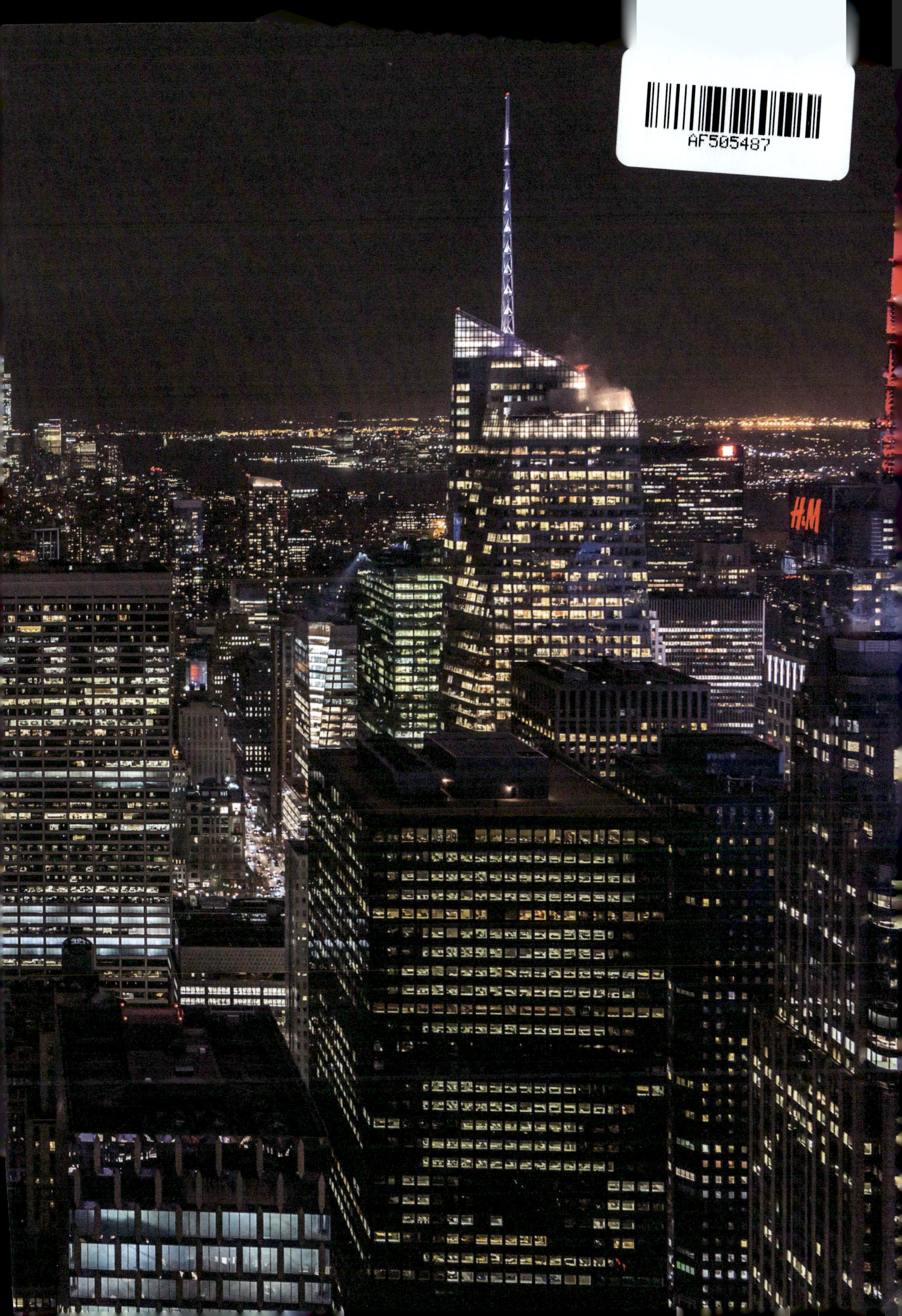
AF505487
H&M

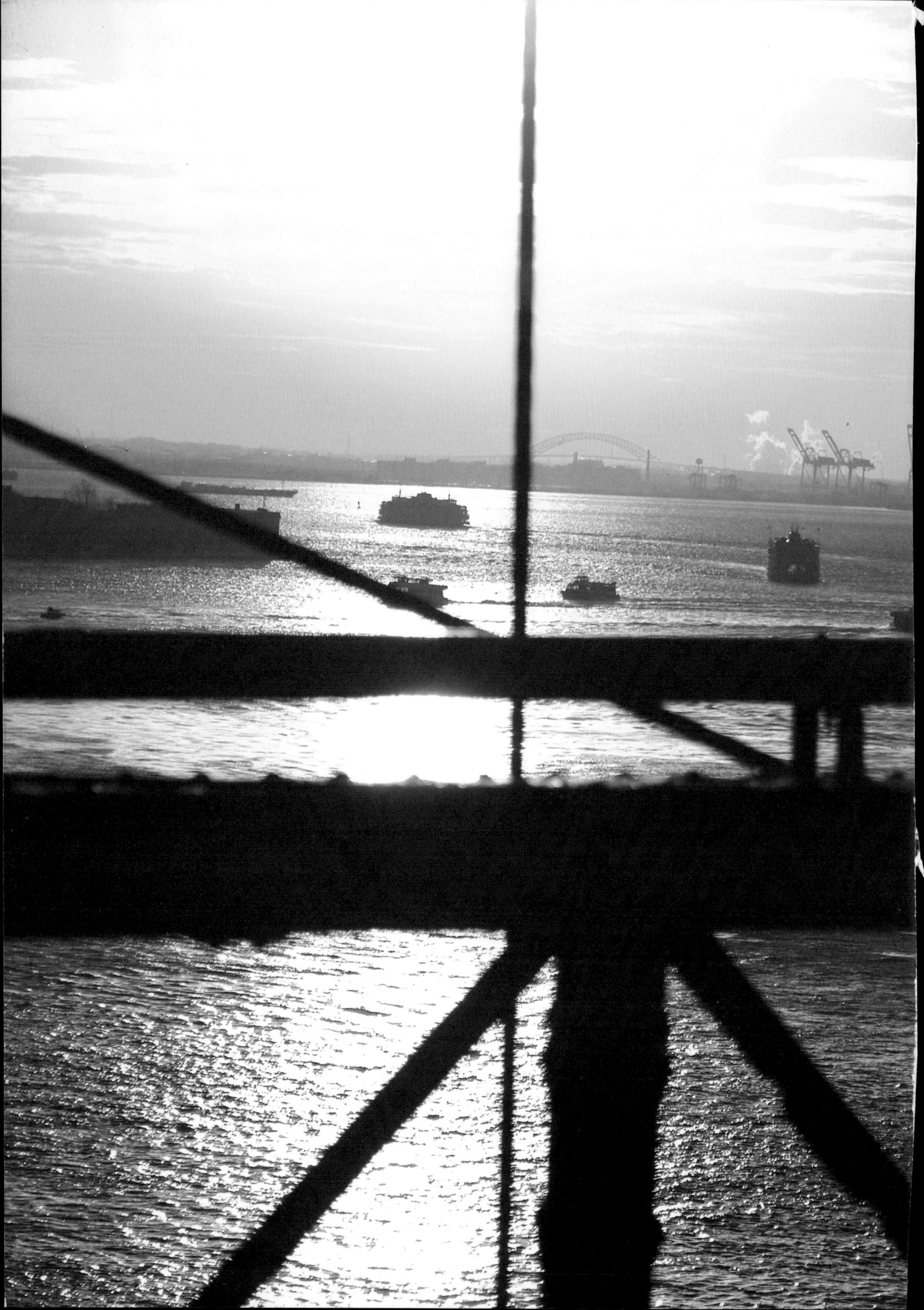

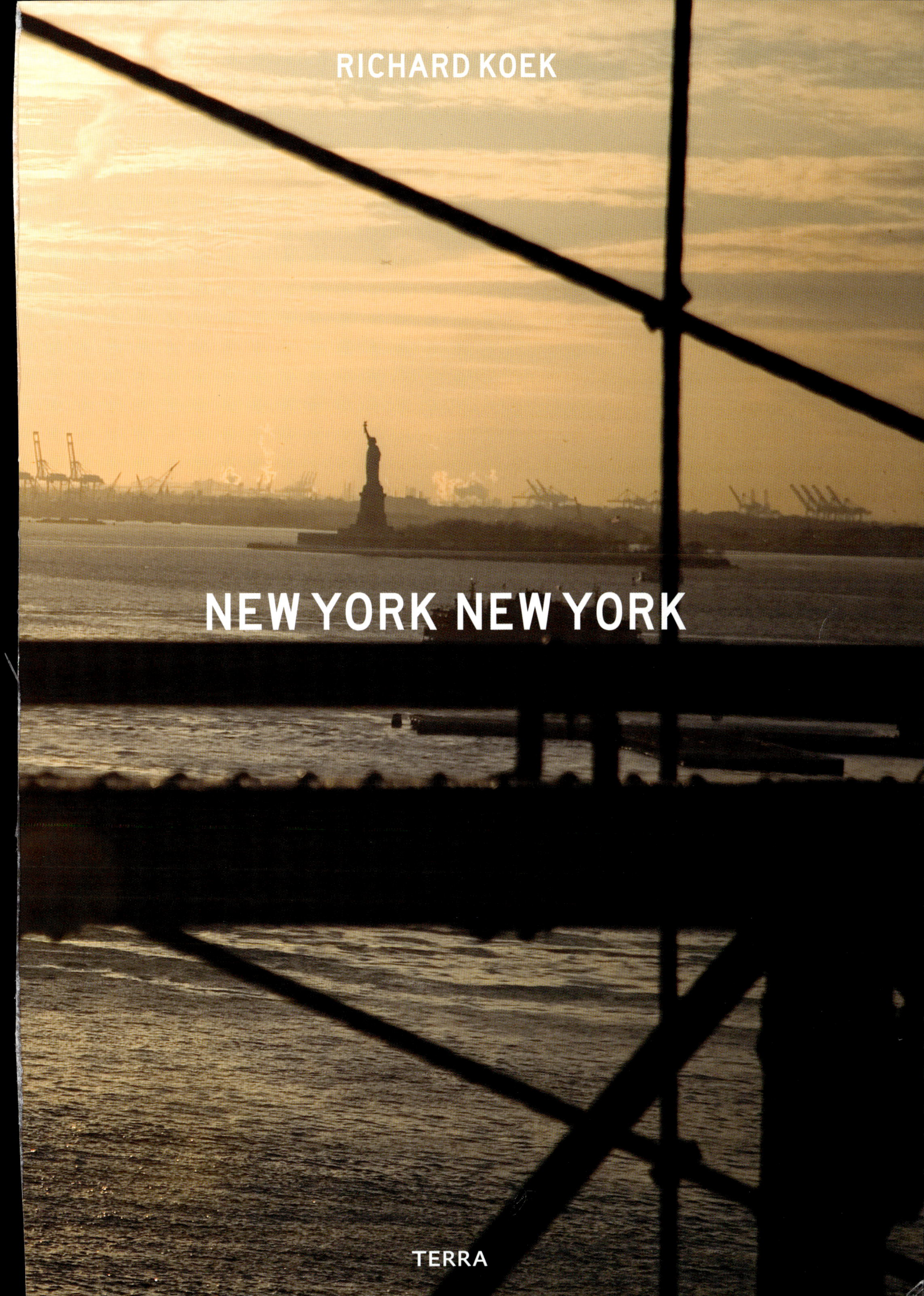

RICHARD KOEK
TERRA
NEW YORK NEW YORK

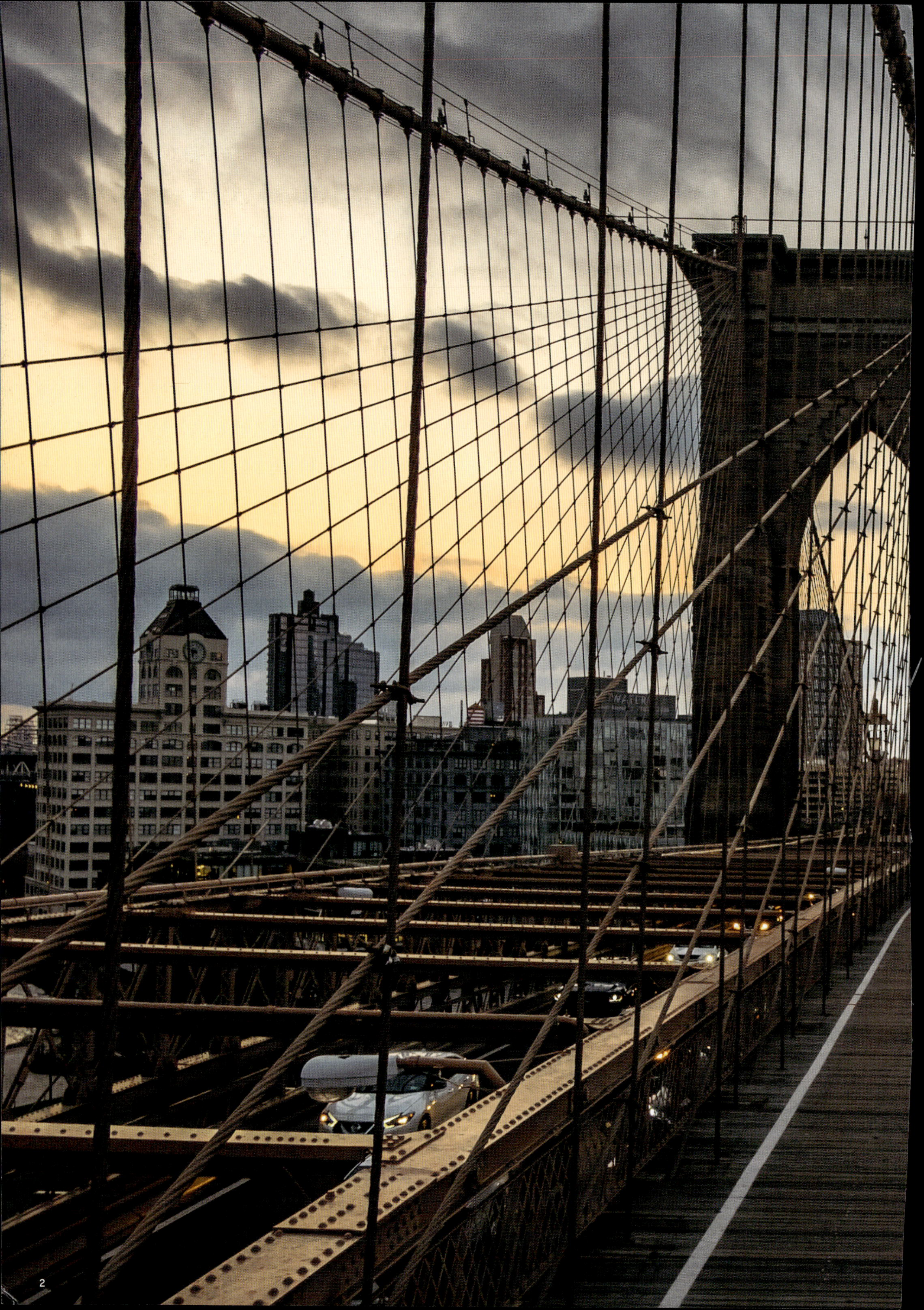

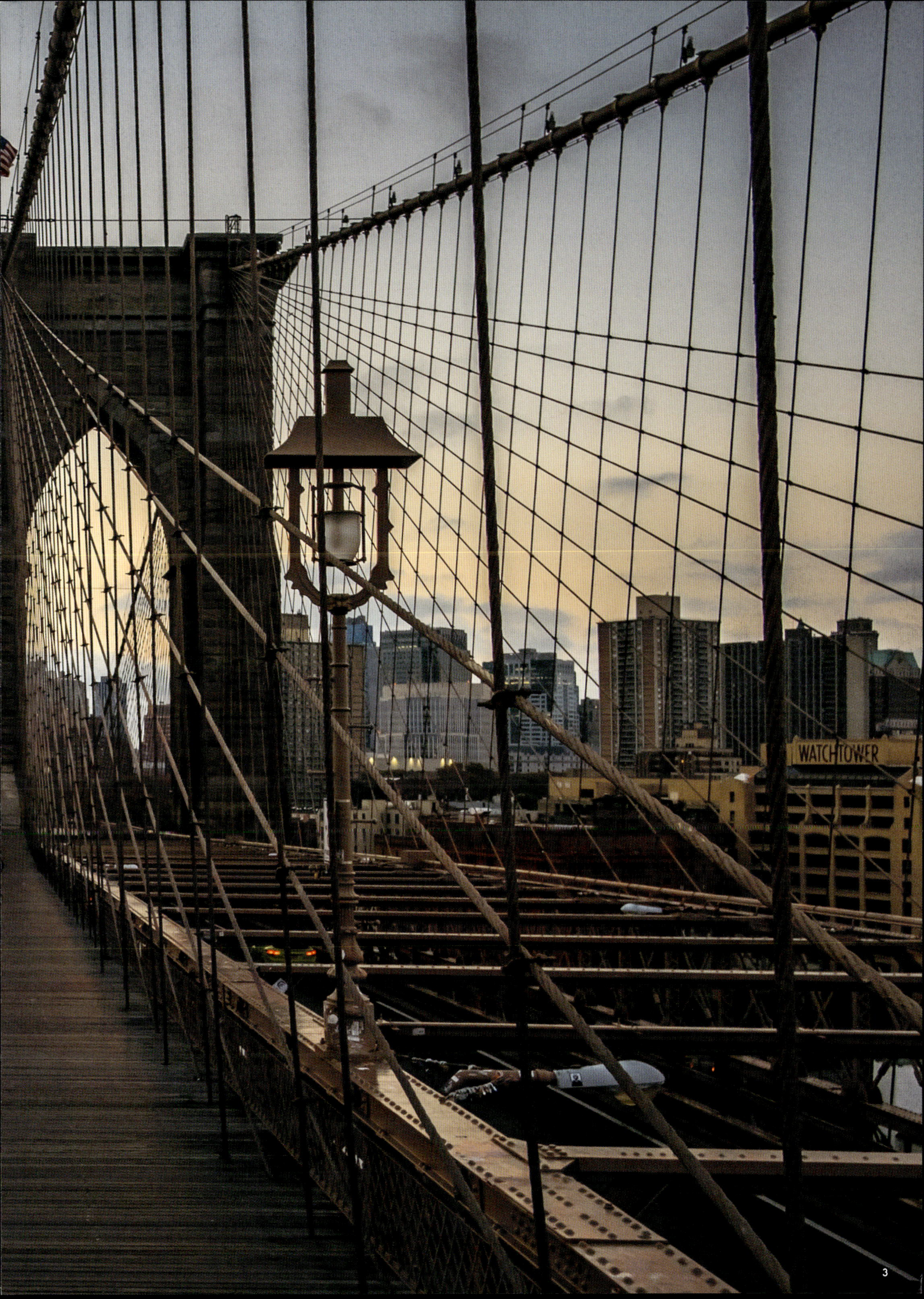

WATCHTOWER

PREFACE

Richard Koek, who took the great majority of the photographs in this book in 2016 and 2017, is a "visual storyteller."

Koek, born in the Netherlands, arrived in New York City in 2000. He had been to the city only once before on a holiday trip, he knew no one in New York, he did not have a job but he was determined to find work as a photographer. "I'm very stubborn," he once said. "I hold on like a pit bull. So, my attitude when I landed in New York was 'I'm here and I'm staying, by any means necessary.'

Not only did he eventually find success, but in the process he also found New York City. And he photographed it. Richard Koek's New York is not just Manhattan's tourist landmarks – the Statue of Liberty, Times Square, or Broadway. He walked through every borough and he "got" it. Stylistically, the photographs should be seen as film stills – after all, they are the result of Koek's active journey through time and space. The images evolve the way a film unfolds and one never knows what will be around the corner. Everyone was a subject and he told the story about the people who define New York City – the barbers, the fishmongers, the auto mechanics, the doormen, subway workers, businesswomen and men, street vendors, cooks, students, the models, dog walkers, firemen, parking attendants, the kids on skateboards, cooks, and invitees to fancy events. He found these people in bodegas, restaurants, in parks throughout the boroughs, in houses of worship, apartment buildings, cemeteries, on the streets, in laundromats and subways. The cacophony of the city was everywhere. New York's buildings as backdrops defined the spaces where these people lived and played. It was a city always on the go.

Now, we see his photographs through the lens of months in quarantine when people only came together at their windows or on their balconies for the "7 o'clock clap" to honor the health care workers who risked their lives to save ours. The streets were empty, there were no cars, trucks, busses, or taxis; the bicycle riders were not there riding in the lanes specially demarked for them; the tourists were gone; no one walked the sidewalks, darted into the streets, and gathered in parks. Restaurants and shops shut down. Where are the people in the photographs? How did they fare in the pandemic? Now, we look at these images and see what we have temporarily lost. We venture out cautiously rather than with abandon, we wear masks everywhere, and we do not yet gather with crowds. Eating inside a restaurant, something that New Yorkers enjoyed without giving it a second thought, now becomes a matter of a conscious decision. Koek's New York has been tamed.

Yet, no doubt, the New York that Richard Koek caught through the lens of his camera will be back. We will gather together, outside and inside, again. We will go to sports events, celebrations, music concerts, museums, school performances, graduations, simple meetings in person, or enjoy visits to our favorite stores, all without fear of consequences. But, we will also look at Koek's views of our city and through them we will experience a new found appreciation and celebrate all that he captured during his walks down the streets and boulevards. And perhaps we will see that we took so much for granted before March 2020 when all of that disappeared. We look with different eyes now and we see the beauty of our city with even more clarity.

Marilyn Satin Kushner
Curator and Head, Department of Prints,
Photographs, and Architectural Collections at
New-York Historical Society

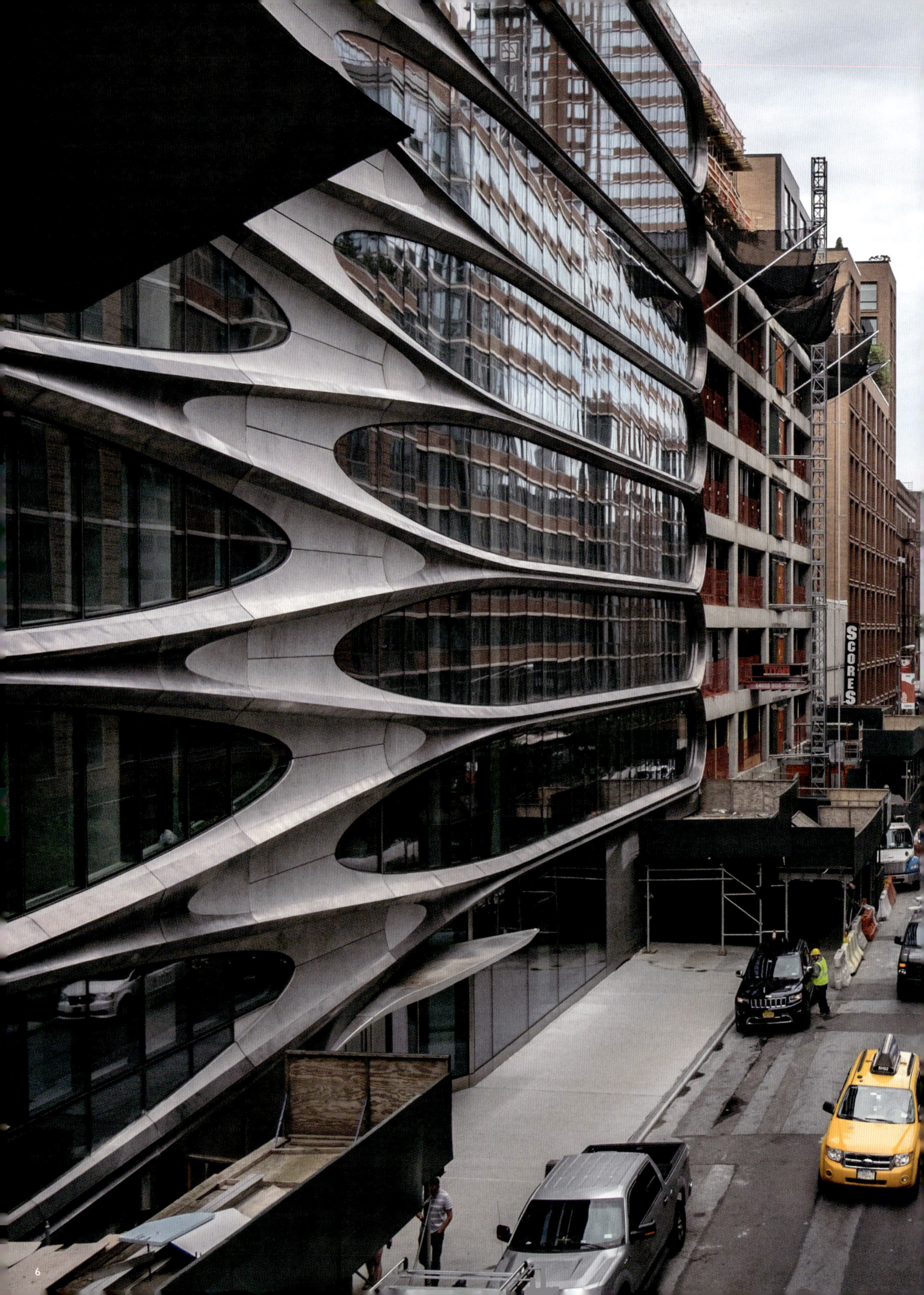

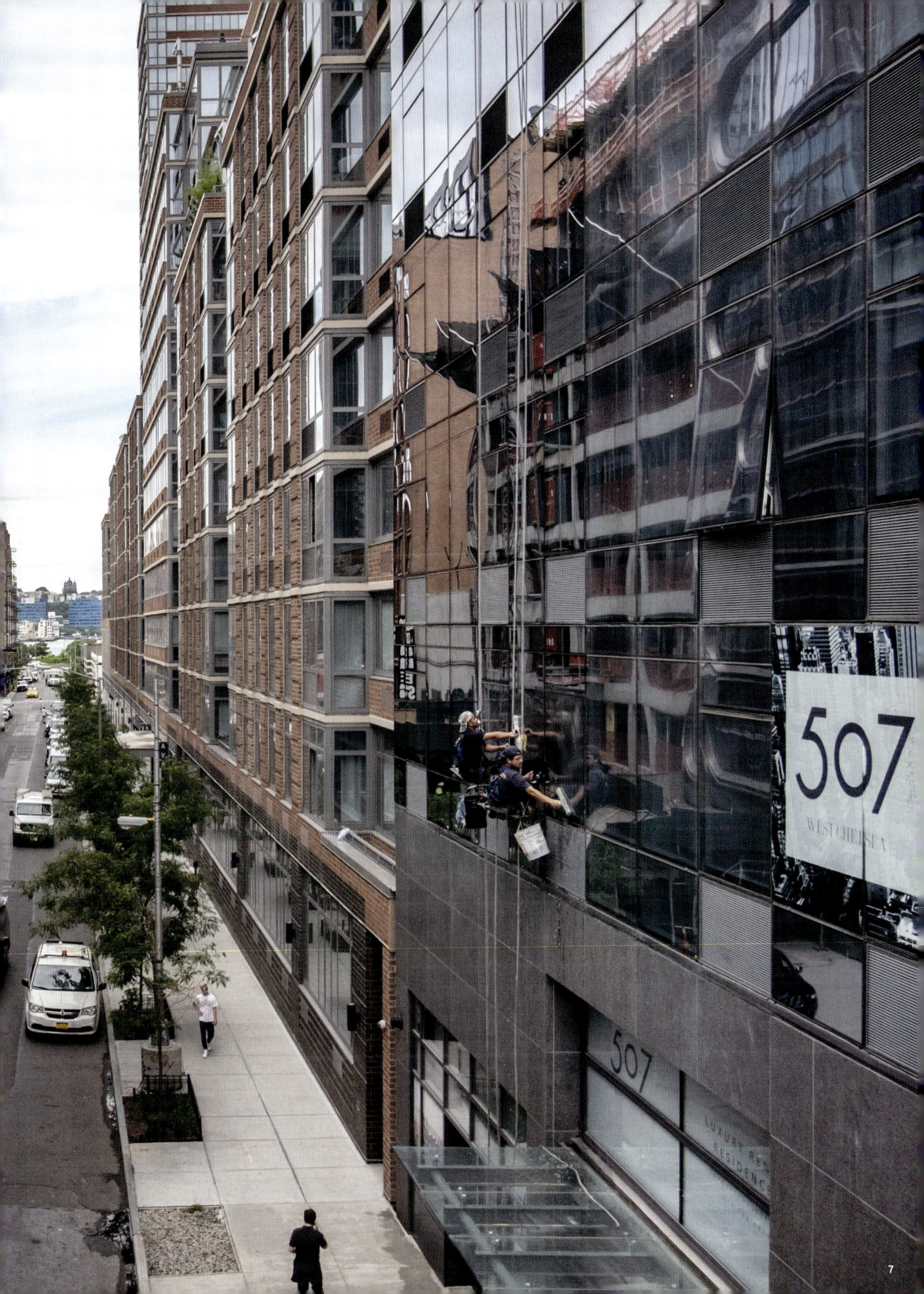

507
WEST CHELSEA
507
LUXURY REN
RESIDENC

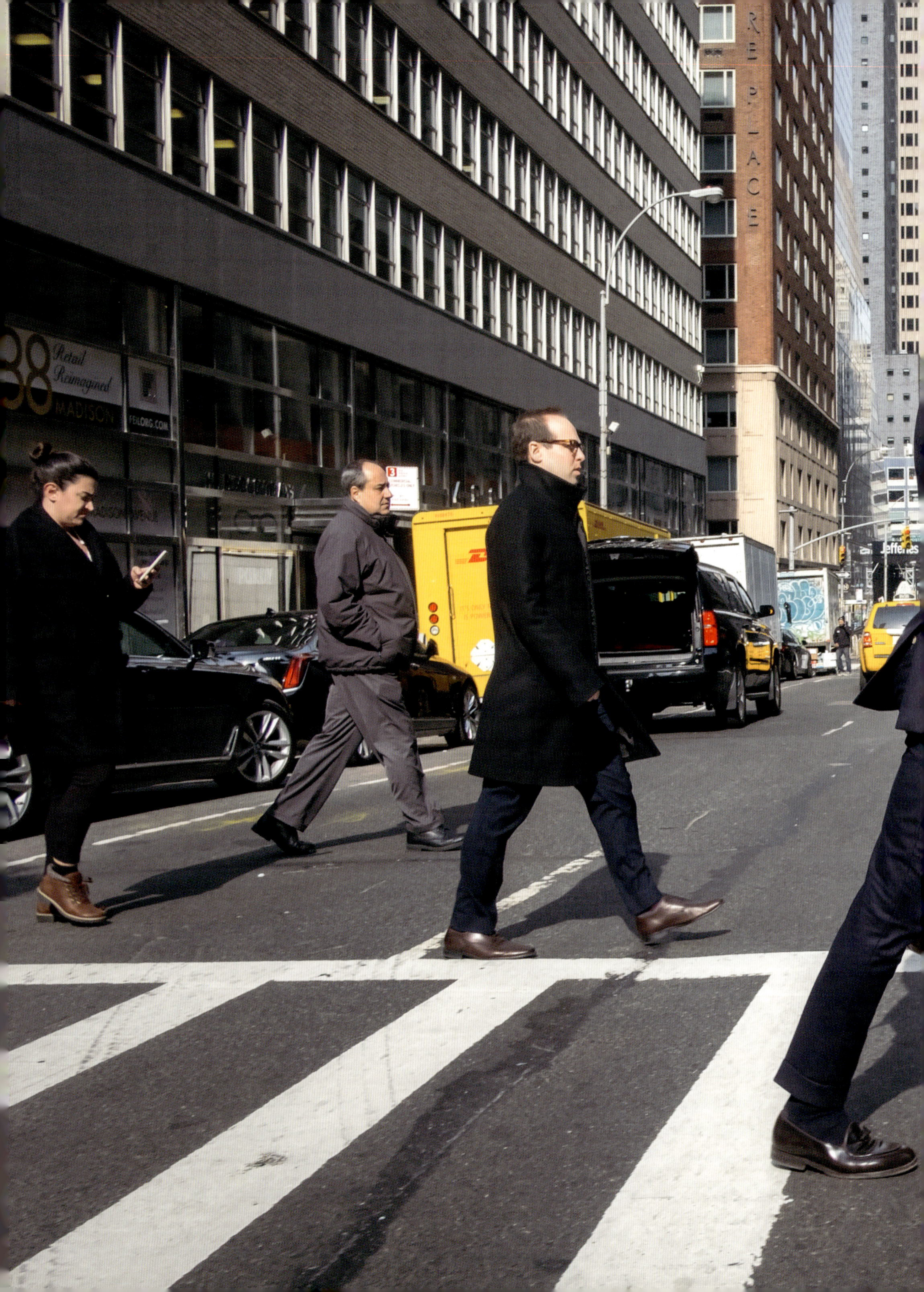

RE PLACE
Retail
Reimagined
MADISON
FEILONG.COM
Jefferies

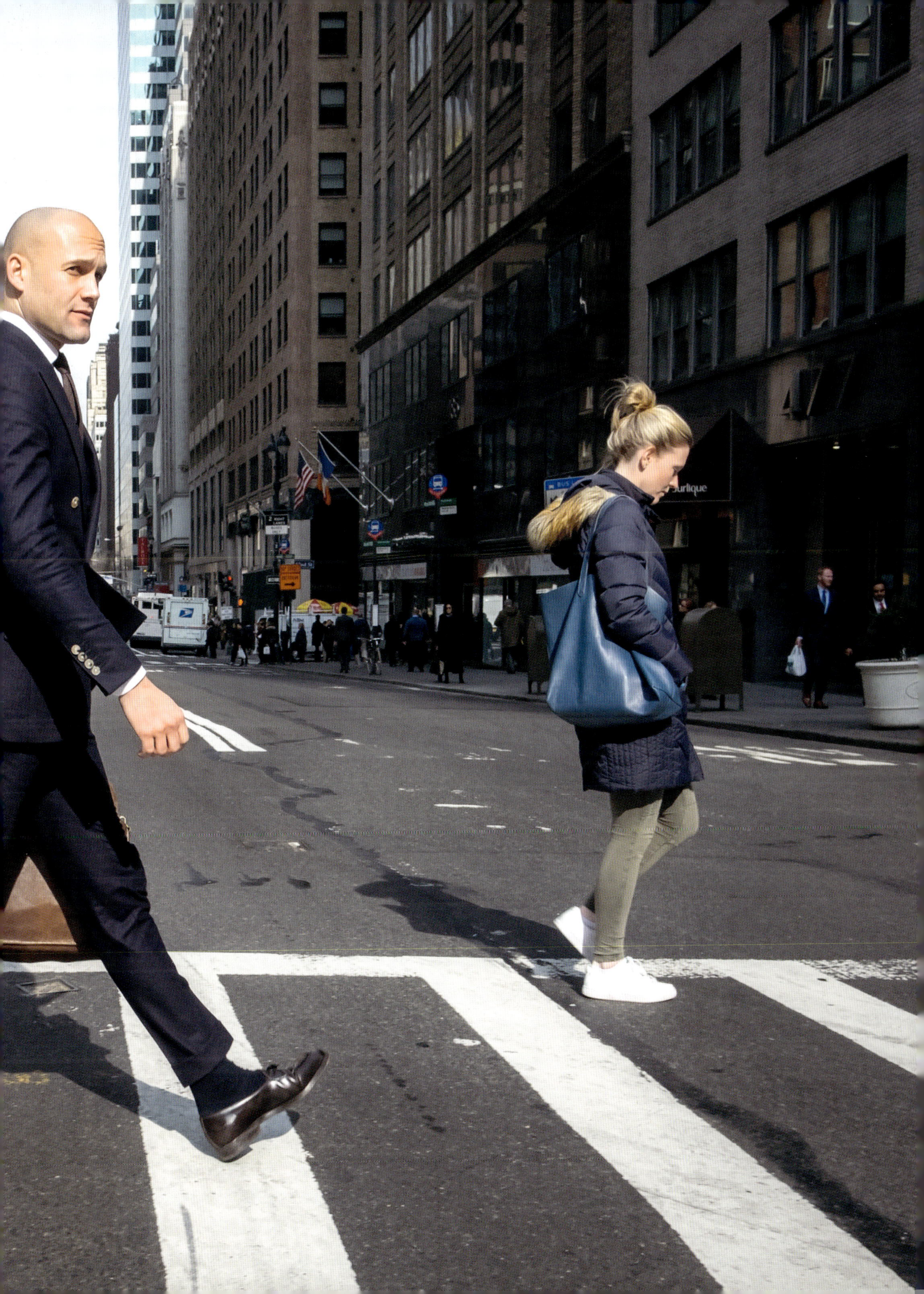

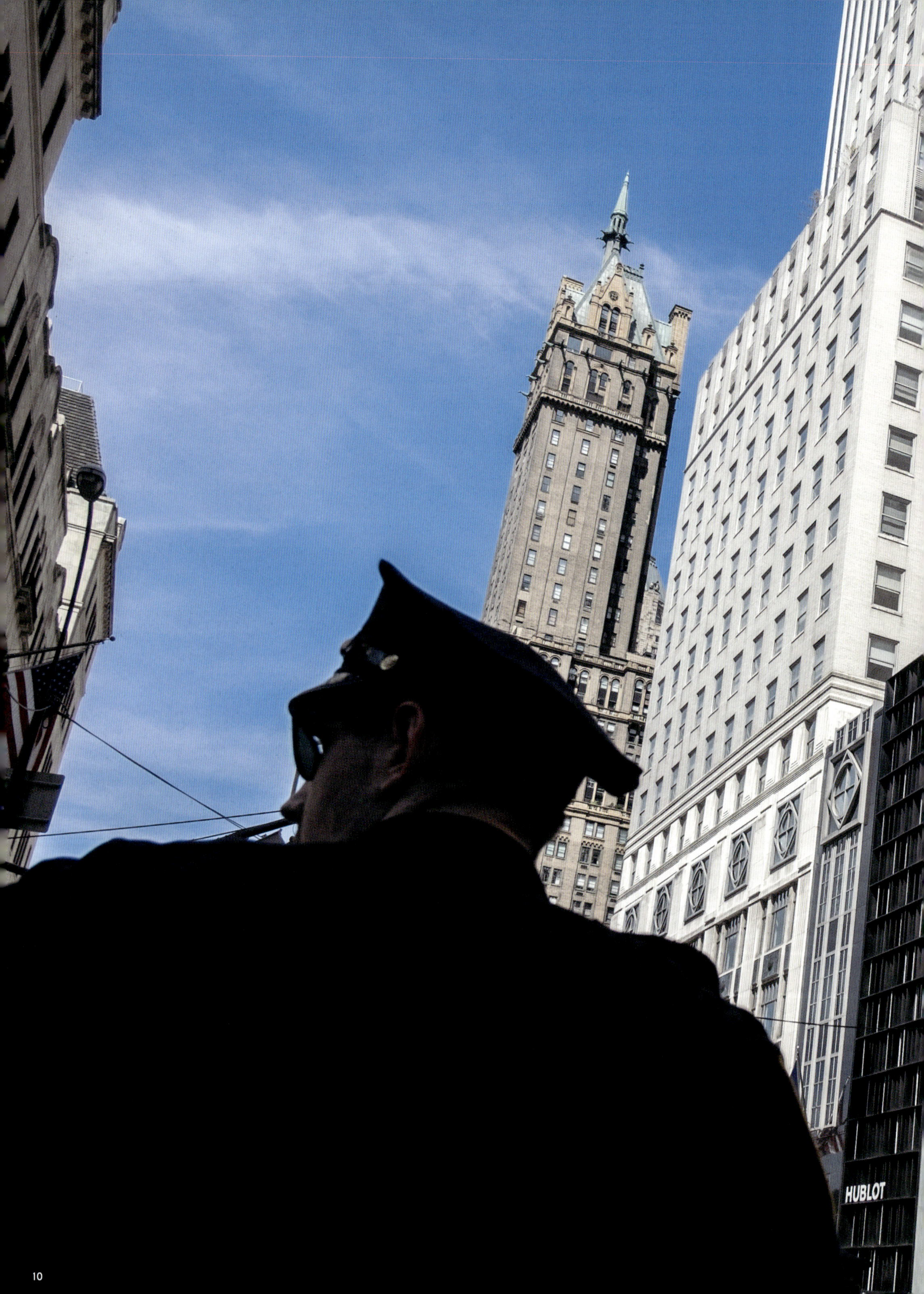

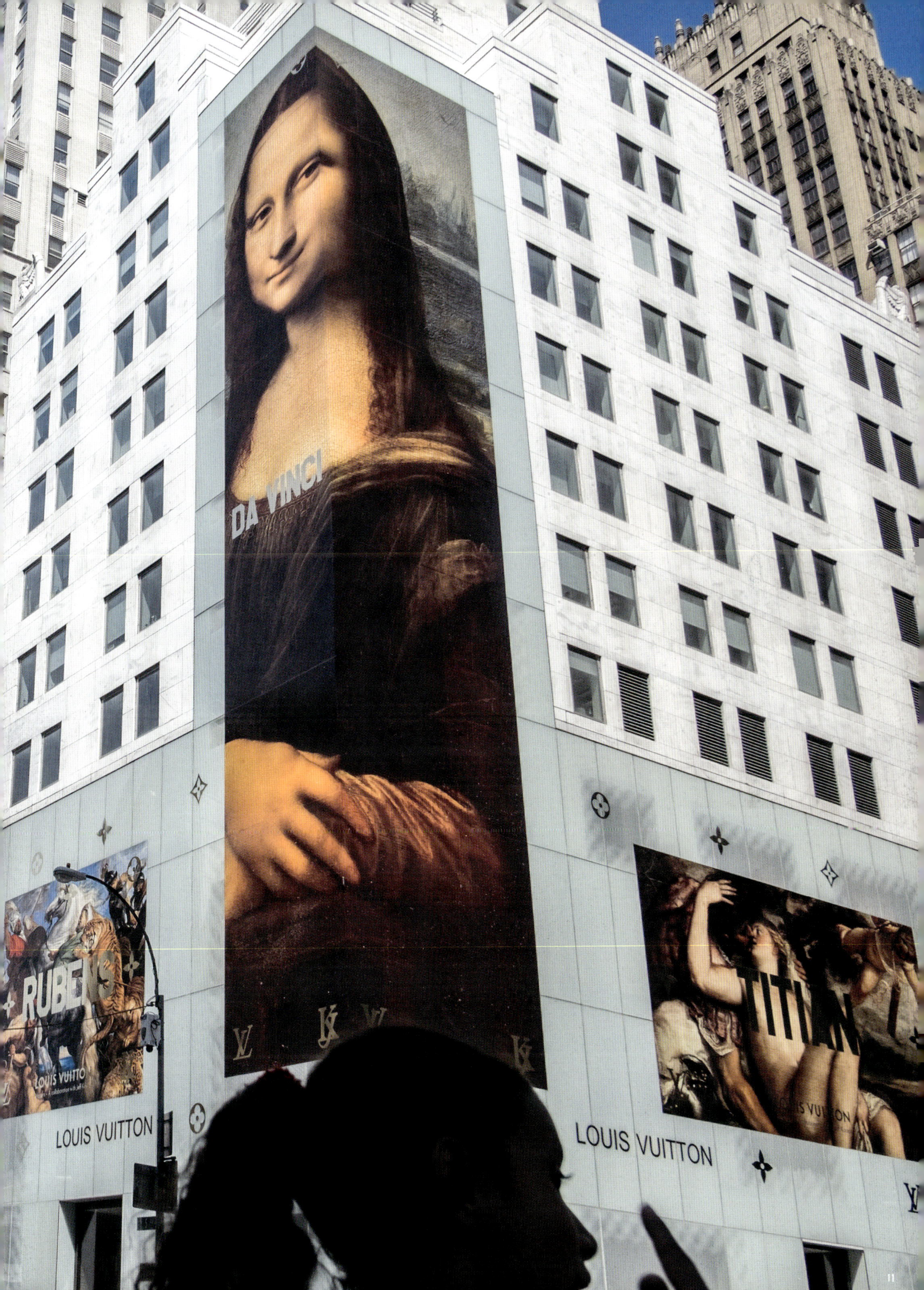

DA VINCI
RUBENS
LOUIS VUITTON
LOUIS VUITTON
TITIAN
LOUIS VUITTON
LOUIS VUITTON

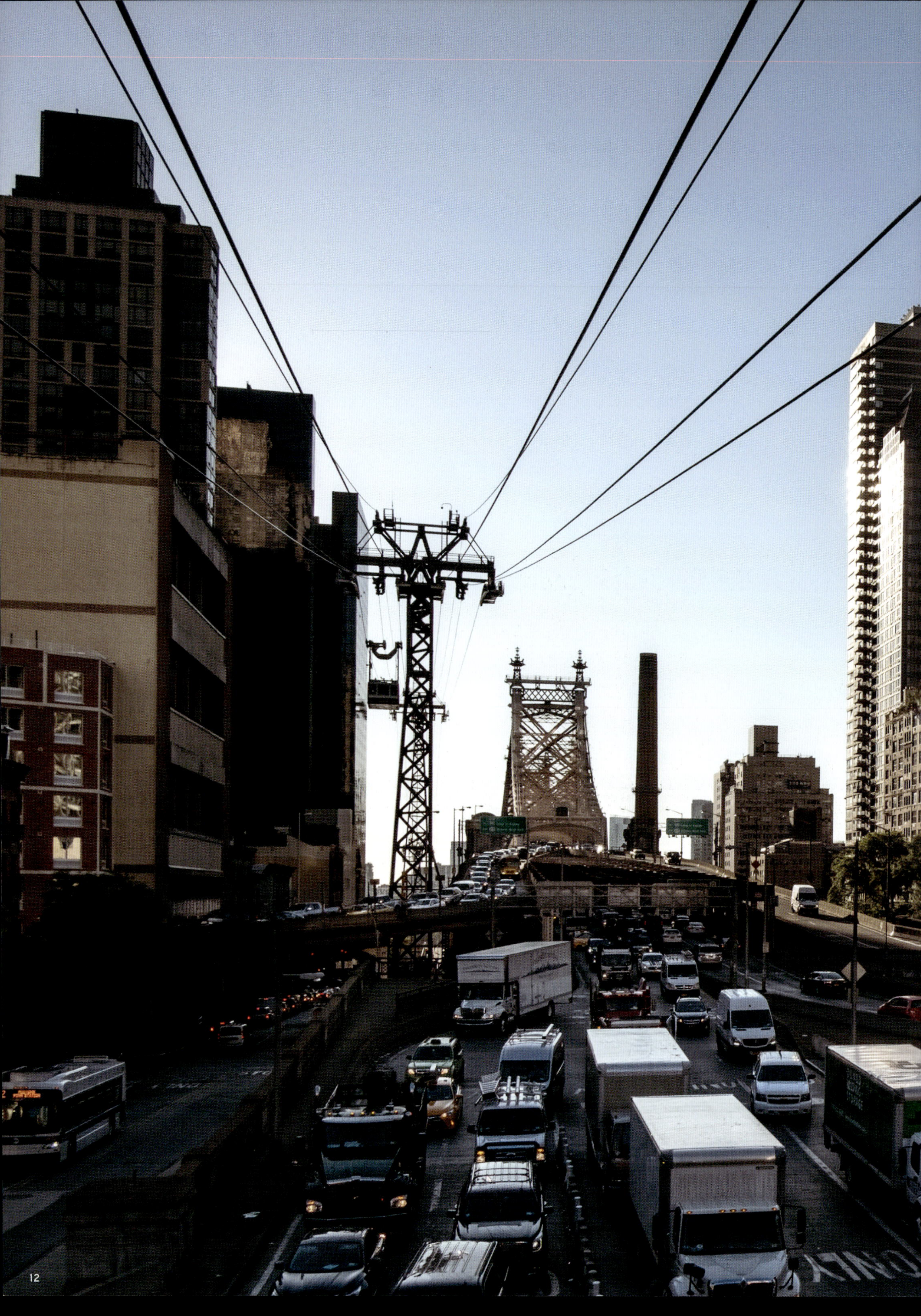

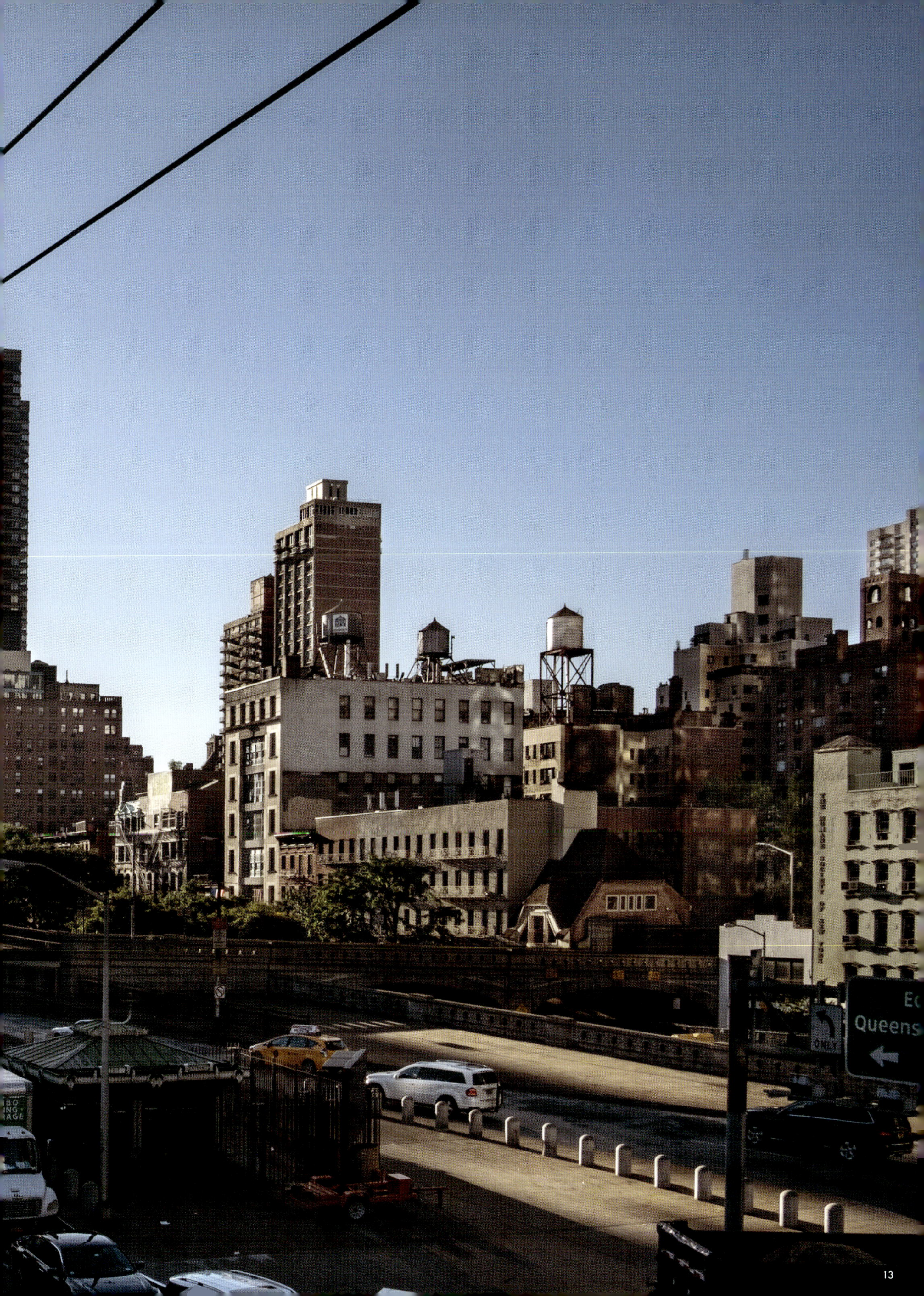

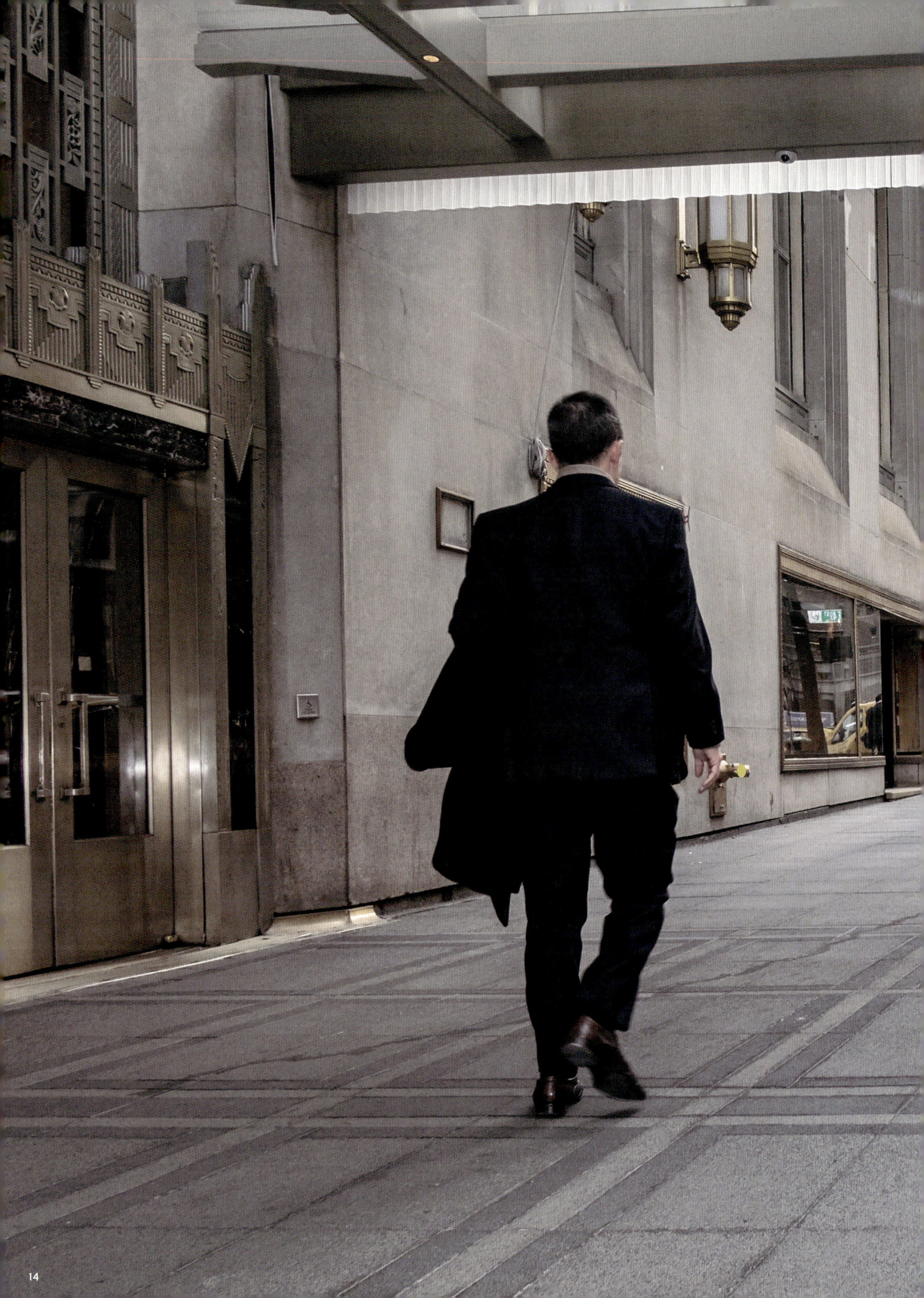

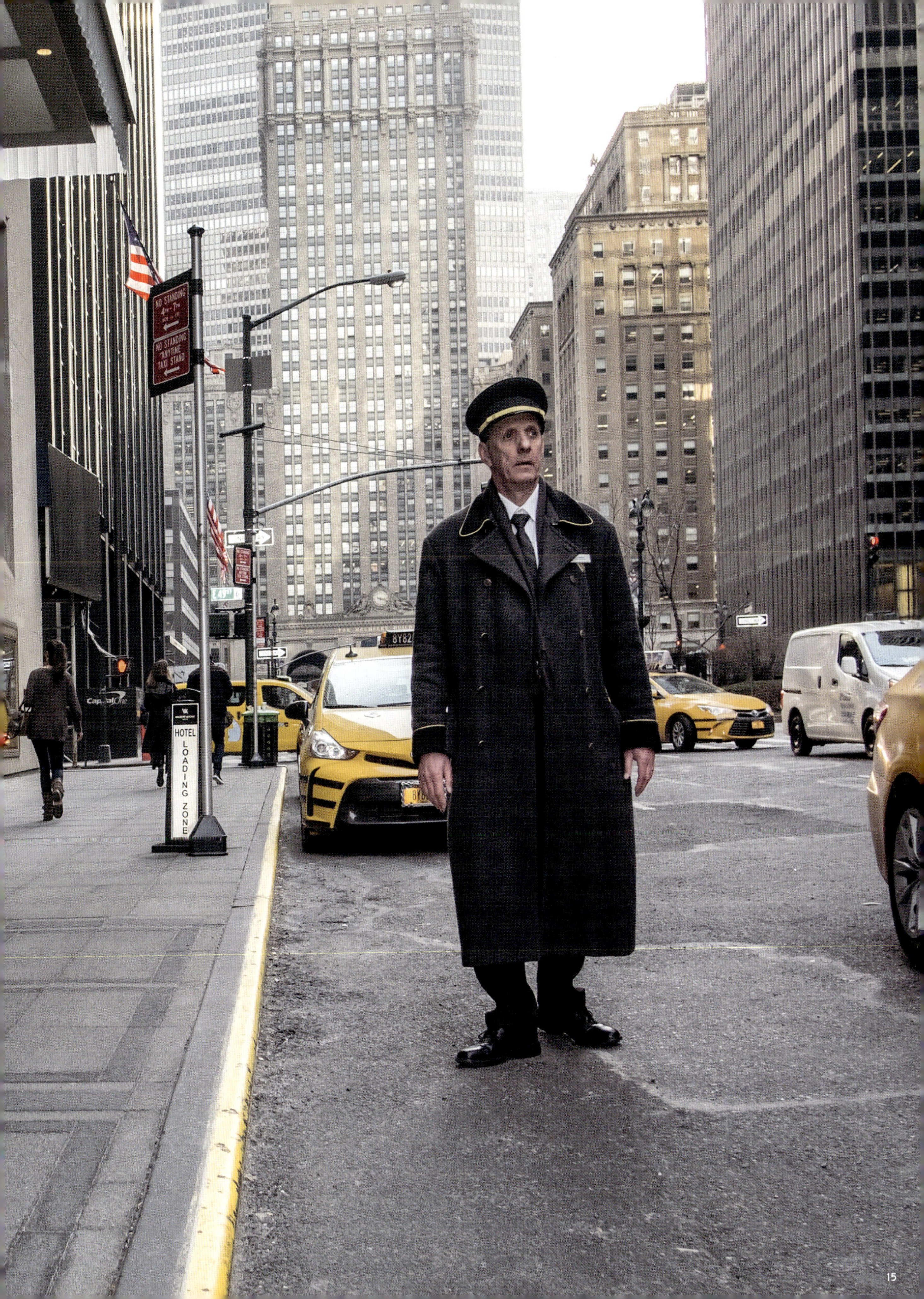

NO STANDING
4PM - 7PM
MON - FRI
NO STANDING
ANYTIME
TAXI STAND
HOTEL
LOADING
ZONE
CapitalOne
8Y82

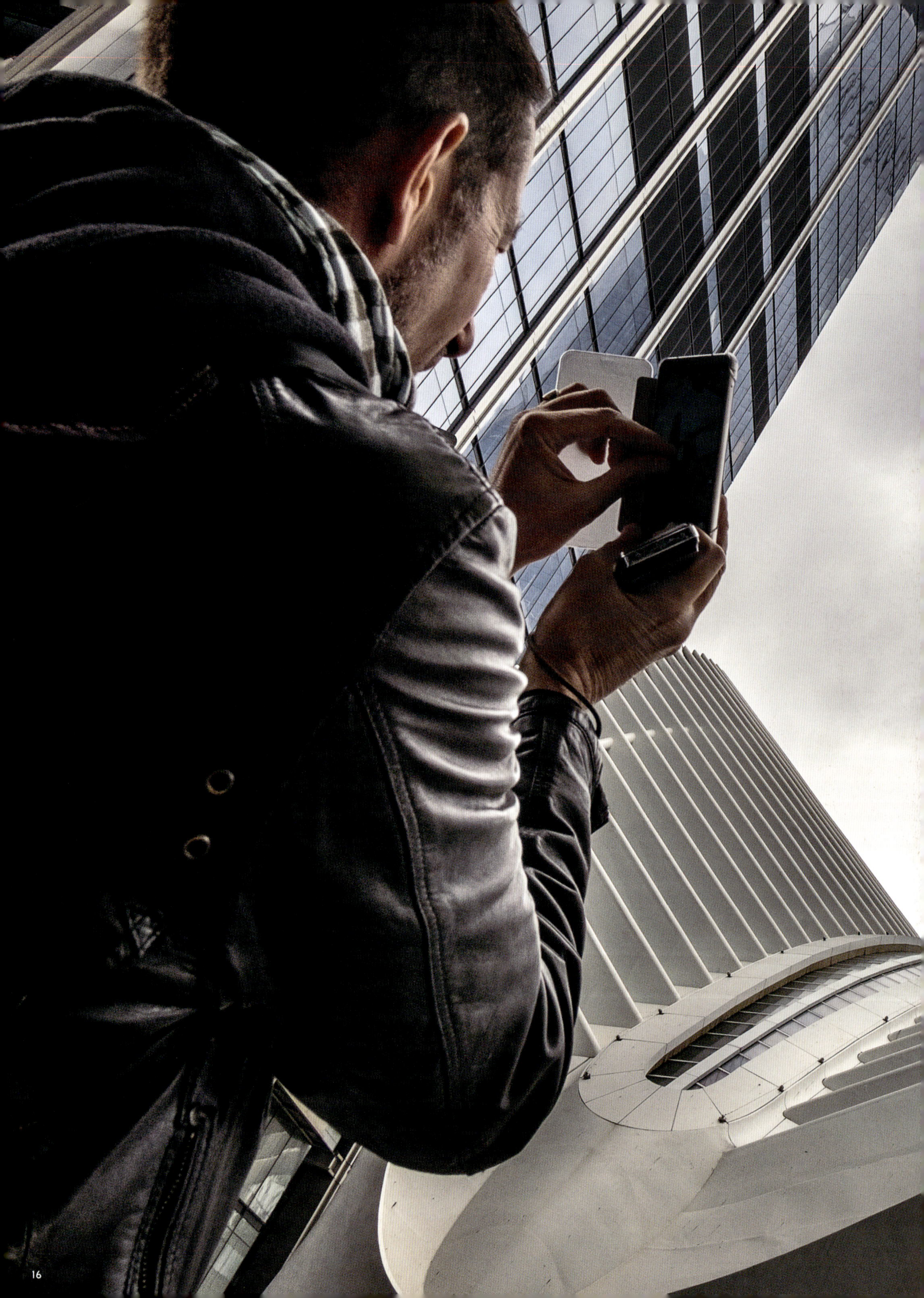

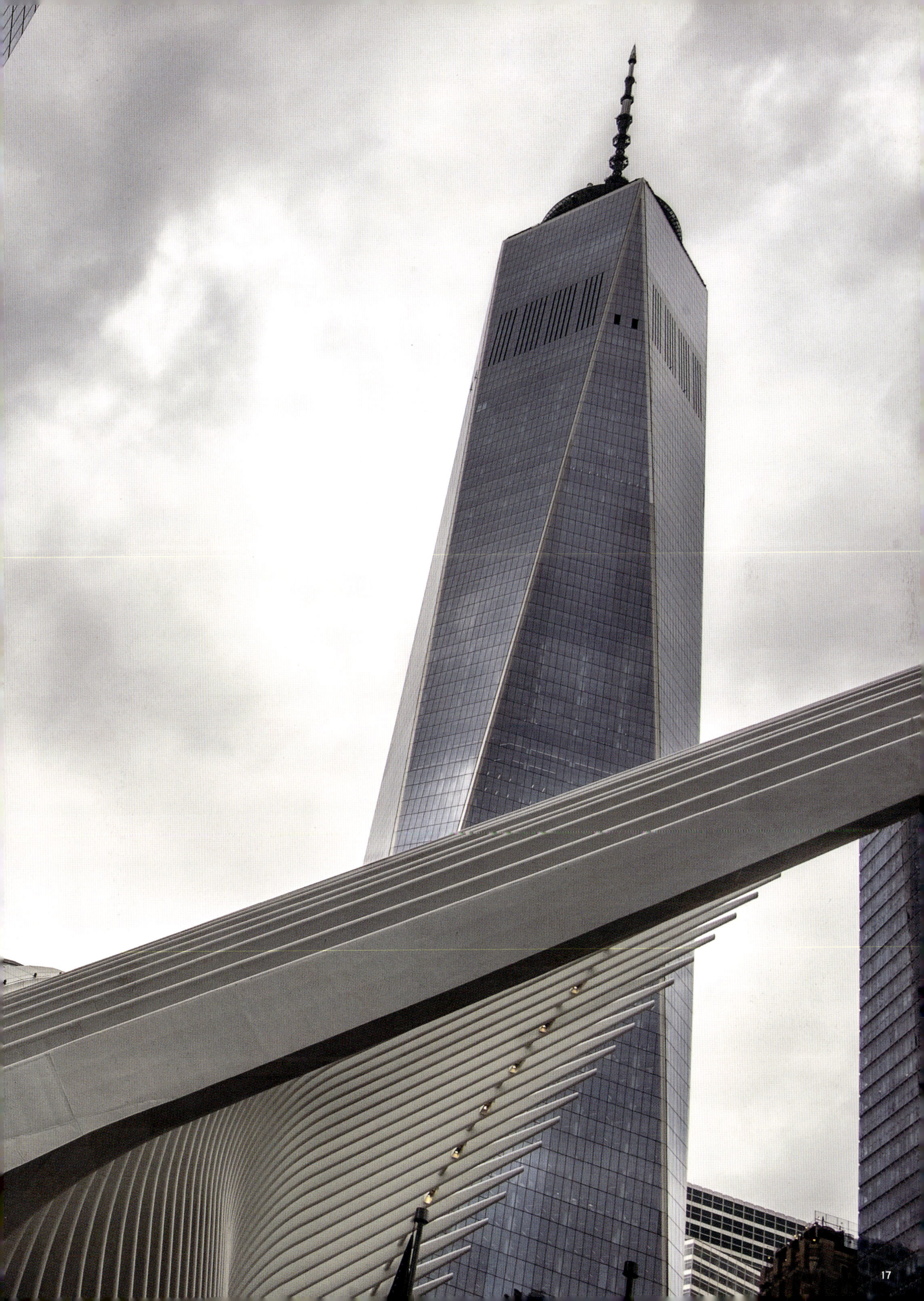

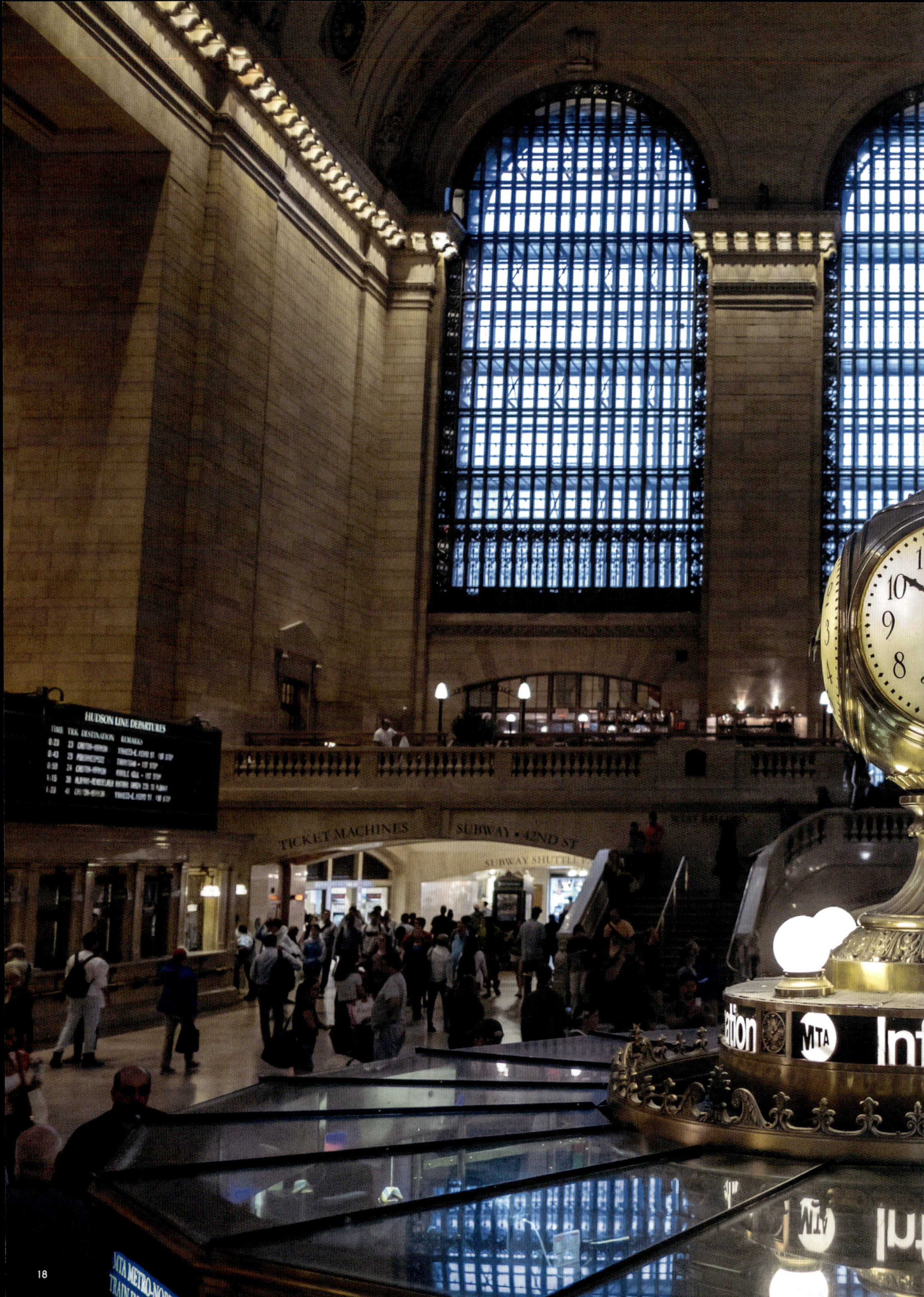
HUDSON LINE DEPARTURES
TICKET MACHINES
SUBWAY • 42ND ST
SUBWAY SHUTTLE
MTA
Inf
tion
MTA METRO-NORTH

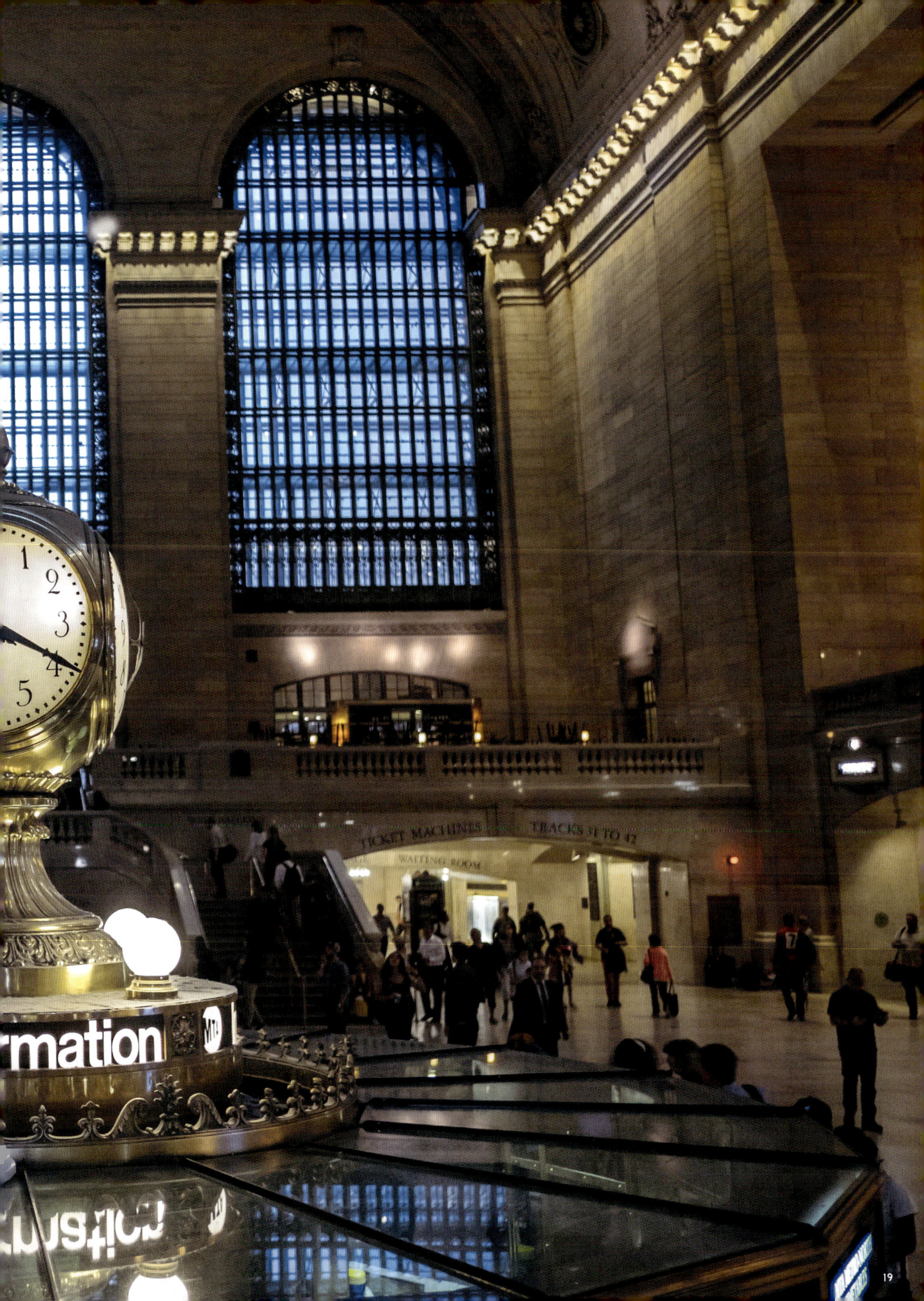

TICKET MACHINES
TRACKS 31 TO 42
WAITING ROOM
mation
MTA

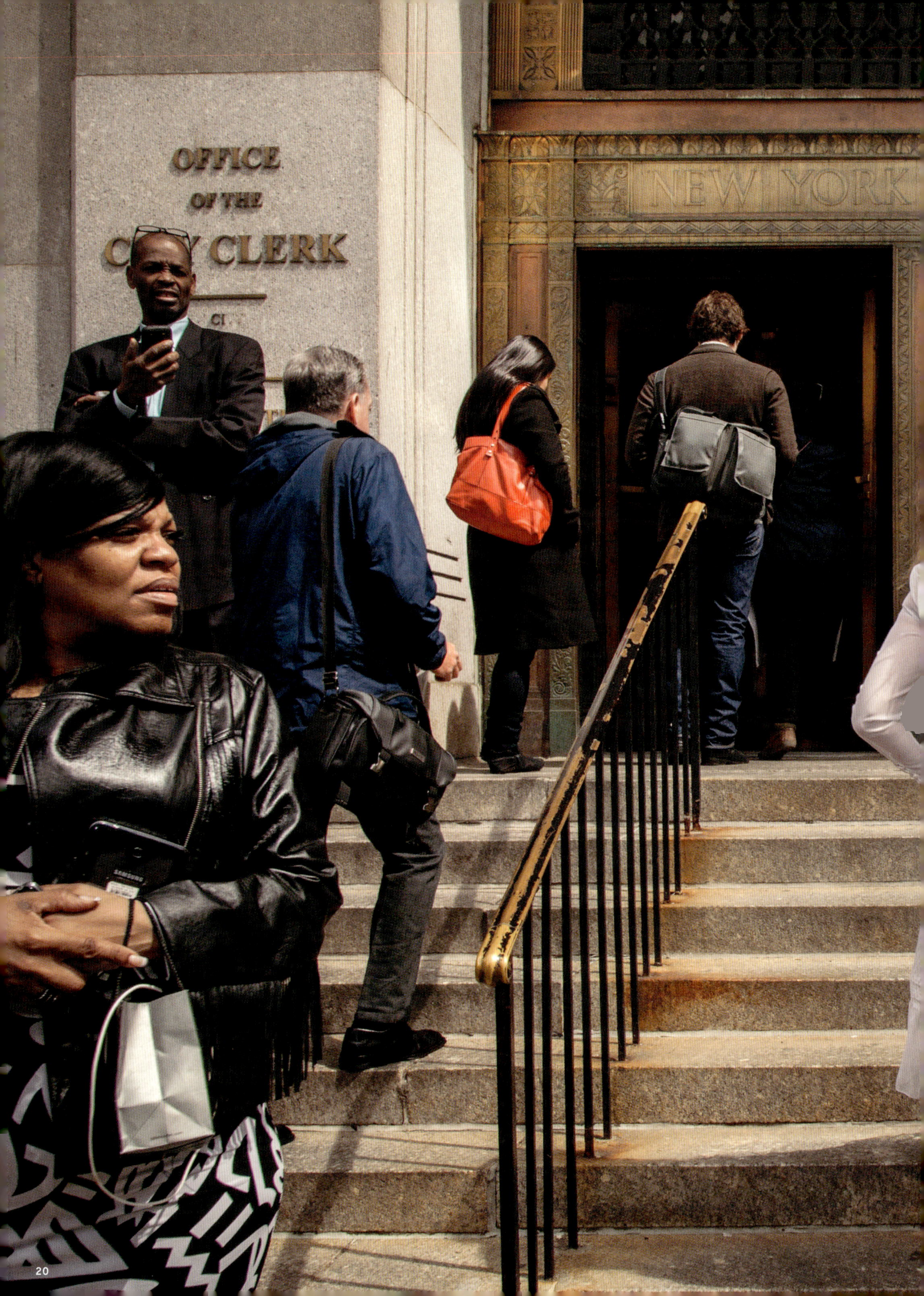

OFFICE
OF THE
CITY CLERK
NEW YORK

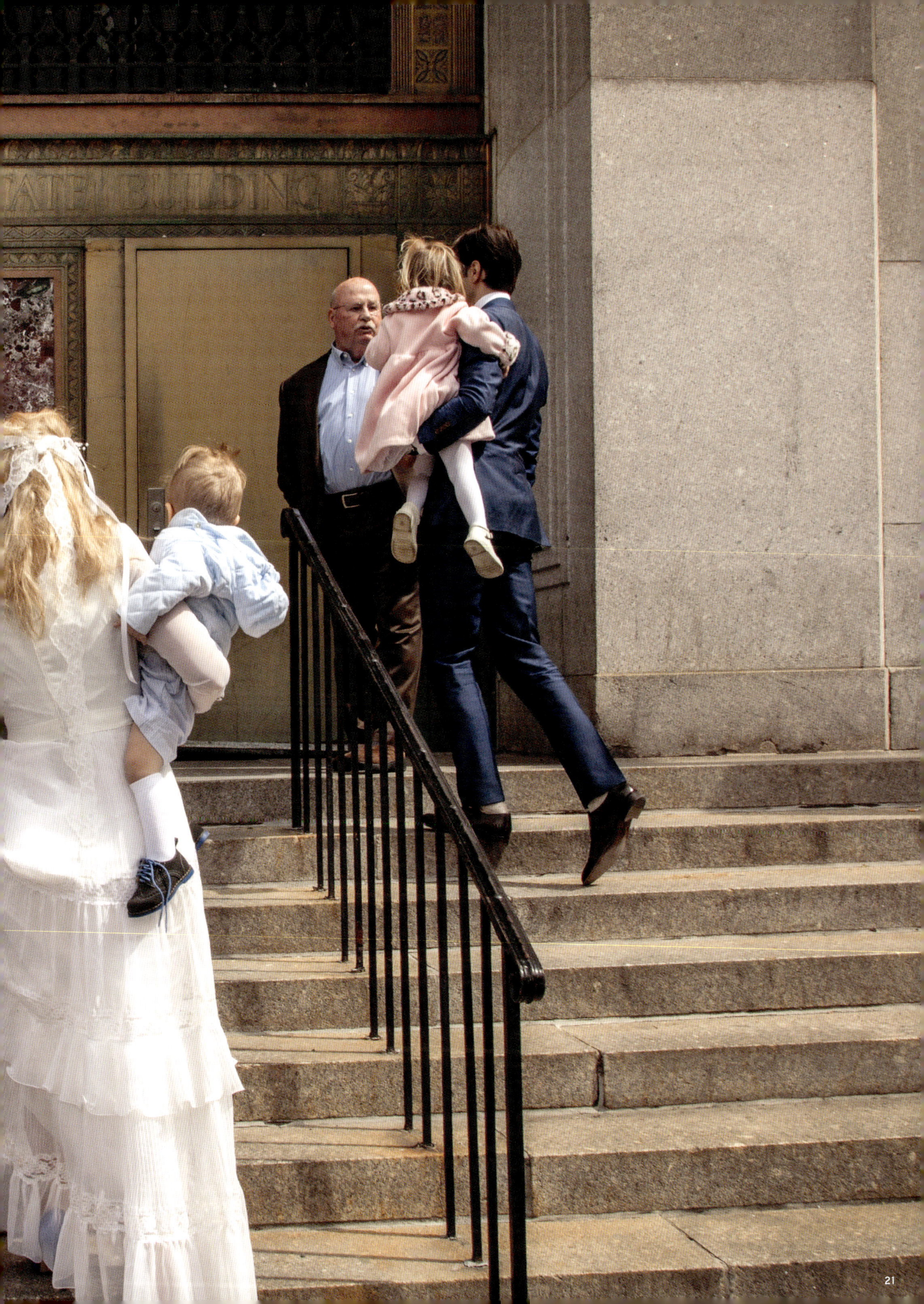
ATE BUILDING

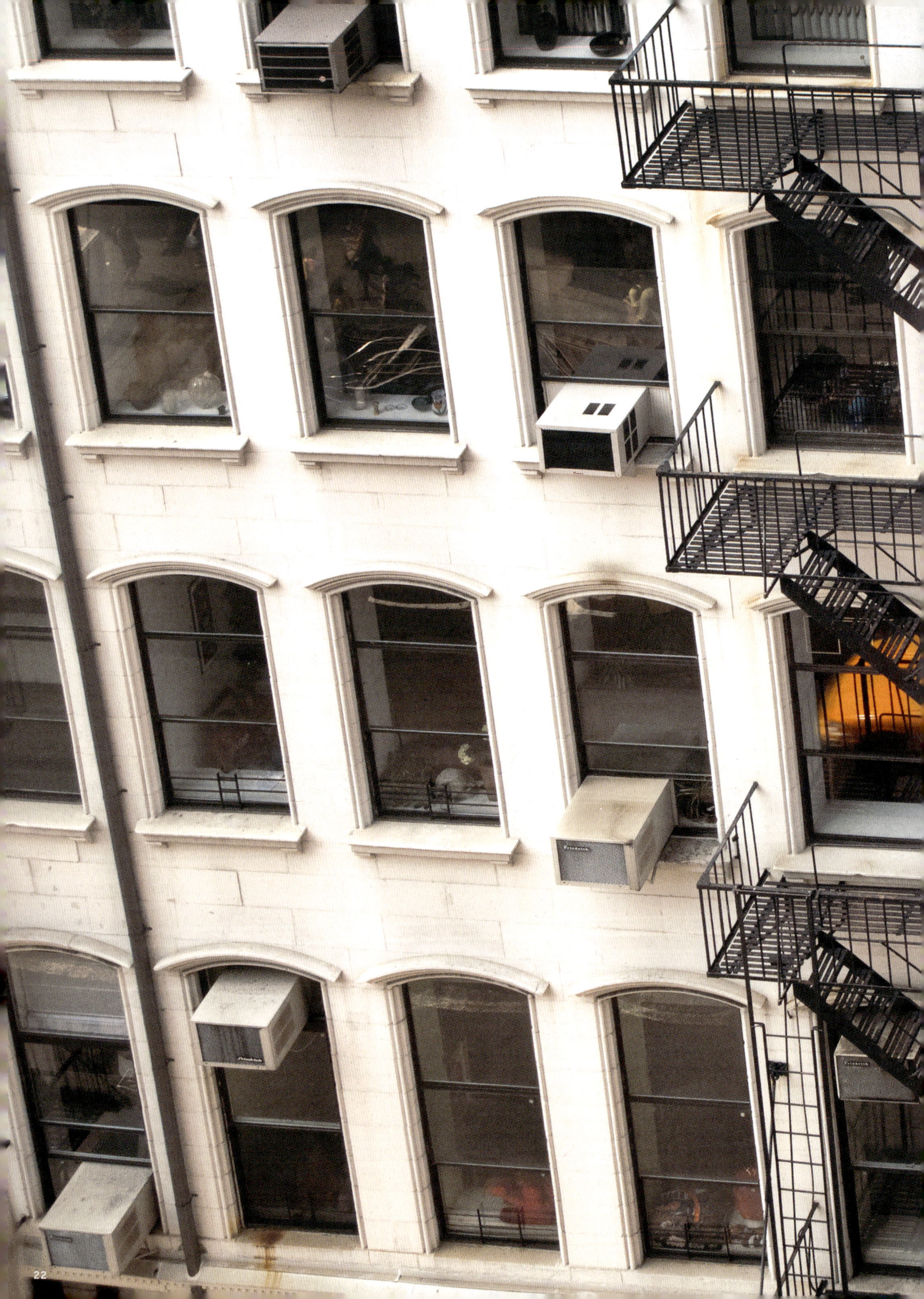

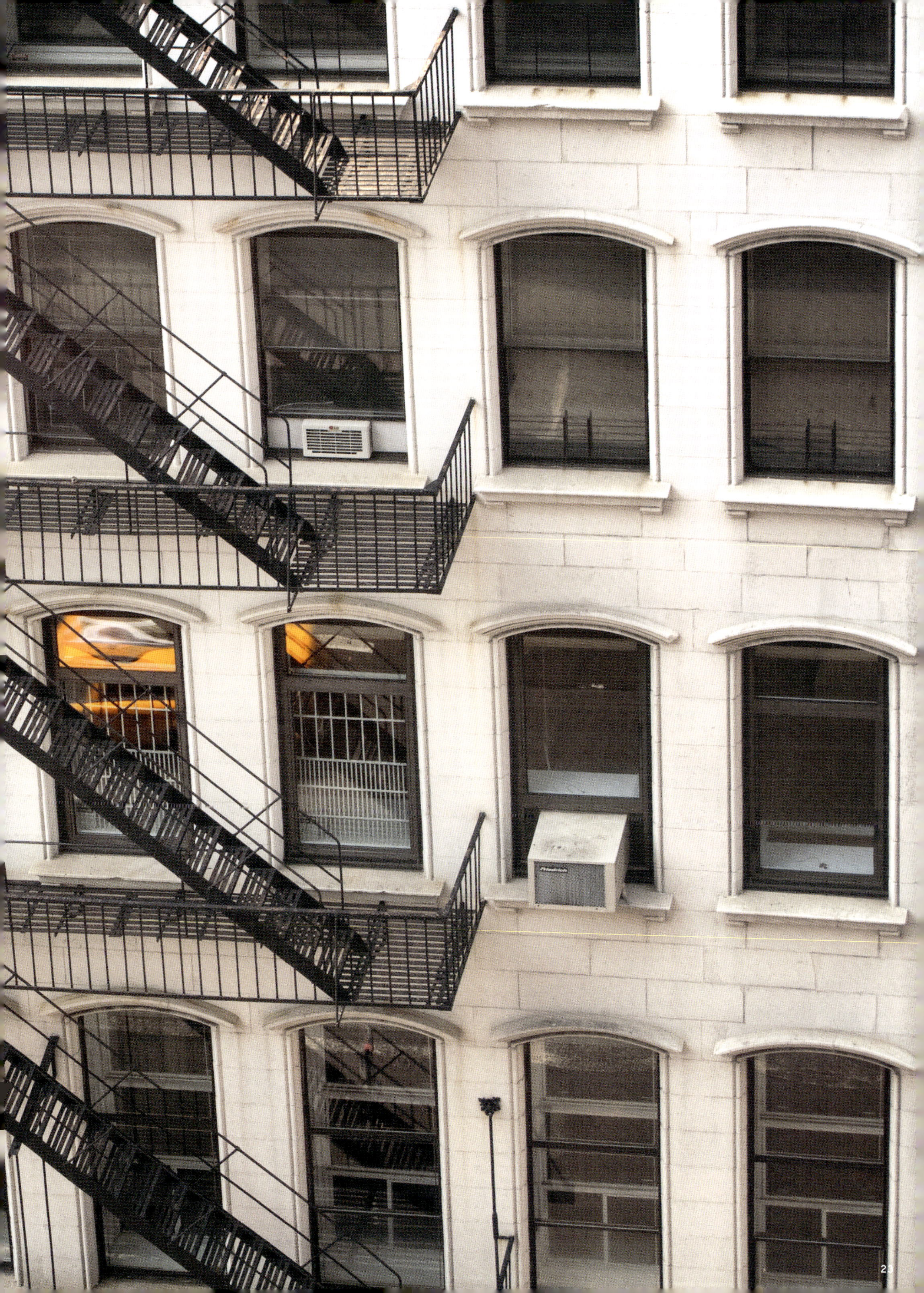

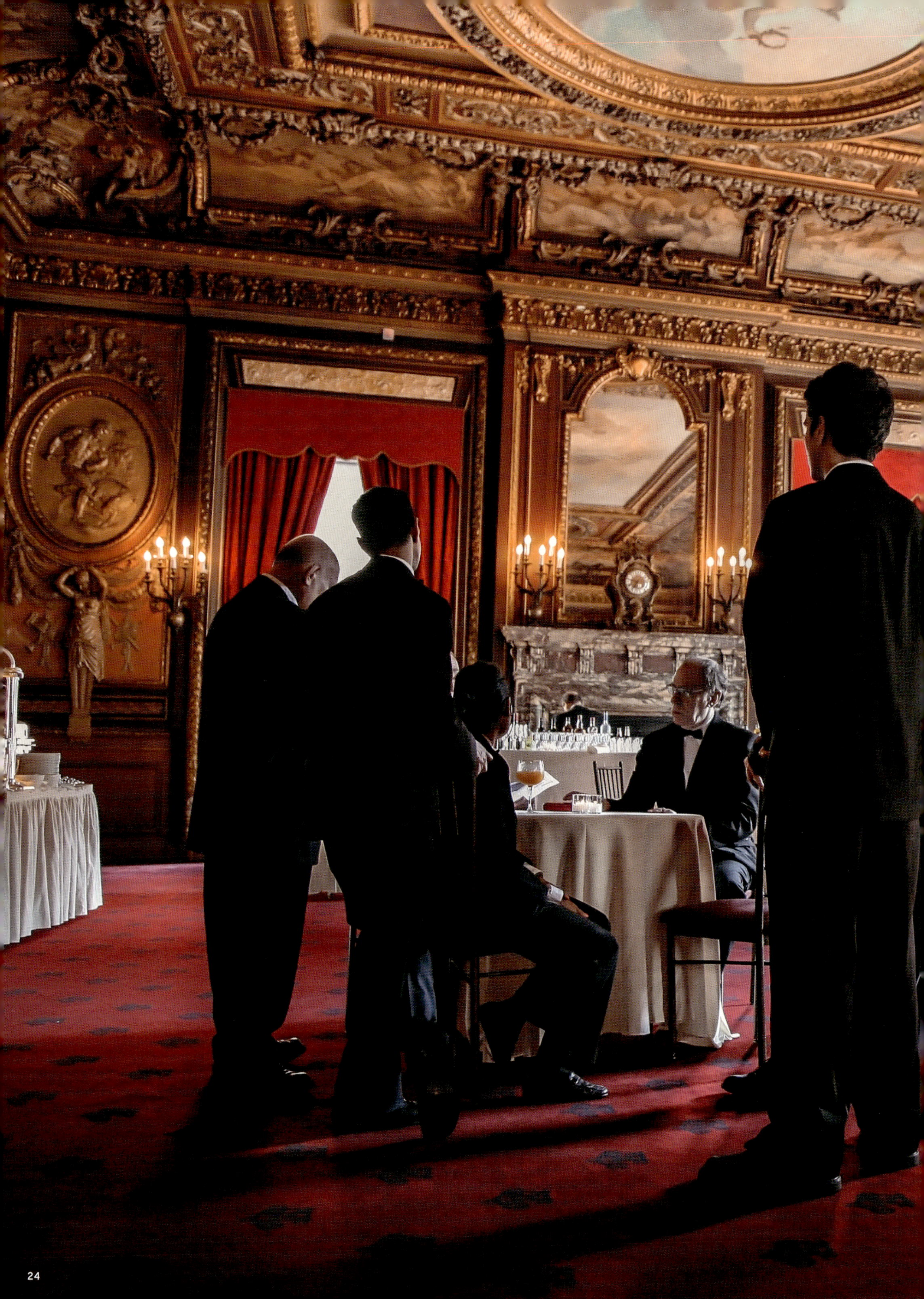

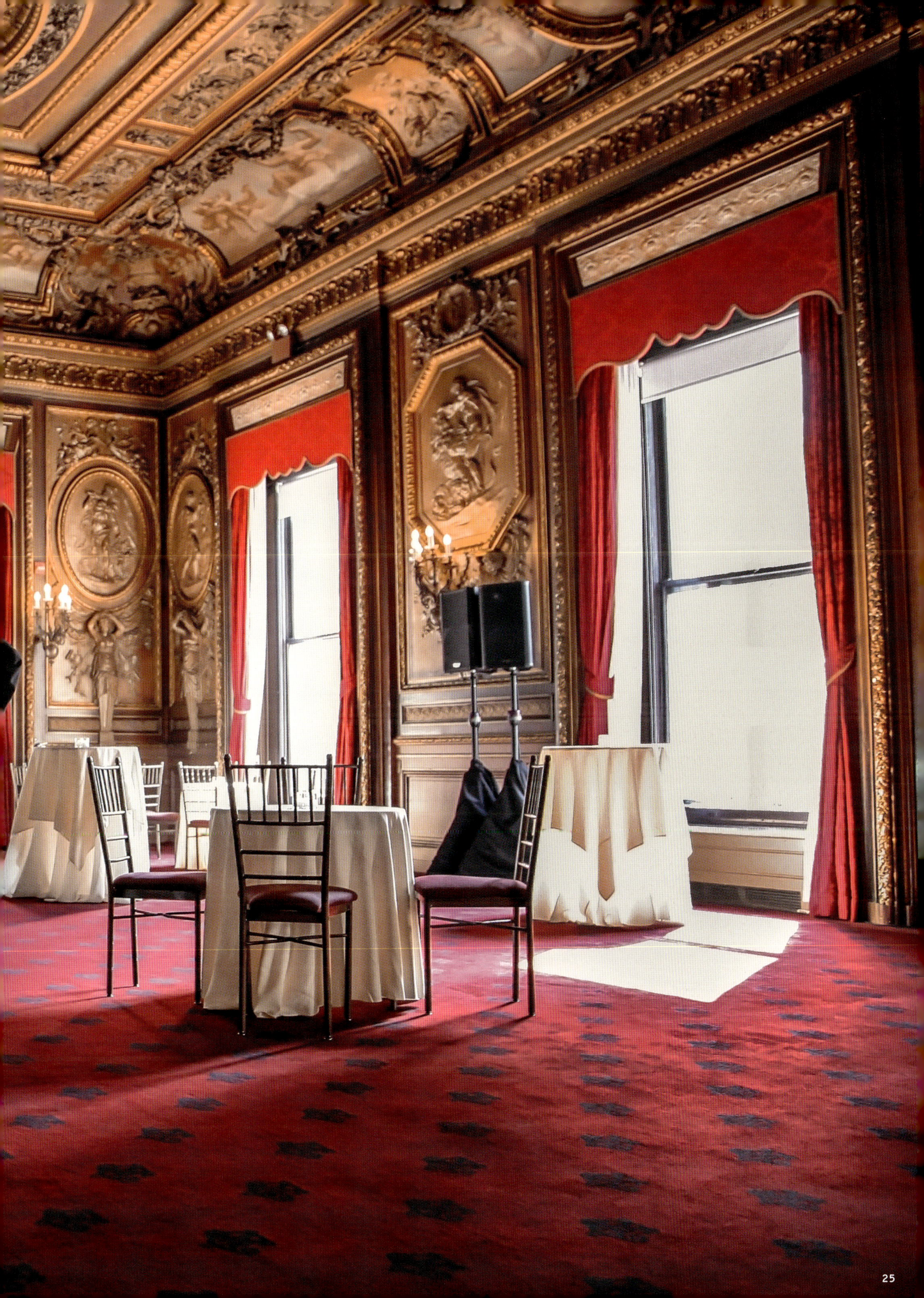

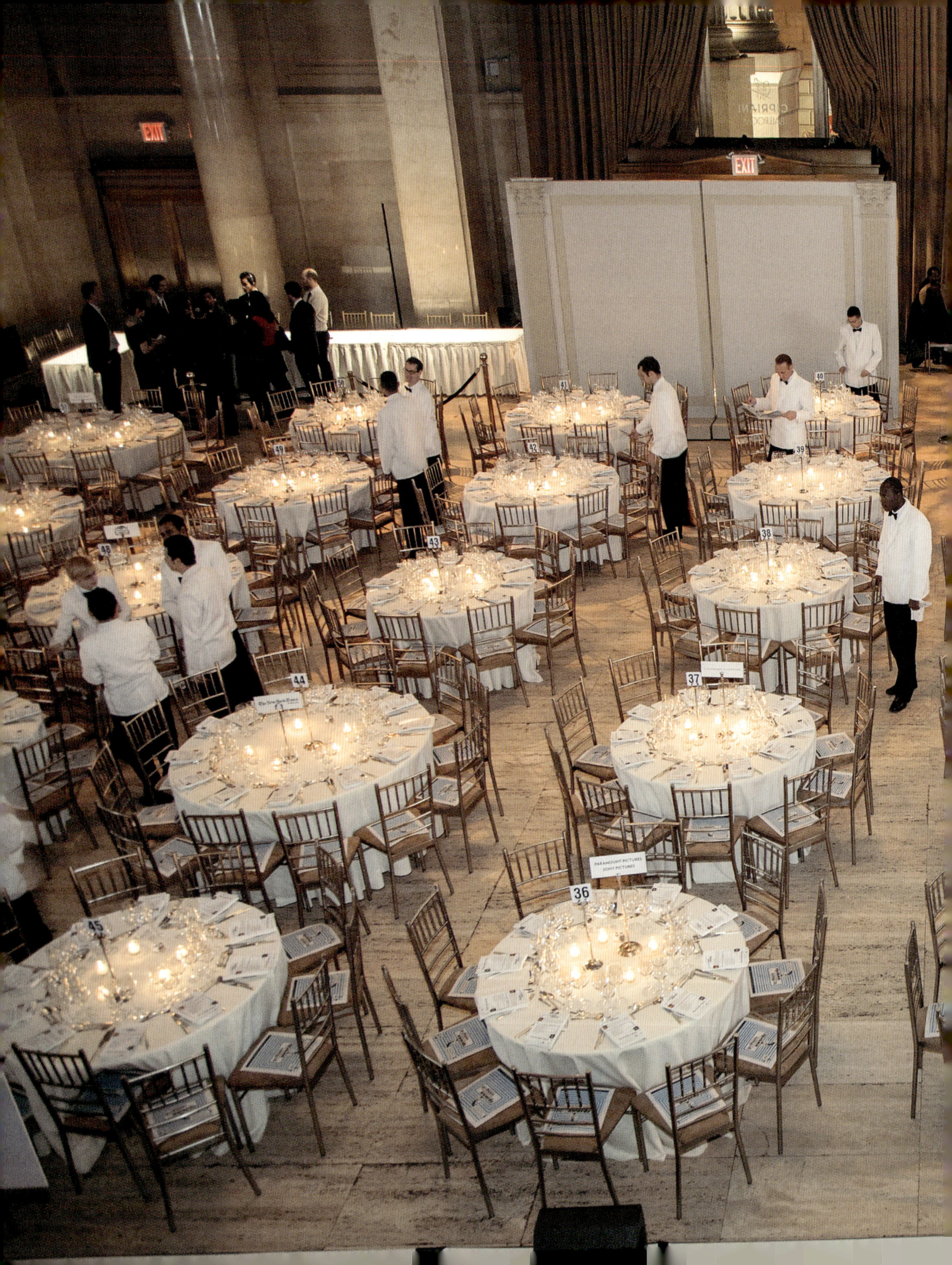

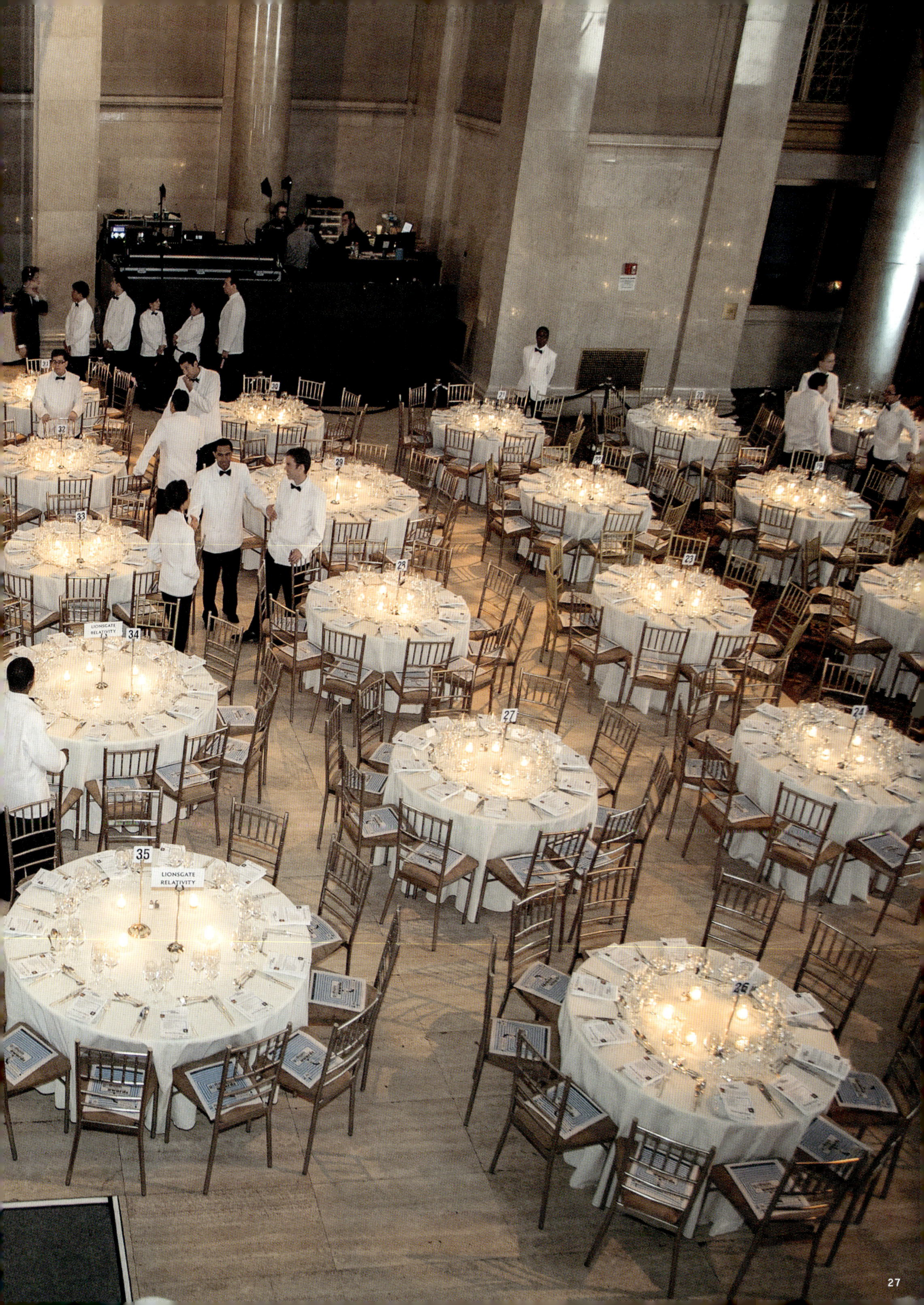

LIONSGATE
RELATIVITY
34
LIONSGATE
RELATIVITY
35
27
26
24
32
33
29
28

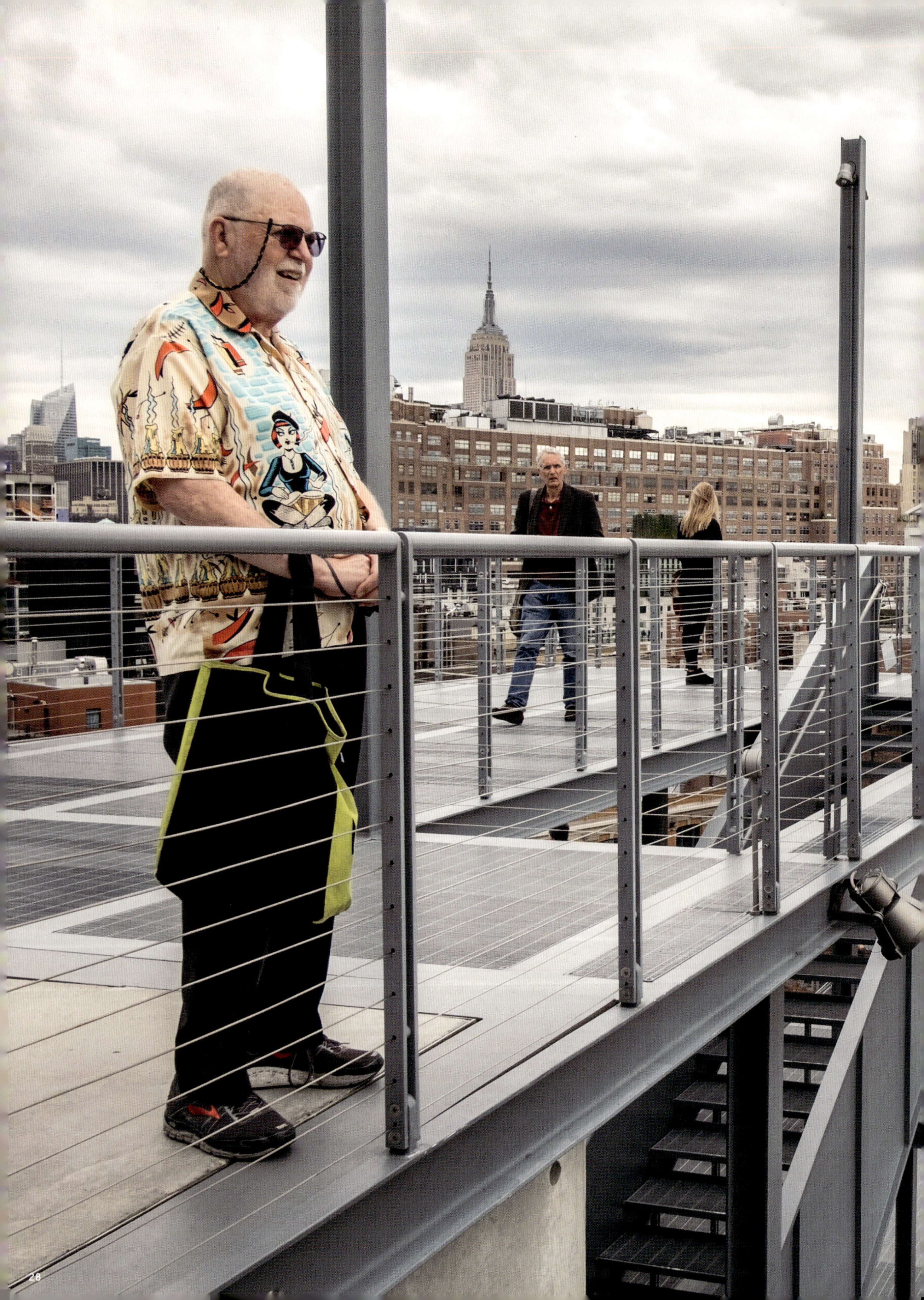

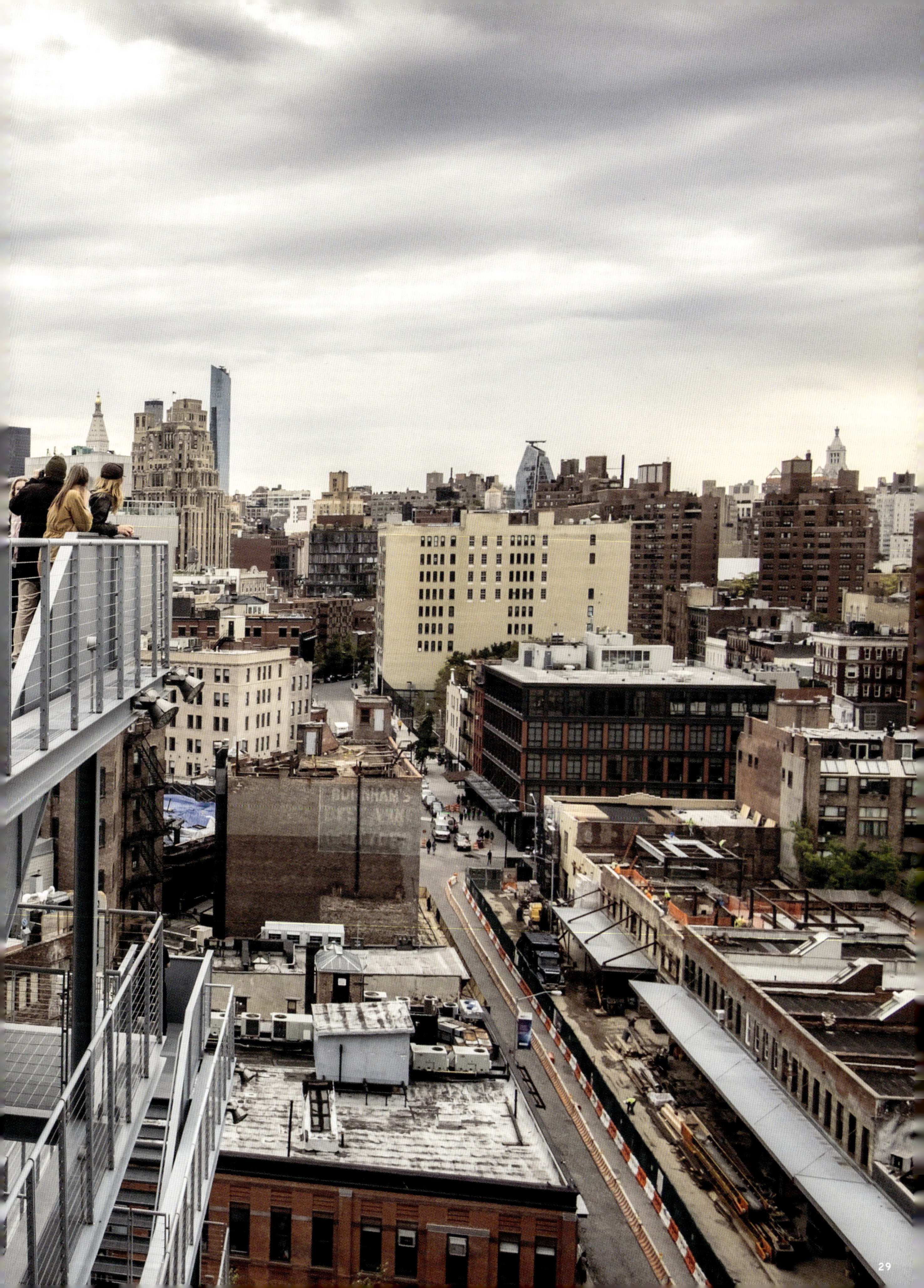

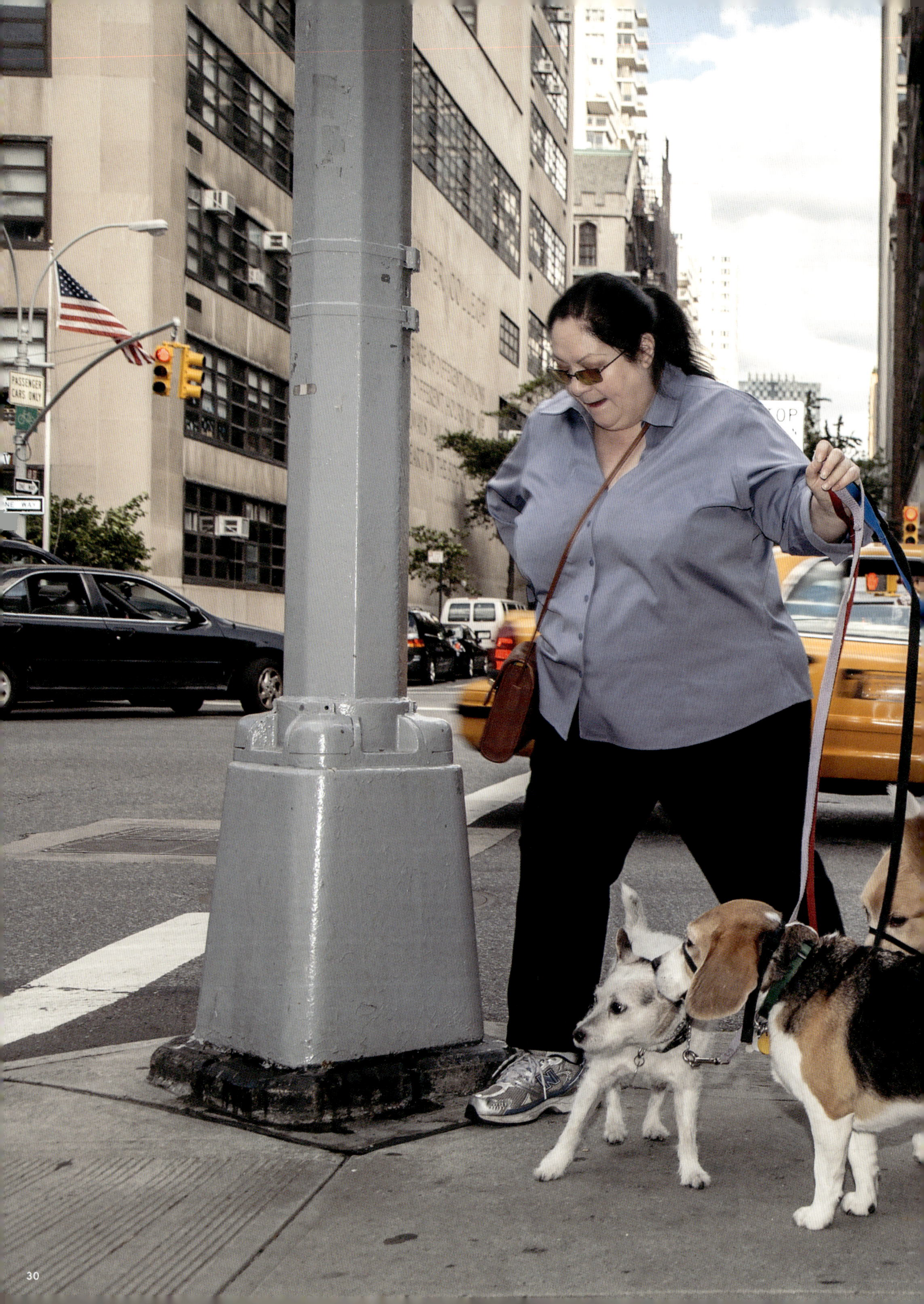

PASSENGER
CARS ONLY
ONE WAY

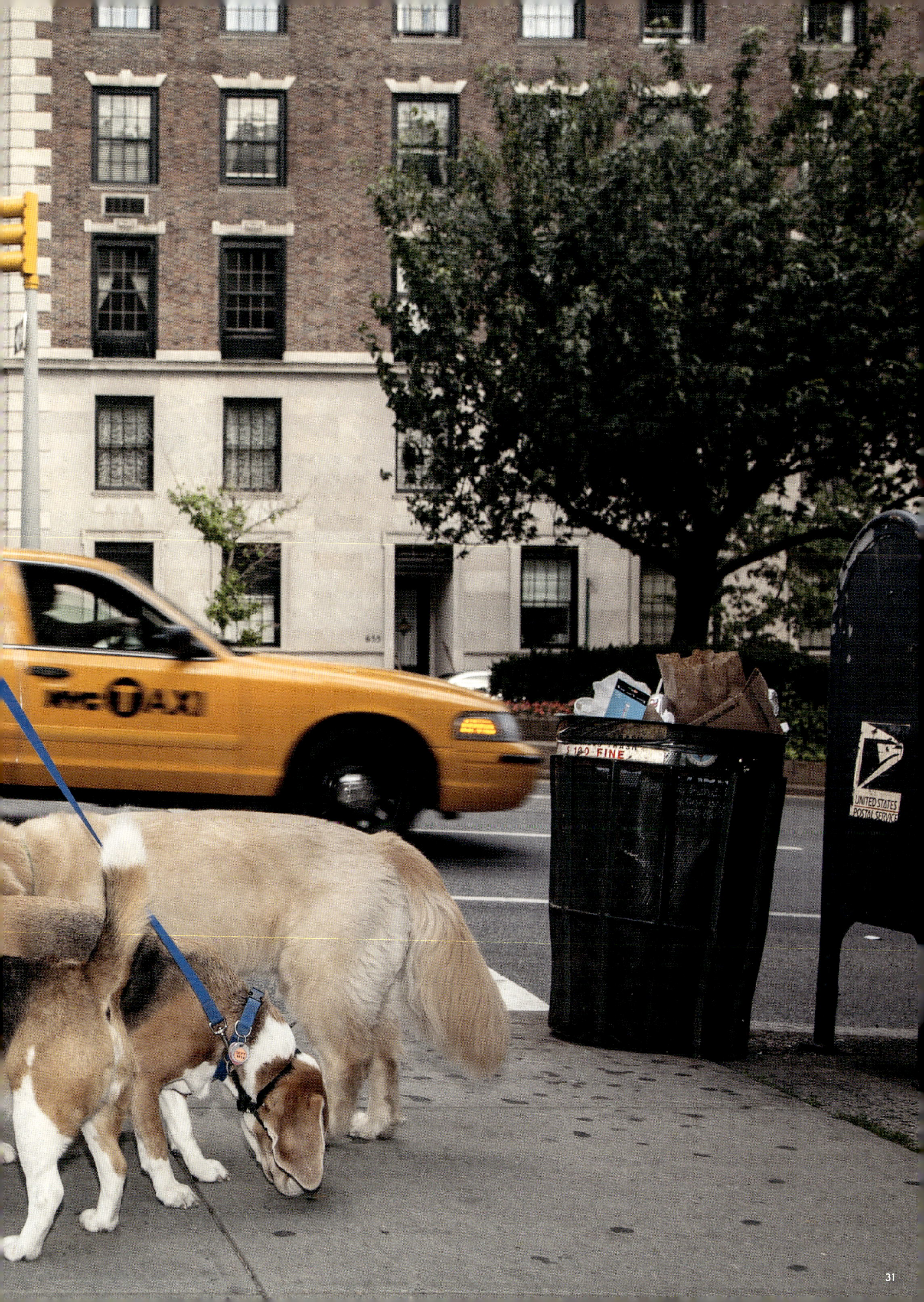

NYC TAXI
$ 100 FINE
UNITED STATES
POSTAL SERVICE

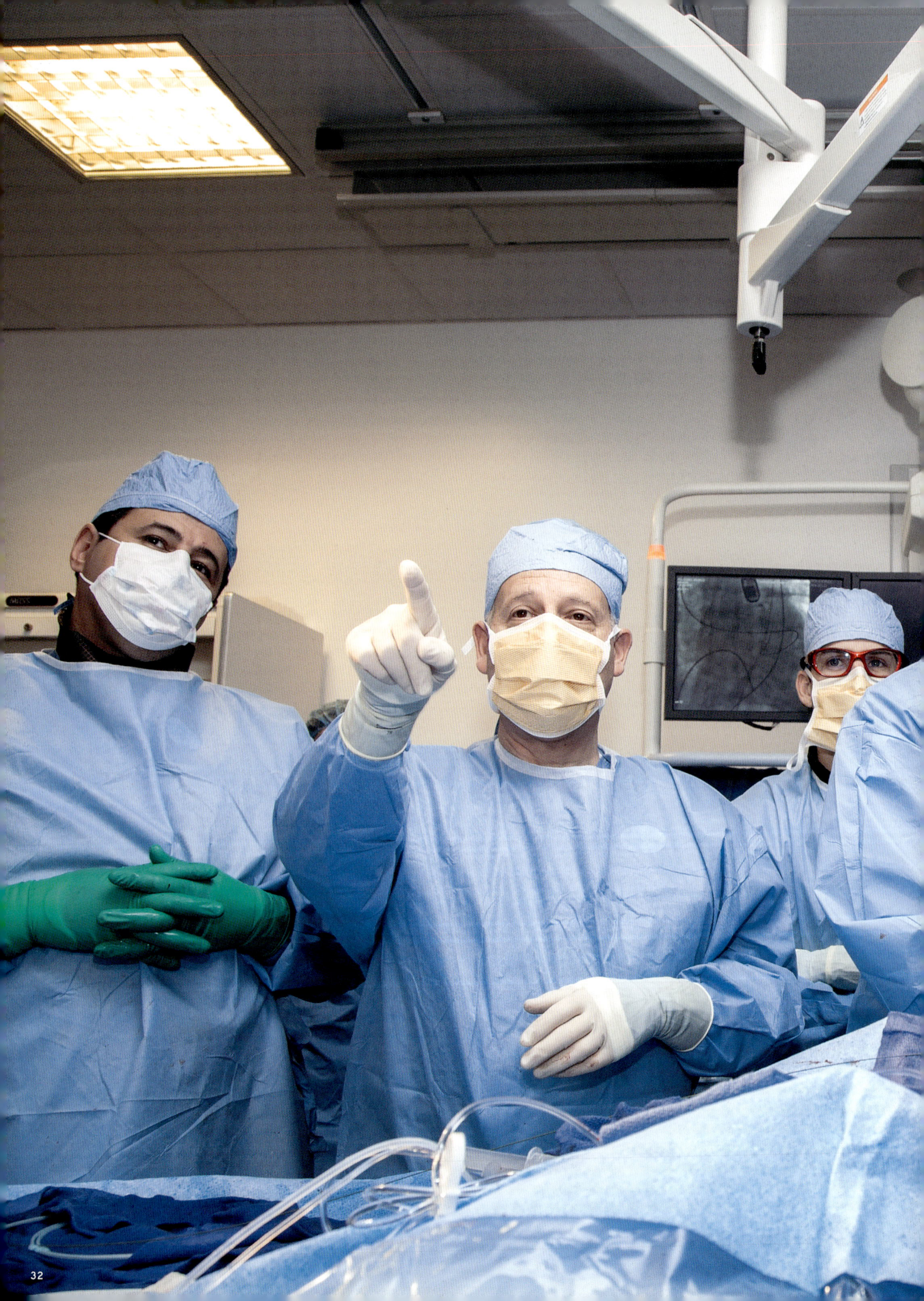

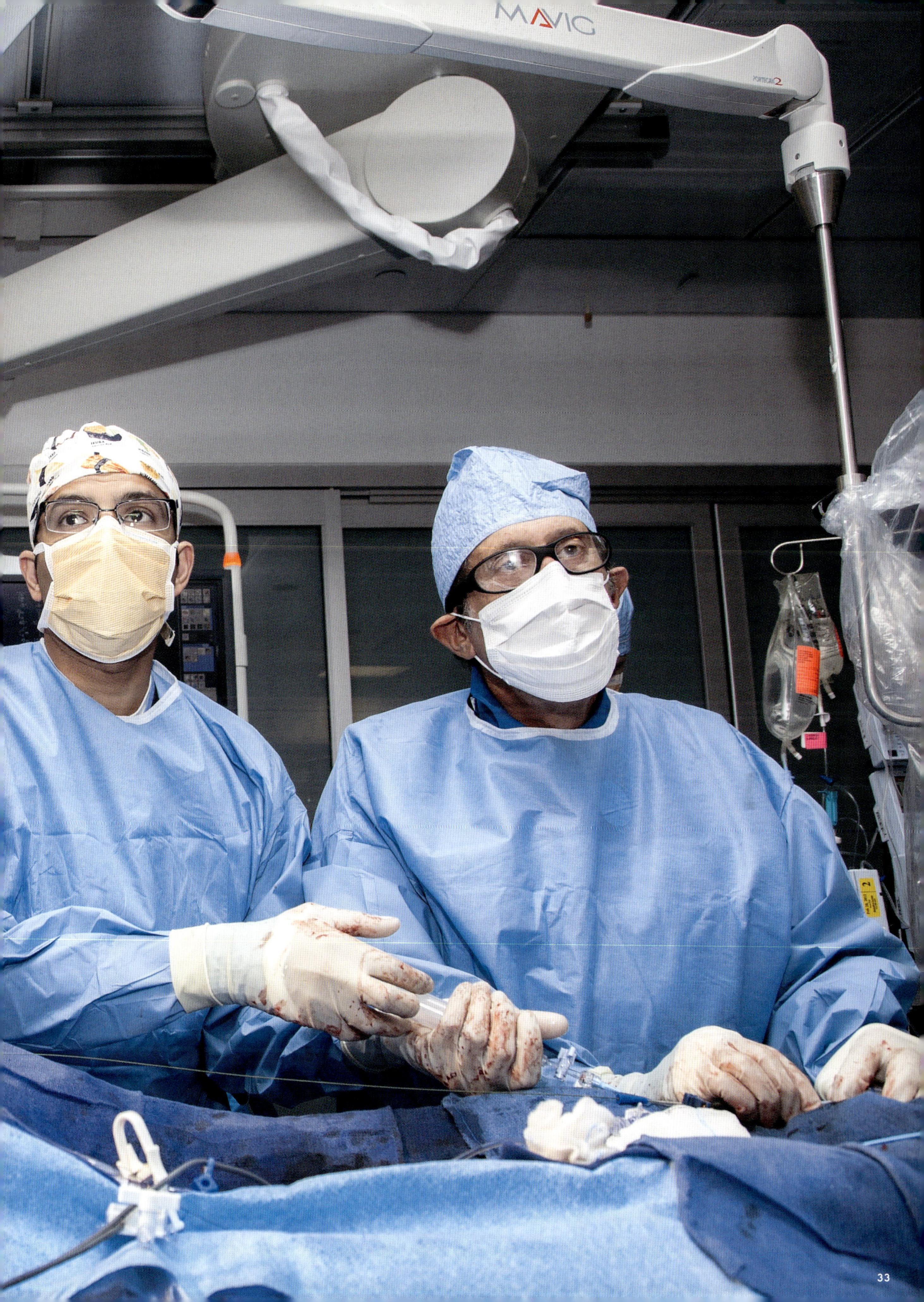

MAVIG

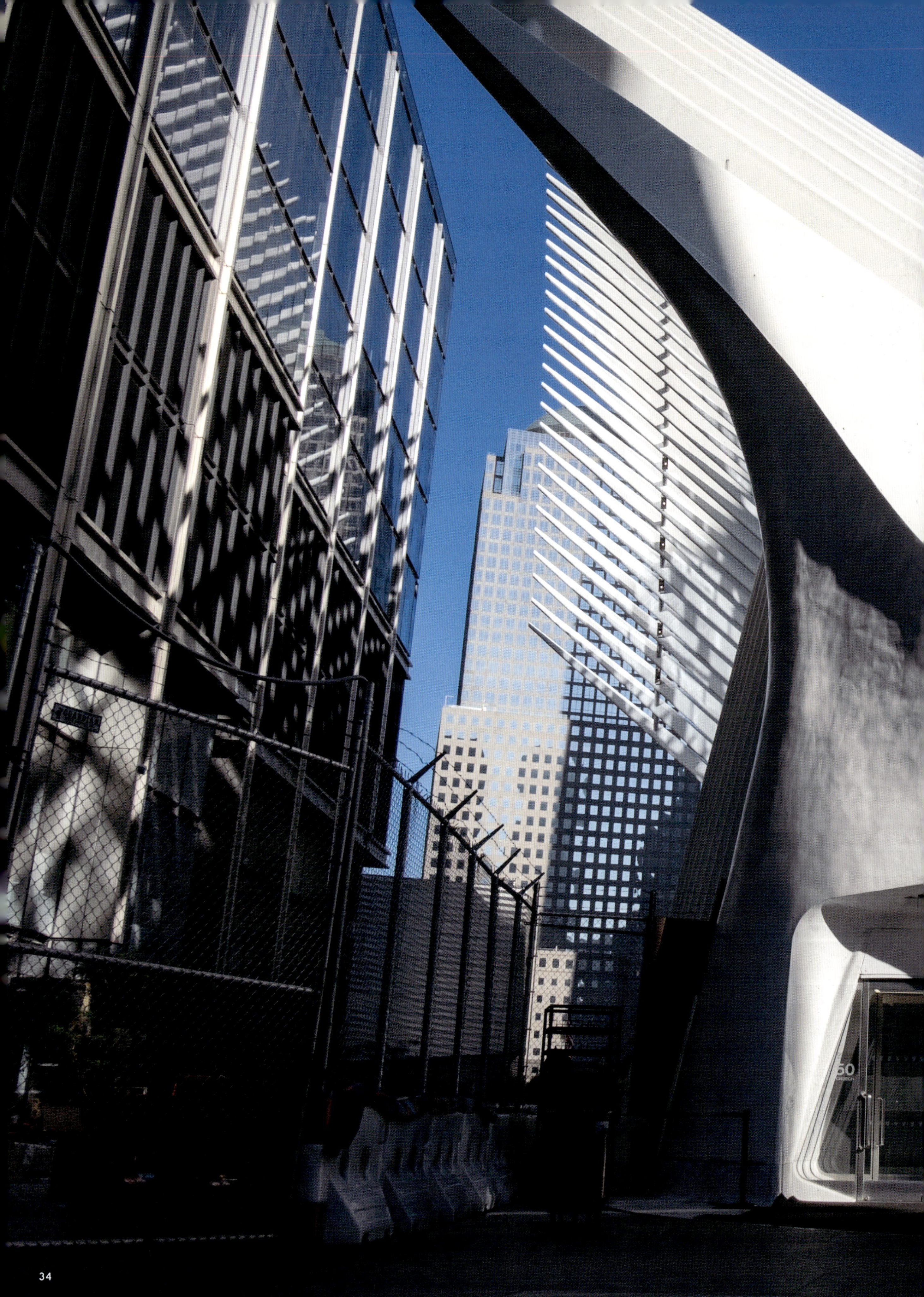

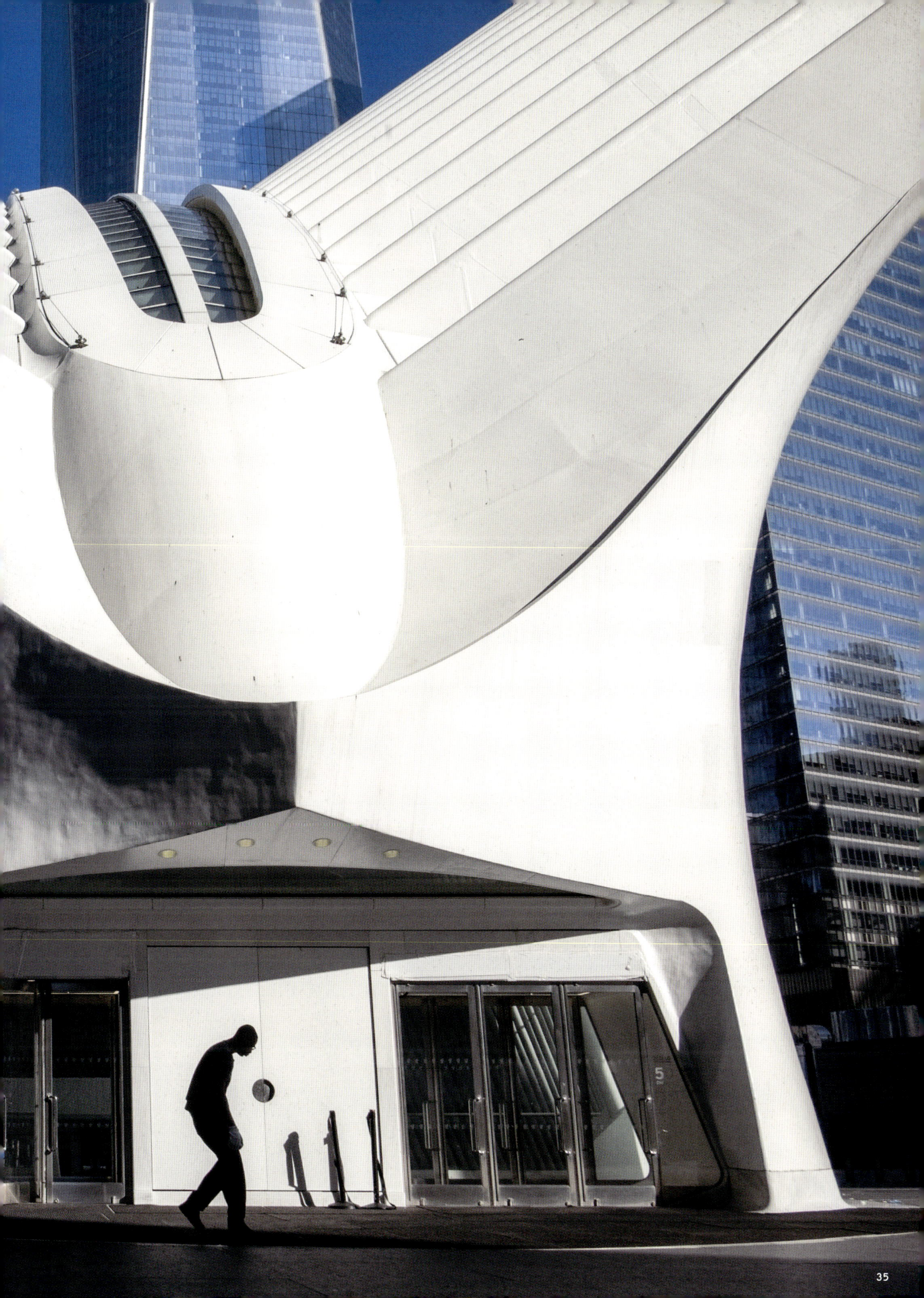

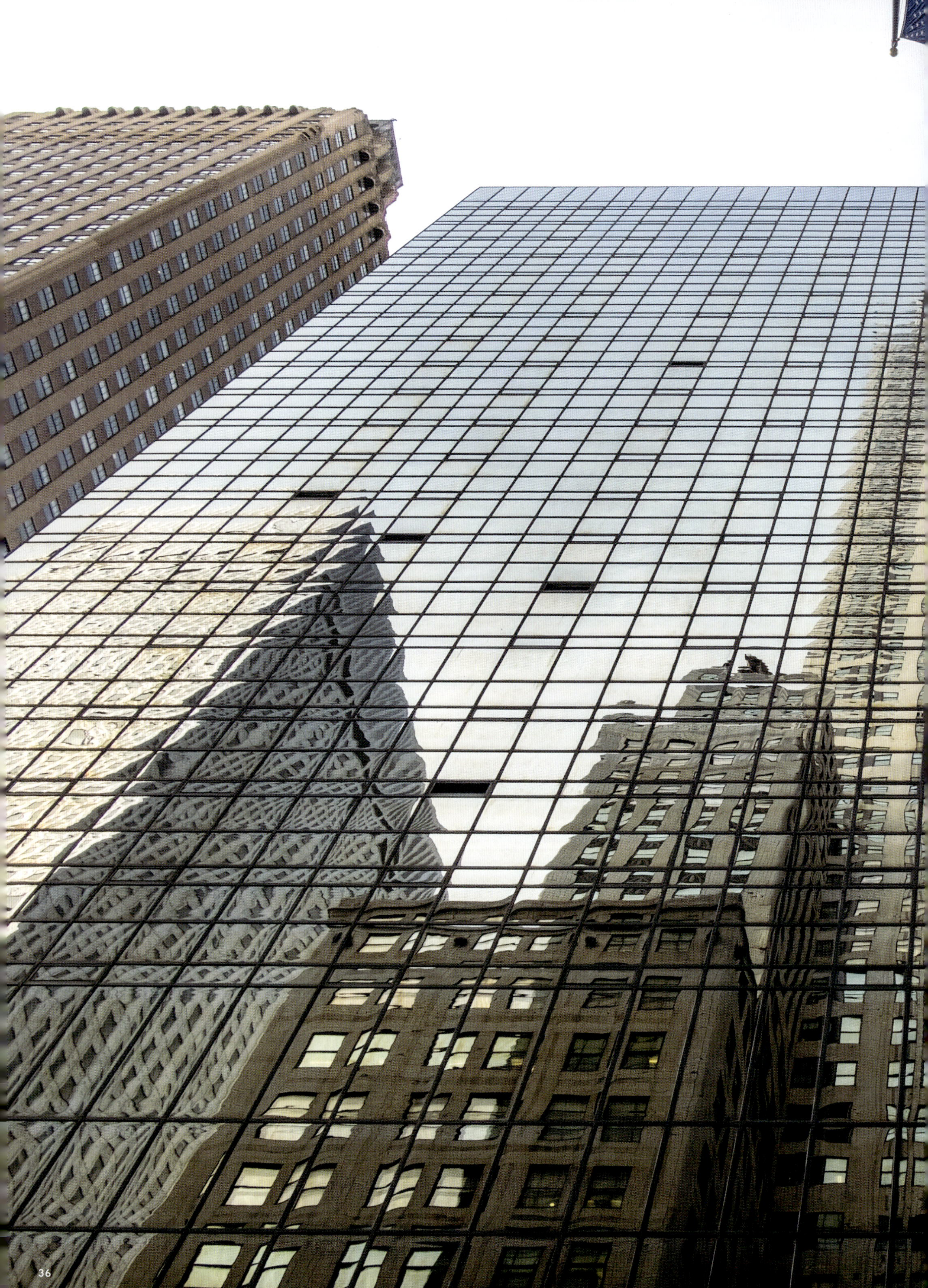

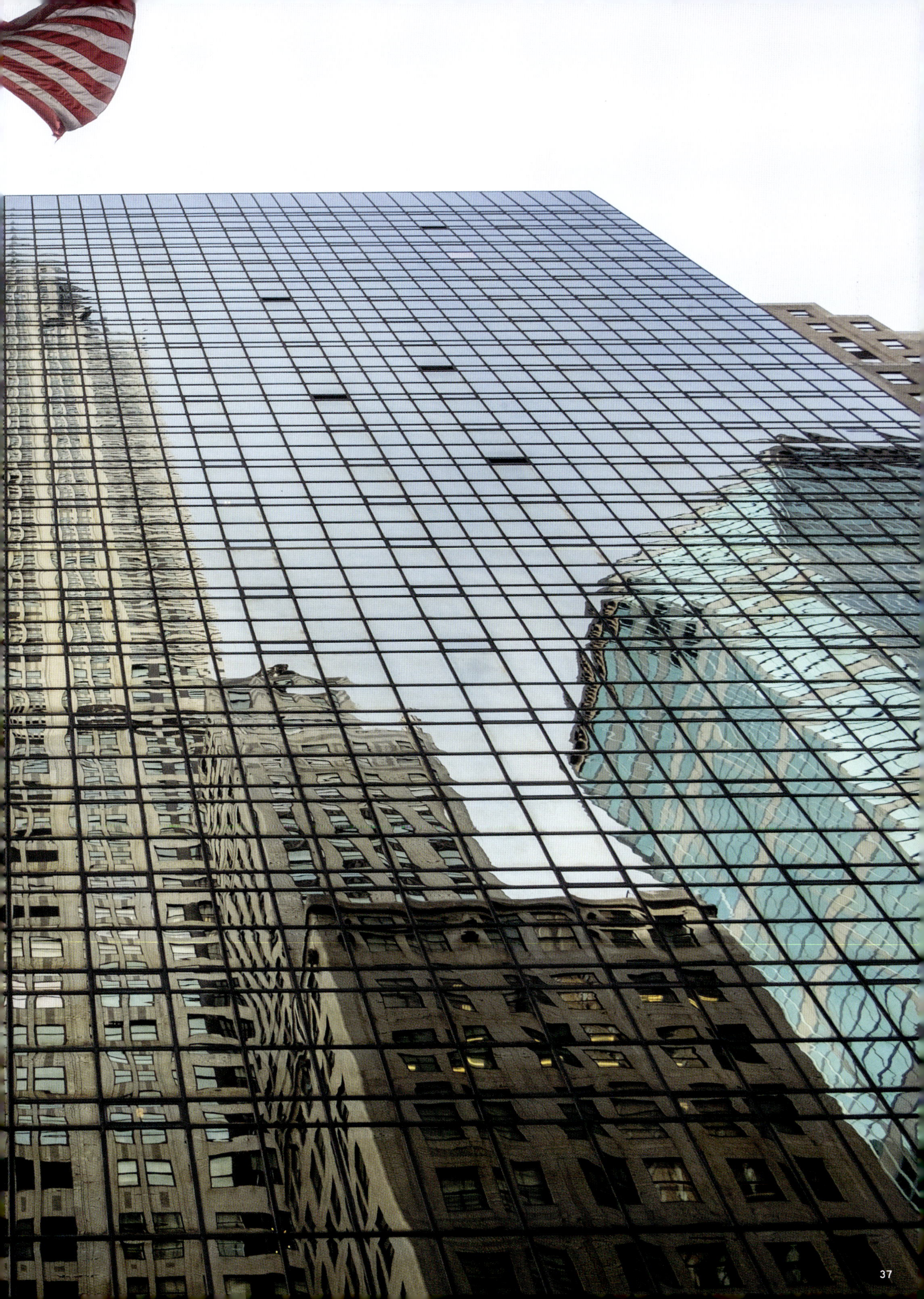

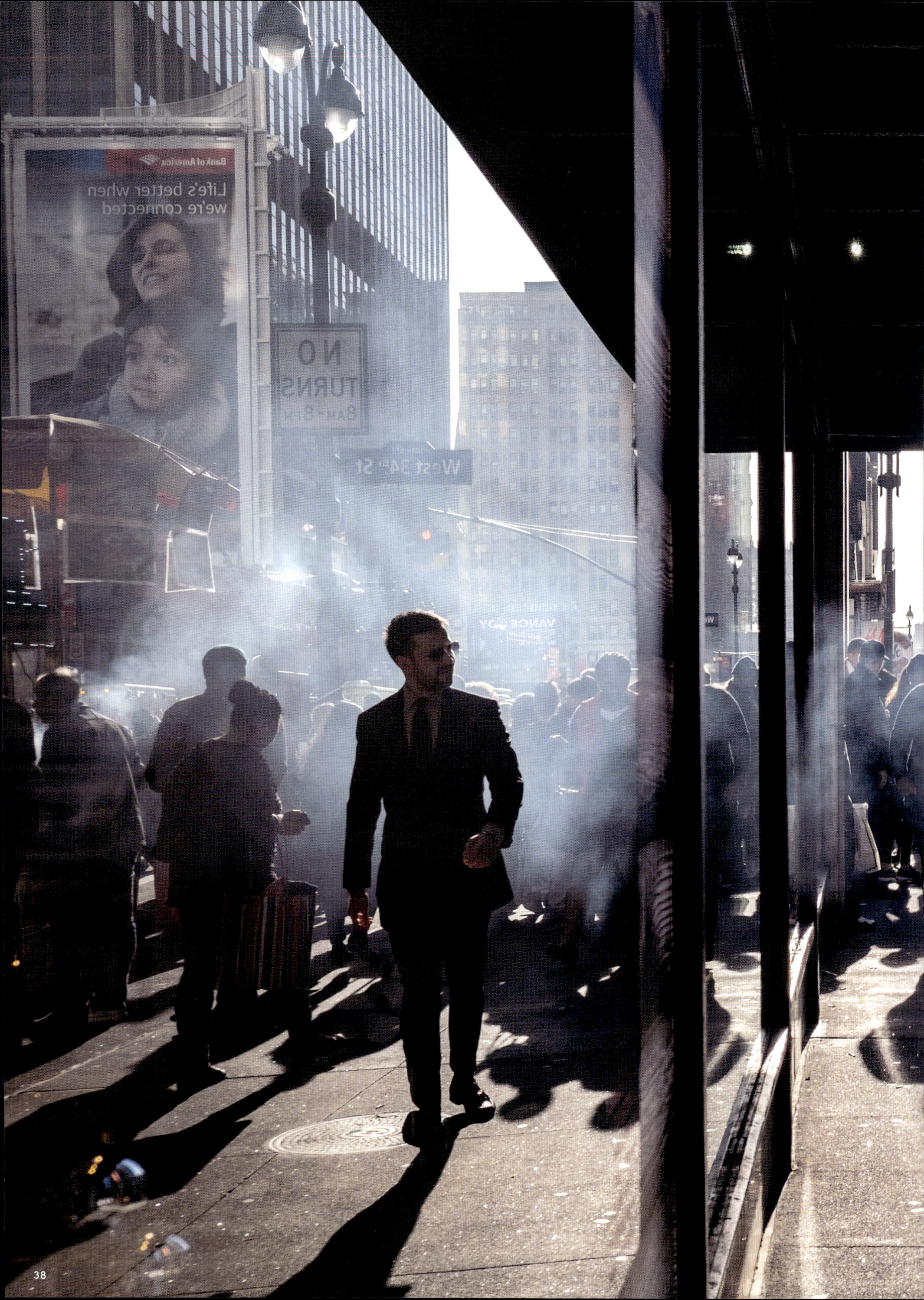

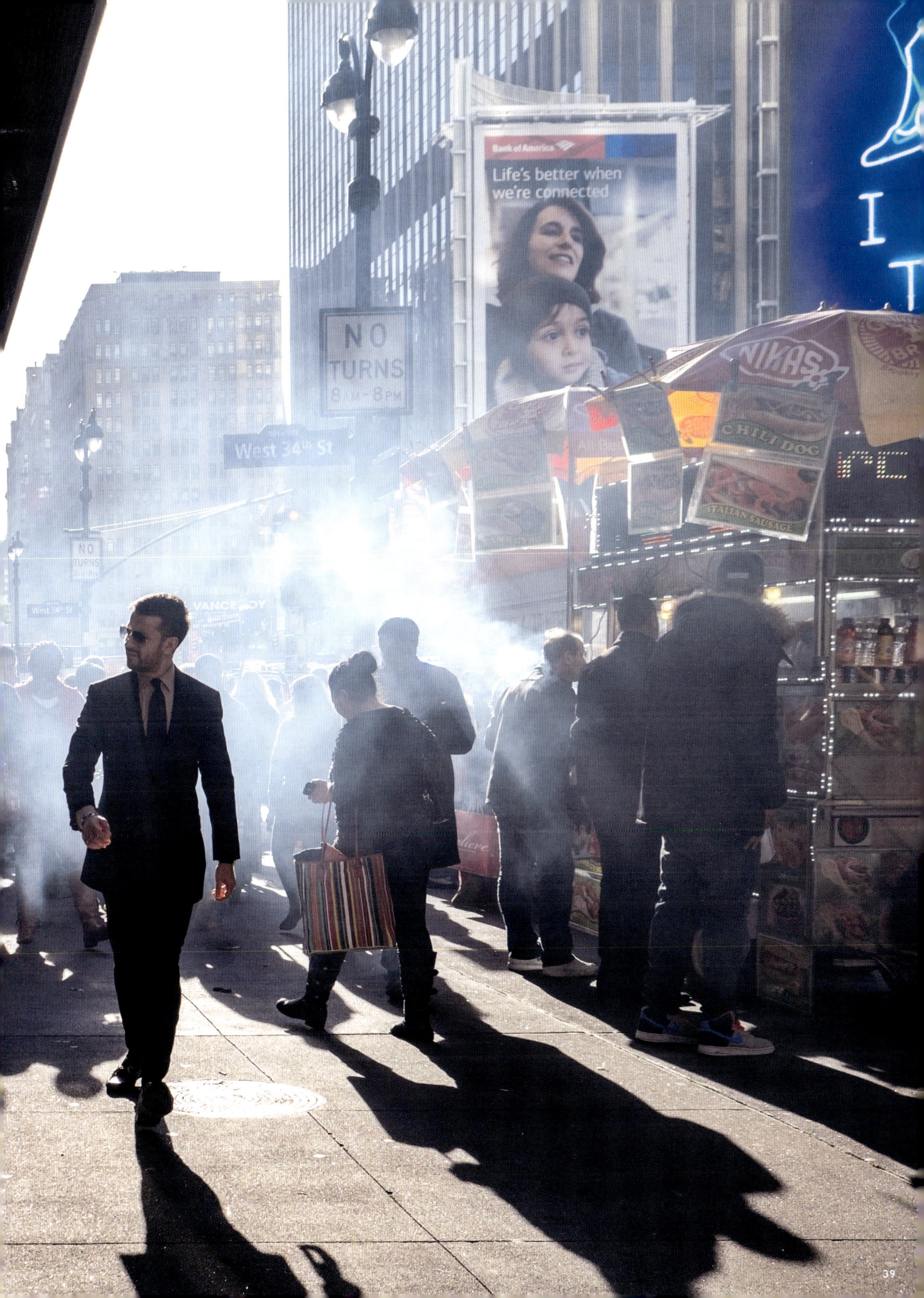

Bank of America
Life's better when
we're connected
NO
TURNS
8 AM – 8 PM
West 34th St
NO
TURNS
West 34th St
NIKAS
CHILI DOG
ITALIAN SAUSAGE

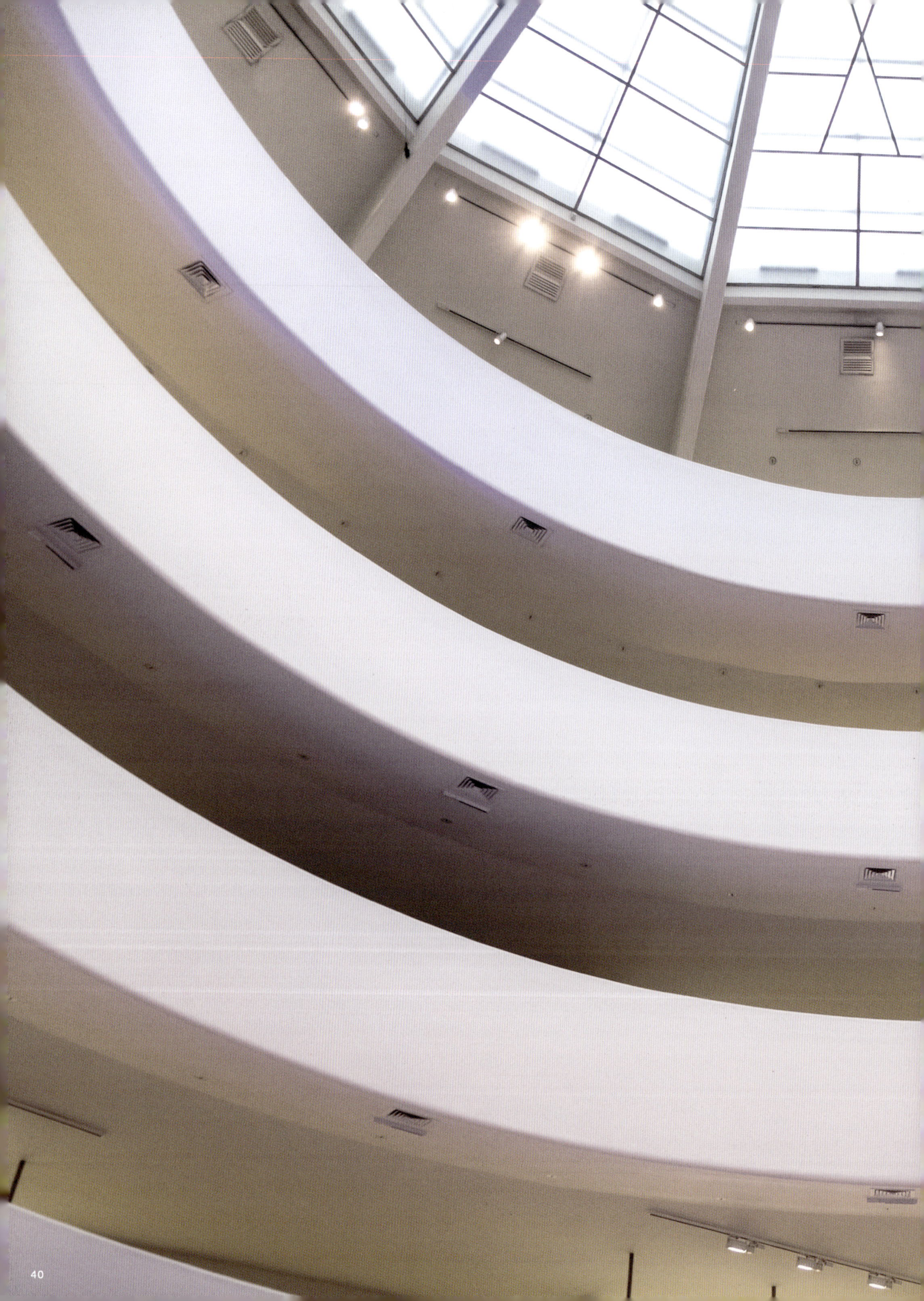

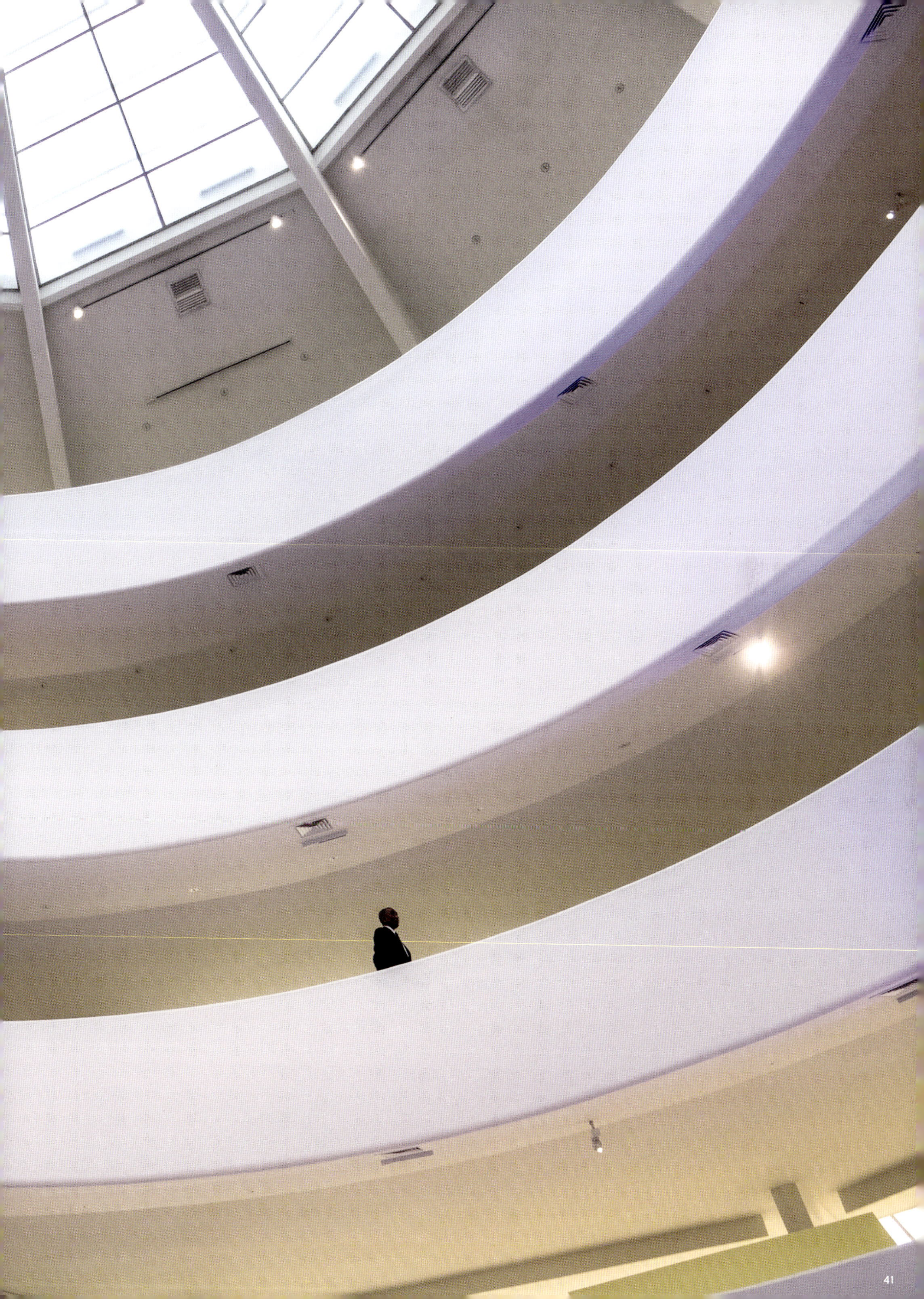

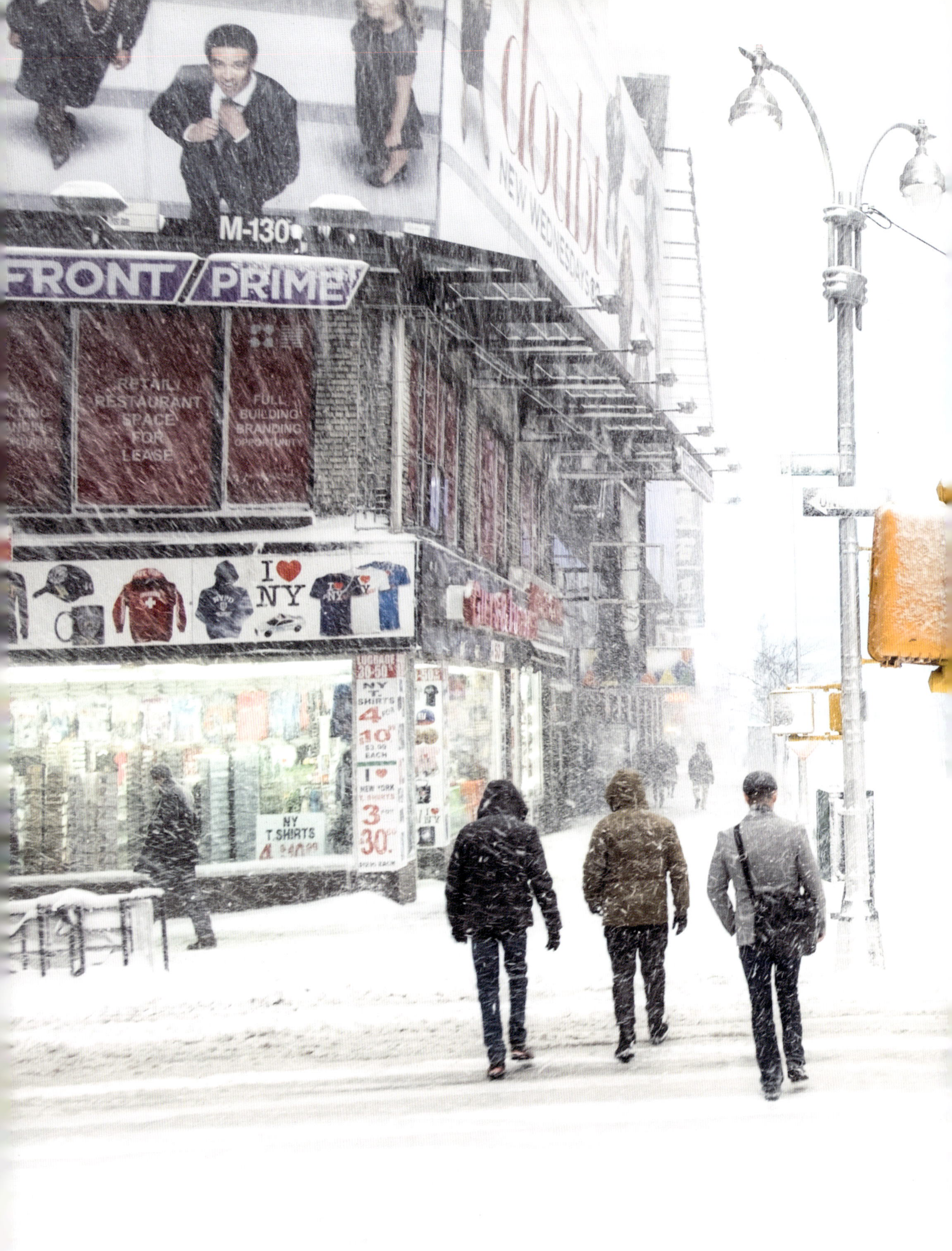
M-130
FRONT / PRIME
RETAIL
RESTAURANT
SPACE
FOR
LEASE
FULL
BUILDING
BRANDING
OPPORTUNITY
I ♥ NY
NY
T-SHIRTS
4 for 10
$3.99 EACH
NEW YORK
T-SHIRTS
3 for 30.
NY
T-SHIRTS

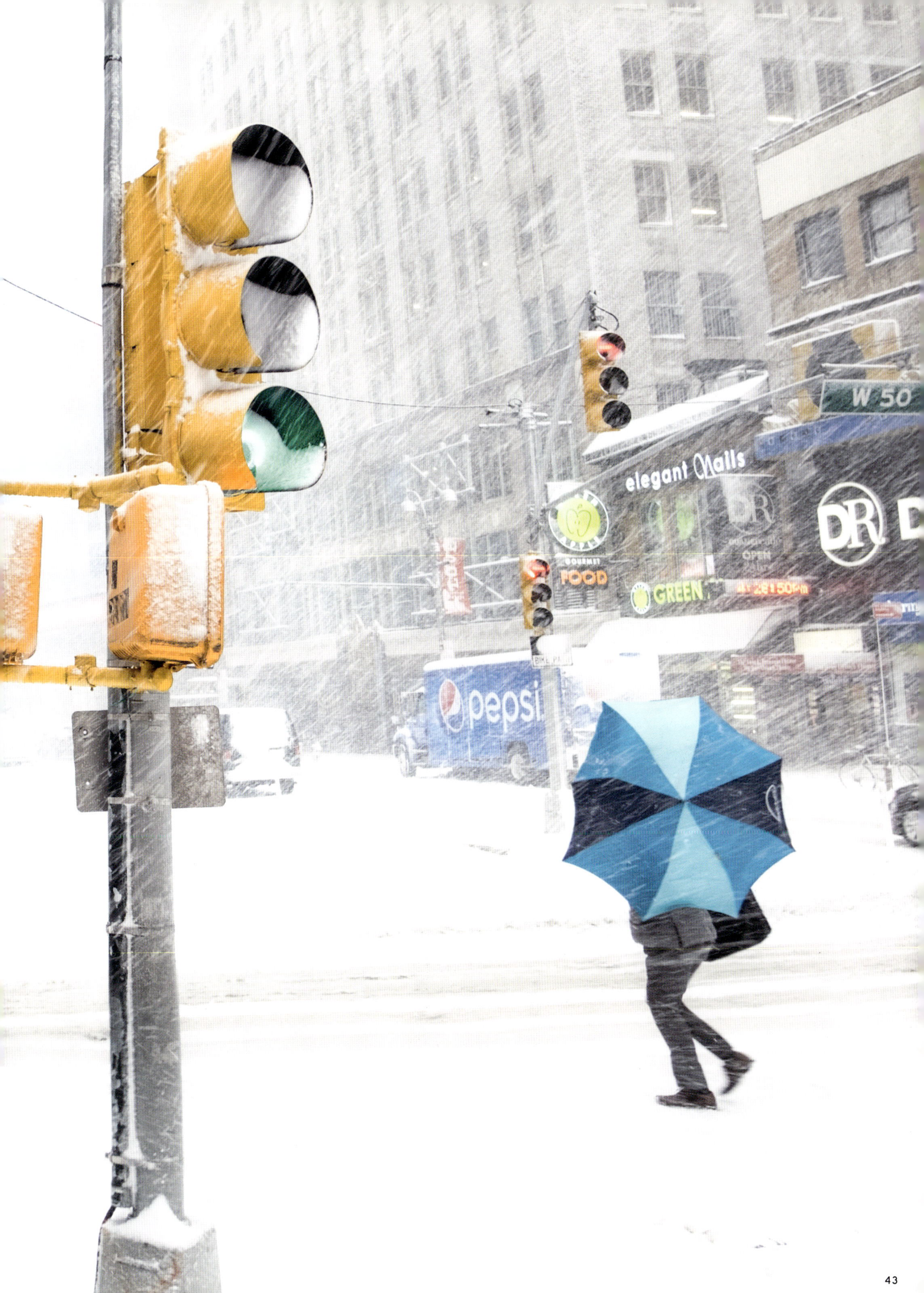

W 50
elegant Nalls
DR
OPEN
GOURMET
FOOD
GREEN
DR
pepsi
BIKE LANE

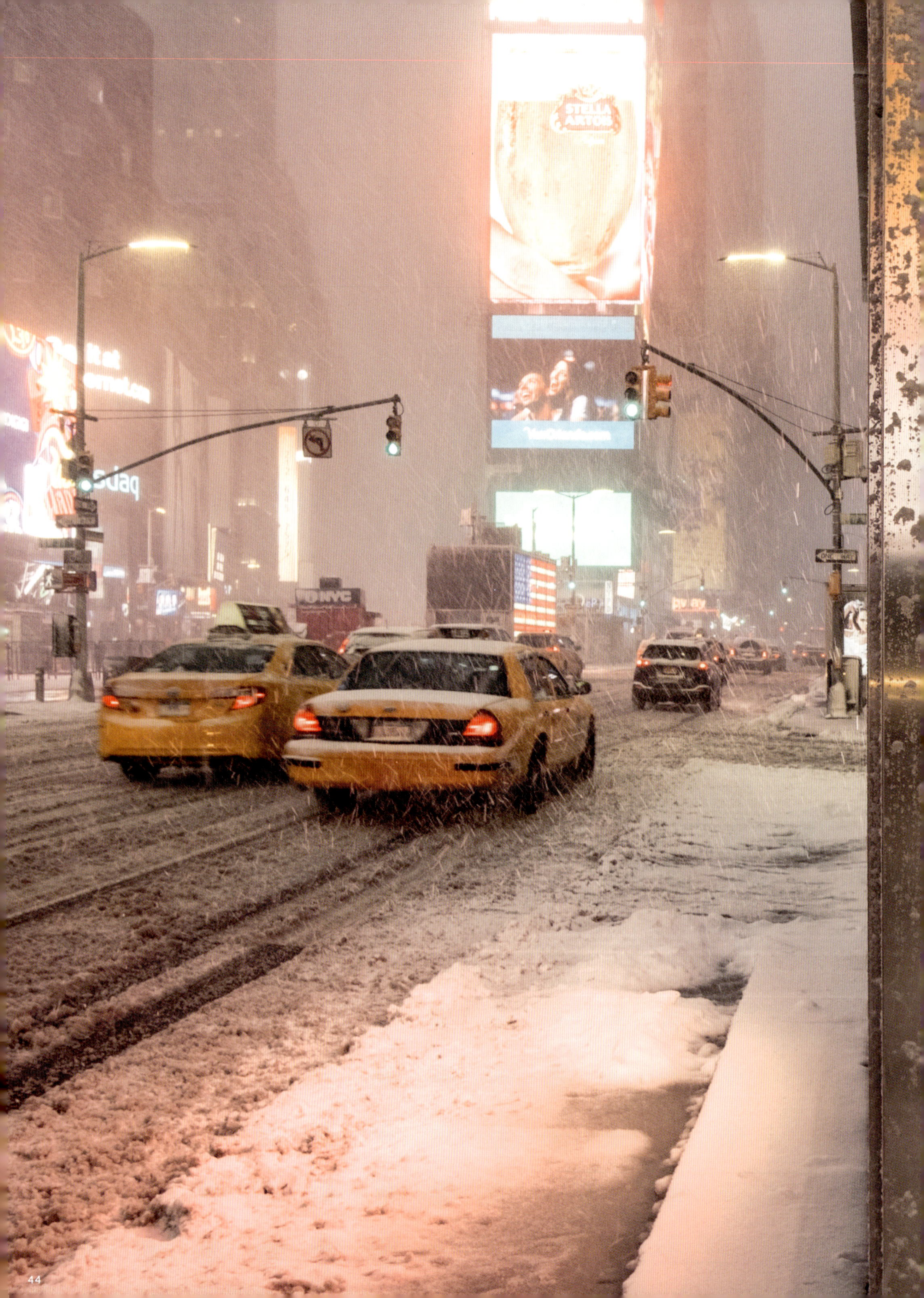

STELLA ARTOIS

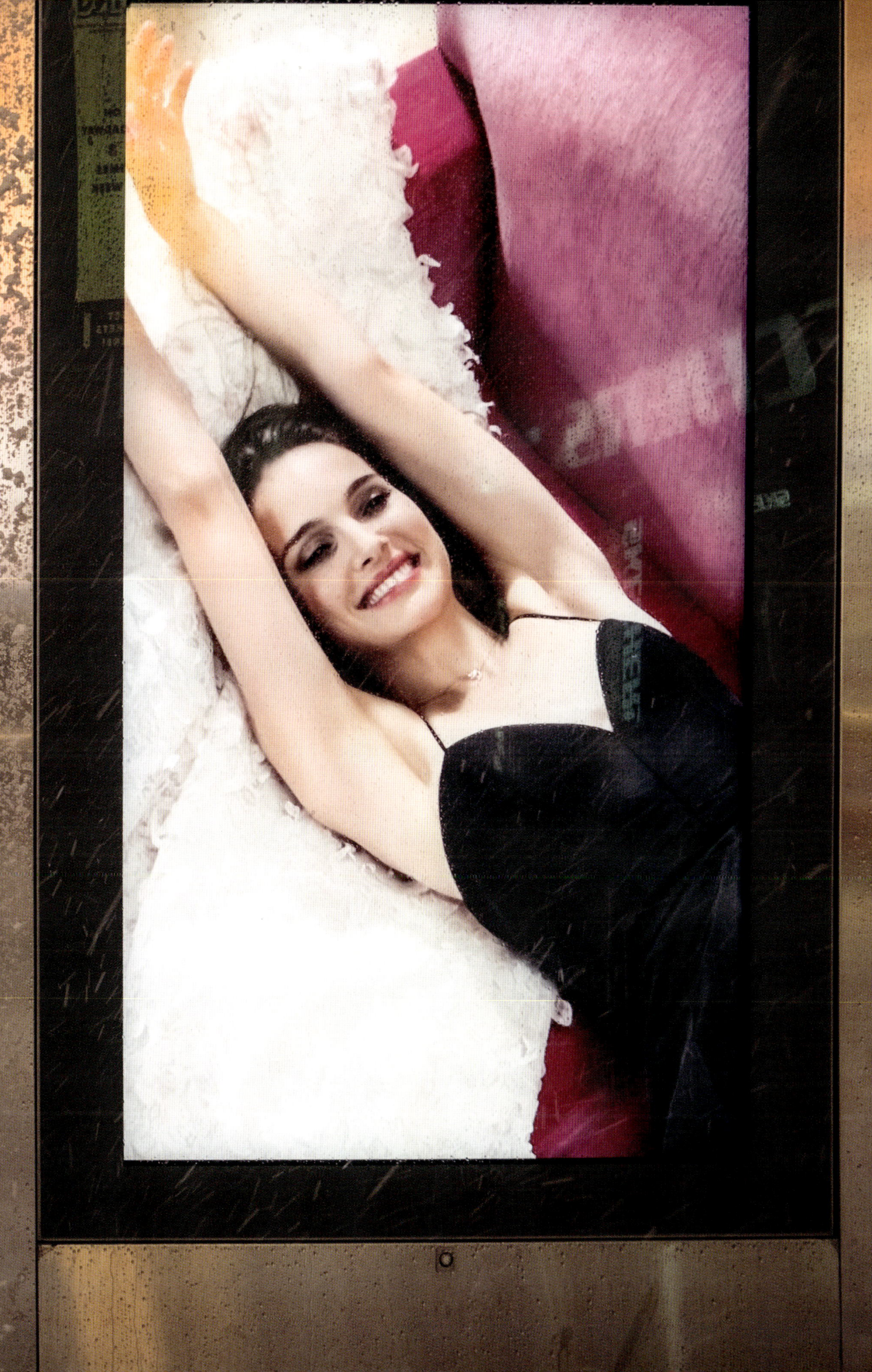

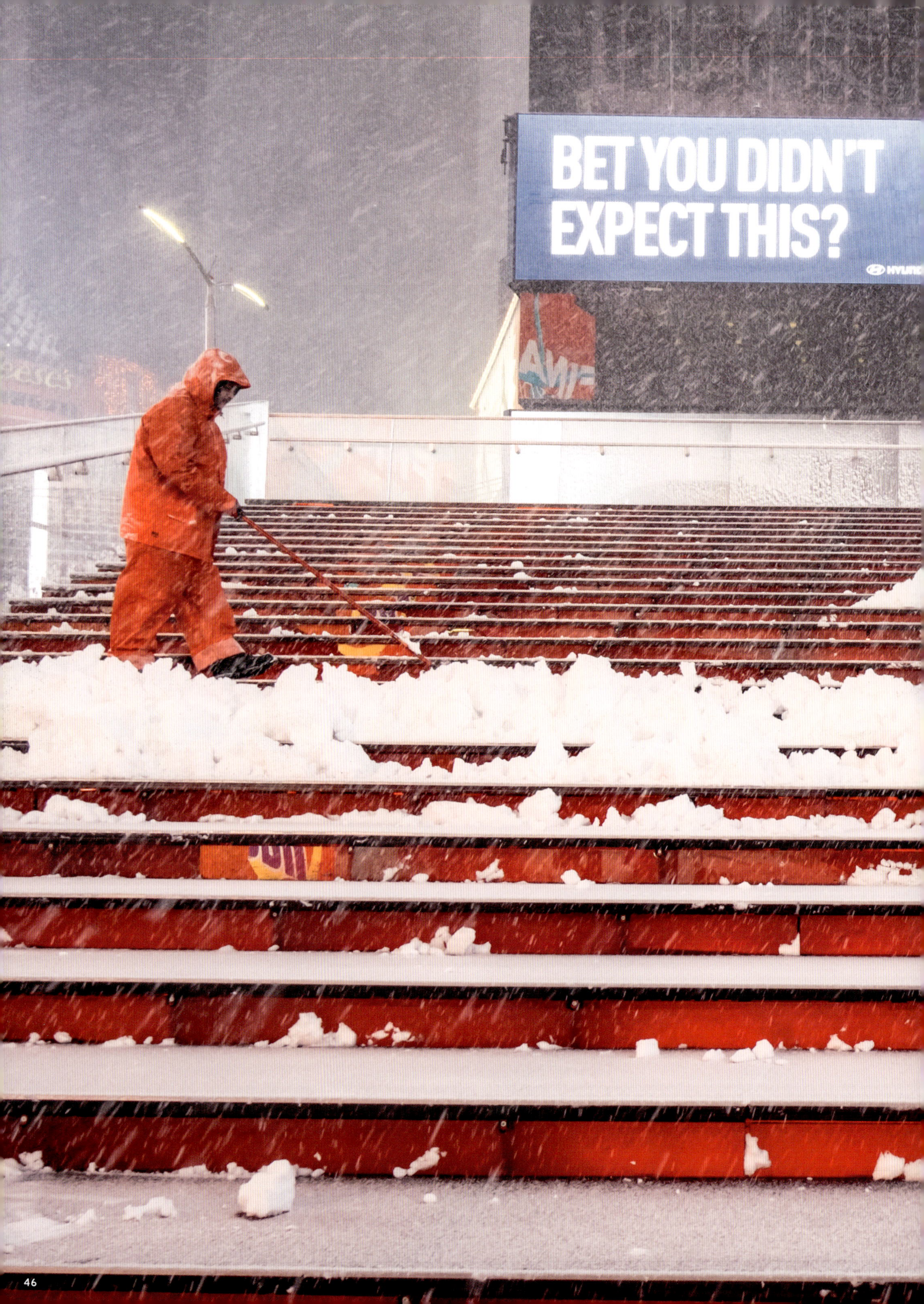

BET YOU DIDN'T
EXPECT THIS?
HYUNDAI

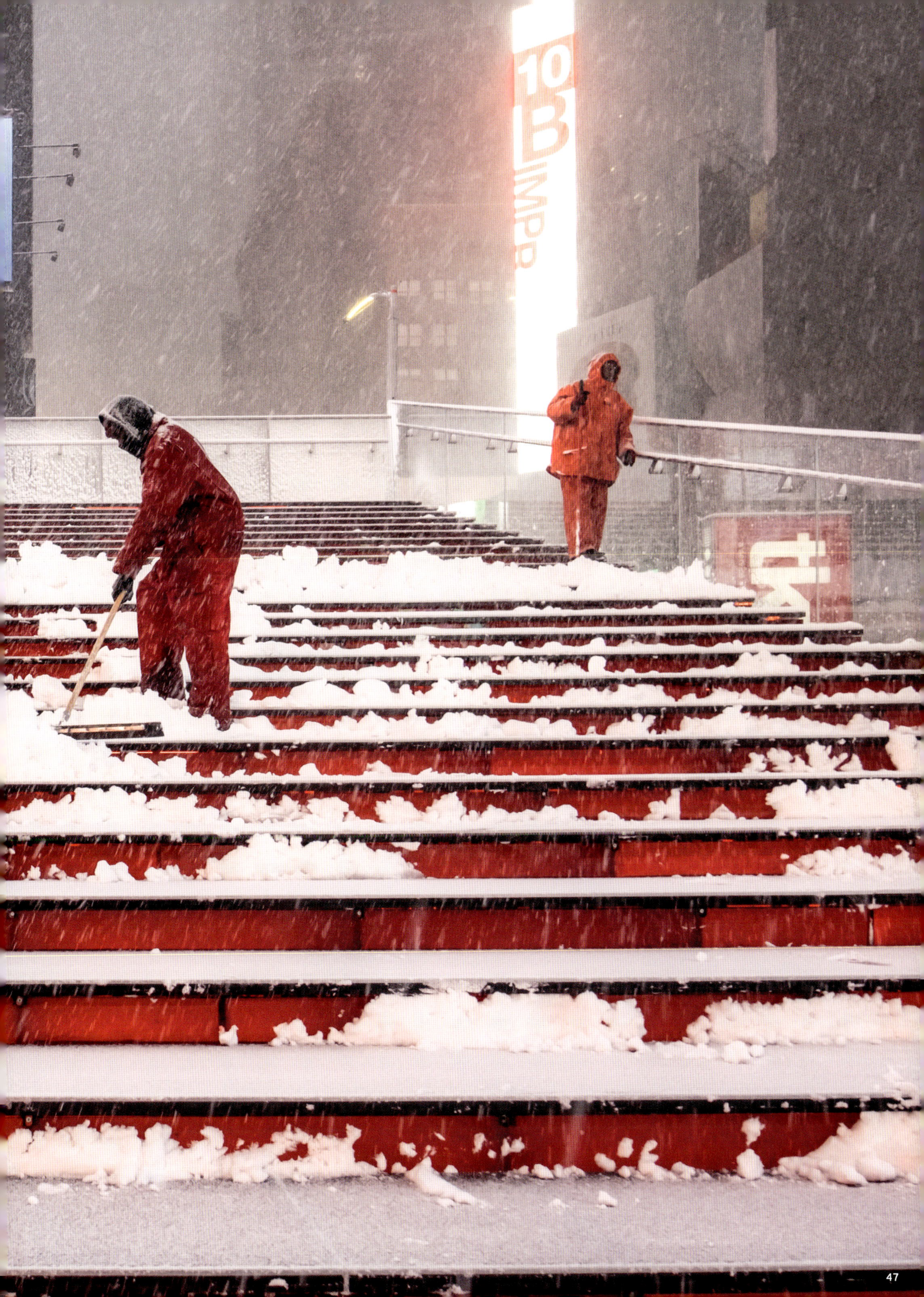

10
B
IMPR

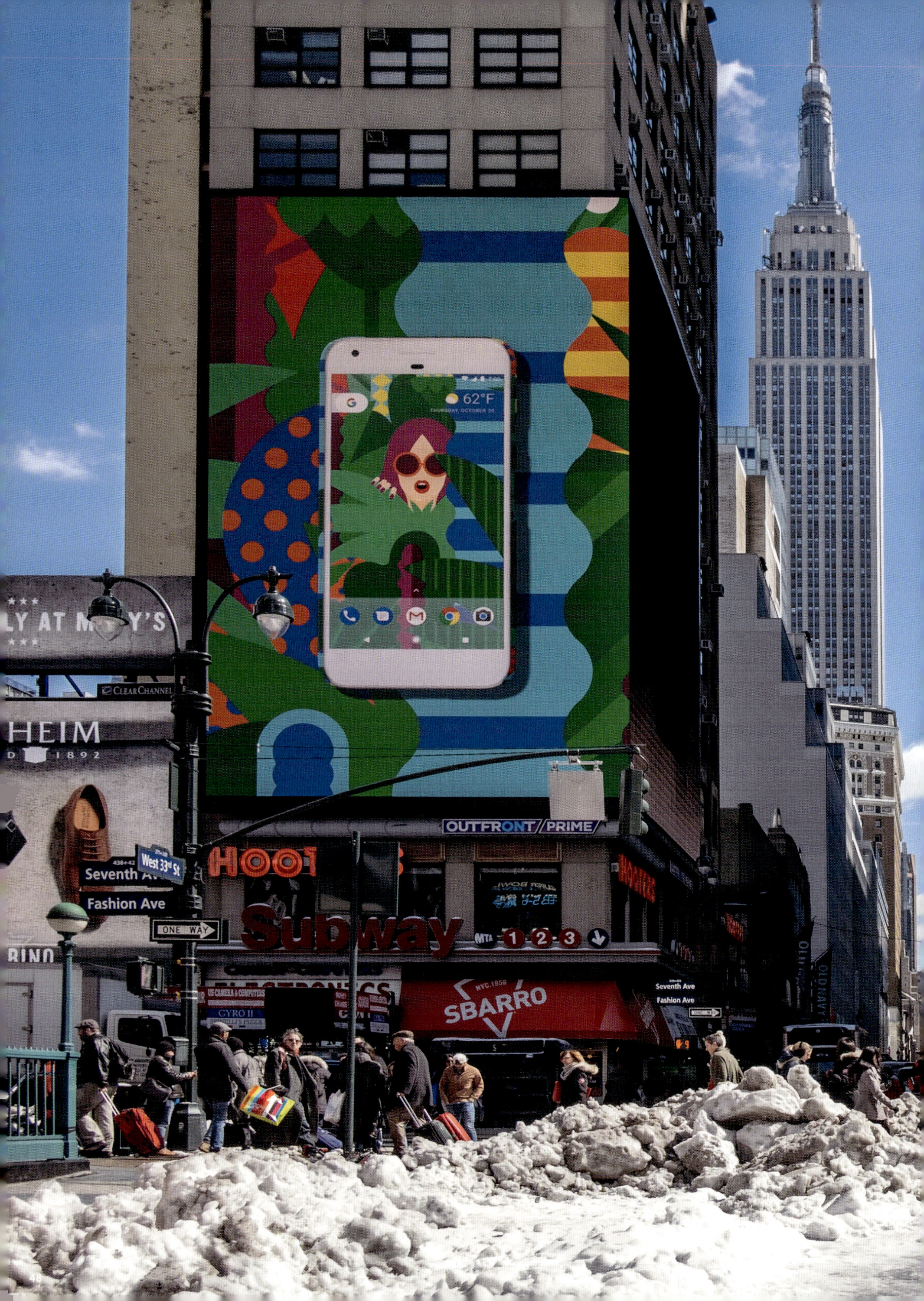

62°F
THURSDAY, OCTOBER 20
Seventh Av
Fashion Ave
West 33rd St
ONE WAY
HOOT
Subway
SBARRO
NYC 1956
OUTFRONT/PRIME
CLEAR CHANNEL
HEIM
1892
LY AT MACY'S
MTA 1 2 3
US CAMERA & COMPUTERS
GYRO II
ELECTRONICS
OLD NAVY

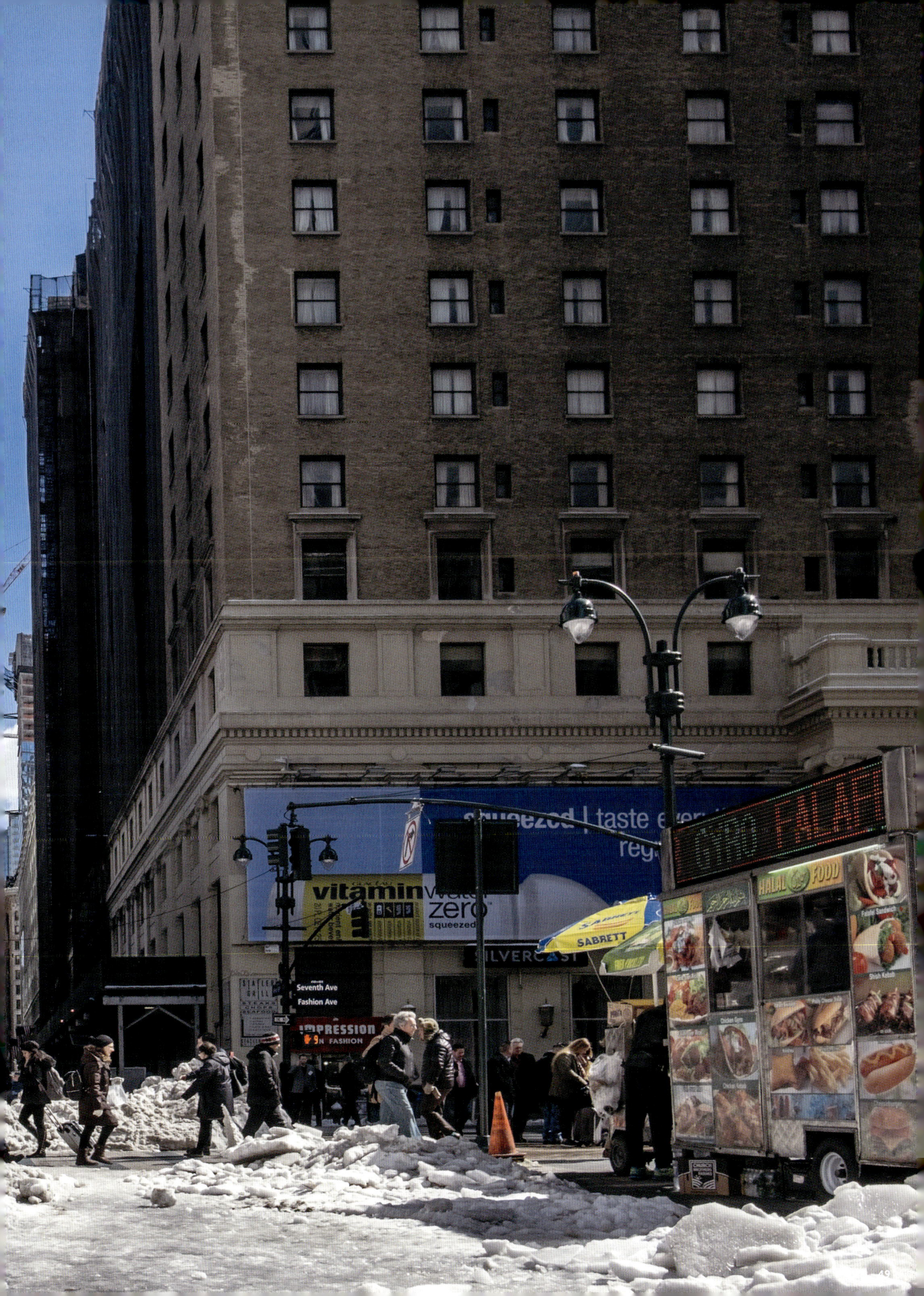

GYRO FALAF
HALAL FOOD
Falafel Sandwich
Shish Kabob
Chicken Gyro
Chicken Kebab
vitamin
water
zero
squeezed
squeezed | taste eve
reg
SABRETT
SILVERCAST
Seventh Ave
Fashion Ave
IMPRESSION
IN FASHION
STATLER
GRILL
STEAKS
CHOPS
SEAFOOD

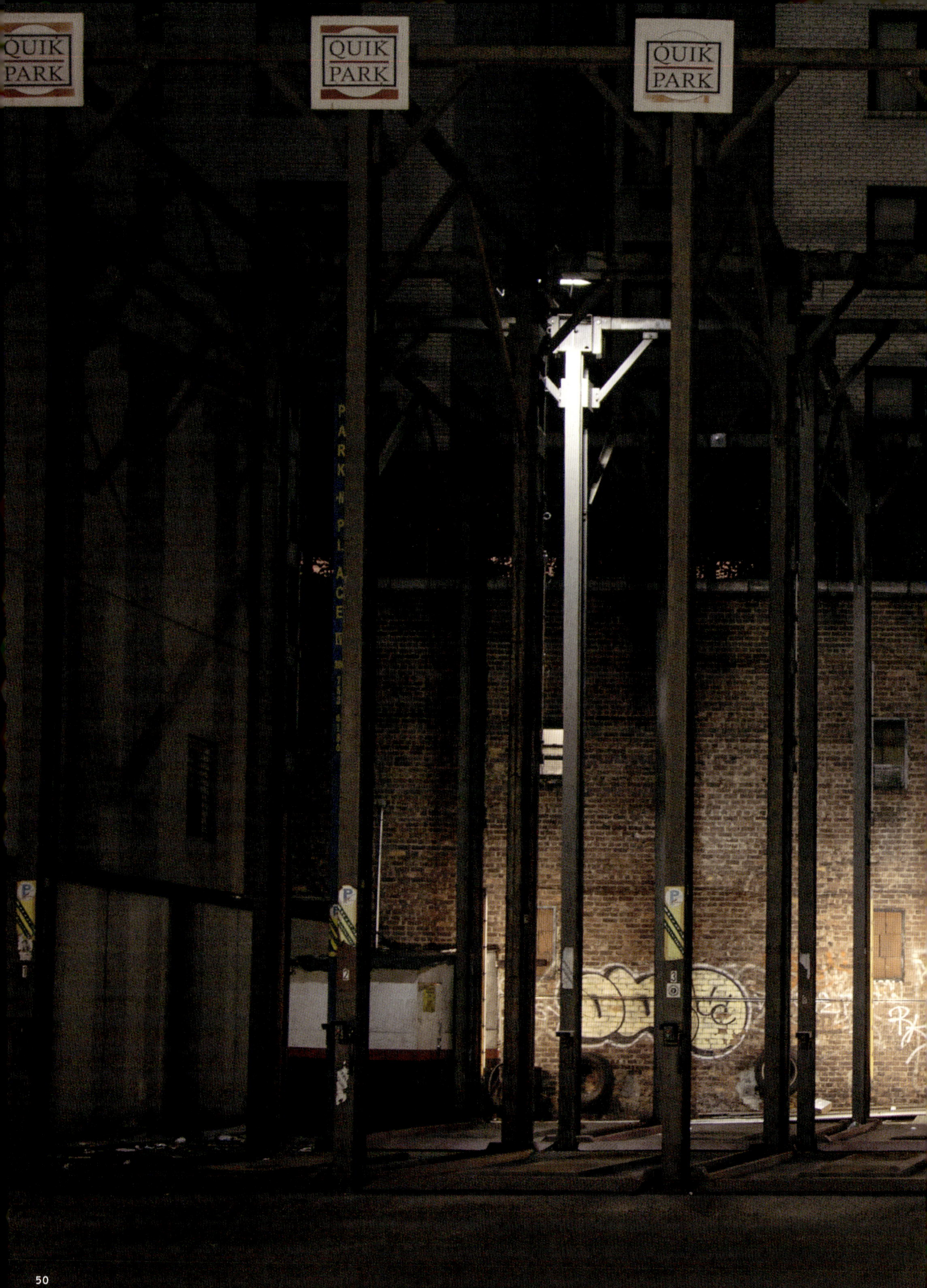

QUIK
PARK
QUIK
PARK
QUIK
PARK
PARK N PLACE

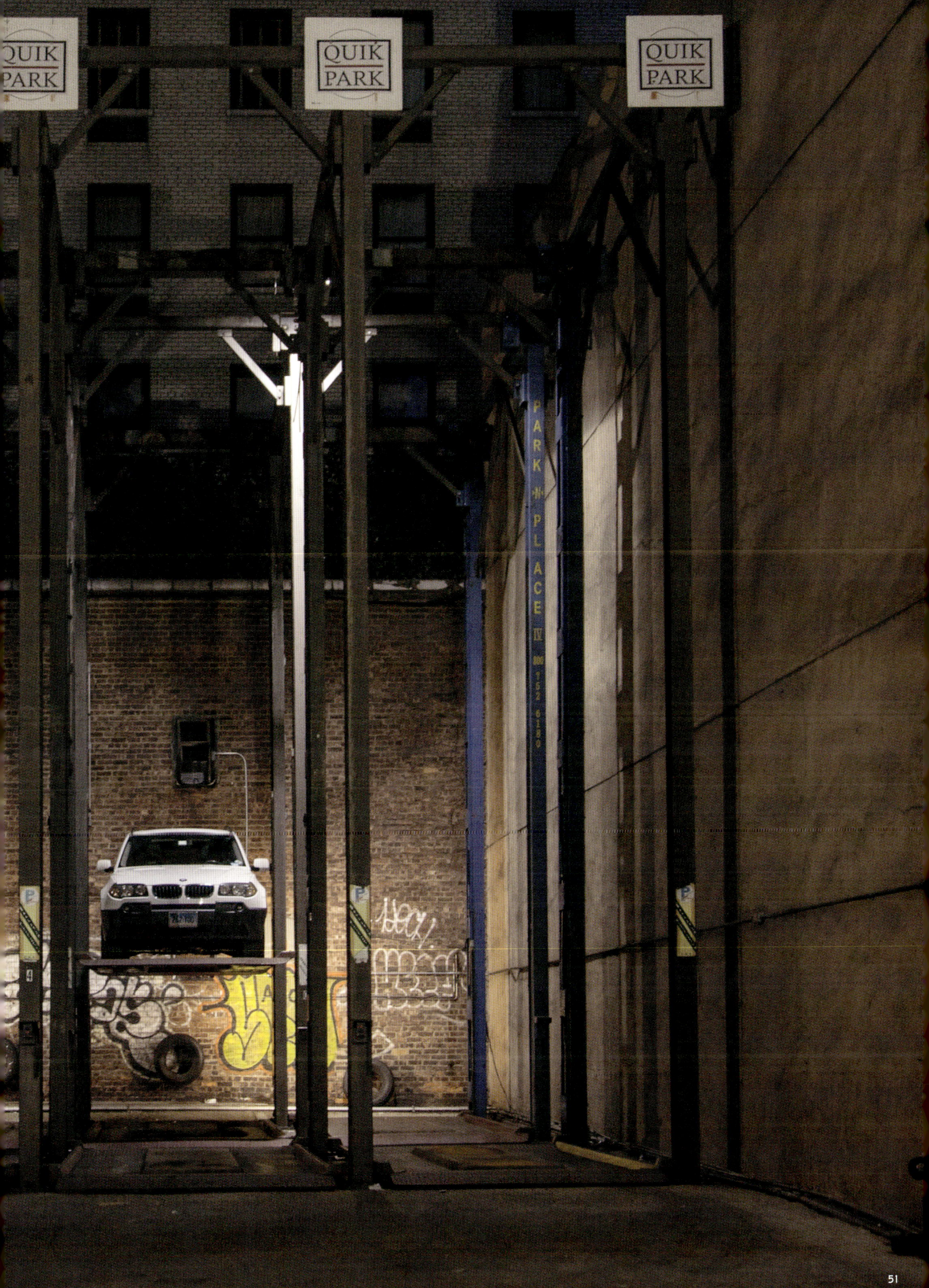

QUIK PARK
QUIK PARK
QUIK PARK
PARK PLACE IV
152
6180

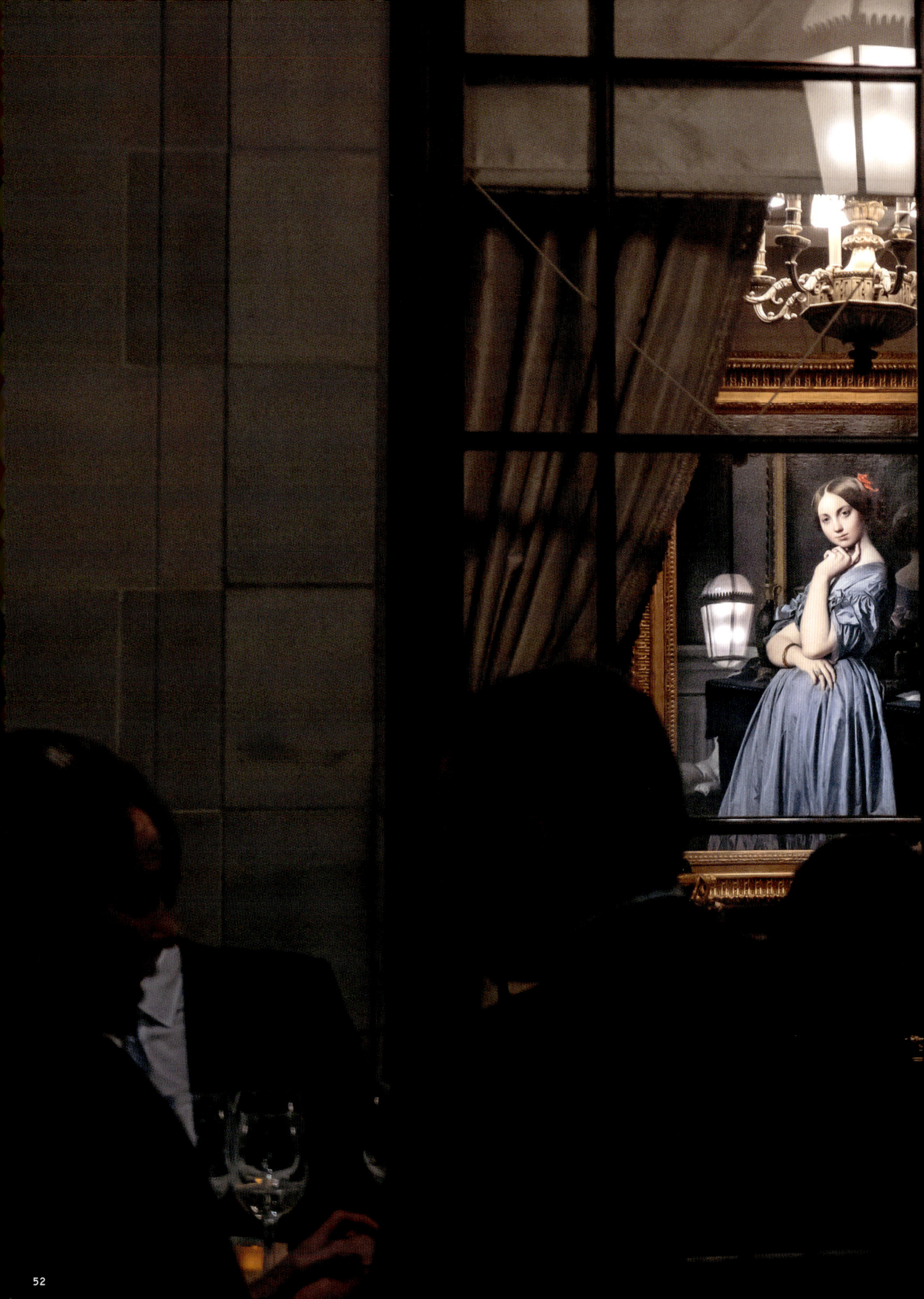

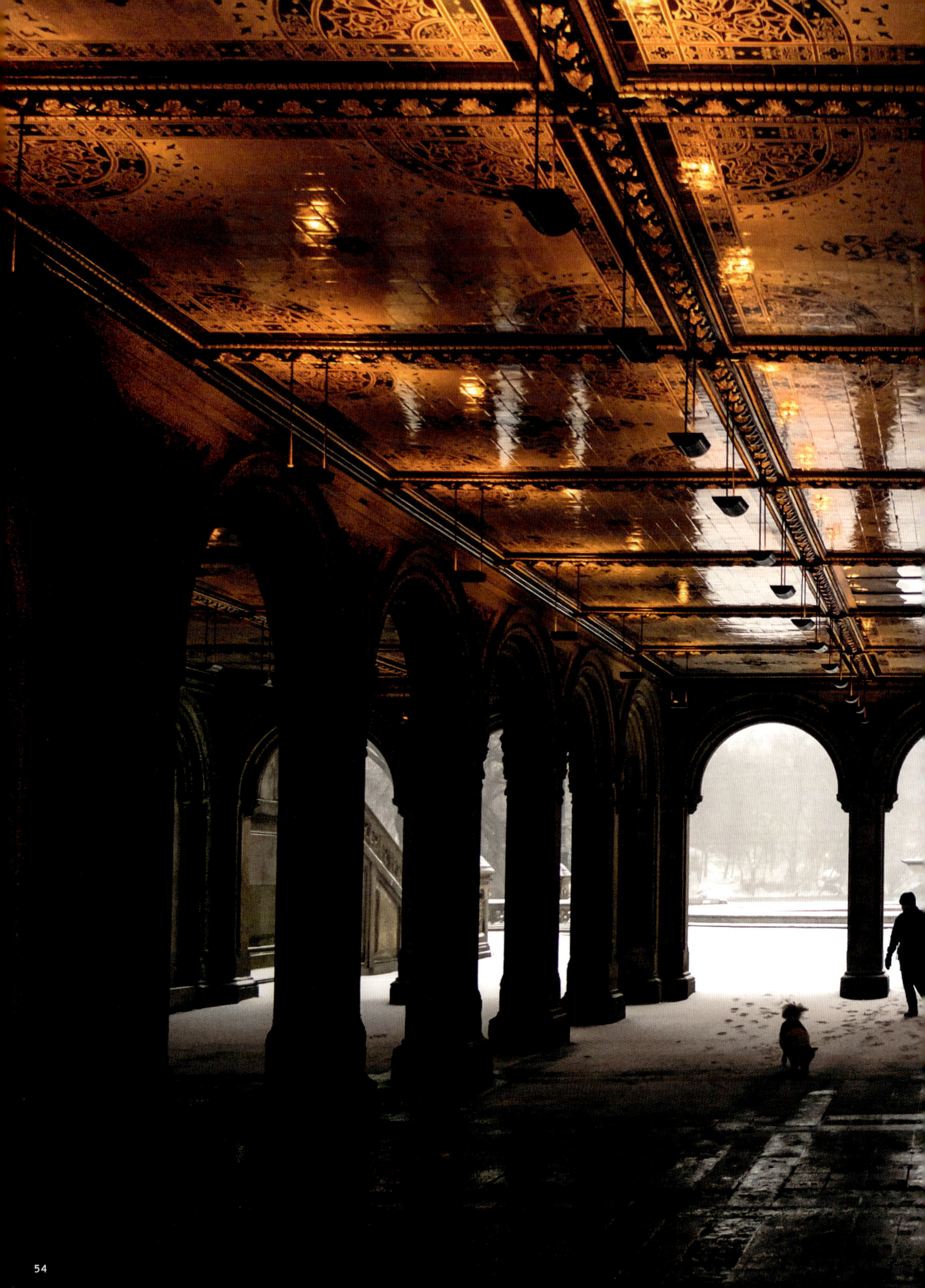

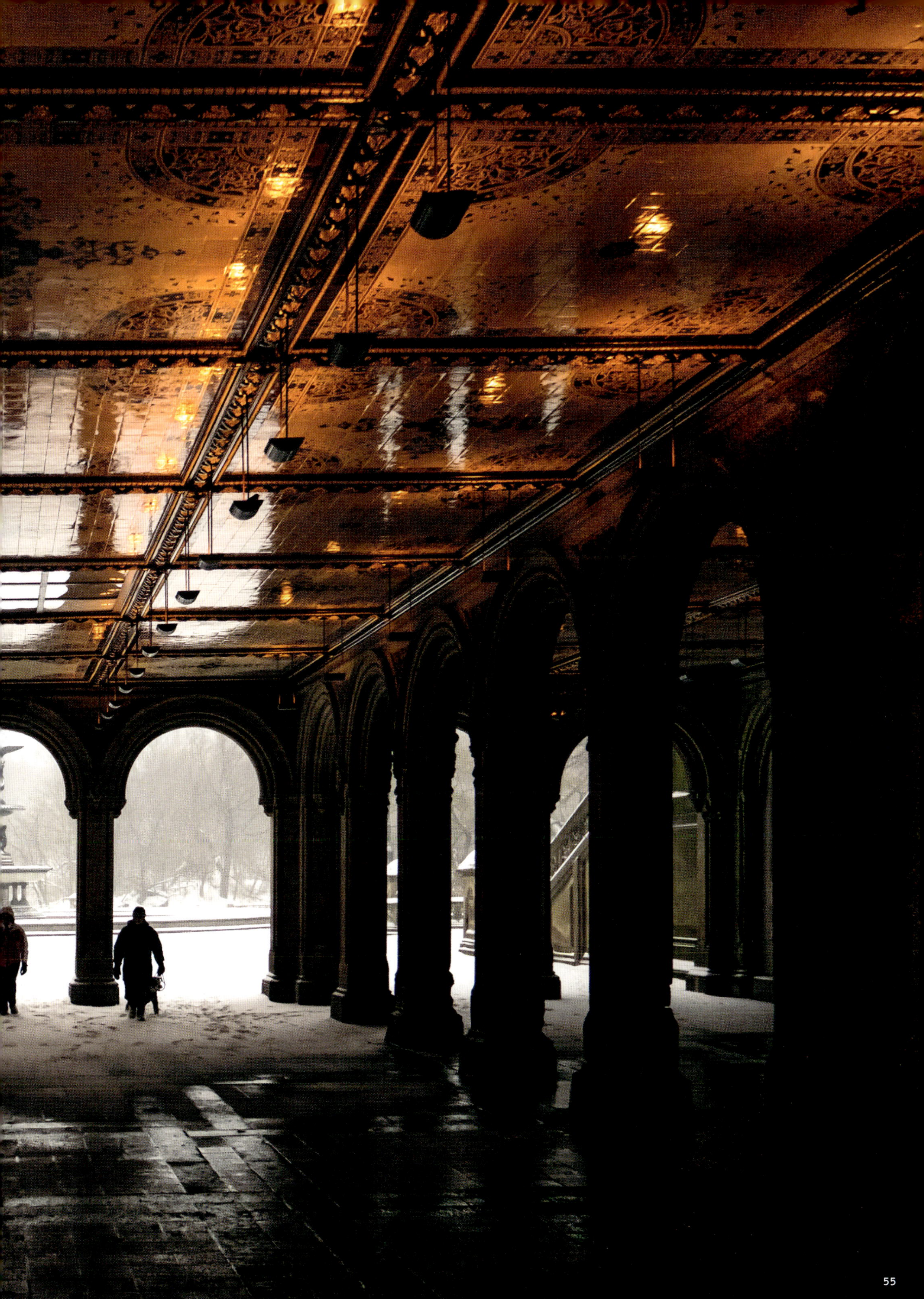

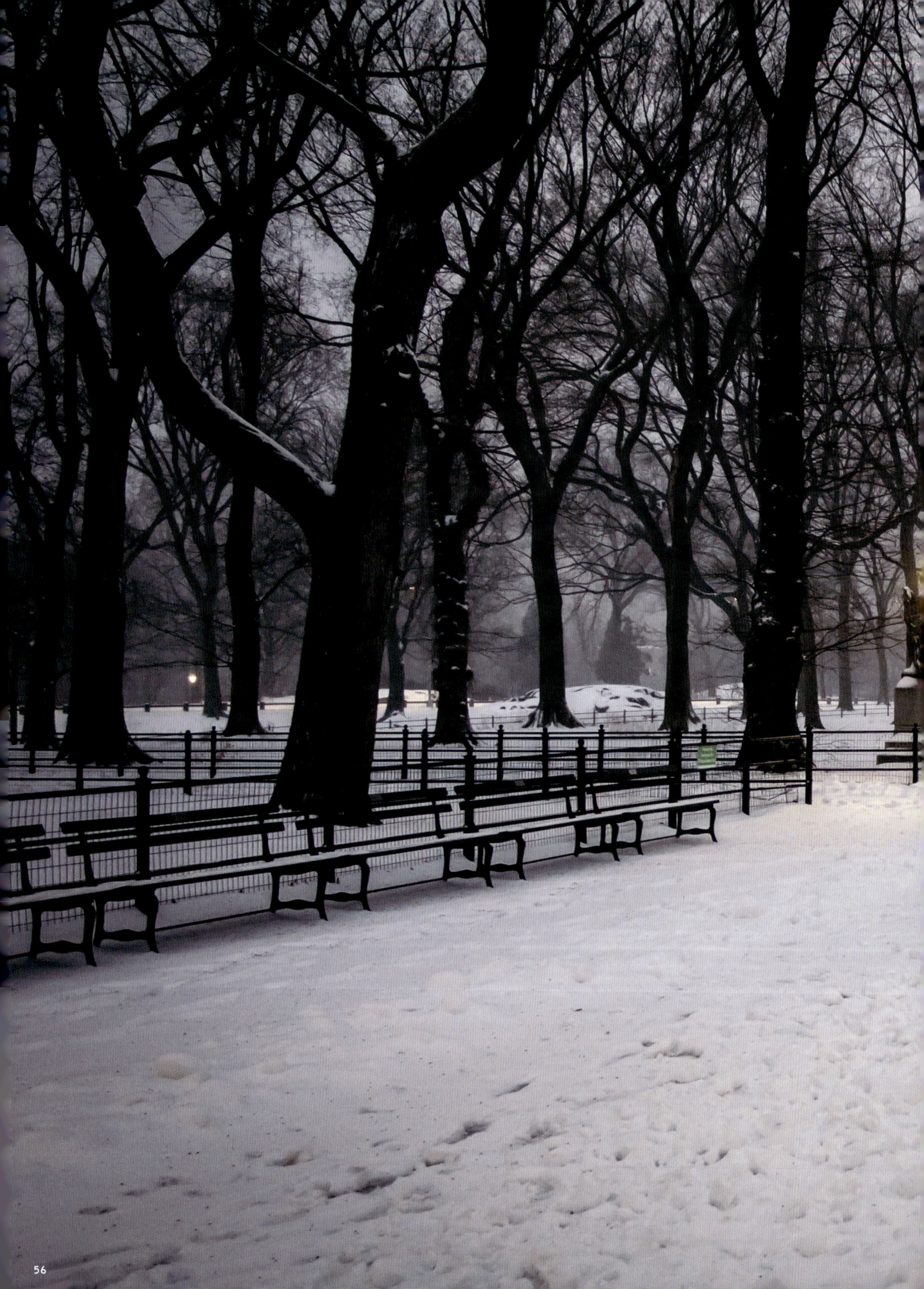

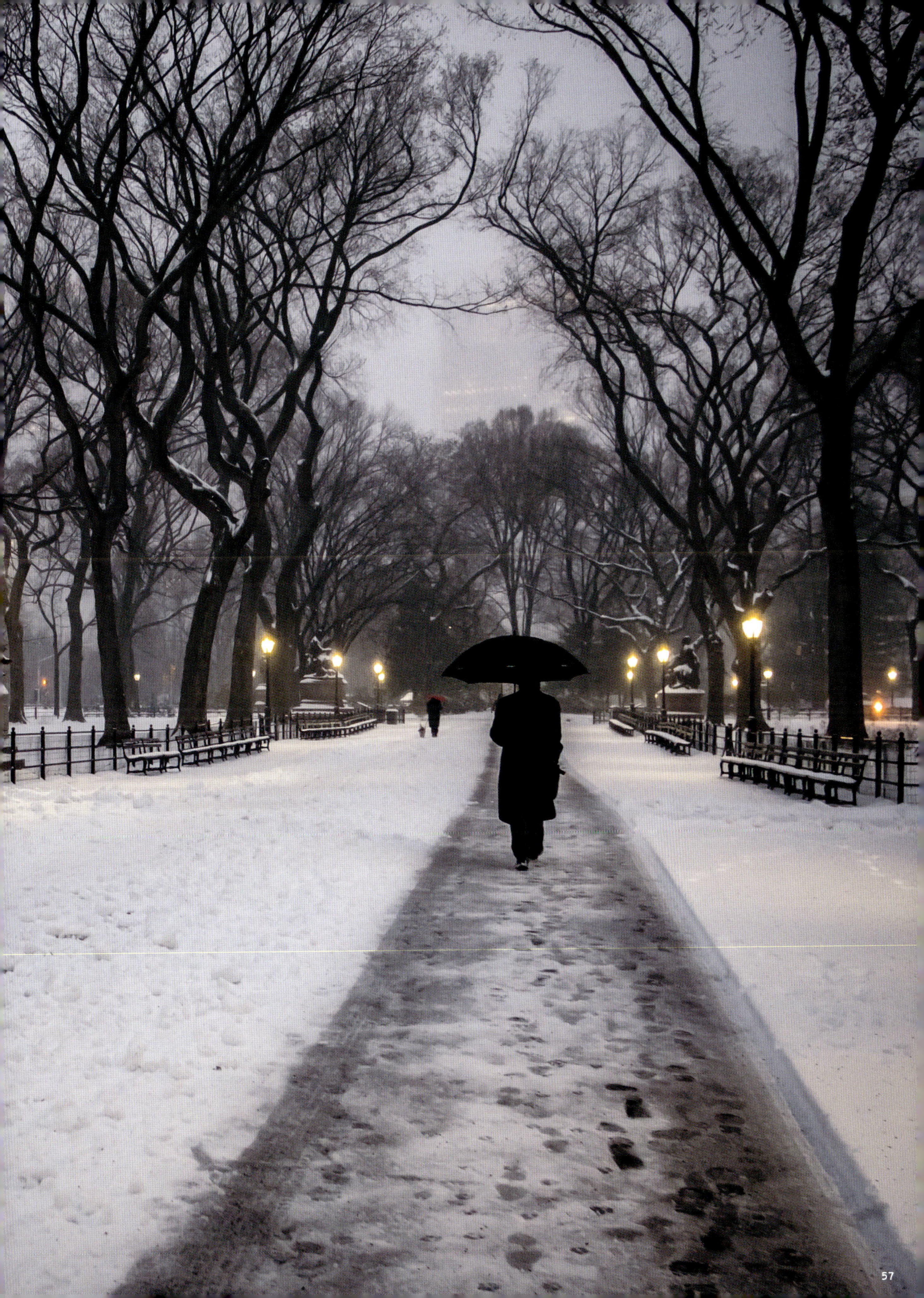

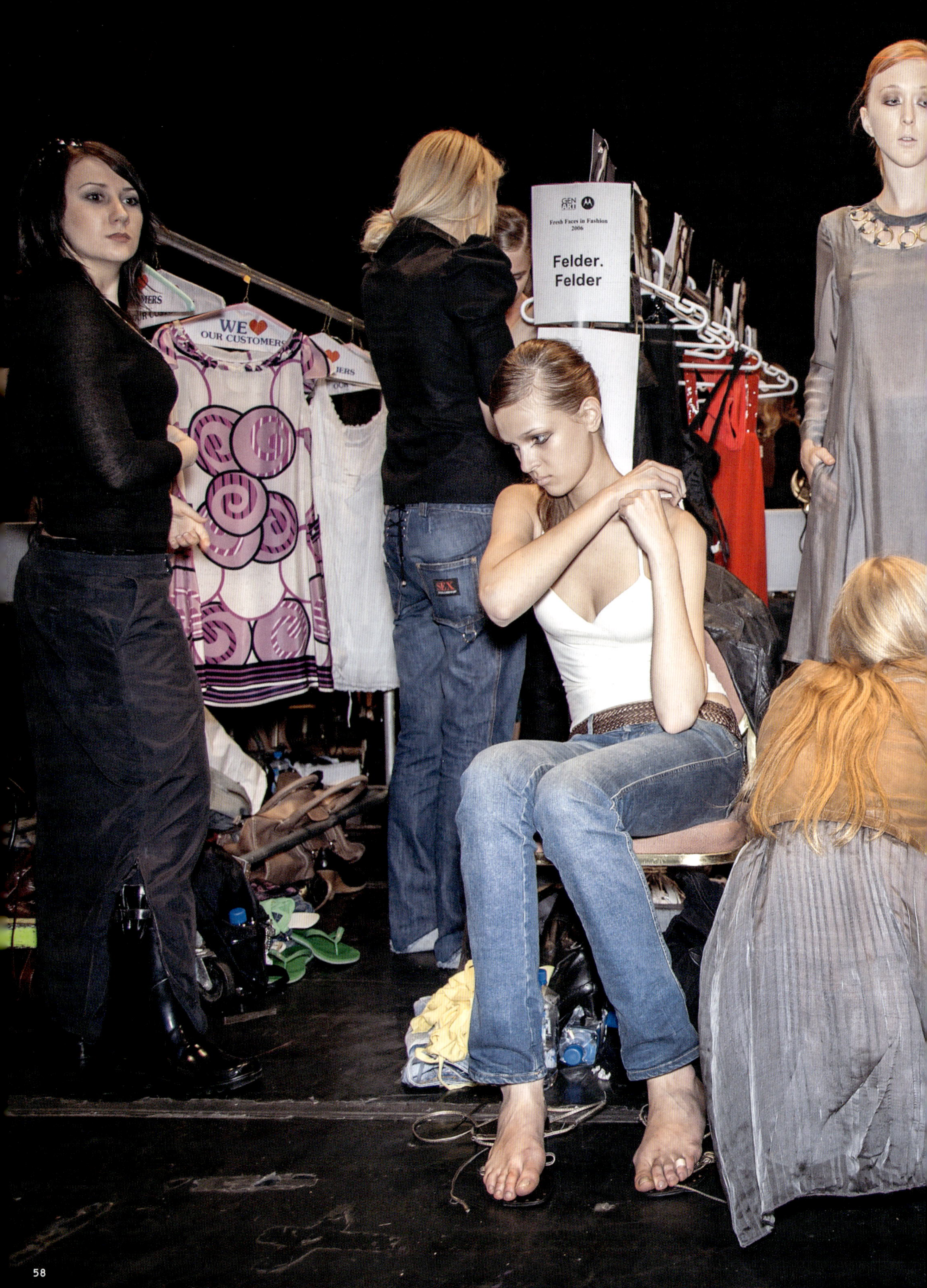
GEN
ART
Fresh Faces in Fashion
2006
Felder.
Felder
WE ♥ OUR CUSTOMERS

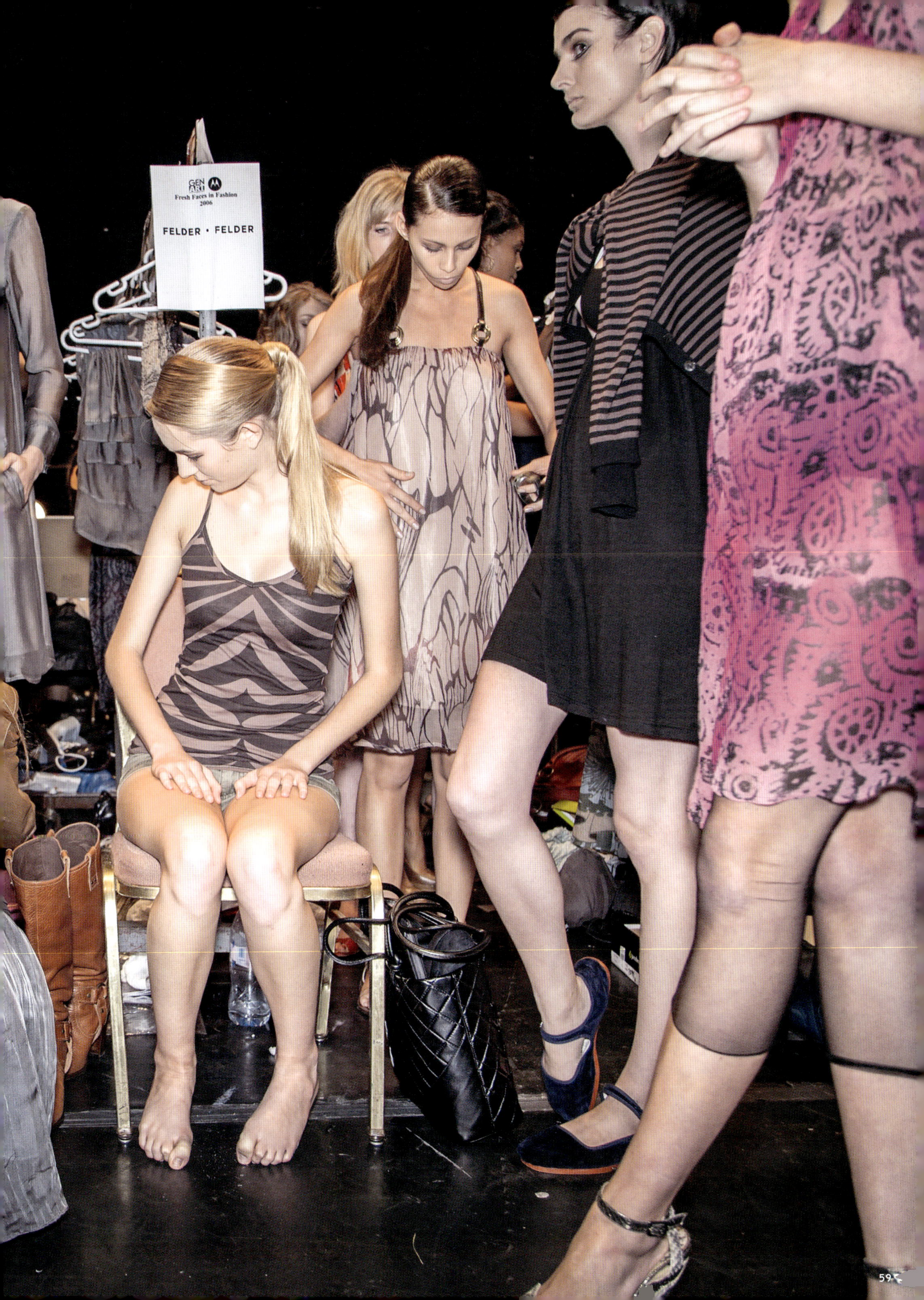

GEN ART
Fresh Faces in Fashion
2006
FELDER • FELDER

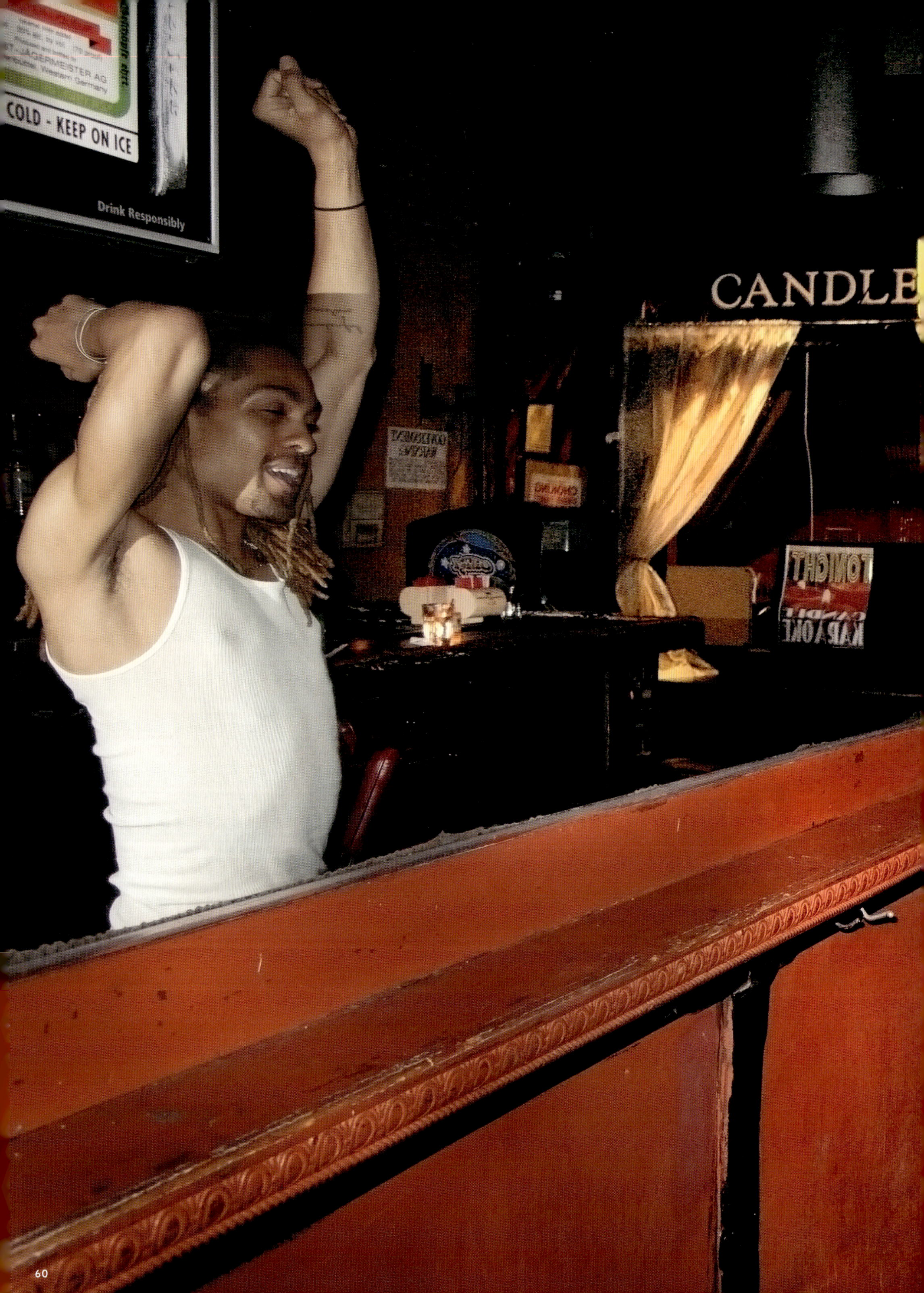
COLD - KEEP ON ICE
Drink Responsibly
CANDLE
TONIGHT

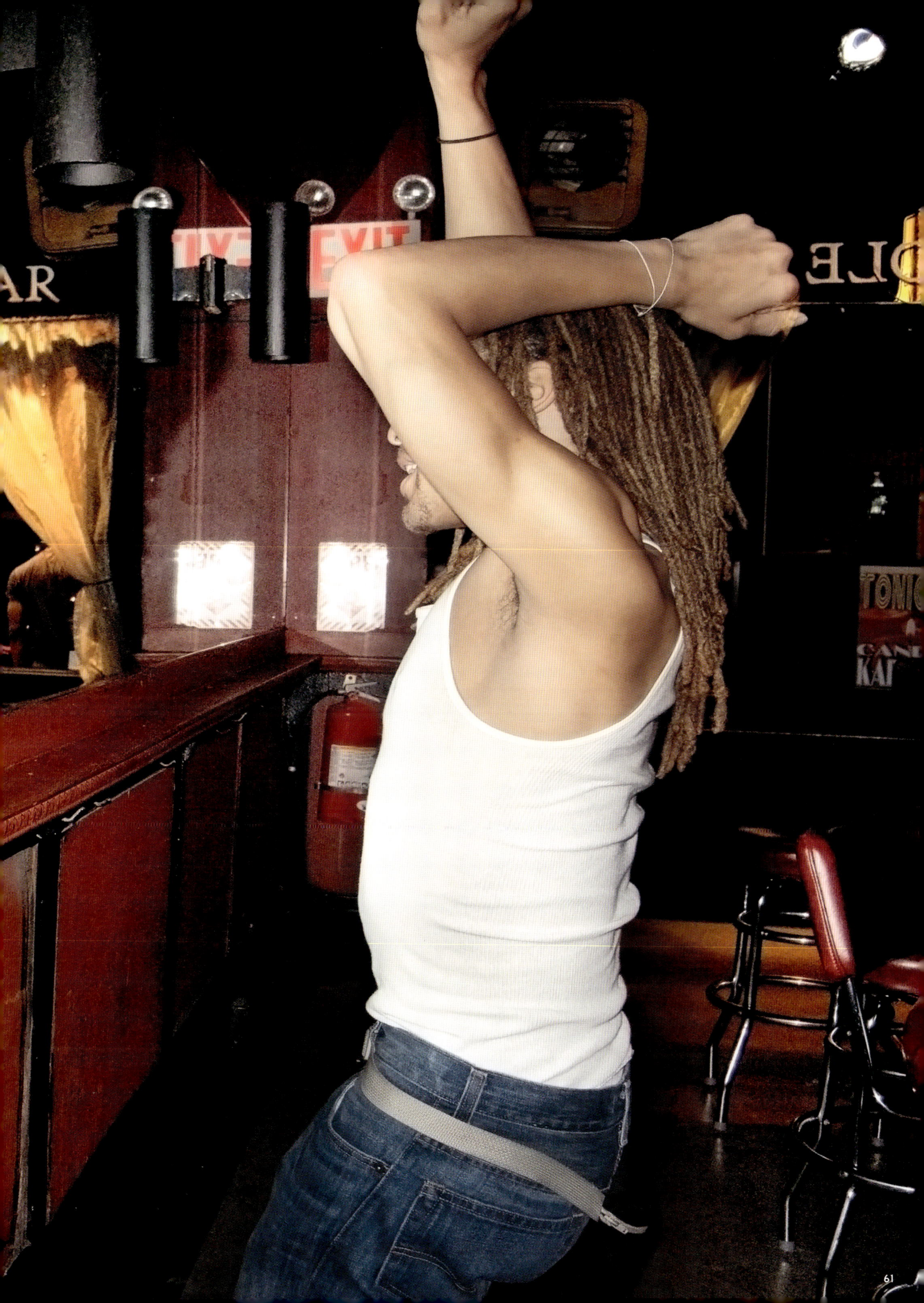
EXIT
EXIT
AR
TONI
KAT

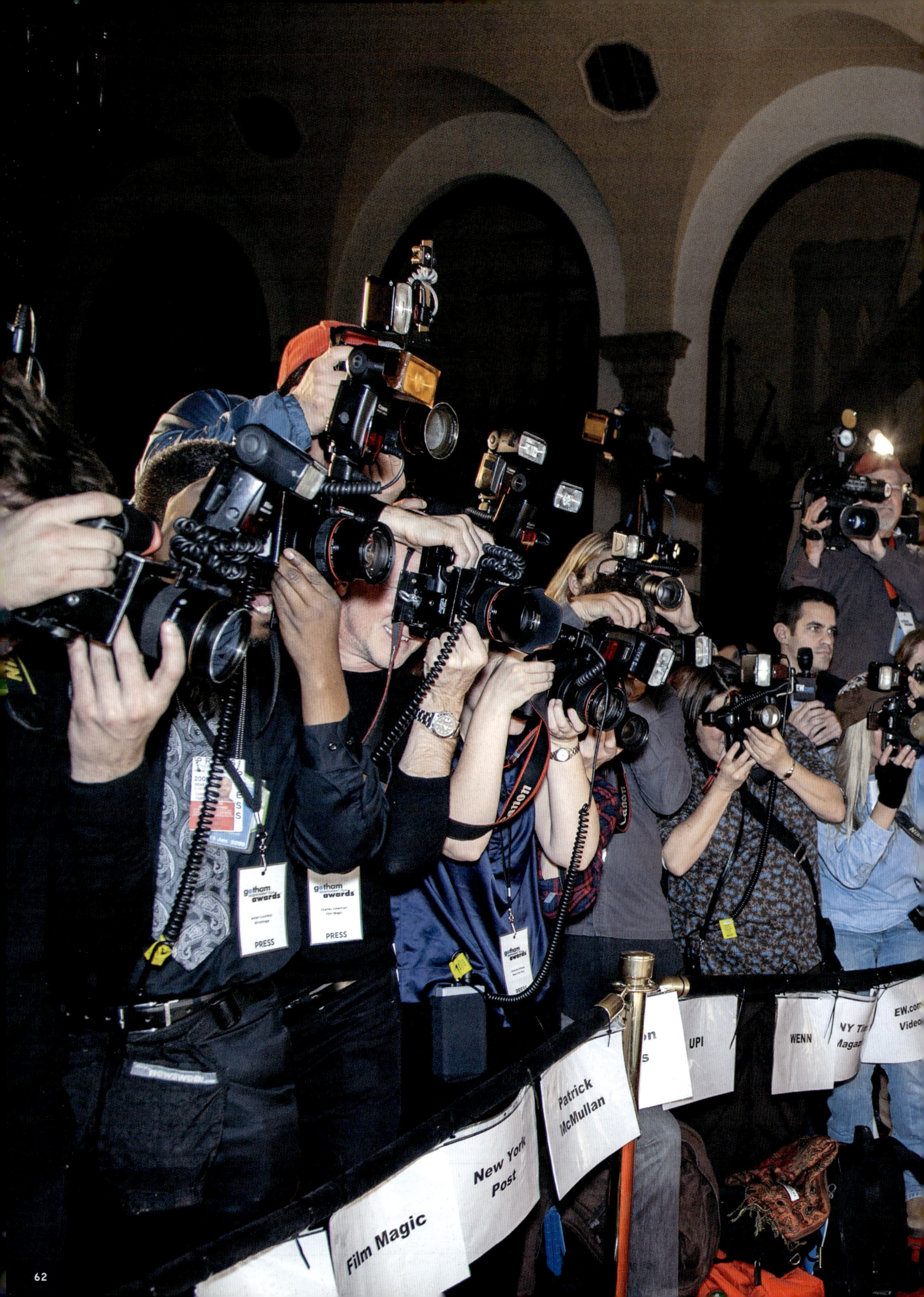

gotham awards
PRESS
gotham awards
PRESS
New York Post
Patrick McMullan
UPI
WENN
EW.com
Film Magic

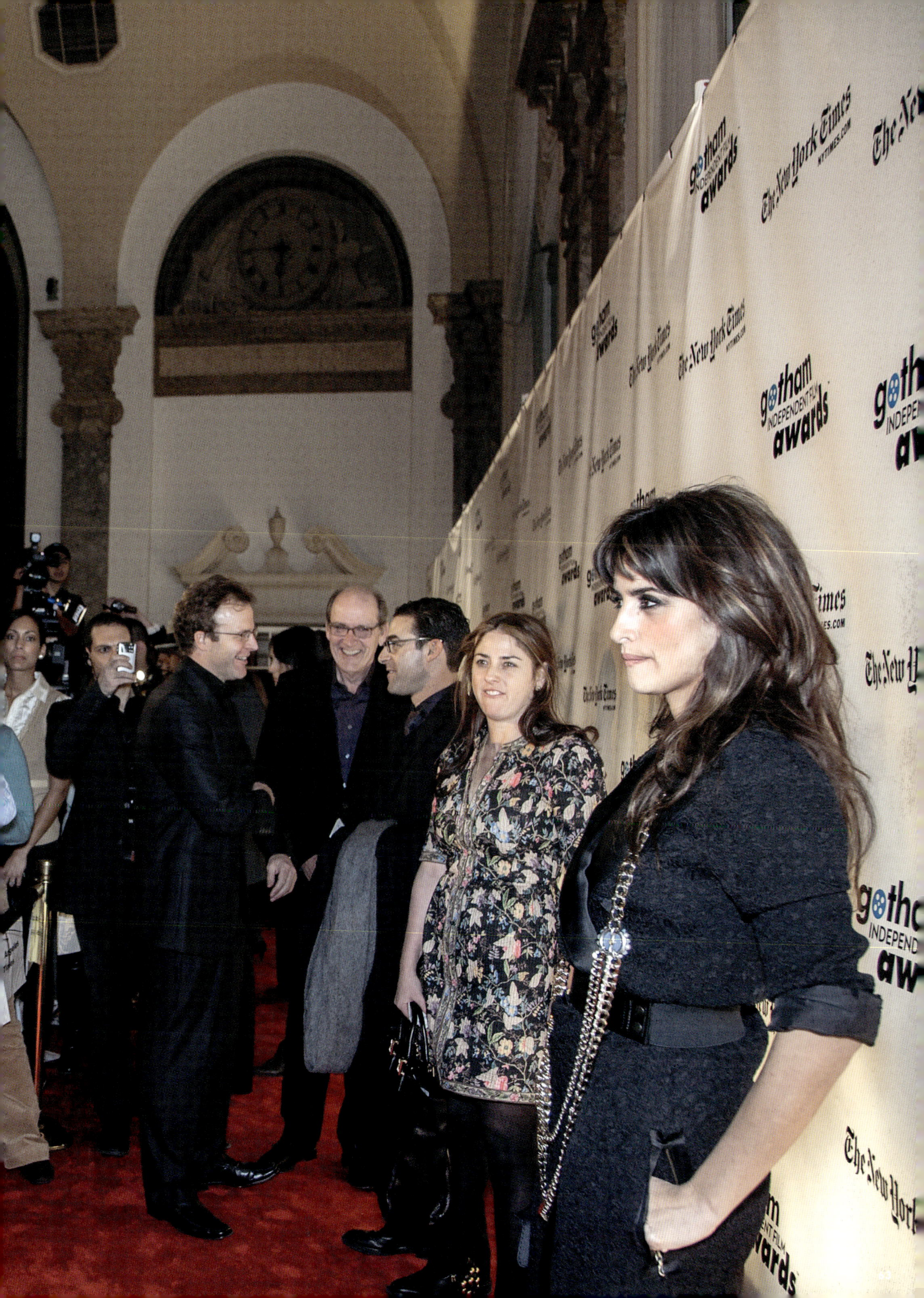

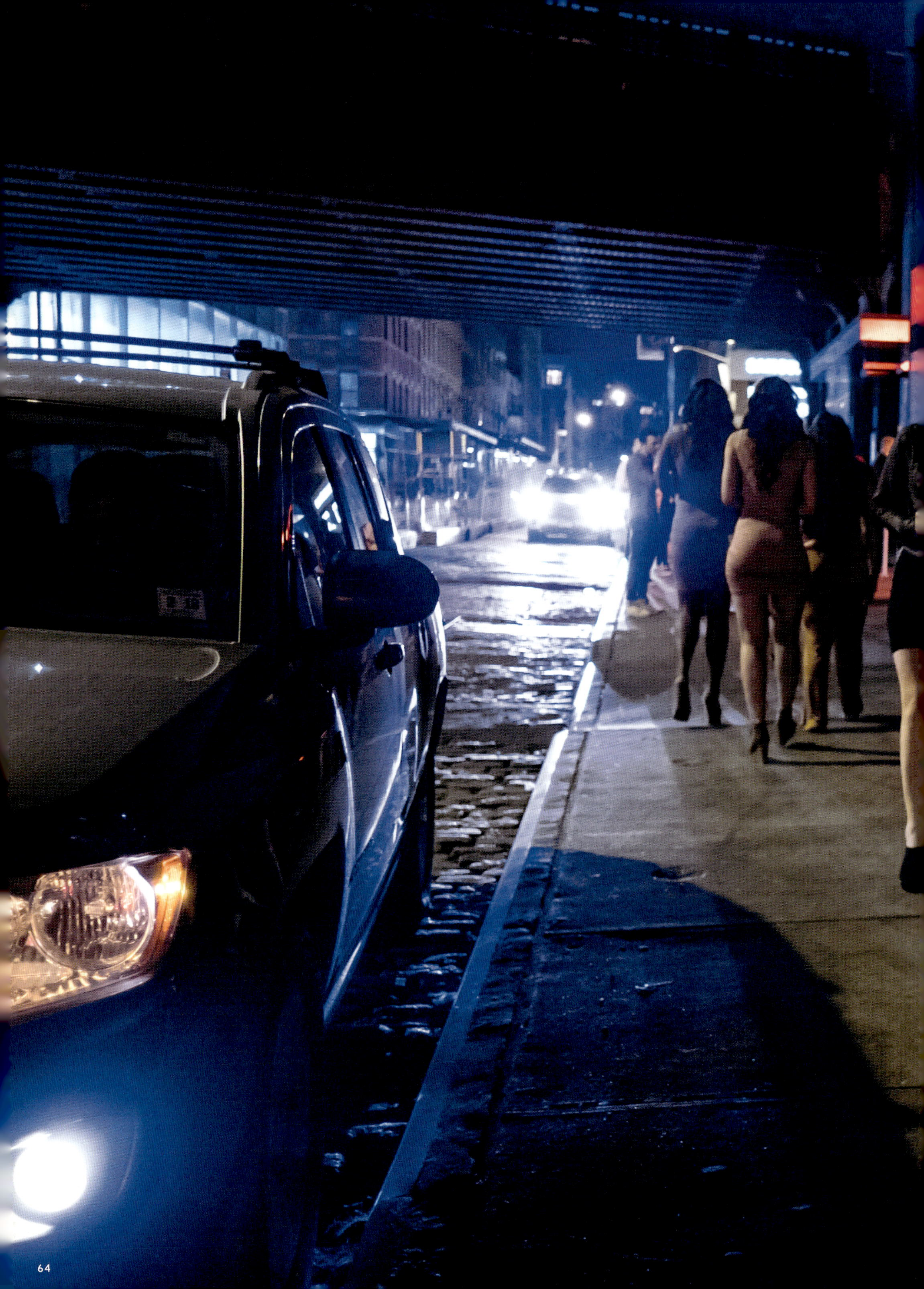

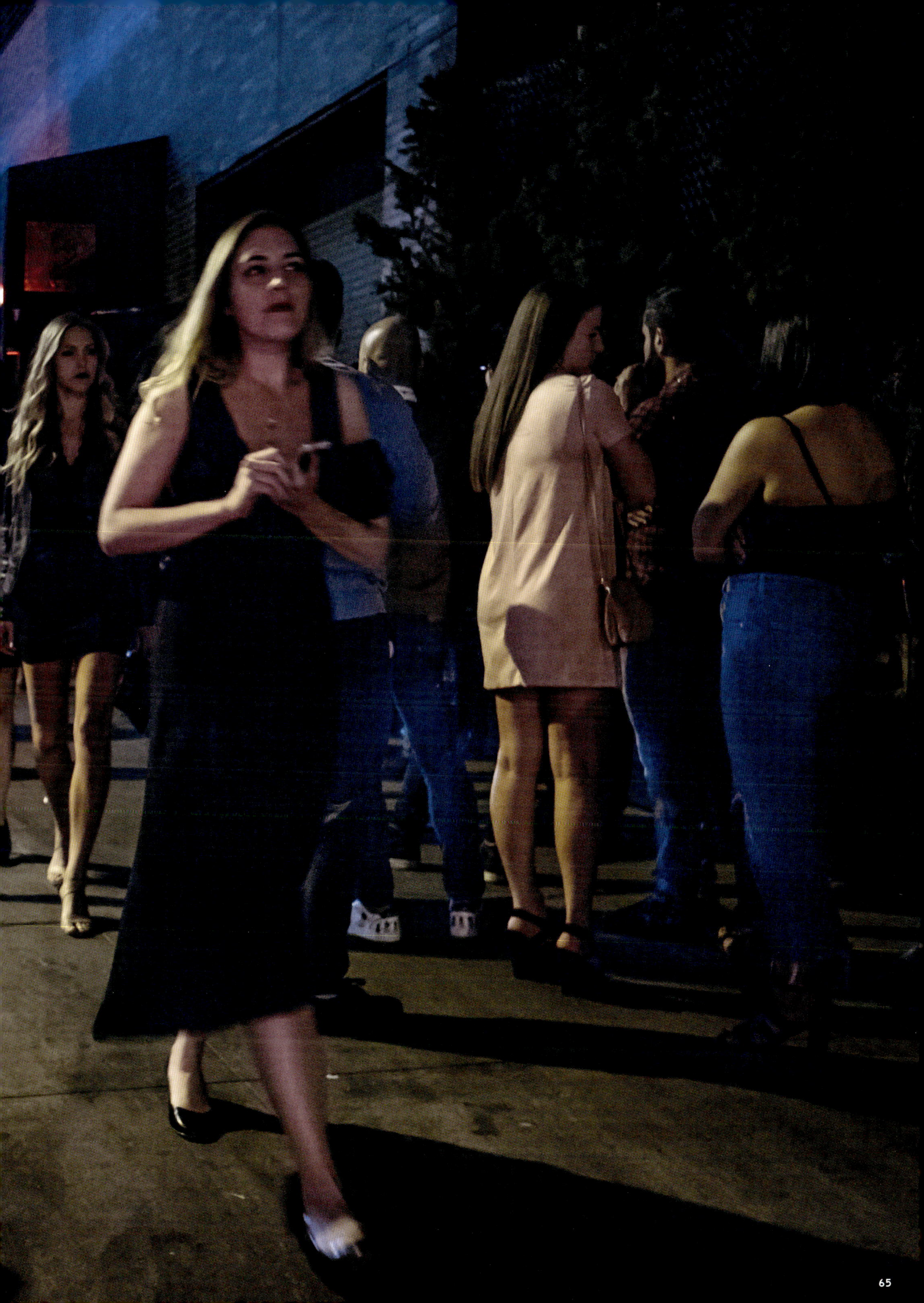

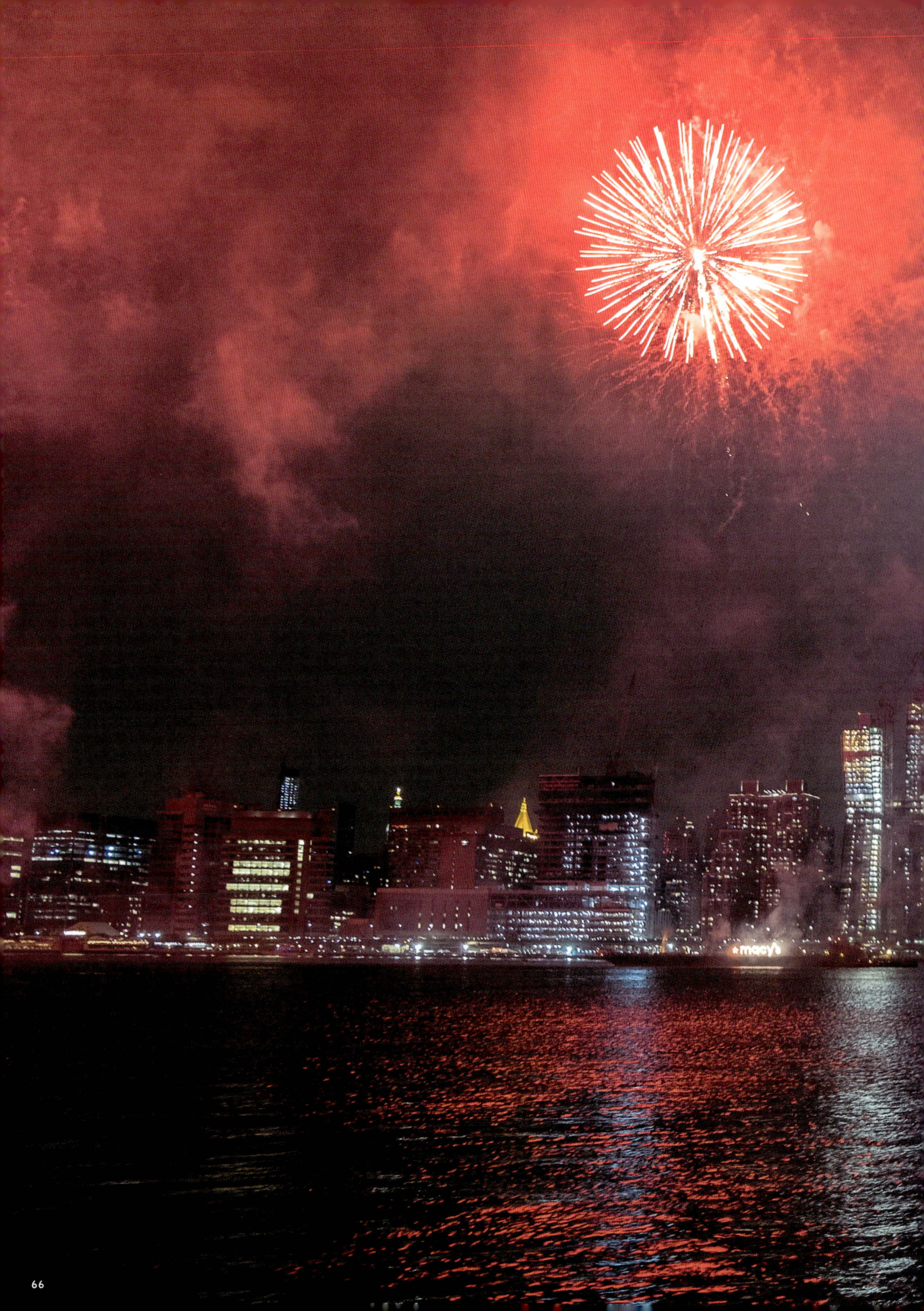

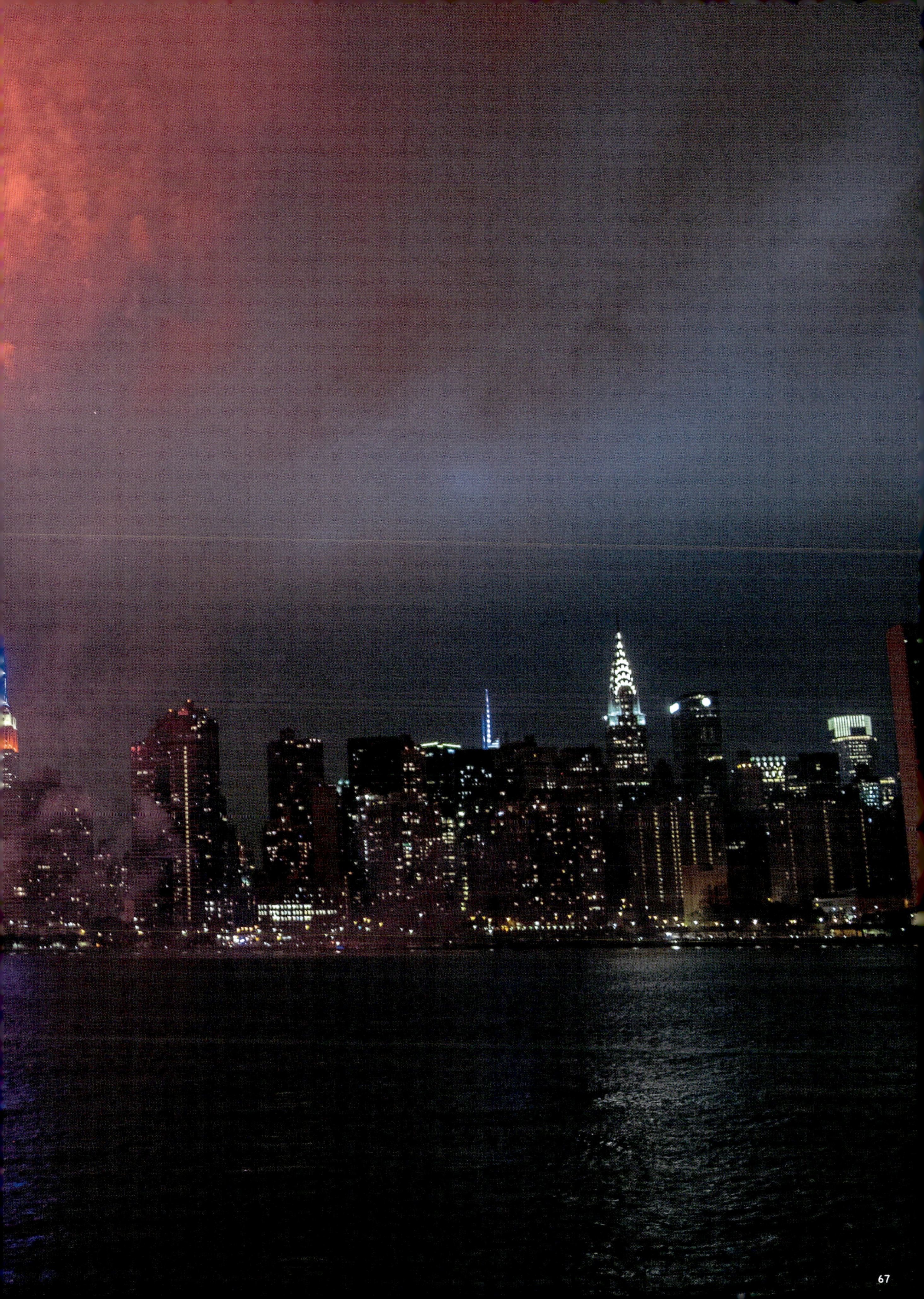

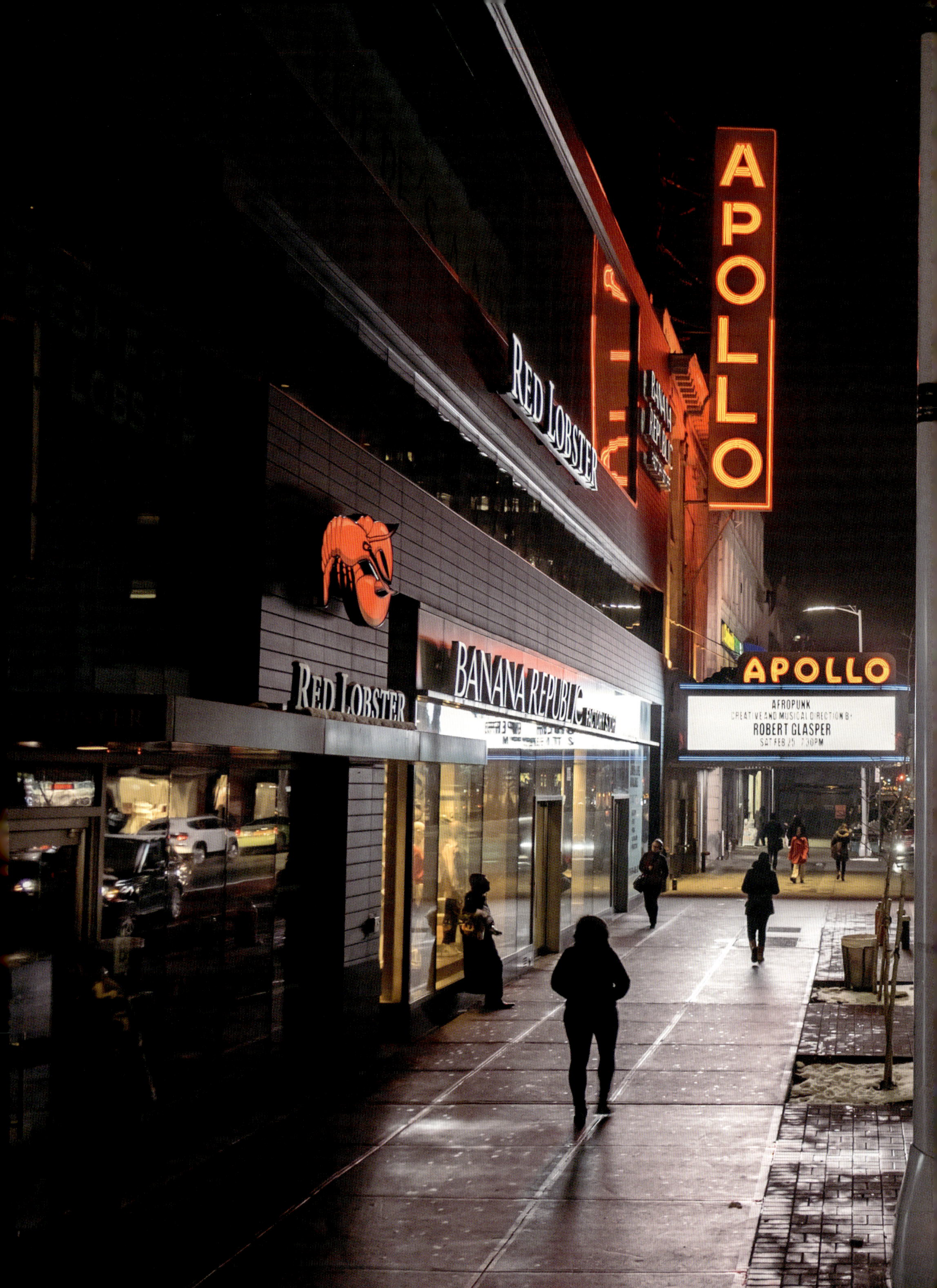

APOLLO
RED LOBSTER
BANANA REPUBLIC
APOLLO
AFROPUNK
CREATIVE AND MUSICAL DIRECTION BY
ROBERT GLASPER
SAT FEB 25 7:30PM

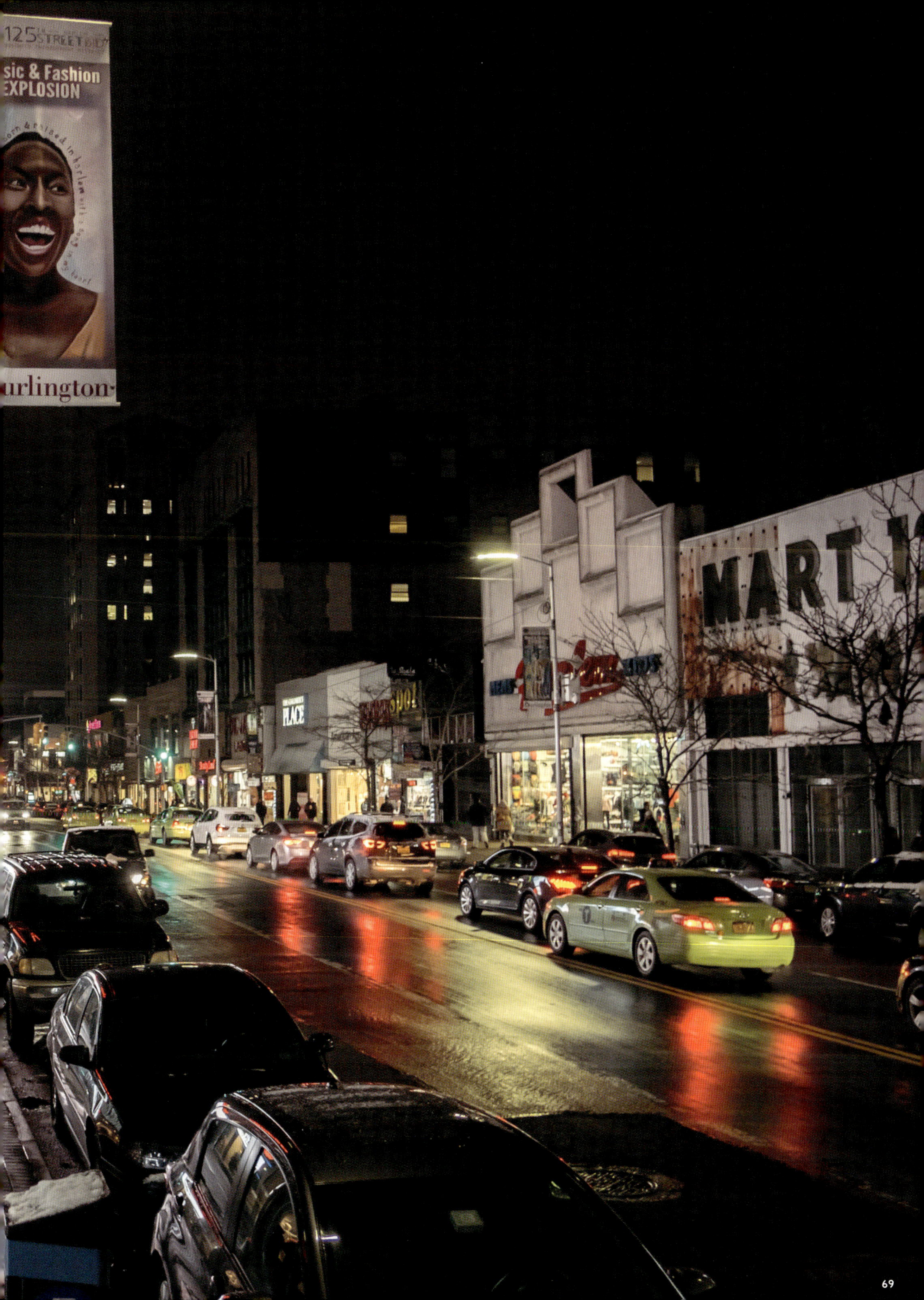
125TH STREET B.I.D
sic & Fashion
EXPLOSION
urlington
PLACE
MART

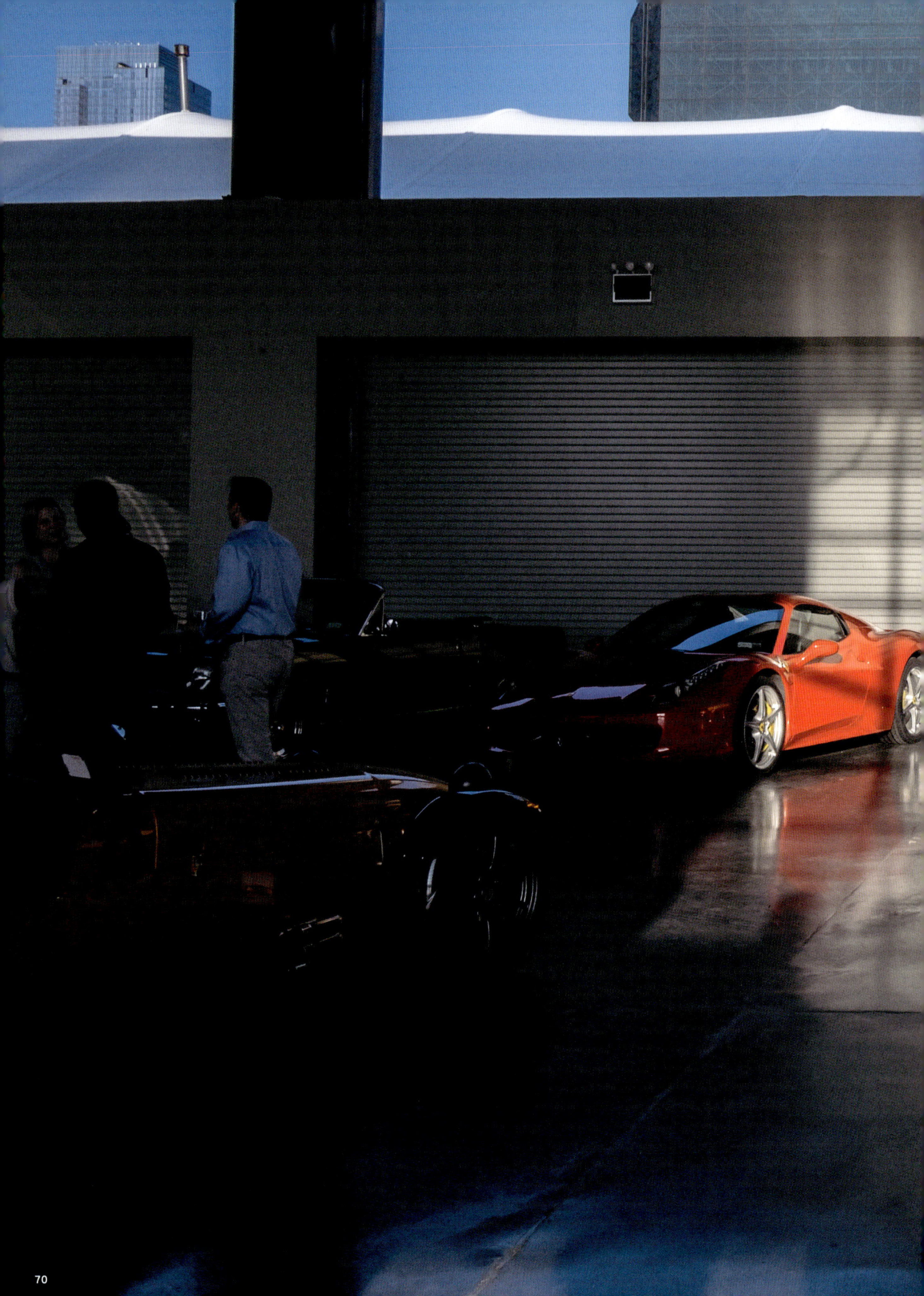

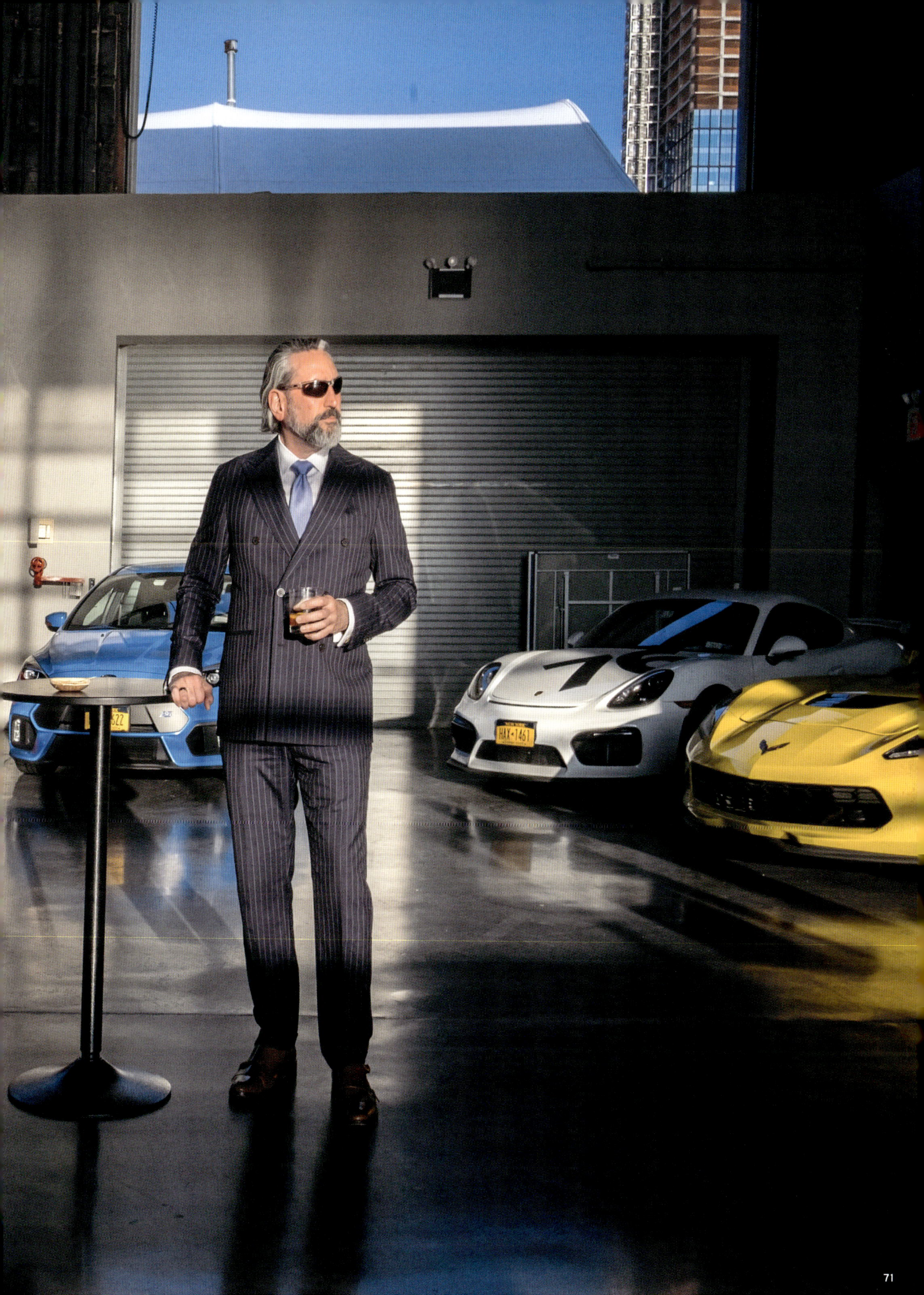

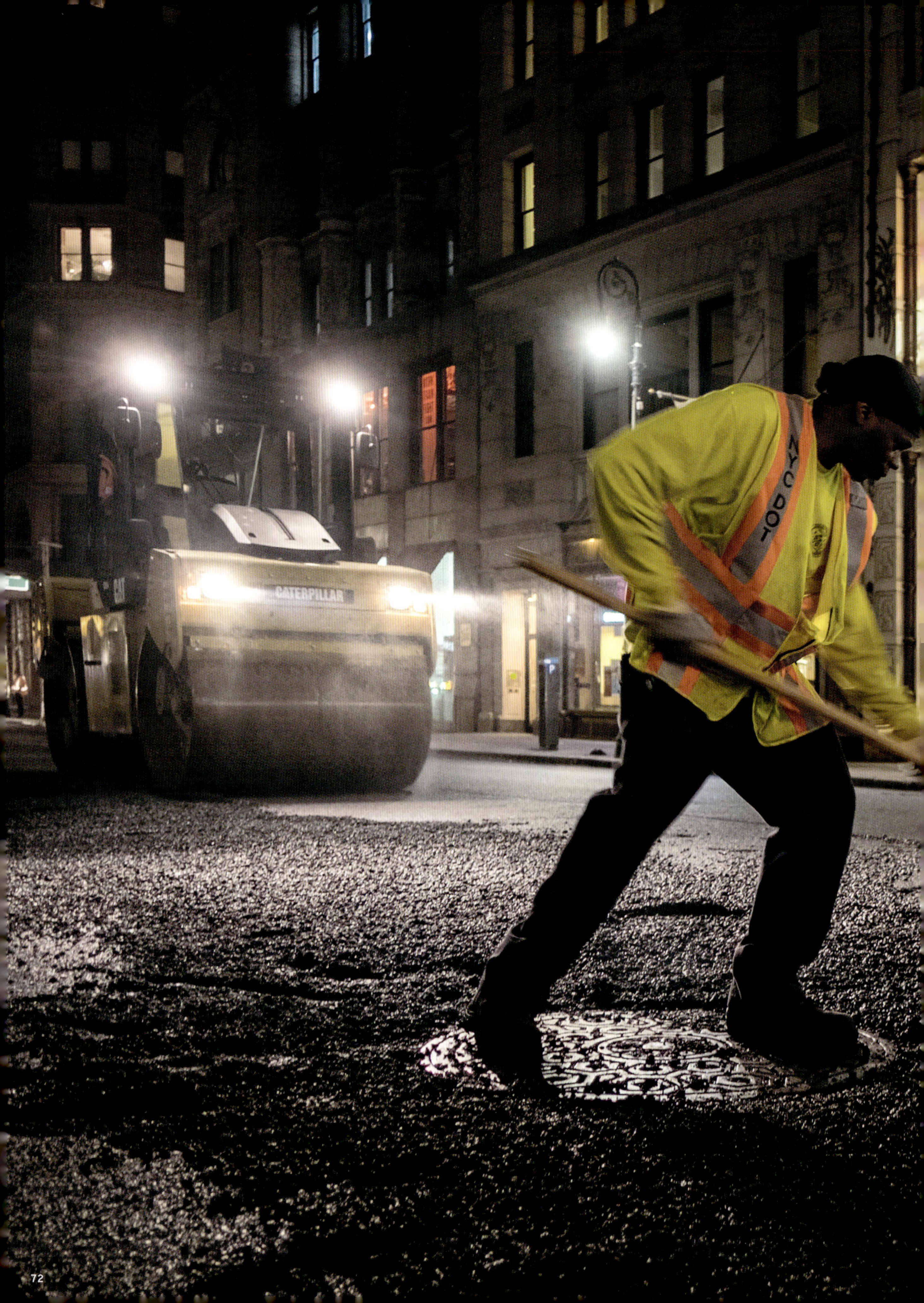

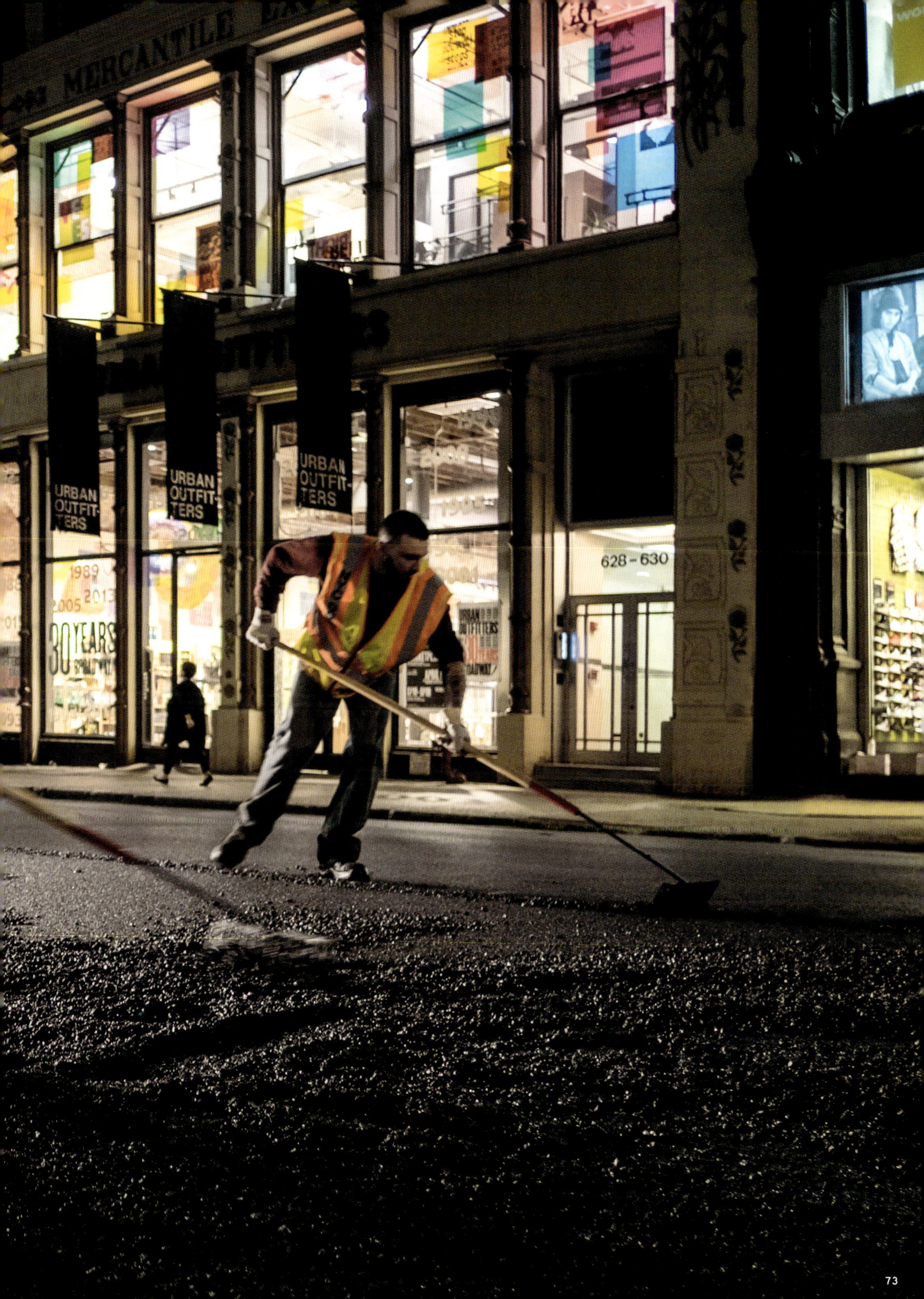

MERCANTILE
URBAN OUTFITTERS
URBAN OUTFIT-TERS
URBAN OUTFIT-TERS
1989
2005 2013
30 YEARS
628 - 630

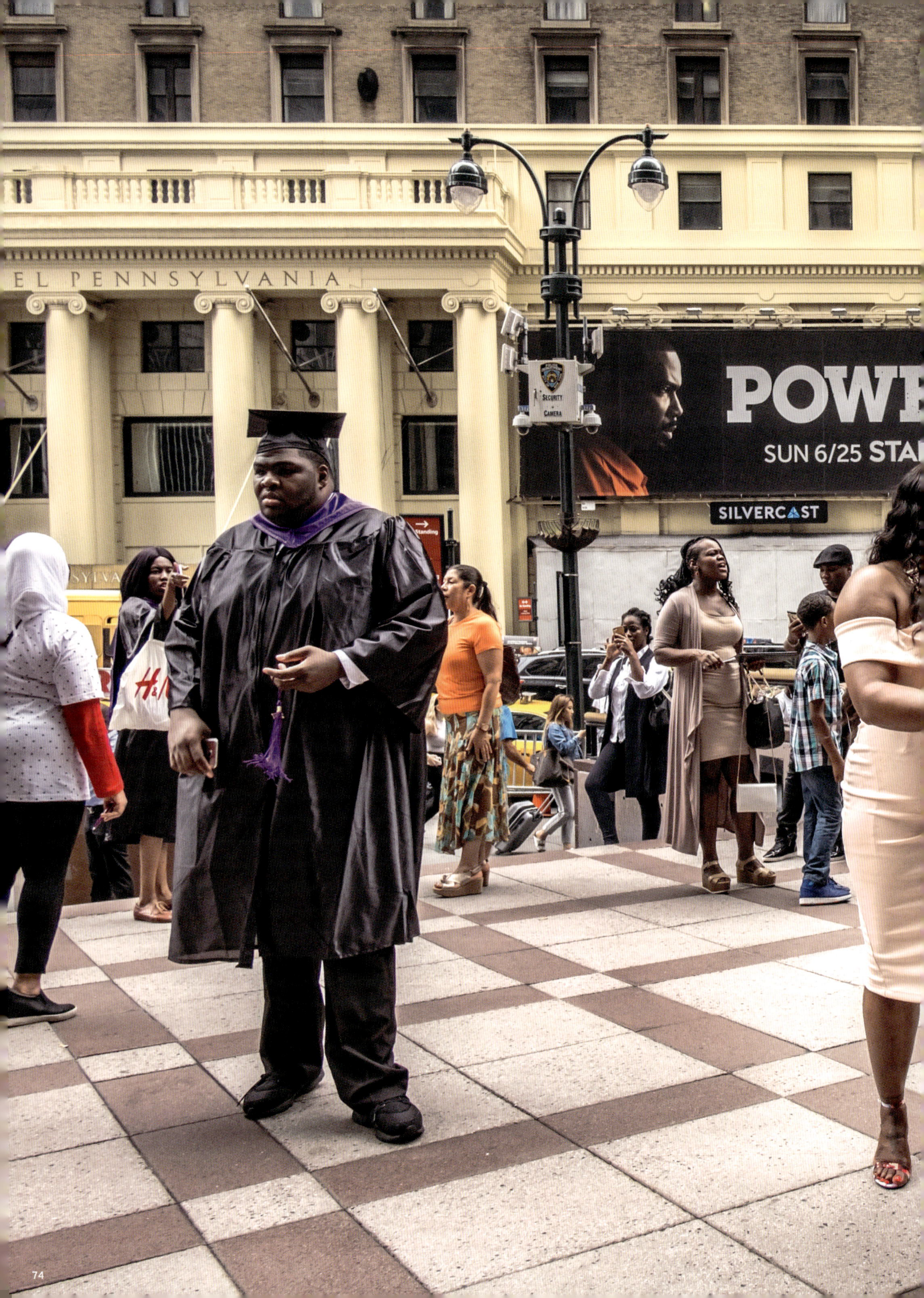
EL PENNSYLVANIA
POWE
SUN 6/25 STA
SILVERCAST
H&M

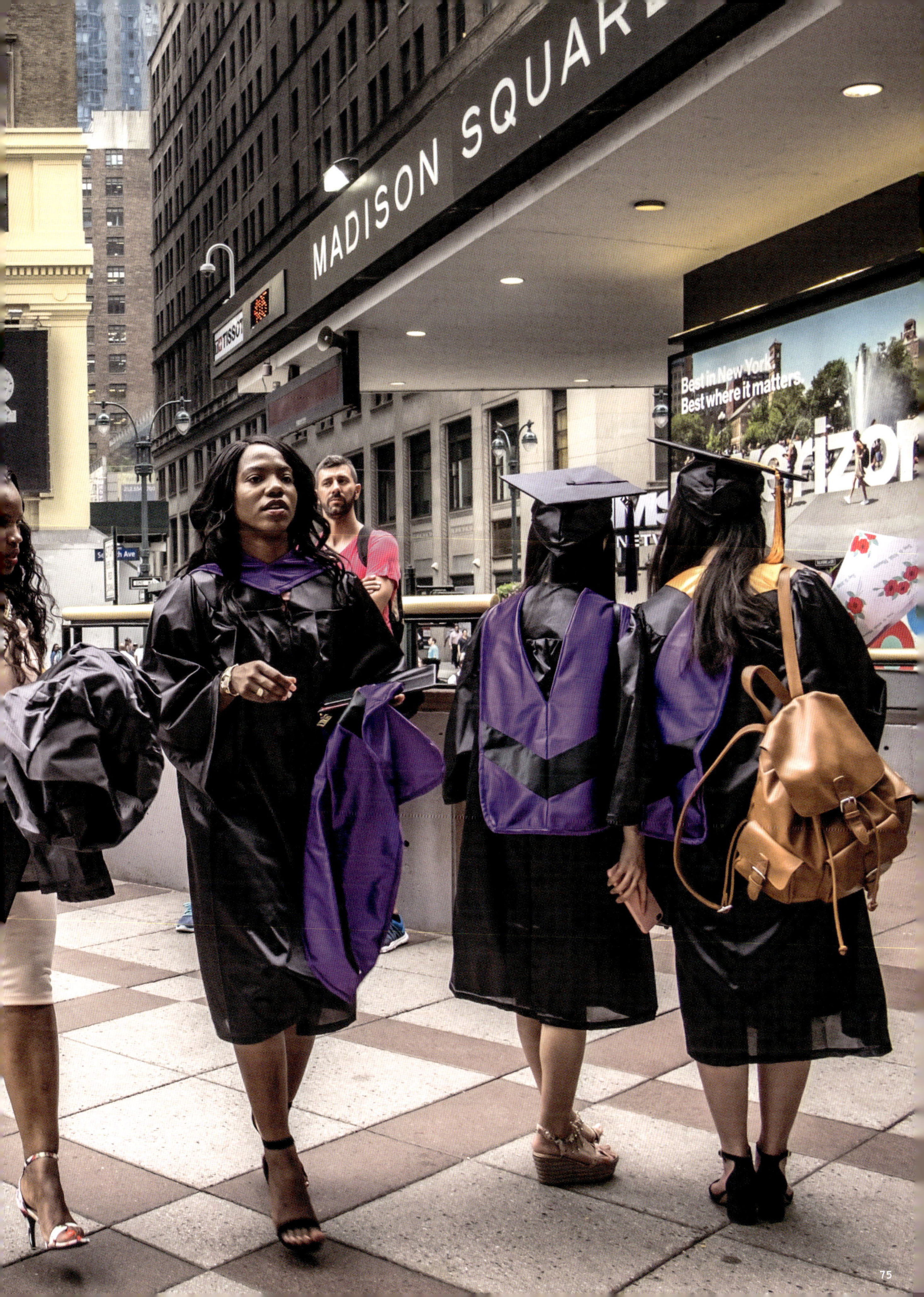

MADISON SQUARE
TISSOT
Best in New York.
Best where it matters.
orizon

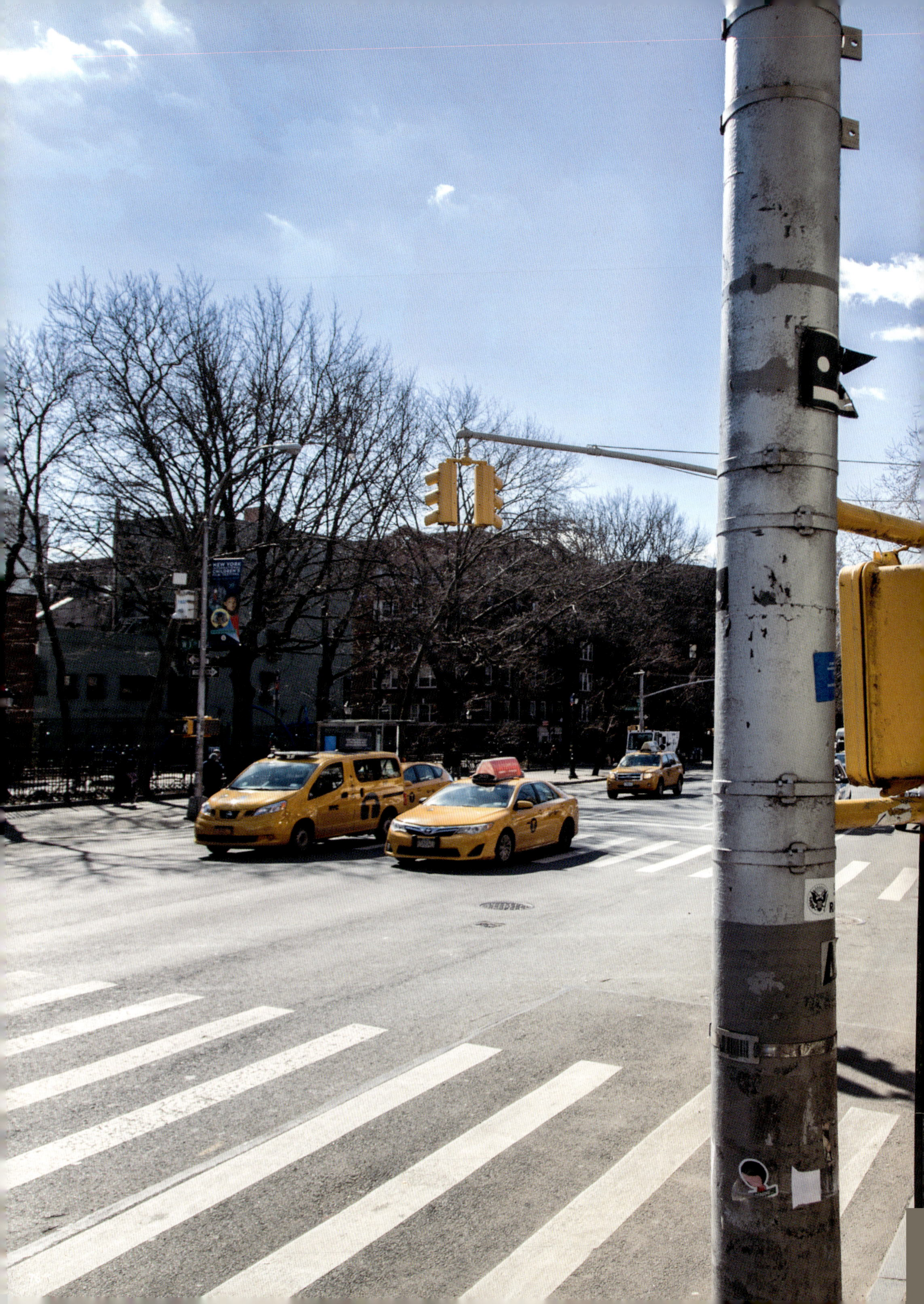

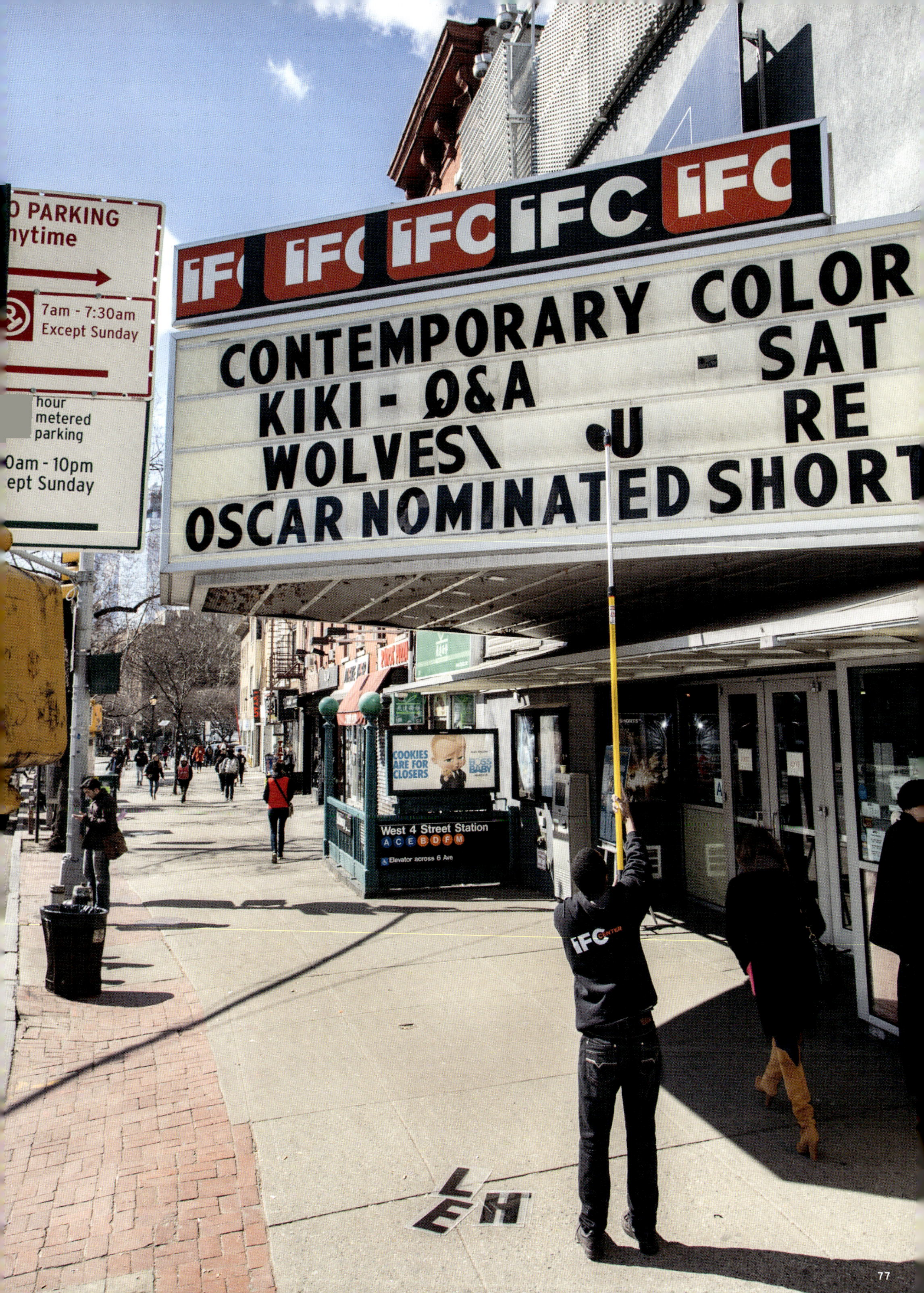
iFC iFC iFC iFC
CONTEMPORARY COLOR
KIKI - Q&A - SAT
WOLVES\ U RE
OSCAR NOMINATED SHORT
NO PARKING
Anytime
7am - 7:30am
Except Sunday
hour
metered
parking
0am - 10pm
ept Sunday
COOKIES
ARE FOR
CLOSERS
BOSS
BABY
West 4 Street Station
A C E B D F M
Elevator across 6 Ave
IFC CENTER

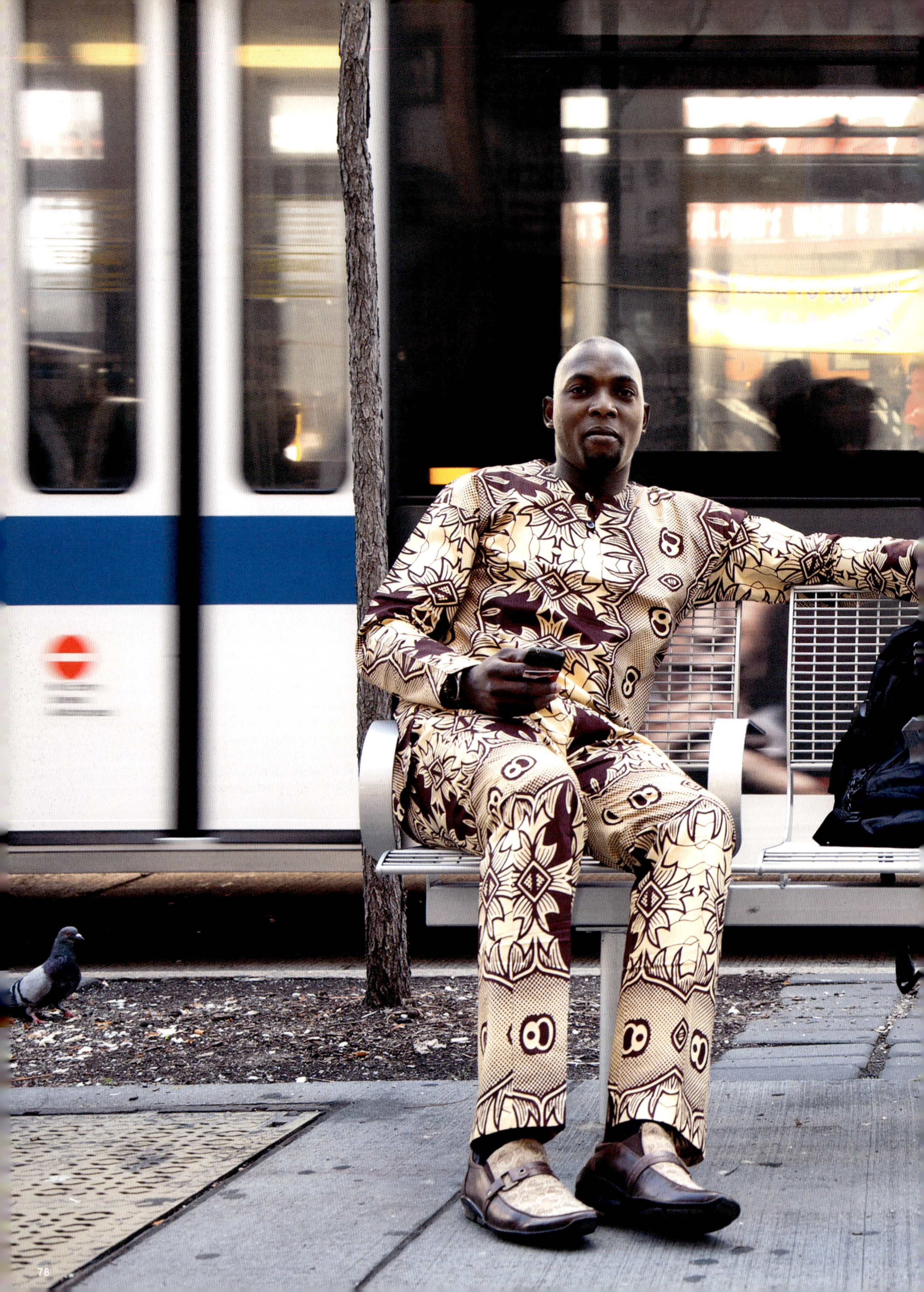

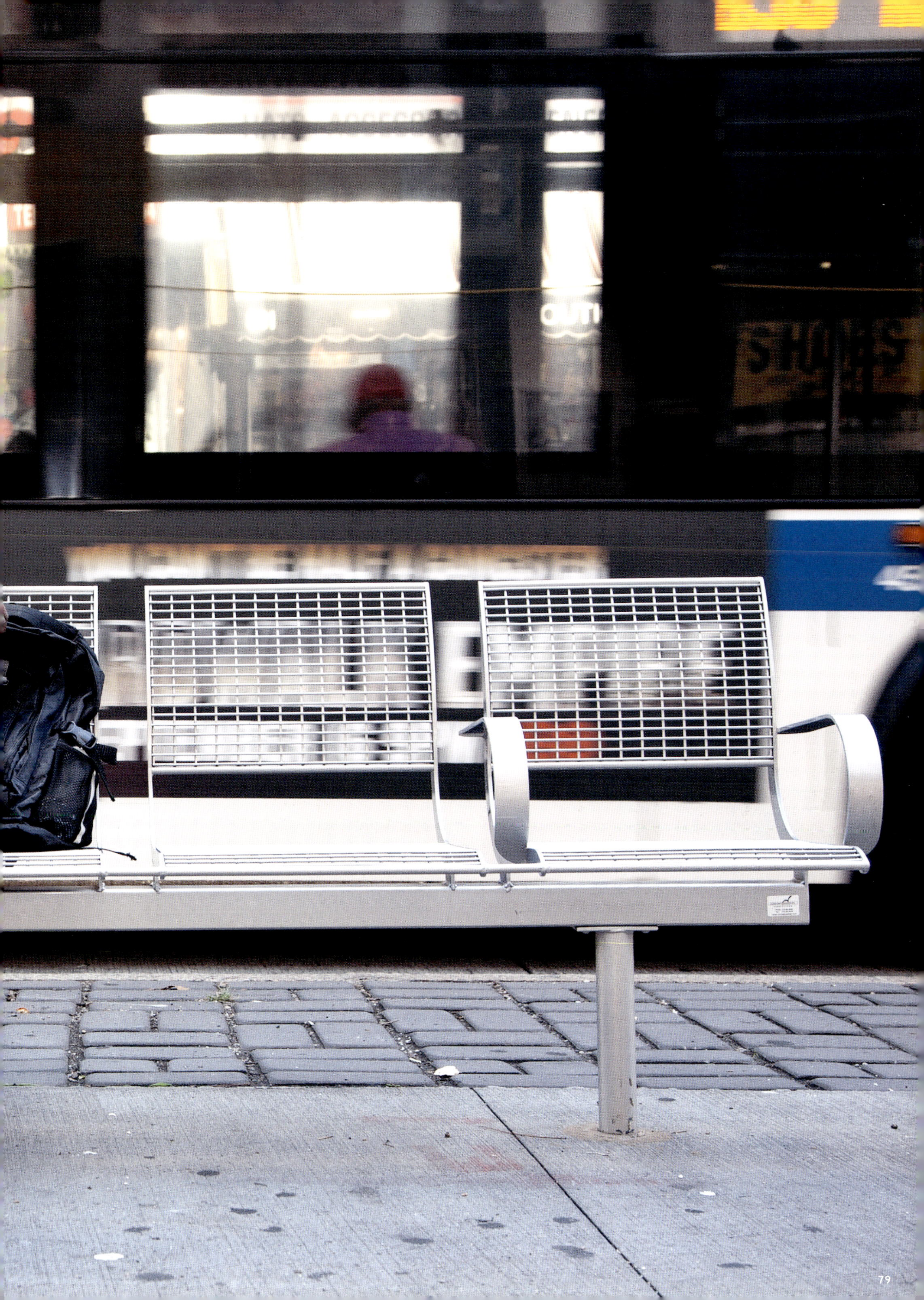

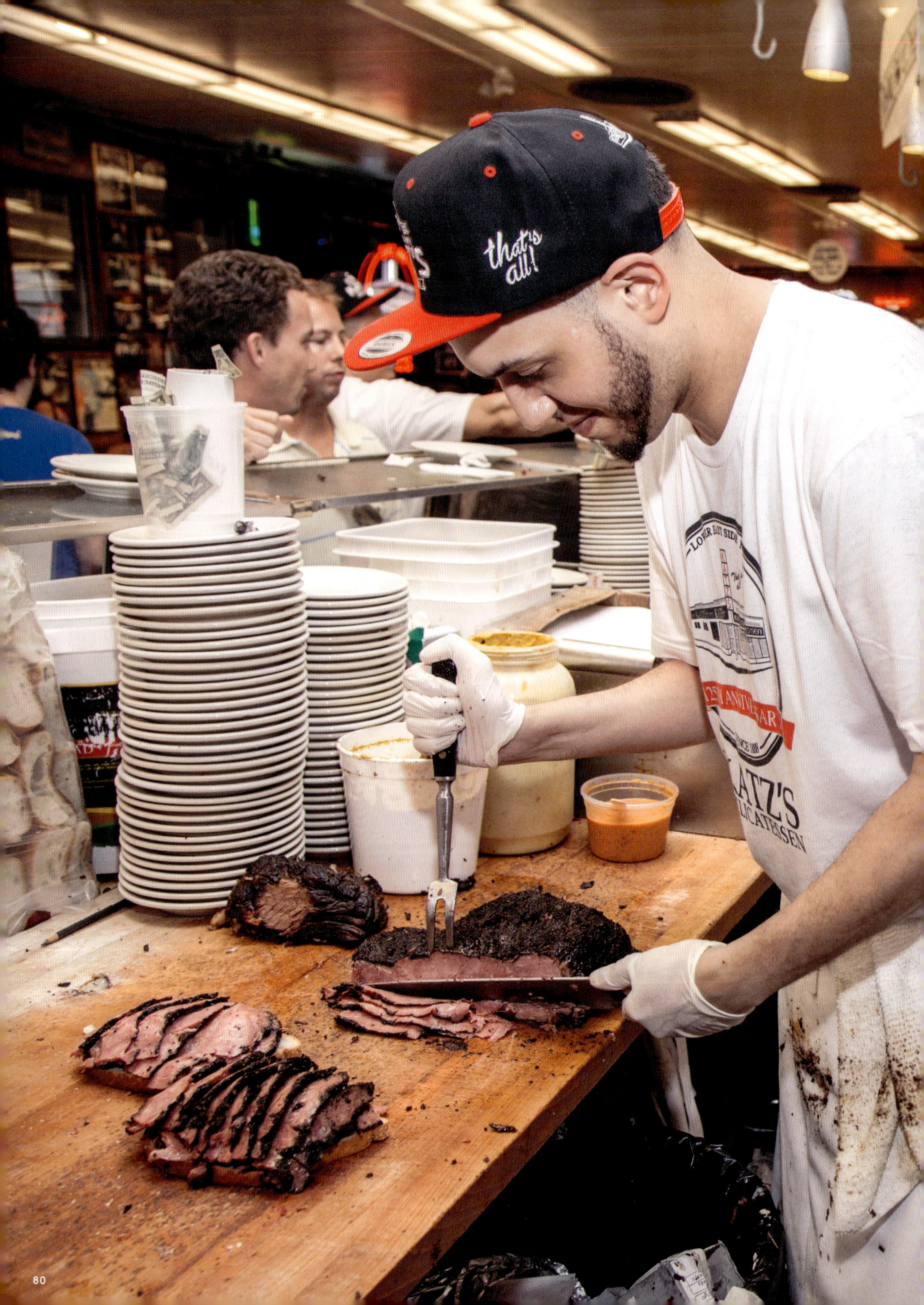

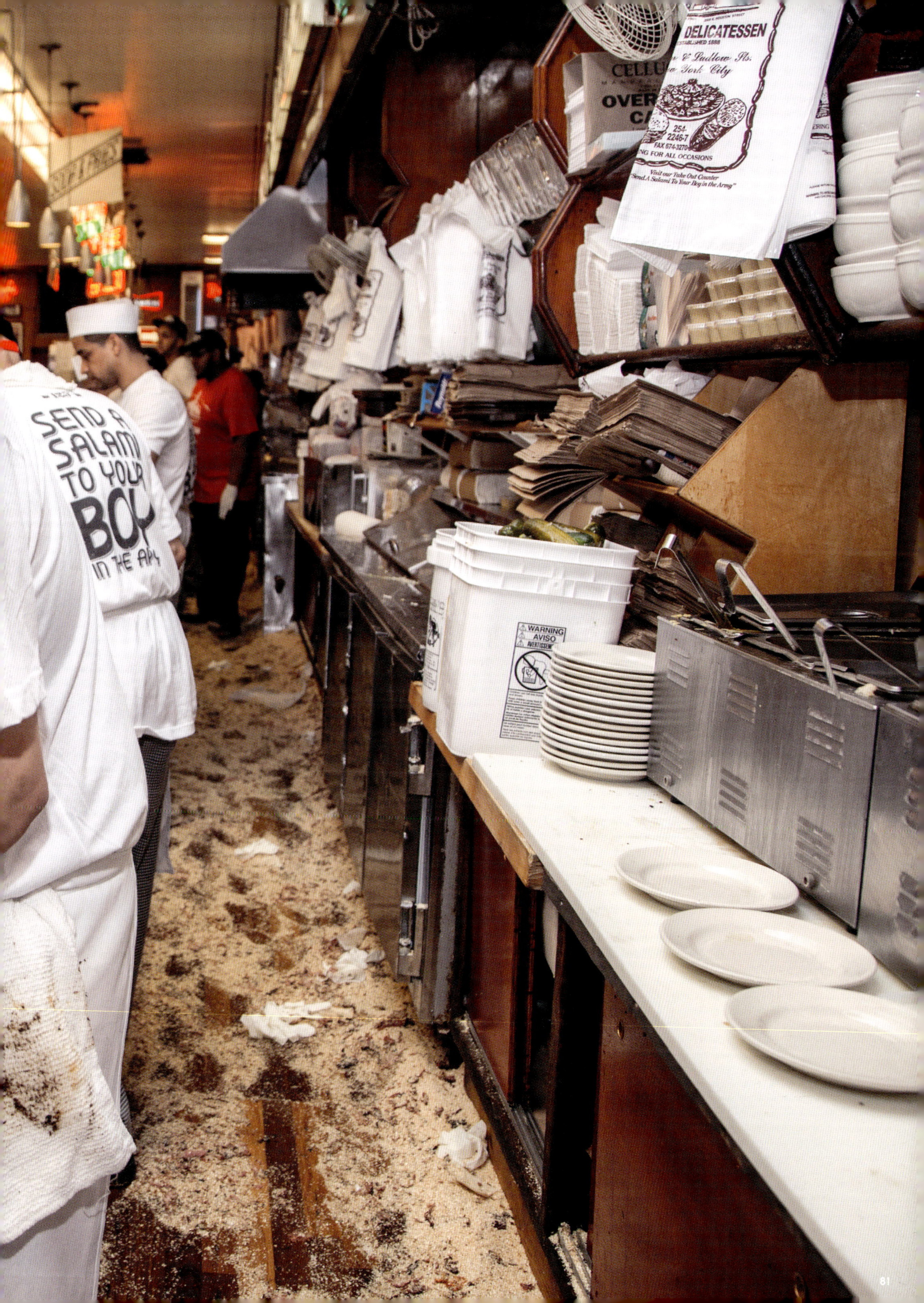

SEND A
SALAMI
TO YOUR
BOY
IN THE ARMY

DELICATESSEN
CELLU
OVER
CA

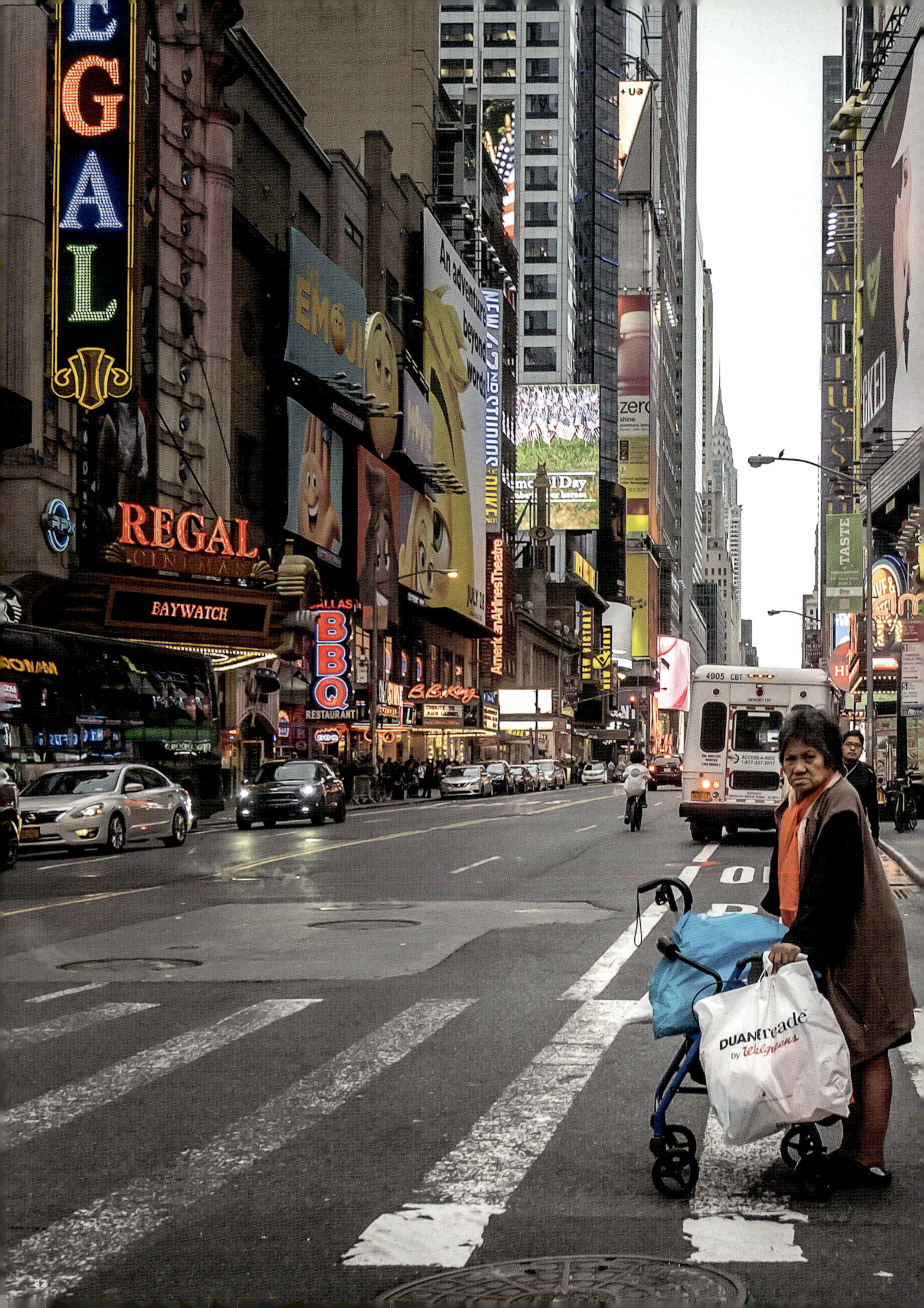

REGAL
REGAL CINEMAS
BAYWATCH
THE EMOJI
DALLAS BBQ RESTAURANT
B.B. King
An adventure beyond words
American Airlines Theatre
TASTE
4905
DUANEreade by Walgreens
ACCESS-A-RIDE

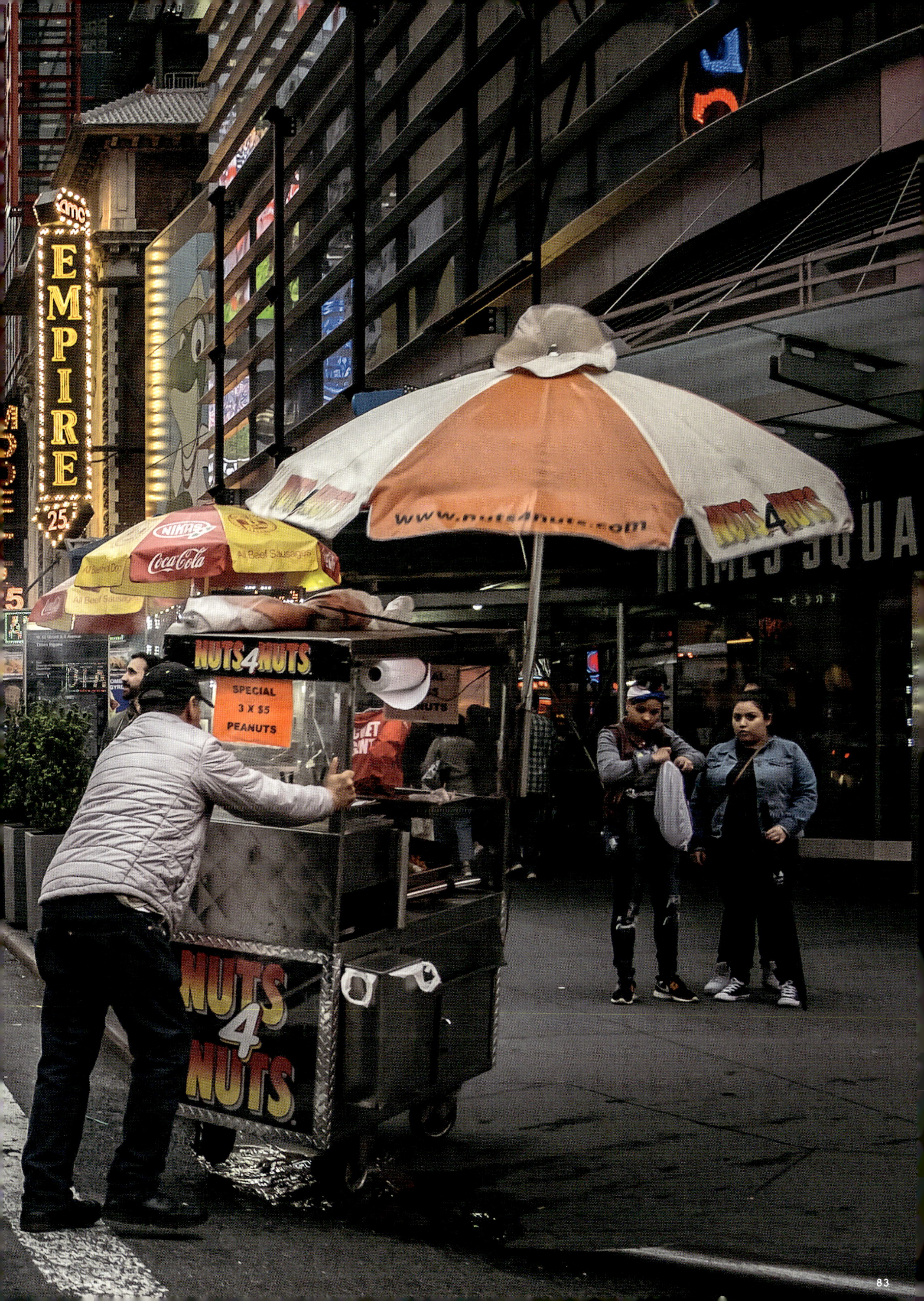

EMPIRE
25
Coca-Cola
All Beef Sausages
NUTS 4 NUTS
SPECIAL
3 X $5
PEANUTS
www.nuts4nuts.com
NUTS 4 NUTS
NUTS 4 NUTS
TIMES SQUA

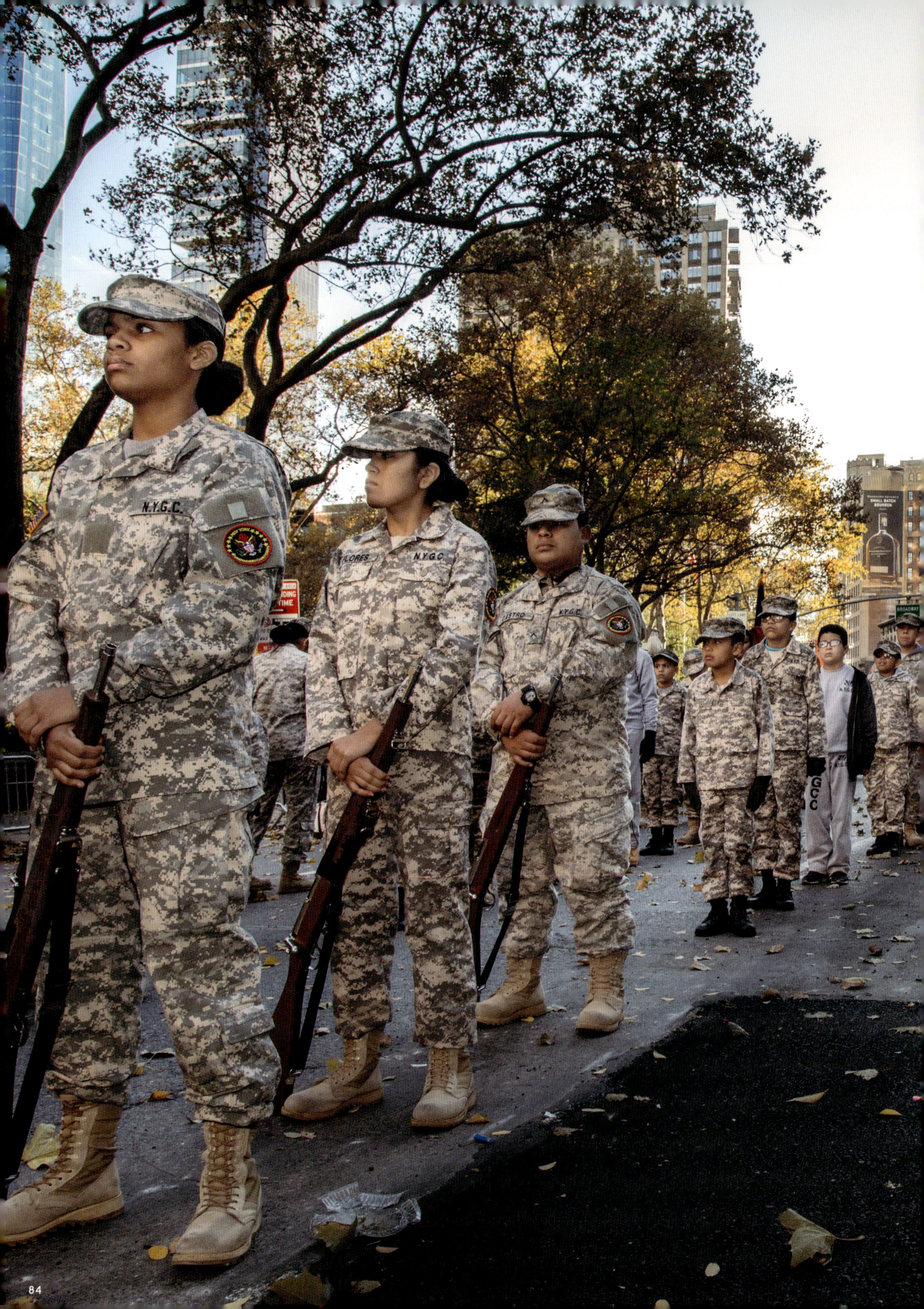

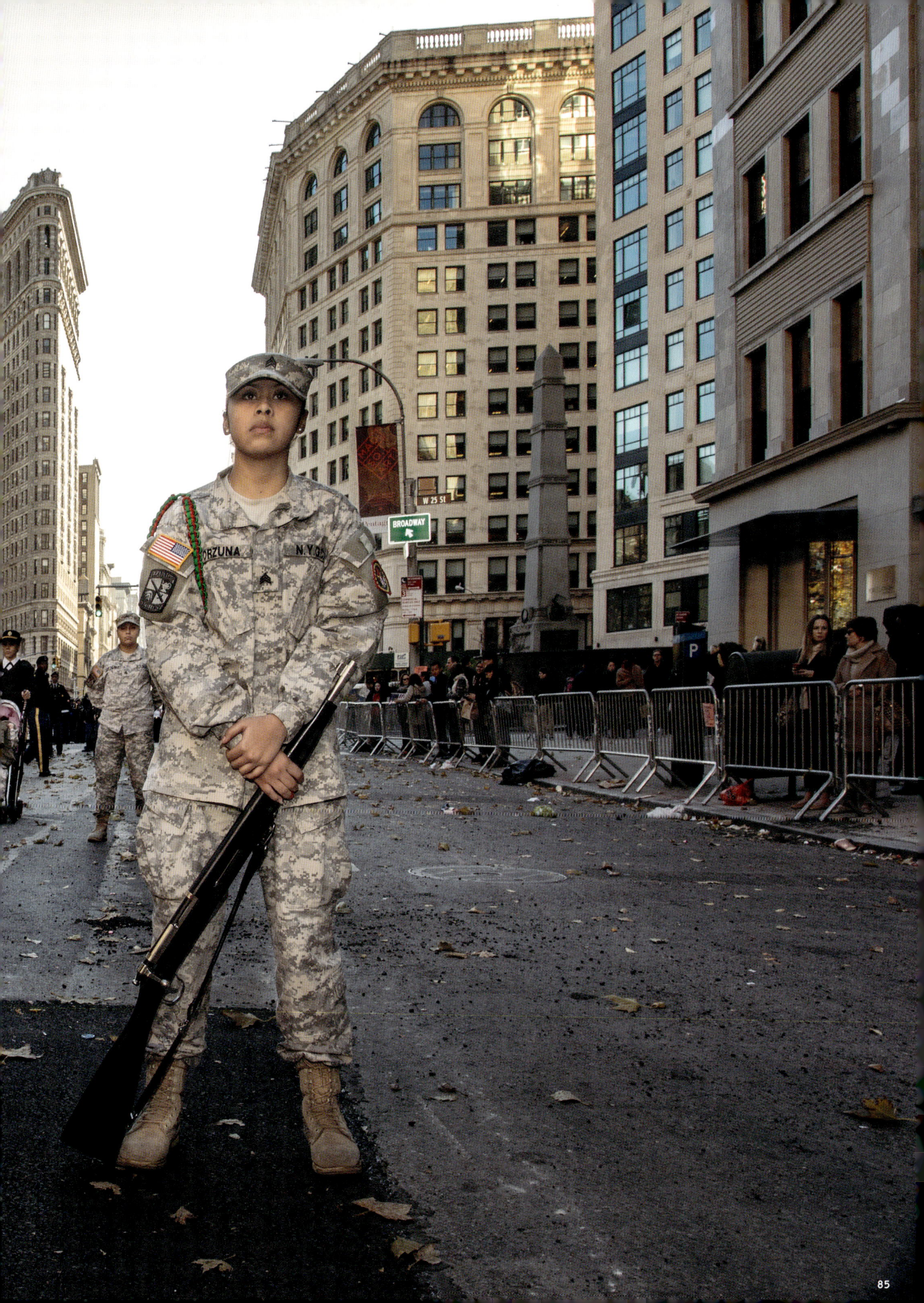
ORZUNA
N.Y.G.
W 25 St
BROADWAY
P

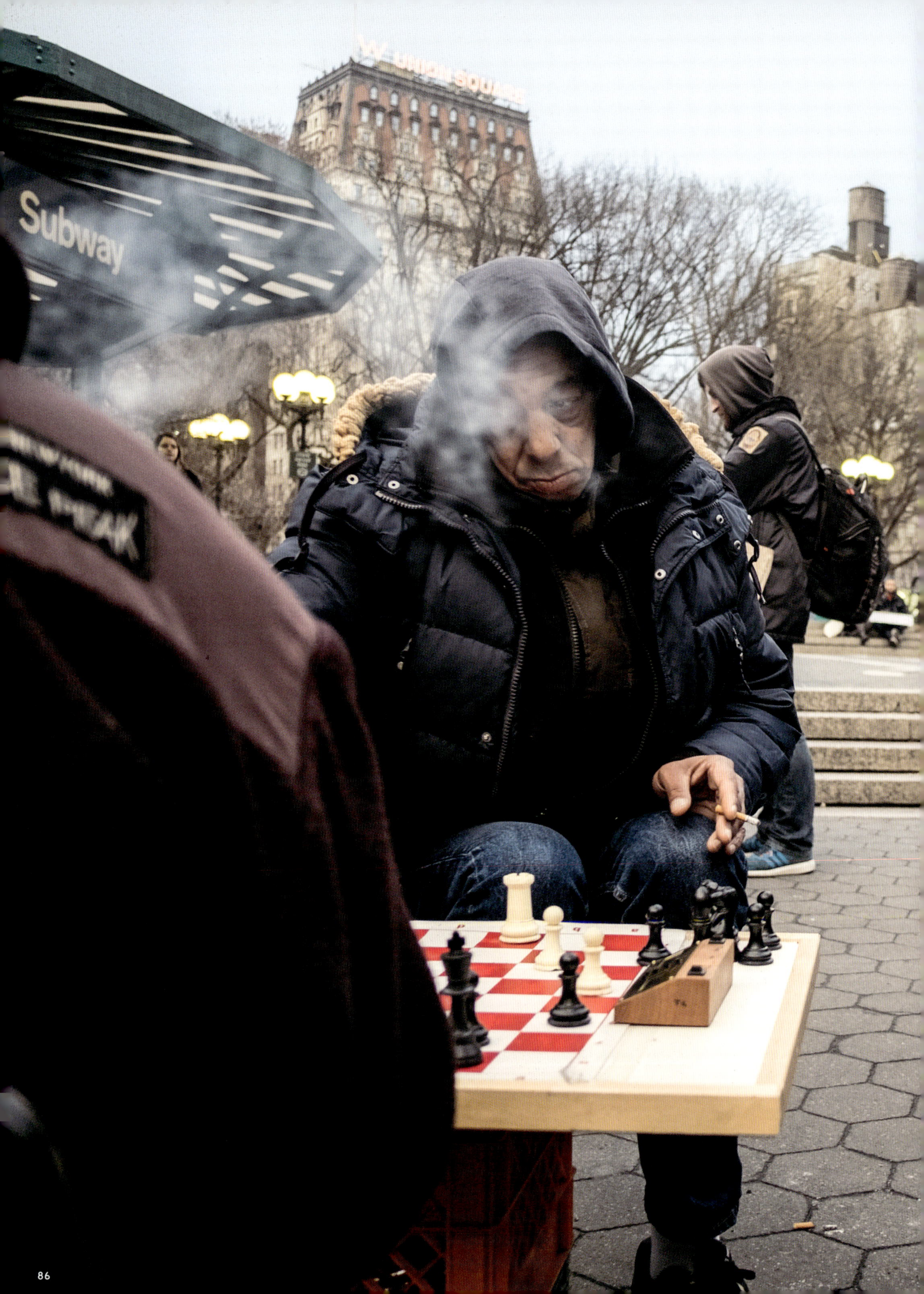

Subway
UNION SQUARE

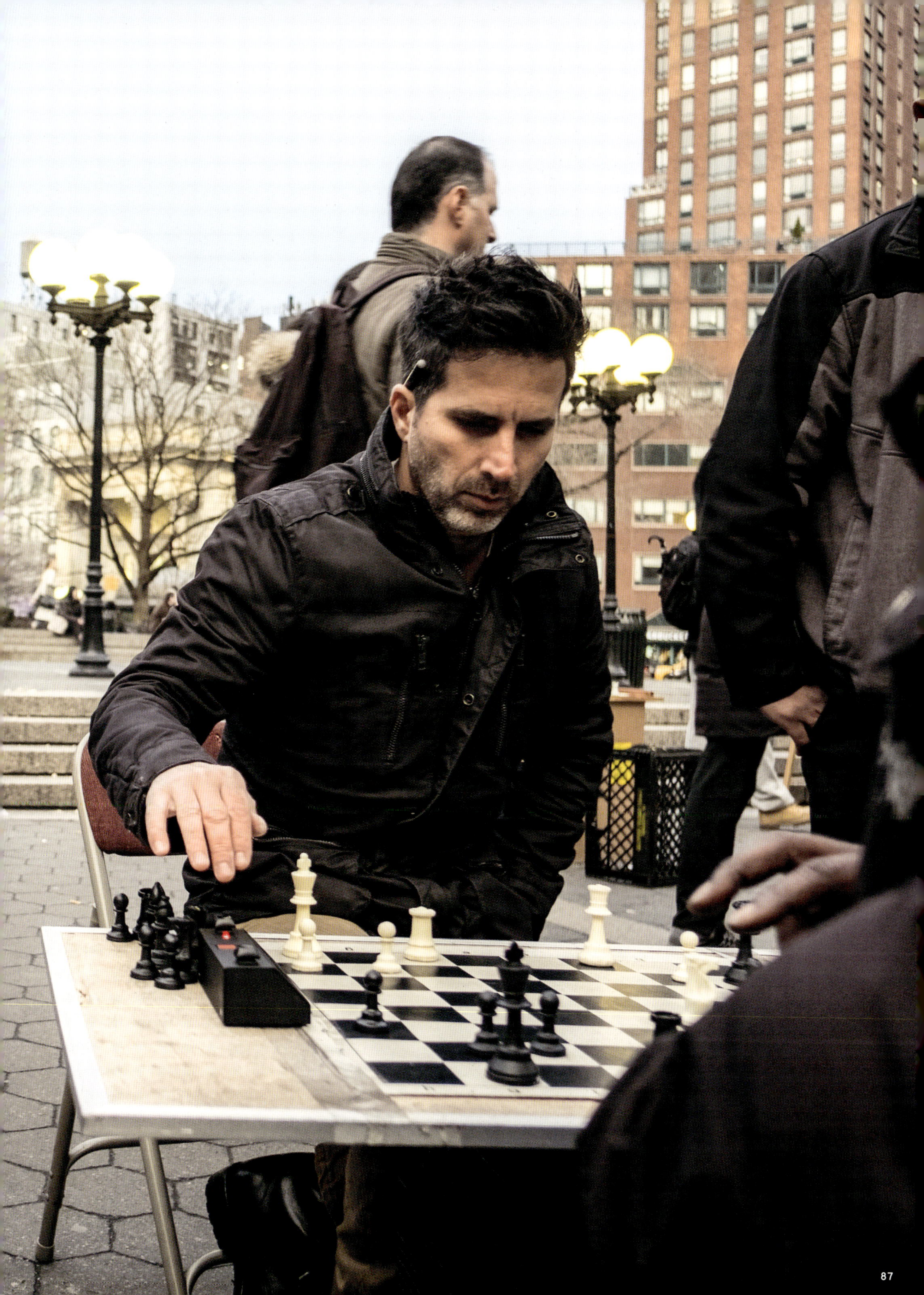

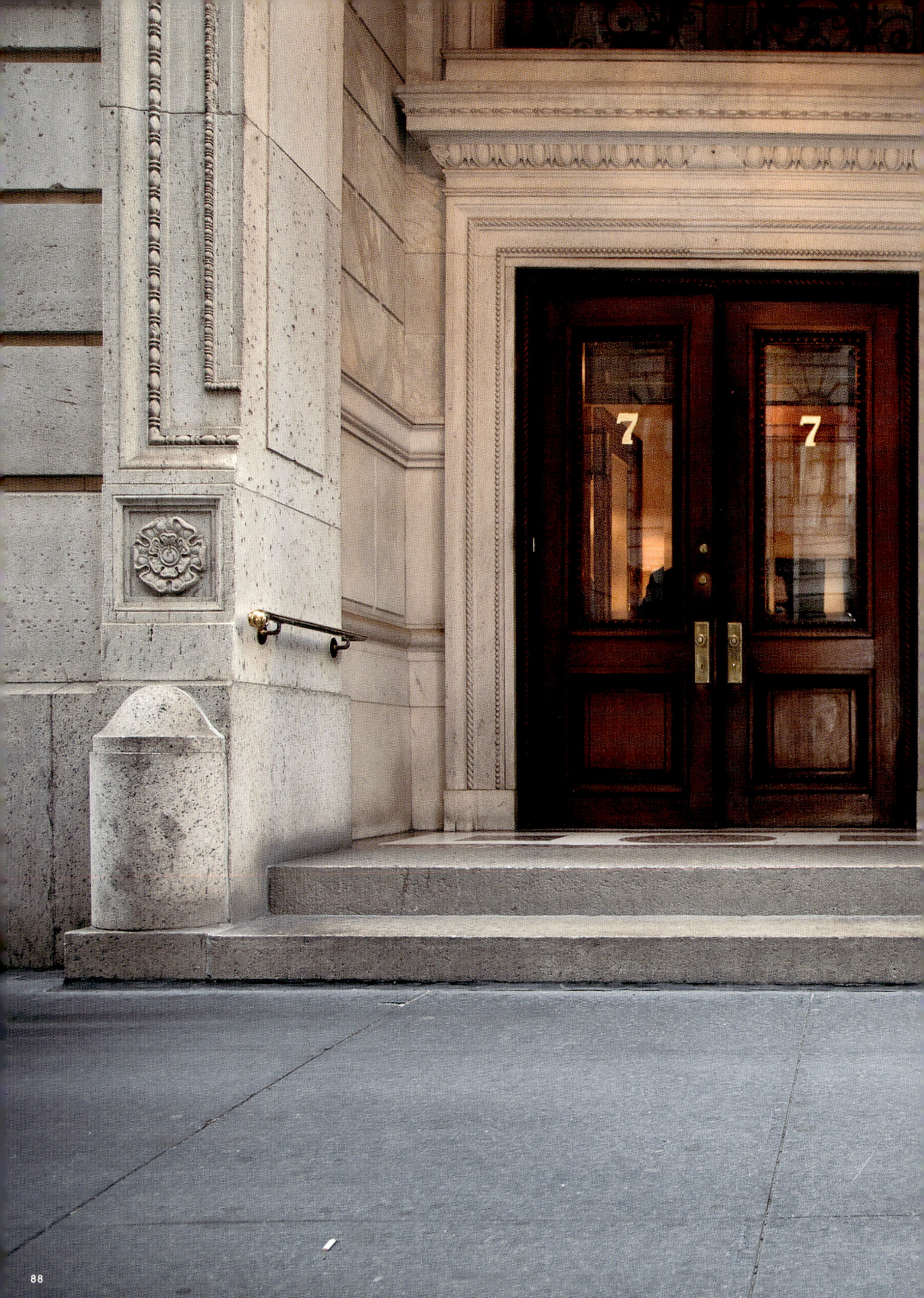

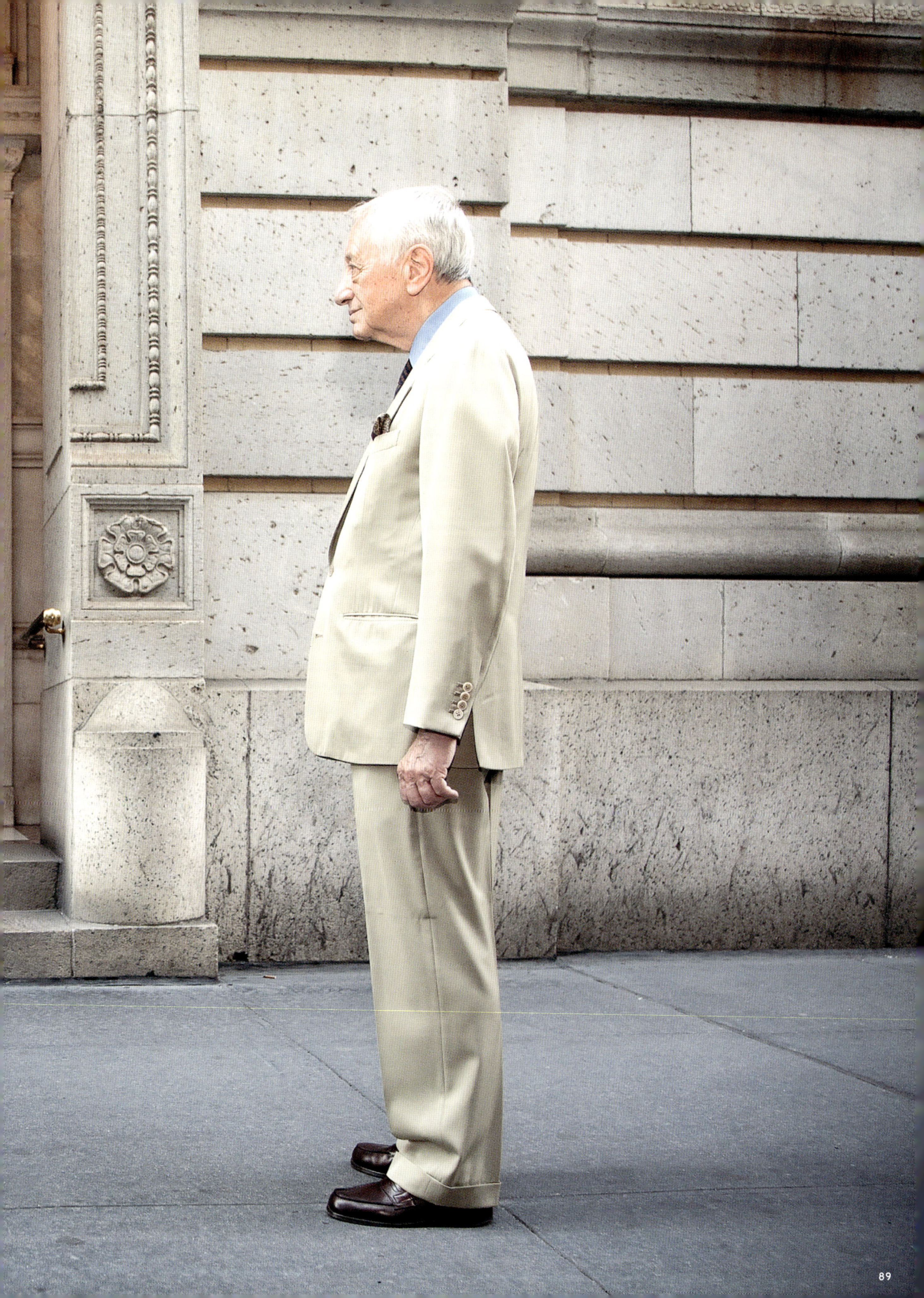

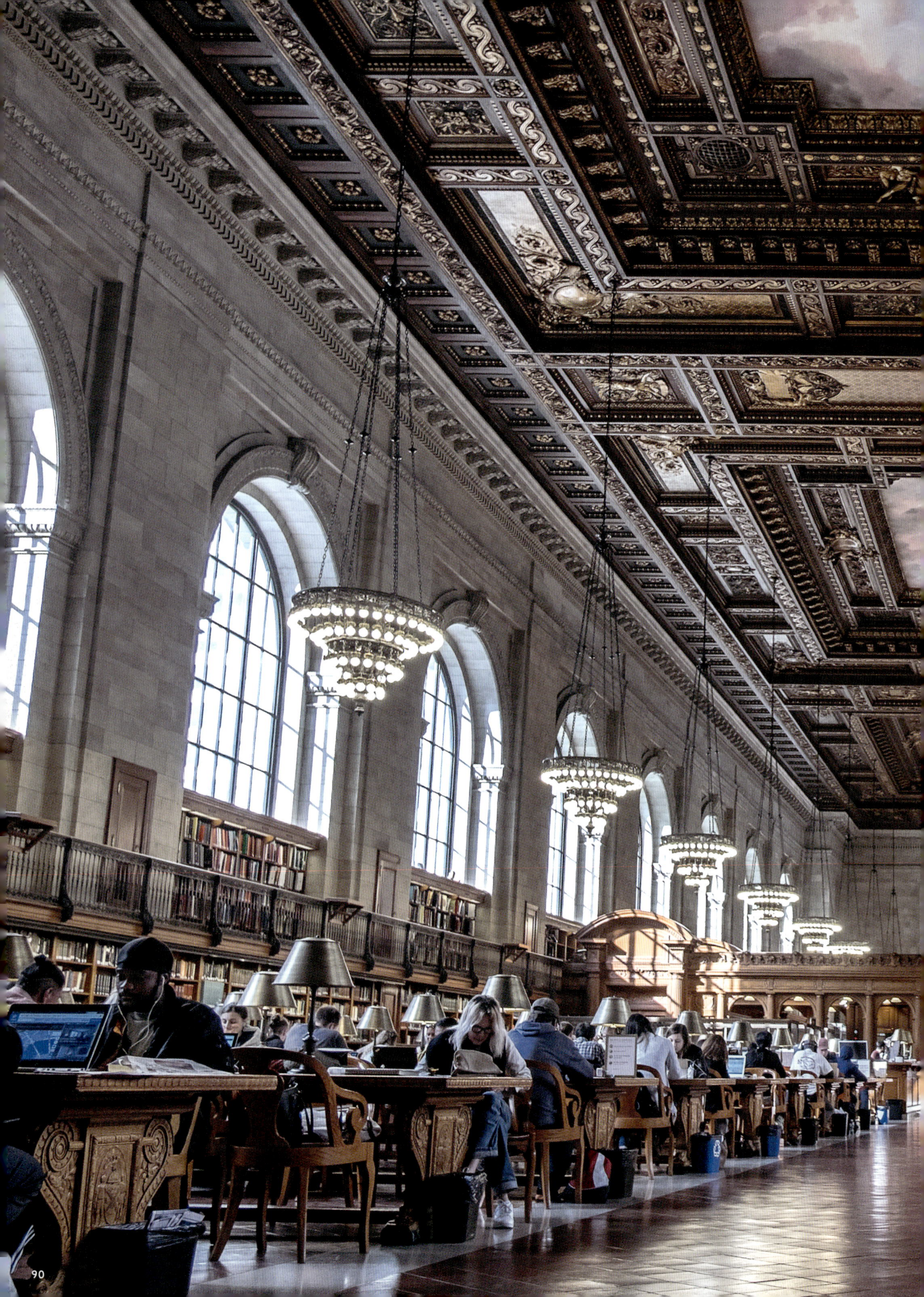

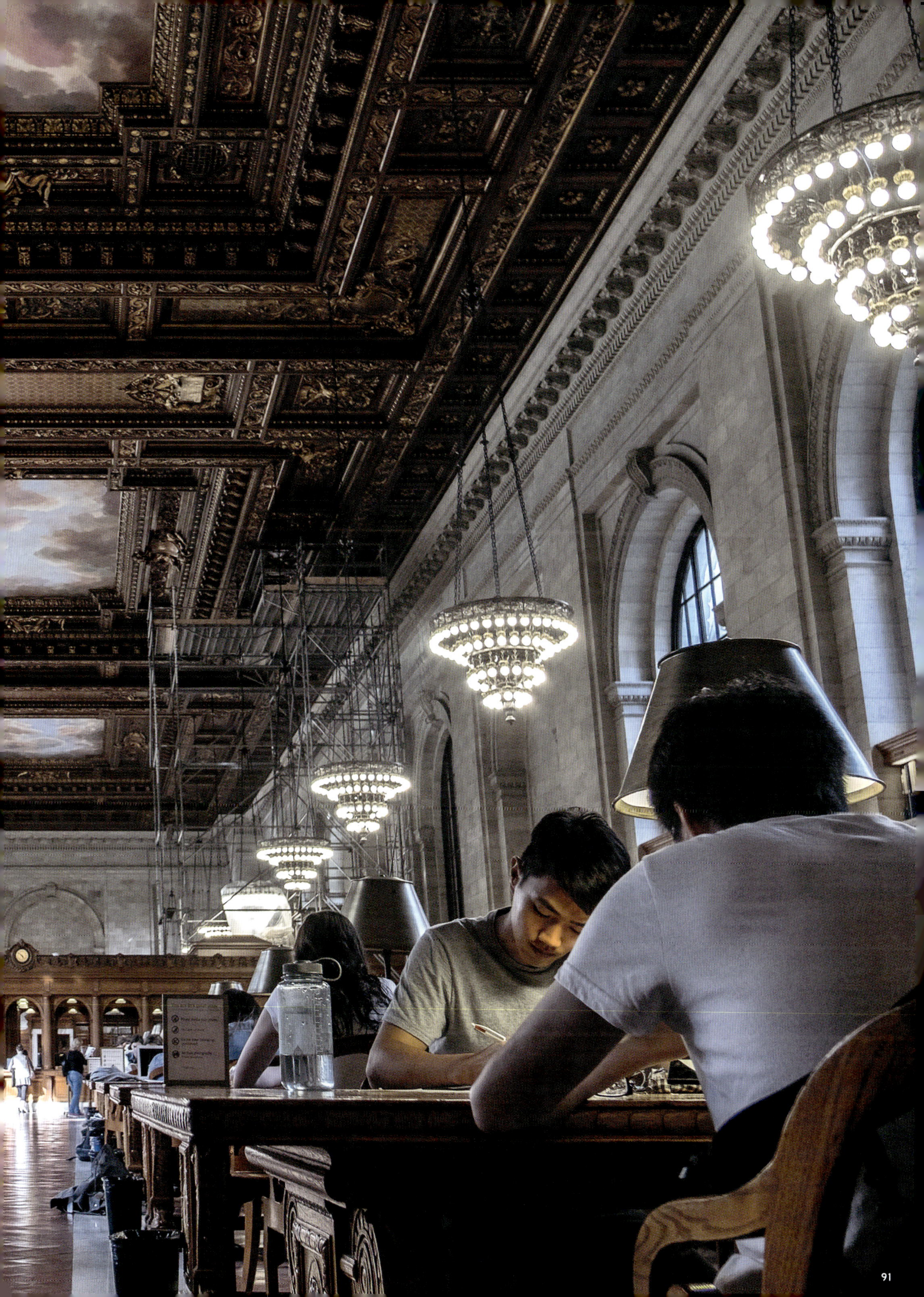

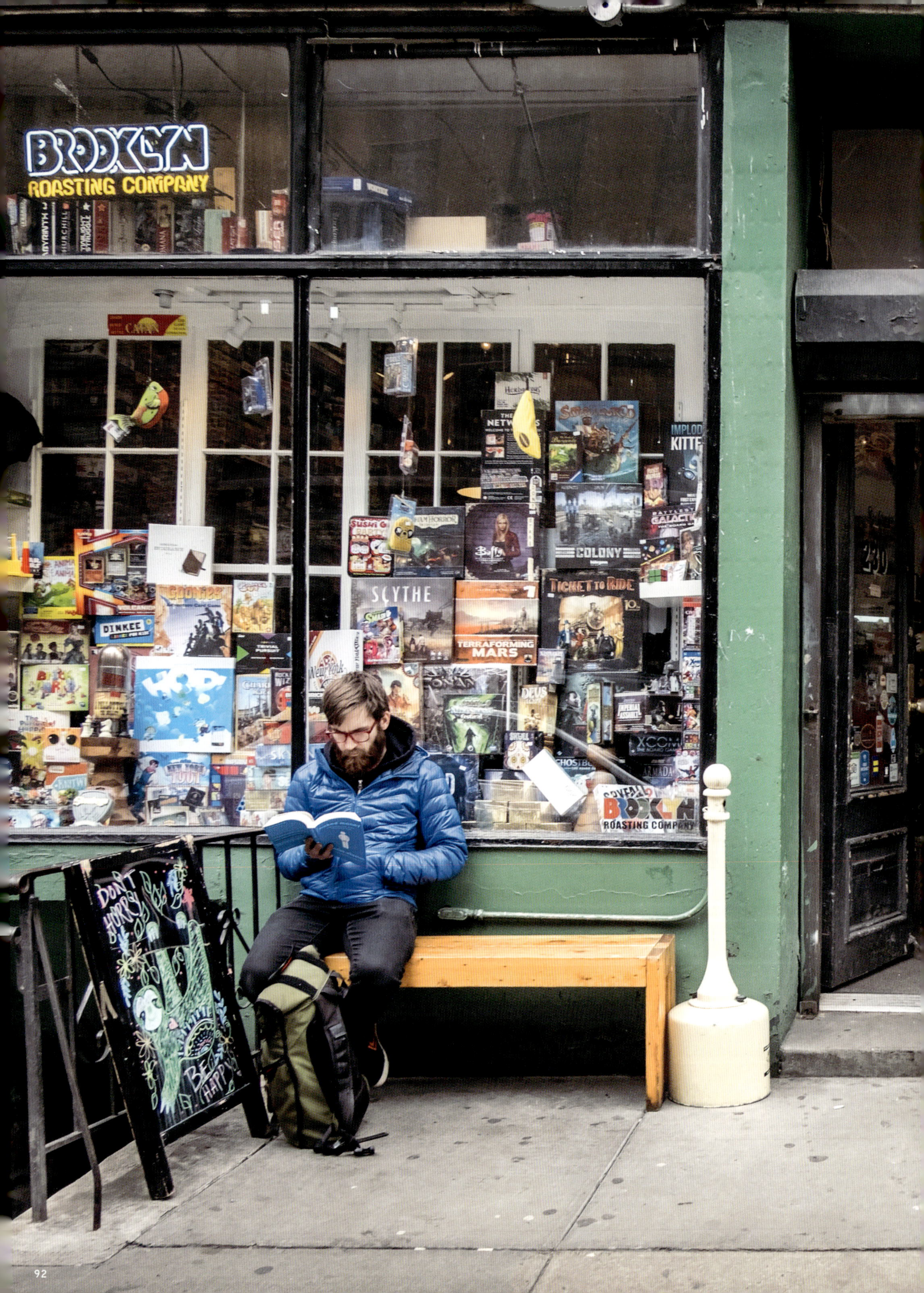

BROOKLYN
ROASTING COMPANY
SCYTHE
TICKET TO RIDE
TERRAFORMING MARS
COLONY
BROOKLYN
ROASTING COMPANY
DON'T WORRY
BE HAPPY

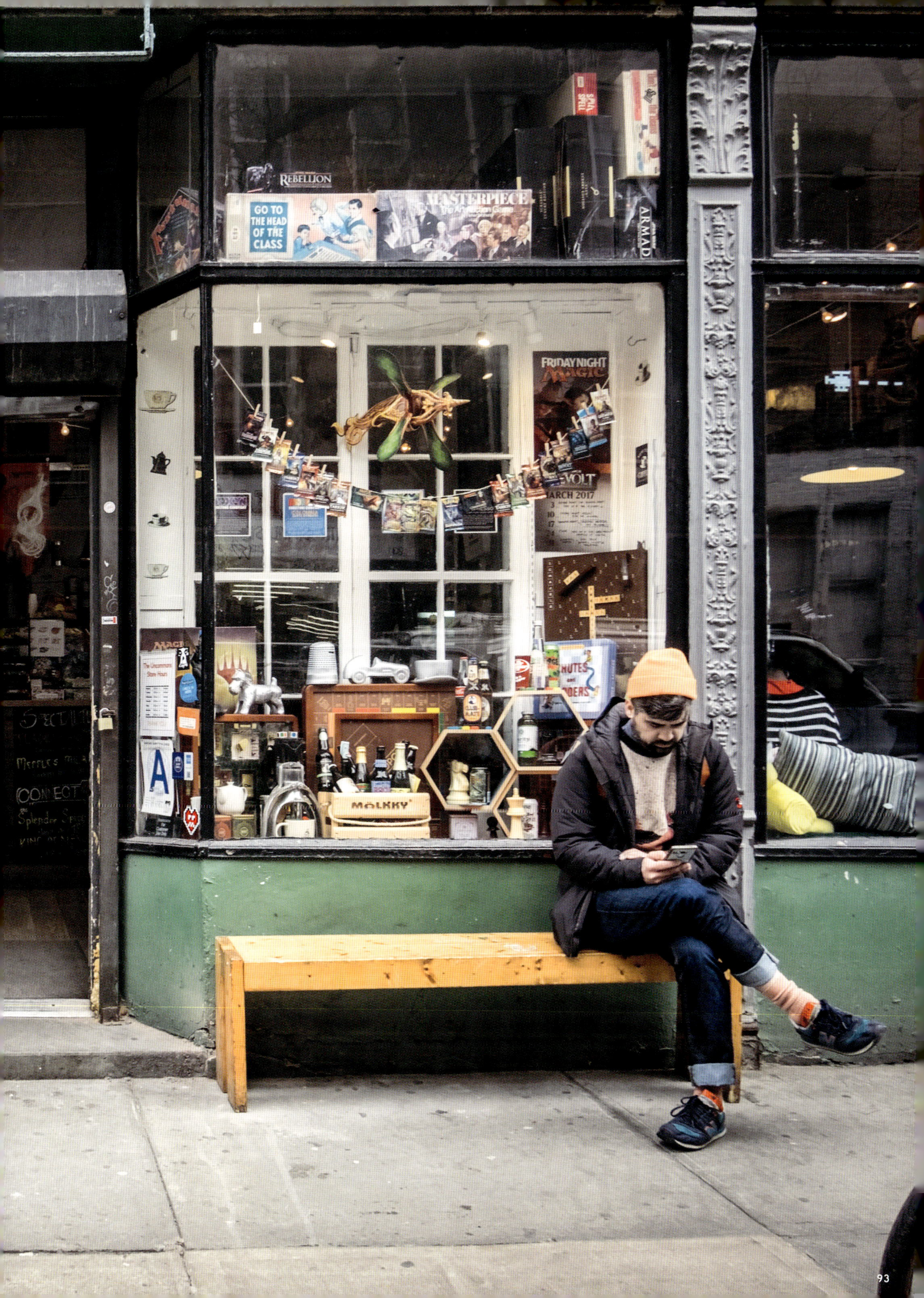

REBELLION
GO TO THE HEAD OF THE CLASS
MASTERPIECE
The American Game
ARMAD
FRIDAY NIGHT MAGIC
MARCH 2017
MAGIC
CHUTES AND LADDERS
MÖLKKY

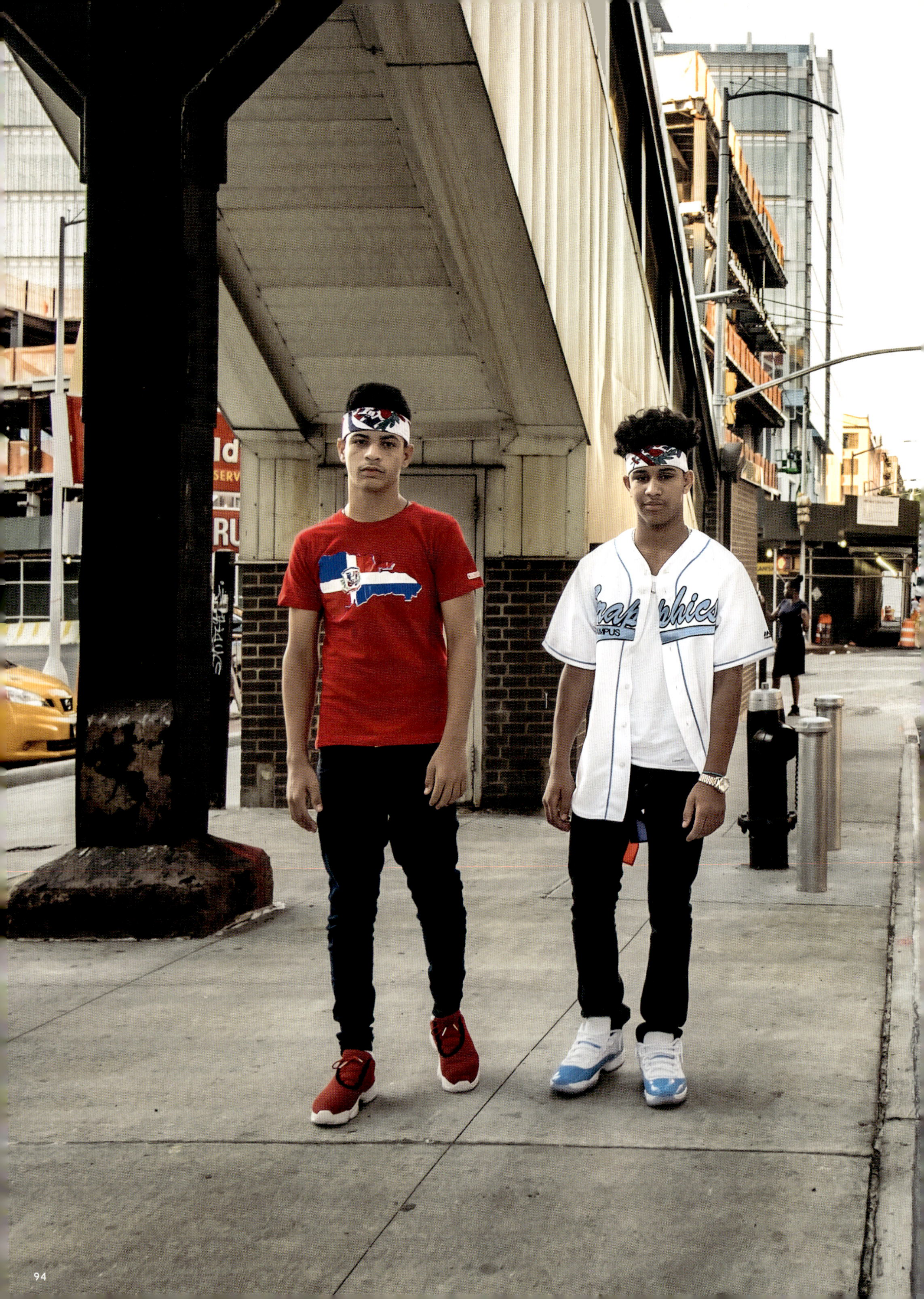

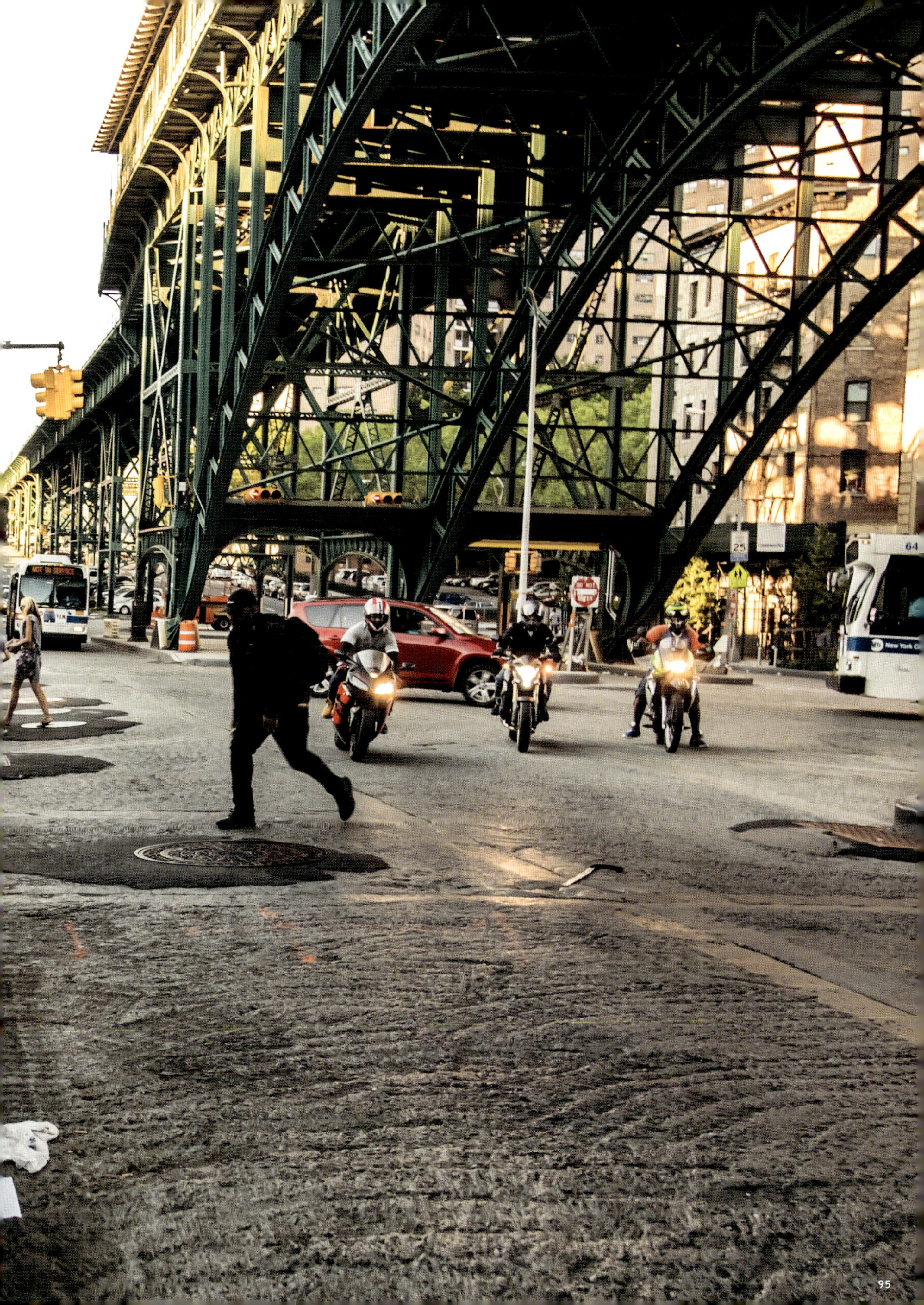

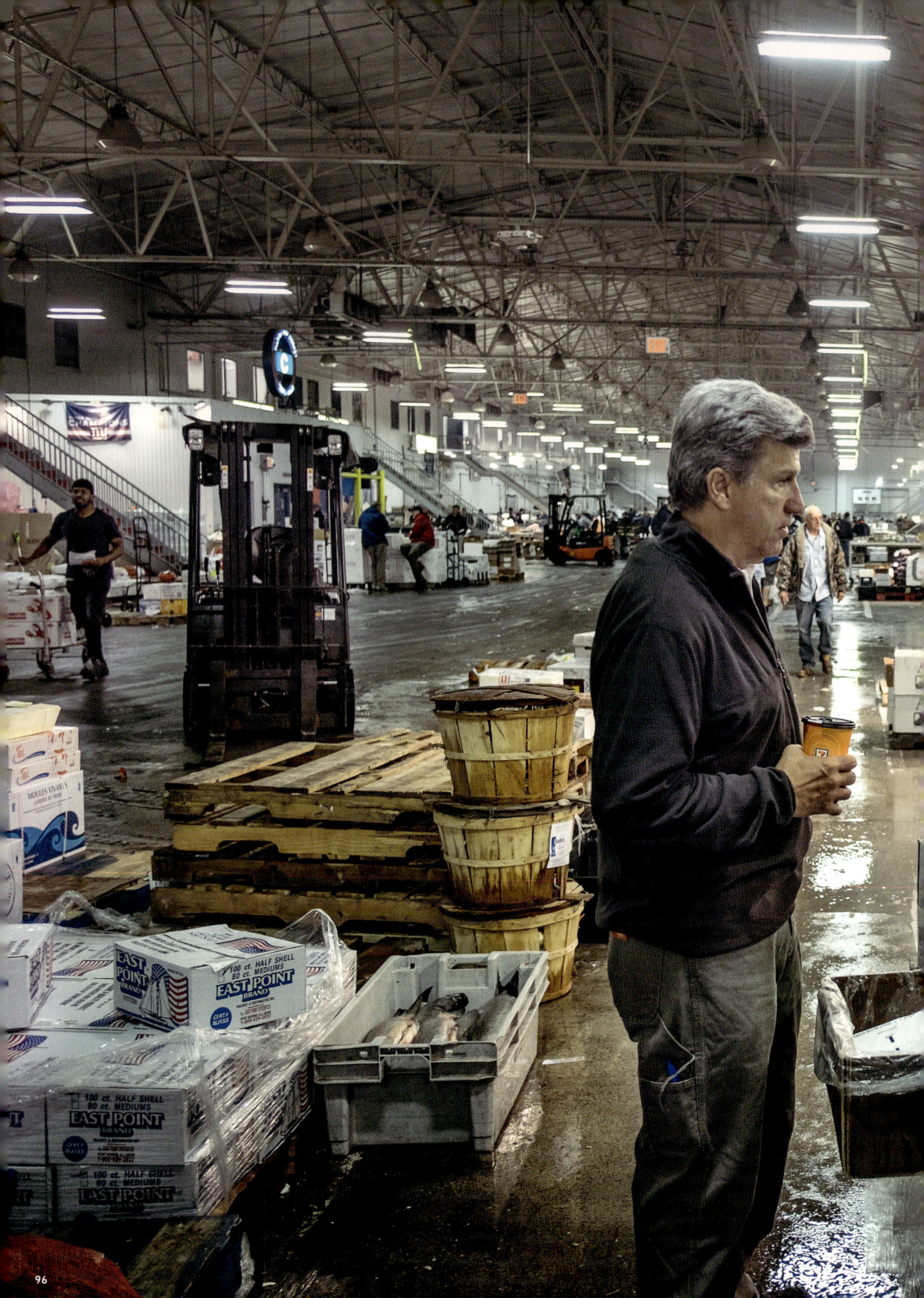
EAST
POINT
BRAND
100 ct. HALF SHELL
80 ct. MEDIUMS
MOLLES VIVANTS

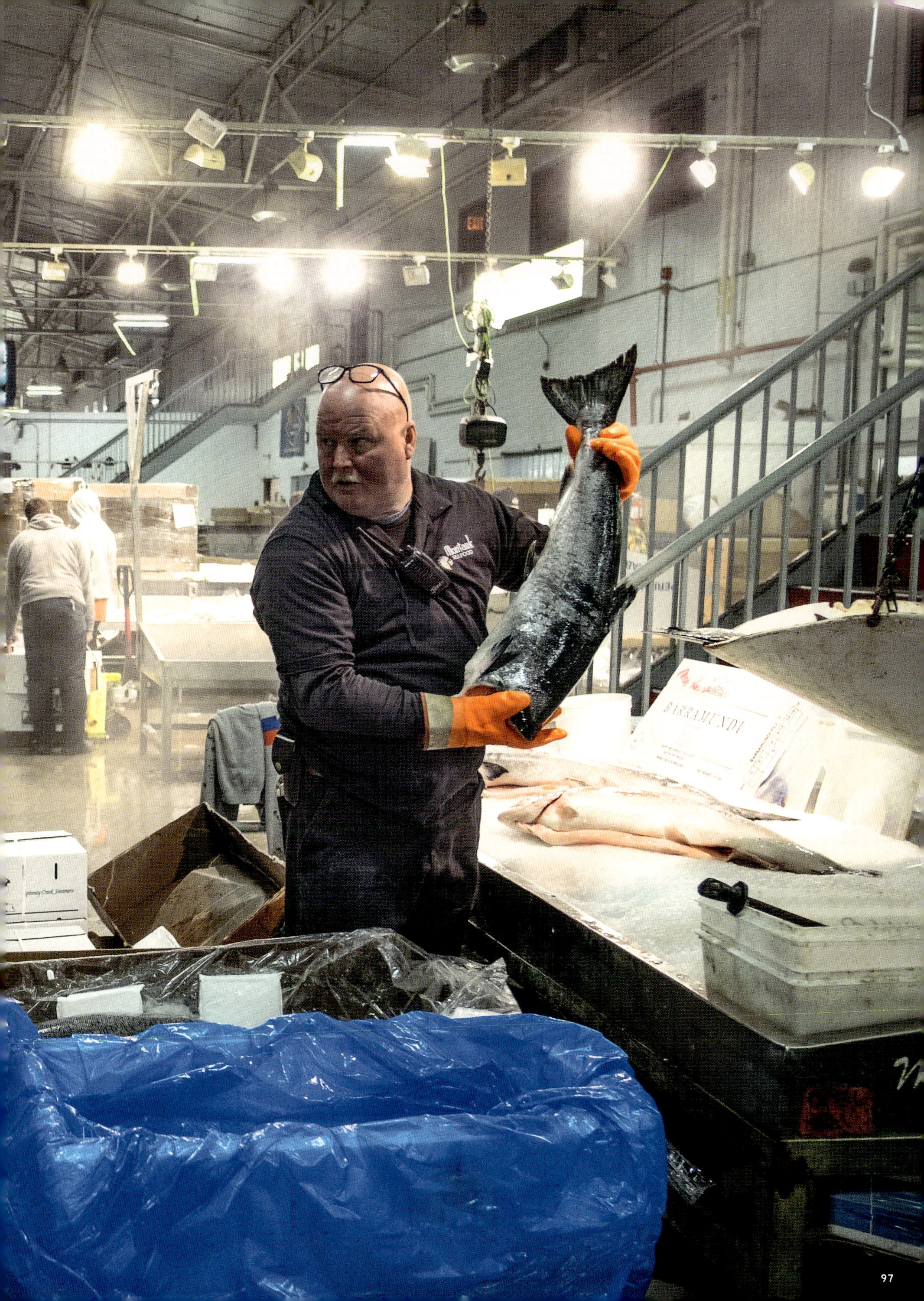

Montauk
SEAFOOD
BARRAMUNDI

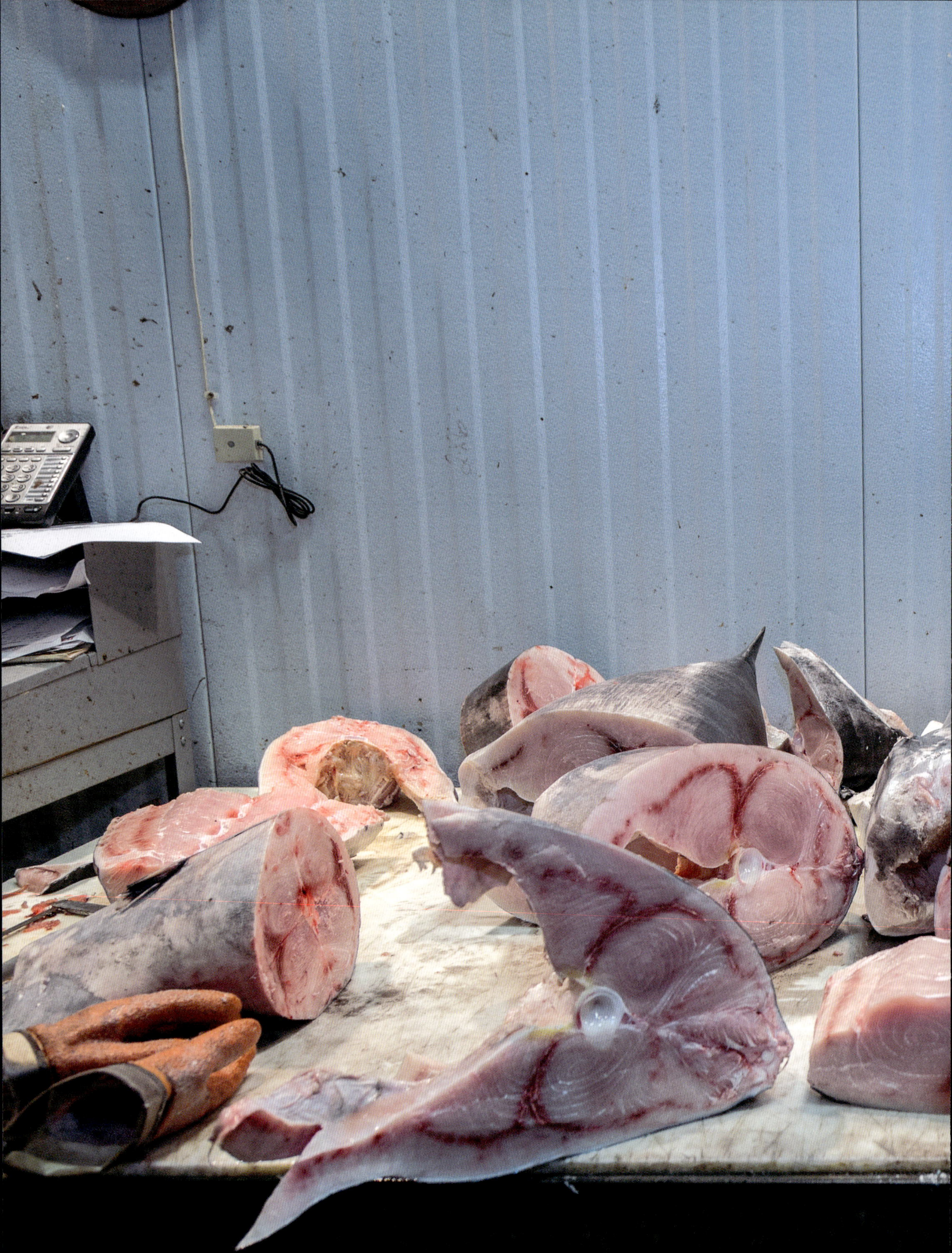

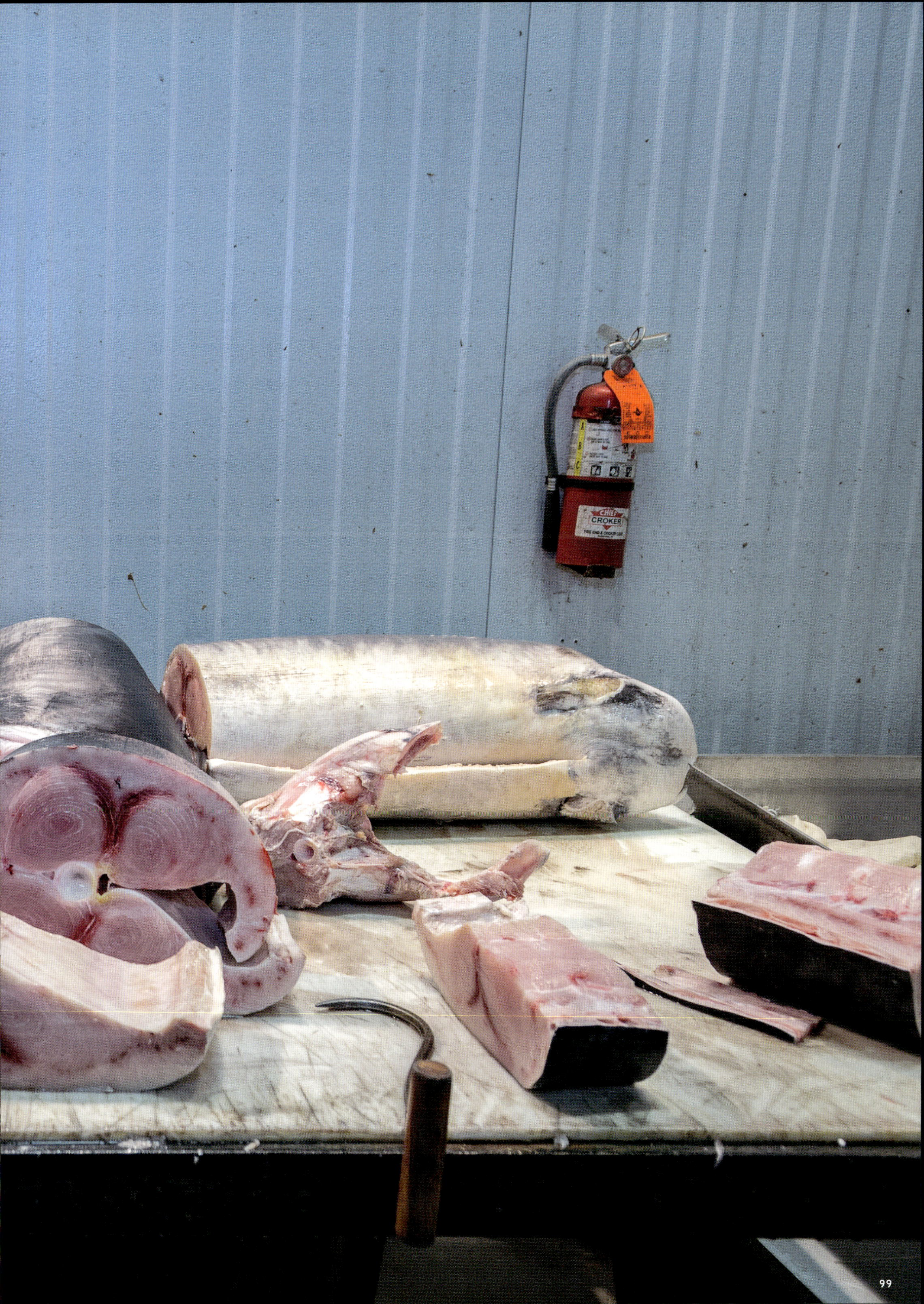

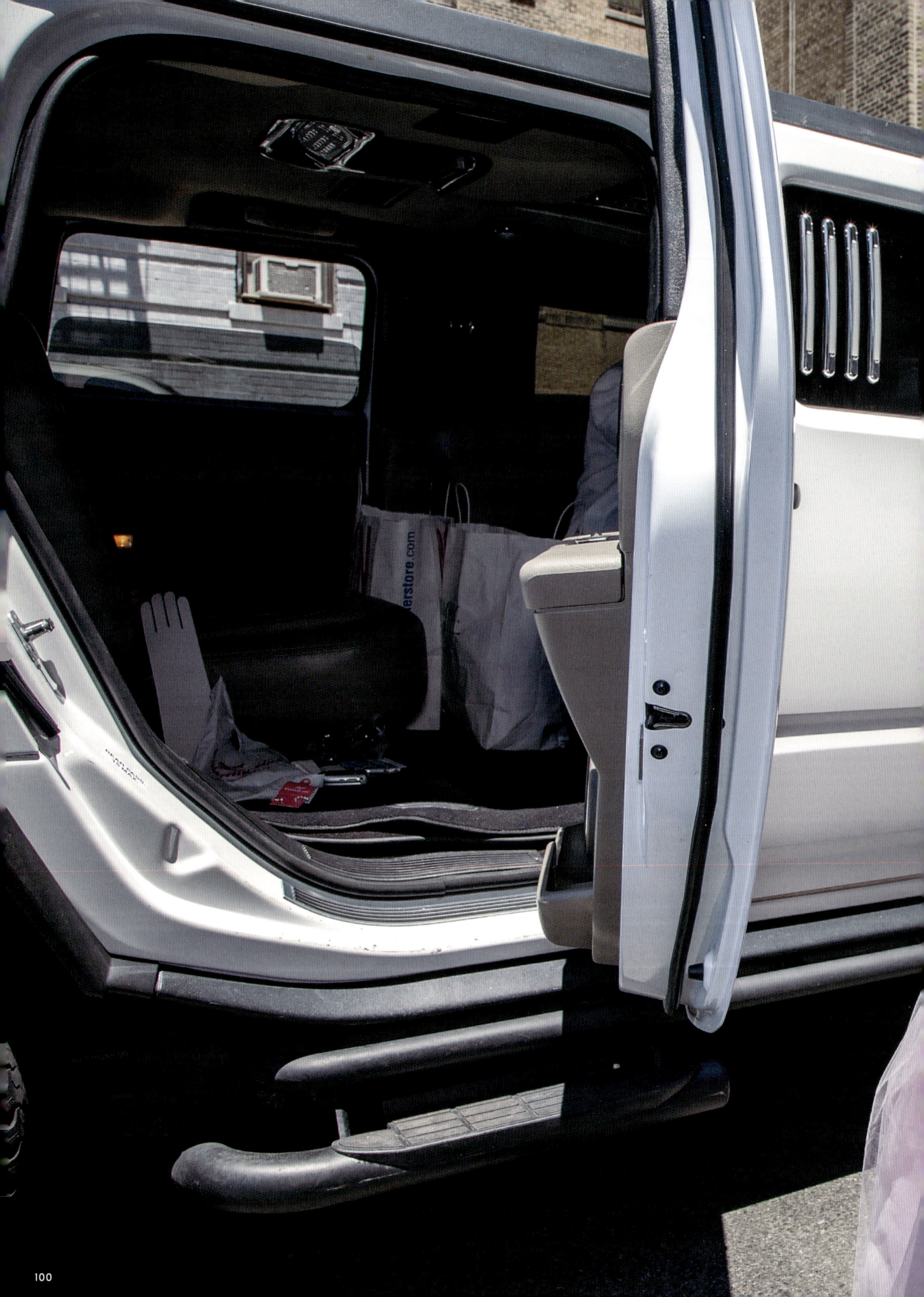

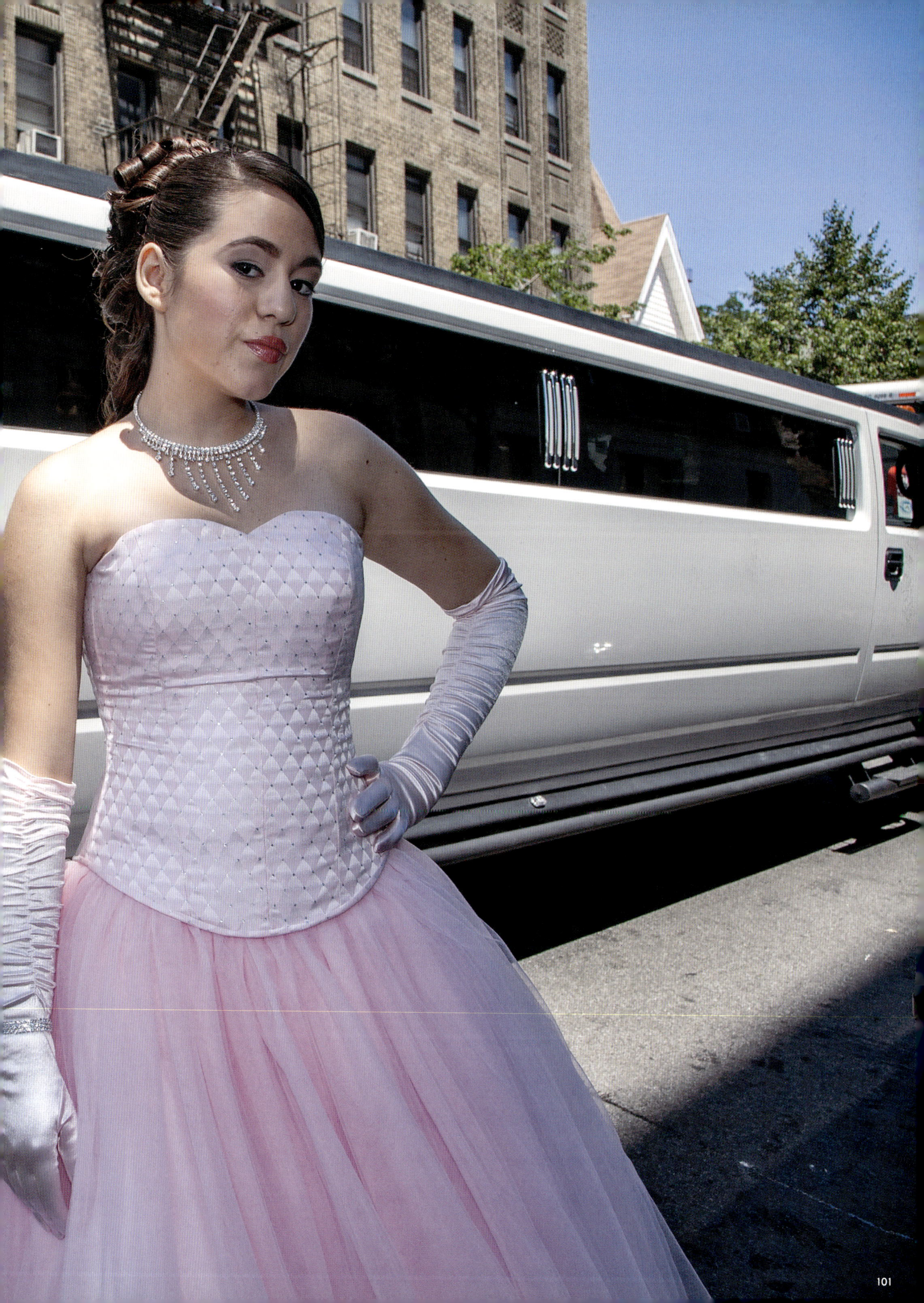

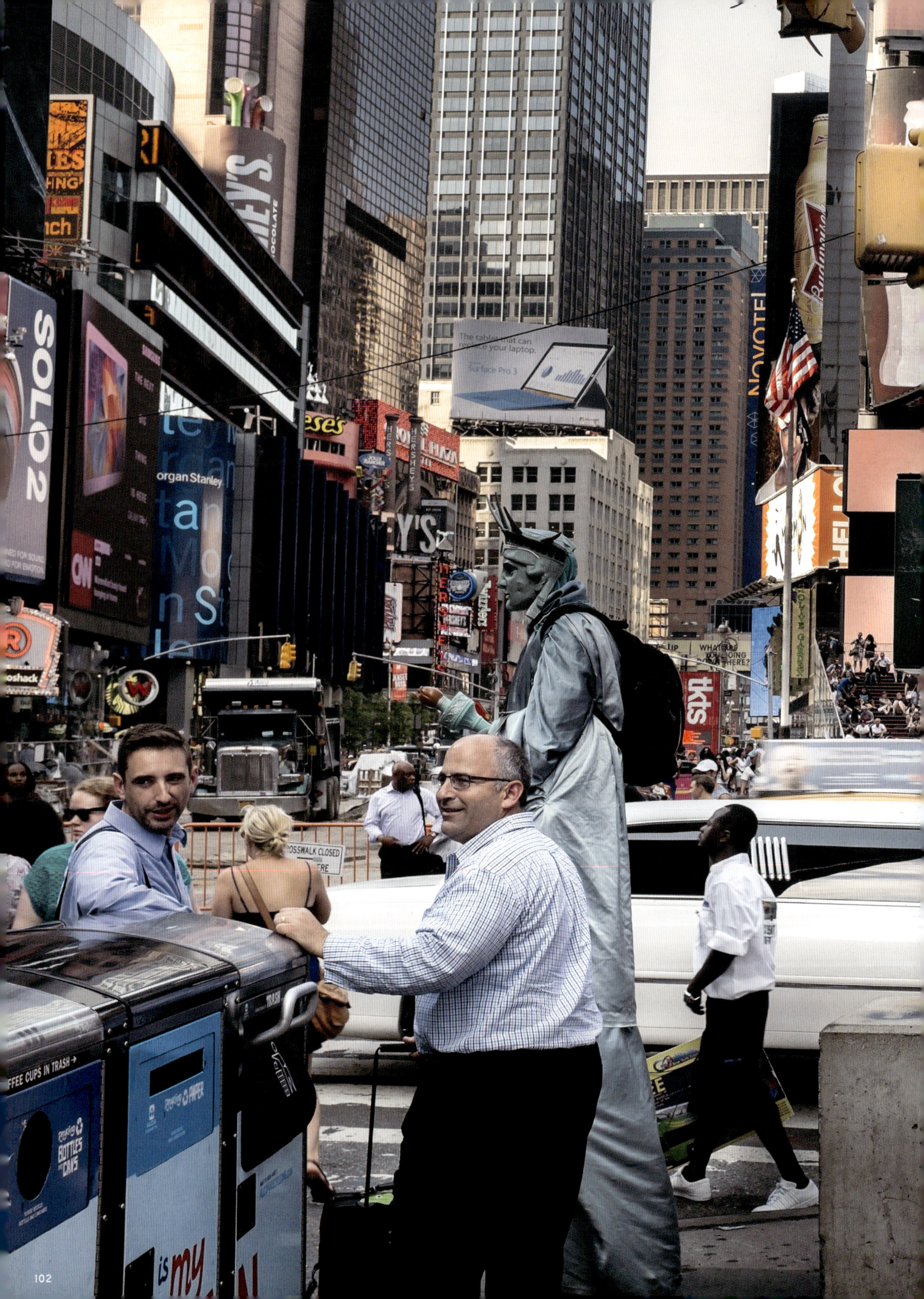

SOLO2
Surface Pro 3
The tablet that can.
replace your laptop.
organ Stanley
tan
Mo
n St
NOVOTEL
HELLO
tkts
CROSSWALK CLOSED
COFFEE CUPS IN TRASH →
BOTTLES
PAPER
TRASH
is my

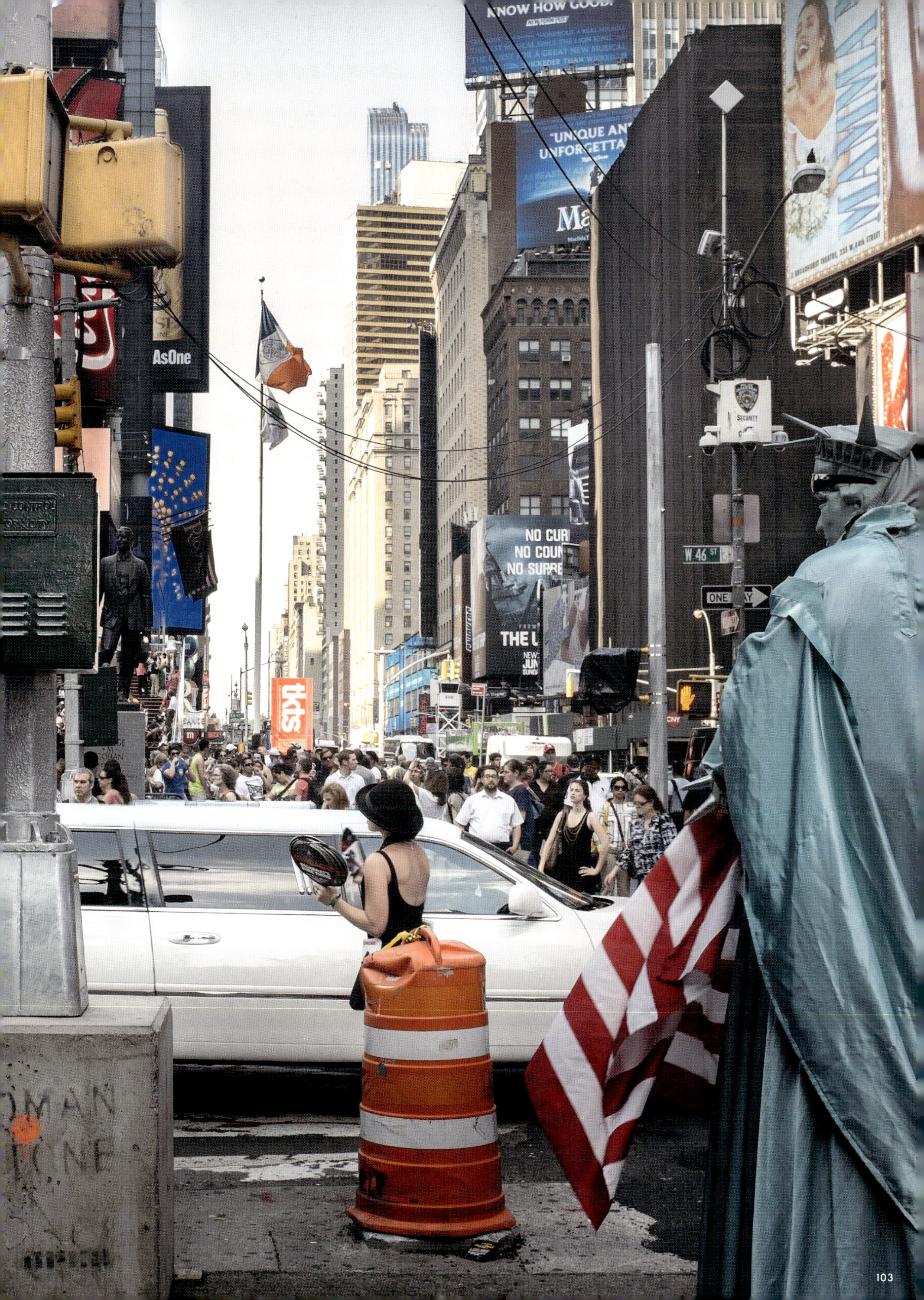

KNOW HOW GOOD!
AsOne
MAMMA
SECURITY
W 46 ST
ONE WAY
tkts
NO CUR
NO COU
NO SURRE
THE U

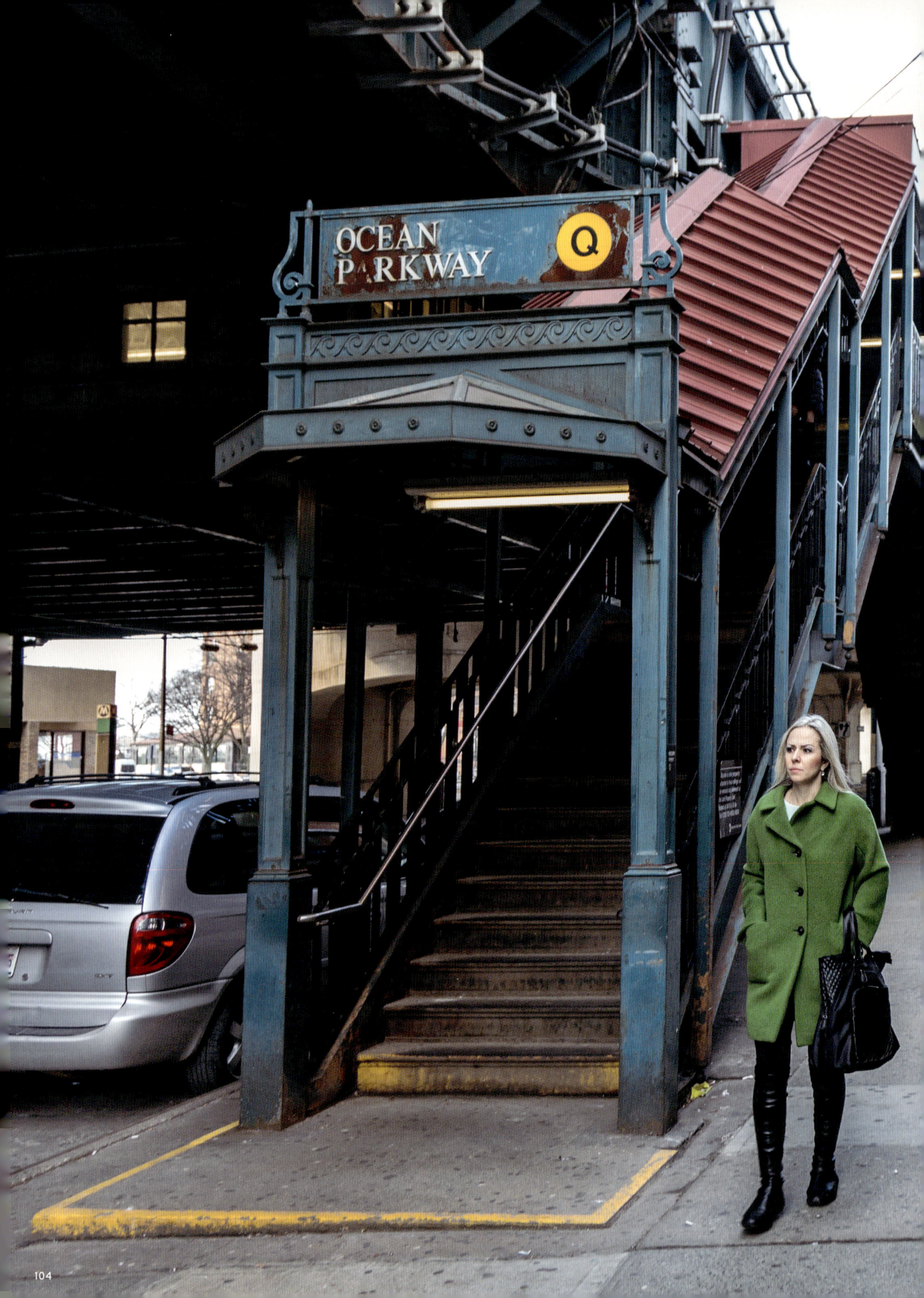

OCEAN
PARKWAY
Q

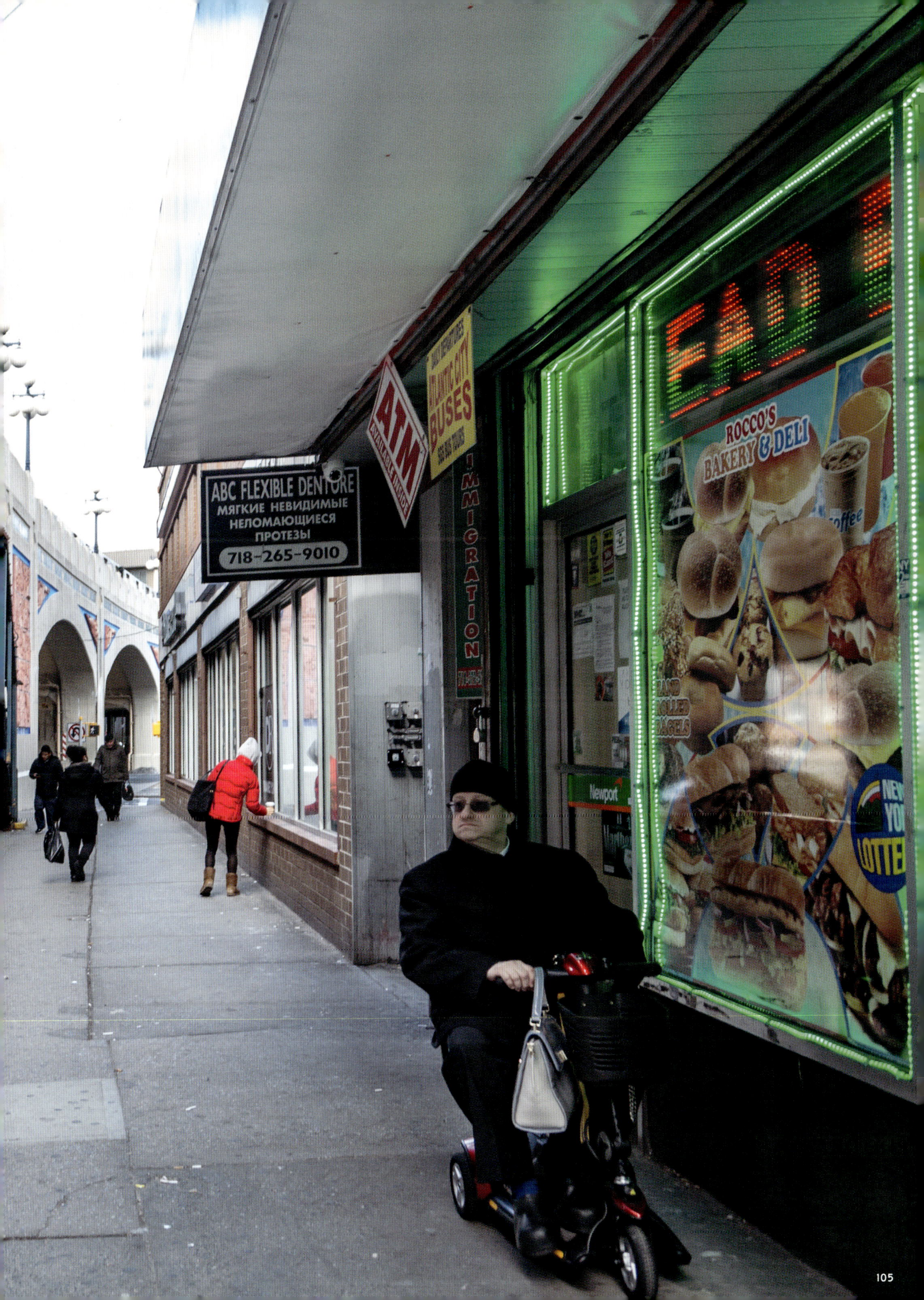
ATM
ATLANTIC CITY
BUSES
IMMIGRATION
ABC FLEXIBLE DENTURE
МЯГКИЕ НЕВИДИМЫЕ
НЕЛОМАЮЩИЕСЯ
ПРОТЕЗЫ
718-265-9010
ROCCO'S
BAKERY & DELI
Coffee
Newport
NEW YORK
LOTTERY

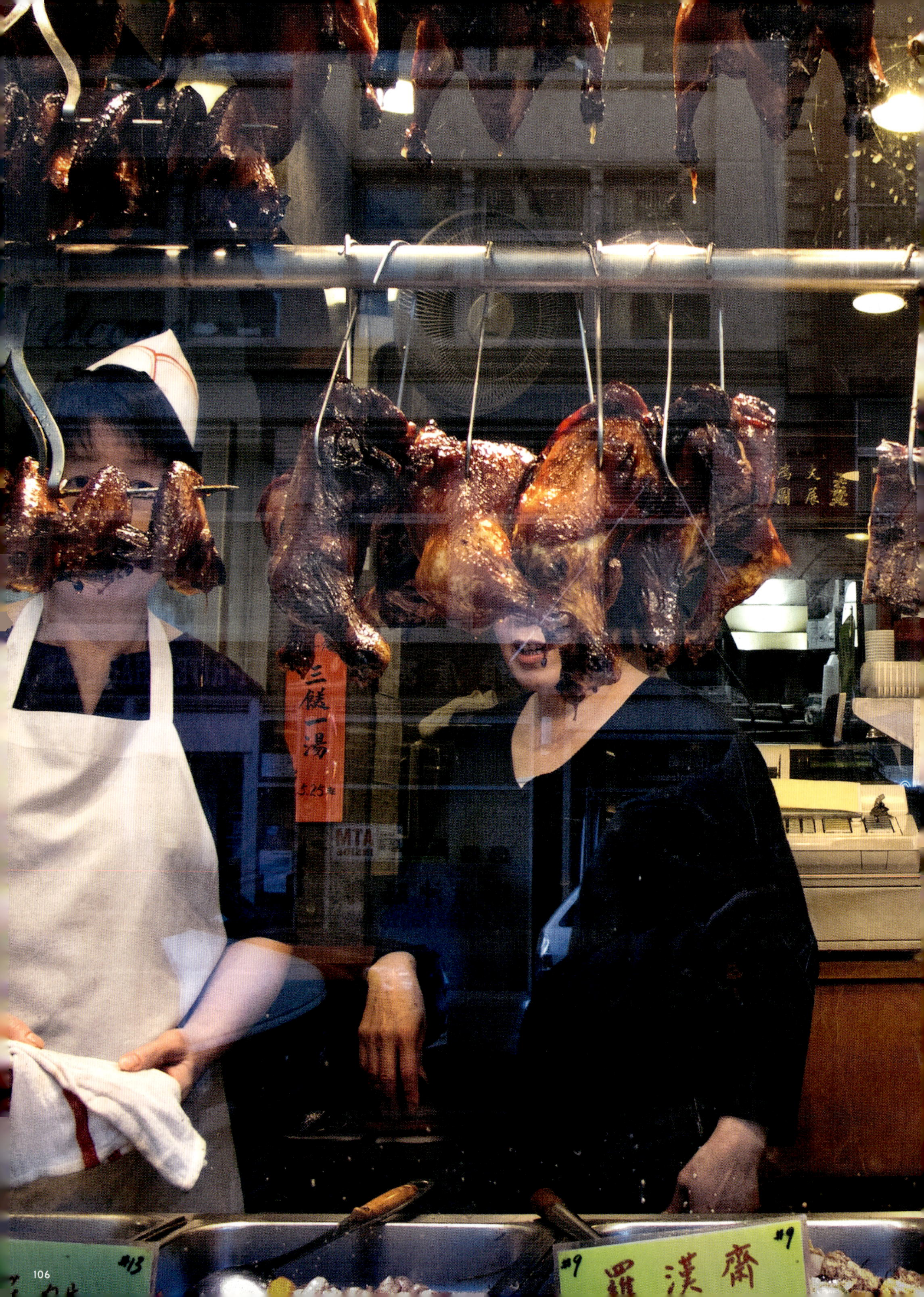

三候一湯
5.25
MTA
#9 羅漢齋
#9

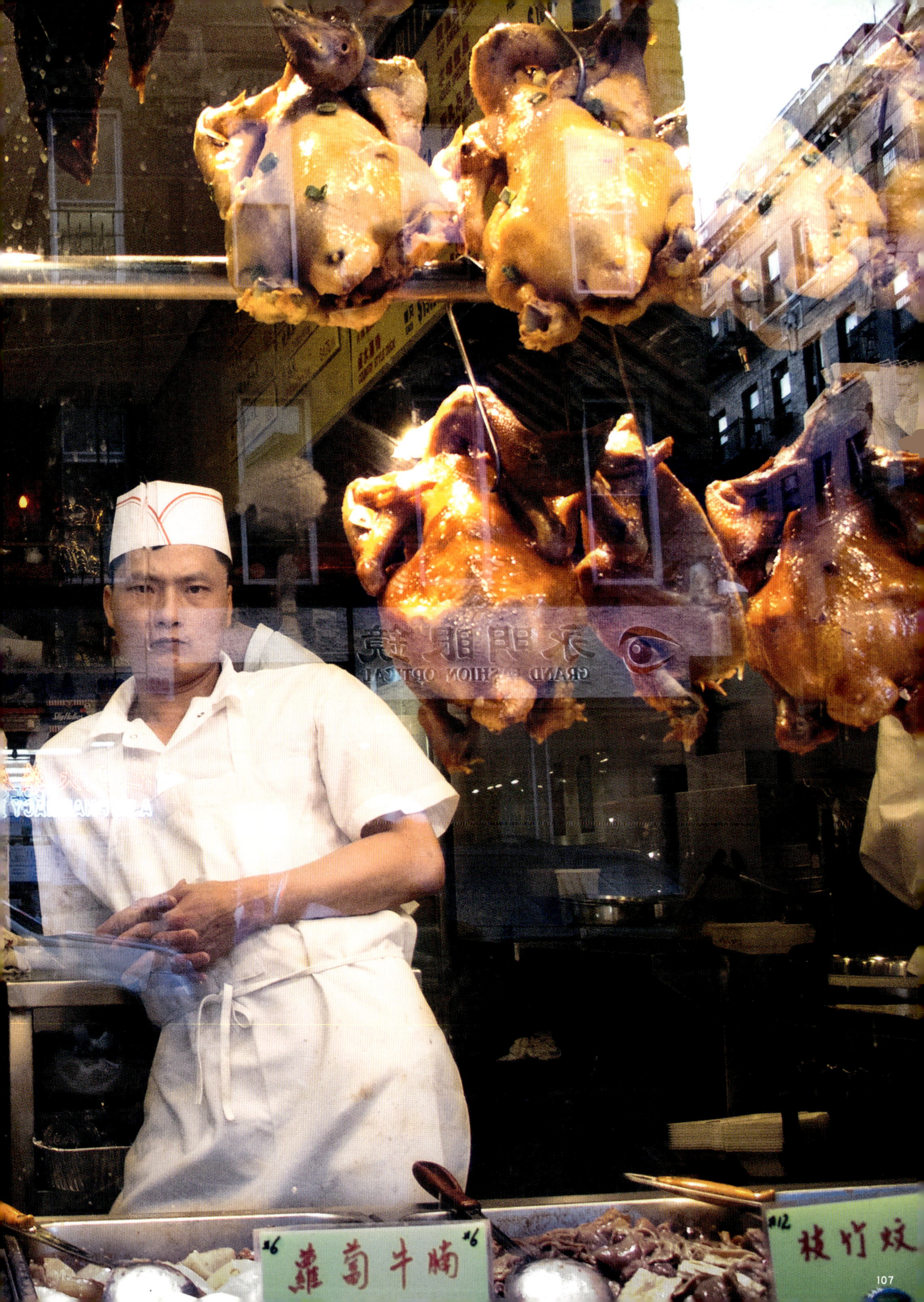
蘿蔔牛腩
枝竹炆

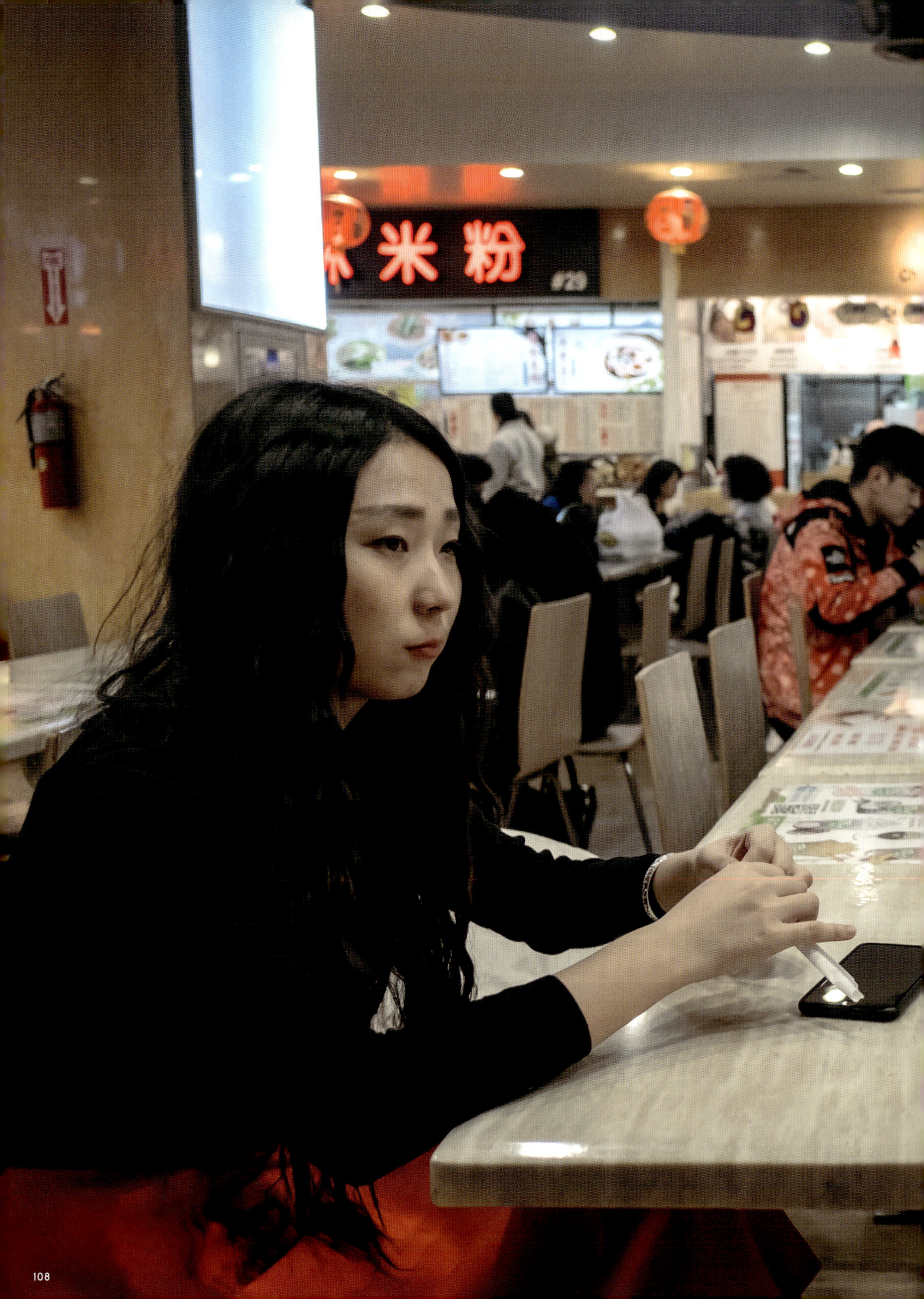

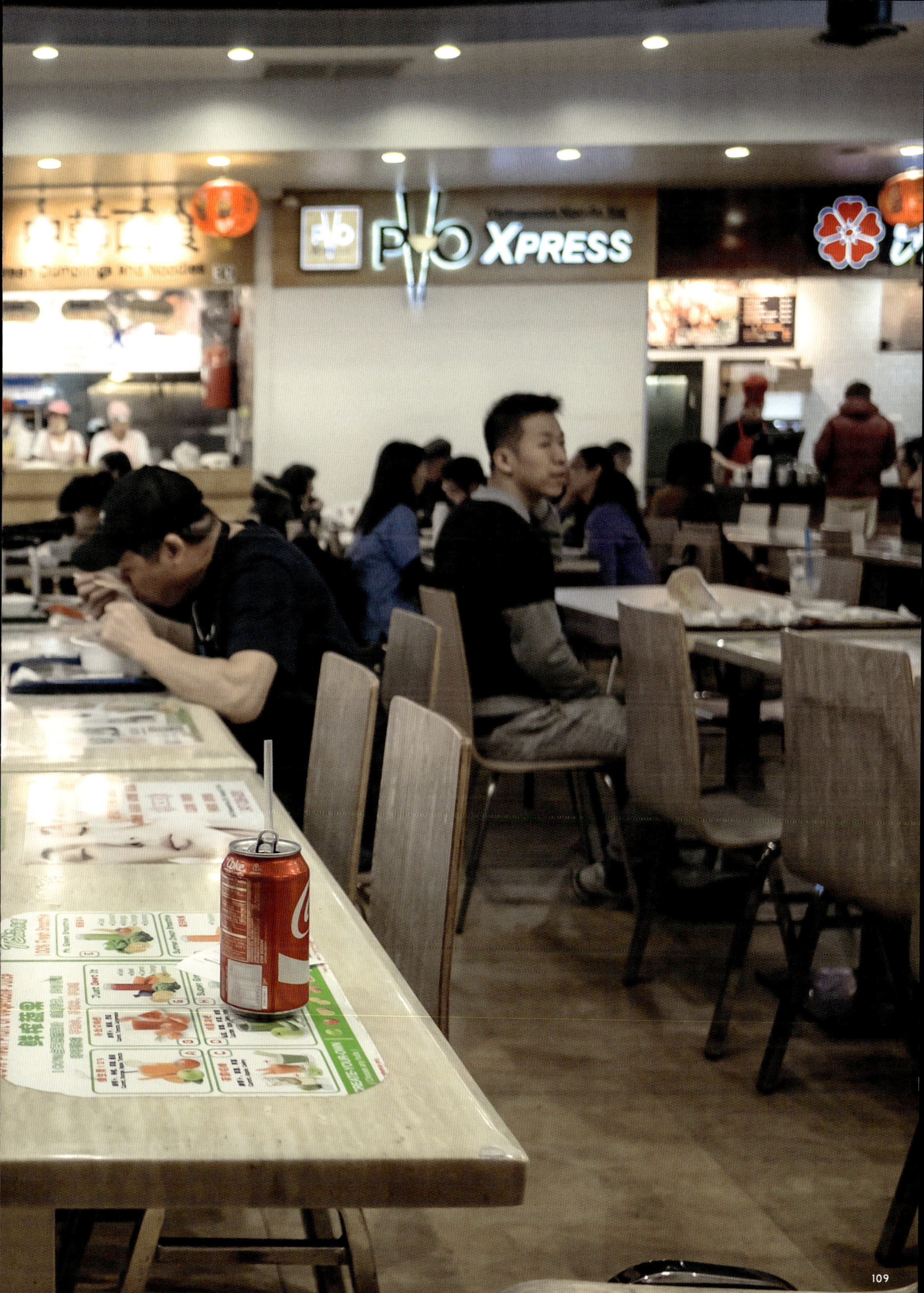

PHO XPRESS

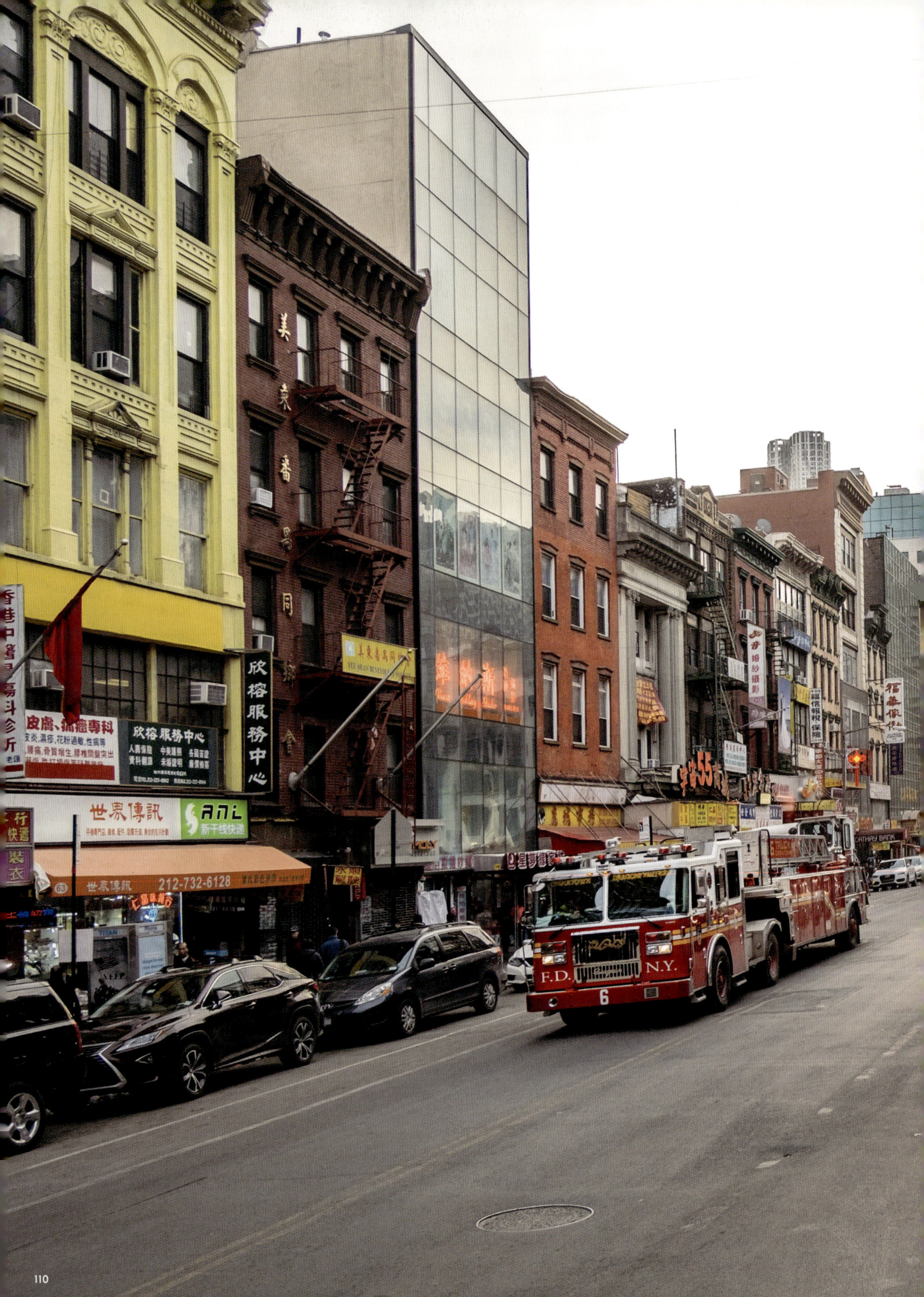

欣榕服務中心
世界傳訊
212-732-6128
F.D. N.Y.
6

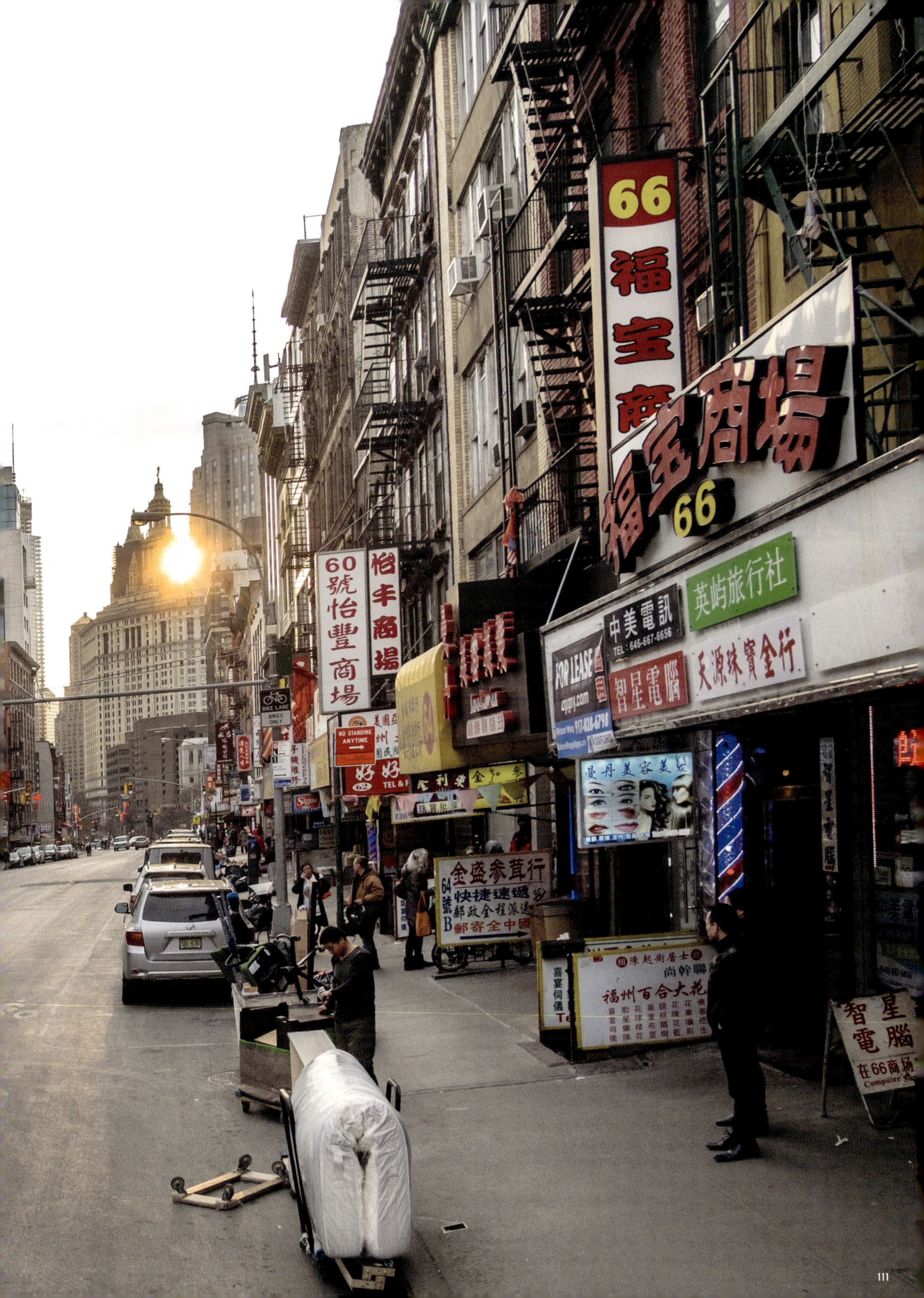

66
福寶商場
66
60號怡豐商場
怡丰商場
英峒旅行社
中美電訊
TEL：646-667-6656
FOR LEASE
智星電腦
天源珠寶金行
曼丹美容美髮
金盛參茸行
64號
B
快捷速遞
郵政全程派送
郵寄全中國
福州百合大花
智星
電腦
在66商場
NO STANDING
ANYTIME
BIKE LANE
BIKES
ONLY

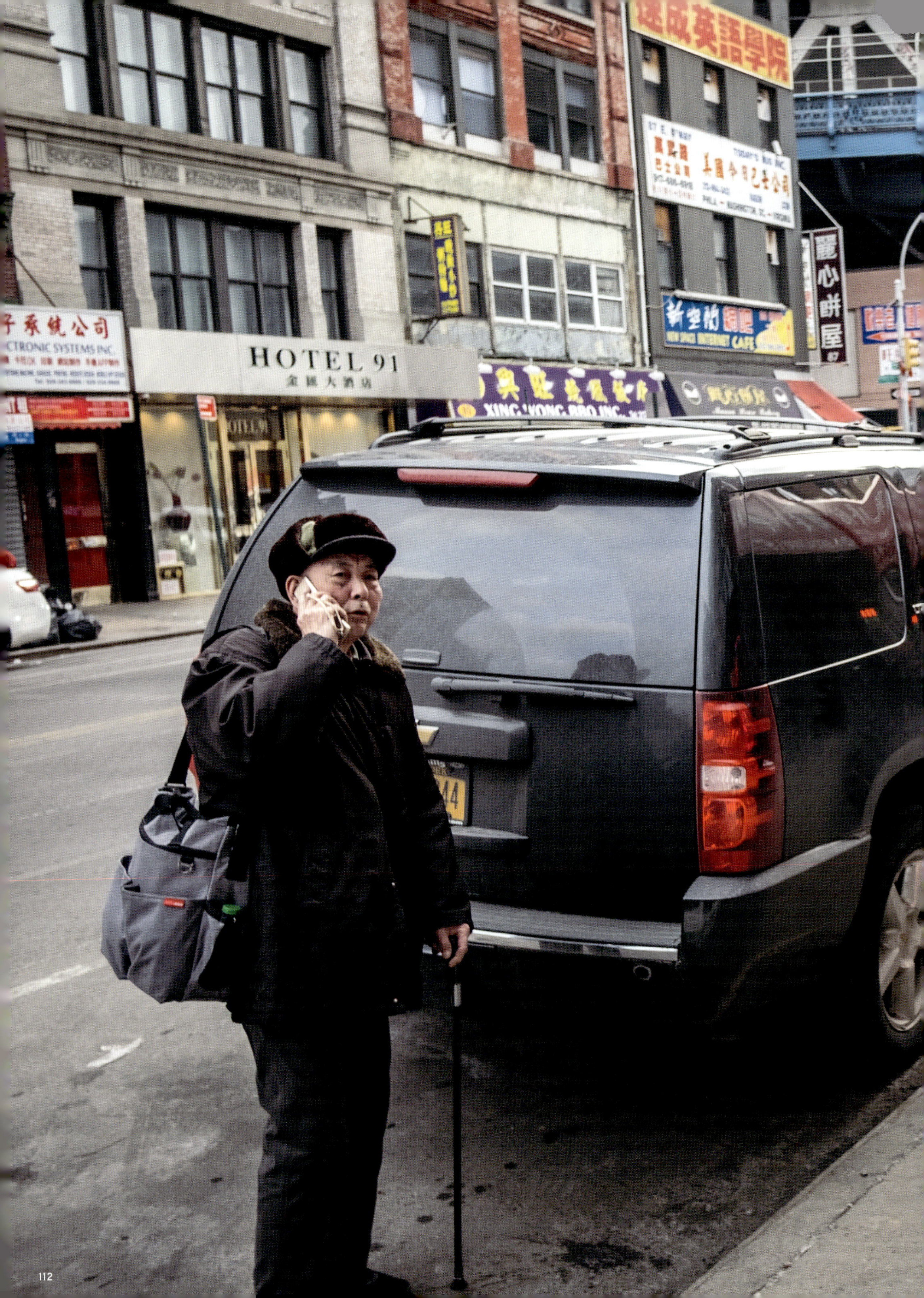
速成英語學院
HOTEL 91
金碧大酒店
麗心餅屋
CTRONIC SYSTEMS INC.
NEW SPACE INTERNET CAFE
XING WONG BBQ INC.

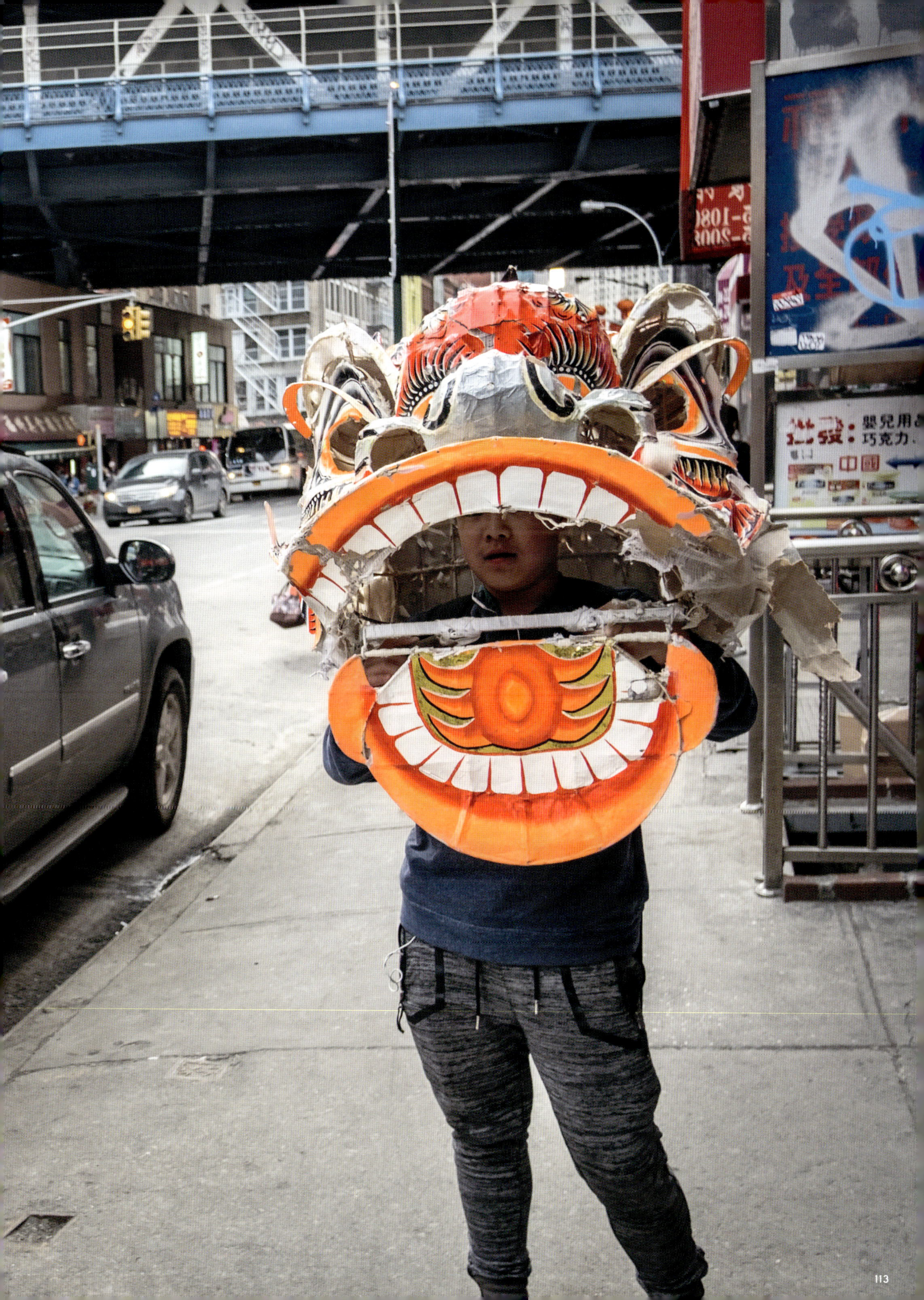

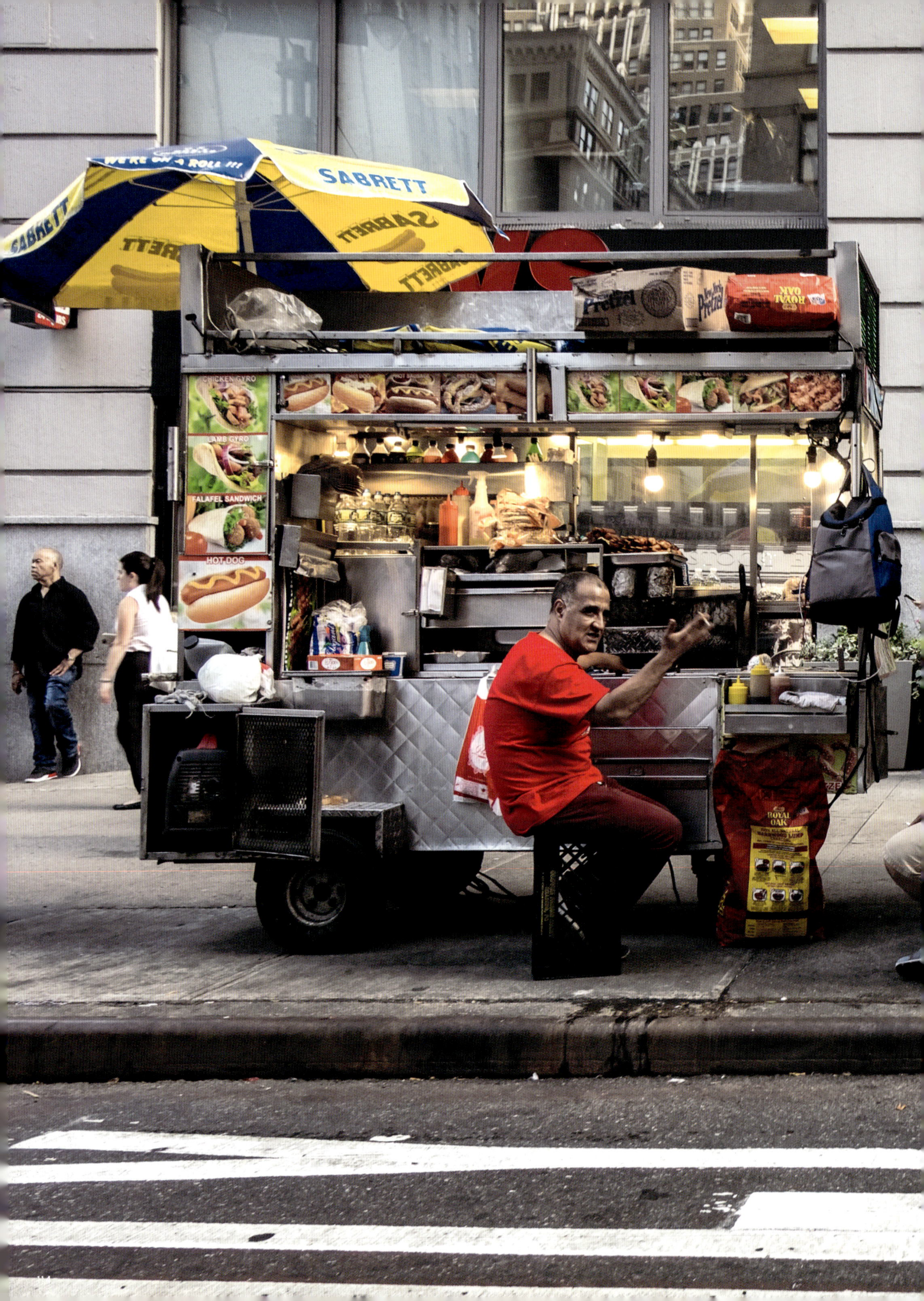
SABRETT
WE'RE ON A ROLL !!!
SABRETT
CHICKEN GYRO
LAMB GYRO
FALAFEL SANDWICH
HOT DOG
Pretzel
New York Pretzel
ROYAL OAK
ROYAL OAK

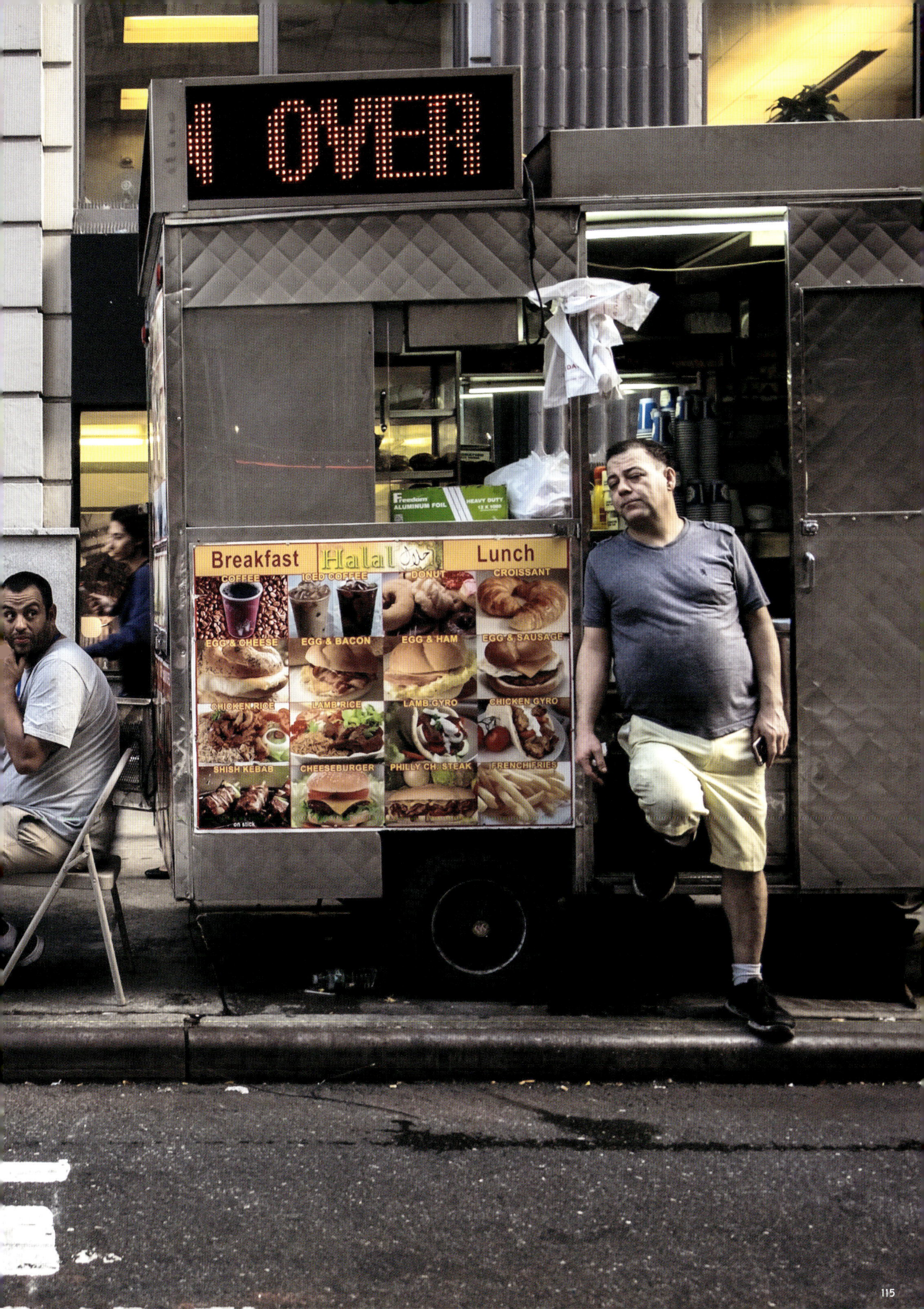
OVER
Breakfast Halal Lunch
COFFEE ICED COFFEE DONUT CROISSANT
EGG & CHEESE EGG & BACON EGG & HAM EGG & SAUSAGE
CHICKEN RICE LAMB RICE LAMB GYRO CHICKEN GYRO
SHISH KEBAB CHEESEBURGER PHILLY CH. STEAK FRENCH FRIES
on stick
ALUMINUM FOIL
HEAVY DUTY

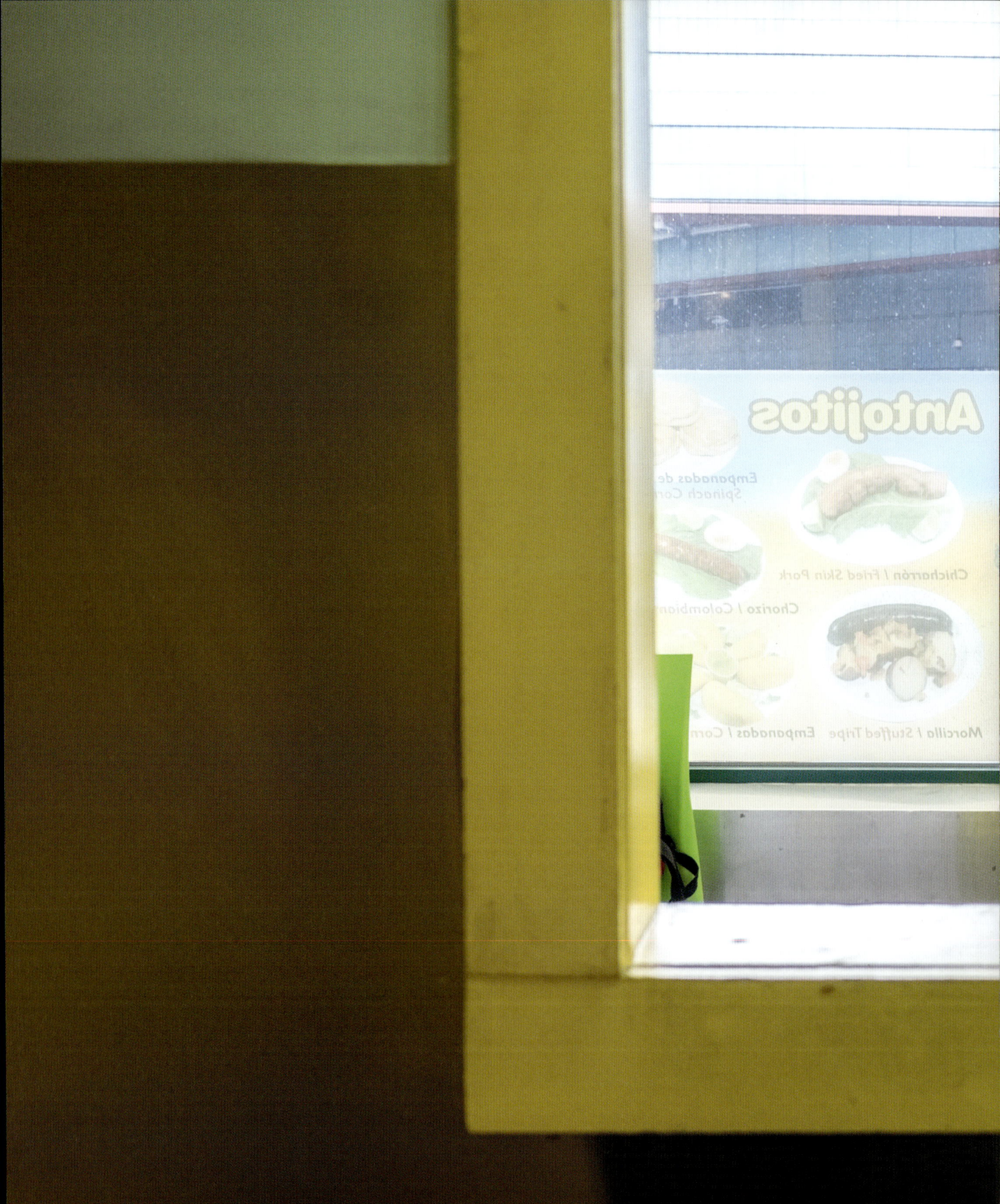

Antojitos

Empanadas de
Spinach Cor...

Chicharrón / Fried Skin Pork

Chorizo / Colombian...

Morcilla / Stuffed Tripe   Empanadas / Cor...

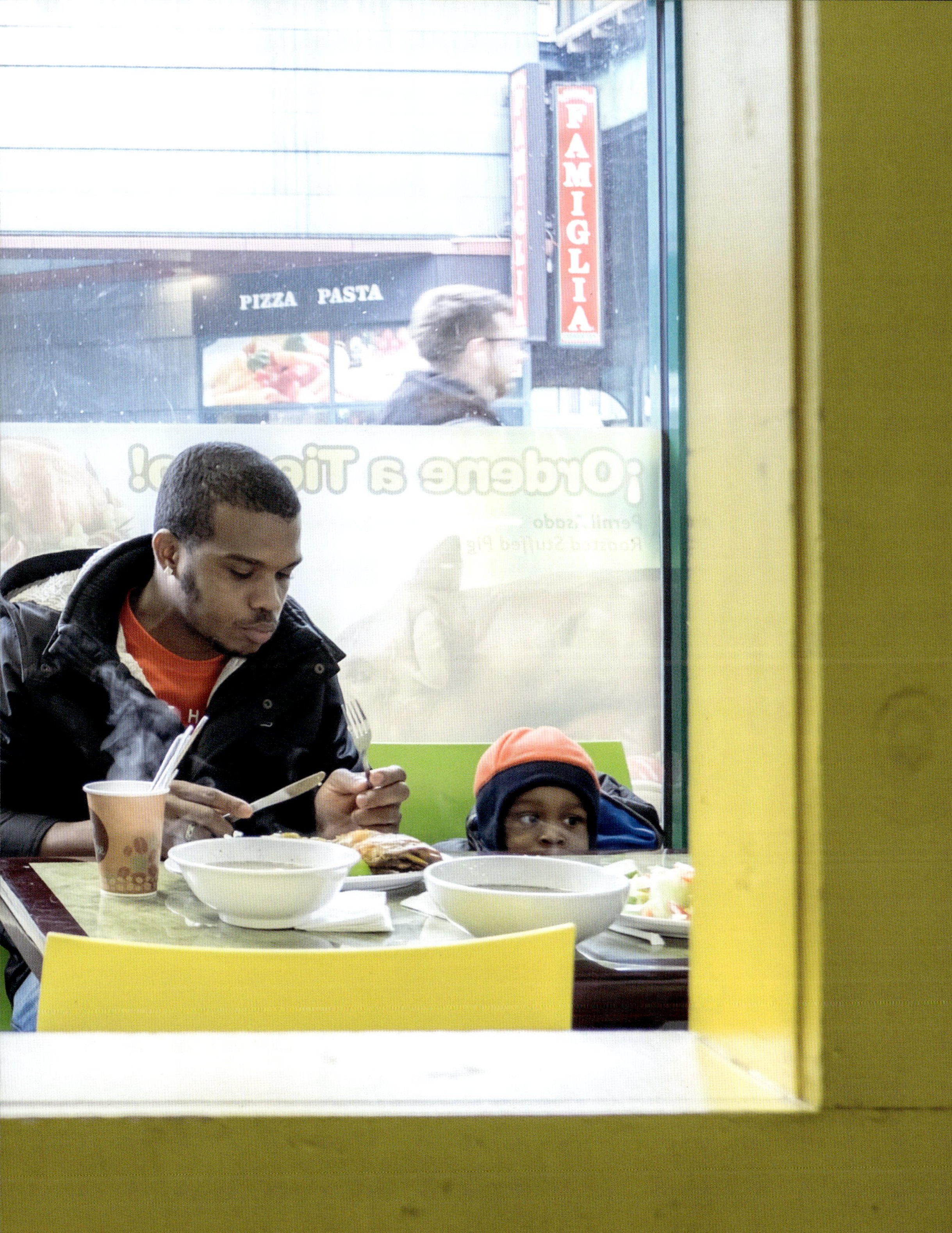
FAMIGLIA
PIZZA   PASTA
¡Ordene a Tiempo!
Pernil Asado
Roasted Stuffed Pig

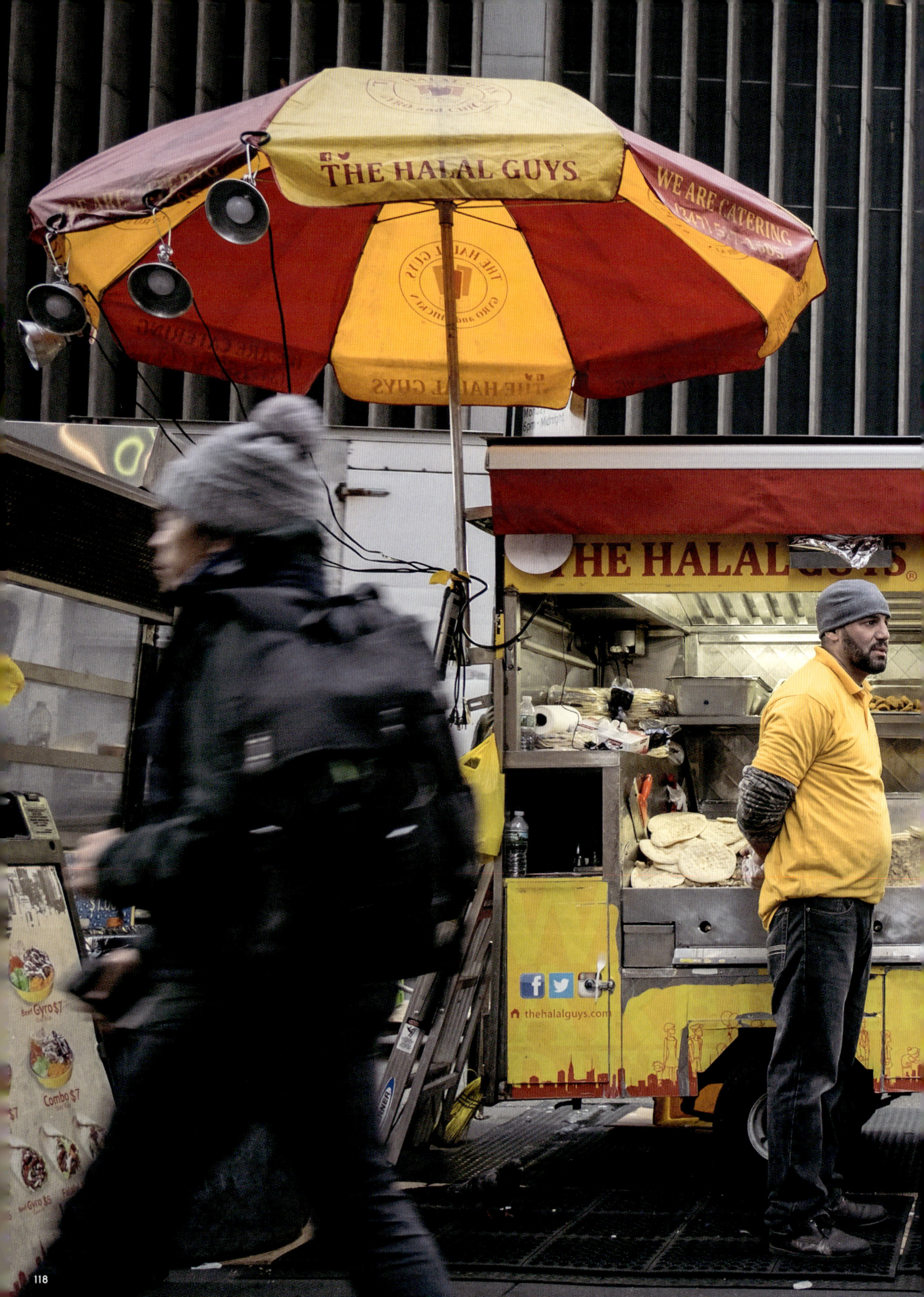
THE HALAL GUYS
WE ARE CATERING
THE HALAL GUYS
THE HALAL GUYS
THE HALAL GUYS
Mon
6pm - Midnight
THE HALAL GUYS
thehalalguys.com
Beef Gyro $7
Combo $7
$7
Gyro $5

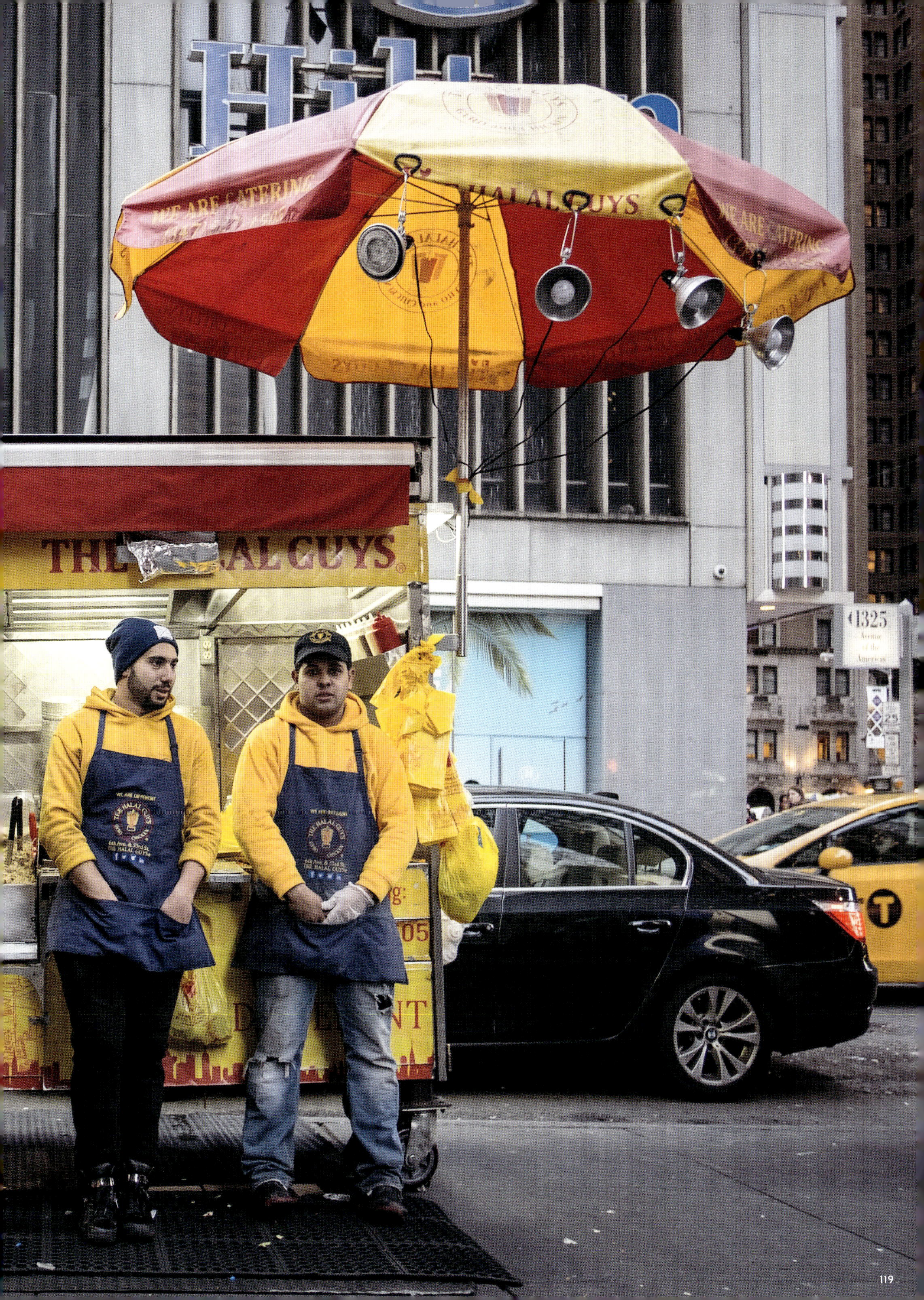

WE ARE CATERING
HALAL GUYS
WE ARE CATERING
THE HALAL GUYS
1325
Avenue of the Americas

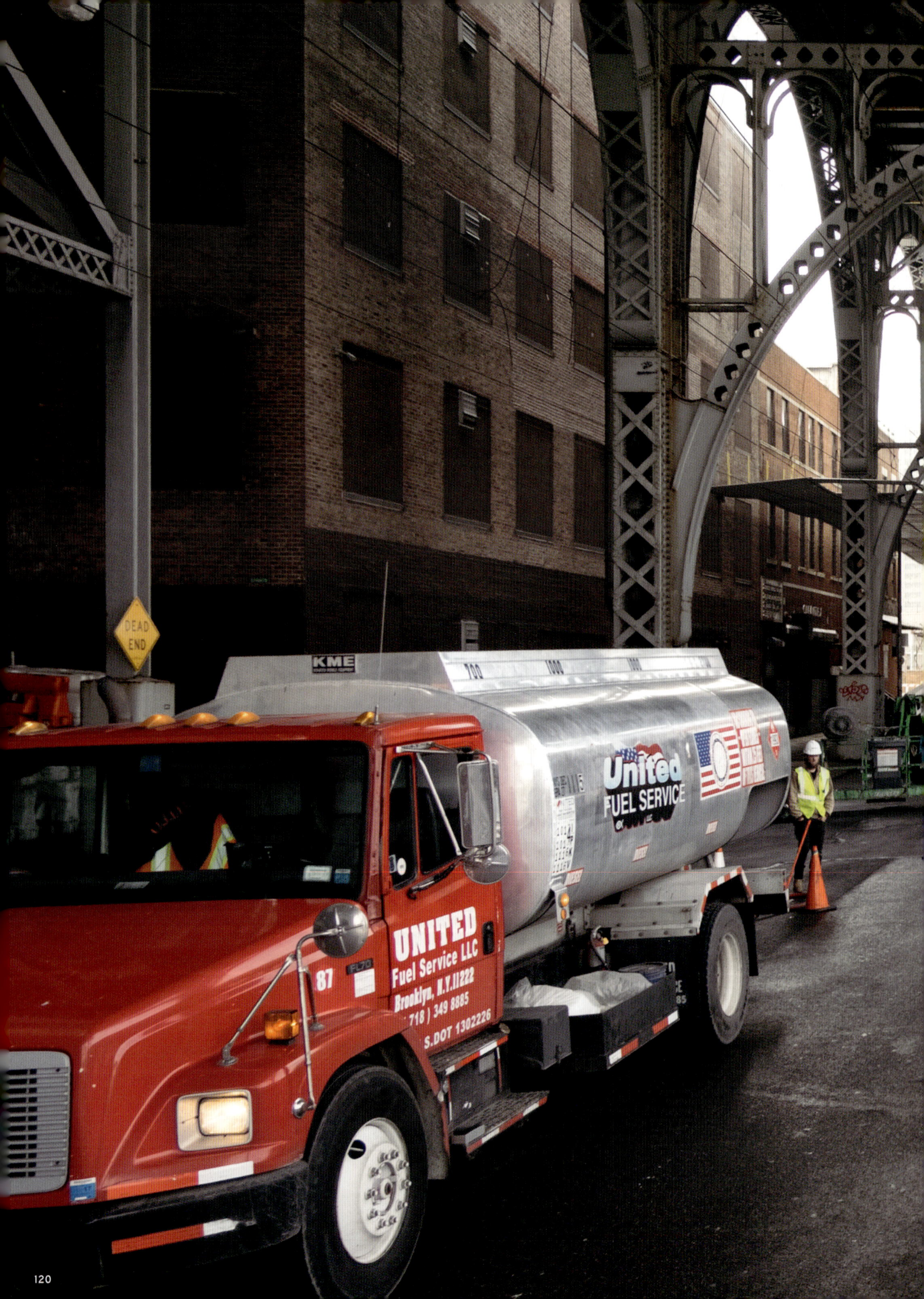
DEAD END
KME
United
FUEL SERVICE
UNITED
Fuel Service LLC
Brooklyn, N.Y. 11222
(718) 349 8885
S.DOT 1302226
87

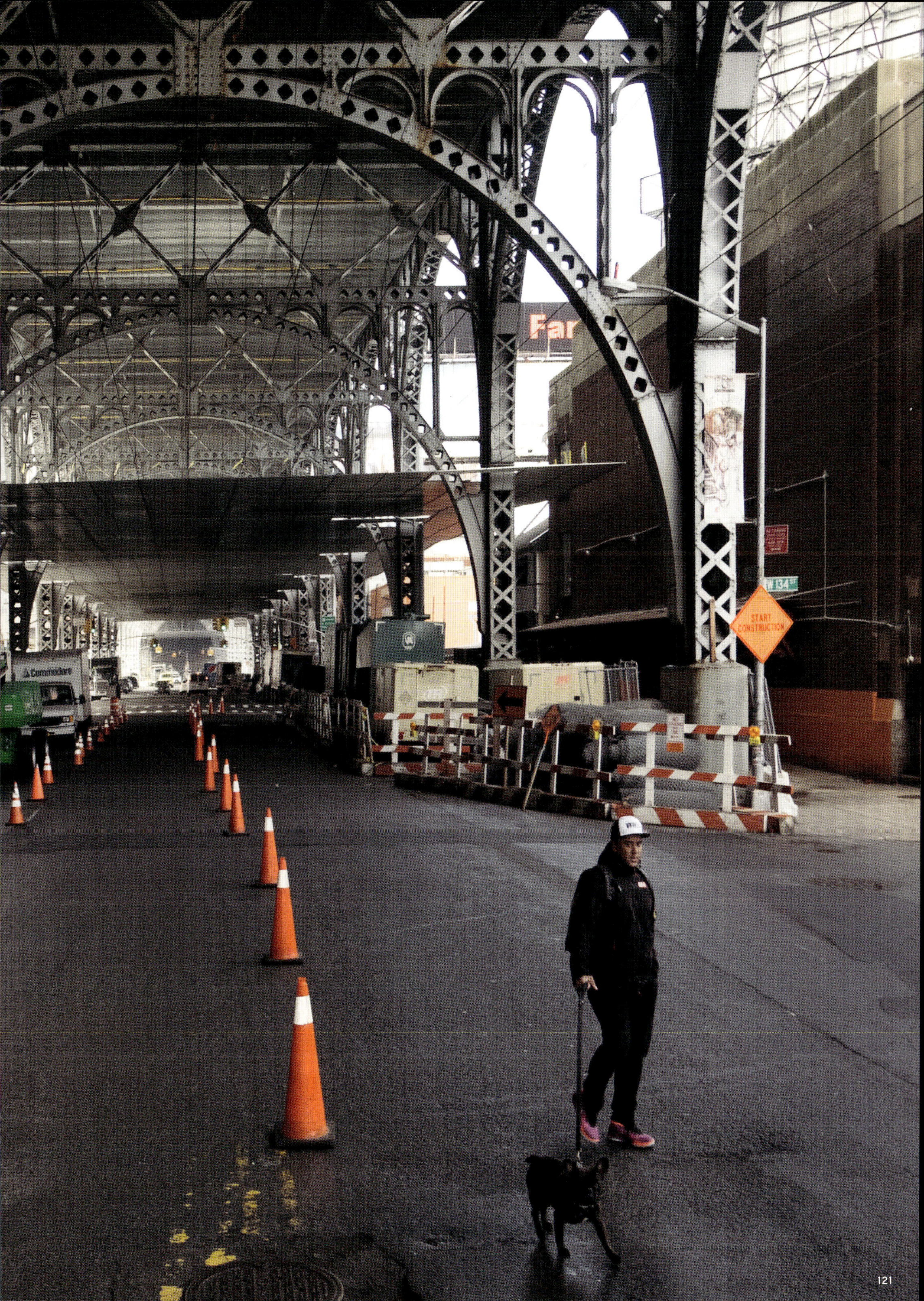

W 134 ST
START CONSTRUCTION
Commodore
Far

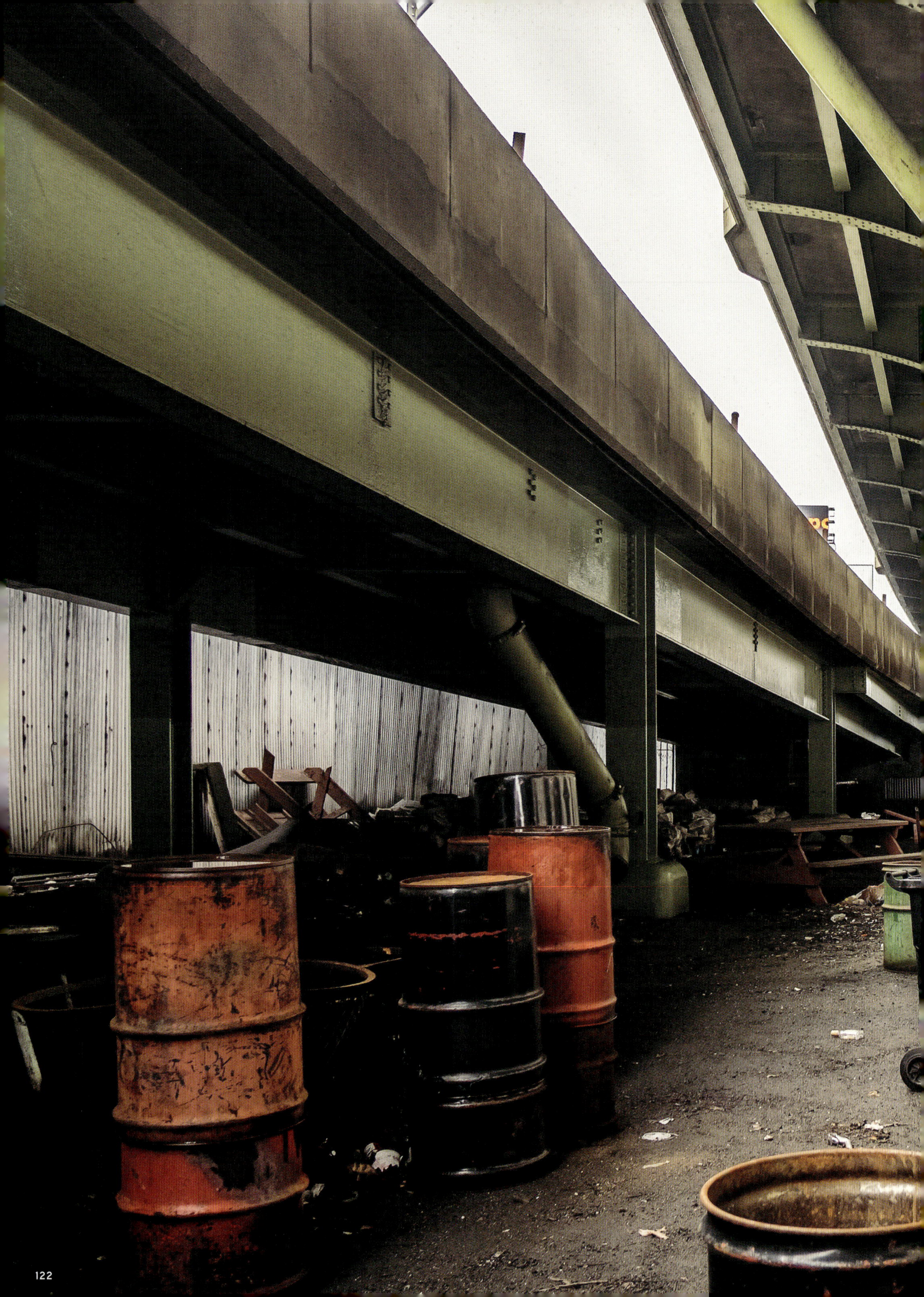

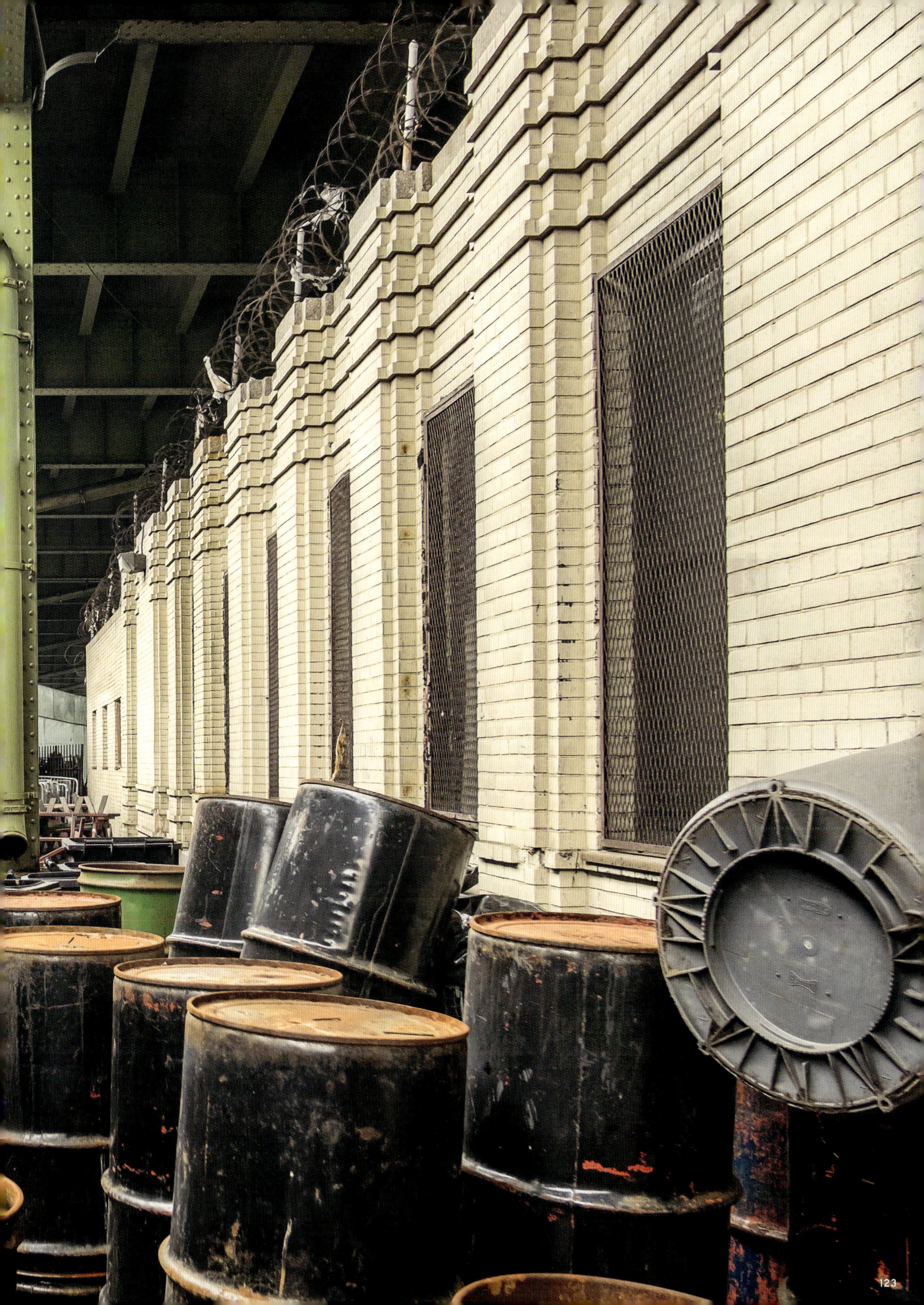

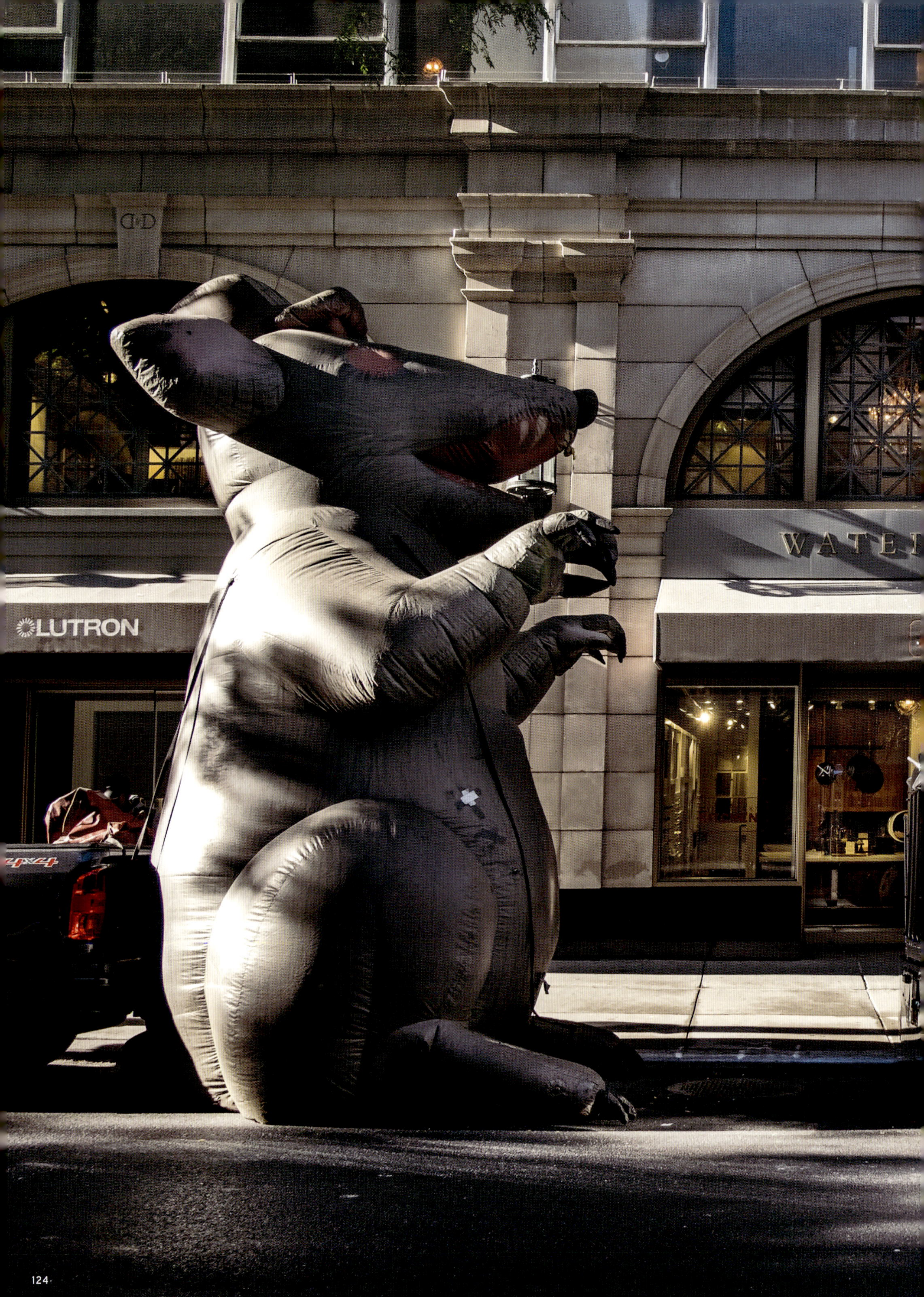
LUTRON
WATE

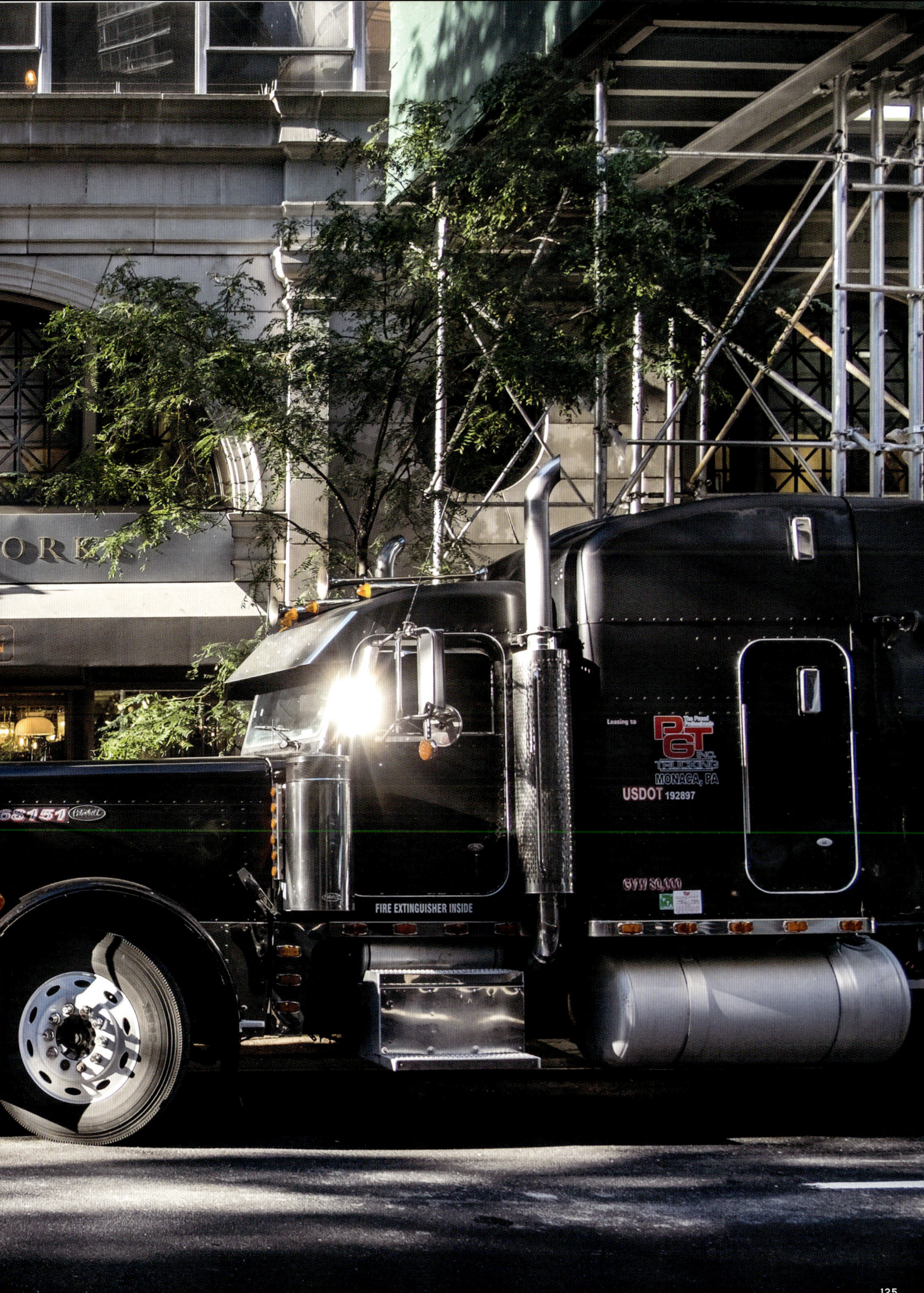

Leasing to
PGT INC. TRUCKING
MONACA, PA
USDOT 192897
FIRE EXTINGUISHER INSIDE

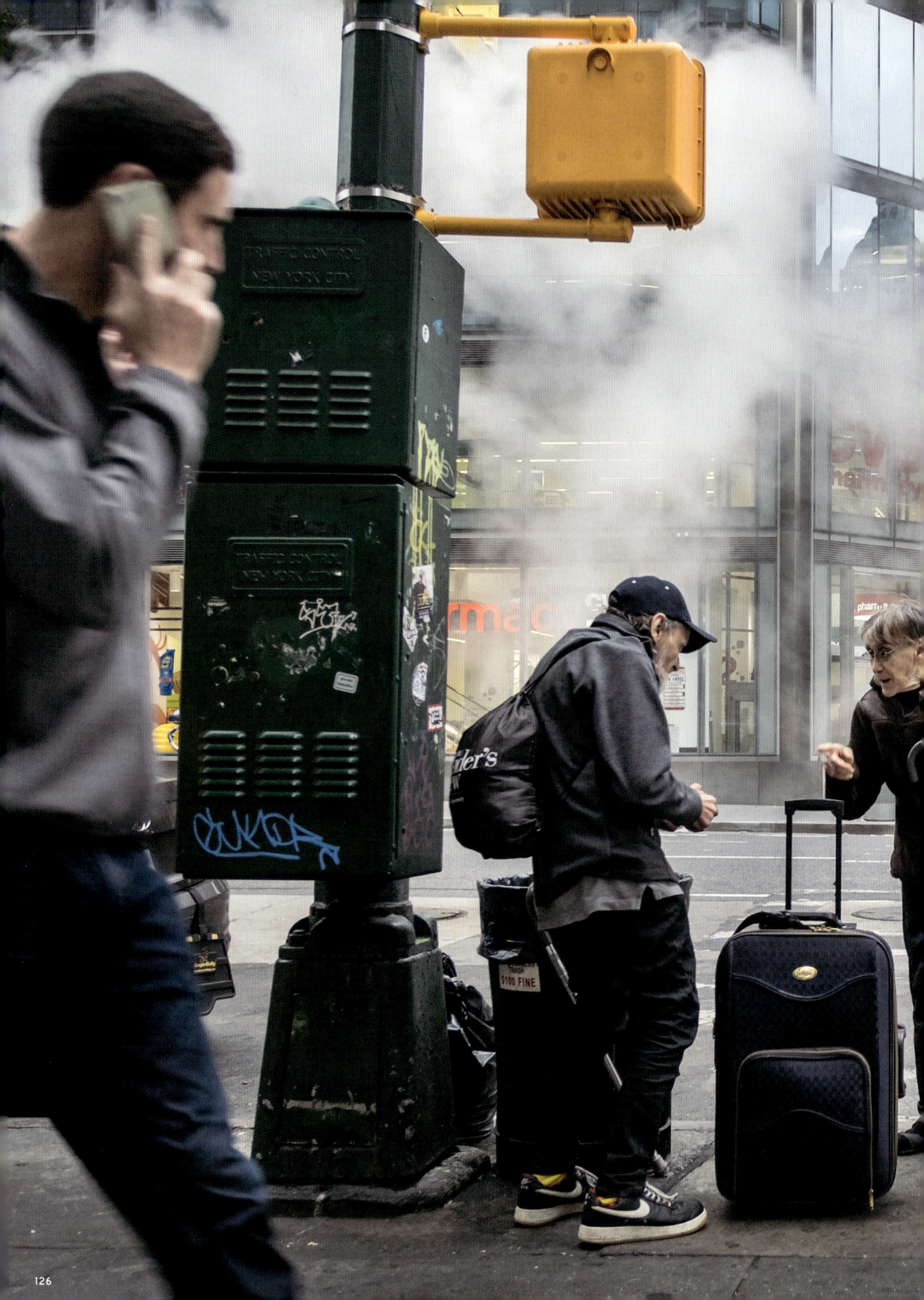
TRAFFIC CONTROL
NEW YORK CITY
TRAFFIC CONTROL
NEW YORK CITY
TRASH
$100 FINE

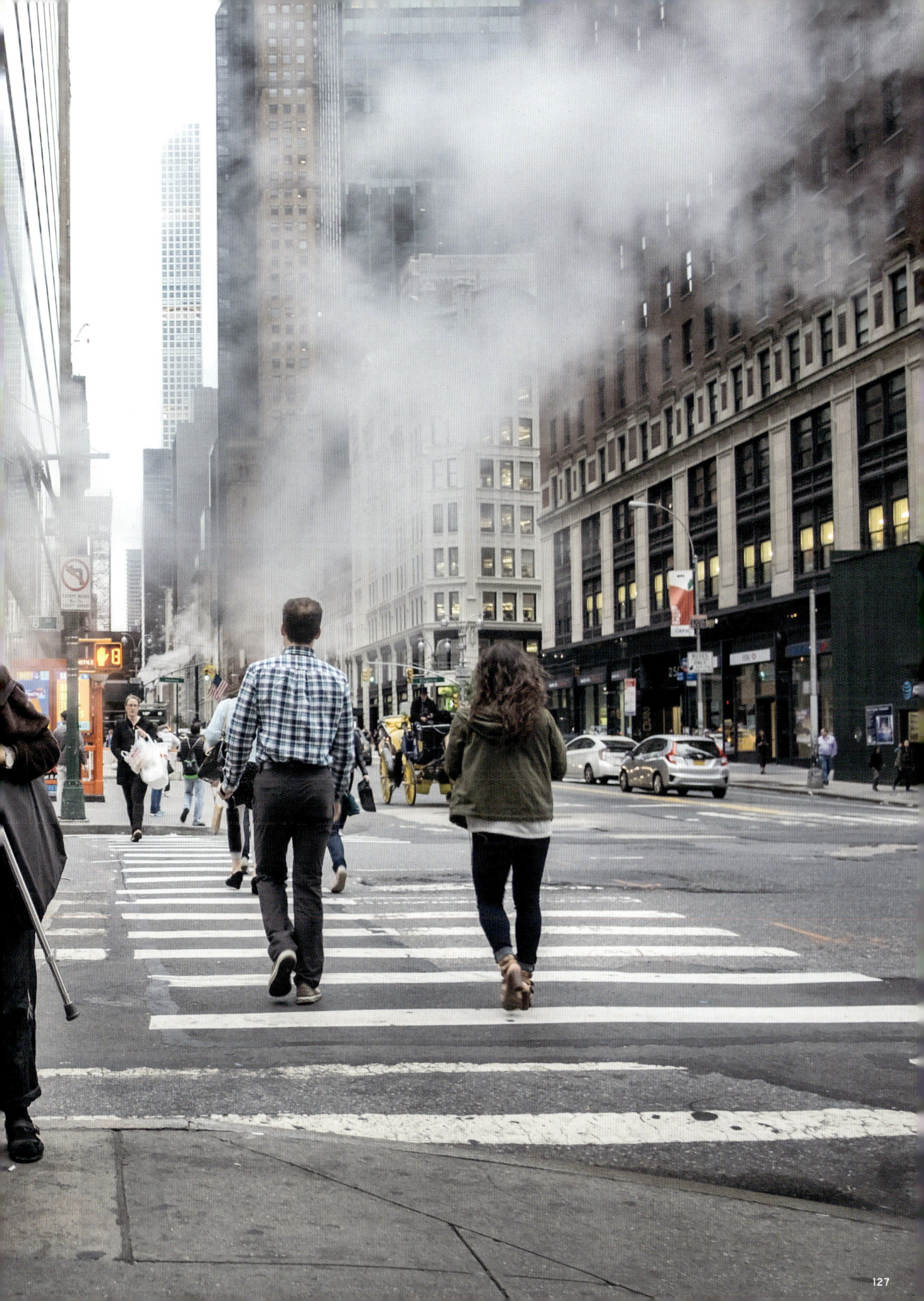

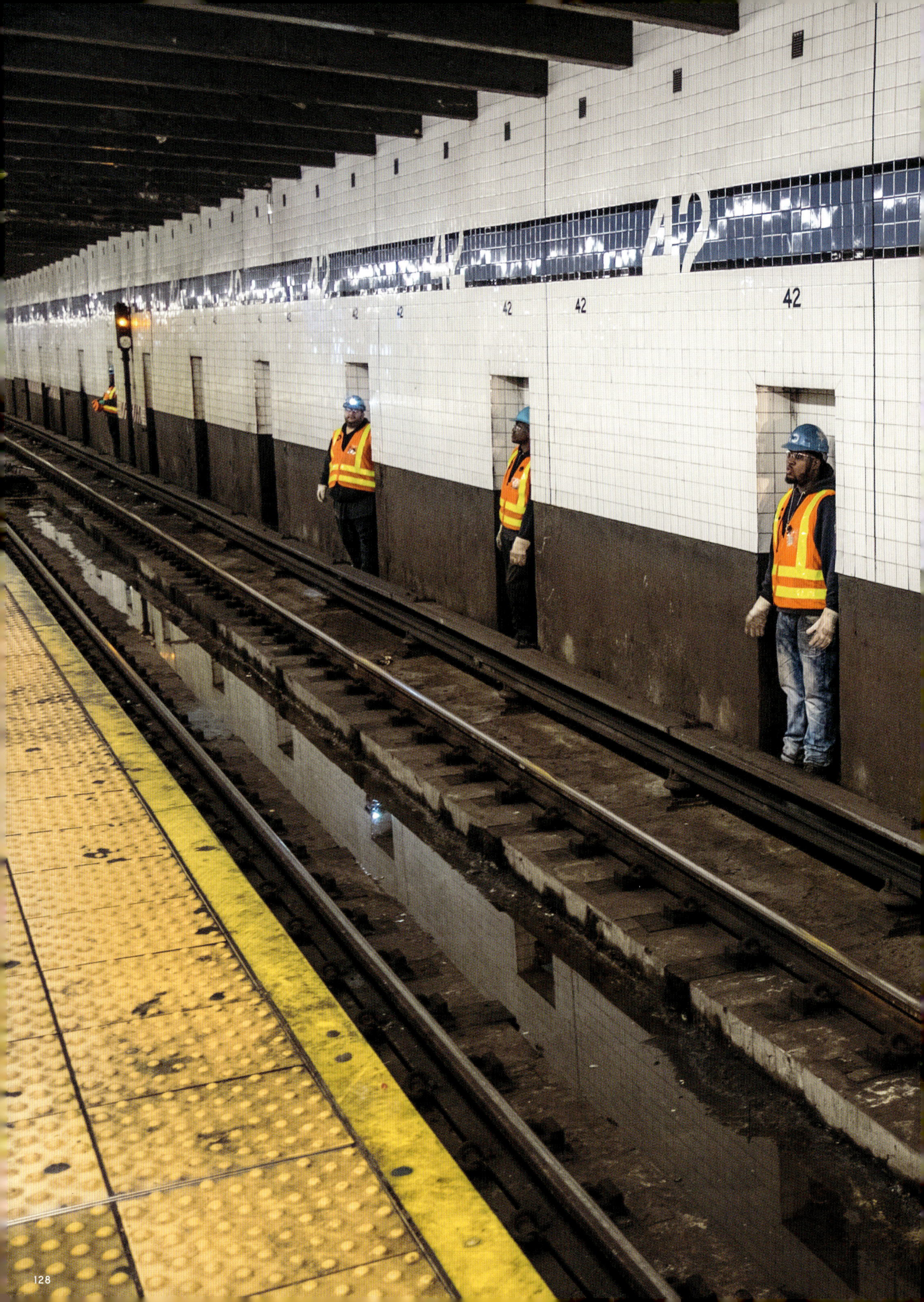

42
42
42
42
42

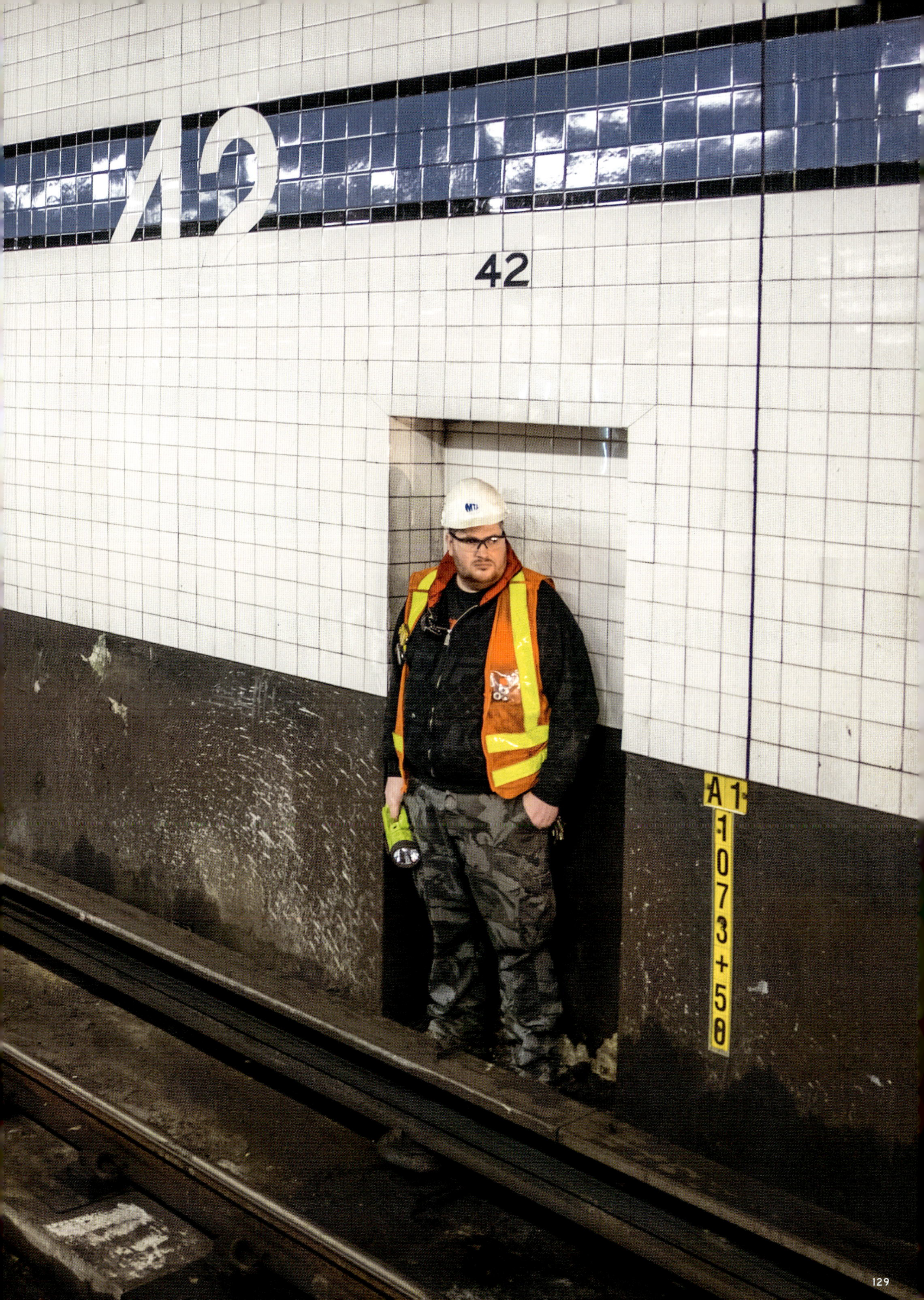

42
42
A 1
1
0
7
3
+
5
0

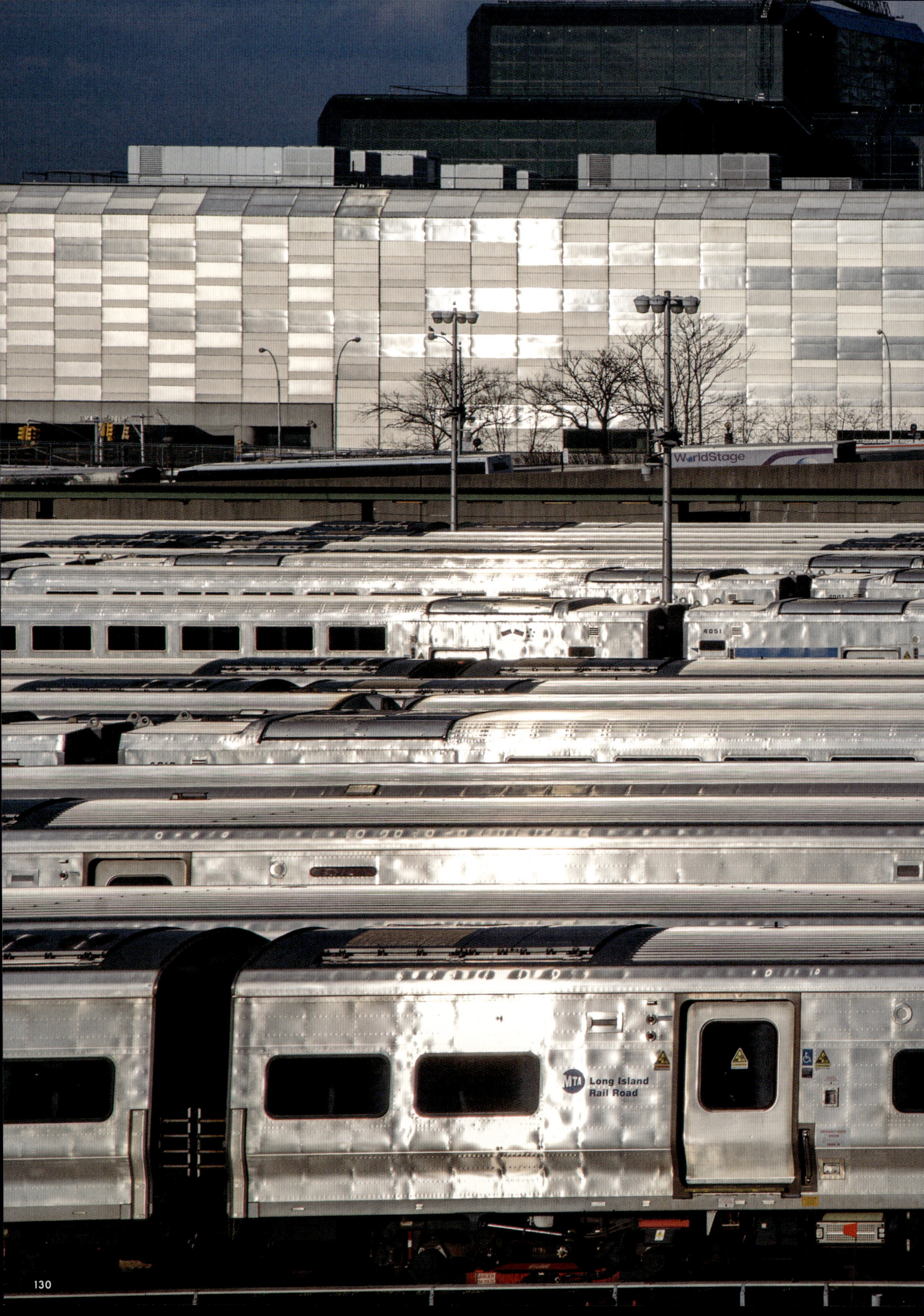

WorldStage
MTA Long Island
Rail Road

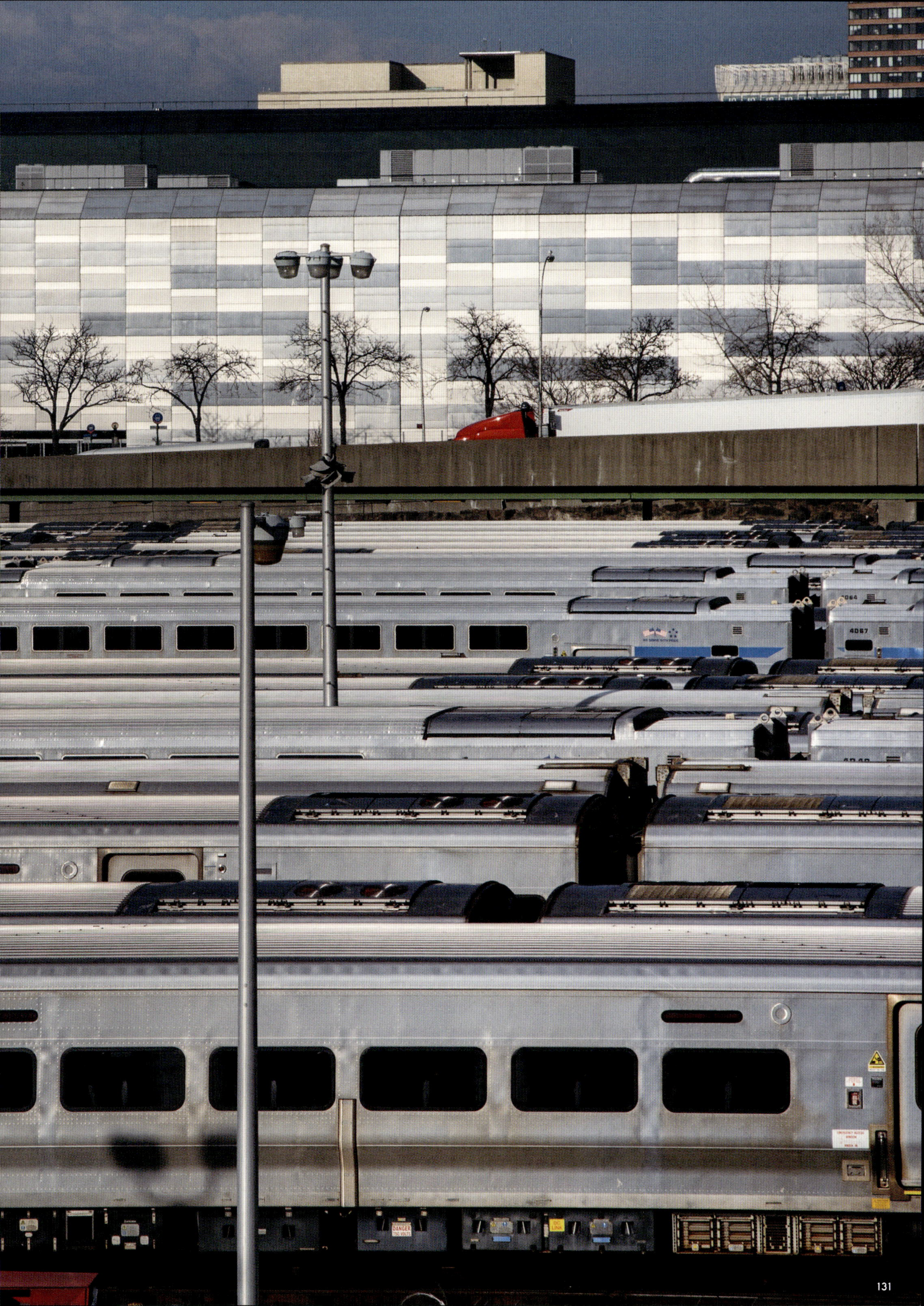

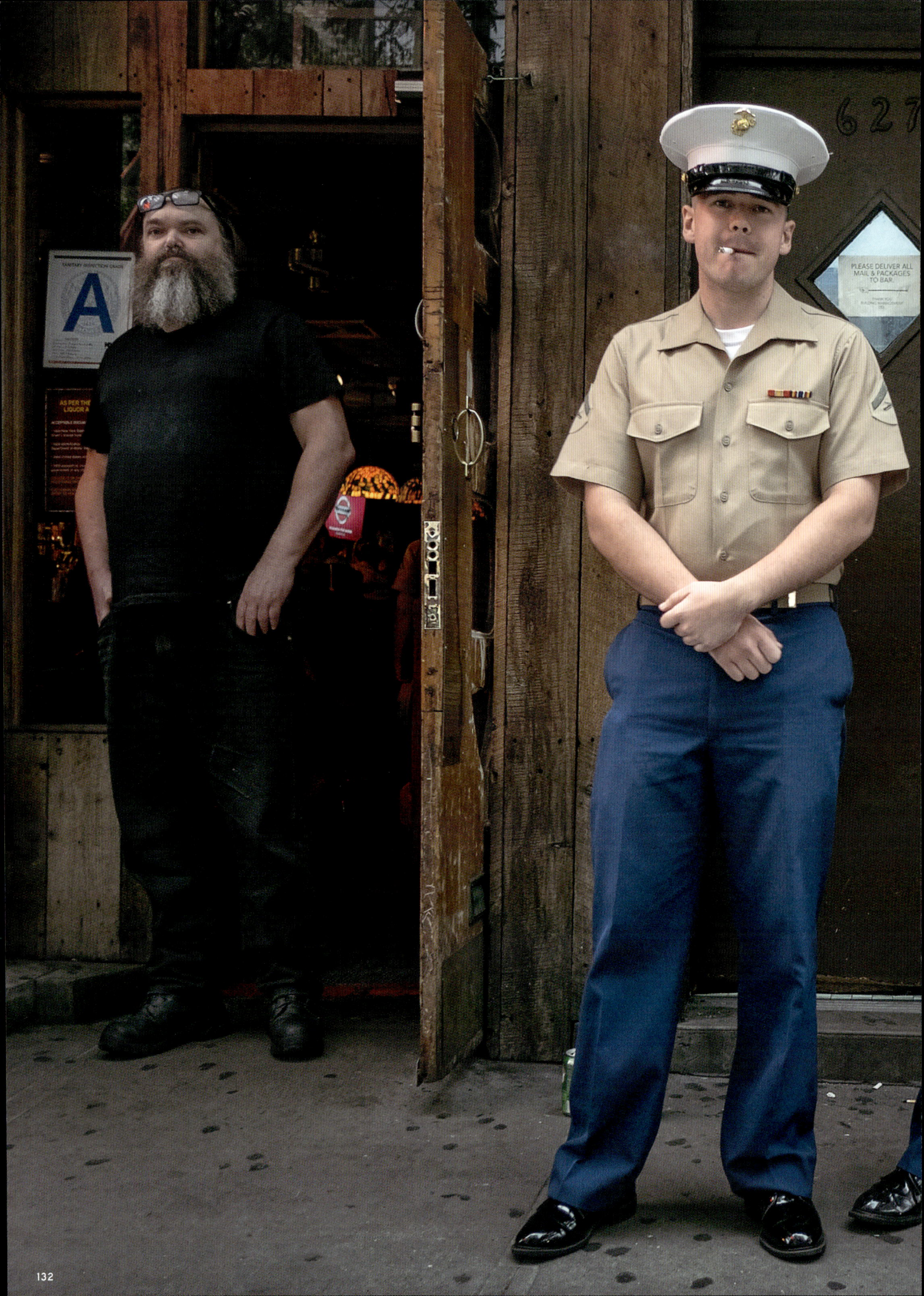

SANITARY INSPECTION GRADE
A
AS PER THE
LIQUOR A
627
PLEASE DELIVER ALL
MAIL & PACKAGES
TO BAR.

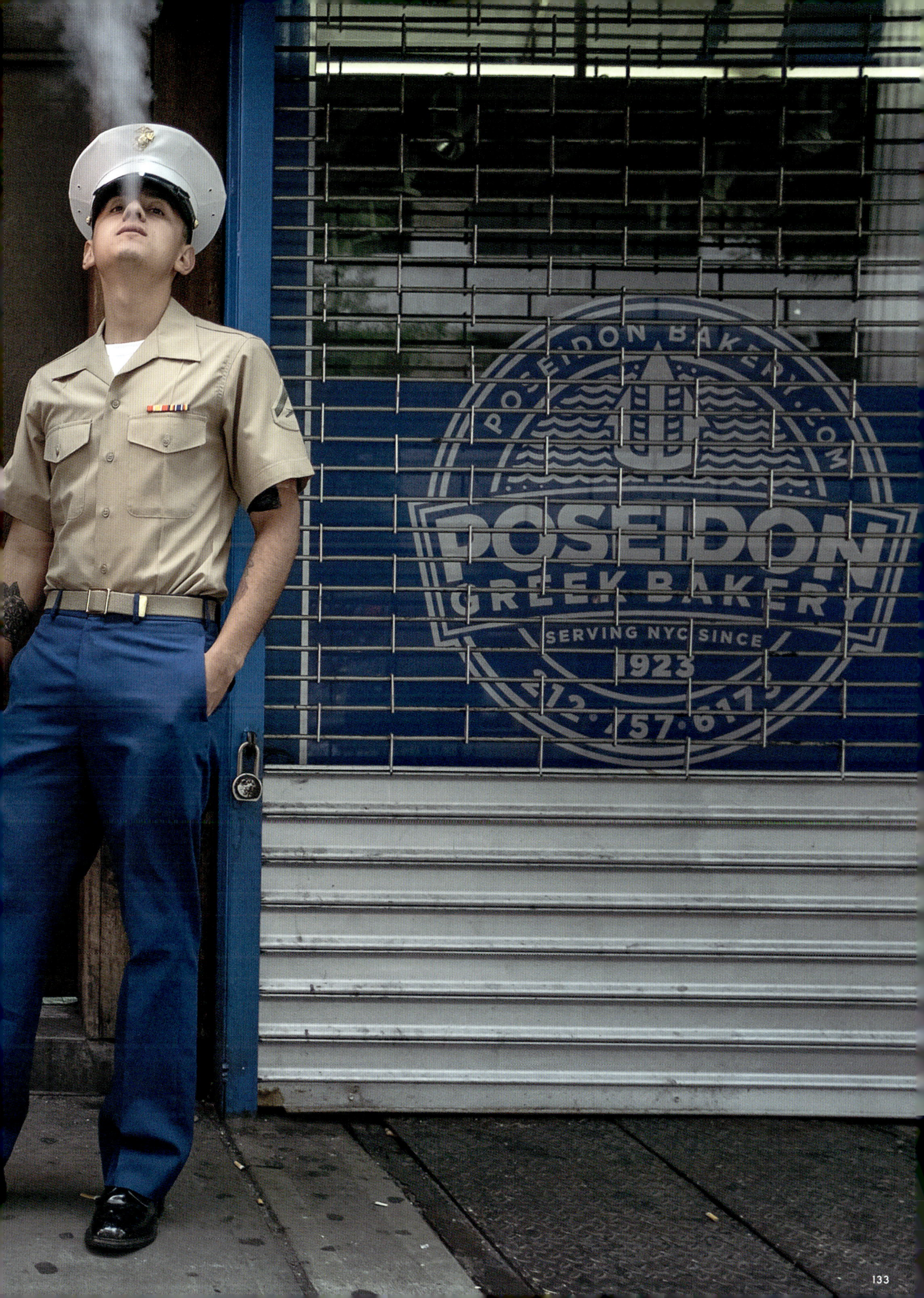
POSEIDON BAKERY.COM
POSEIDON
GREEK BAKERY
SERVING NYC SINCE
1923
212·757·611

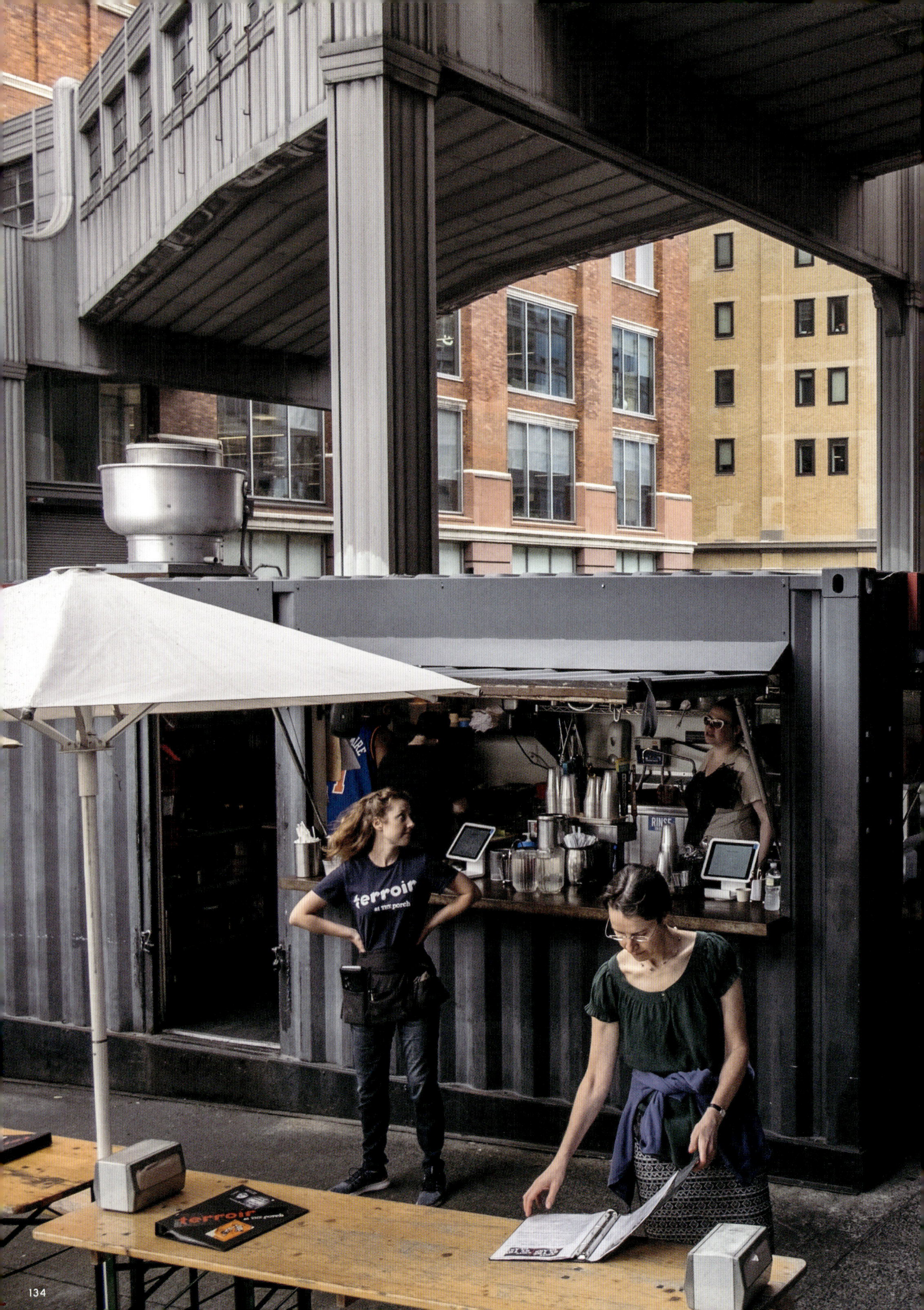

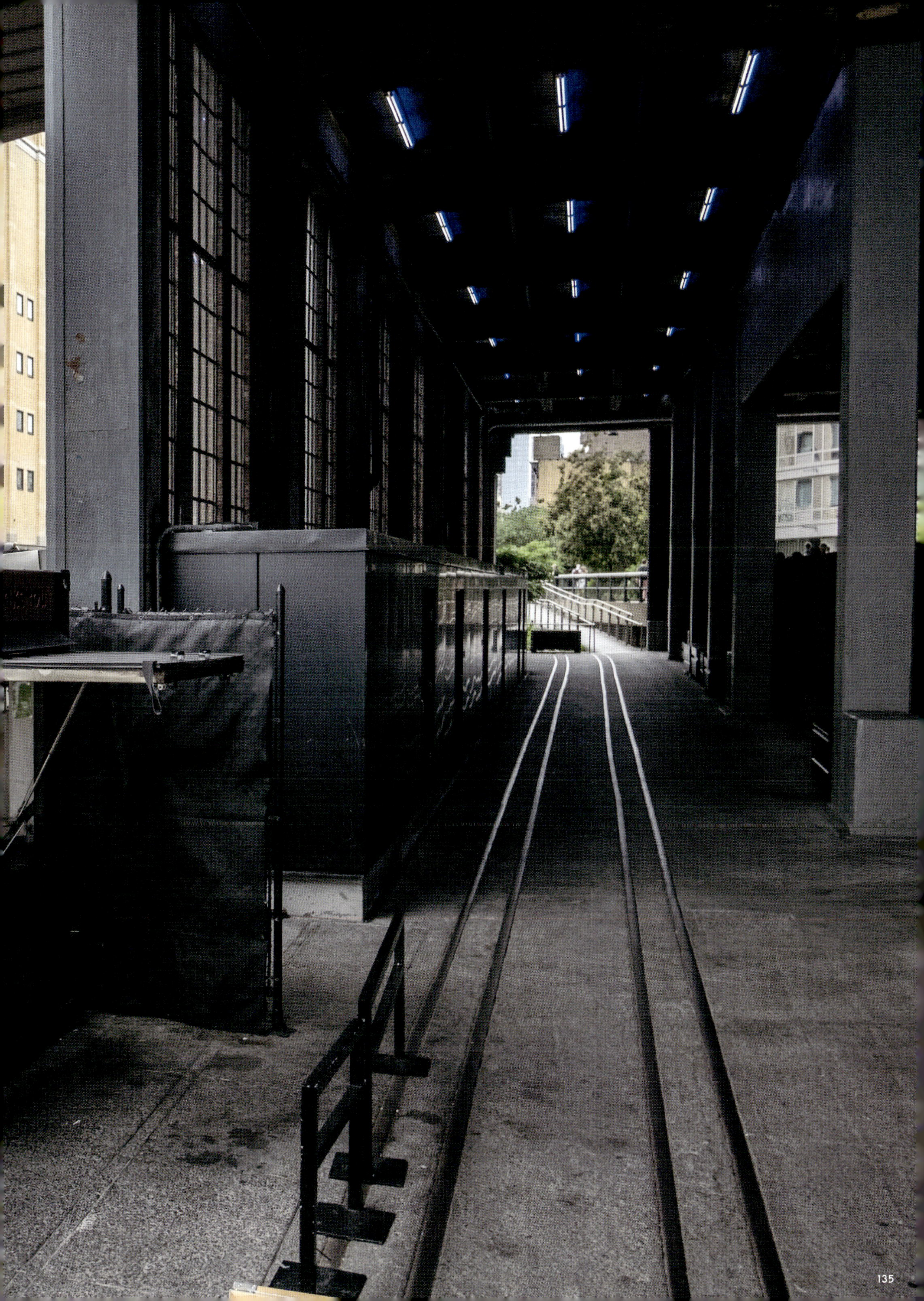

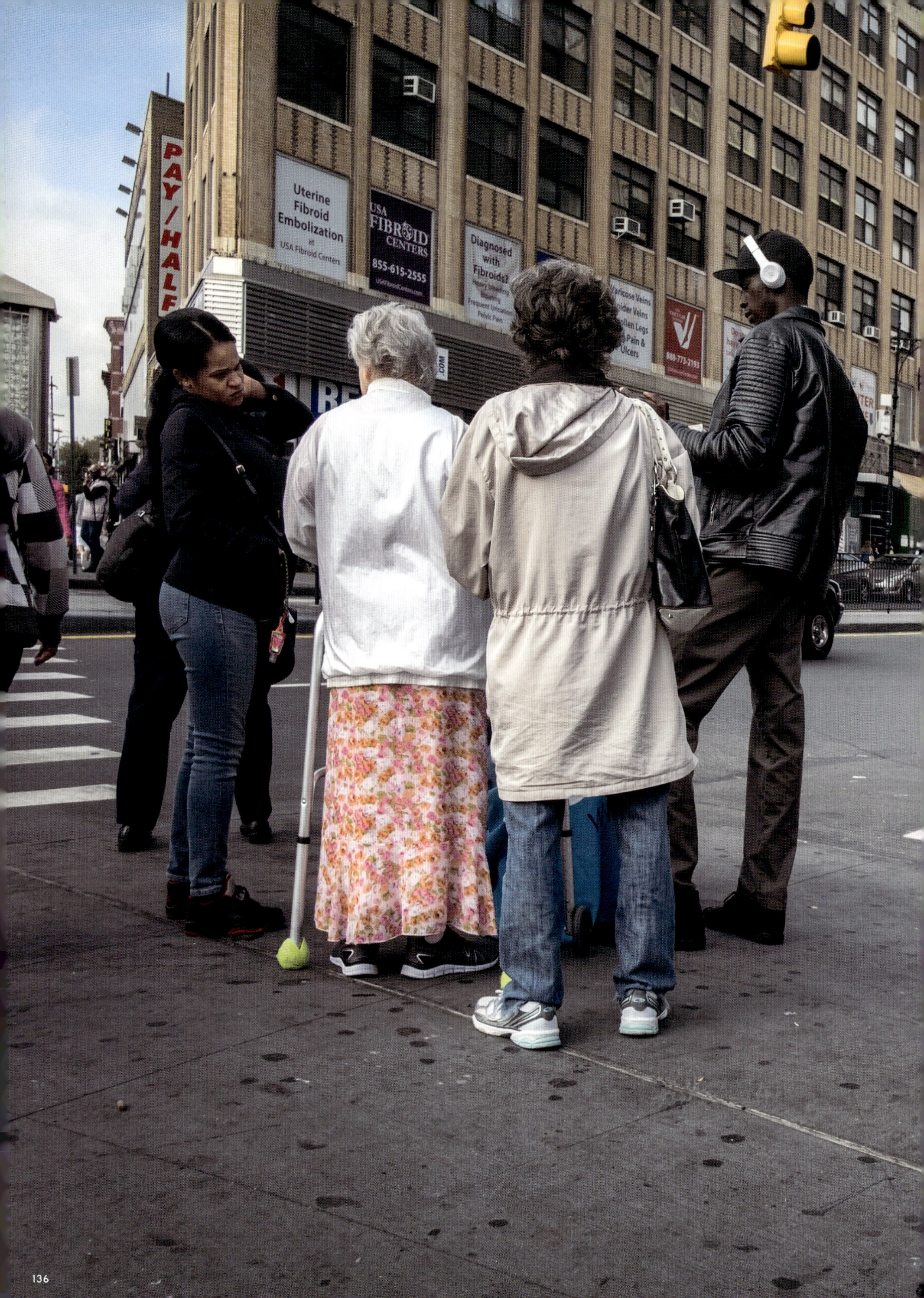

PAY / HALF
Uterine
Fibroid
Embolization
at
USA Fibroid Centers
USA
FIBROID
CENTERS
855-615-2555
USAFibroidCenters.com
Diagnosed
with
Fibroids?
Heavy bleeding
Bloating
Frequent Urination
Pelvic Pain
Varicose Veins
Spider Veins
Swollen Legs
Leg Pain &
Ulcers
888-773-2193

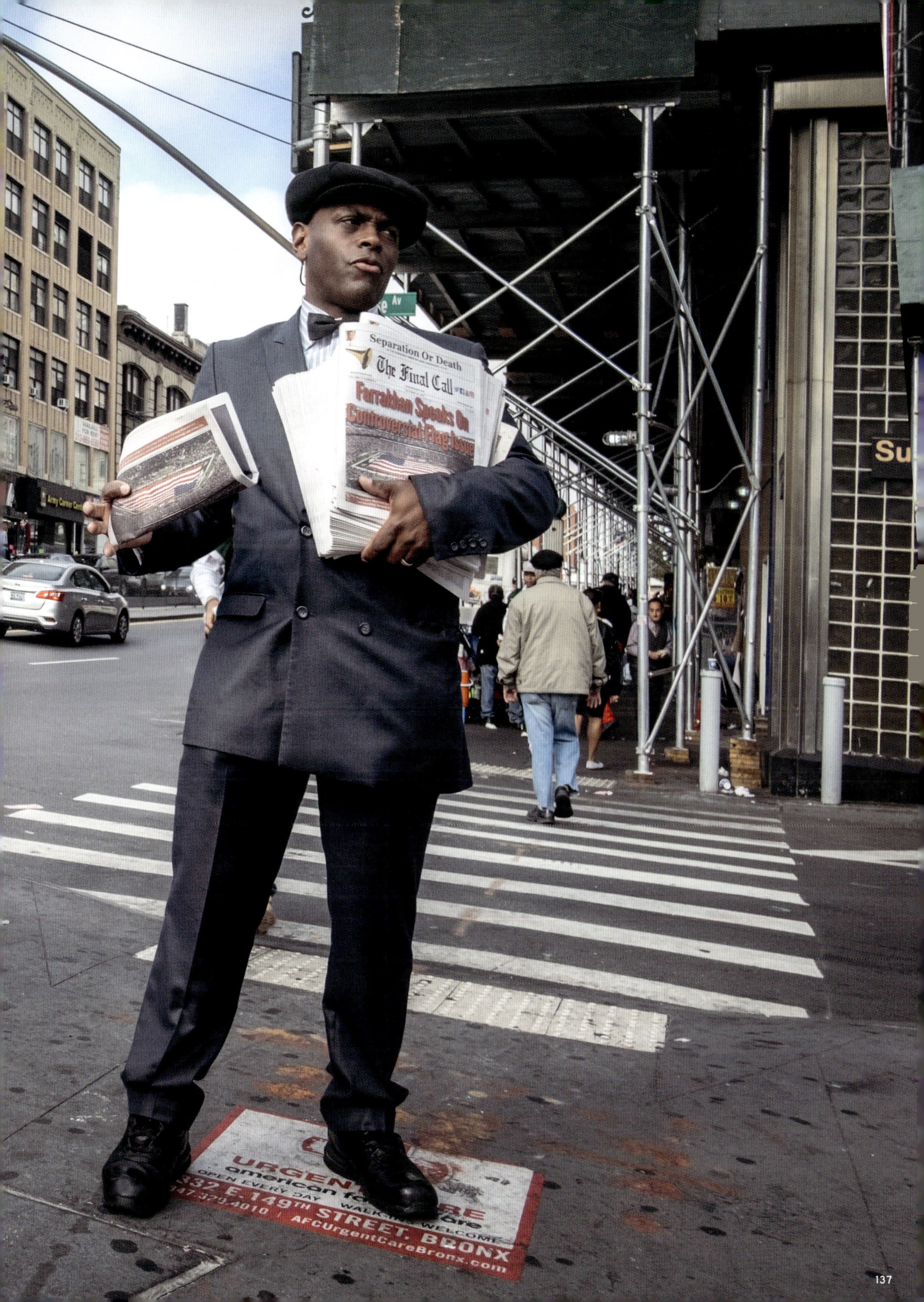

Separation Or Death
The Final Call
Farrakhan Speaks On
Controversial Flag Issue
URGENT CARE
american for...
332 E. 149TH STREET, BRONX
347-320-4010 AFCurgentCareBronx.com
OPEN EVERY DAY WALK-INS WELCOME
Army Career Center

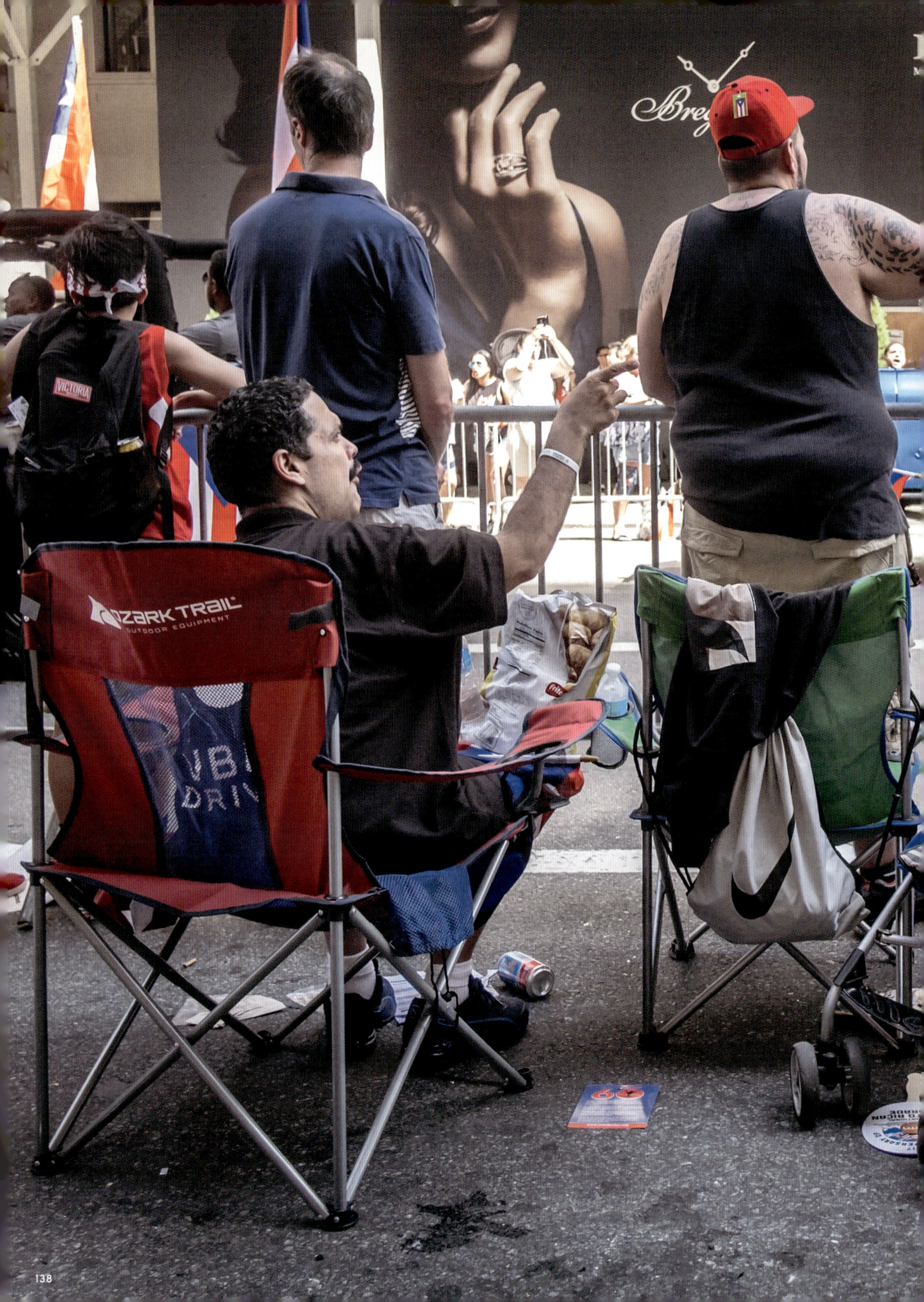

OZARK TRAIL
OUTDOOR EQUIPMENT
VICTORIA
Breg

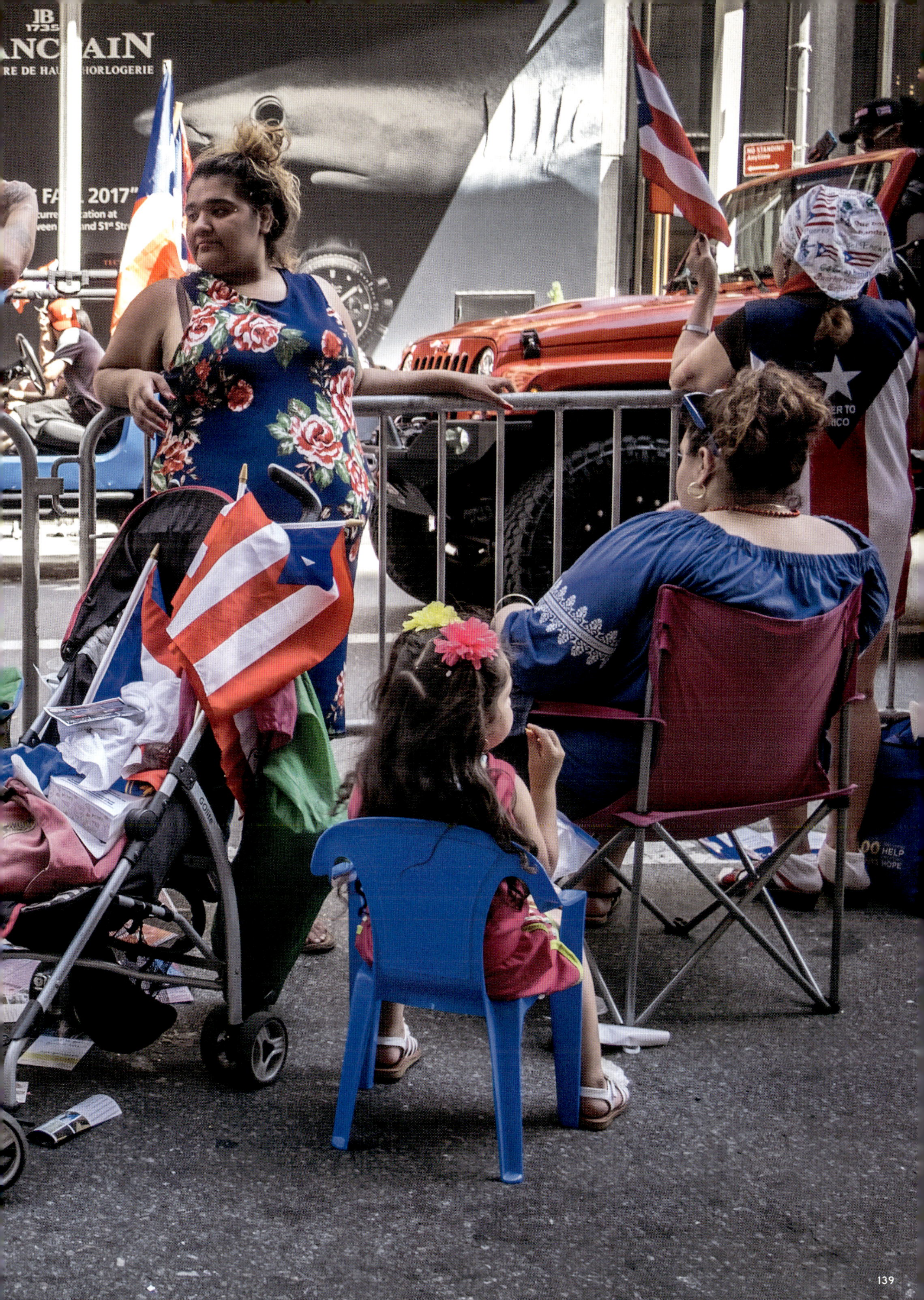

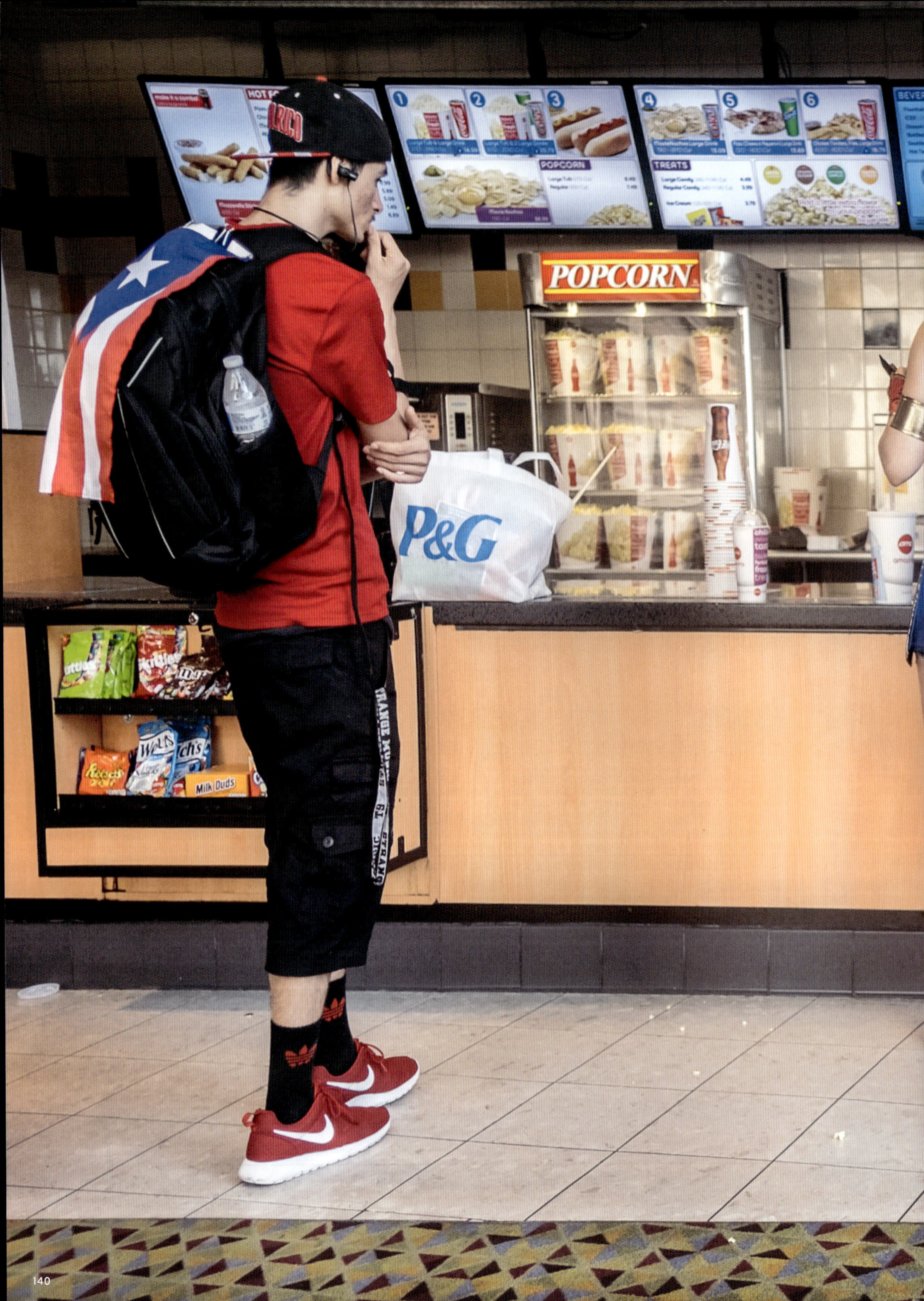

POPCORN
HOT FO
POPCORN
Large Tub
Regular
TREATS
Large Candy
Regular Candy
Ice Cream
BEVER
P&G
Milk Duds
Welch's
Reese's

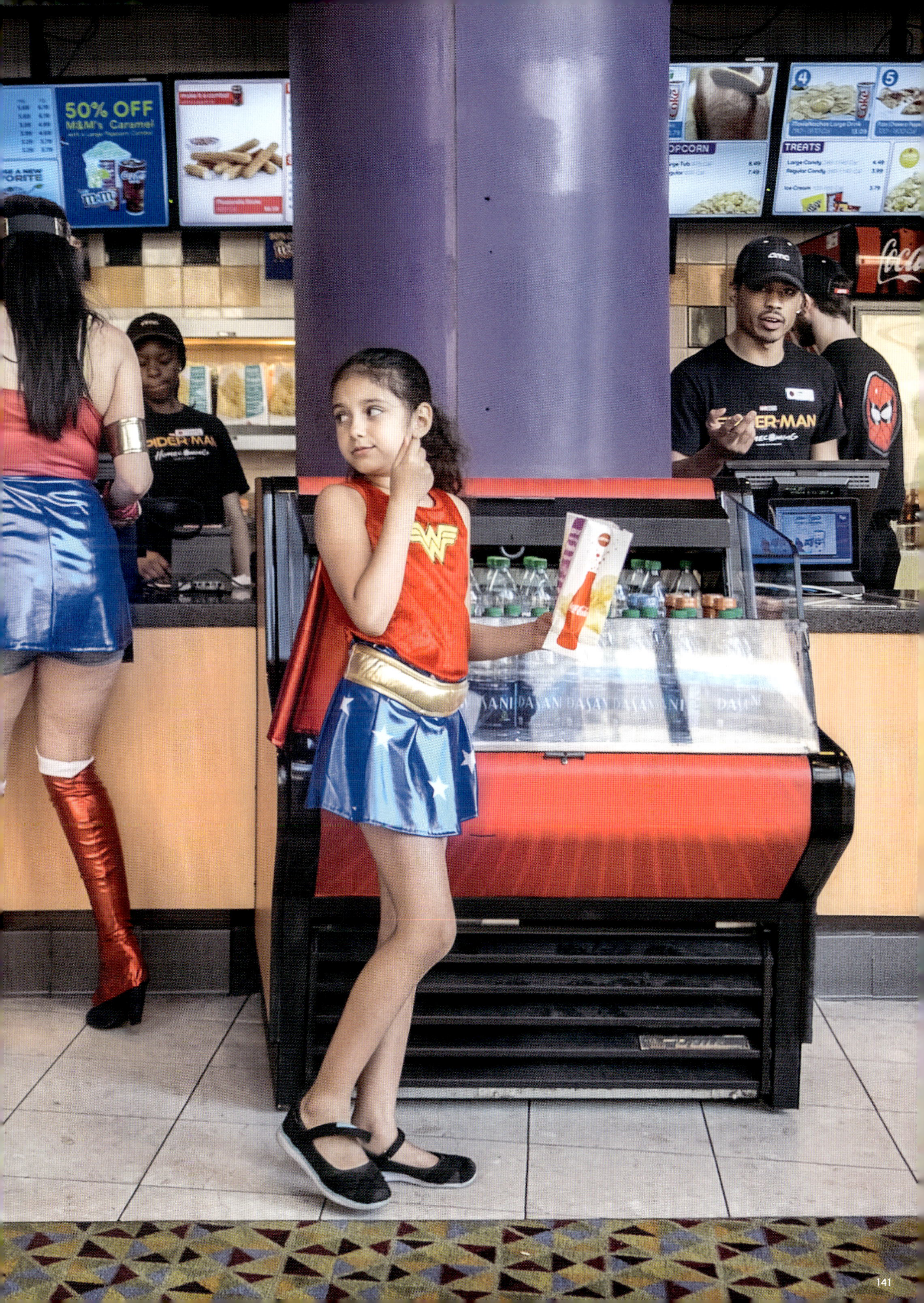
50% OFF
M&M's Caramel
POPCORN
TREATS
Large Candy   4.49
Regular Candy   3.99
Ice Cream   3.79
Coca-Cola
SPIDER-MAN
HOMECOMING

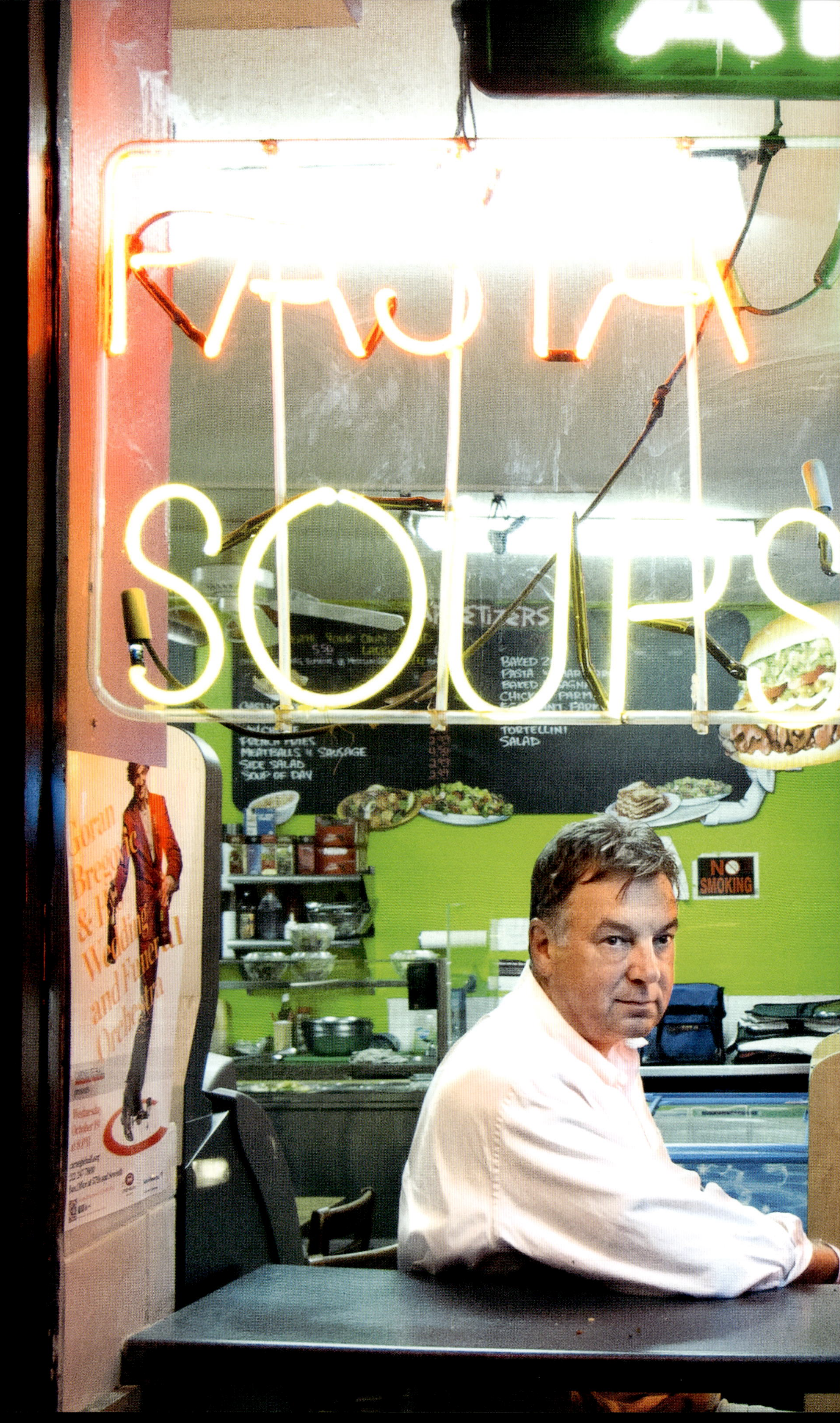

PASTA
SOUP'S
NO
SMOKING
APPETIZERS
TORTELLINI
SALAD
FRENCH FRIES
MEATBALLS & SAUSAGE
SIDE SALAD
SOUP OF DAY
Goran
Bregovic
& his
Wedding
and Funeral
Orchestra

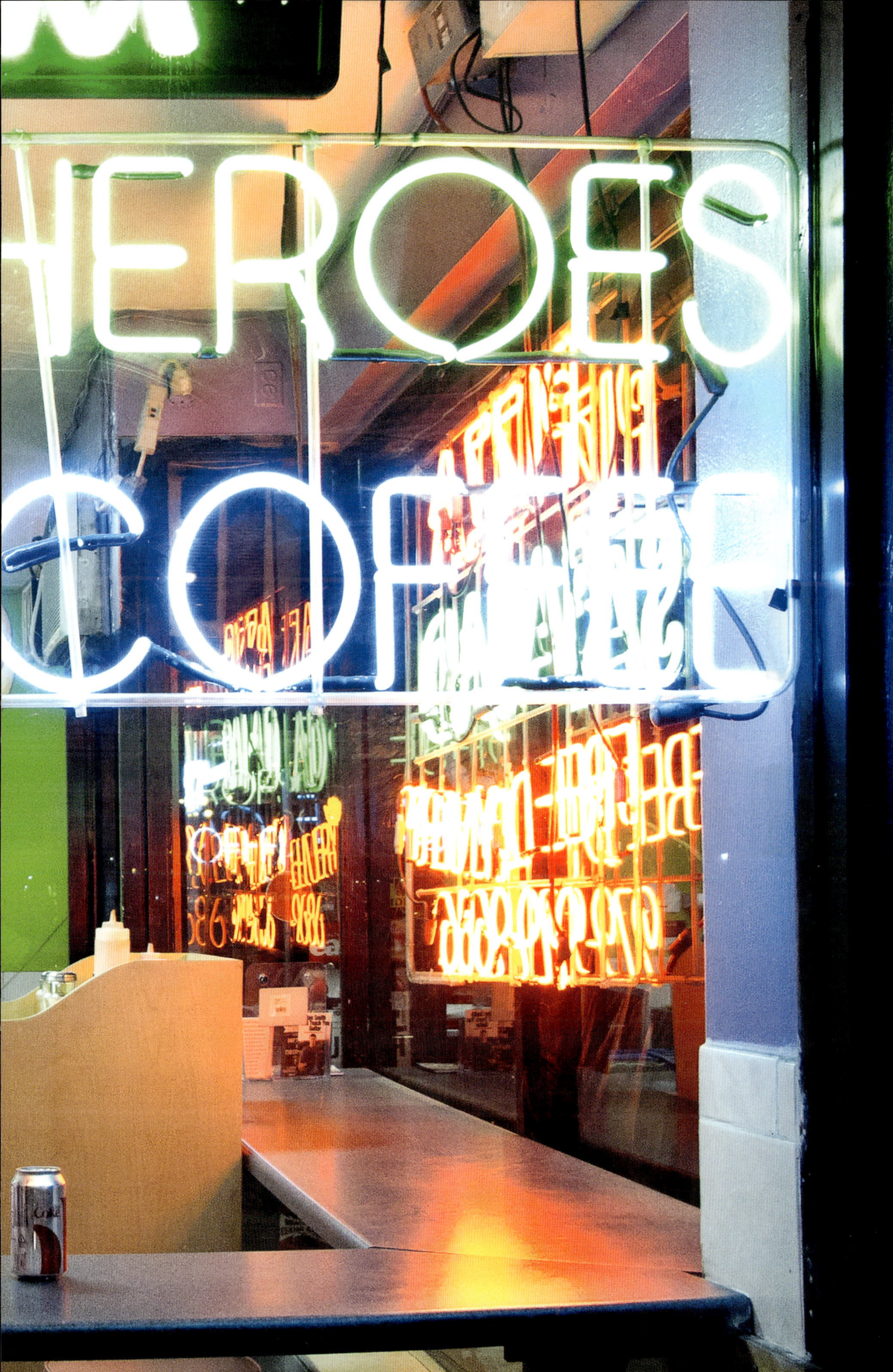
HEROES
COFFEE

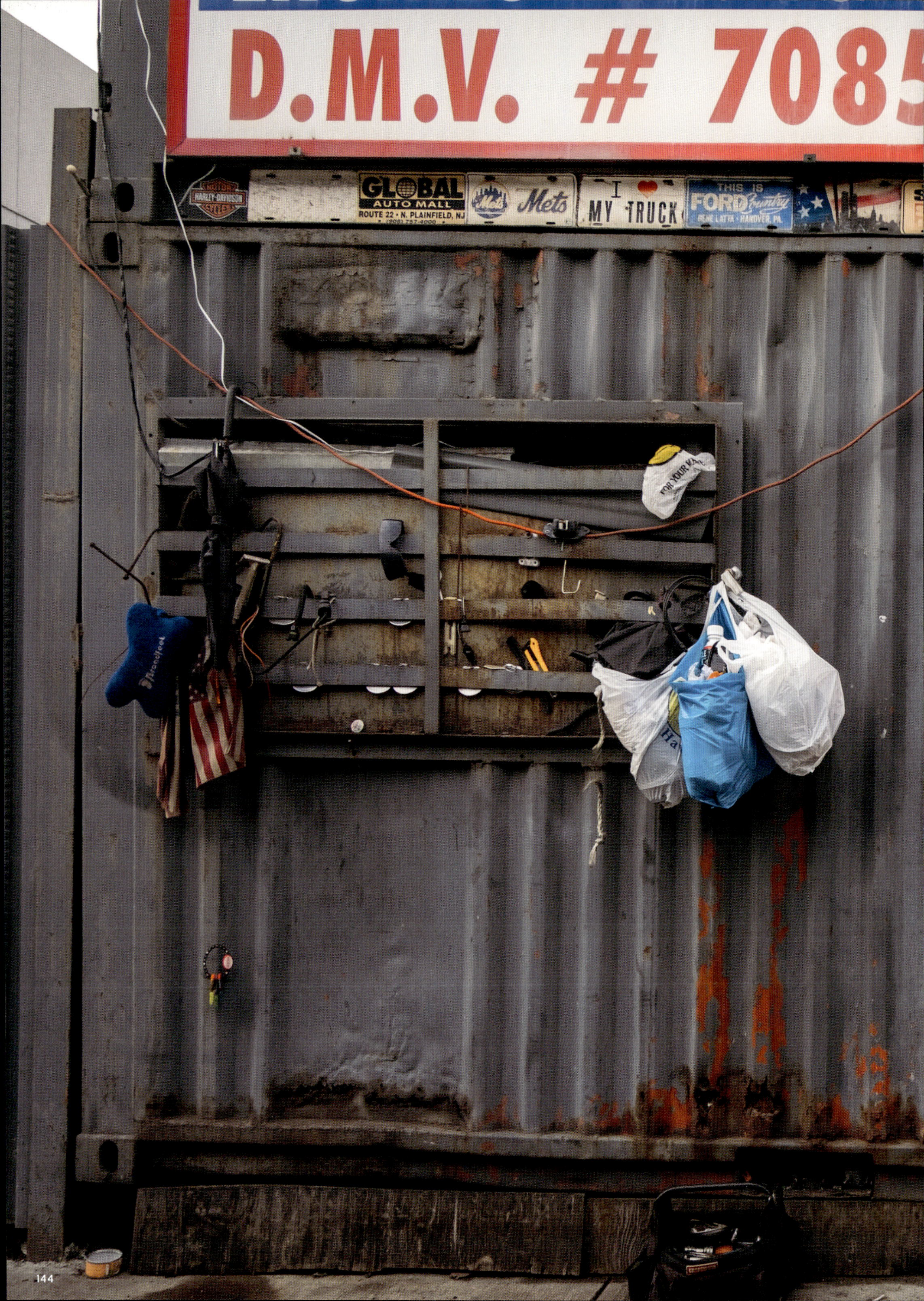

D.M.V. # 7085
HARLEY-DAVIDSON MOTOR CYCLES
GLOBAL AUTO MALL
ROUTE 22 • N. PLAINFIELD, NJ
(908) 757-4000
Mets Mets
I ♥ MY TRUCK
THIS IS FORD Country
RENE LATTA • HANOVER, PA.

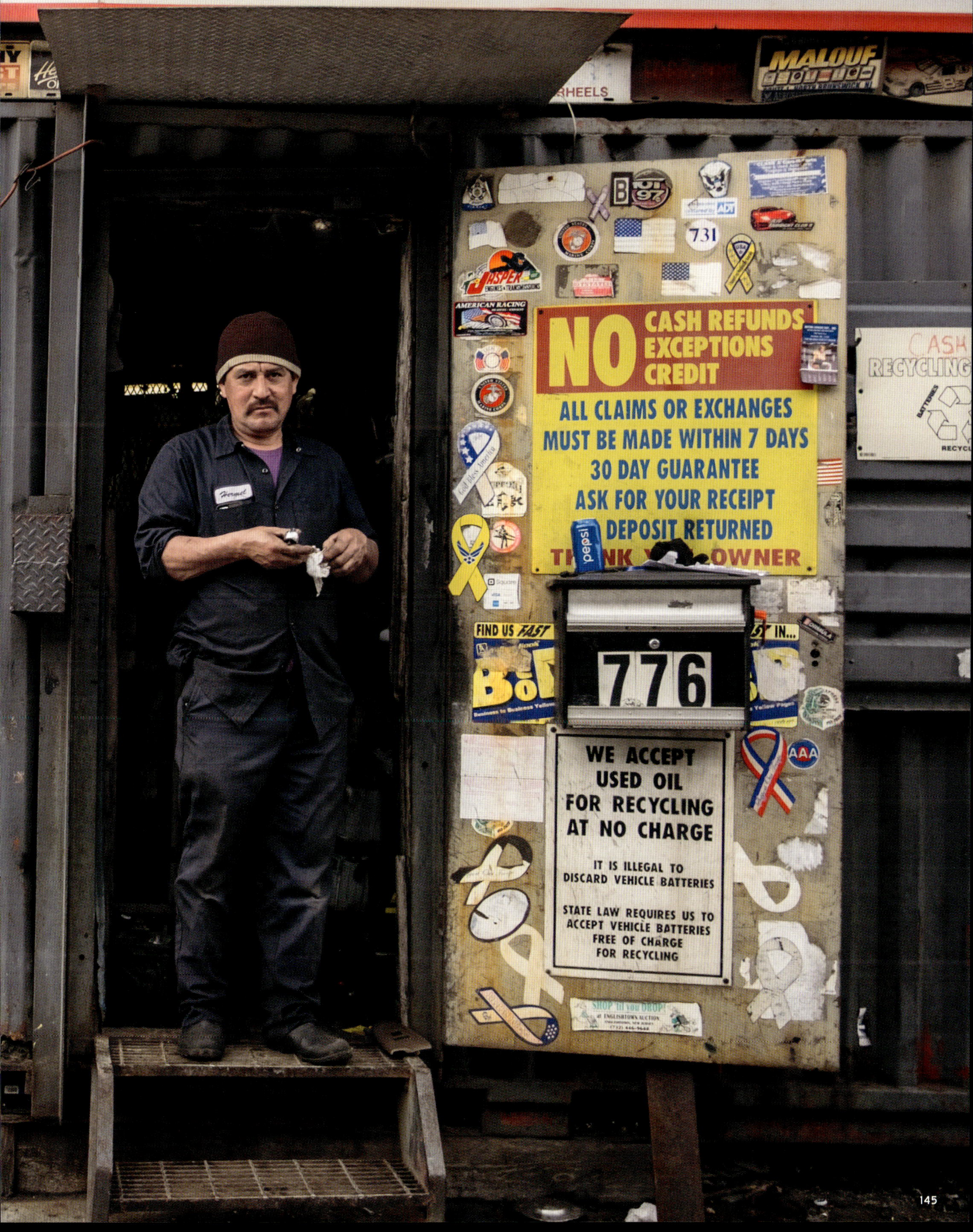
636 Tel. 718 768
MALOUF
731
NO CASH REFUNDS
EXCEPTIONS
CREDIT
ALL CLAIMS OR EXCHANGES
MUST BE MADE WITHIN 7 DAYS
30 DAY GUARANTEE
ASK FOR YOUR RECEIPT
DEPOSIT RETURNED
THANK YOU OWNER
CASH
RECYCLING
FIND US FAST
776
WE ACCEPT
USED OIL
FOR RECYCLING
AT NO CHARGE
IT IS ILLEGAL TO
DISCARD VEHICLE BATTERIES
STATE LAW REQUIRES US TO
ACCEPT VEHICLE BATTERIES
FREE OF CHARGE
FOR RECYCLING
AAA
AMERICAN RACING
JASPER

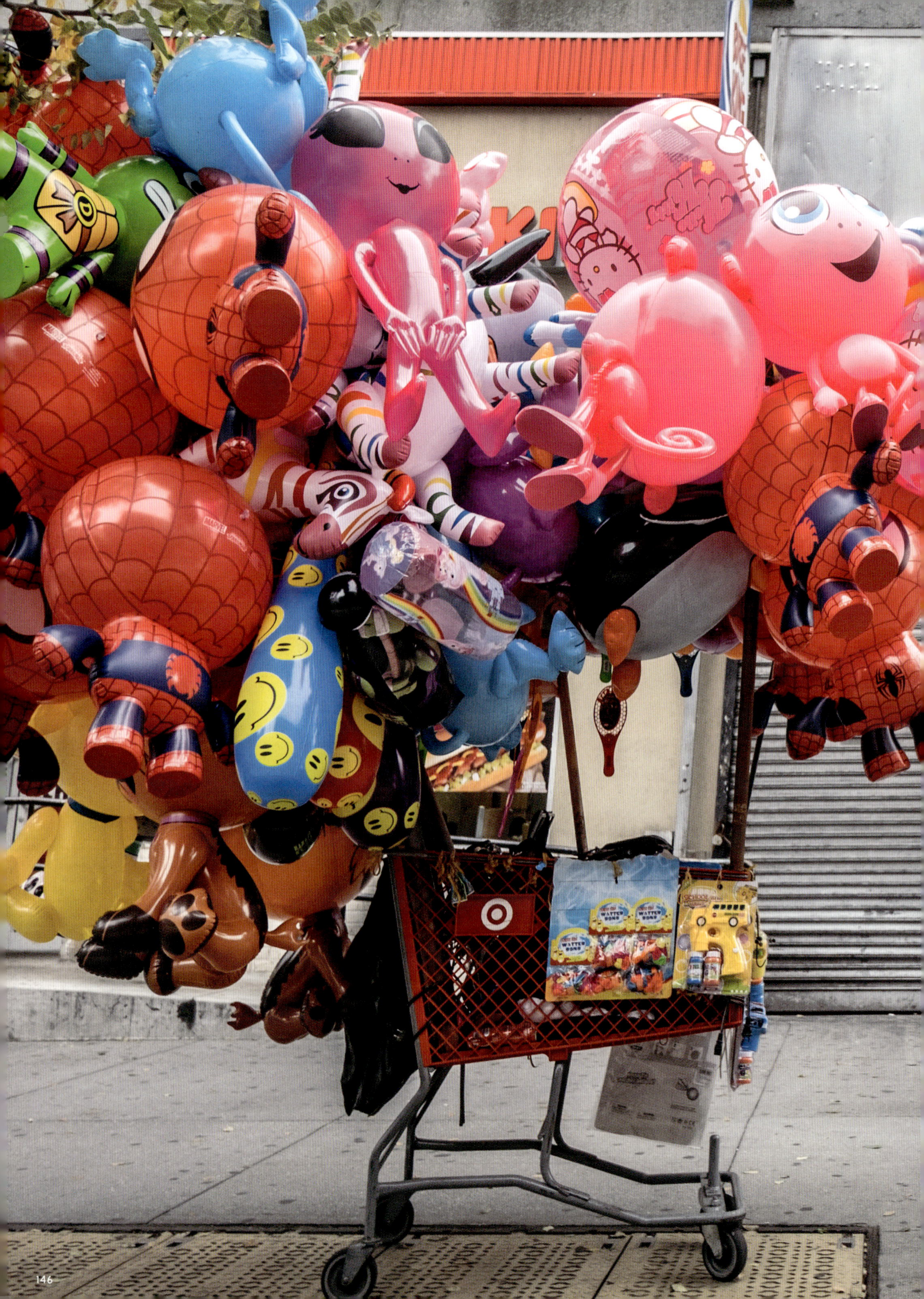

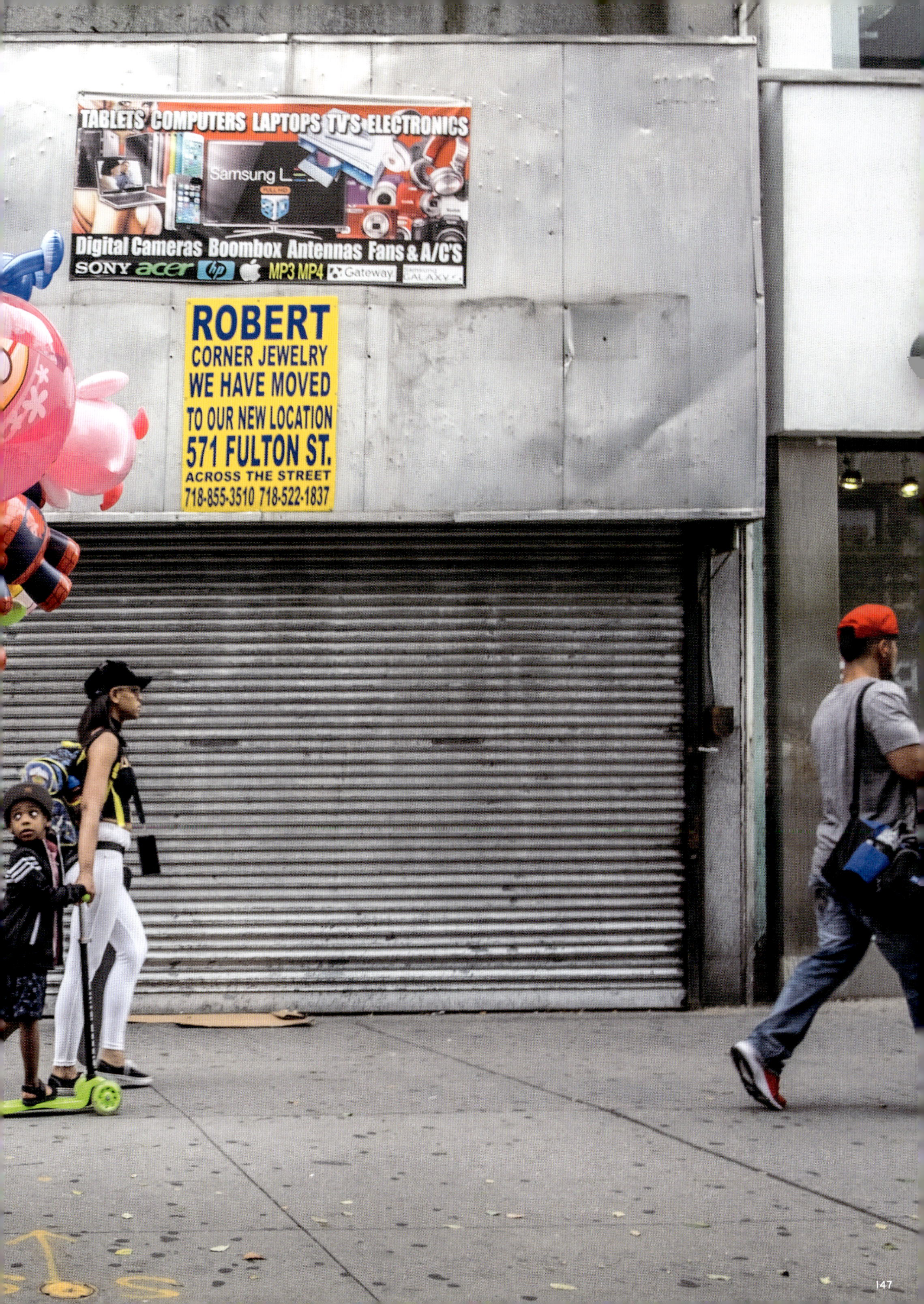
TABLETS COMPUTERS LAPTOPS TVS ELECTRONICS
Samsung L
Digital Cameras Boombox Antennas Fans & A/C'S
SONY acer hp MP3 MP4 Gateway GALAXY
ROBERT
CORNER JEWELRY
WE HAVE MOVED
TO OUR NEW LOCATION
571 FULTON ST.
ACROSS THE STREET
718-855-3510 718-522-1837

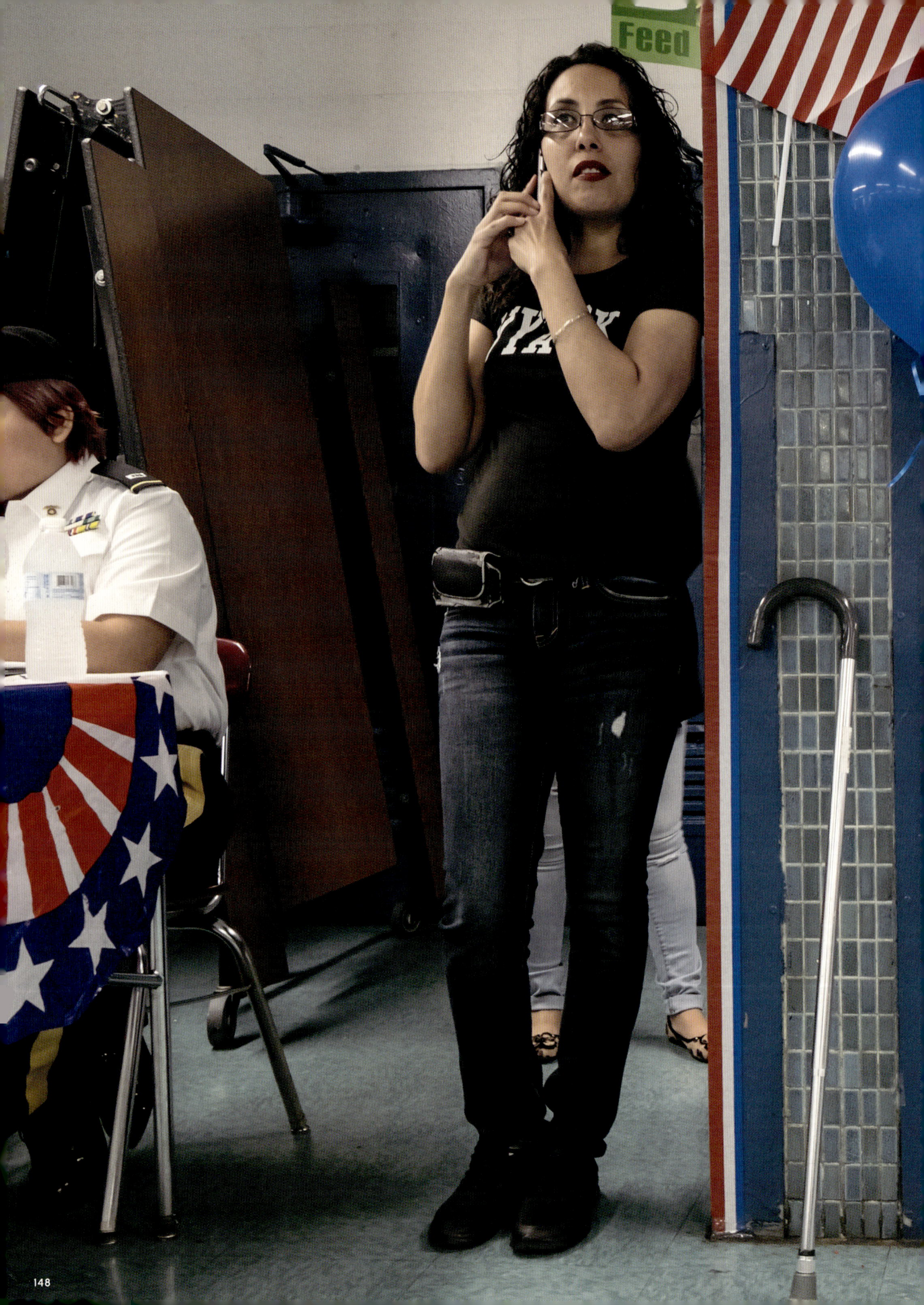

Feed

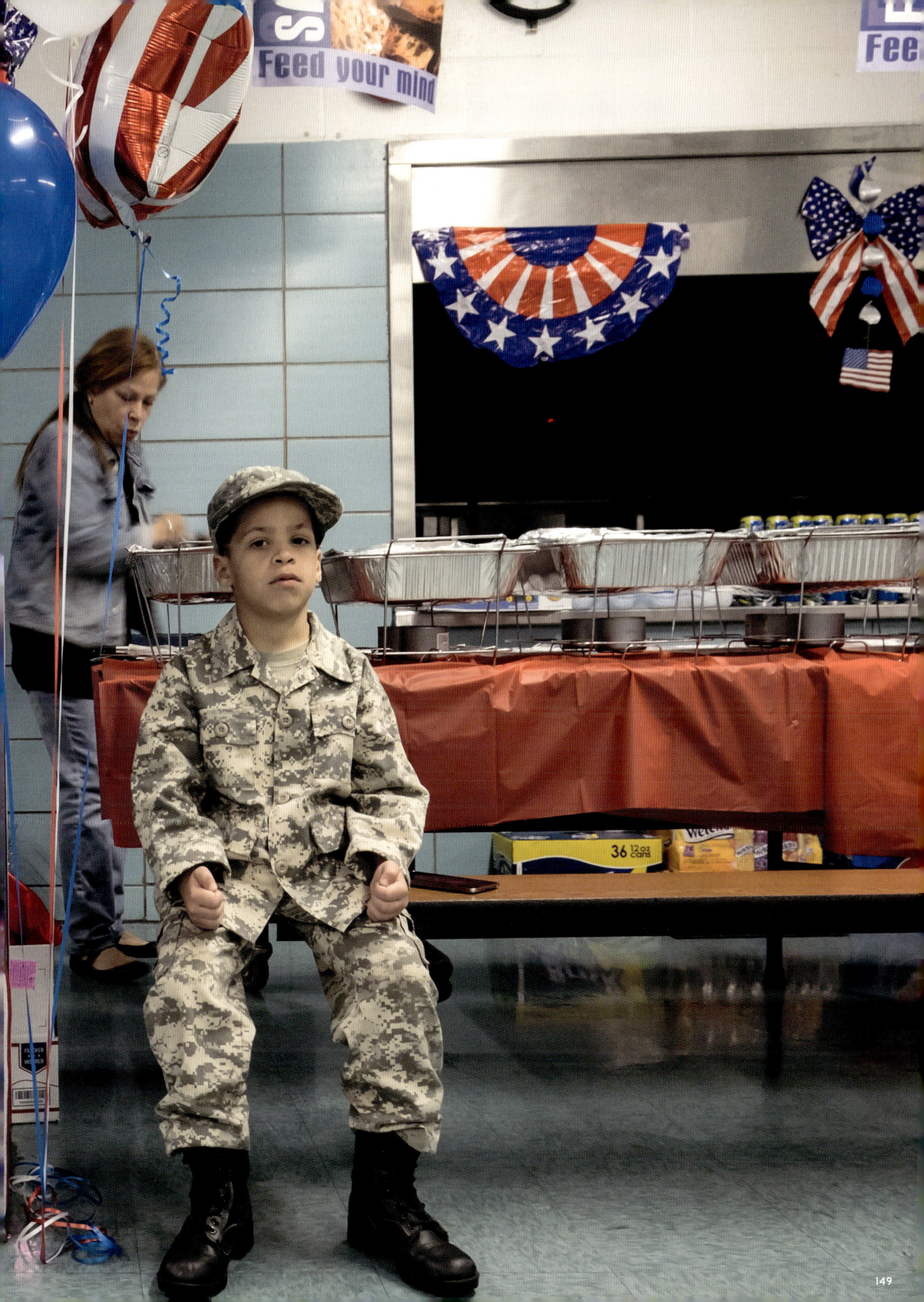
Feed your mind
Feed
36 12oz cans
Welch's

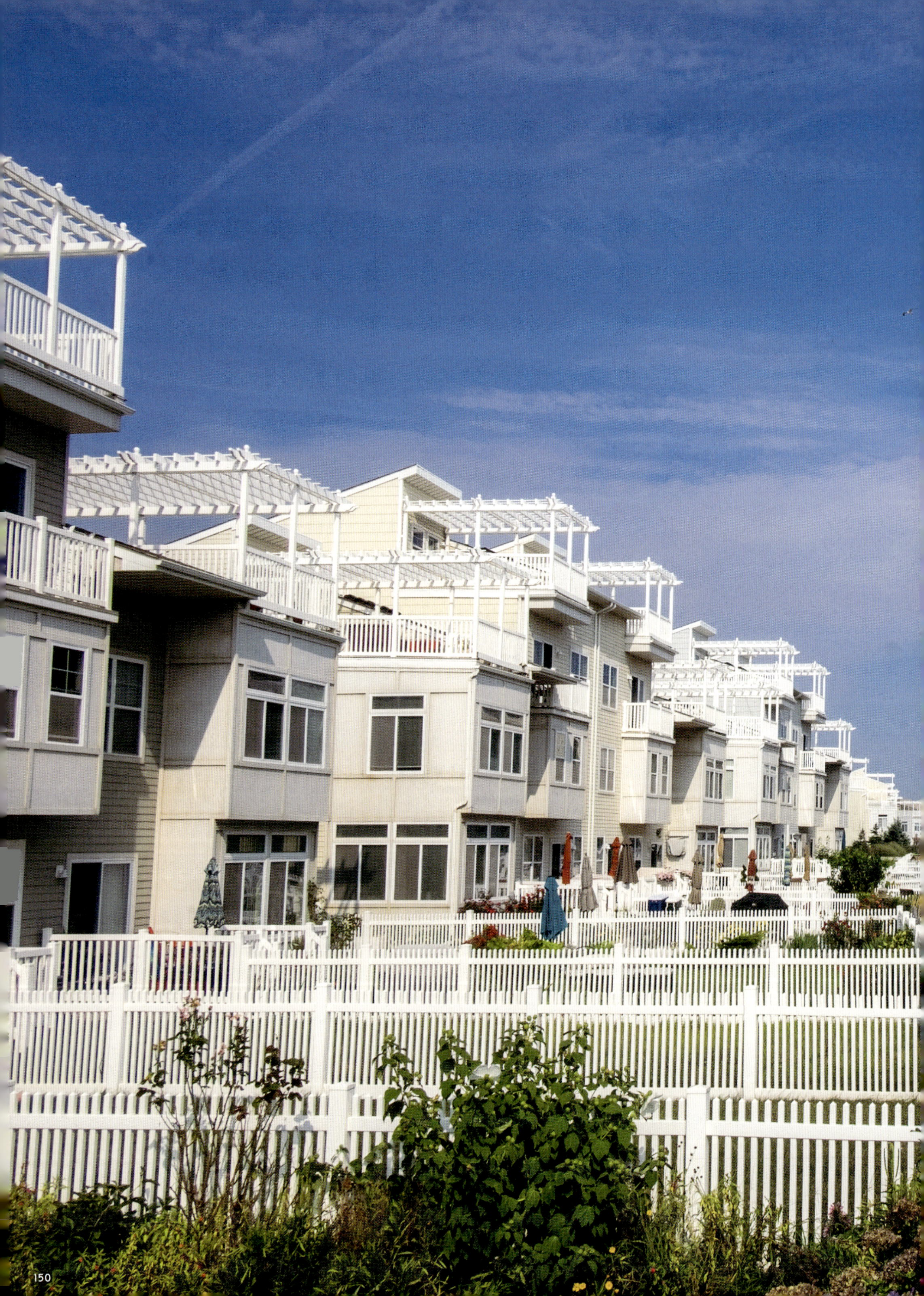

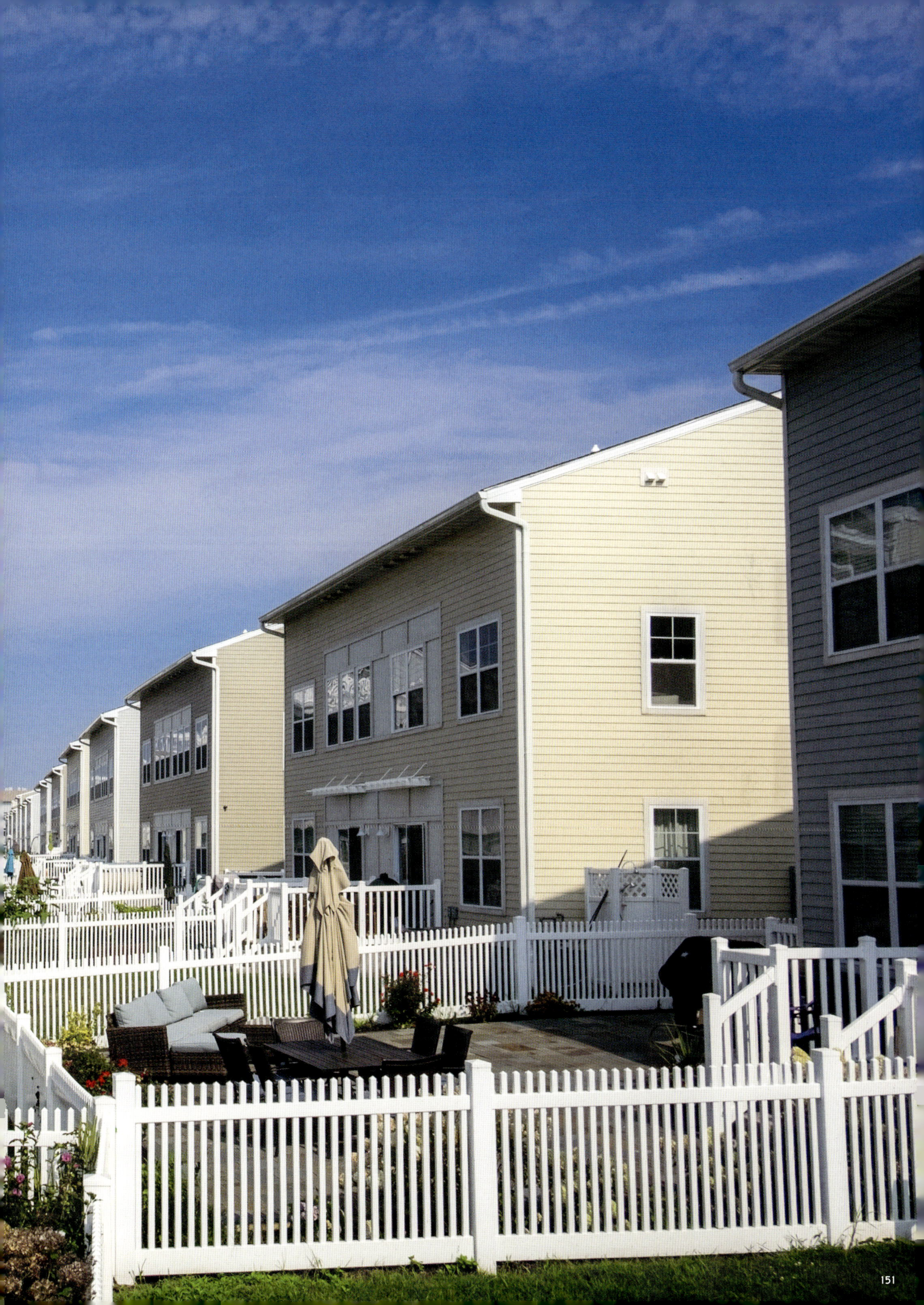

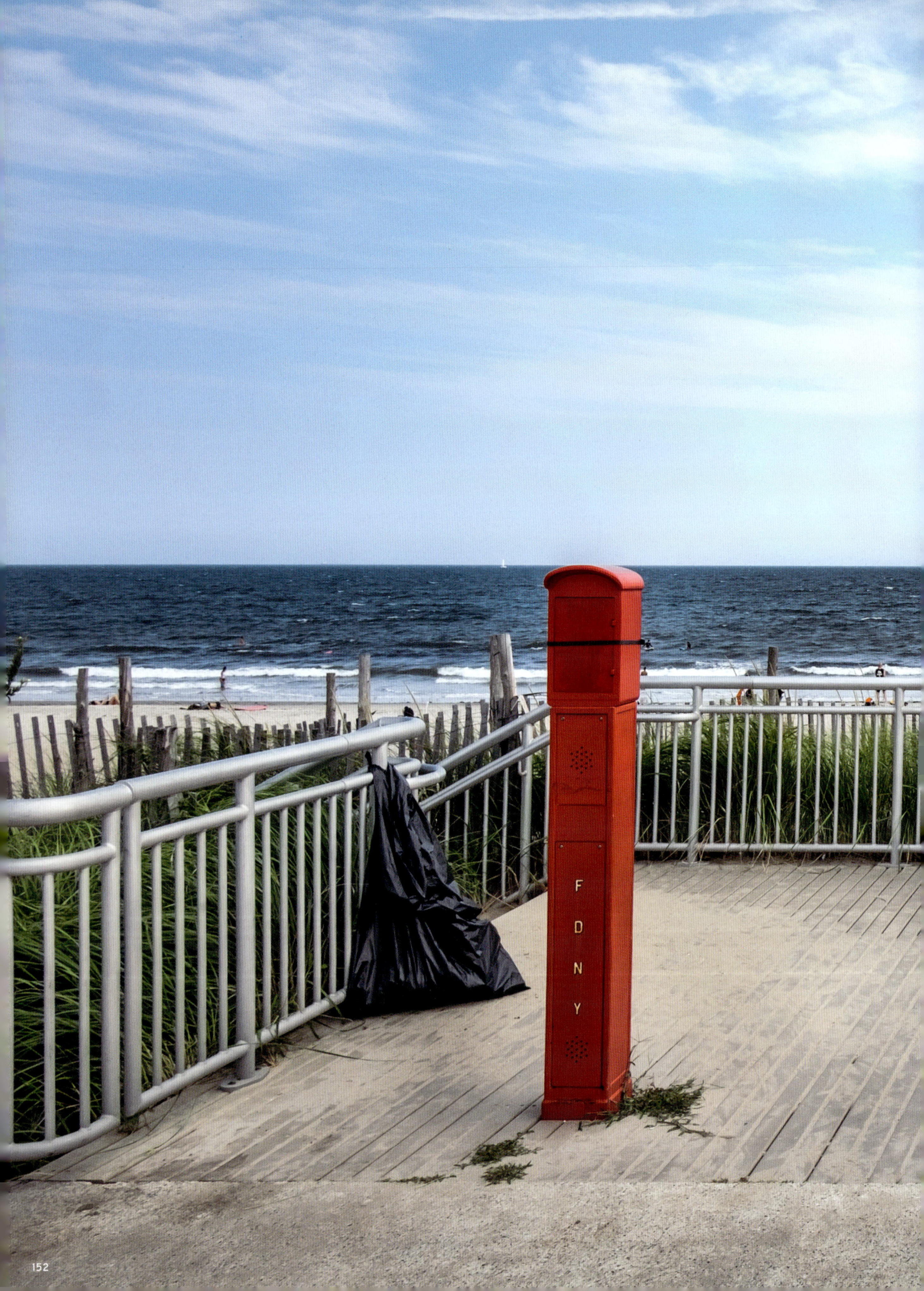

F
D
N
Y

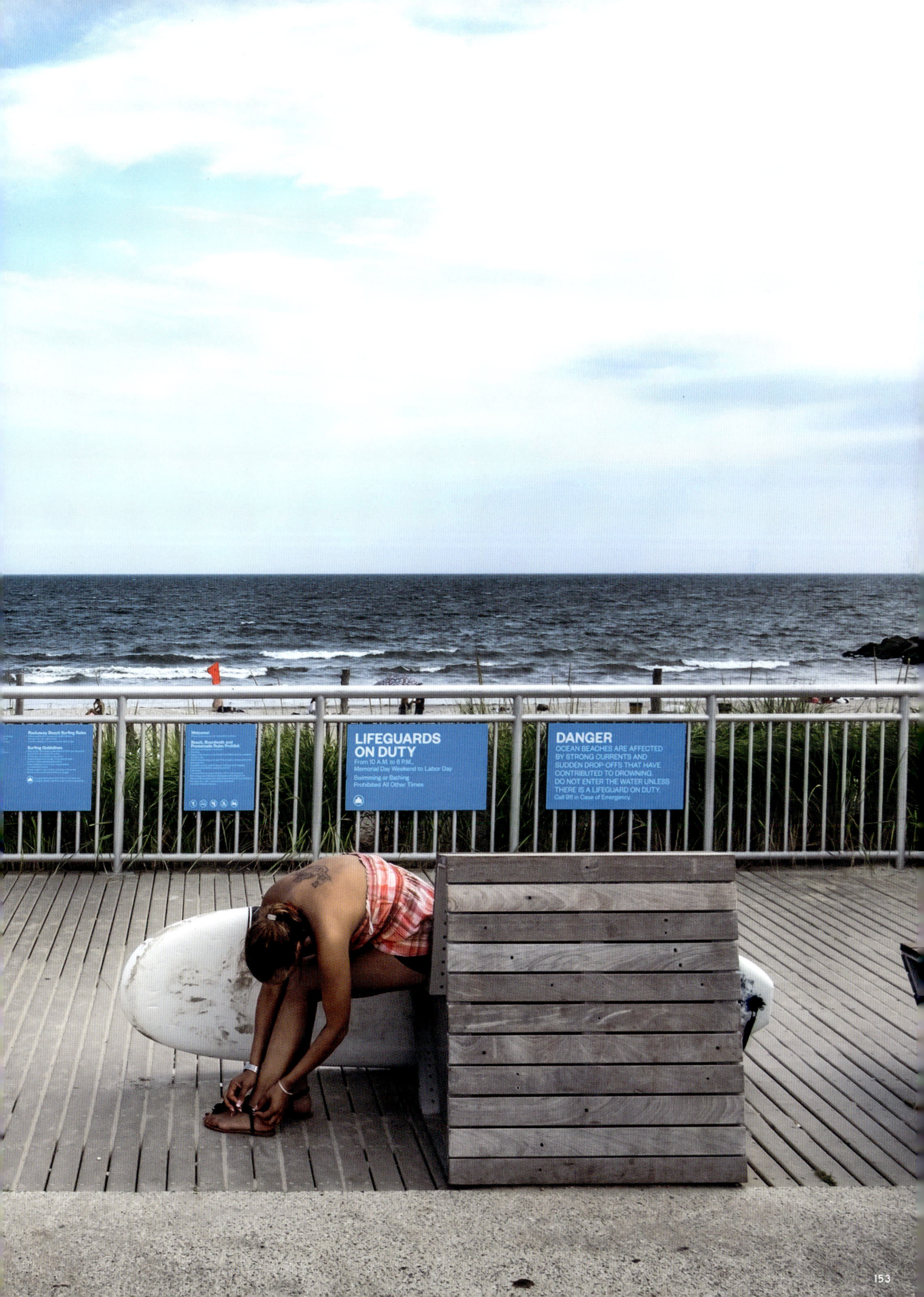
LIFEGUARDS
ON DUTY
From 10 A.M. to 6 P.M.
Memorial Day Weekend to Labor Day
Swimming or Bathing
Prohibited All Other Times
DANGER
OCEAN BEACHES ARE AFFECTED
BY STRONG CURRENTS AND
SUDDEN DROP-OFFS THAT HAVE
CONTRIBUTED TO DROWNING
DO NOT ENTER THE WATER UNLESS
THERE IS A LIFEGUARD ON DUTY.
Call 911 in Case of Emergency.

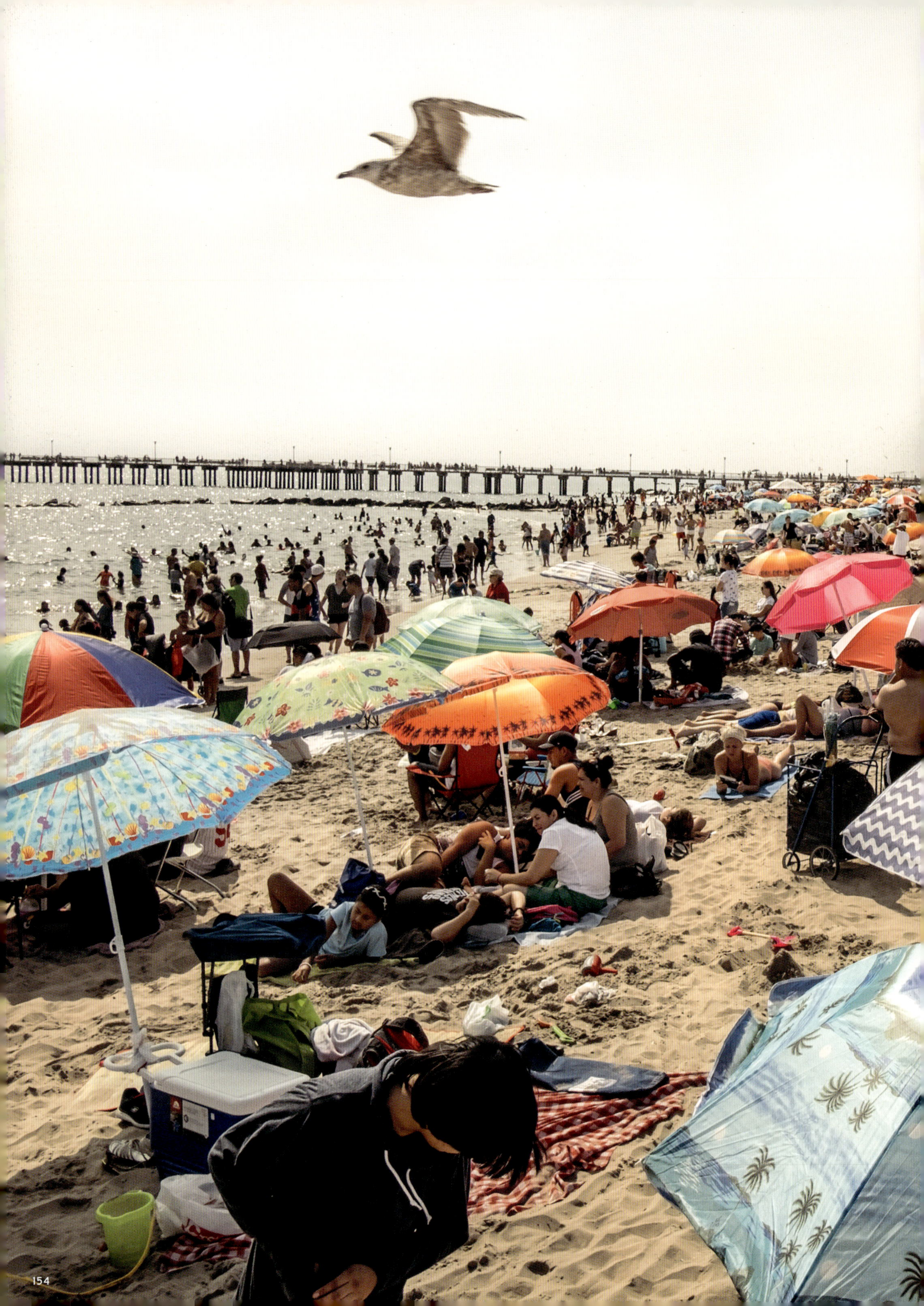

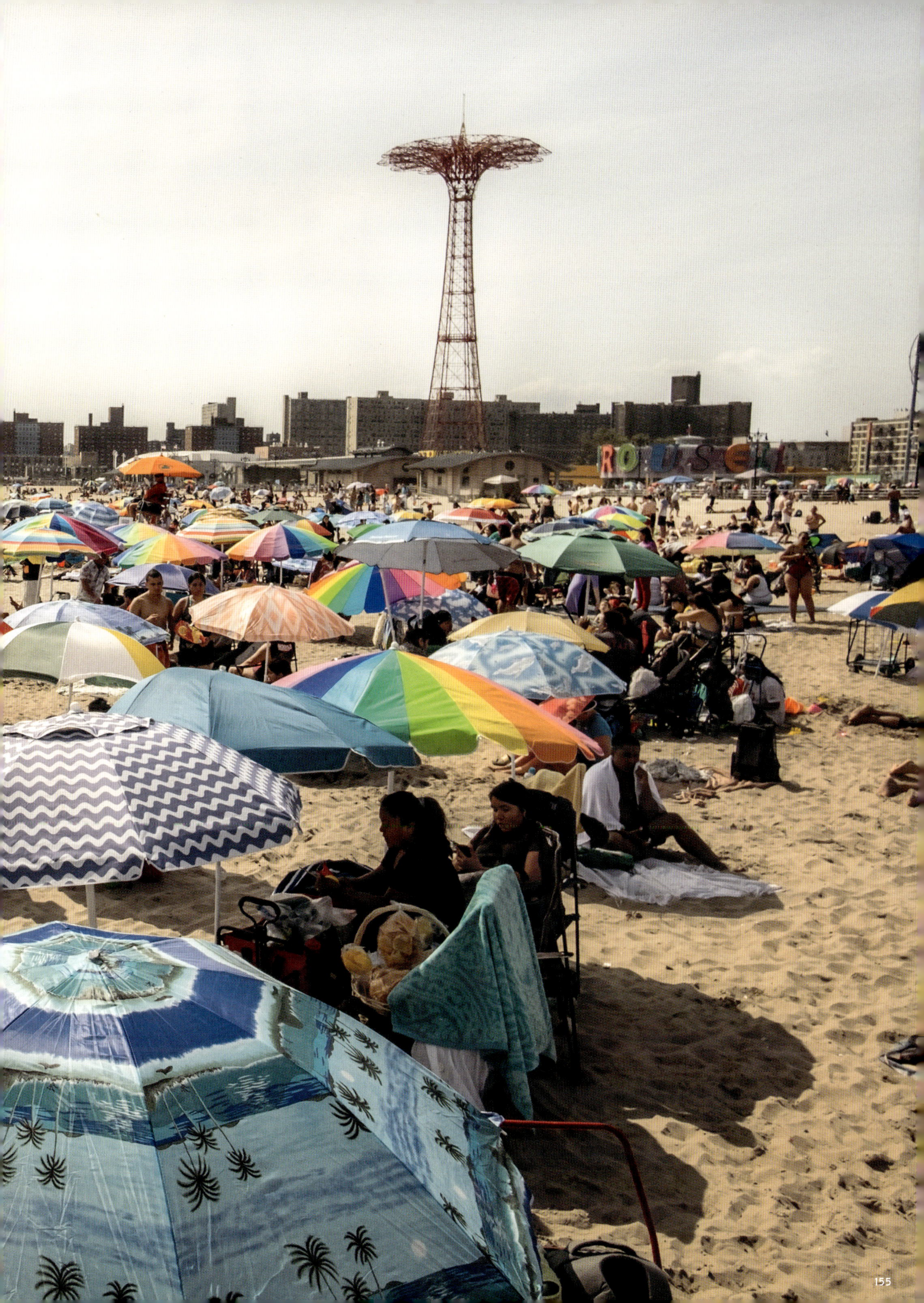

ROXSCL

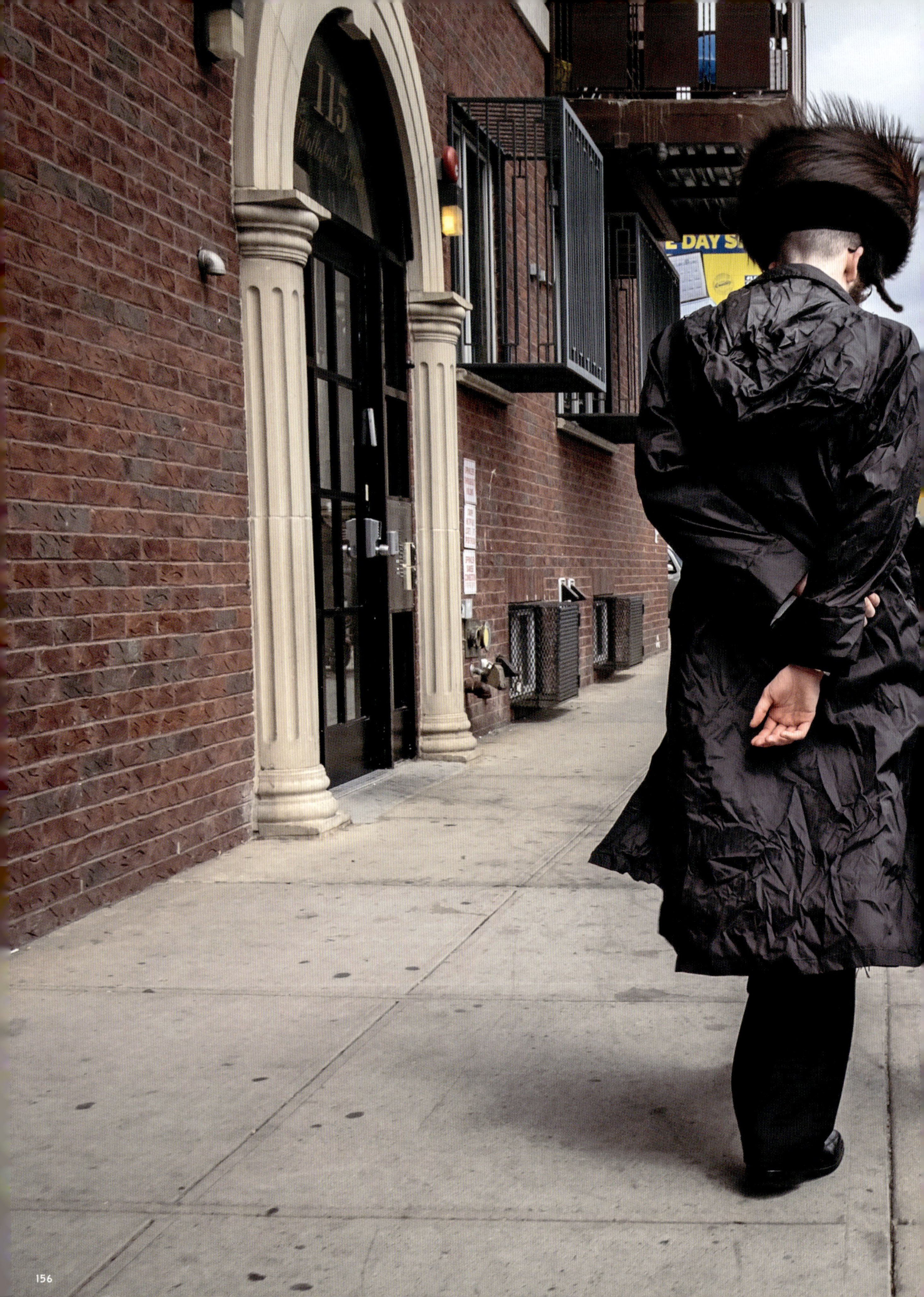
E DAY S

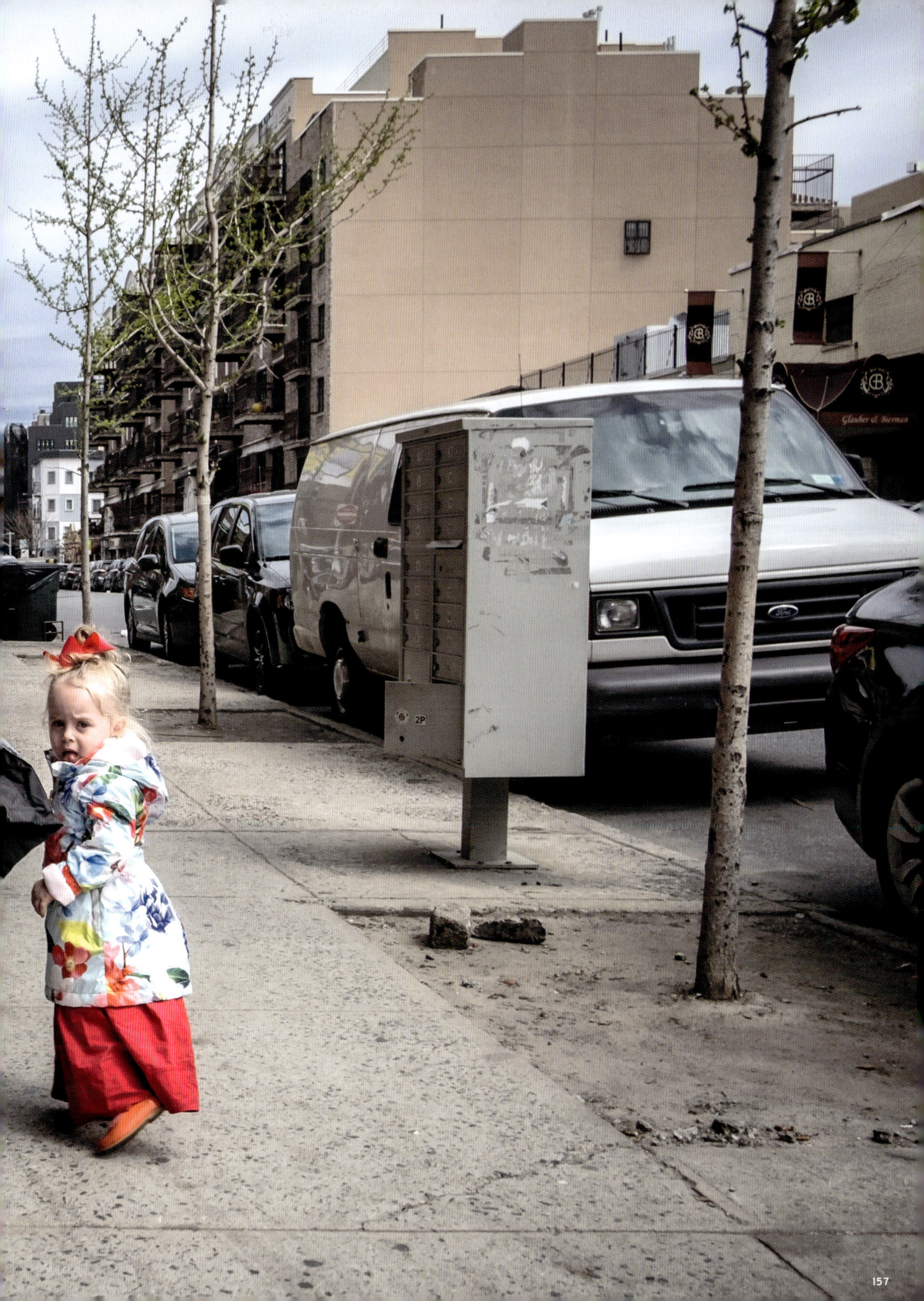

Glauber & Bierman
Ford
2P

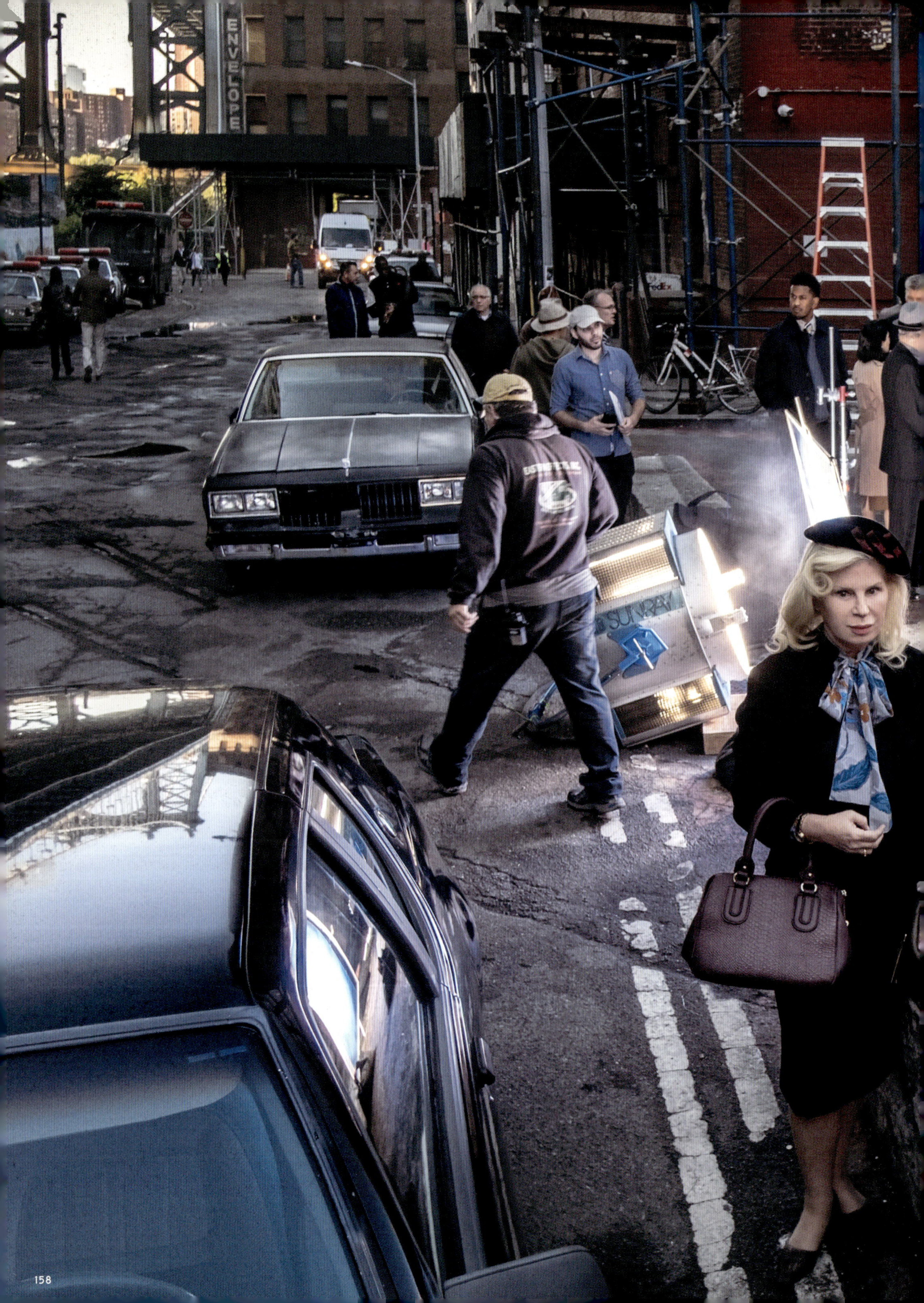

ENVELOPE

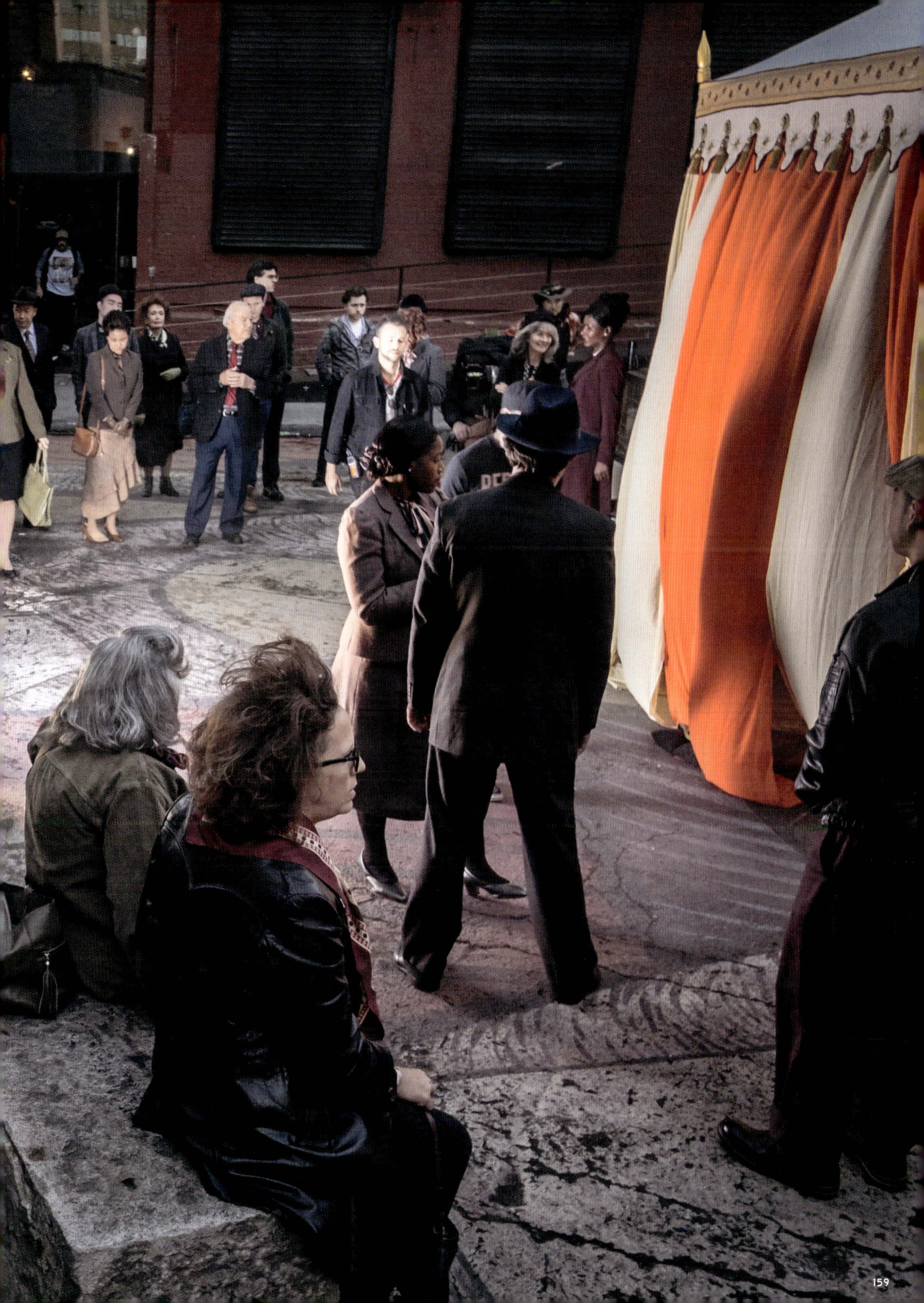

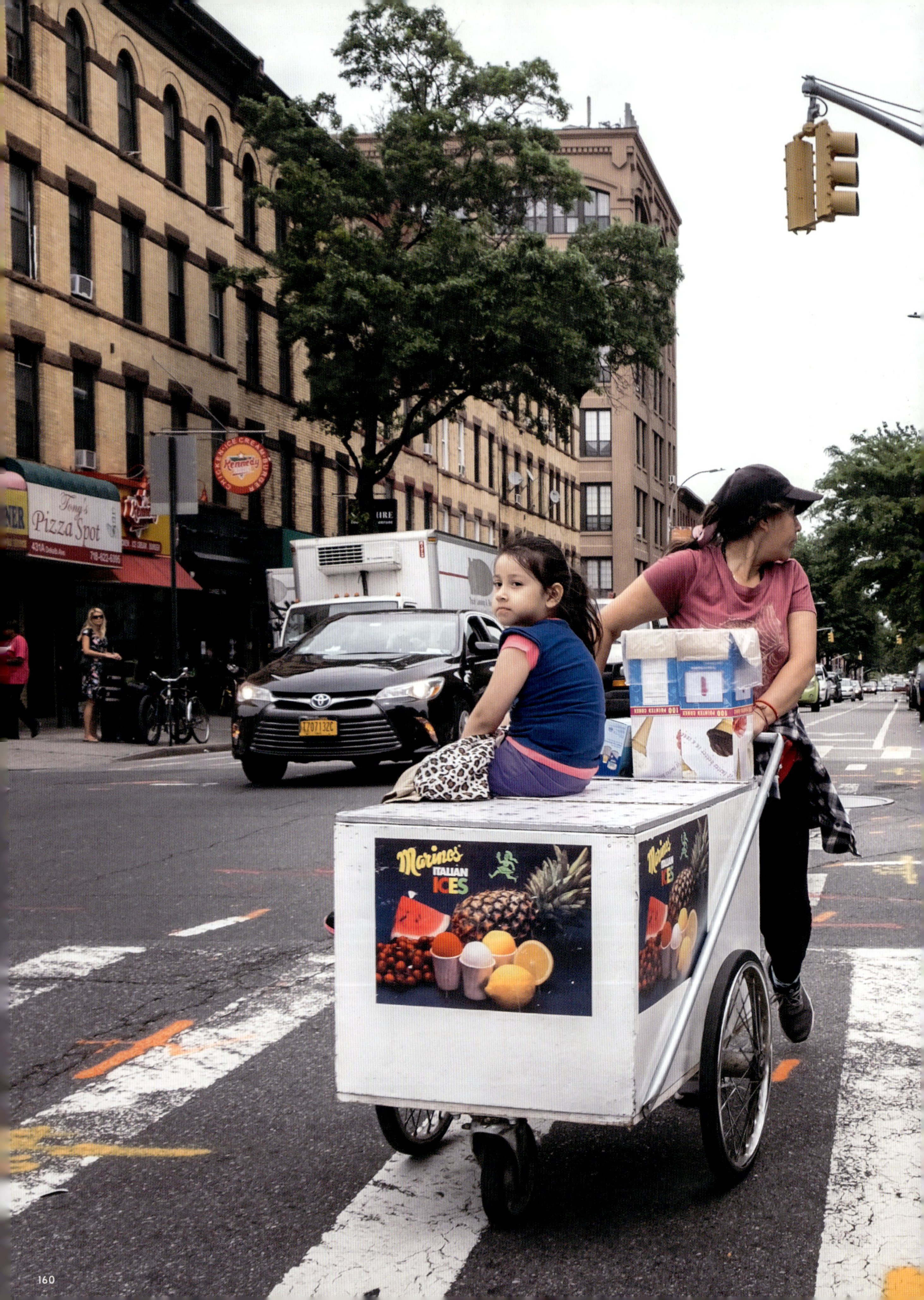
Tony's
Pizza Spot
431A DeKalb Ave.
718-622-6365
Marinos
ITALIAN
ICES
Marinos
ICES
100 POINTED SHEET

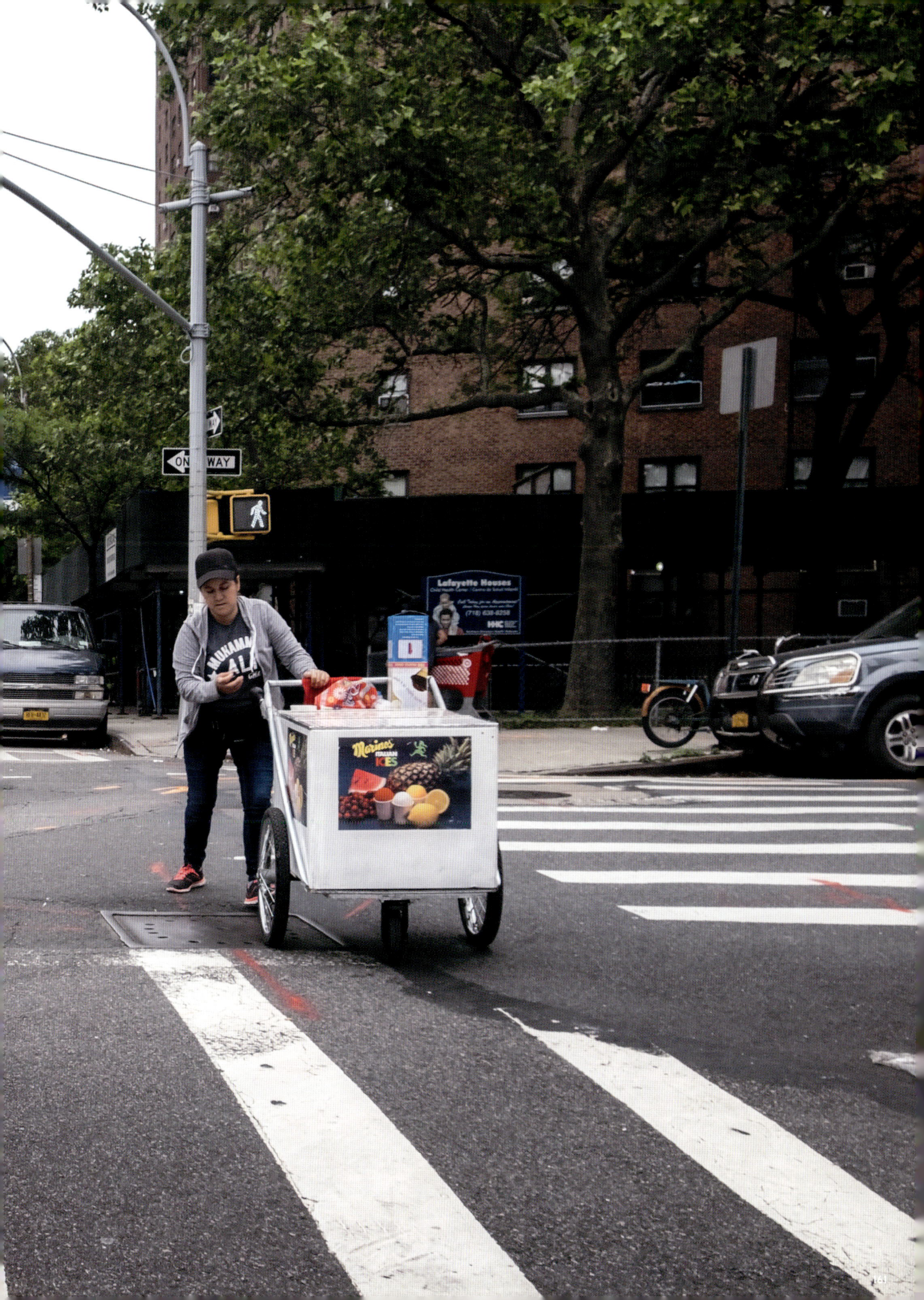

ONE WAY
Lafayette Houses
Child Health Center · Centro de Salud Infantil
(718) 638-8258
HHC
Marino's
ITALIAN ICES

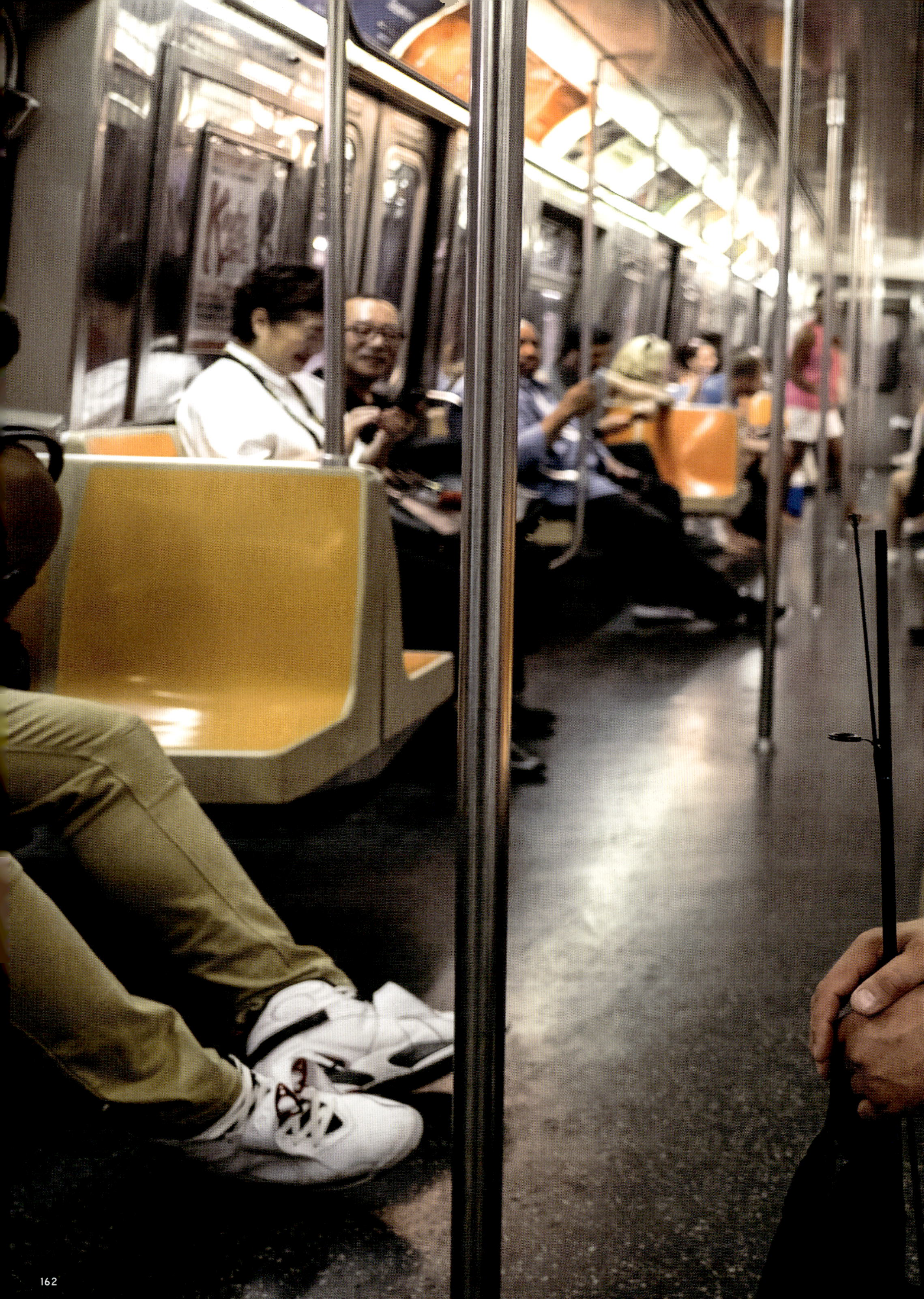

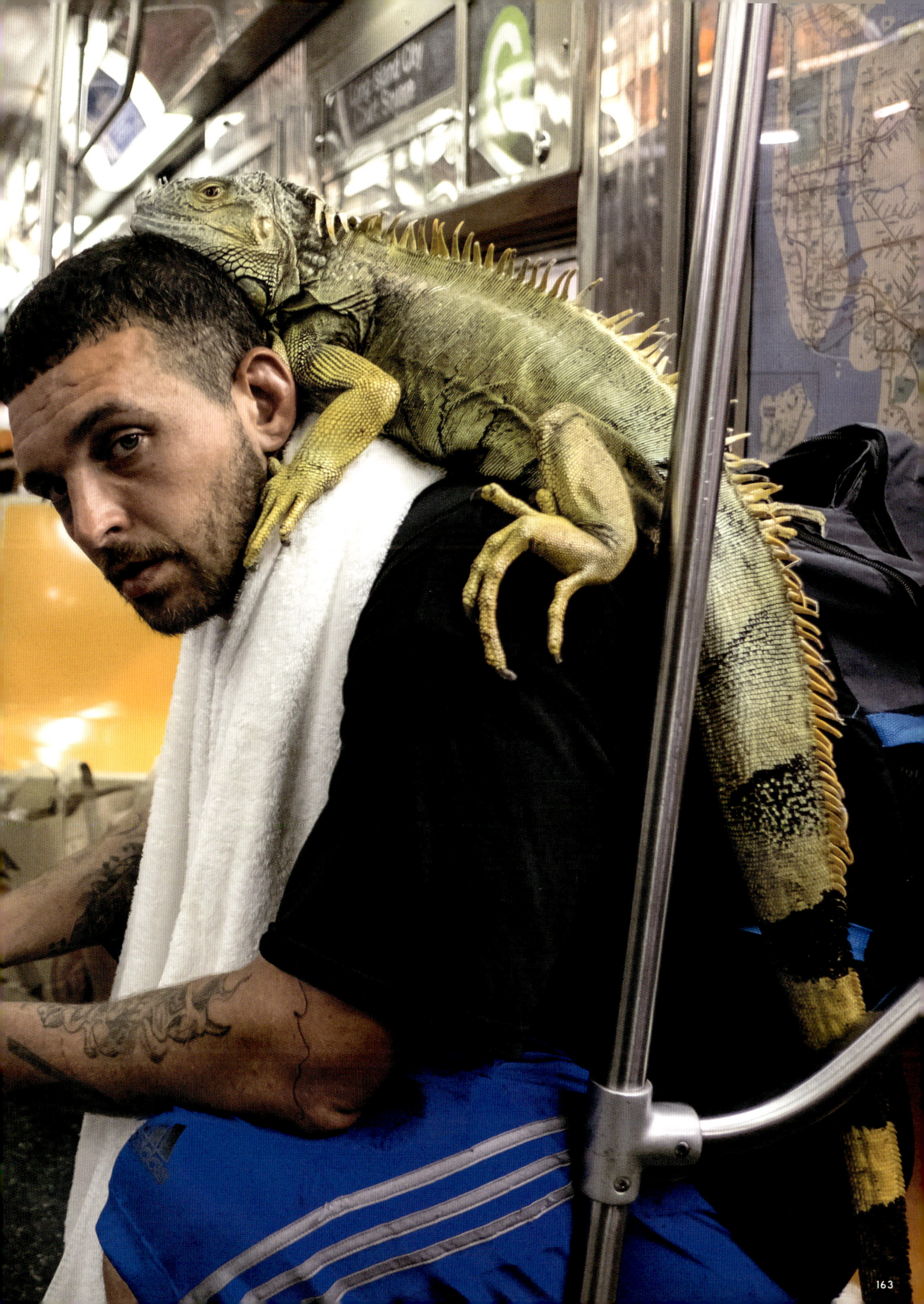

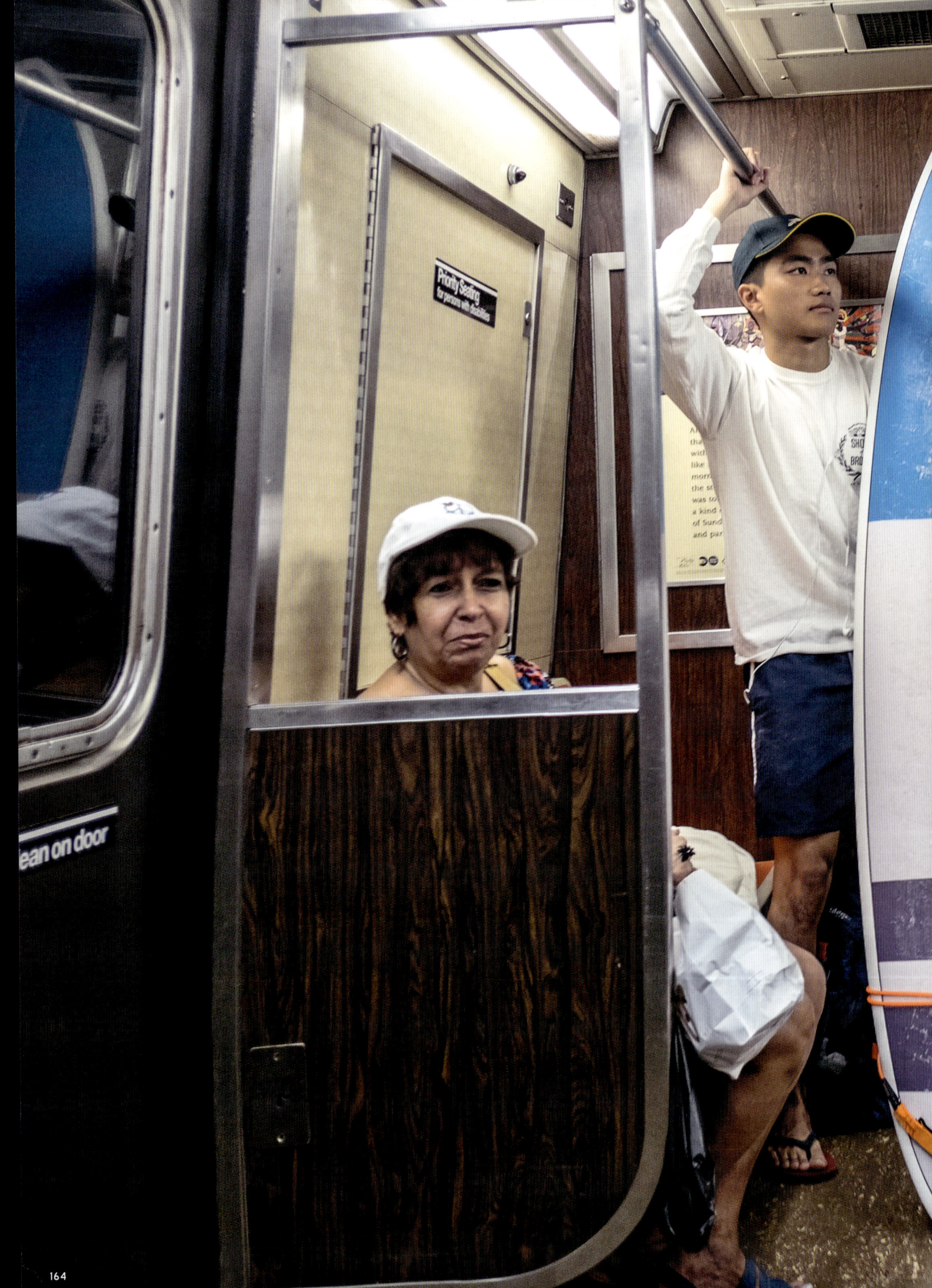

Priority Seating
for persons with disabilities
ean on door

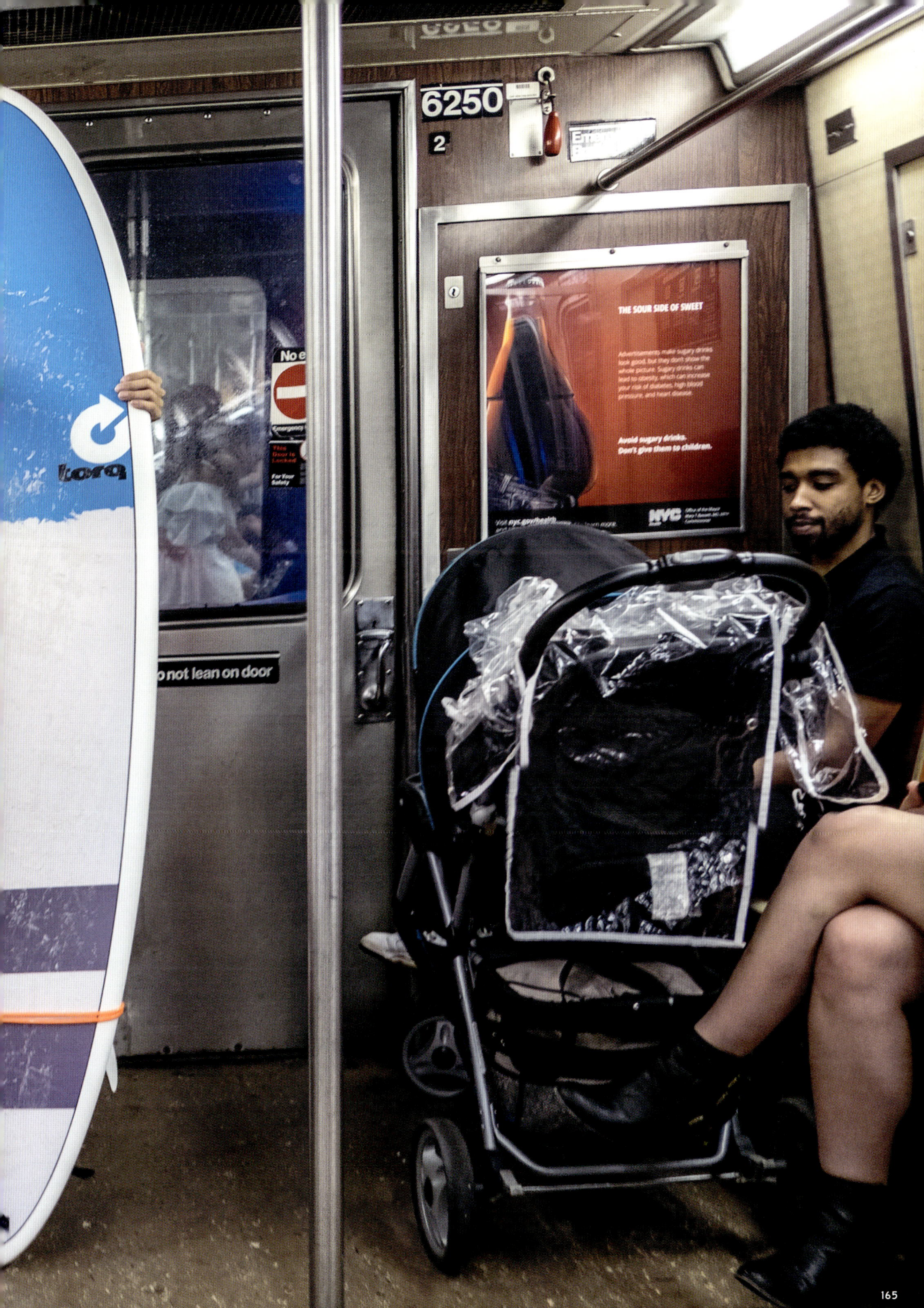

6250
2
THE SOUR SIDE OF SWEET
Avoid sugary drinks.
Don't give them to children.
NYC
No e
For Your Safety
Do not lean on door

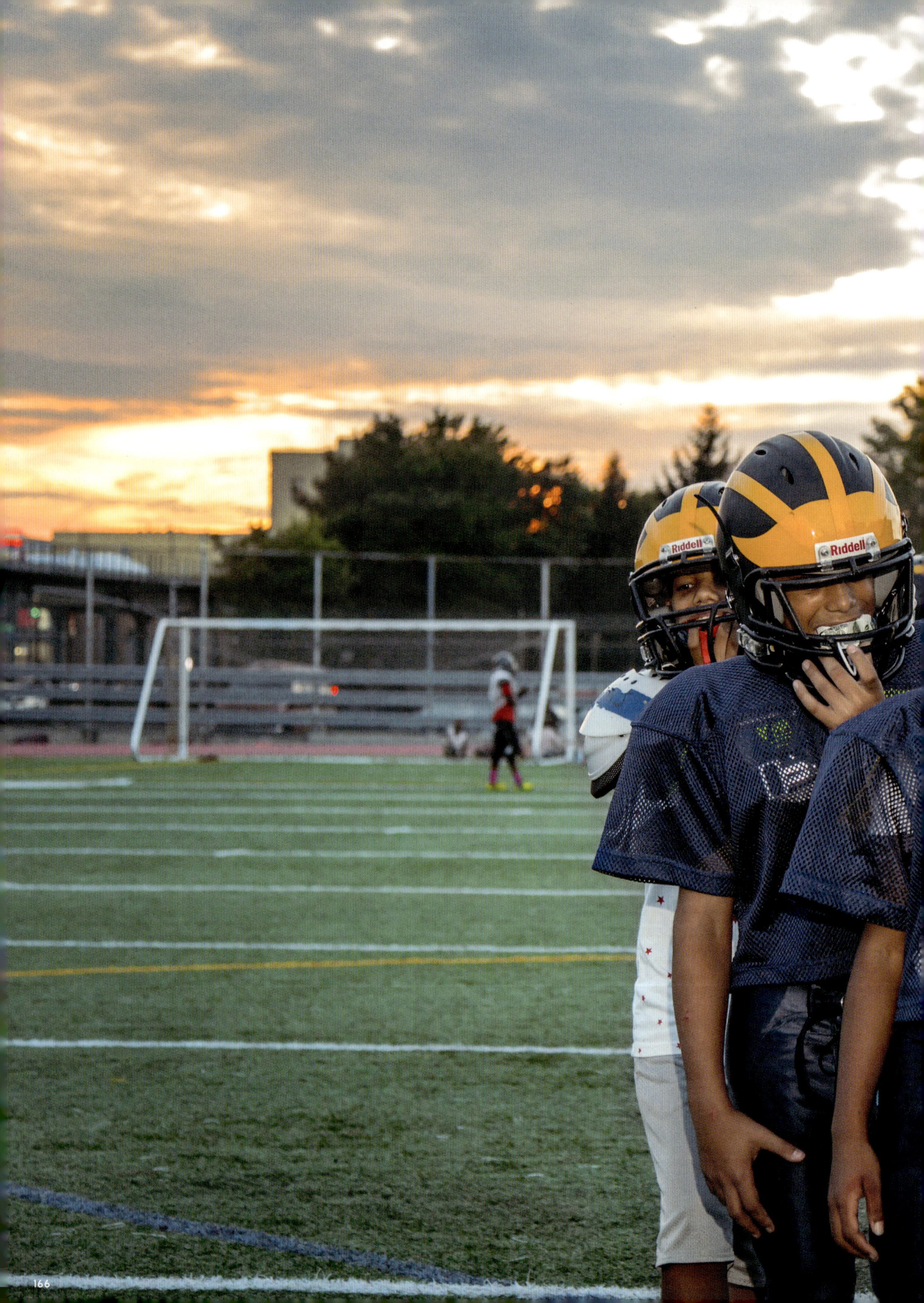

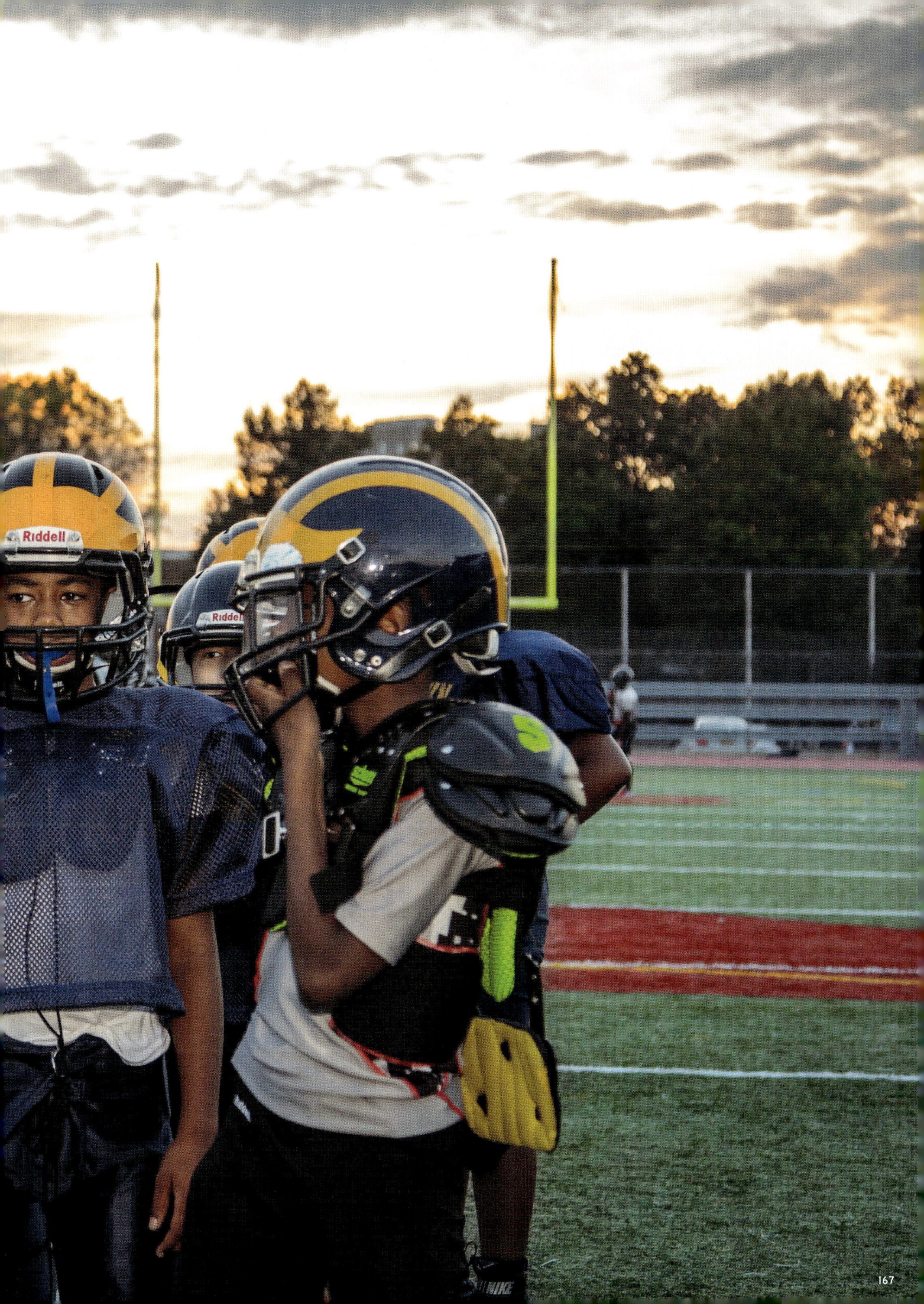
Riddell
Riddell
NIKE

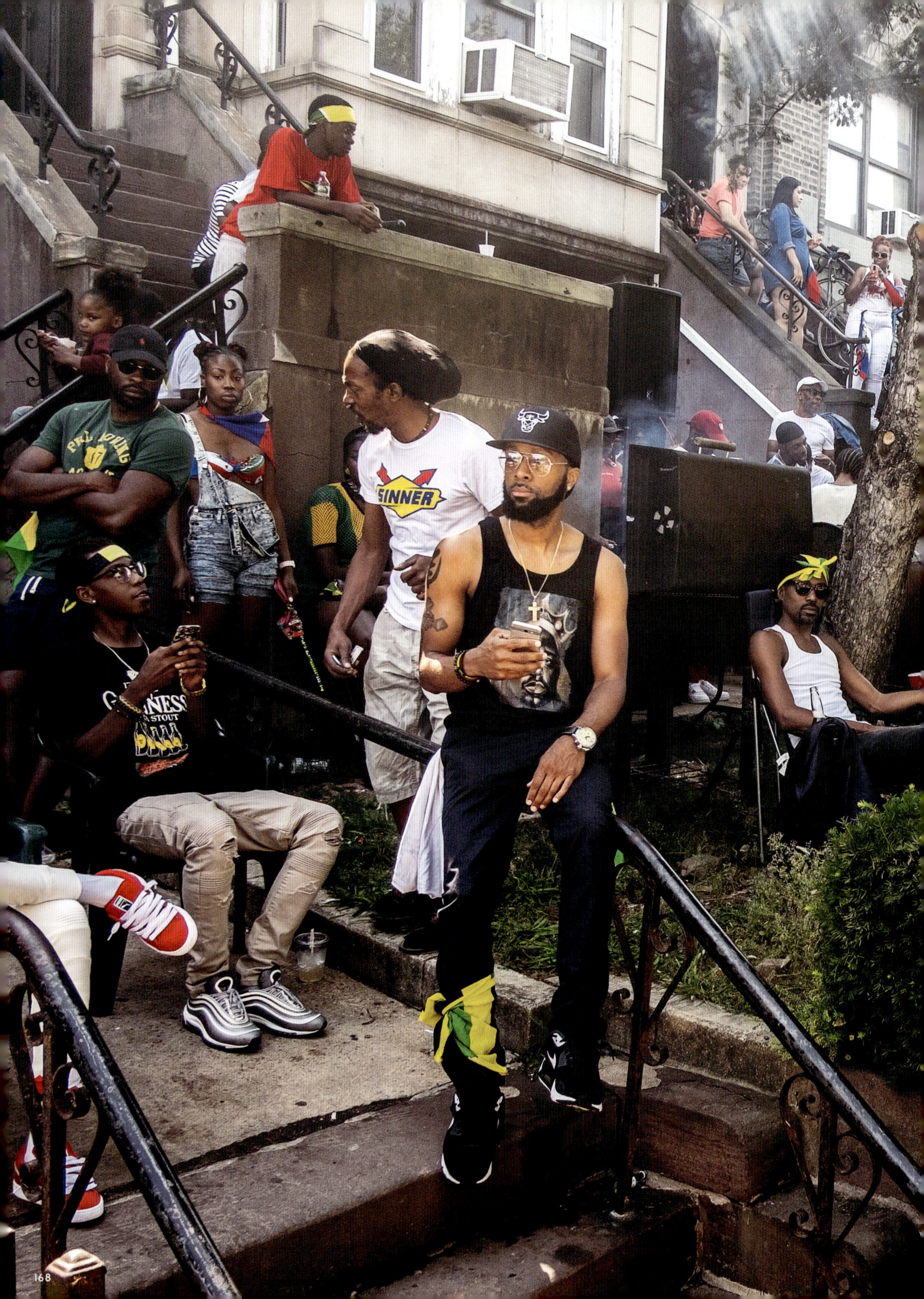

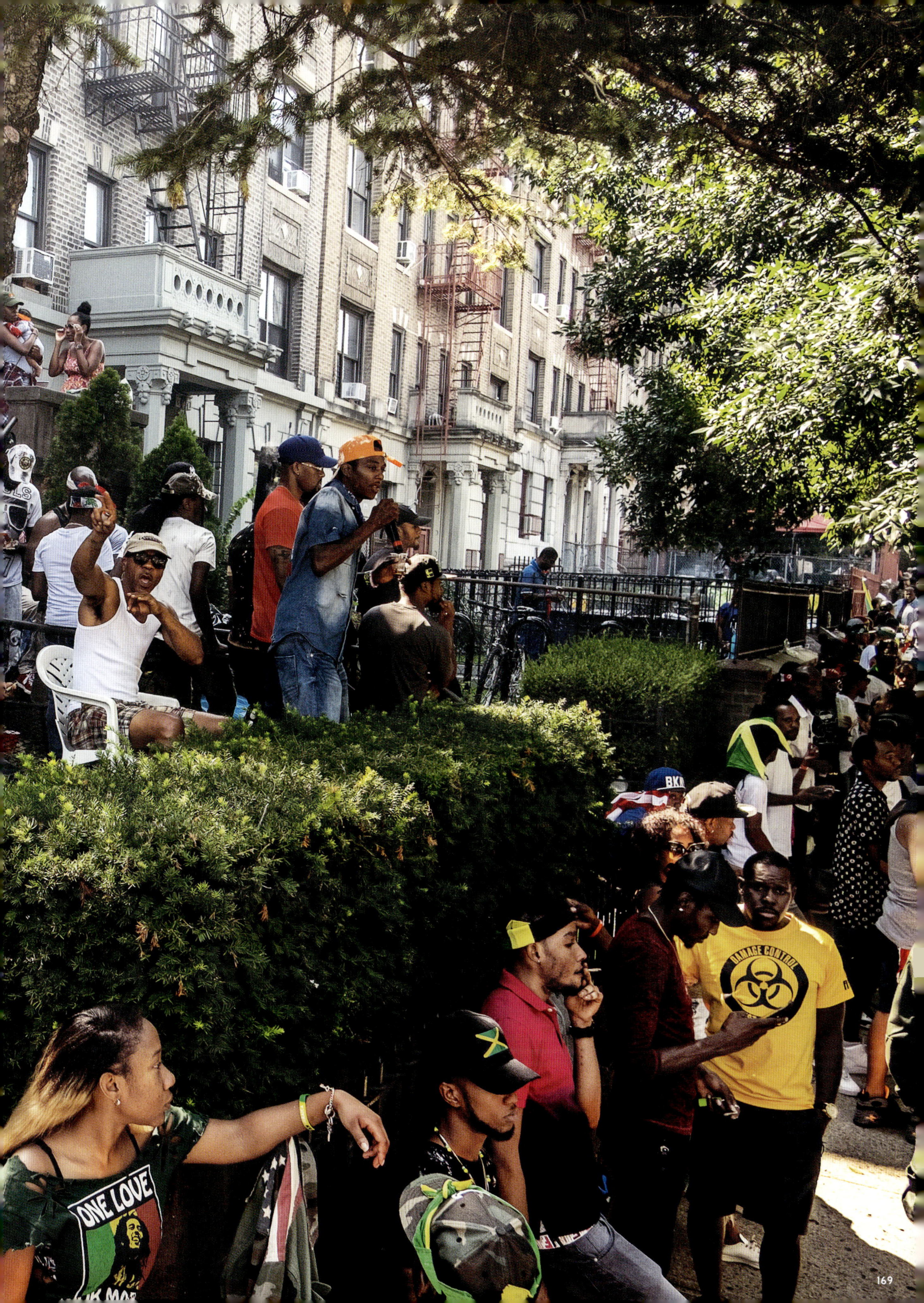

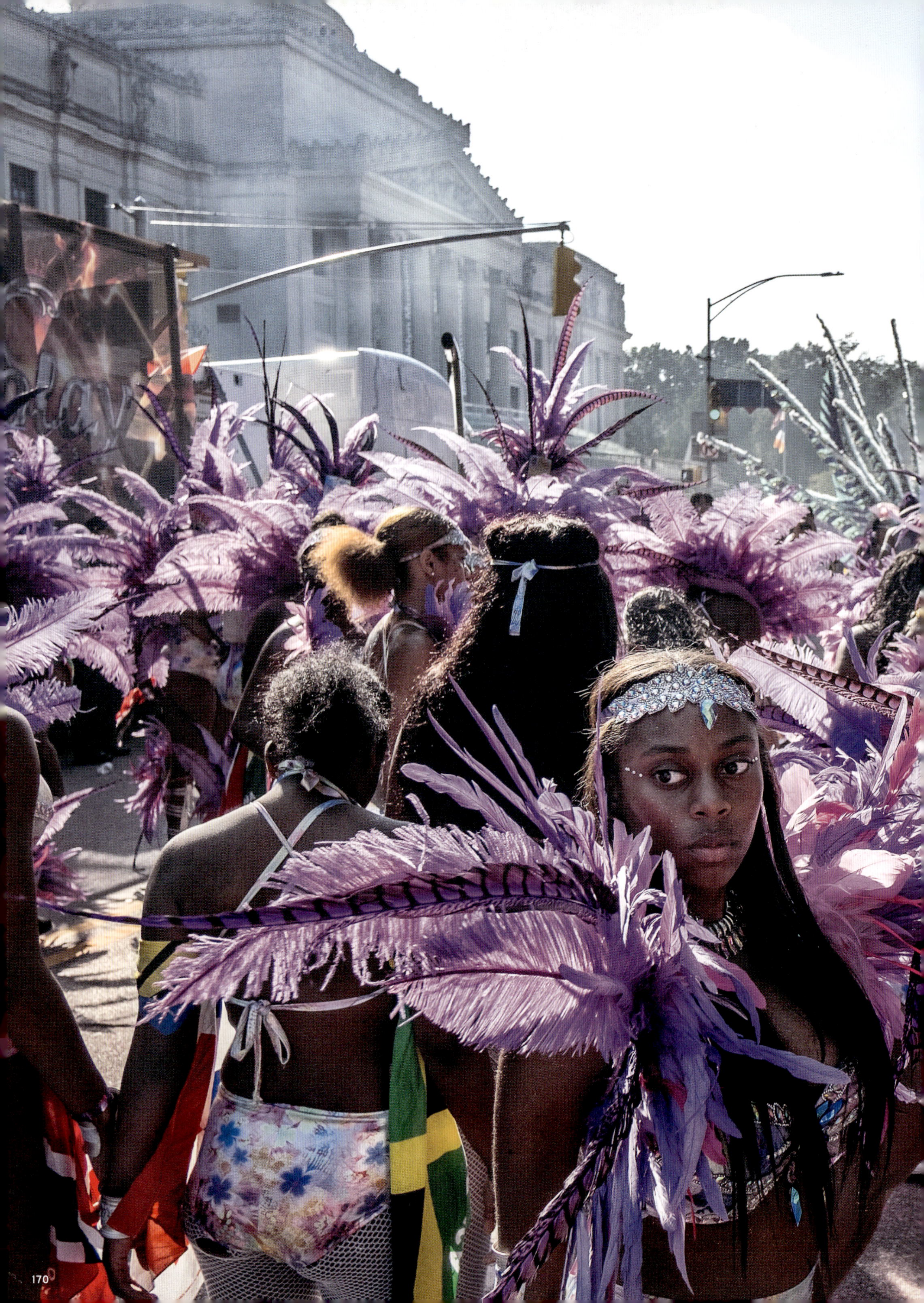

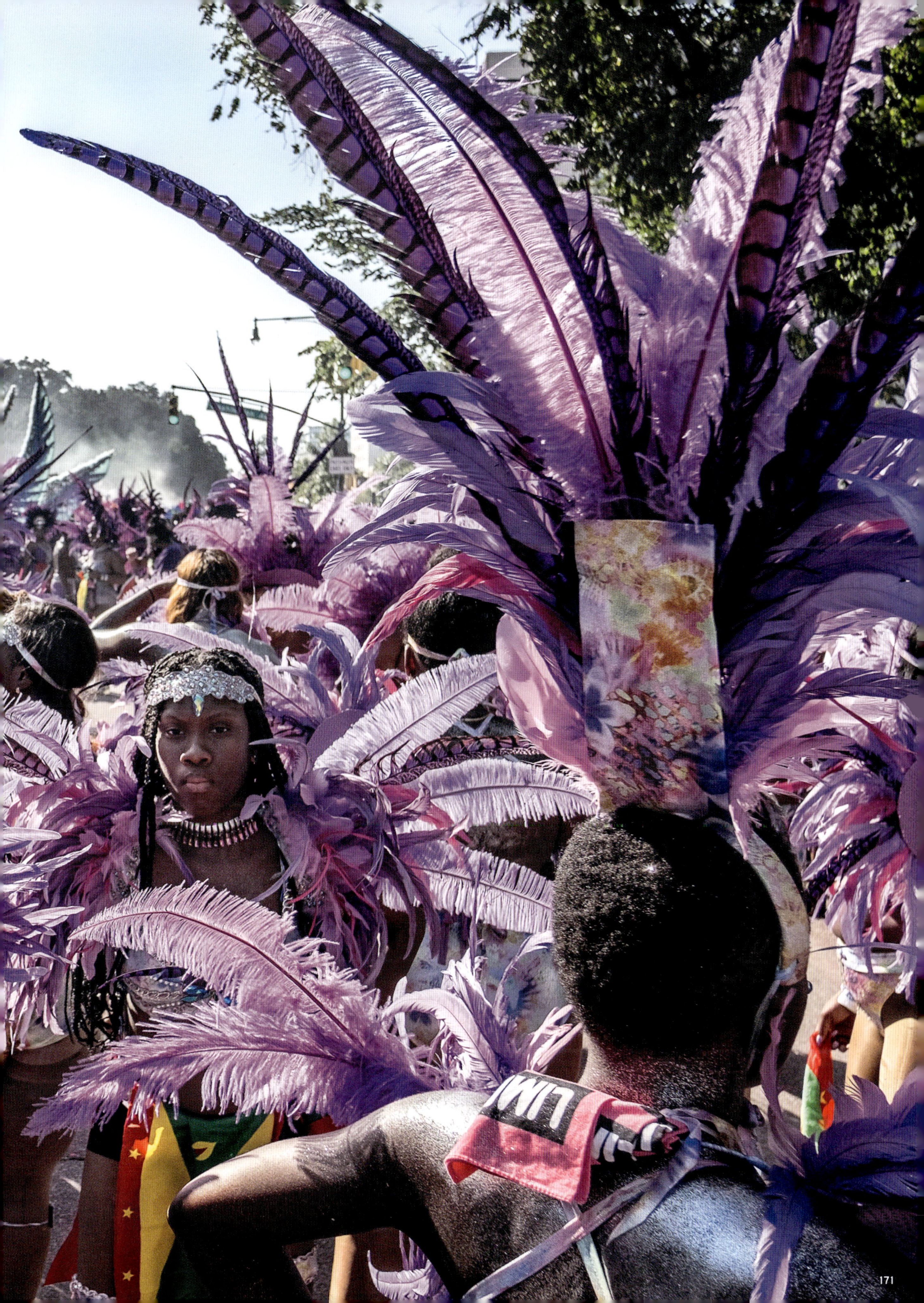

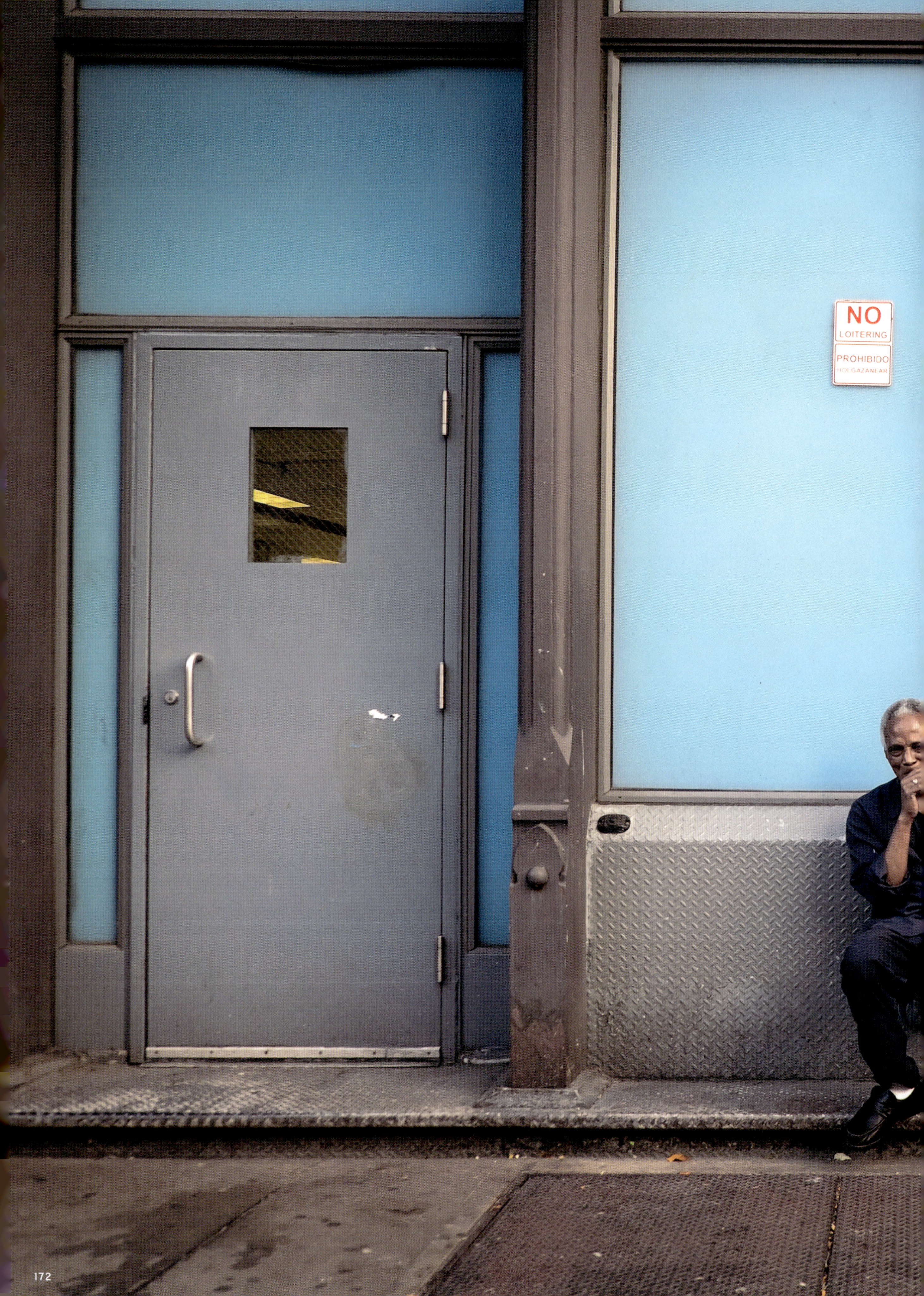

NO
LOITERING
PROHIBIDO
HOLGAZANEAR

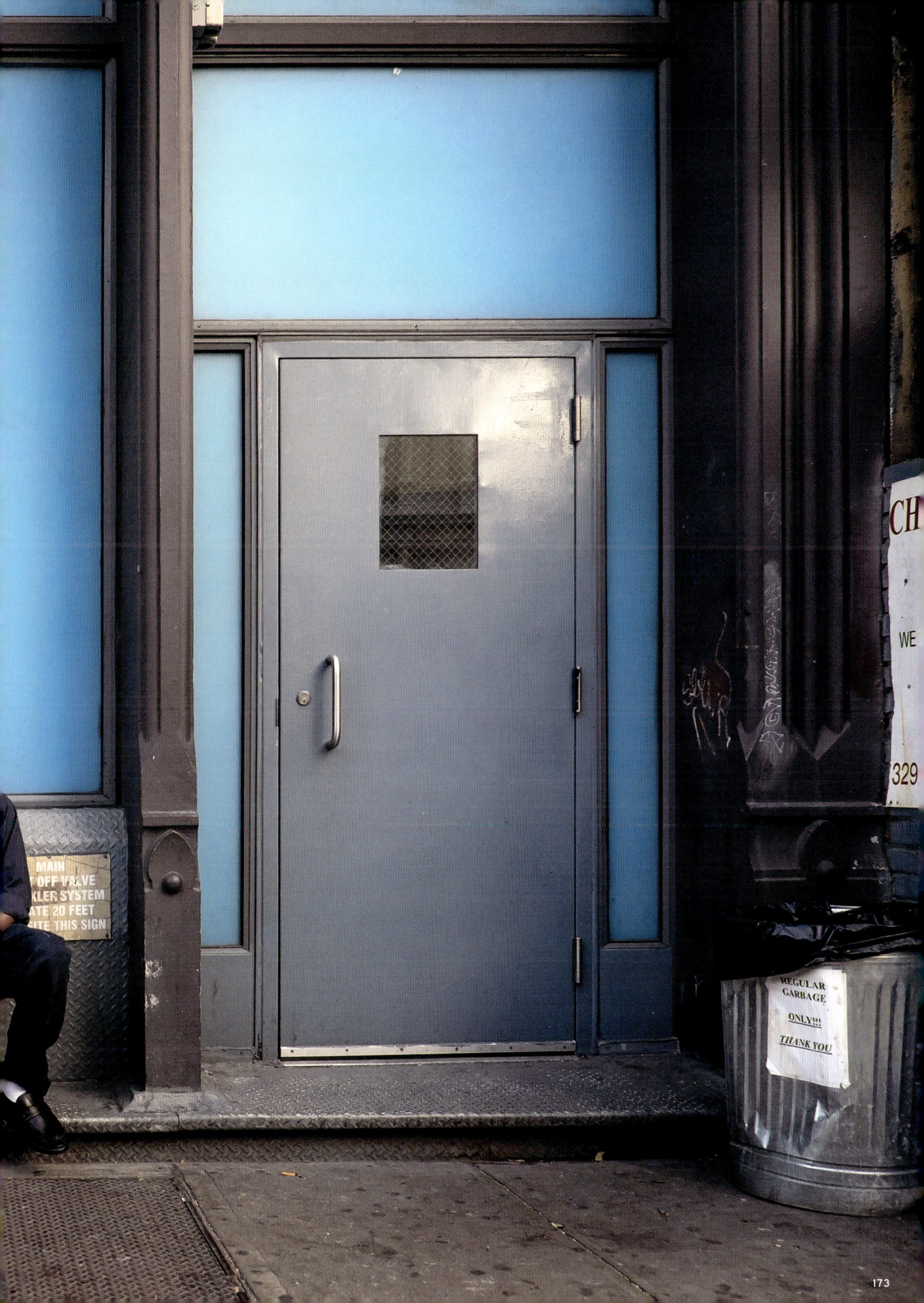
MAIN
OFF VALVE
KLER SYSTEM
ATE 20 FEET
ITE THIS SIGN
CH
WE
329
REGULAR
GARBAGE
ONLY!!!
THANK YOU

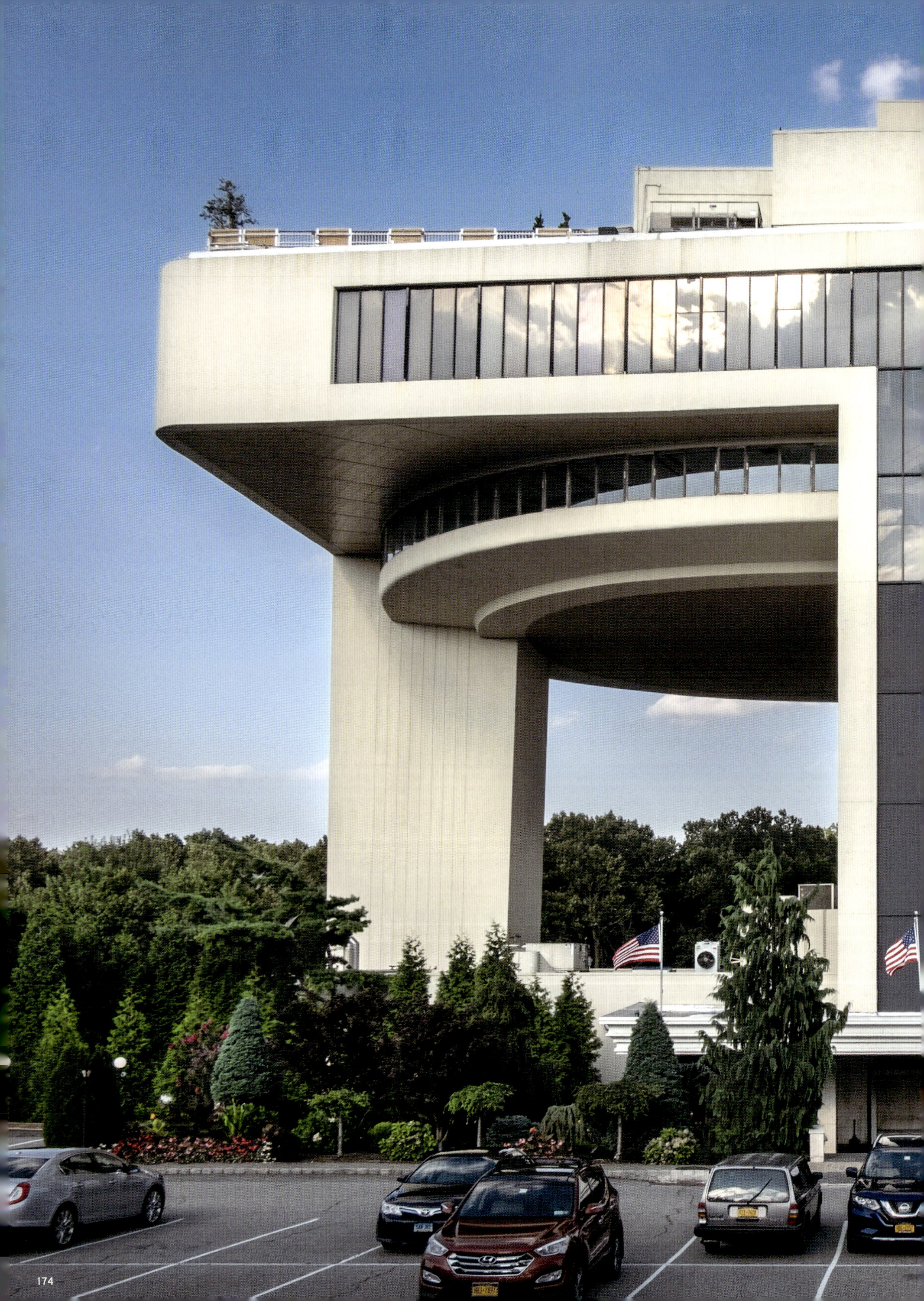

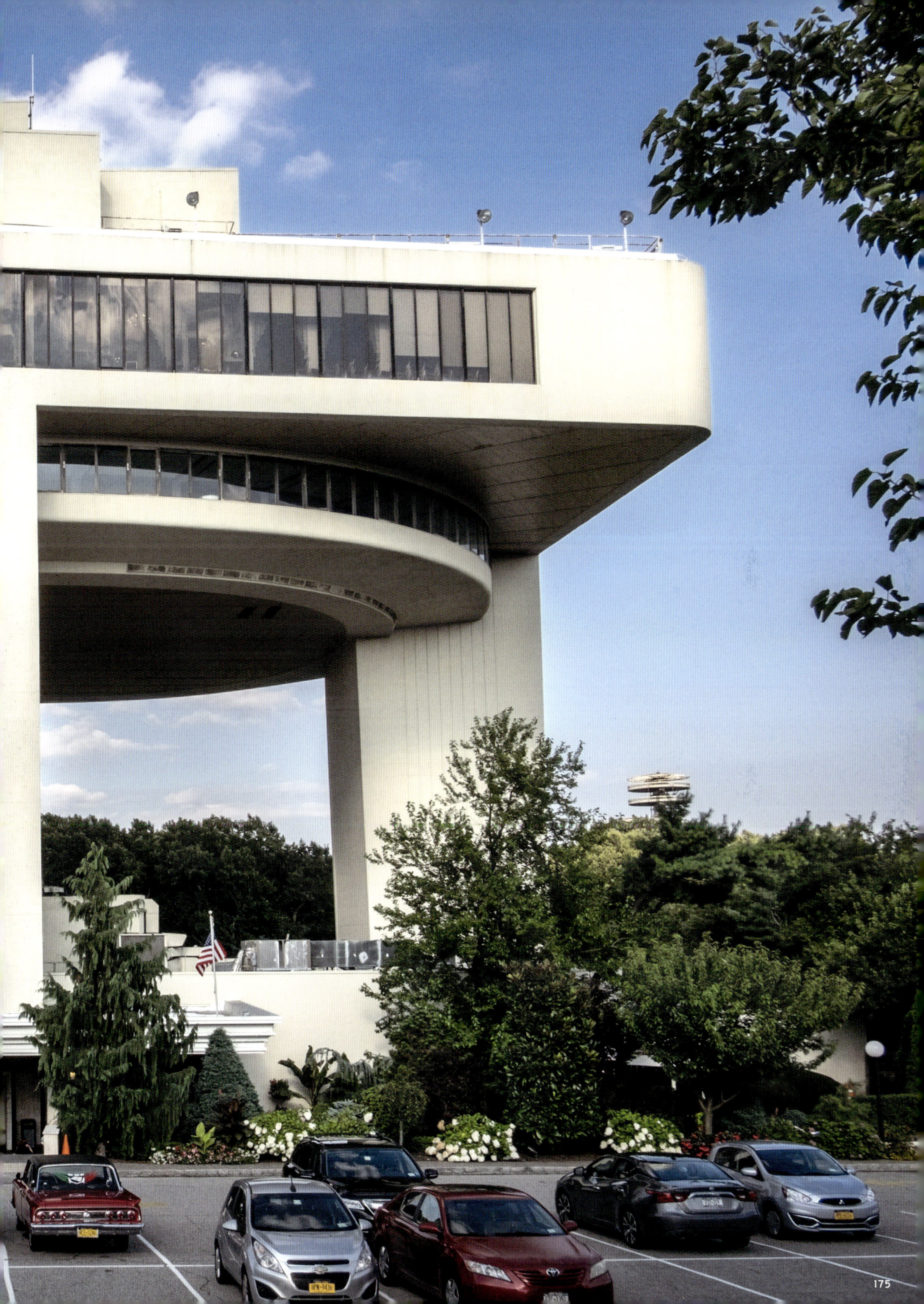

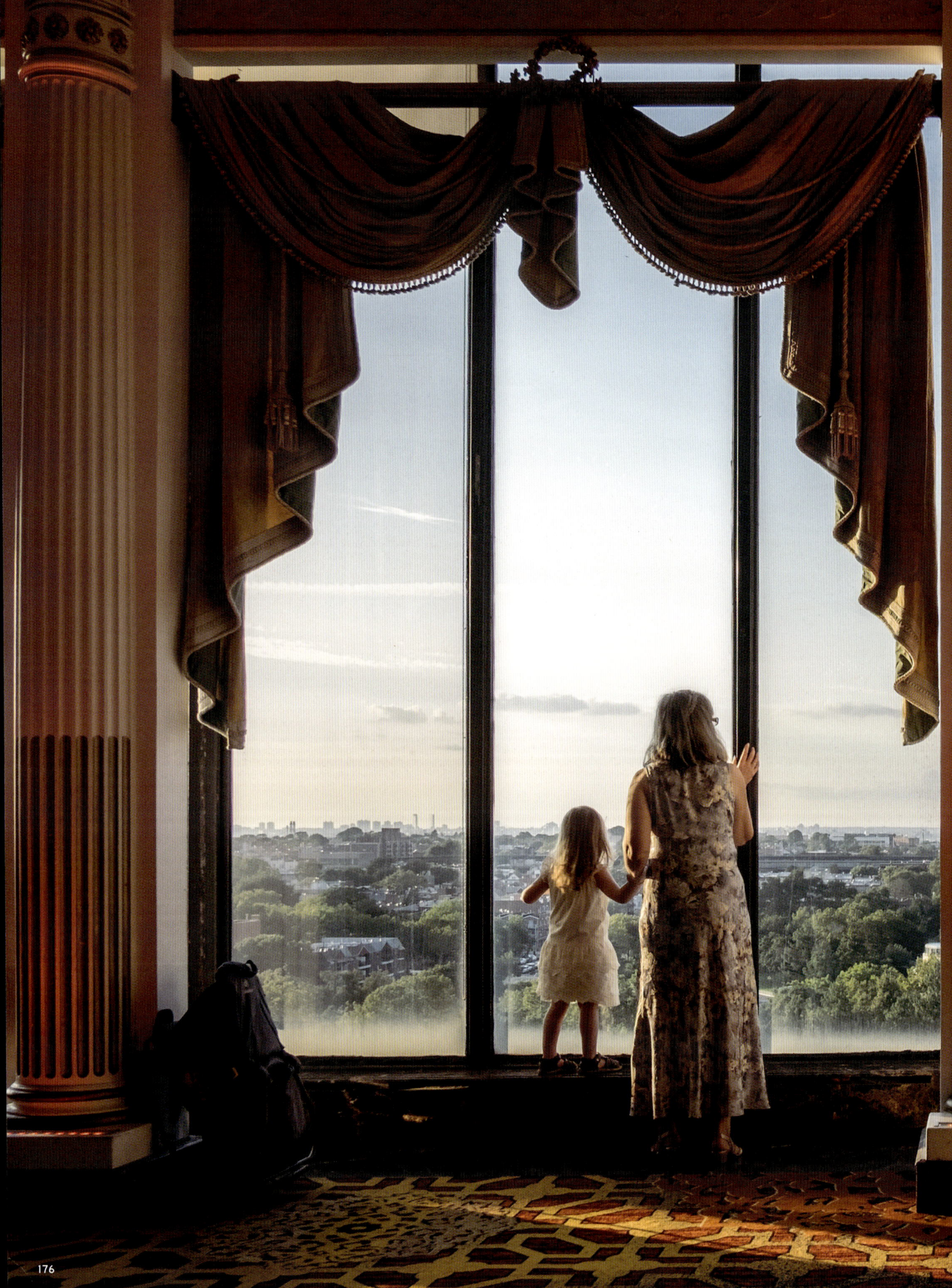

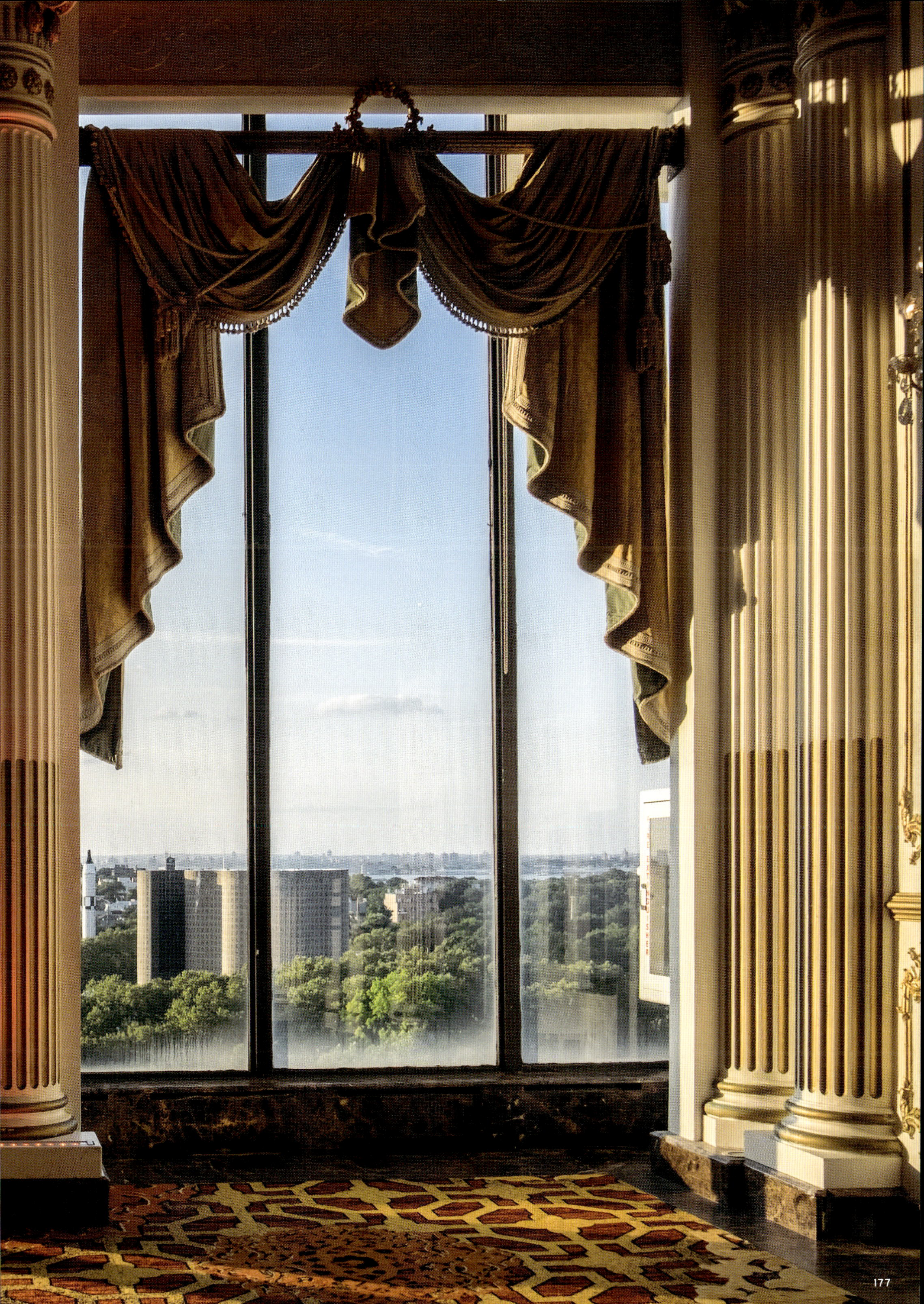

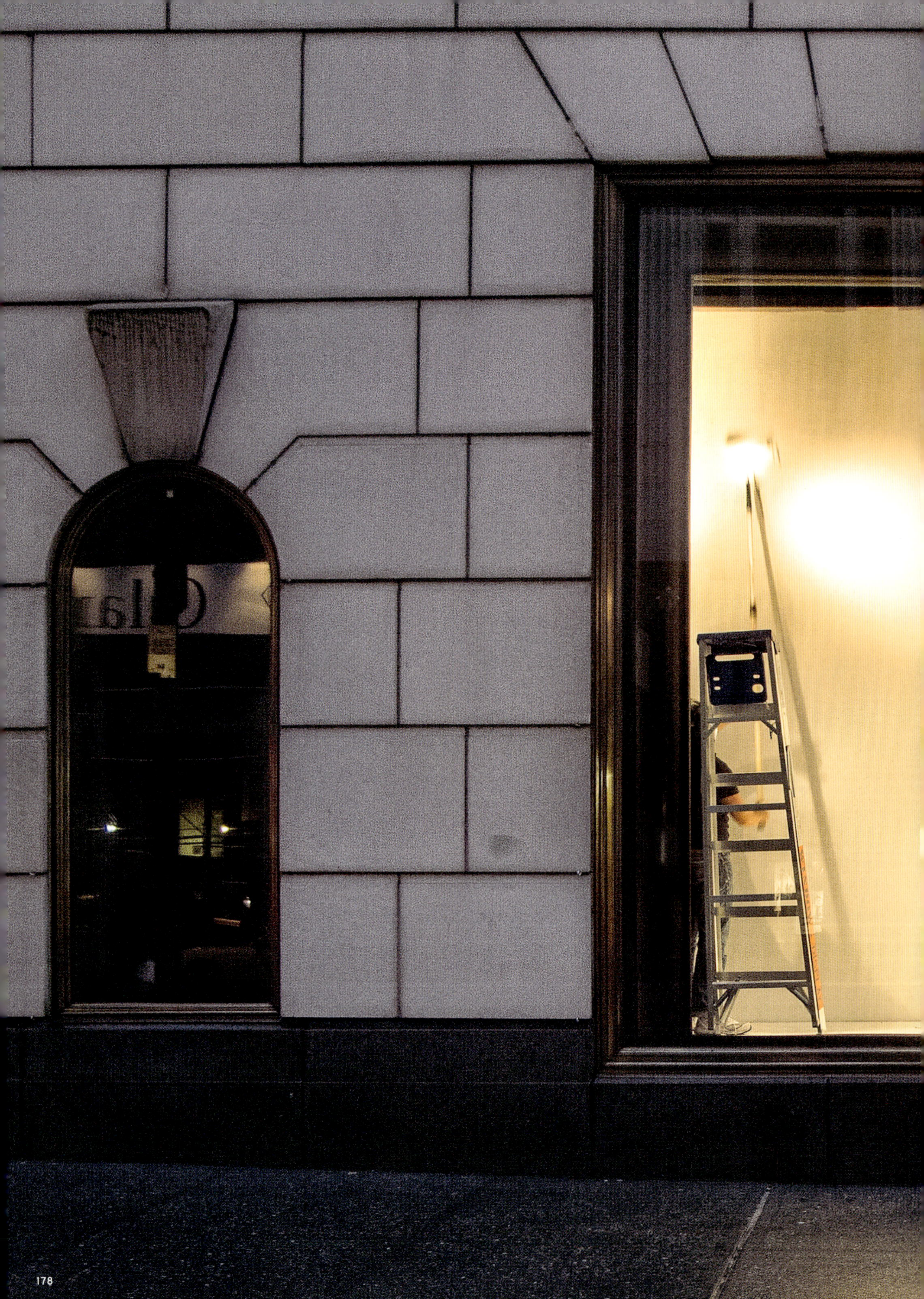

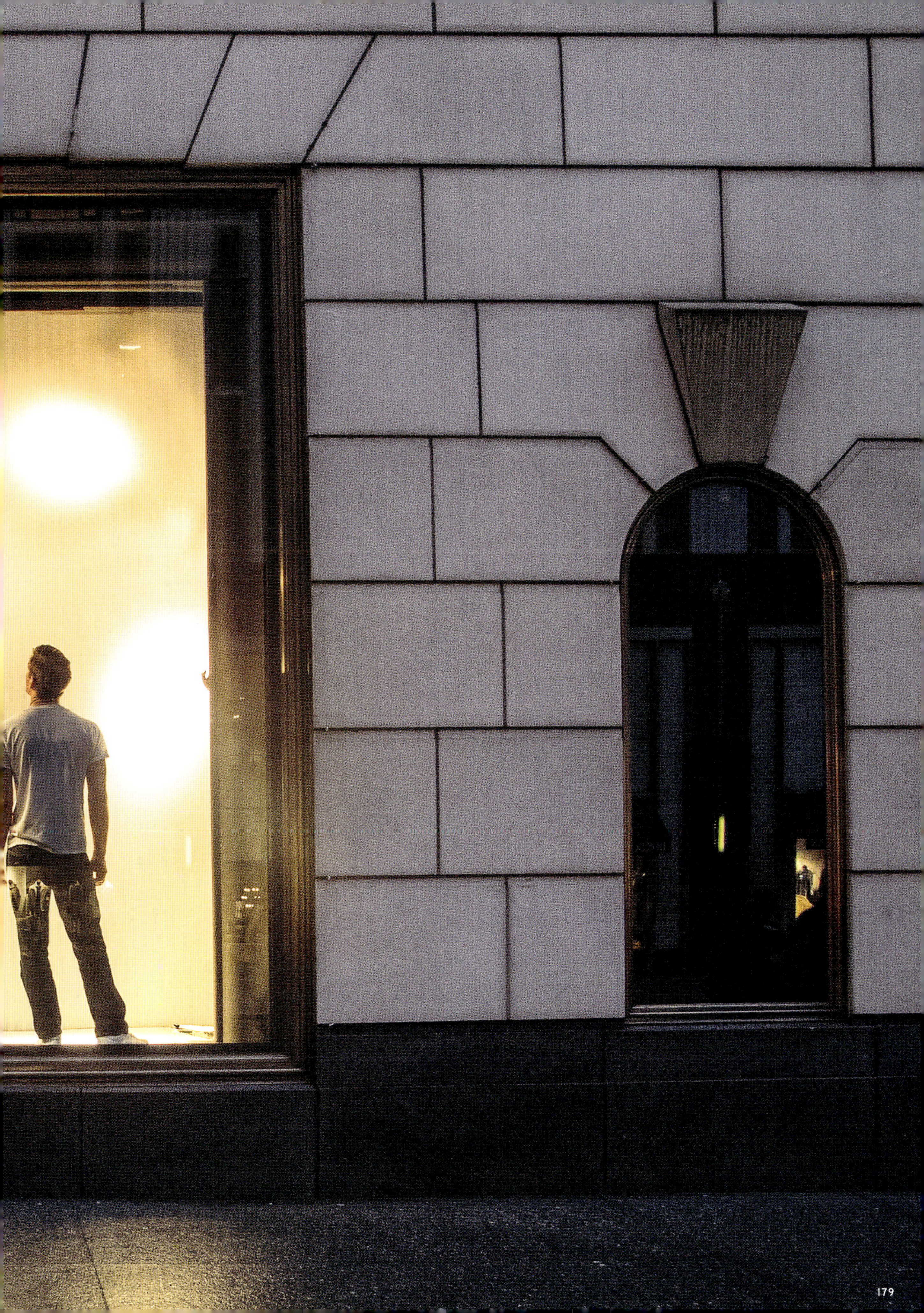

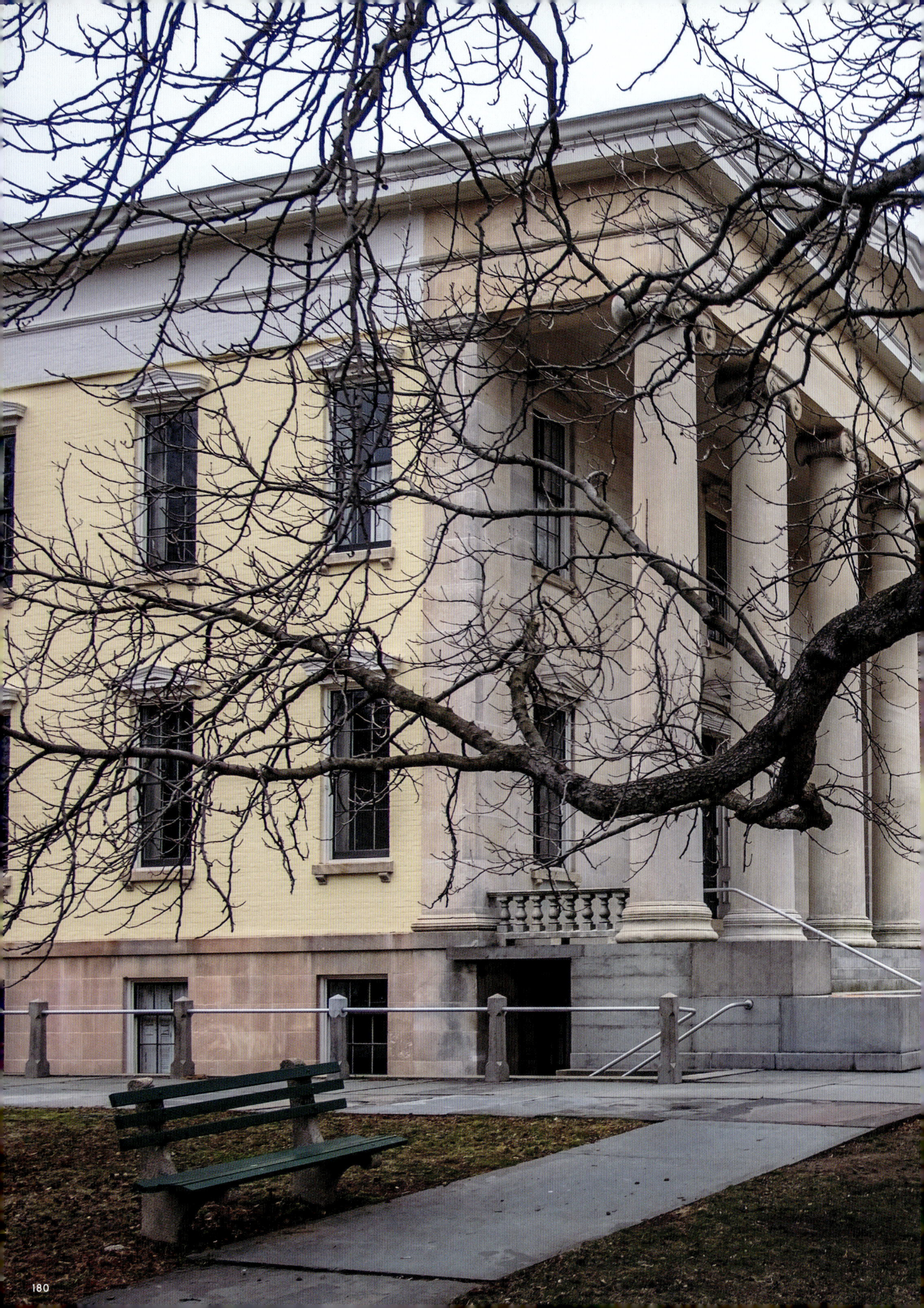

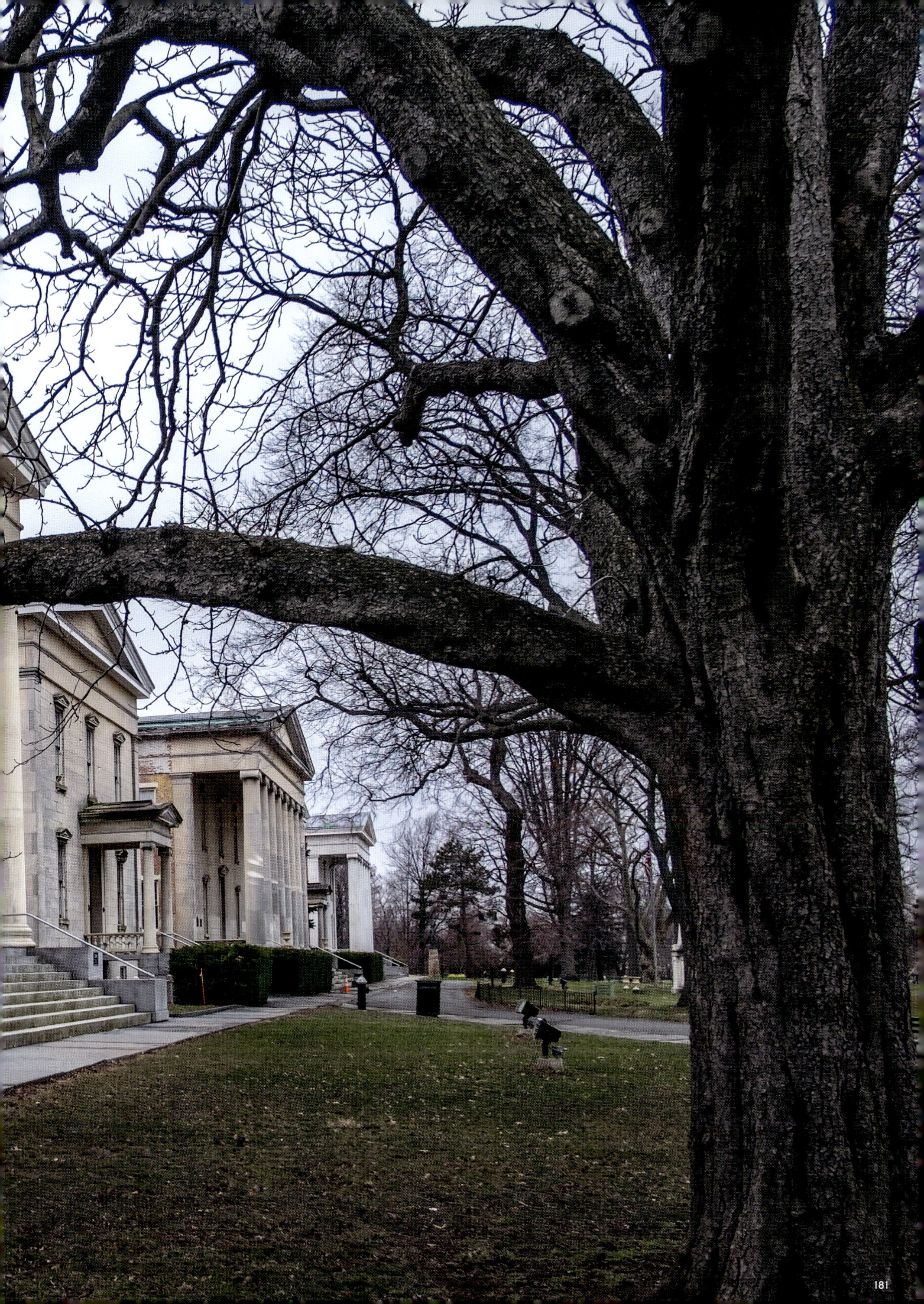

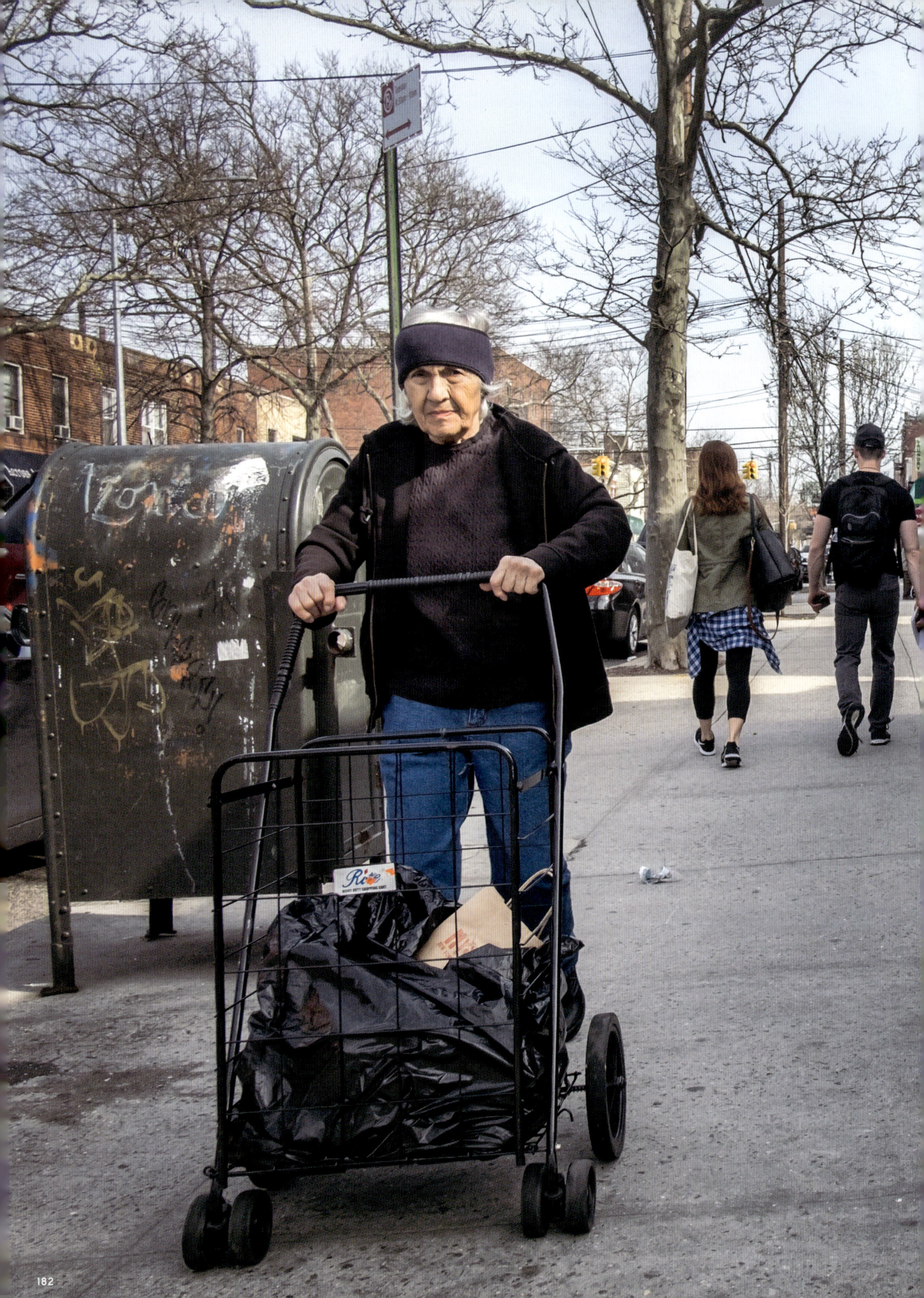

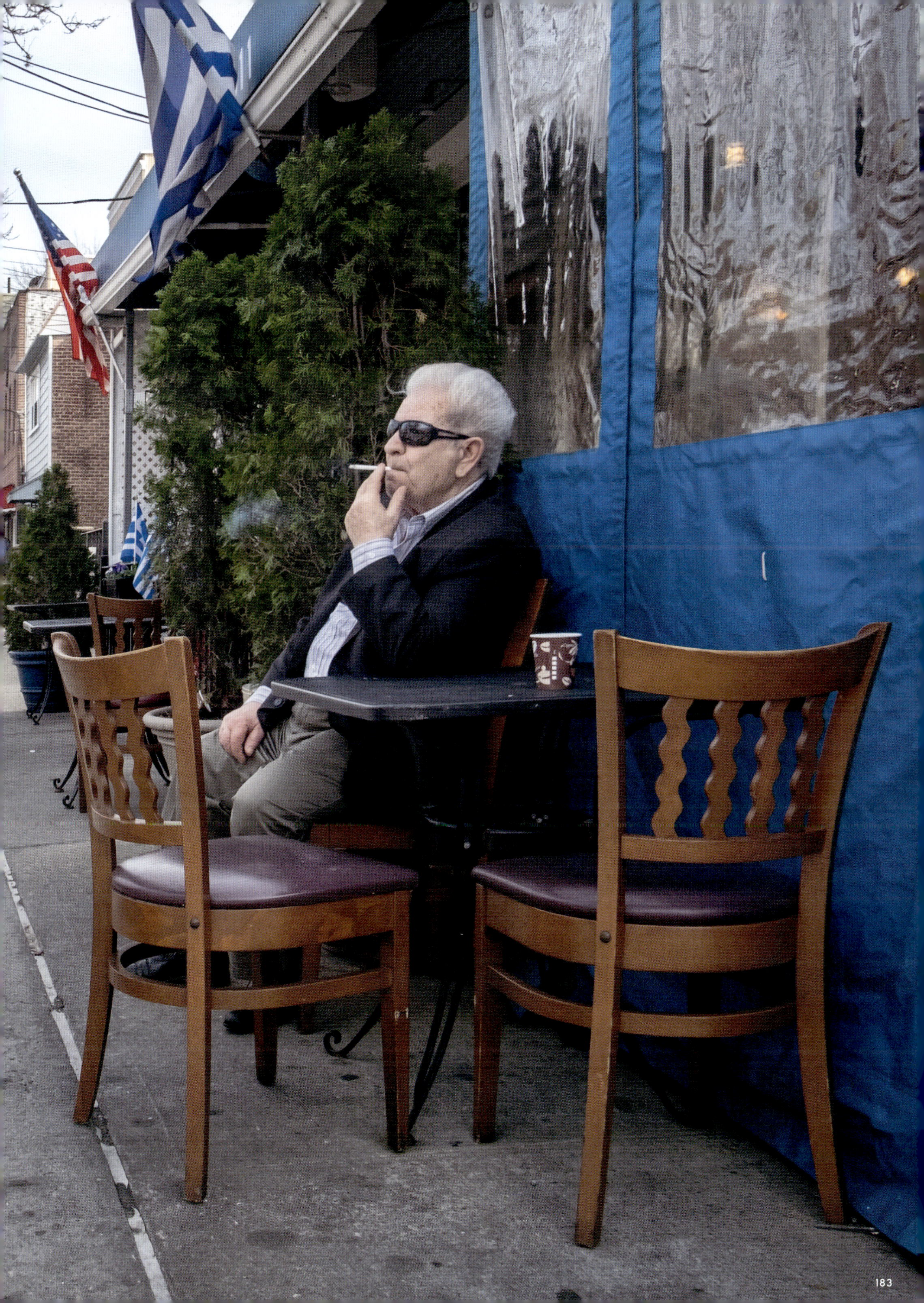

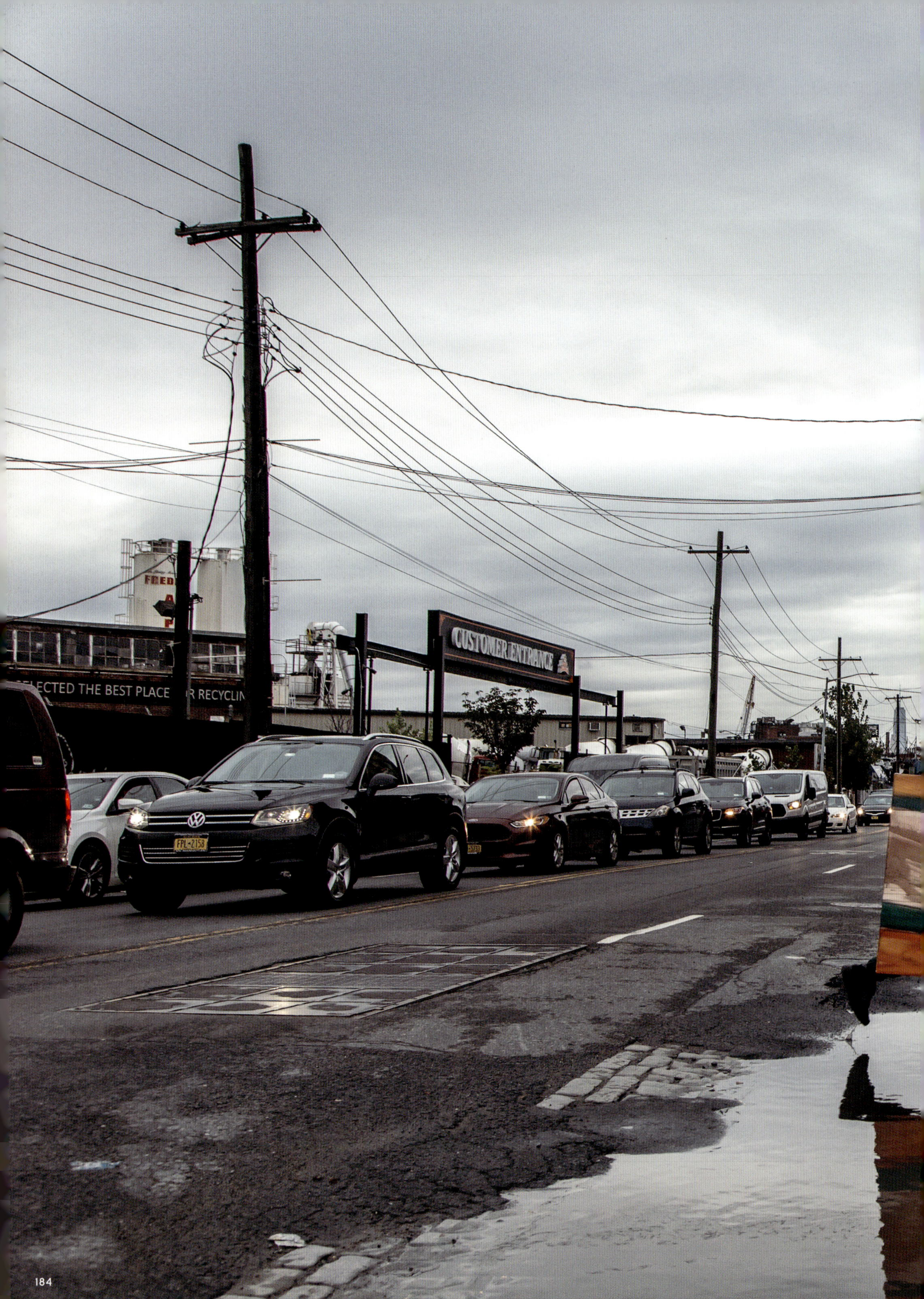

CUSTOMER ENTRANCE
SELECTED THE BEST PLACE FOR RECYCLIN
FRED
VW
FPL-2158

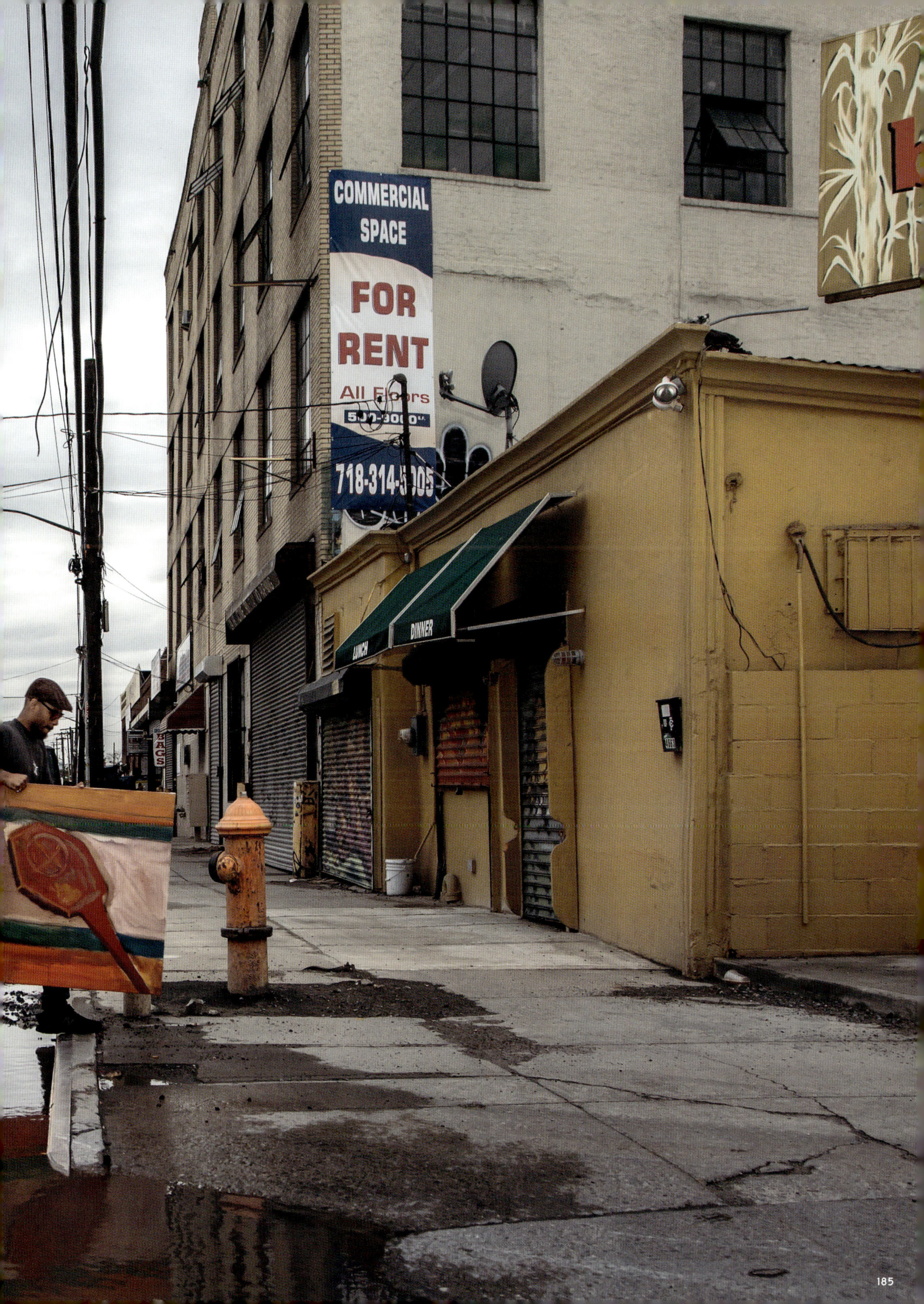

COMMERCIAL SPACE
FOR RENT
All Floors
718-314-5305
LUNCH
DINNER

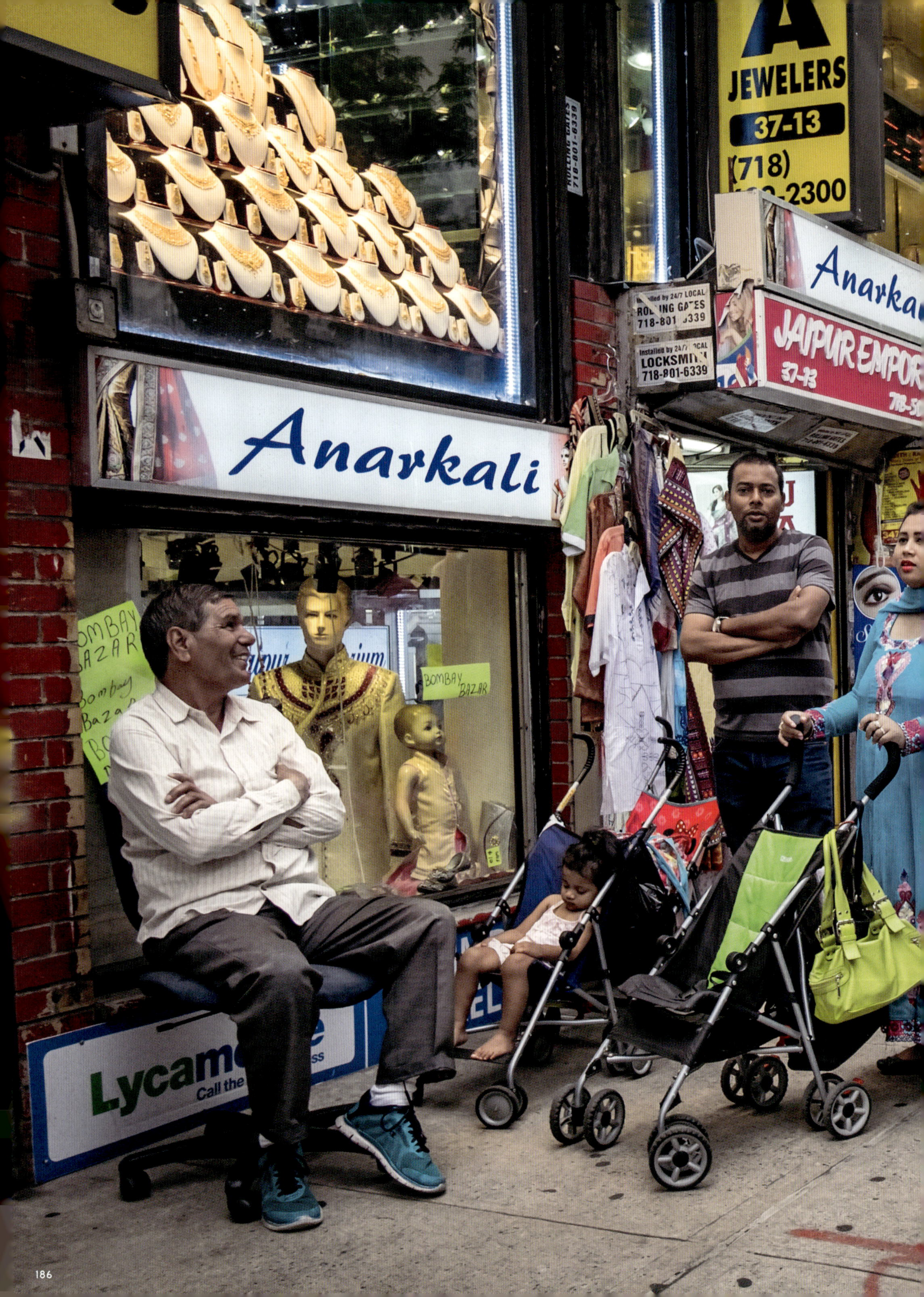

A
JEWELERS
37-13
(718)
2300
Anarka
JAIPUR EMPOR
37-13
Anarkali
Installed by 24/7 LOCAL
ROLLING GATES
718-801-6339
Installed by 24/7 LOCAL
LOCKSMITH
718-801-6339
BOMBAY
BAZAR
Bombay
Bazar
BOMBAY
BAZAR
Lycamobile

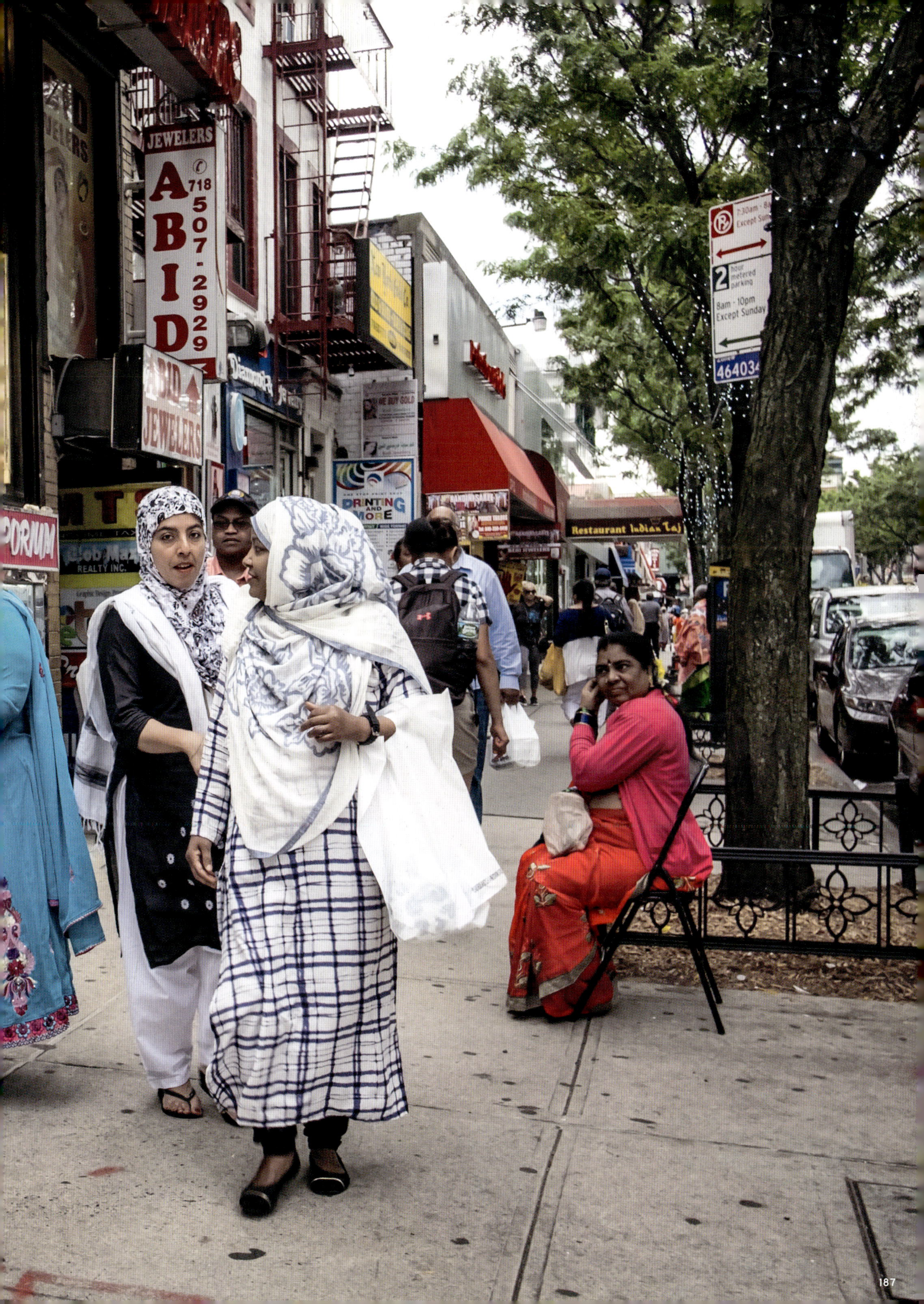
JEWELERS
ABID
718
507-2929
ABID
JEWELERS
Diamond
WE BUY GOLD
ONE STOP PRINT SHOP
PRINTING
AND
MORE
Restaurant Indian Taj
REALTY INC.
2 hour metered parking
8am - 10pm
Except Sunday
464034

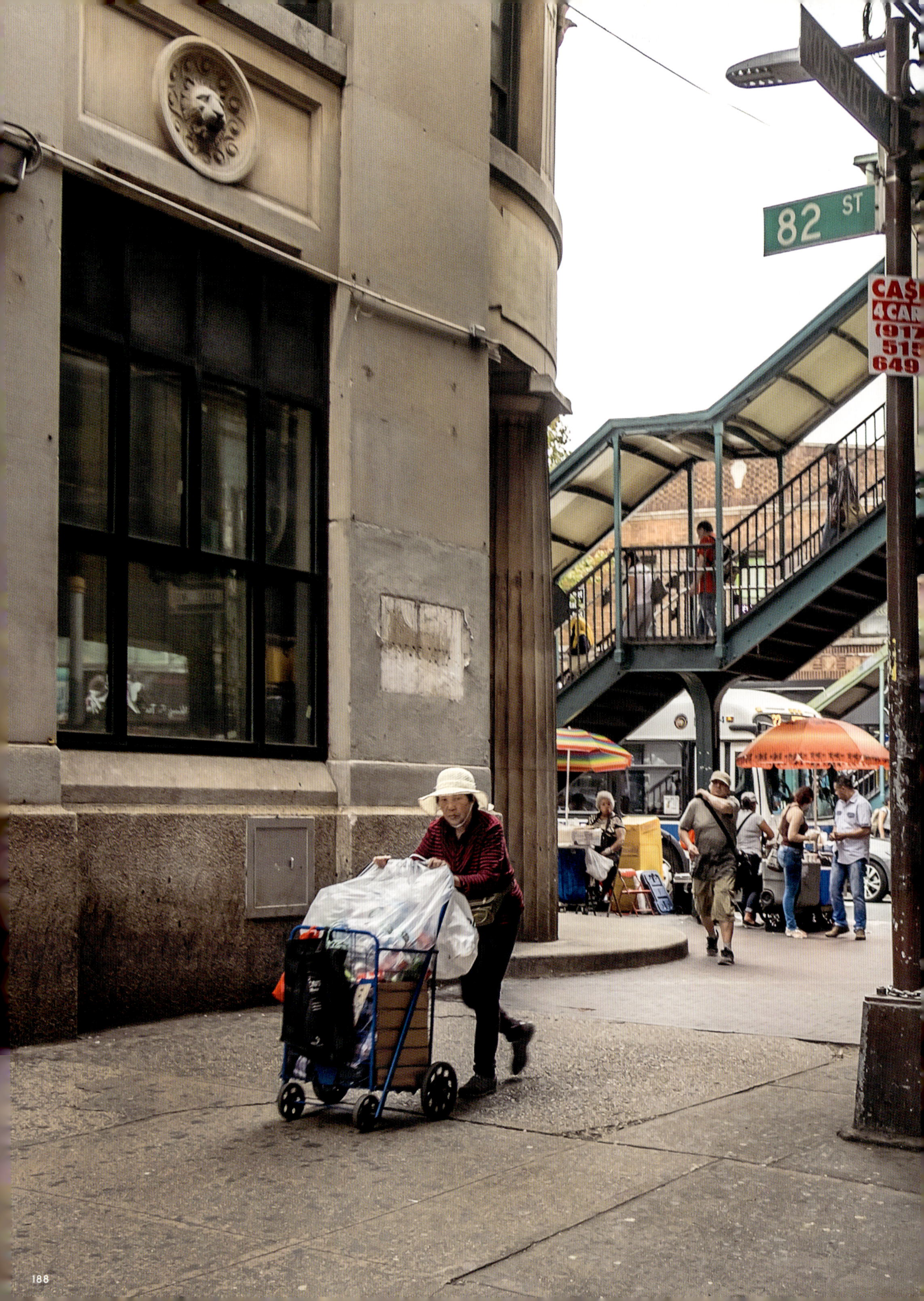

82 ST
CA$H
4 CAR
(917)
515
649

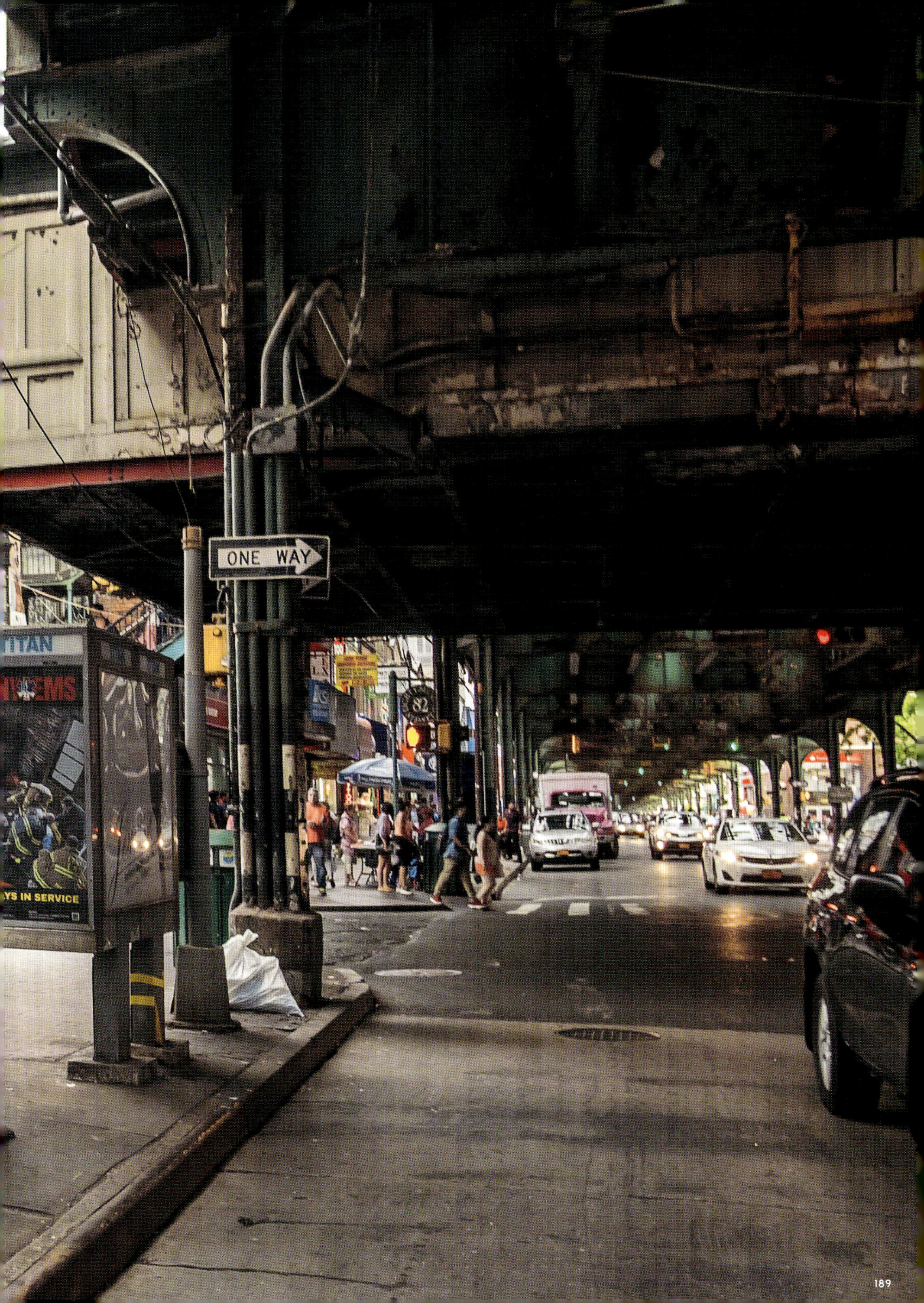

ONE WAY
TITAN
82

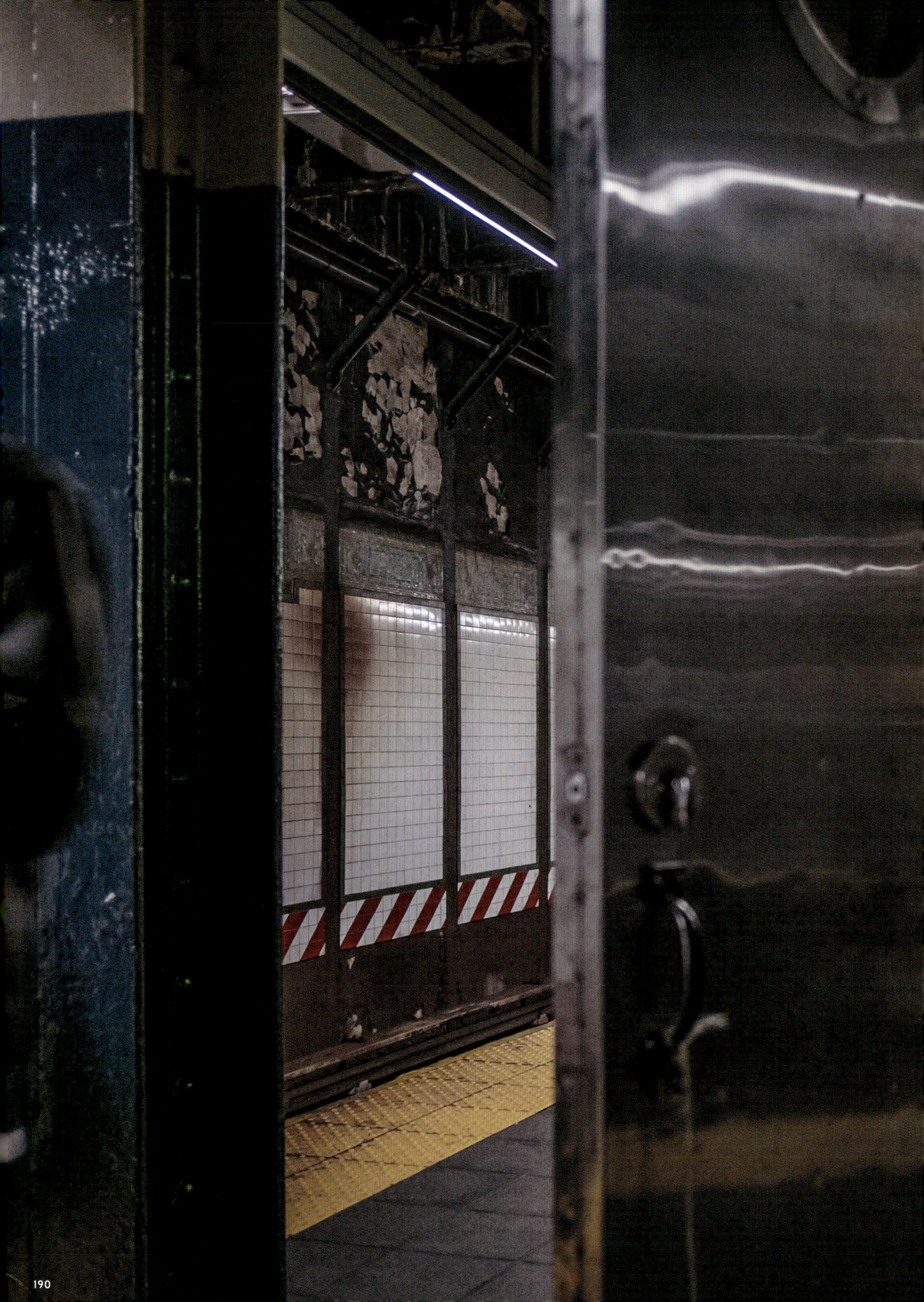

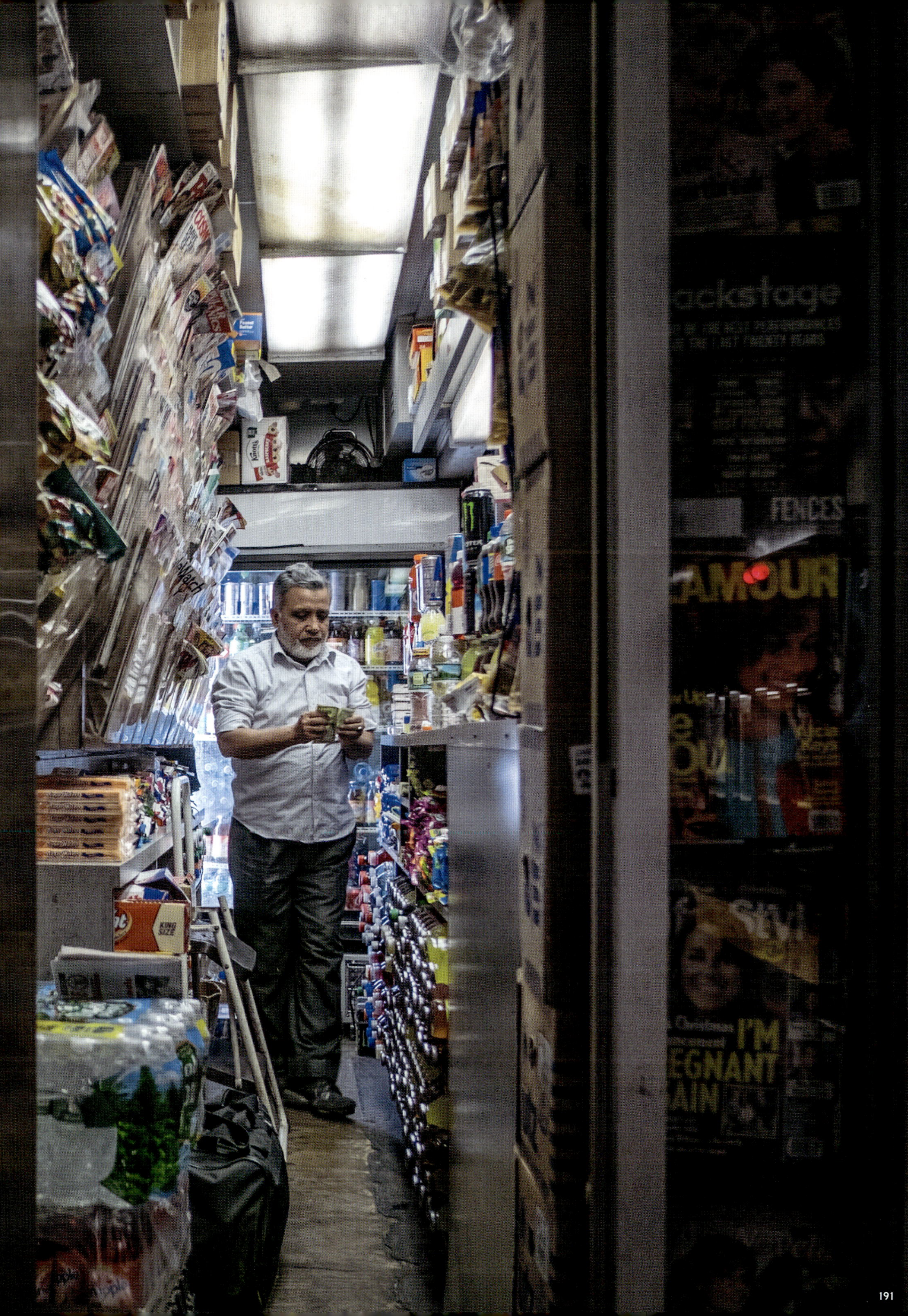
Backstage
FENCES
GLAMOUR
STYLE
I'M PREGNANT
AGAIN

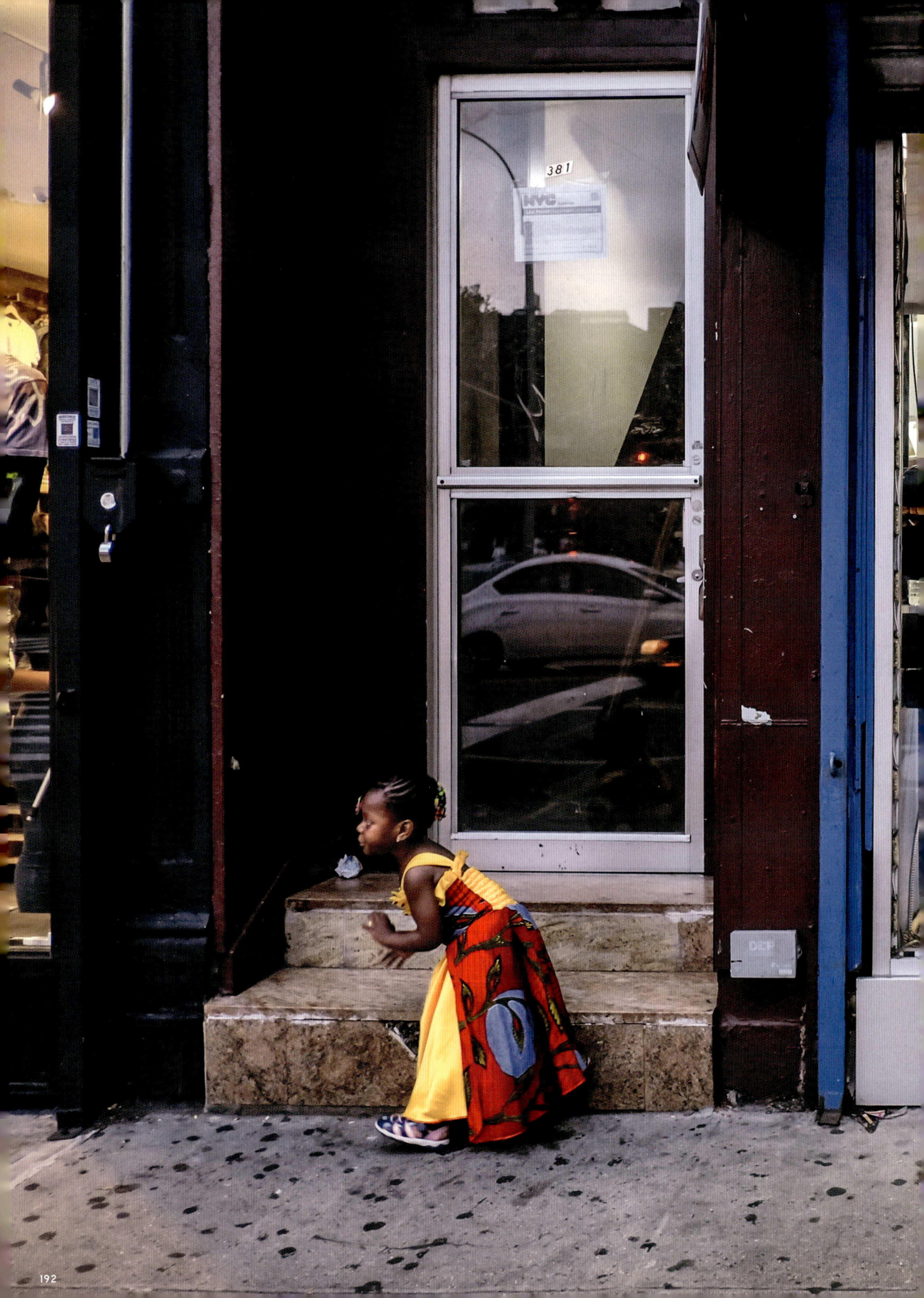
381

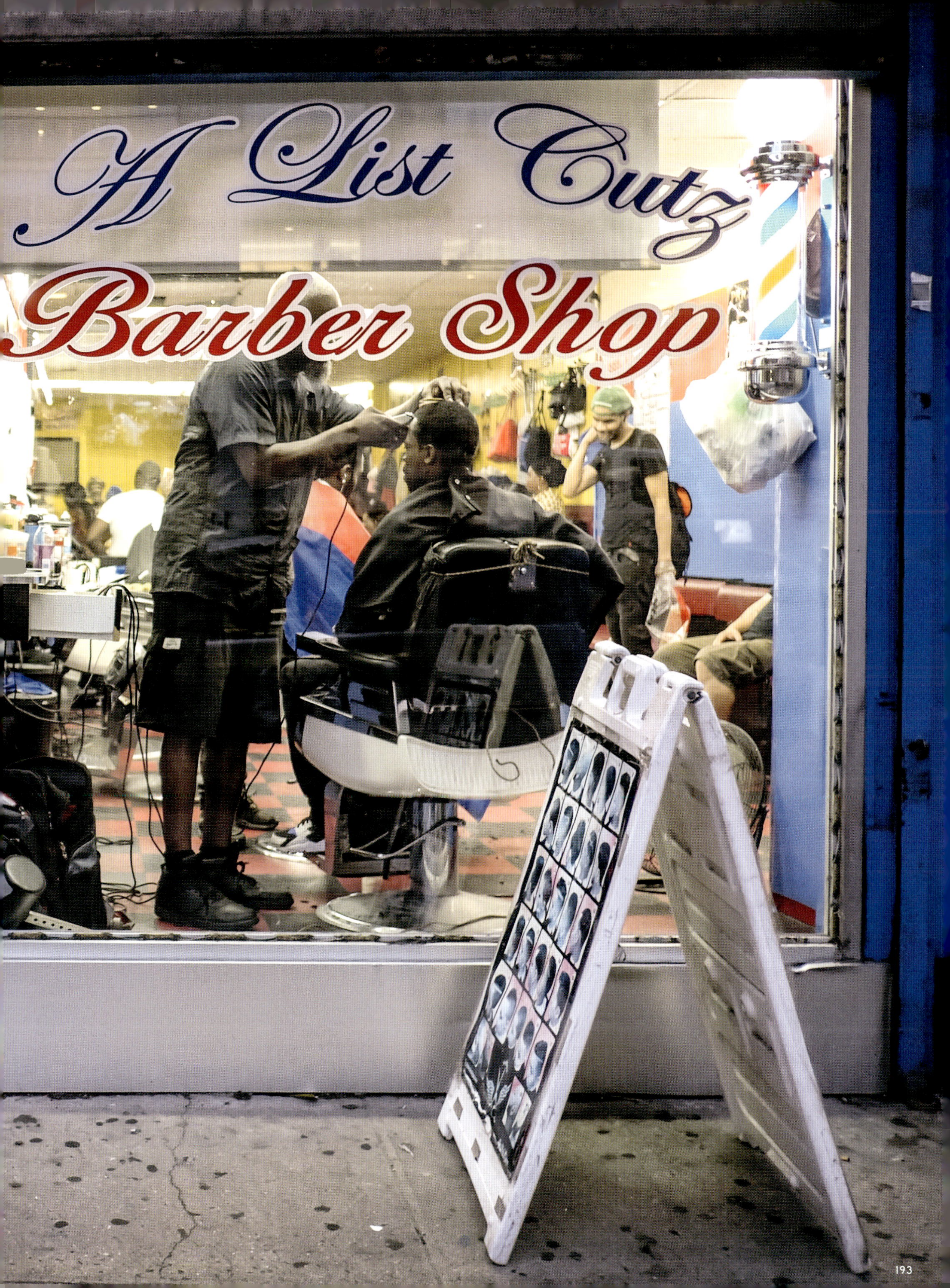

A List Cutz
Barber Shop

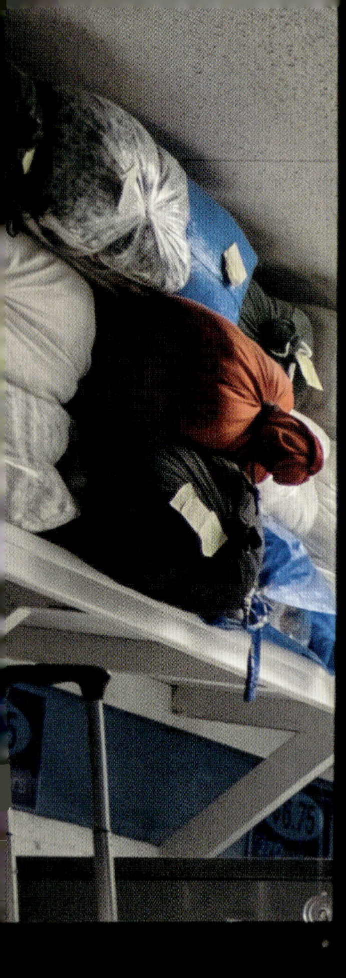
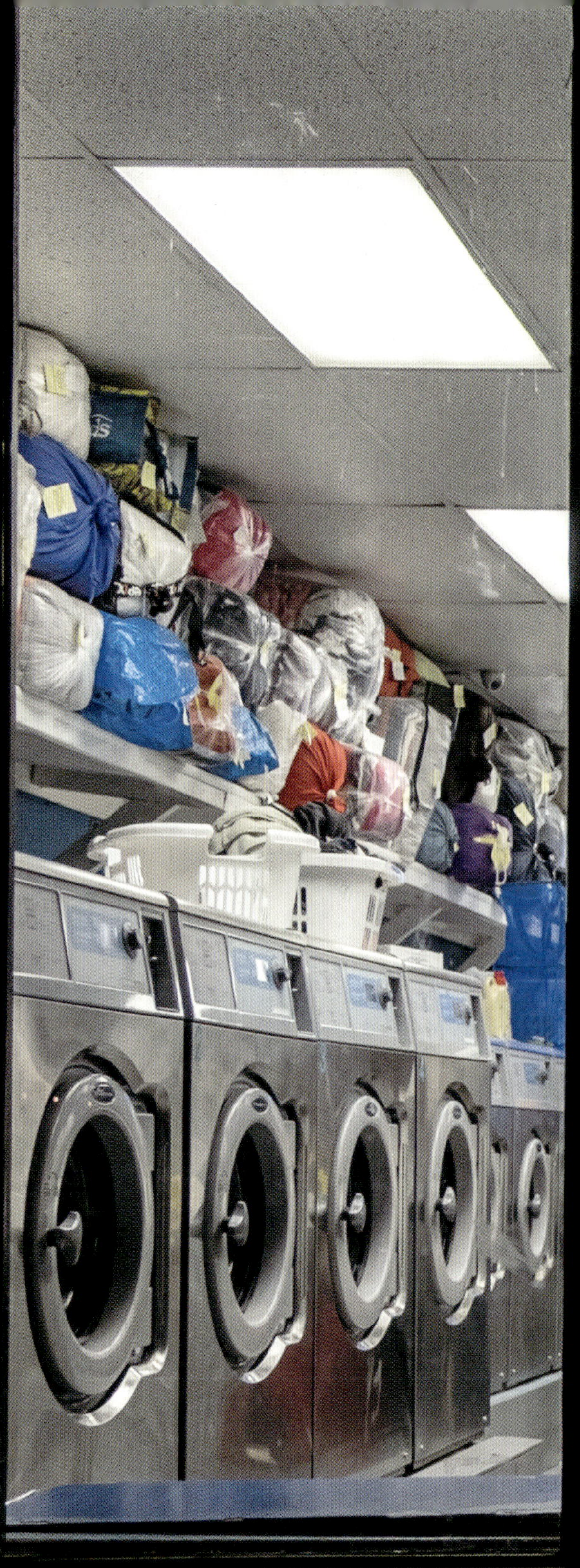
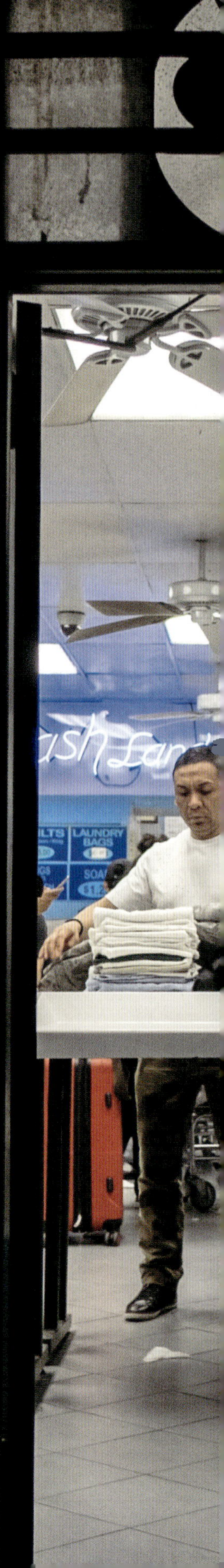
ash Land
LTS
LAUNDRY BAGS
SOA

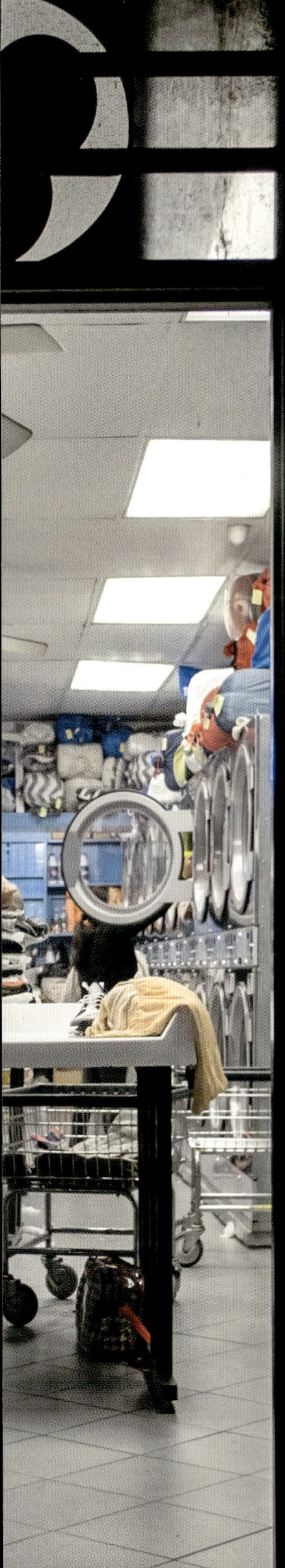
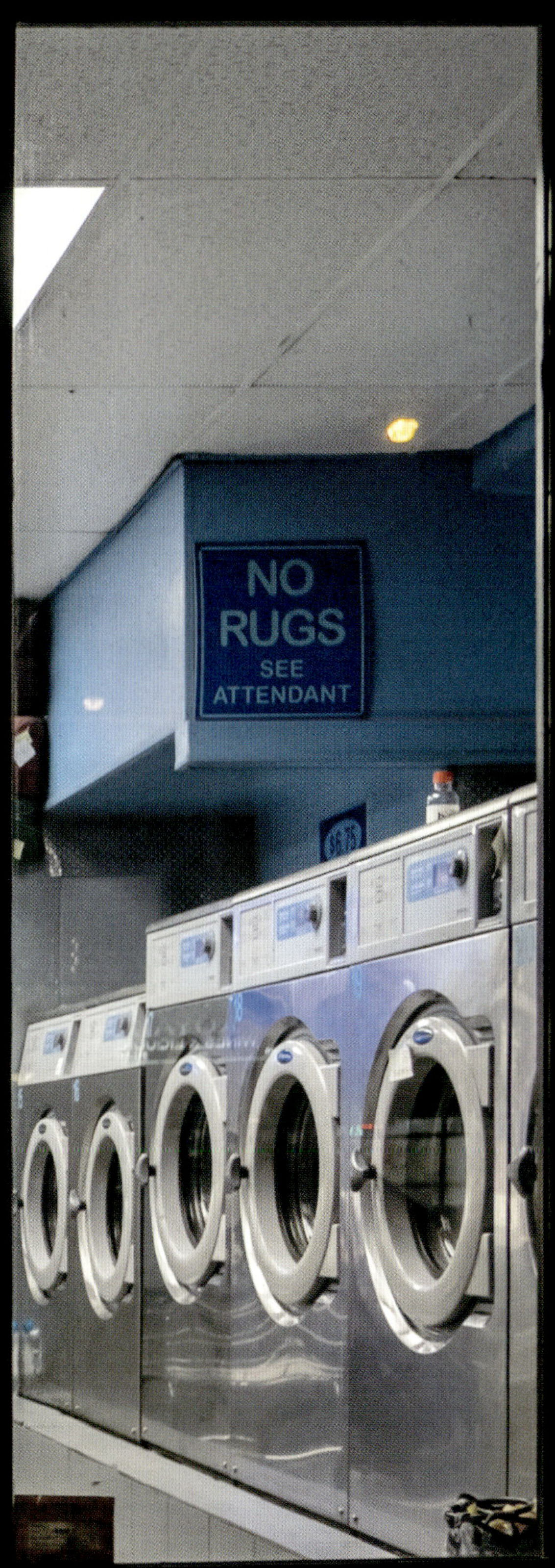
NO
RUGS
SEE
ATTENDANT
$1.75
$1 Quarters
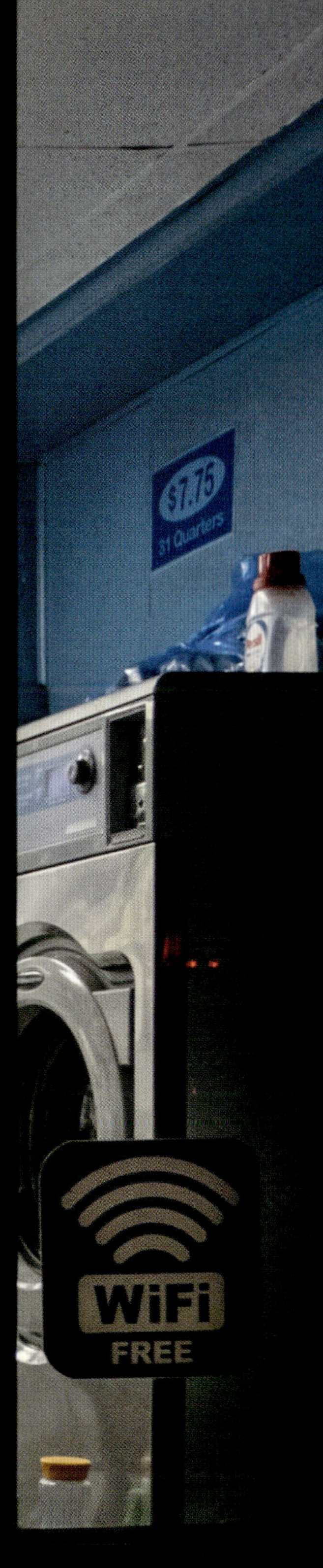
WiFi
FREE

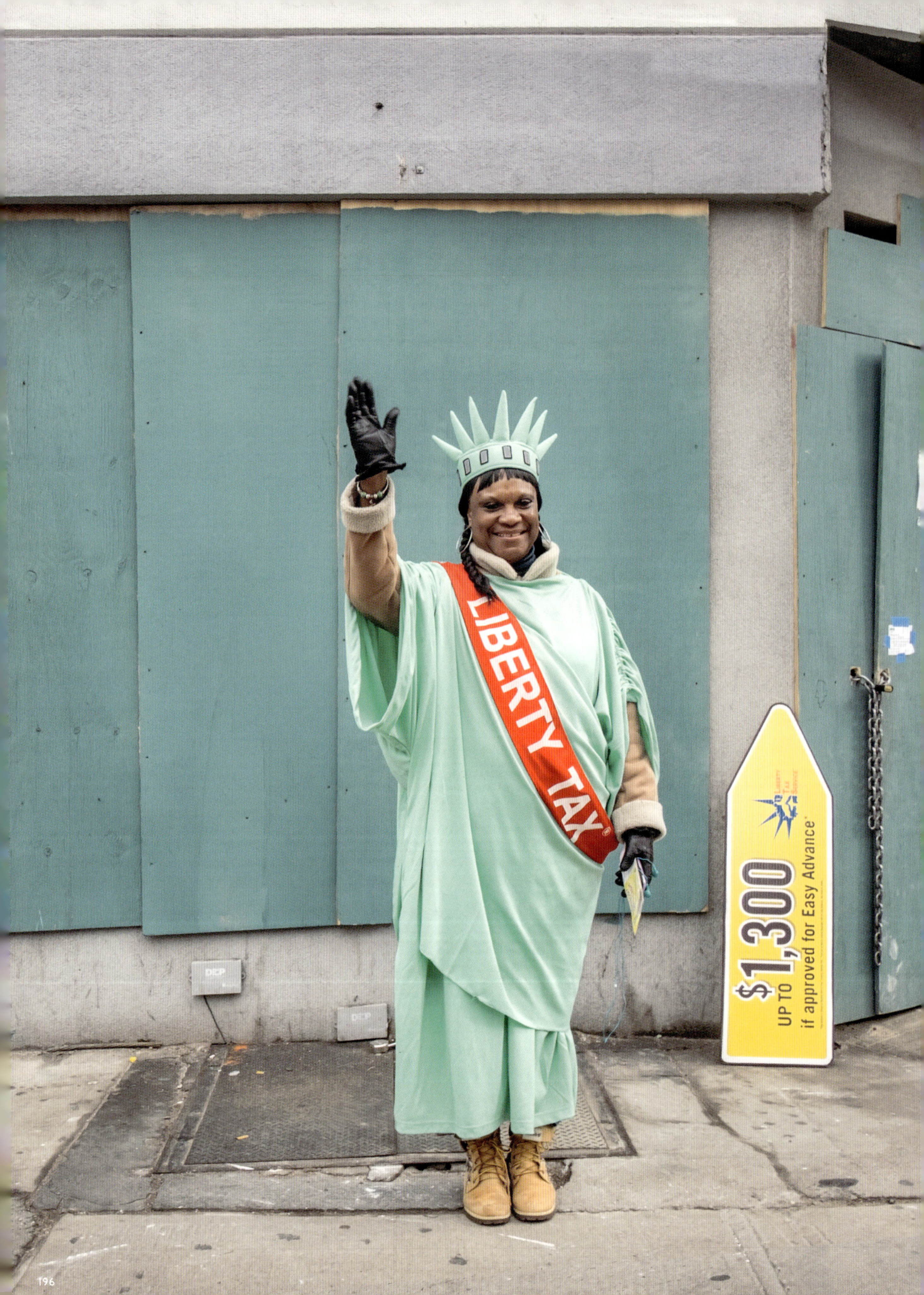

LIBERTY TAX
$1,300
UP TO
if approved for Easy Advance

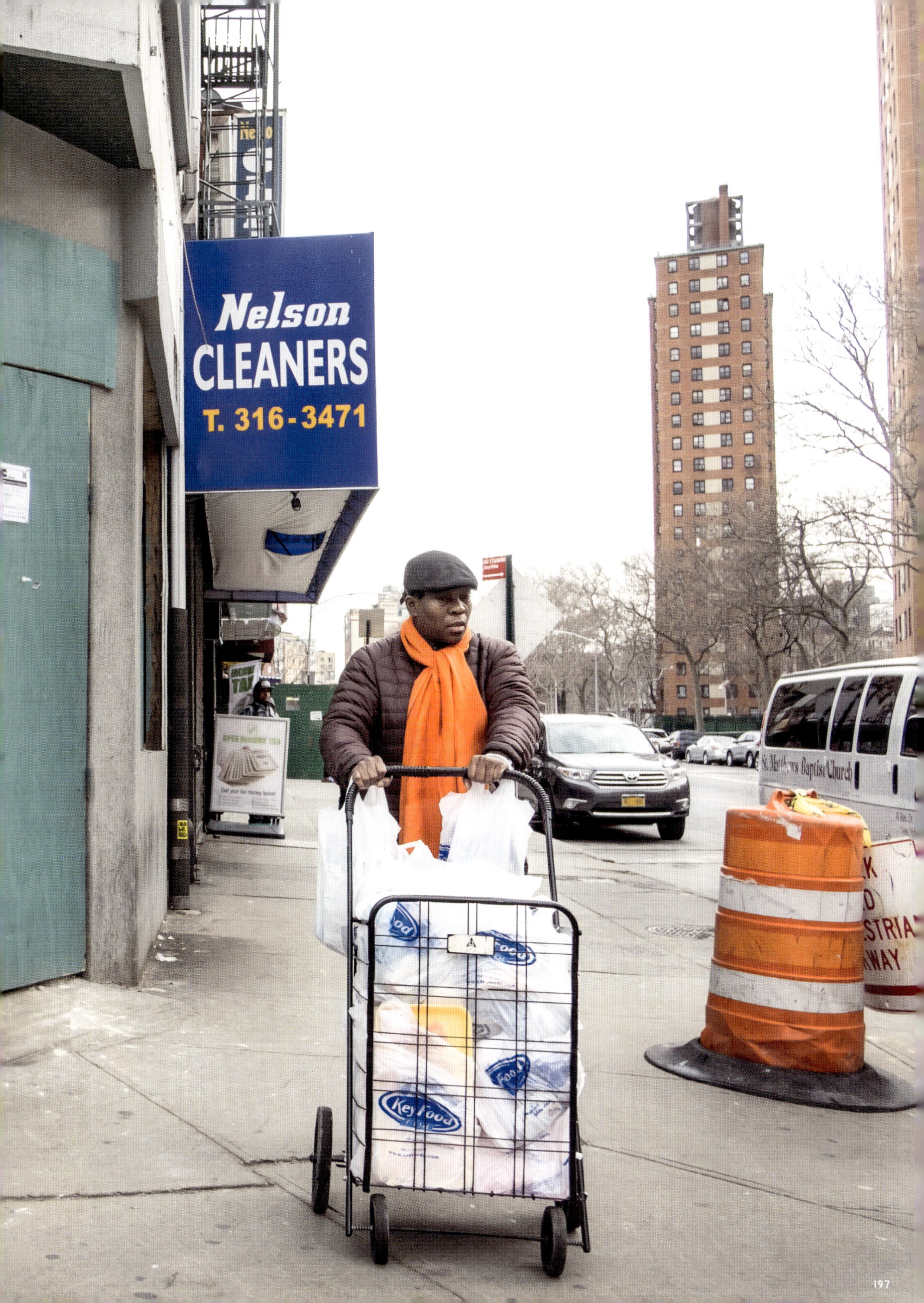
Nelson
CLEANERS
T. 316-3471
Key Food
St. Matthews Baptist Church

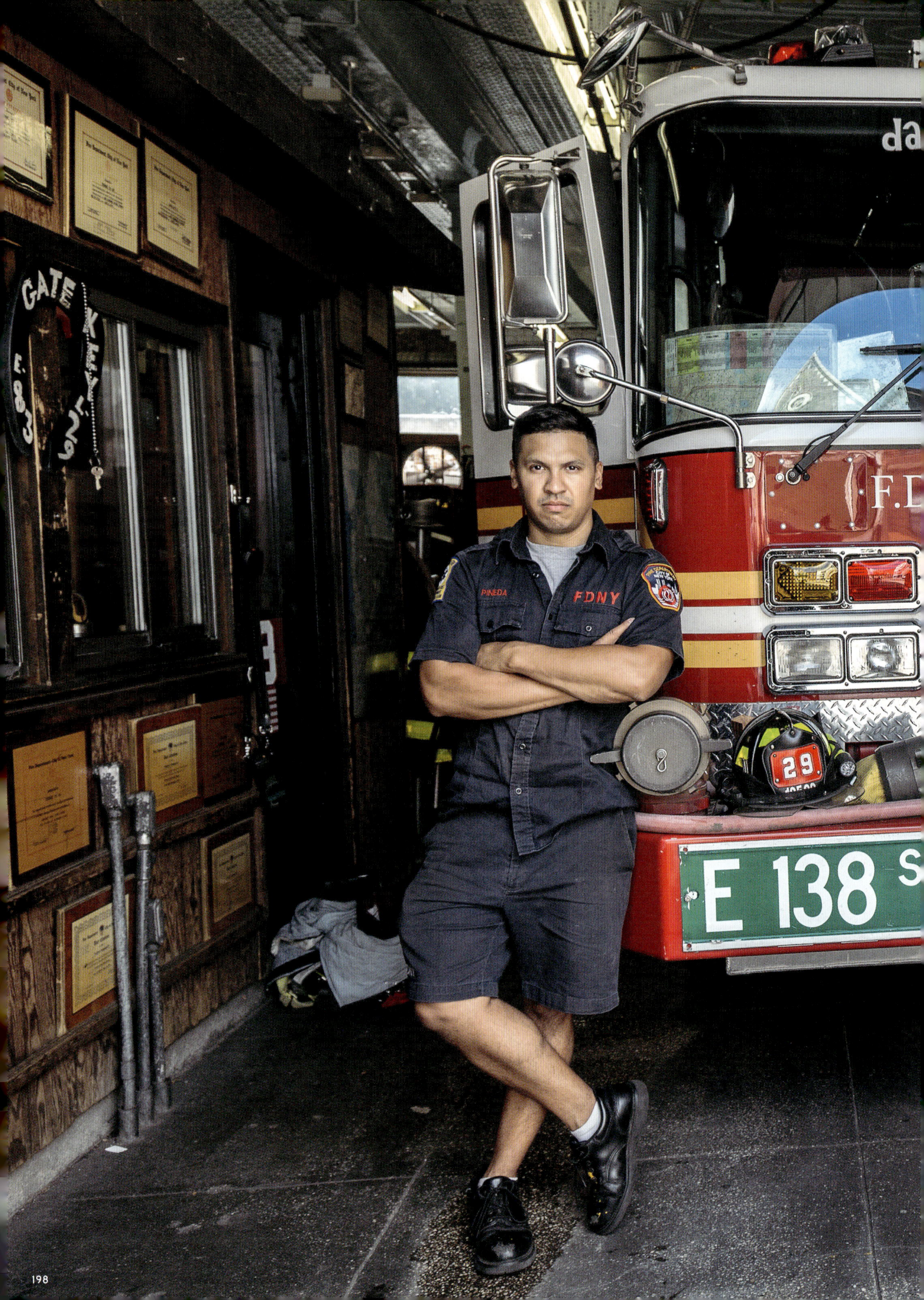
FDNY
PINEDA
29
E 138 S

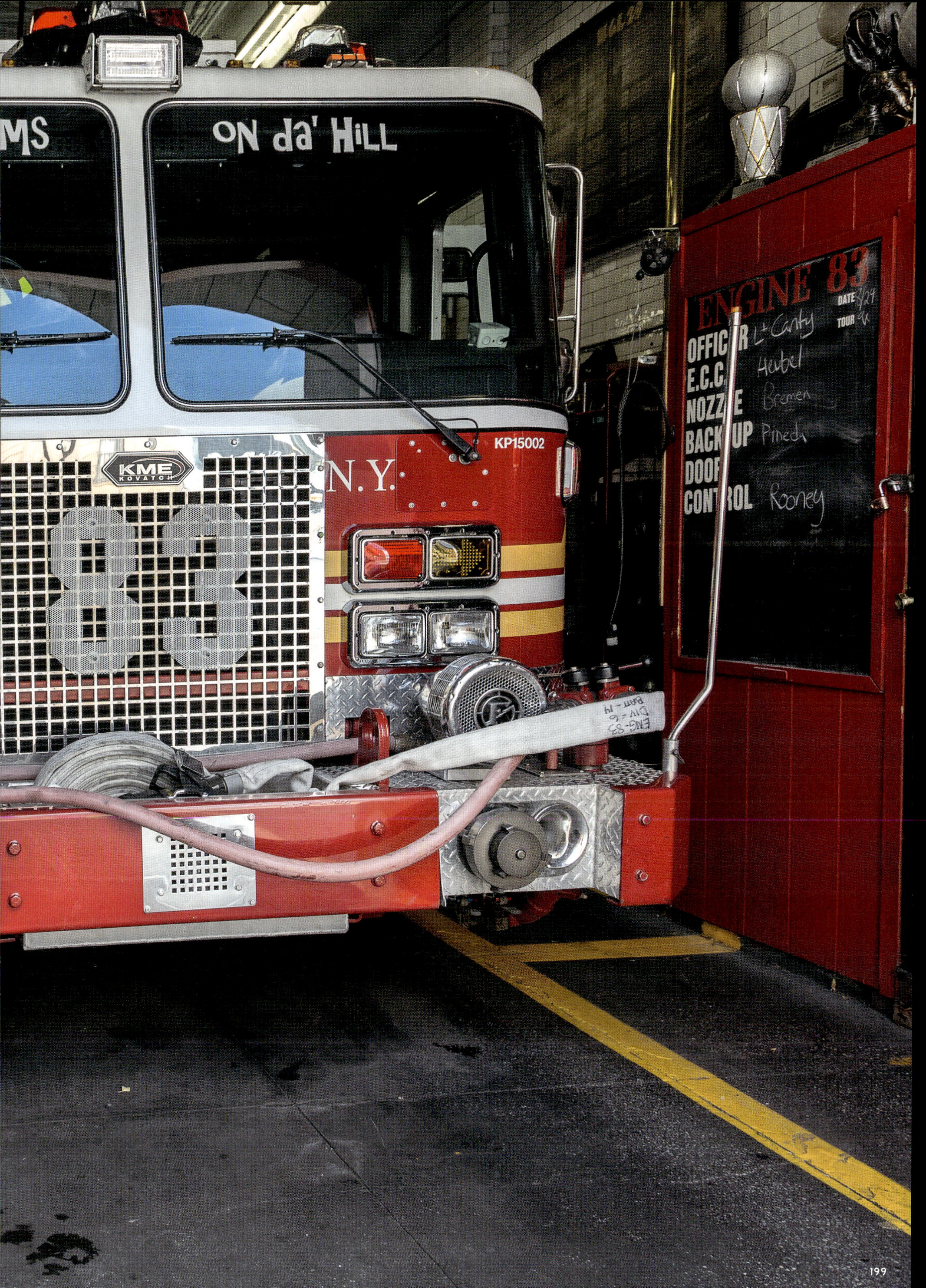
MS
ON da' HiLL
KME
KOVATCH
N.Y.
KP15002
ENGINE 83
DATE
TOUR
OFFICER   Lt Canty
E.C.C.   Heubel
NOZZLE   Bremen
BACKUP   Pineda
DOOR
CONTROL   Rooney
ENG-83
Div-6
Bat'n-19

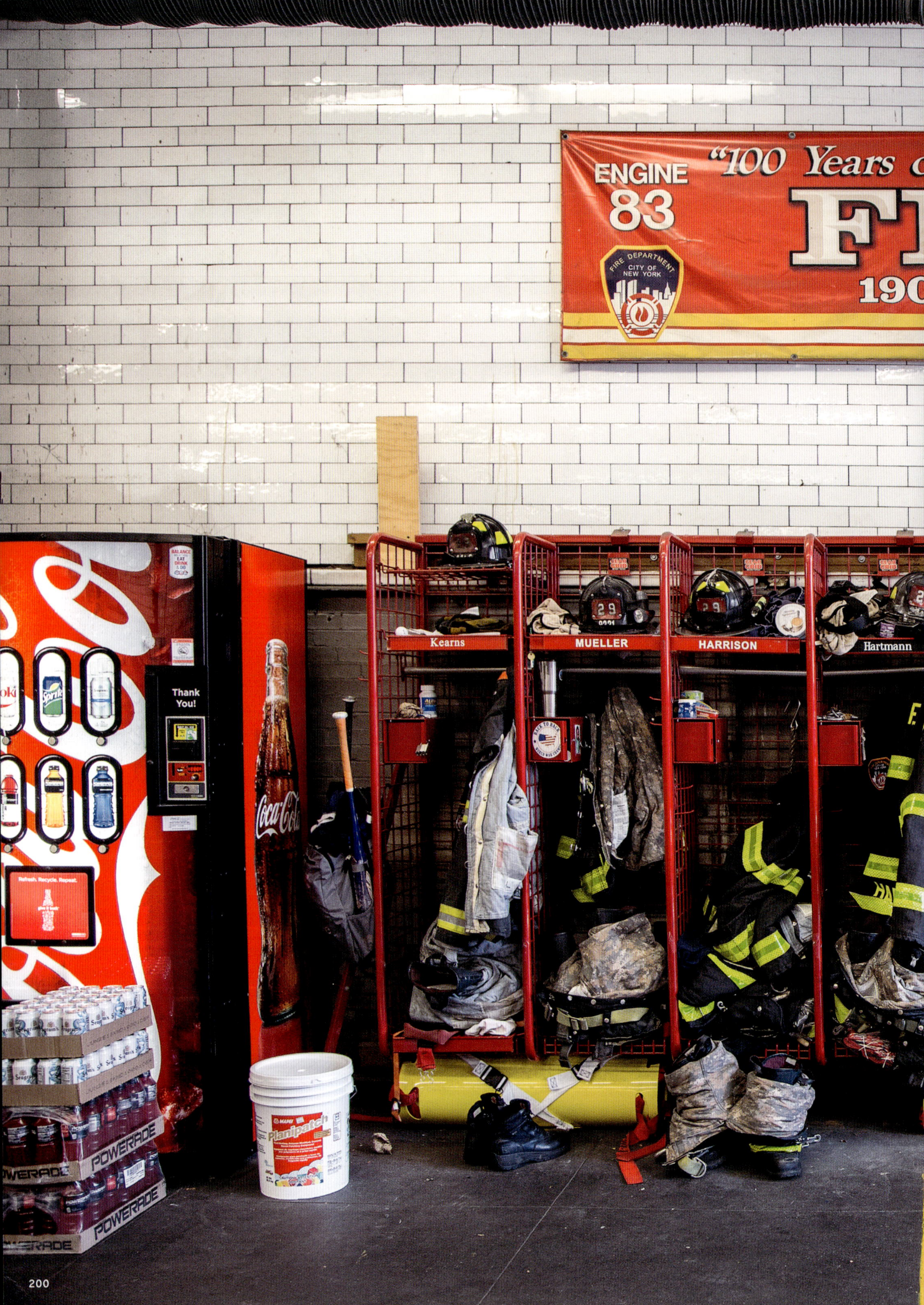

ENGINE
83
FIRE DEPARTMENT
CITY OF
NEW YORK
"100 Years o
FI
190
Kearns
MUELLER
HARRISON
Hartmann
Coca-Cola
Thank
You!

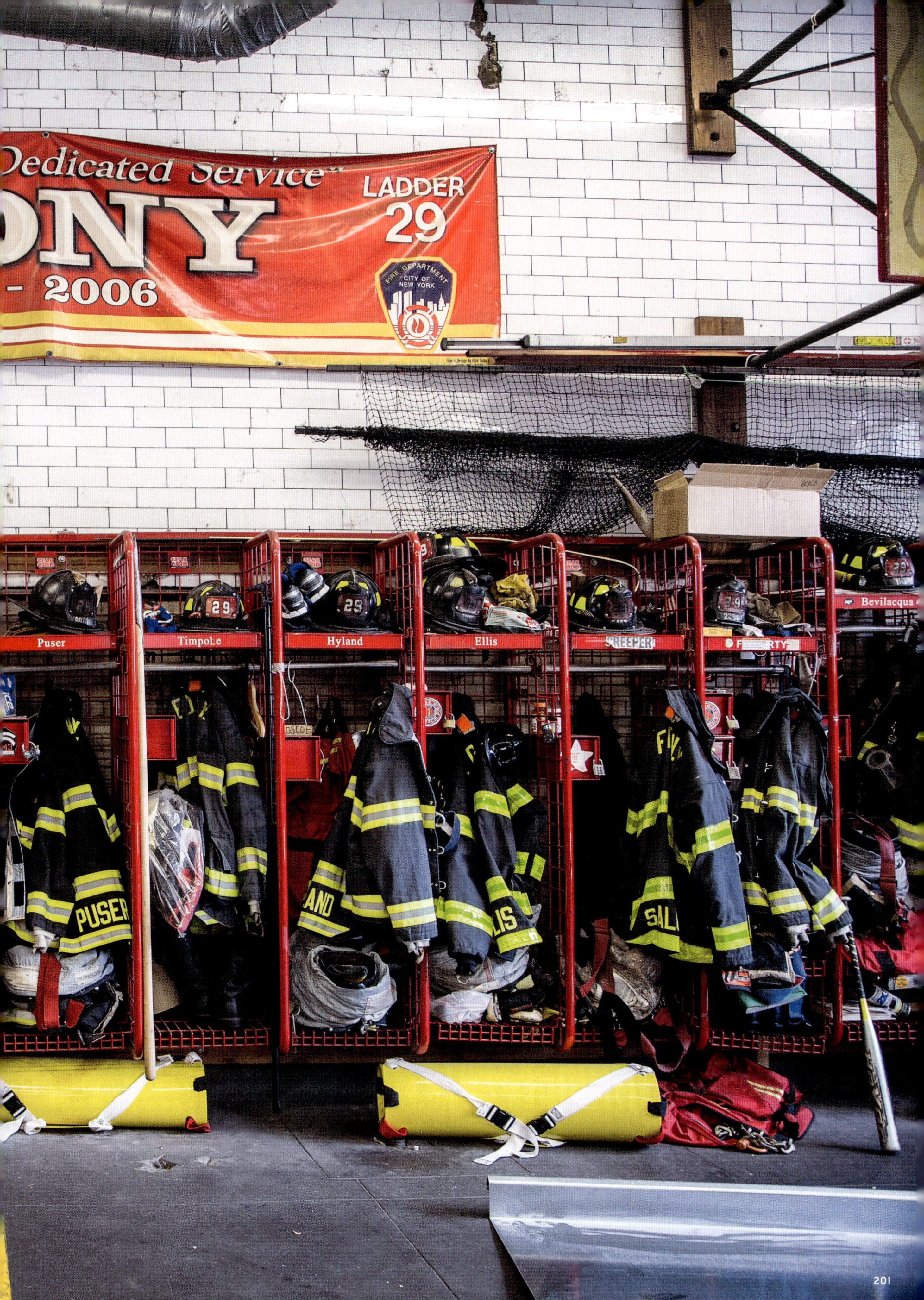
Dedicated Service
FDNY
- 2006
LADDER
29
FIRE DEPARTMENT
CITY OF
NEW YORK
Puser
TimpoLe
Hyland
Ellis
CREEPER
FLAHERTY
Bevilacqua
PUSER
AND
LIS
SAL

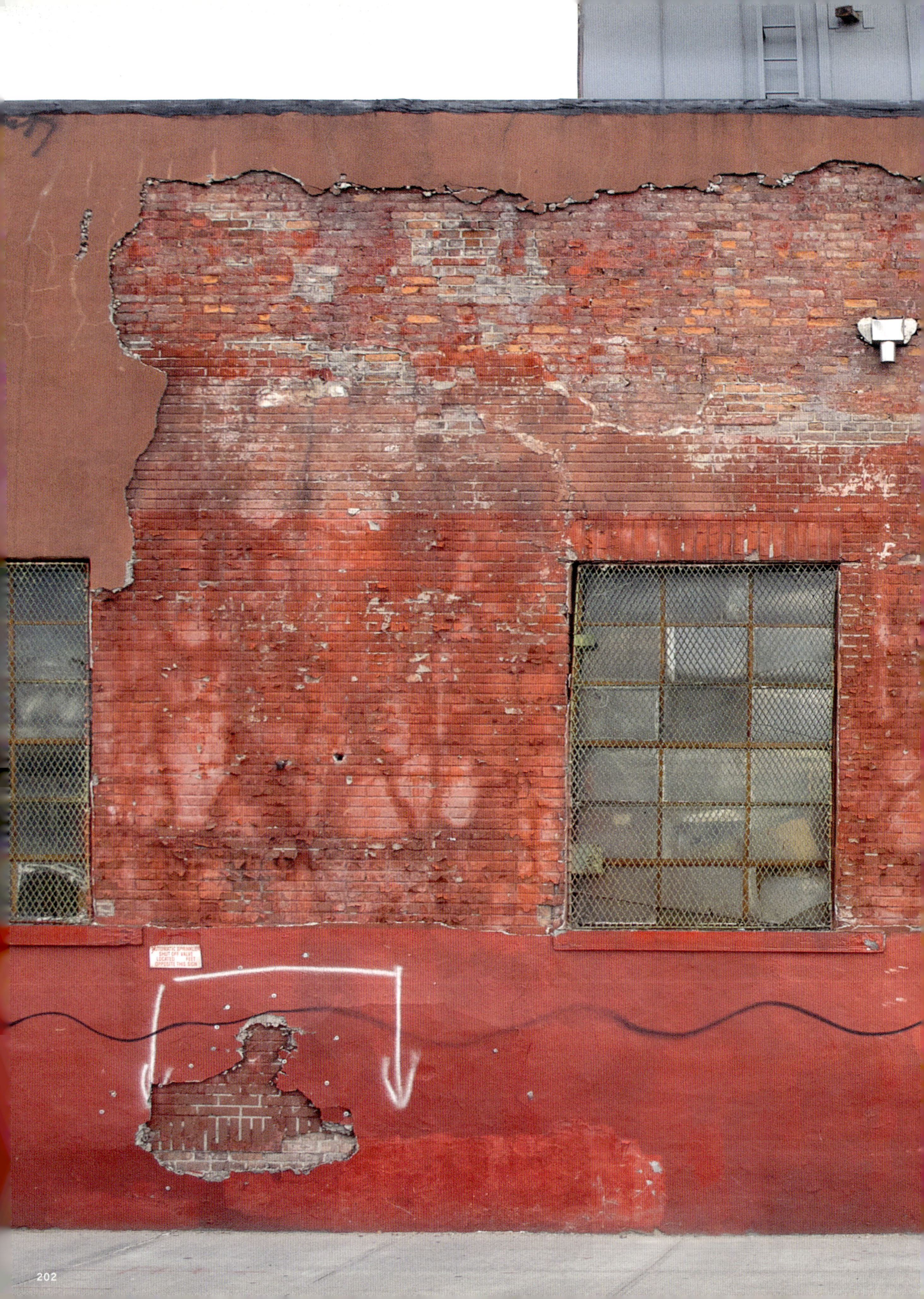

AUTOMATIC SPRINKLER
SHUT OFF VALVE
LOCATED ___ FEET
OPPOSITE THIS SIGN

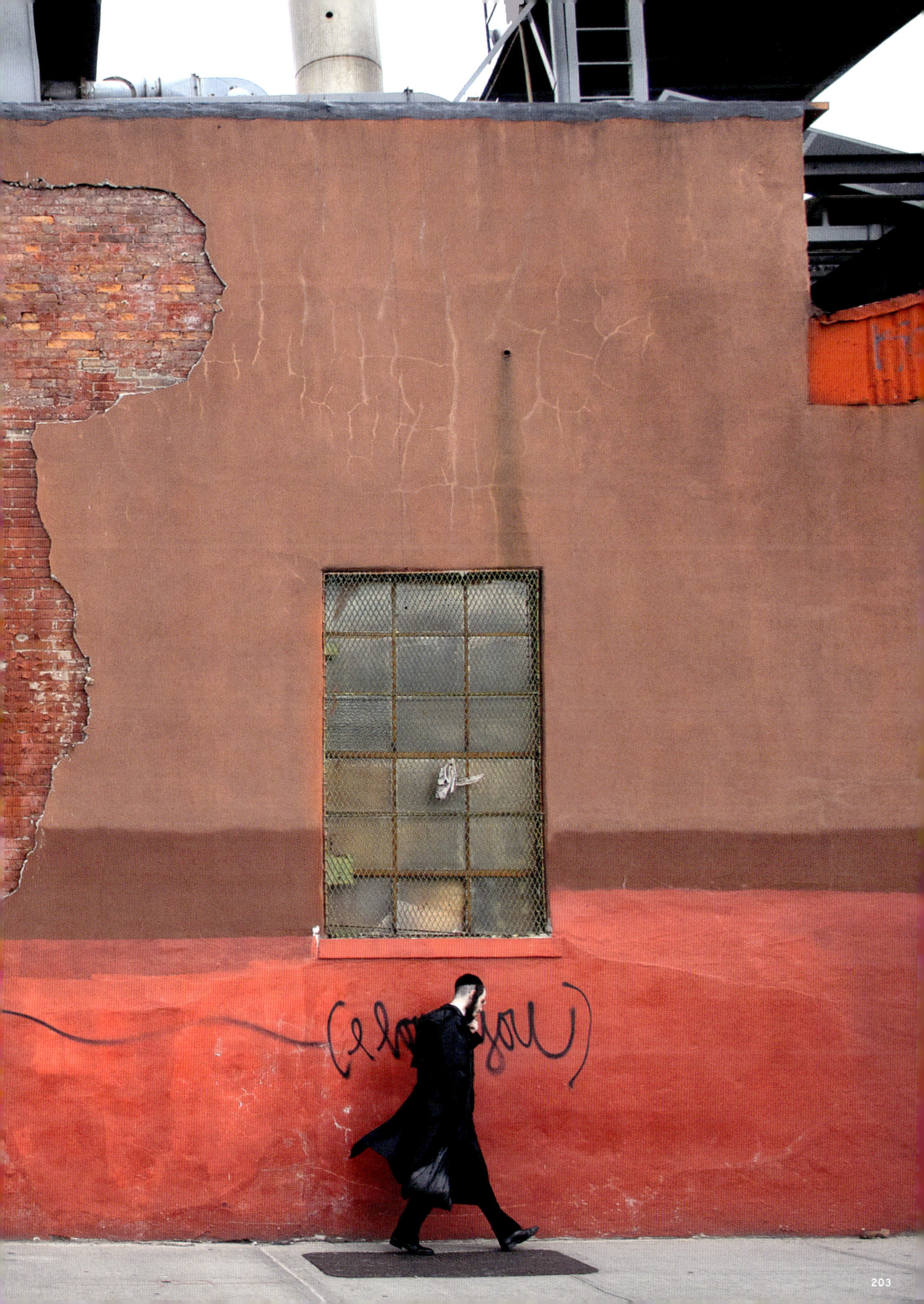
(I love you)

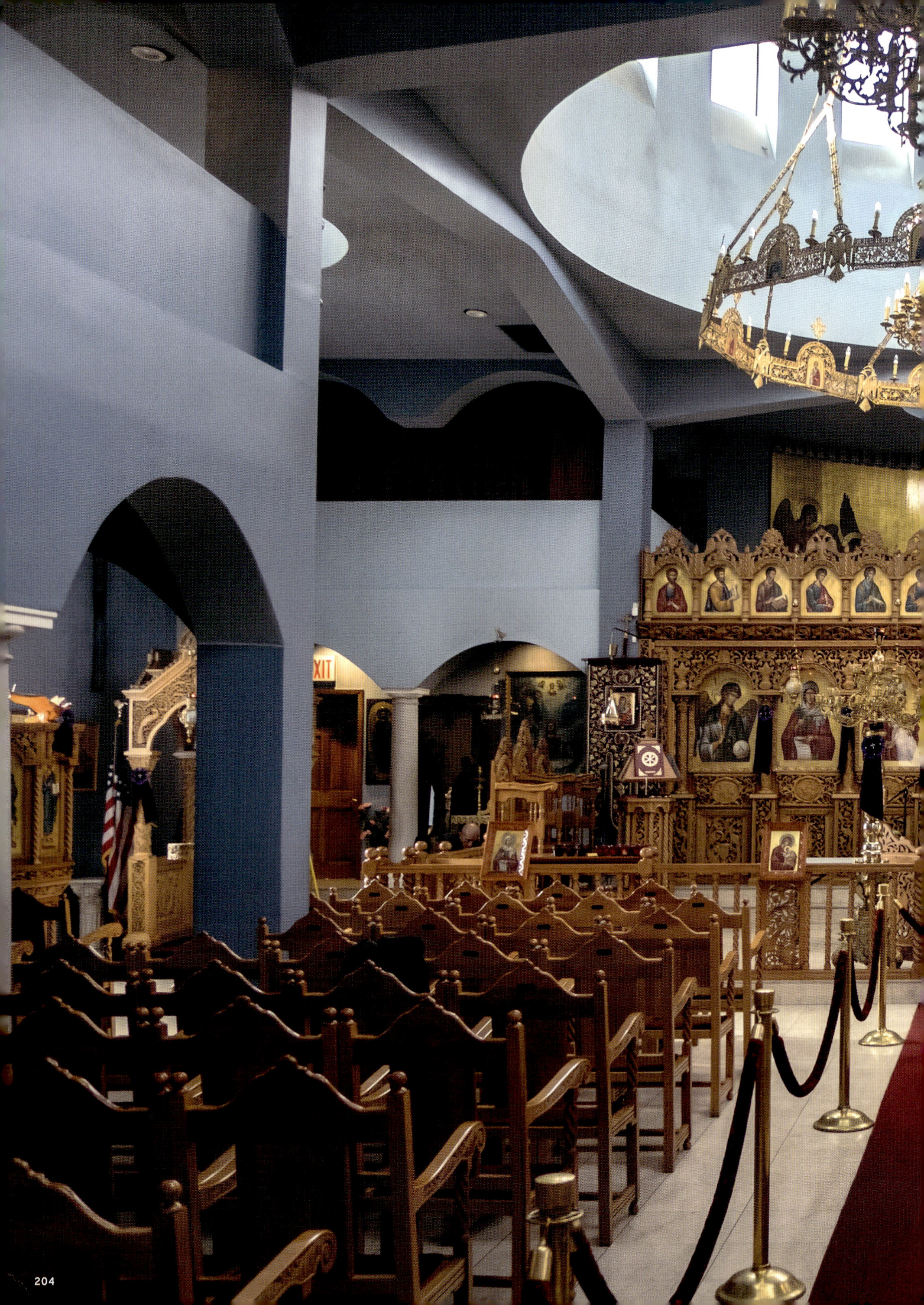

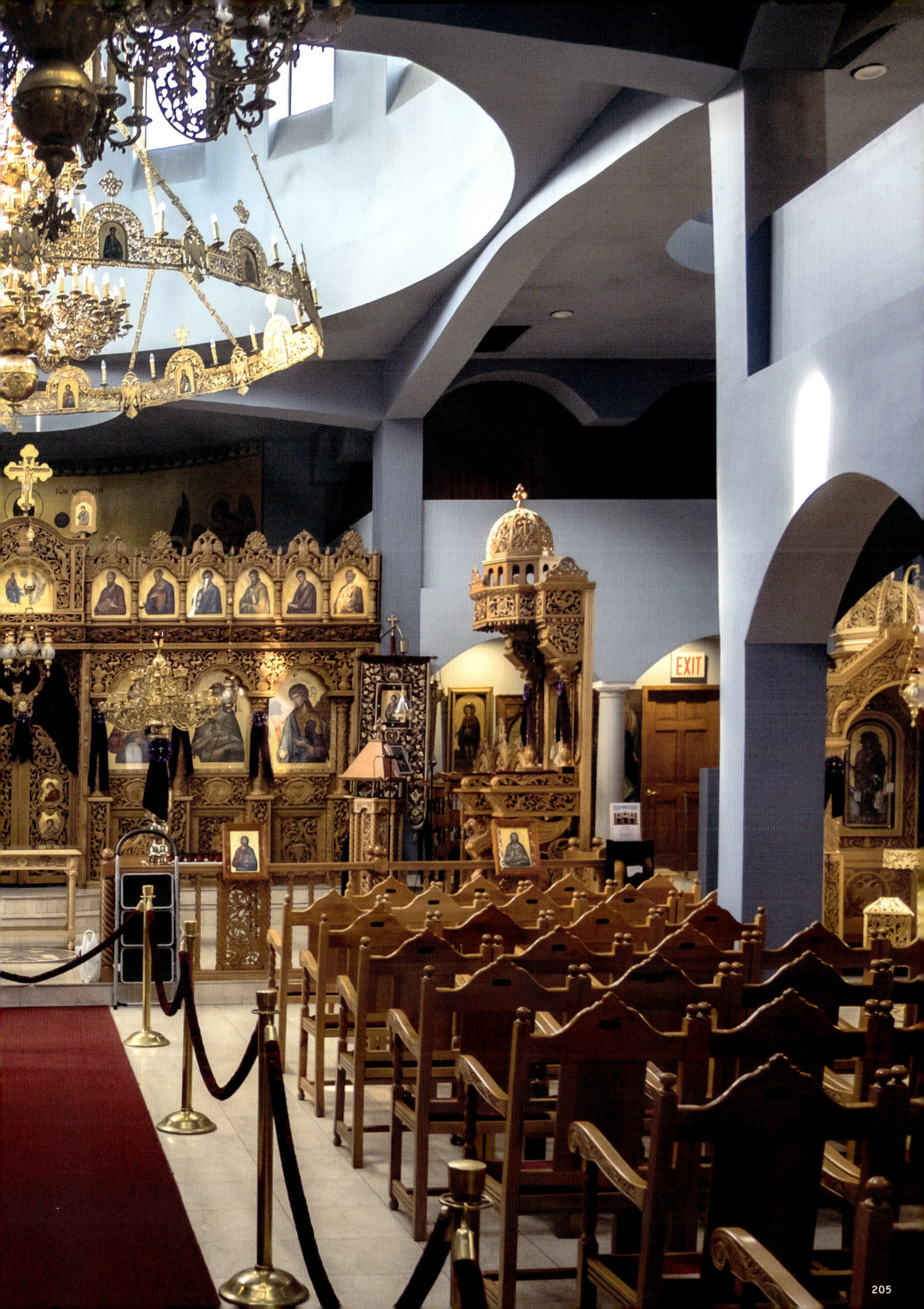

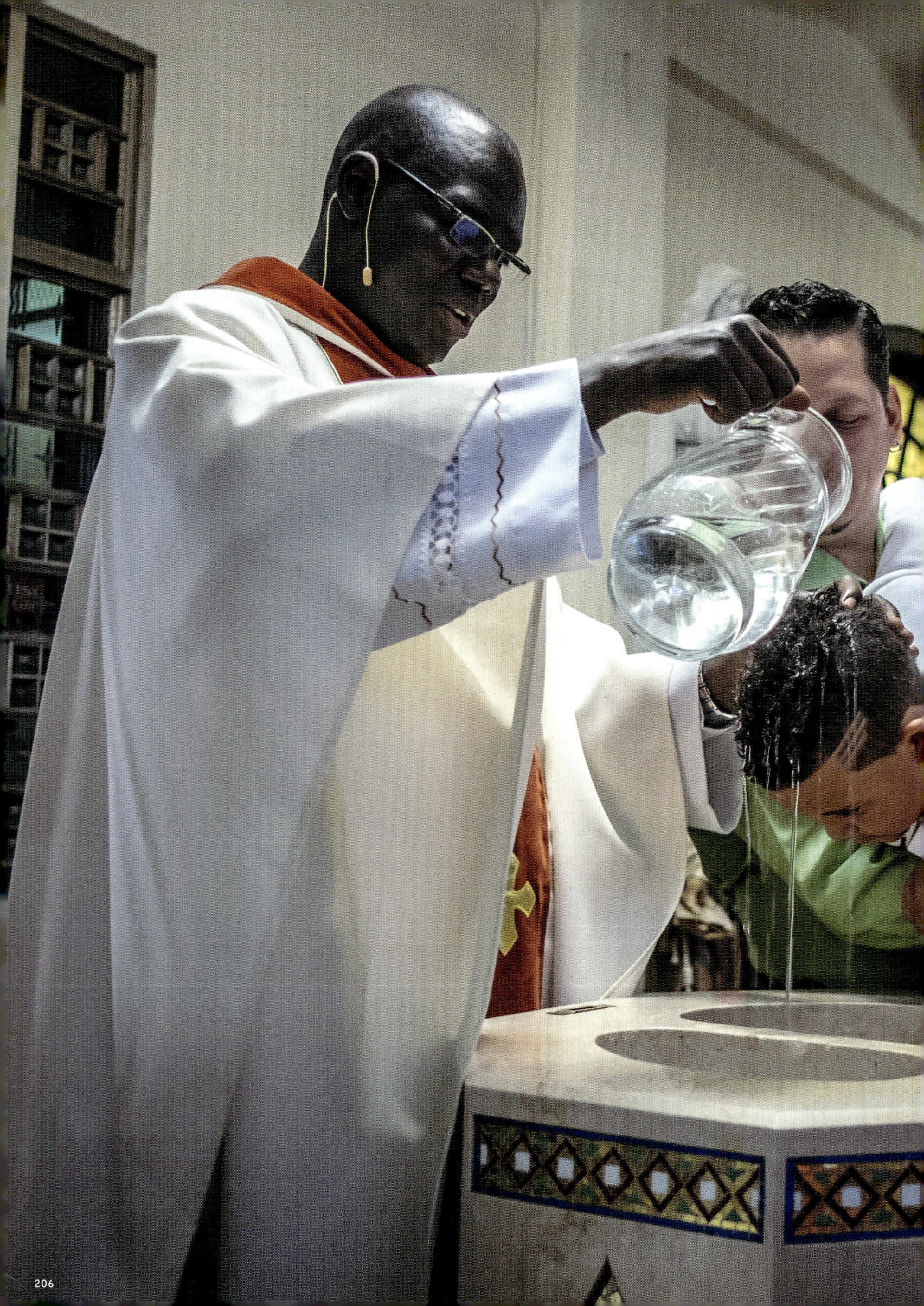

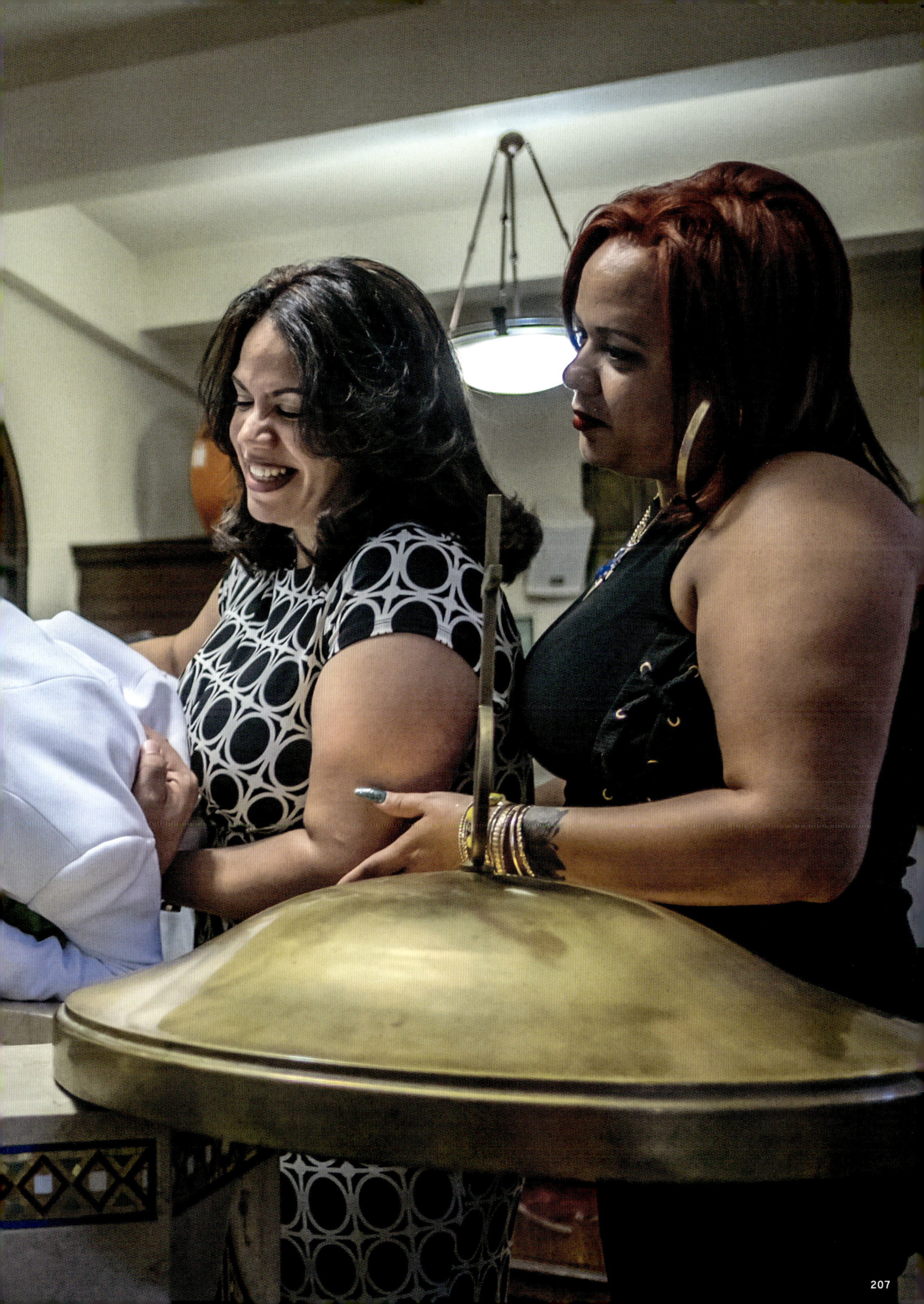

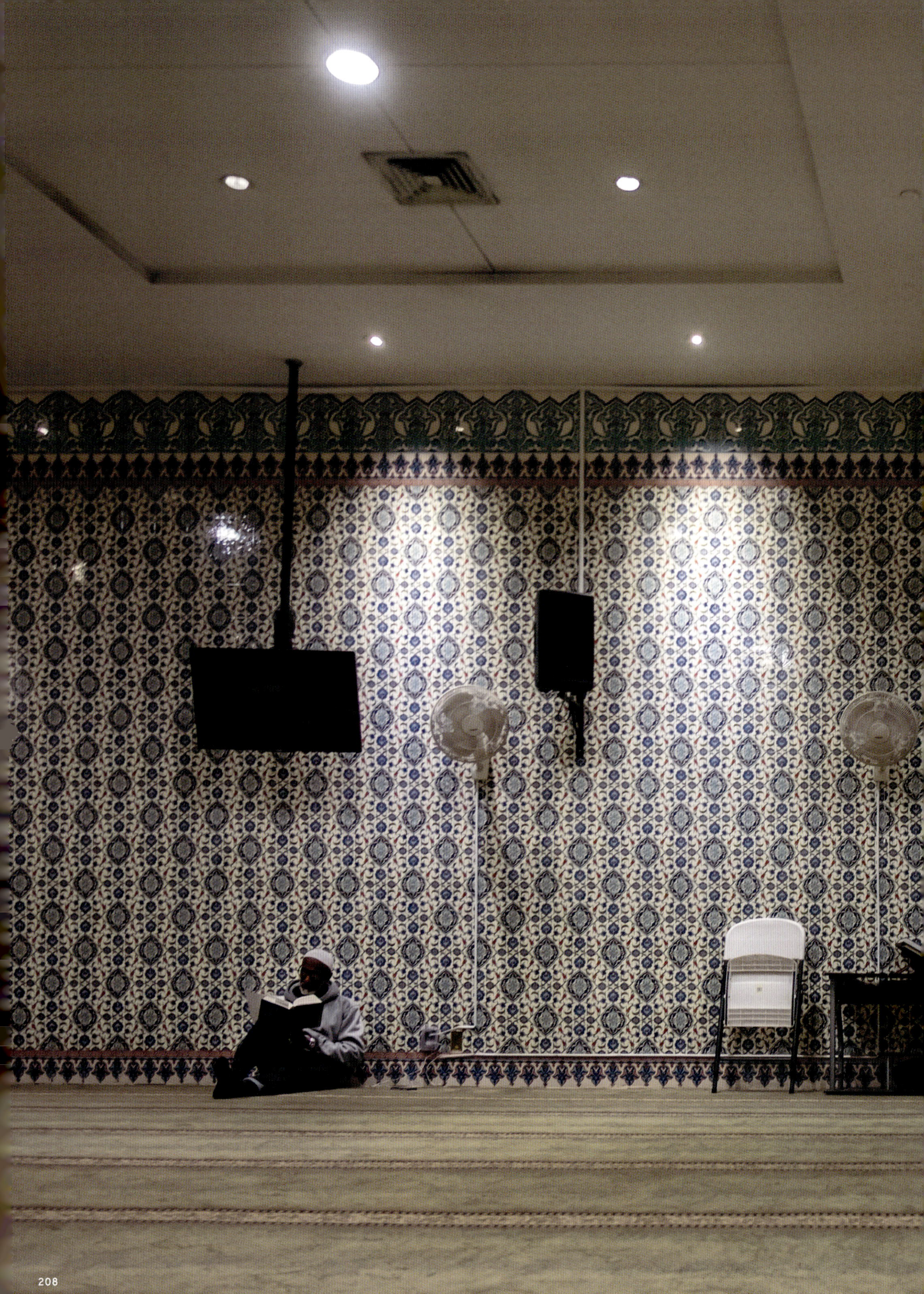

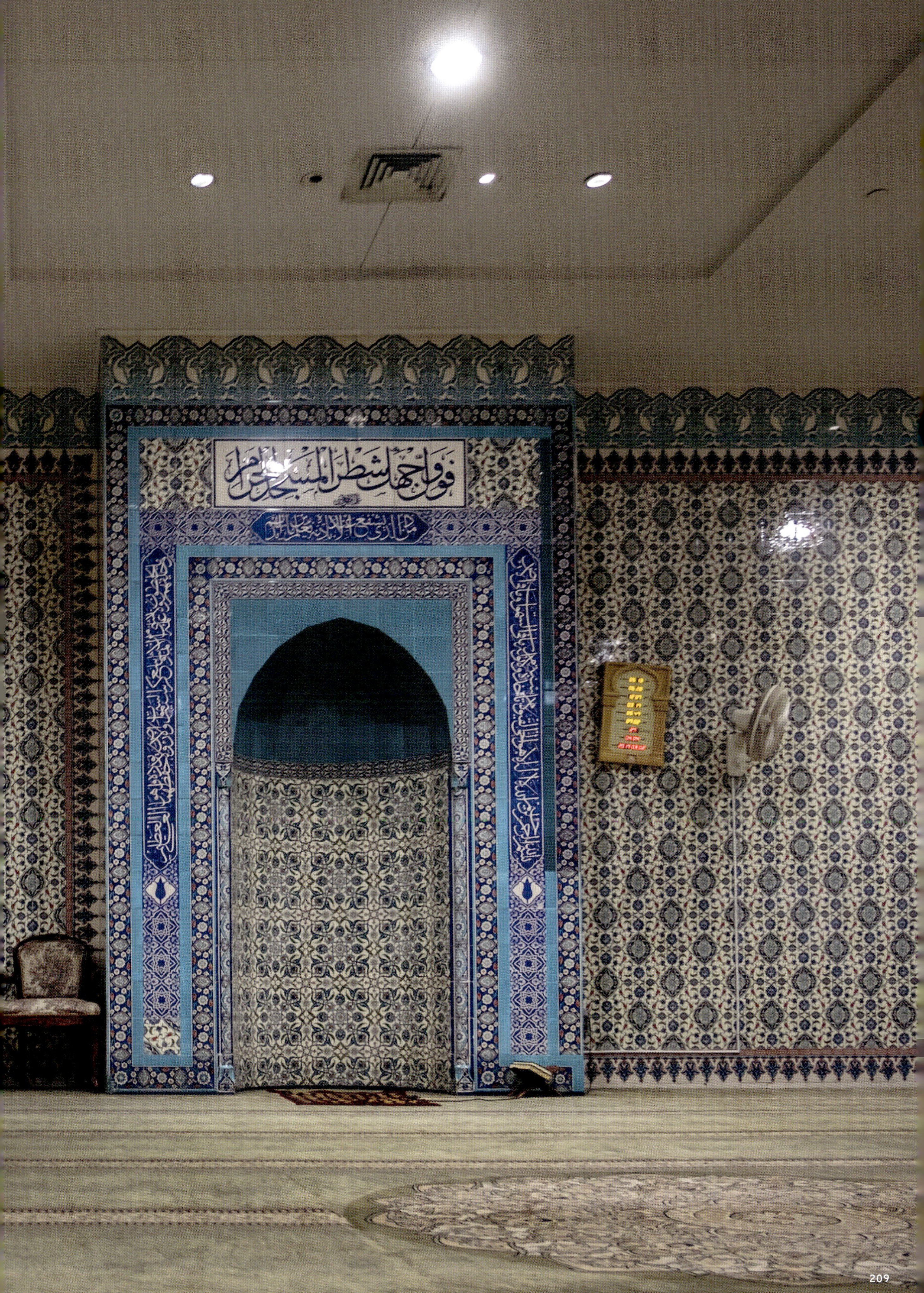

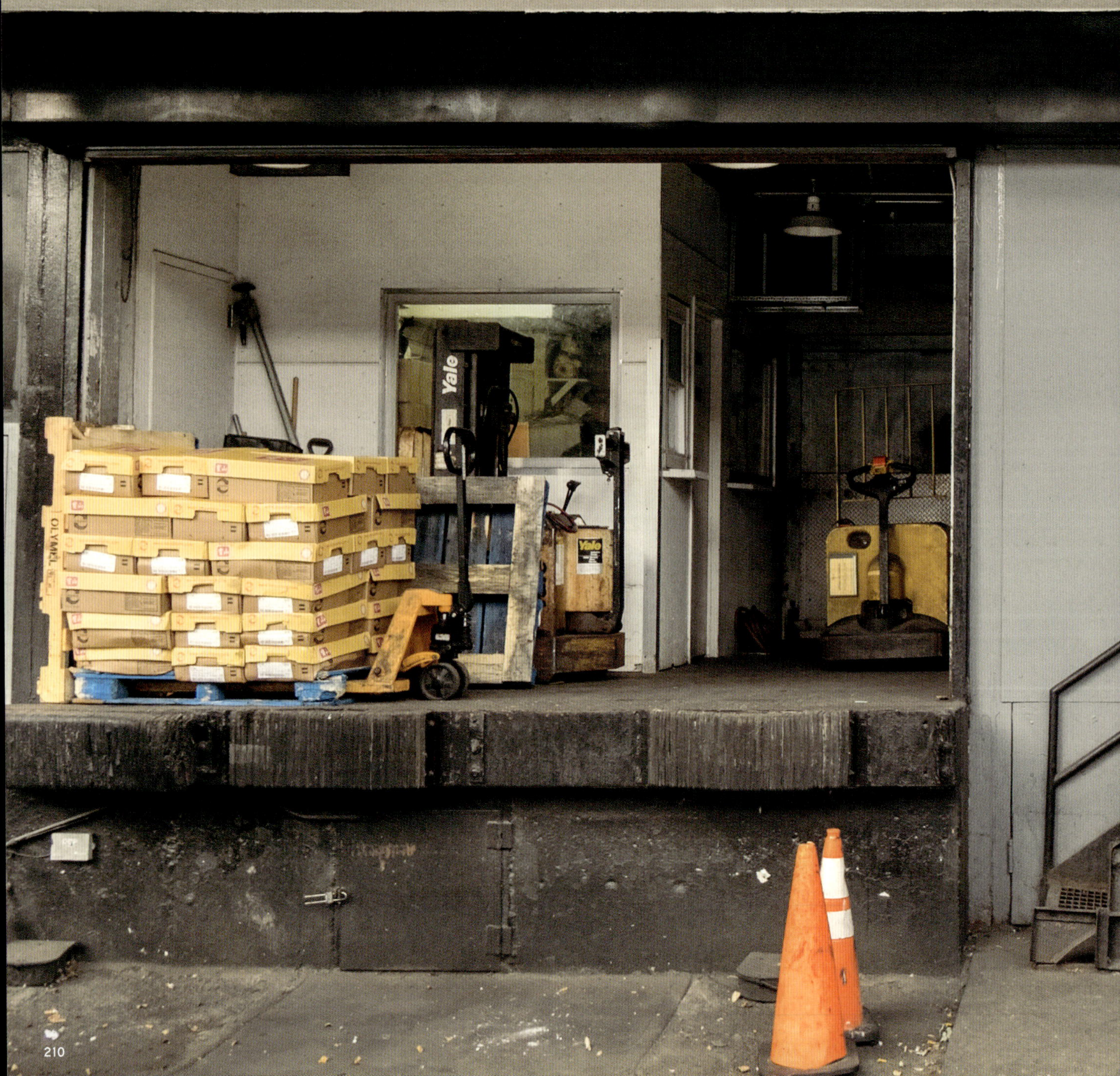

LOUIS ZUC
Hatfield
DISTRIBUTOR
& I.B.P. P
212
Yale

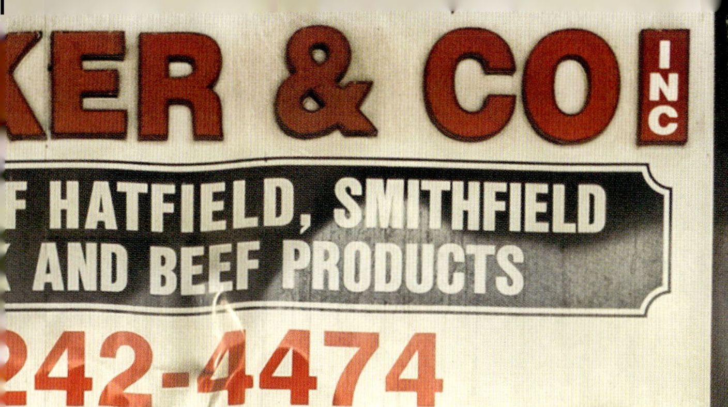
KER & CO INC
F HATFIELD, SMITHFIELD
K AND BEEF PRODUCTS
242-4474

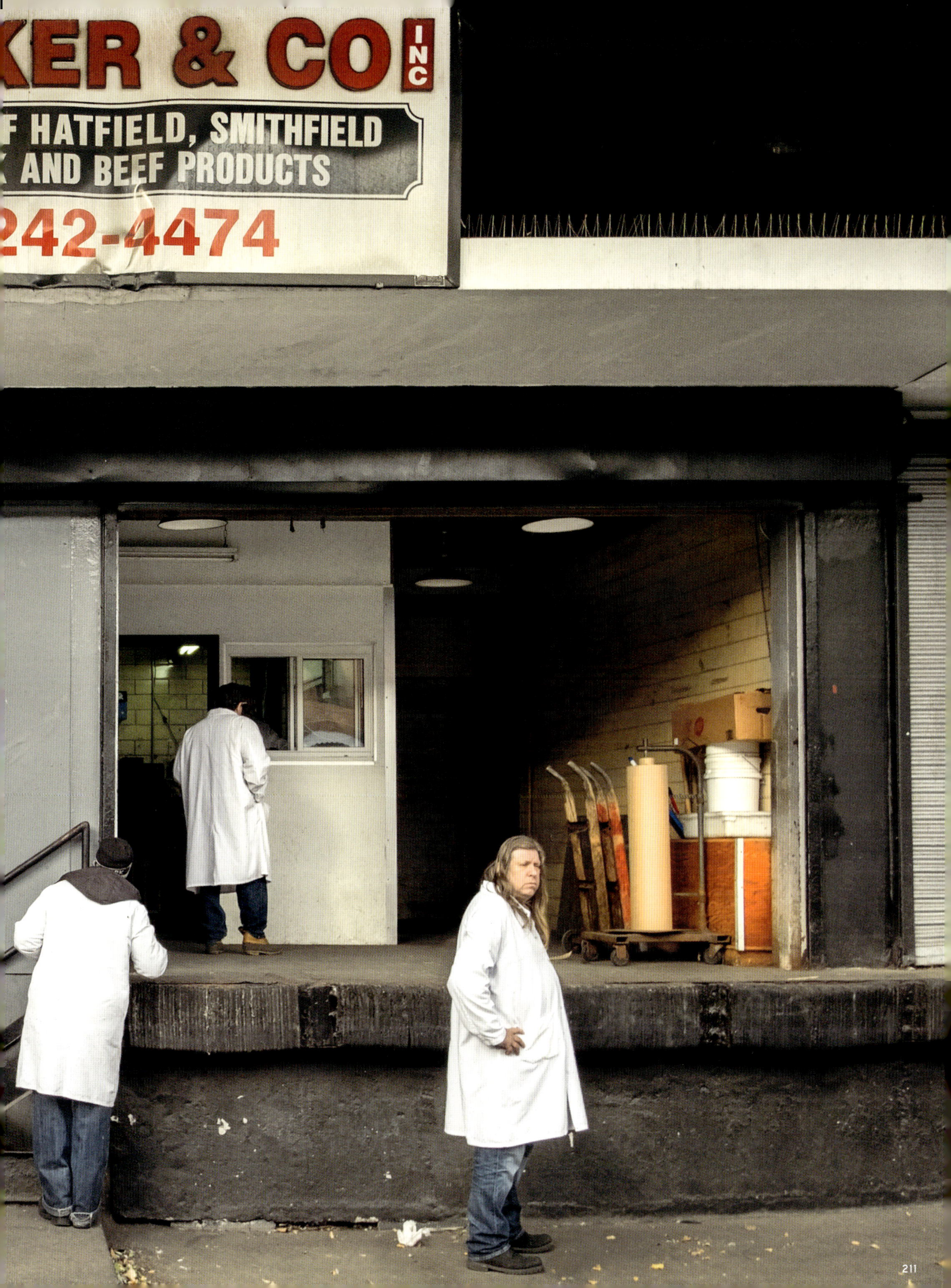

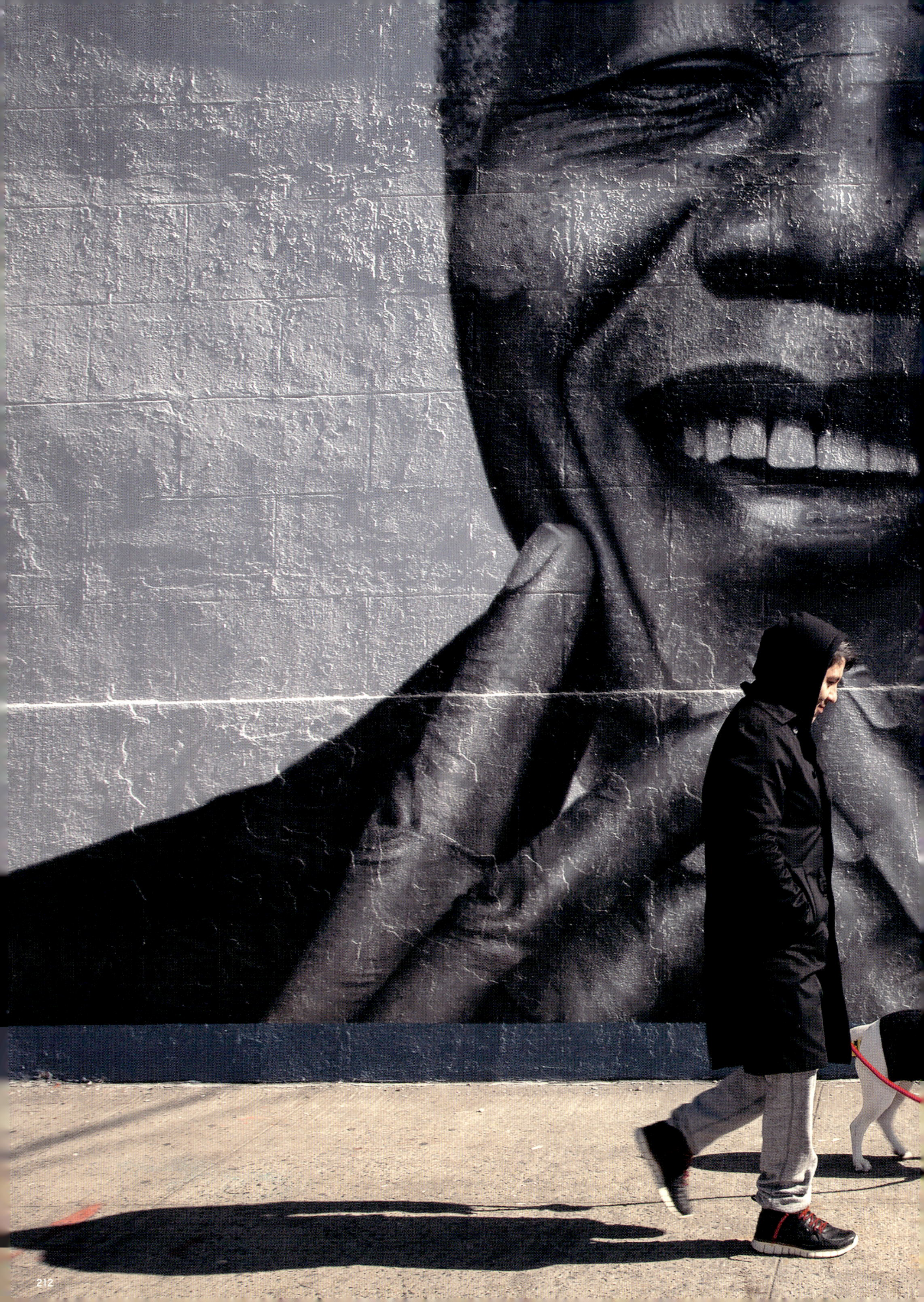

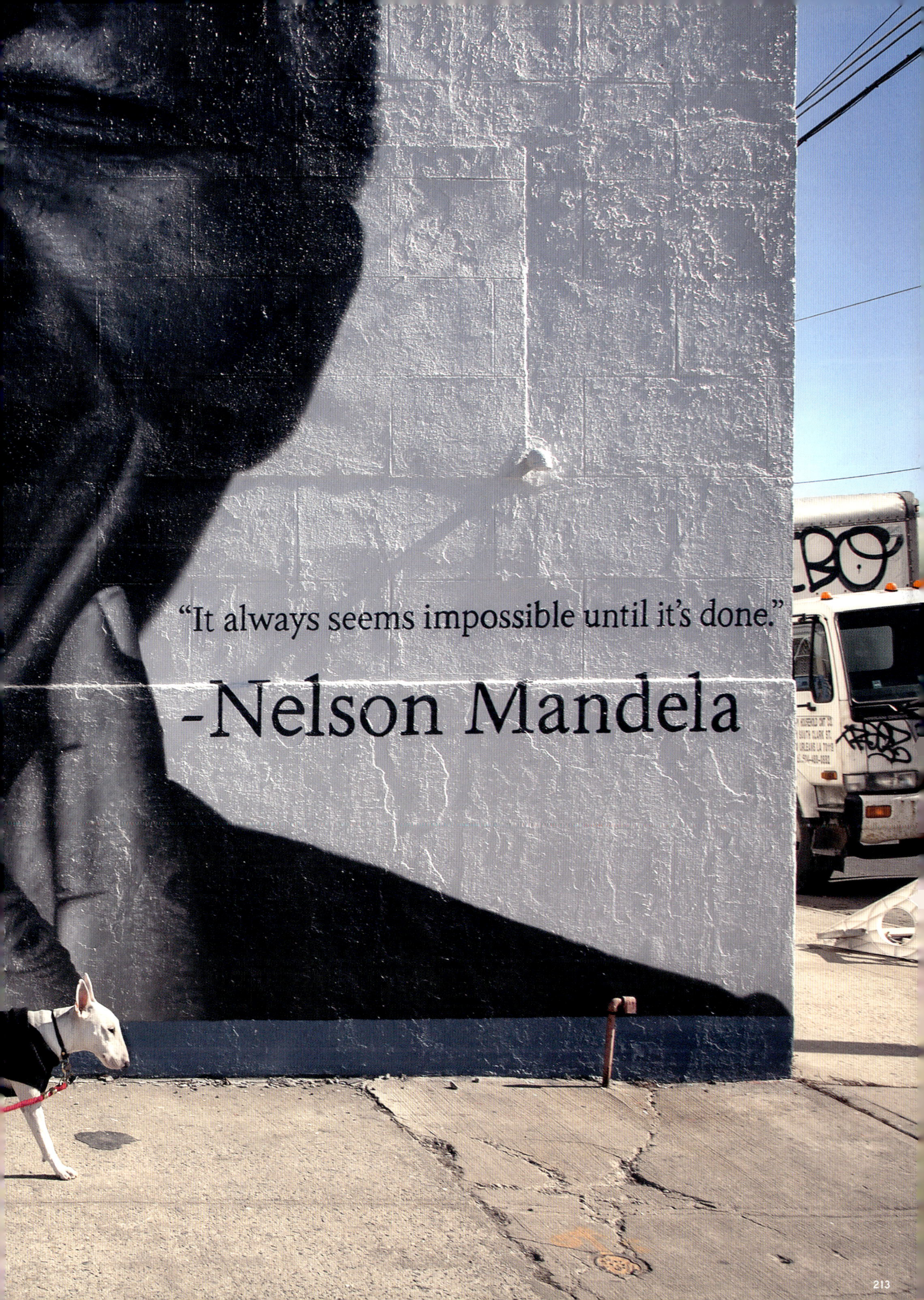

"It always seems impossible until it's done."
-Nelson Mandela

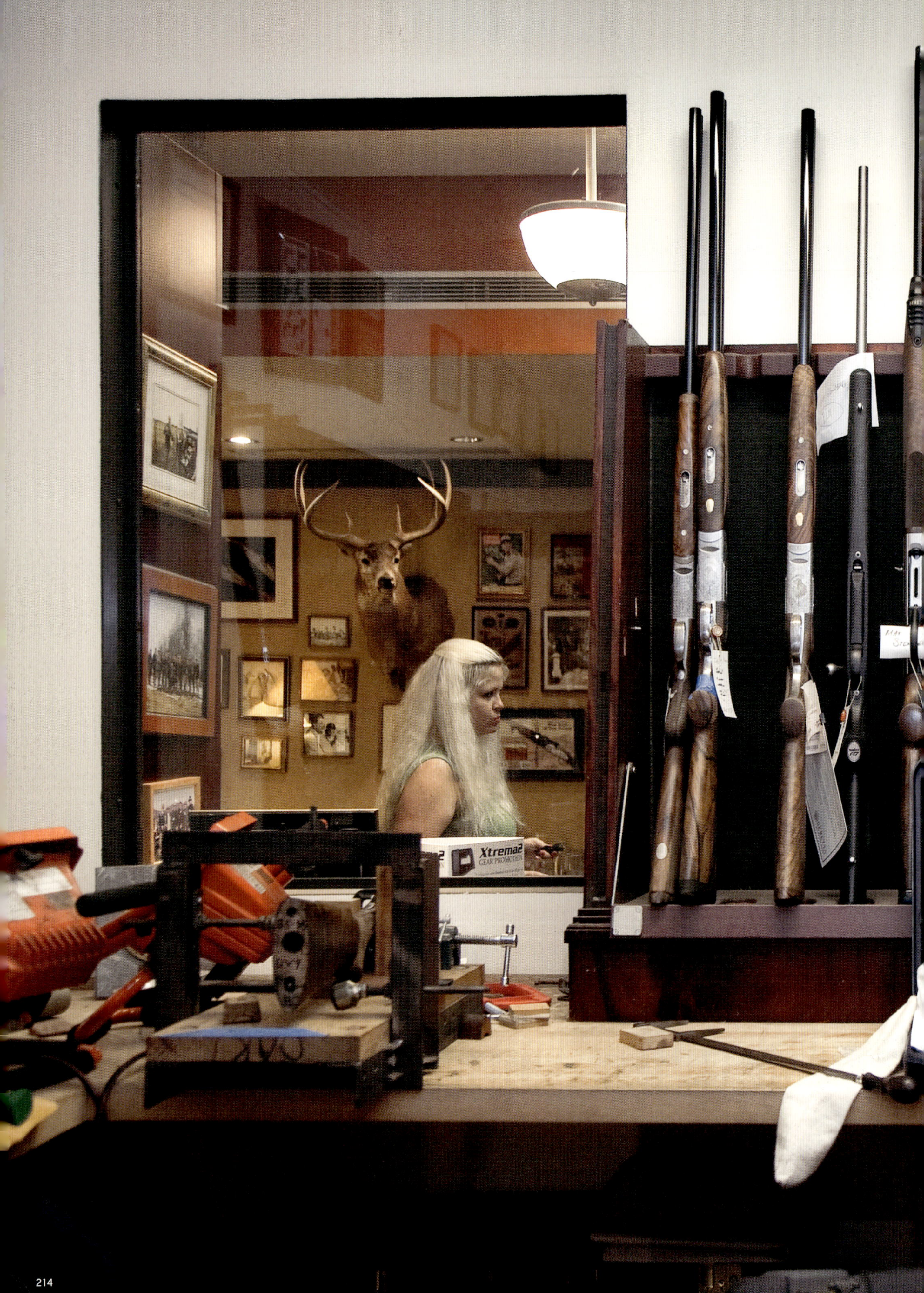

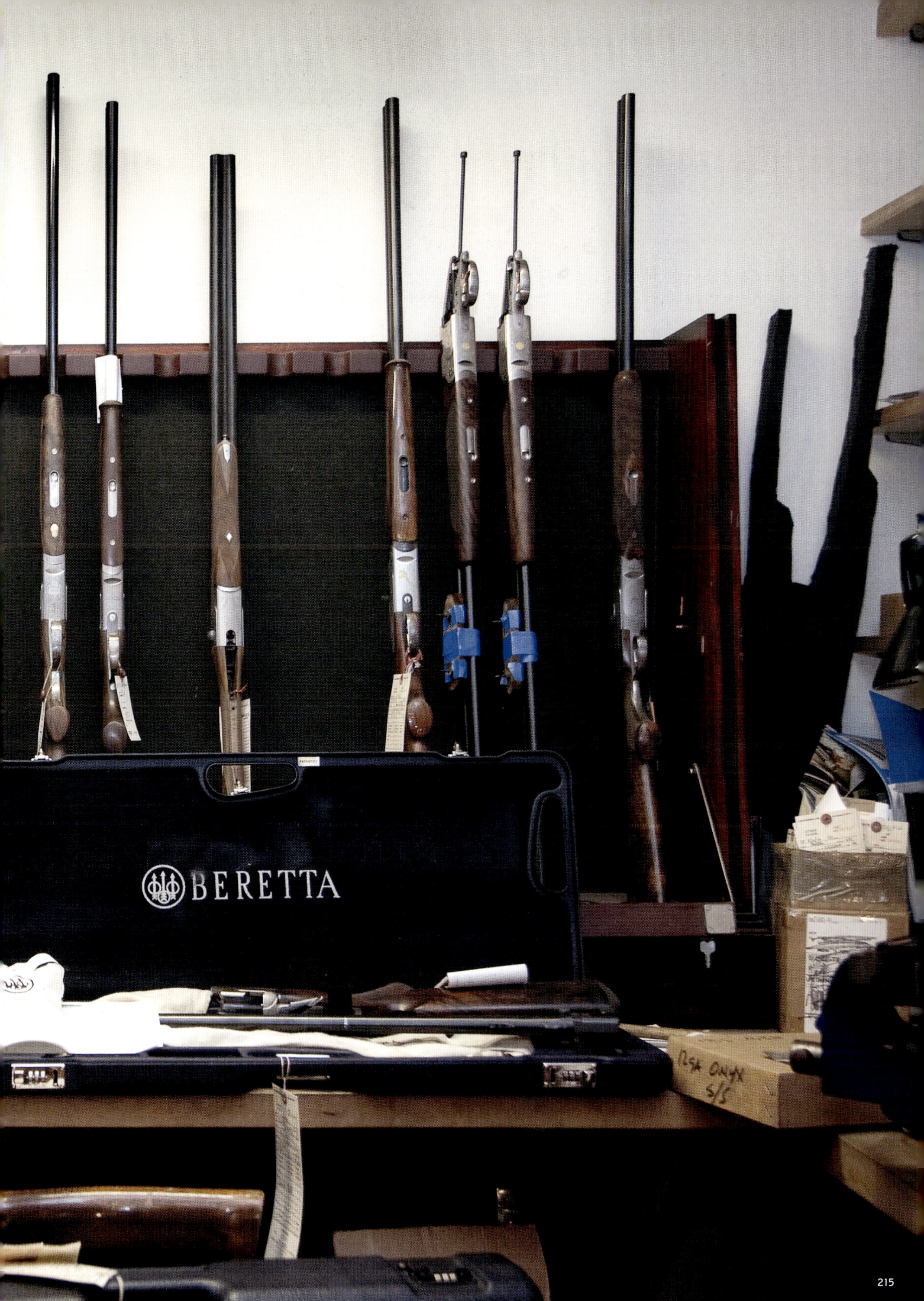

BERETTA

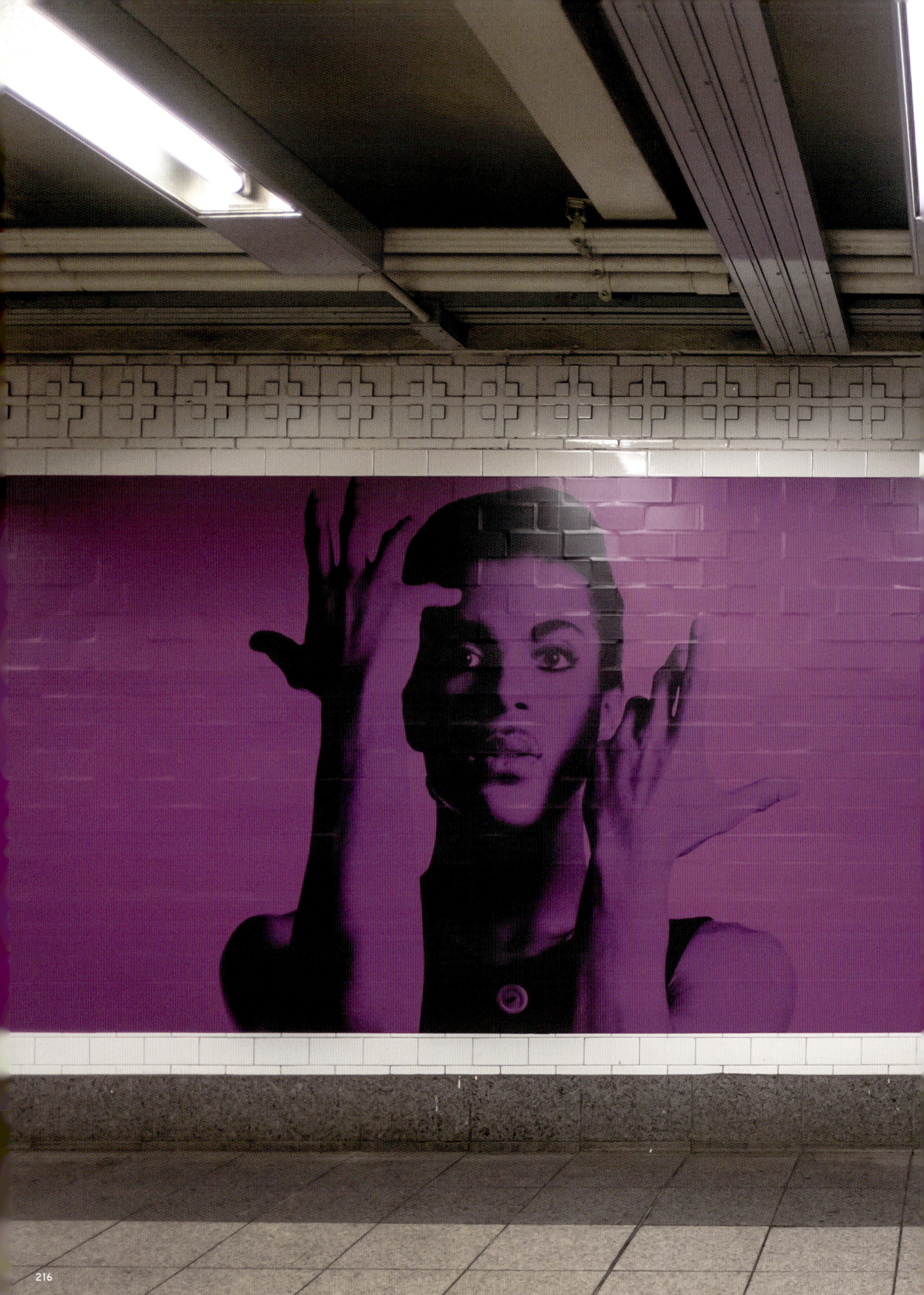

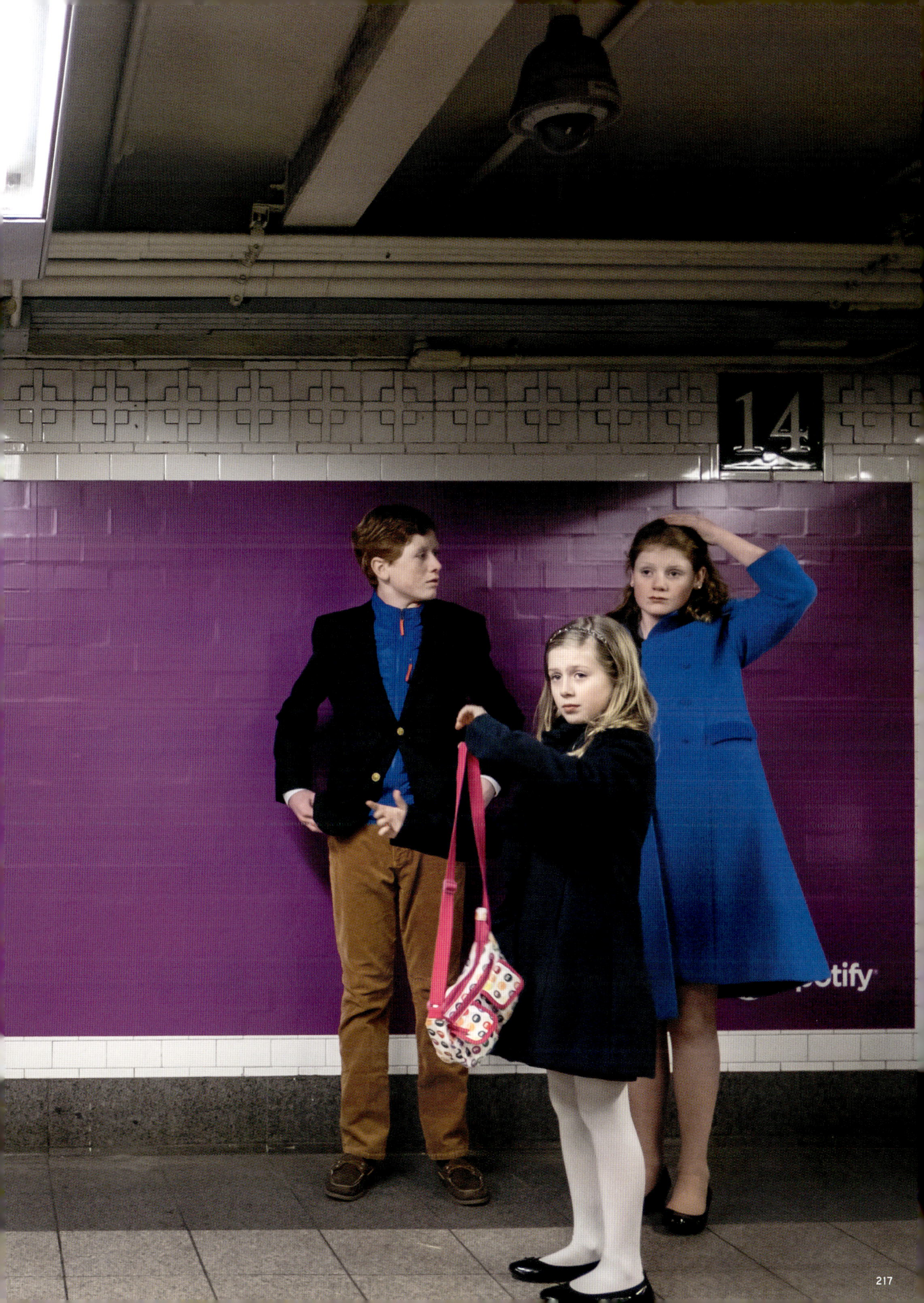
14
tify

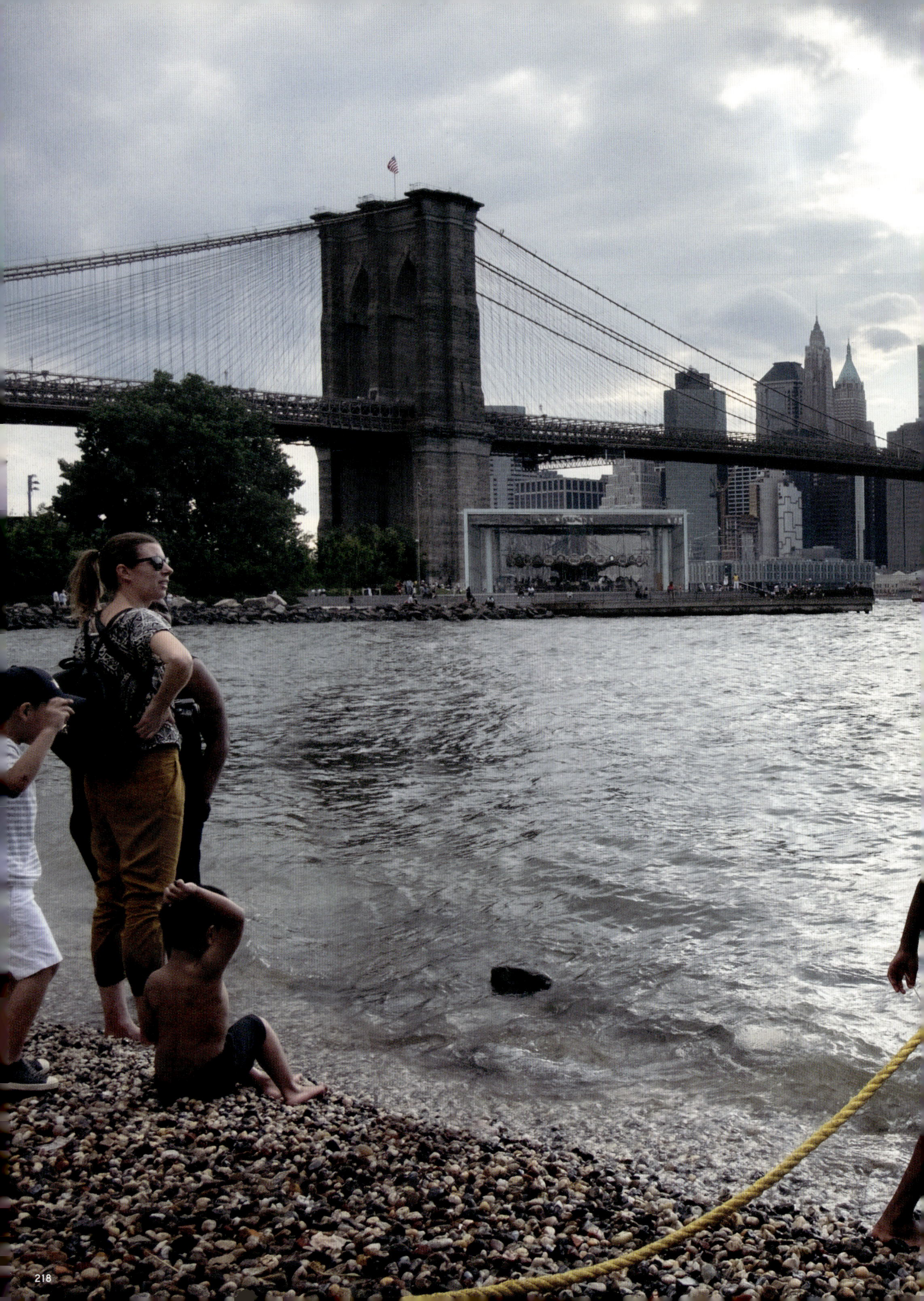

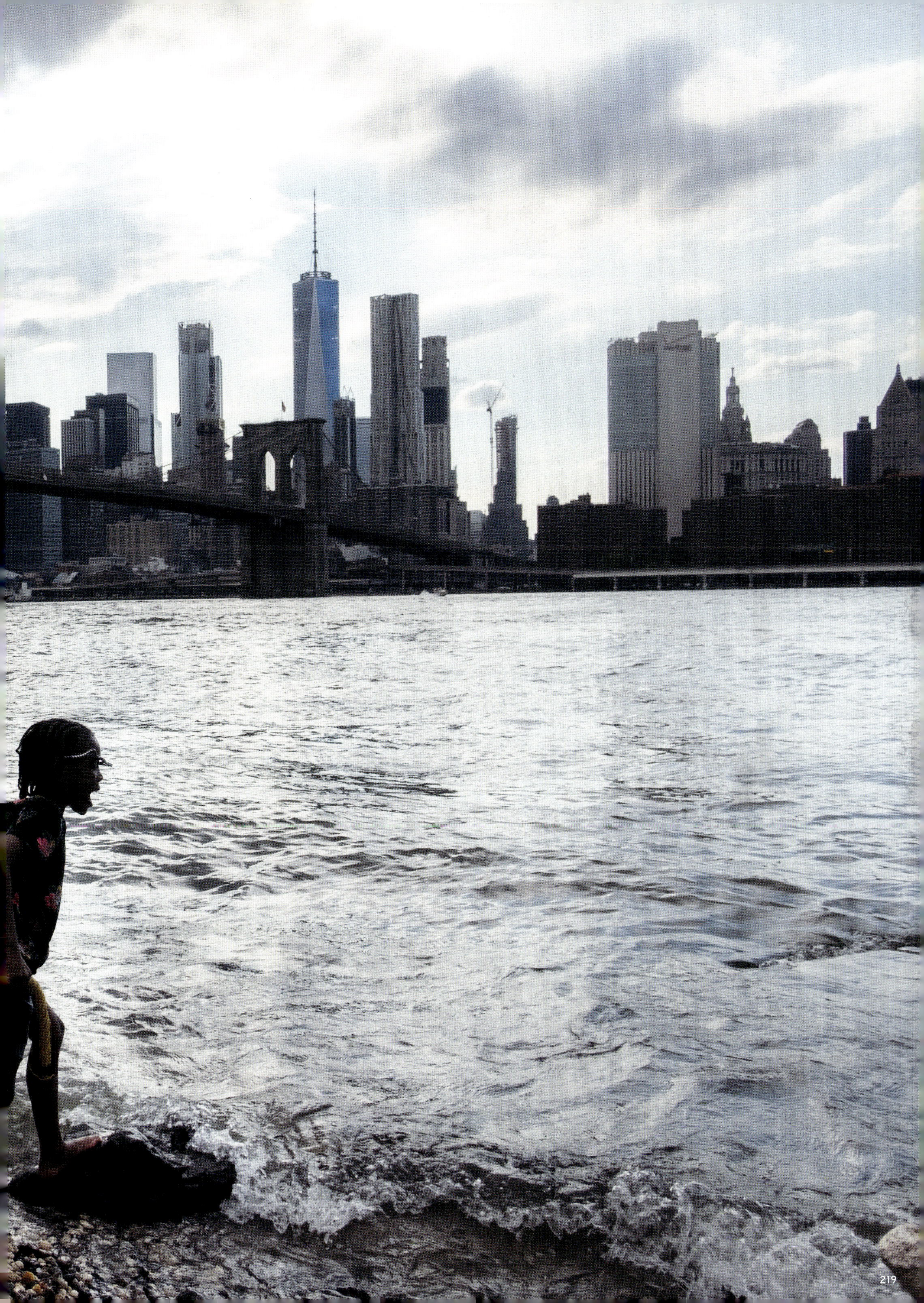

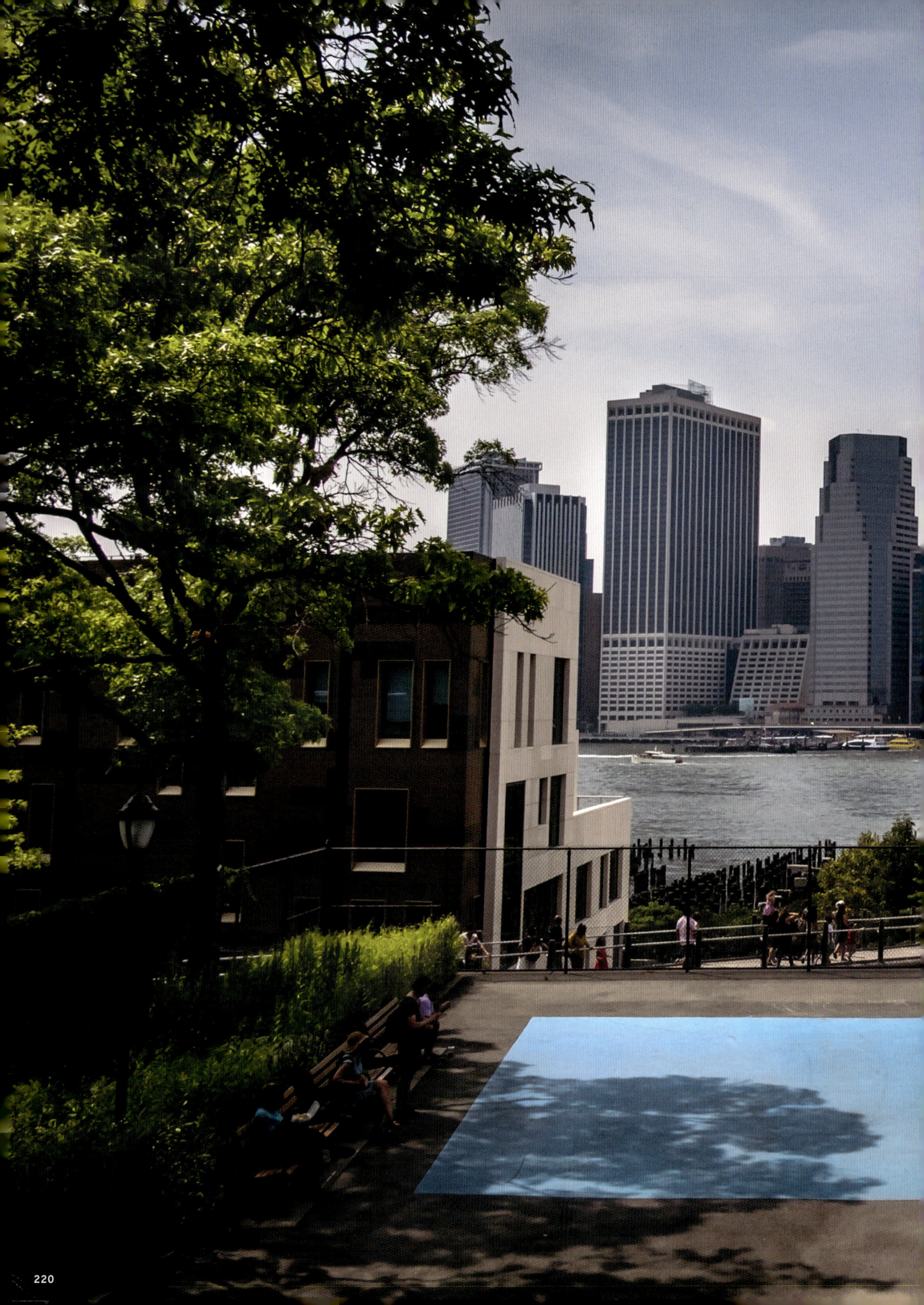

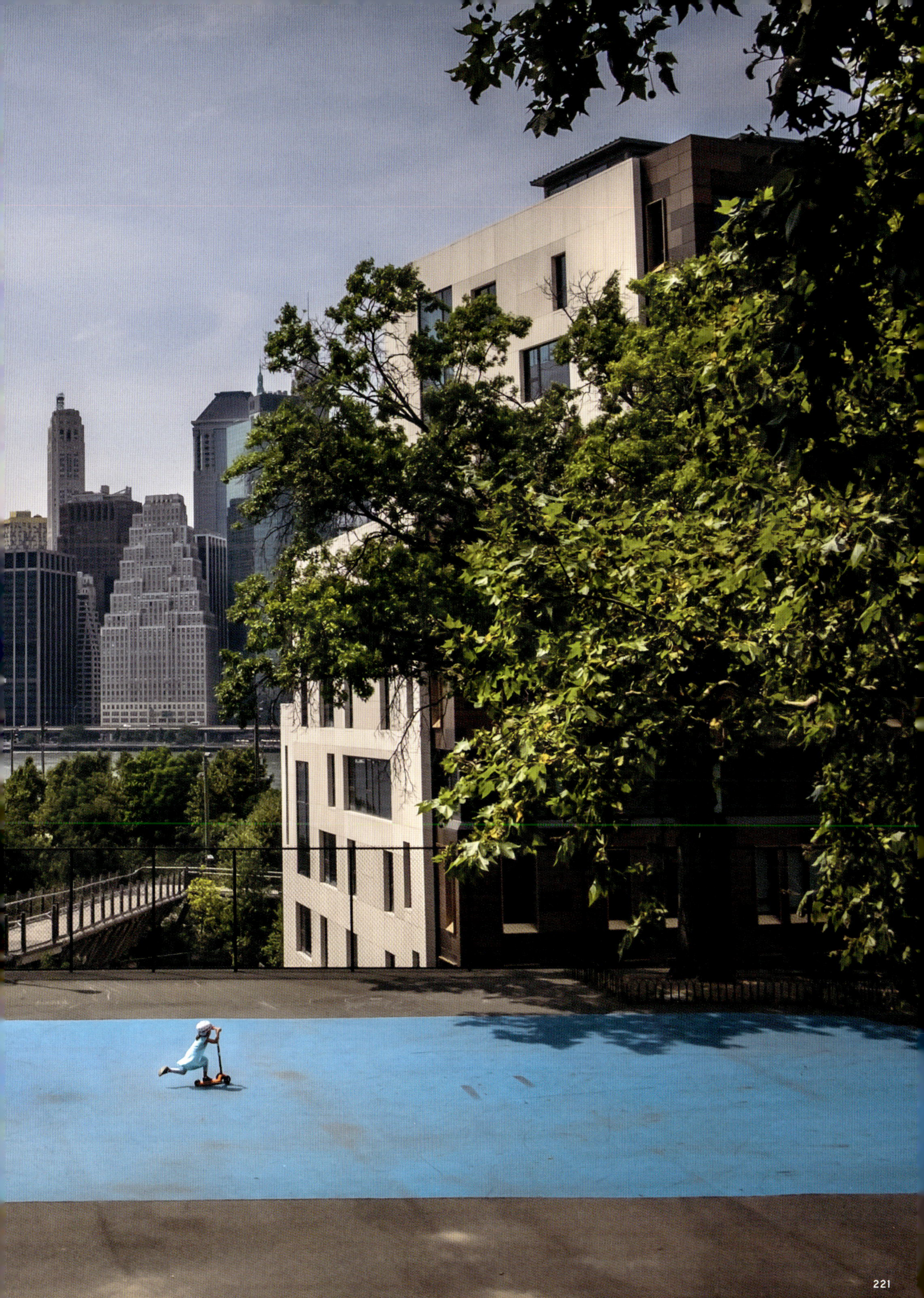

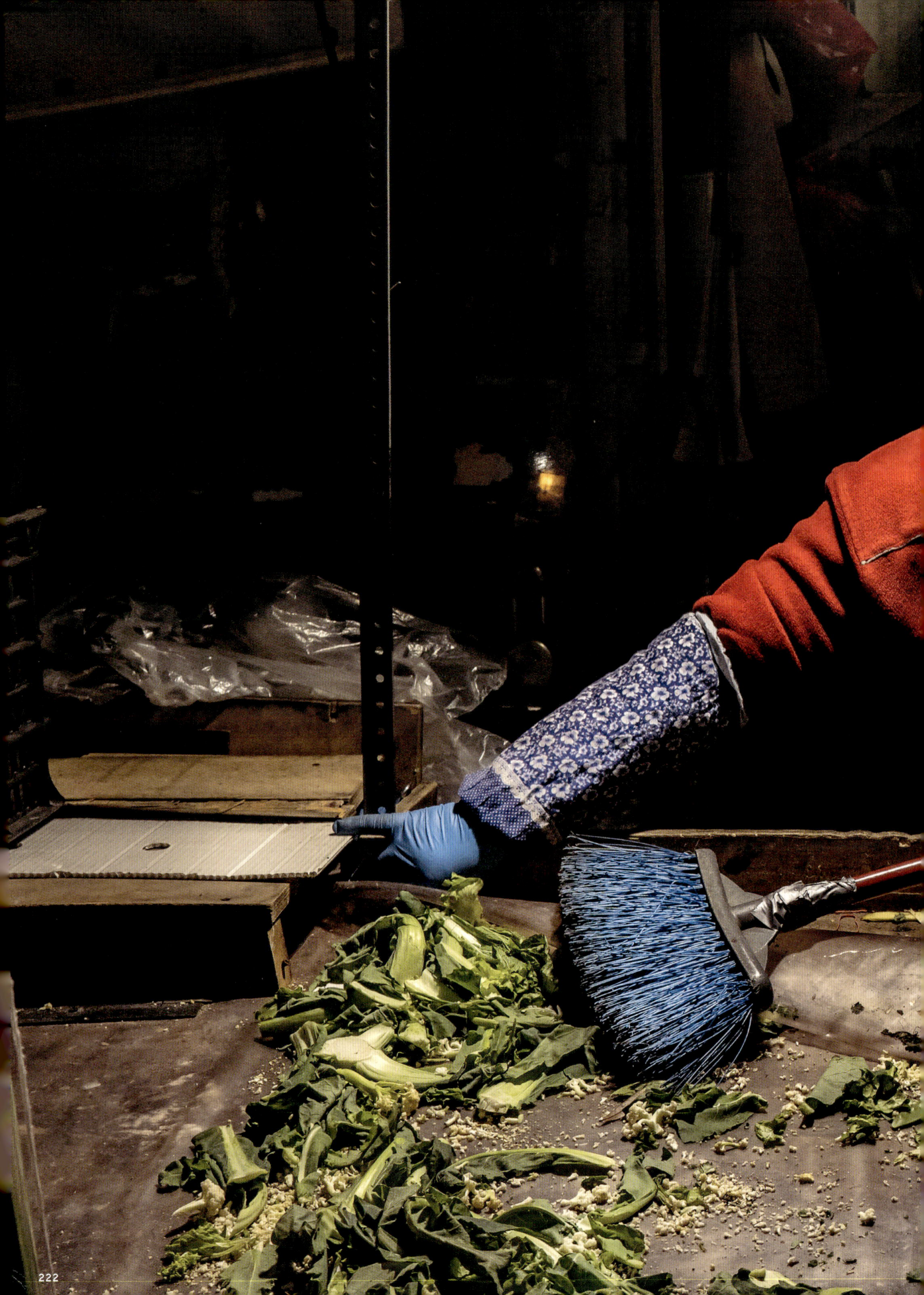

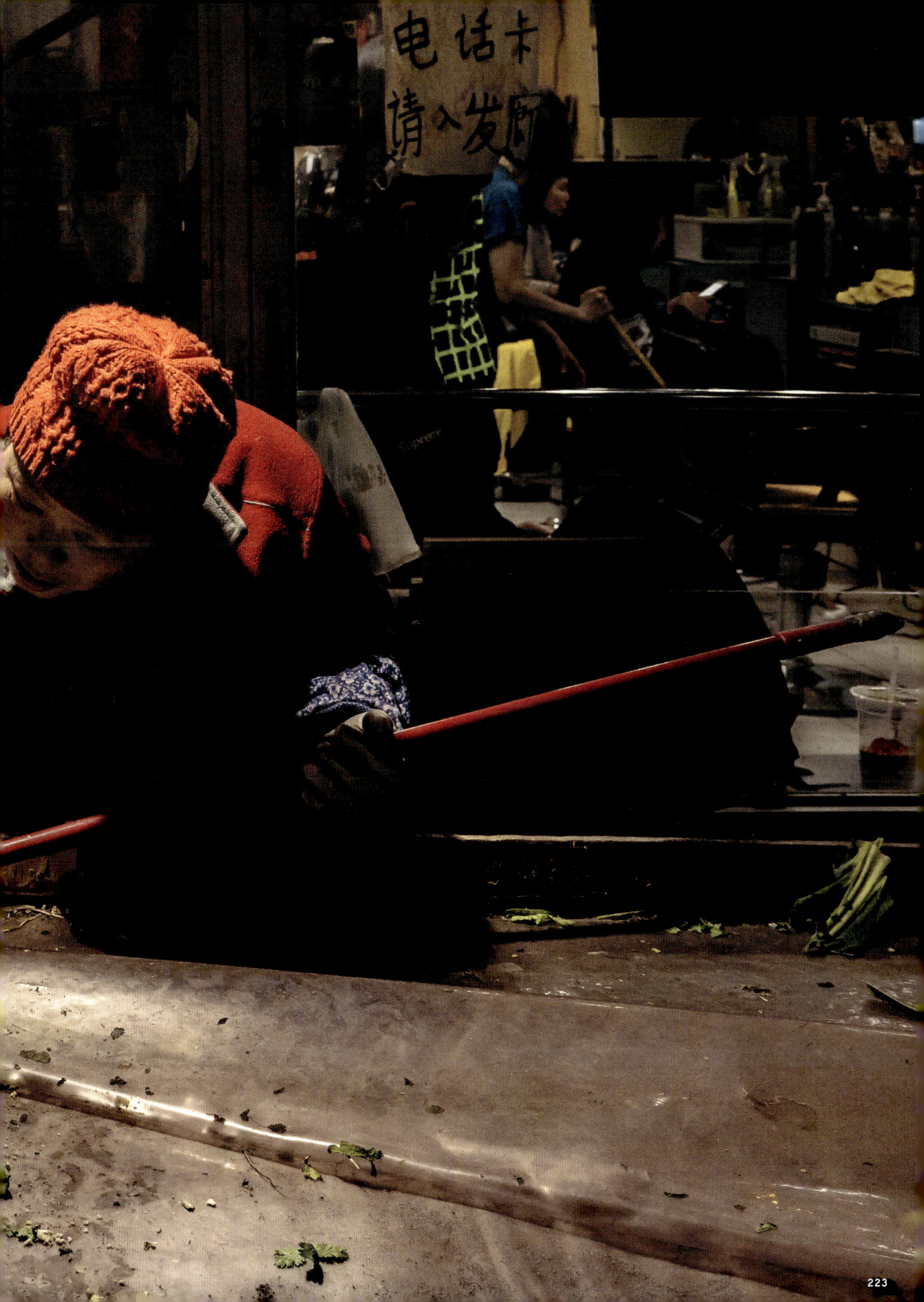

电话卡
请入发廊

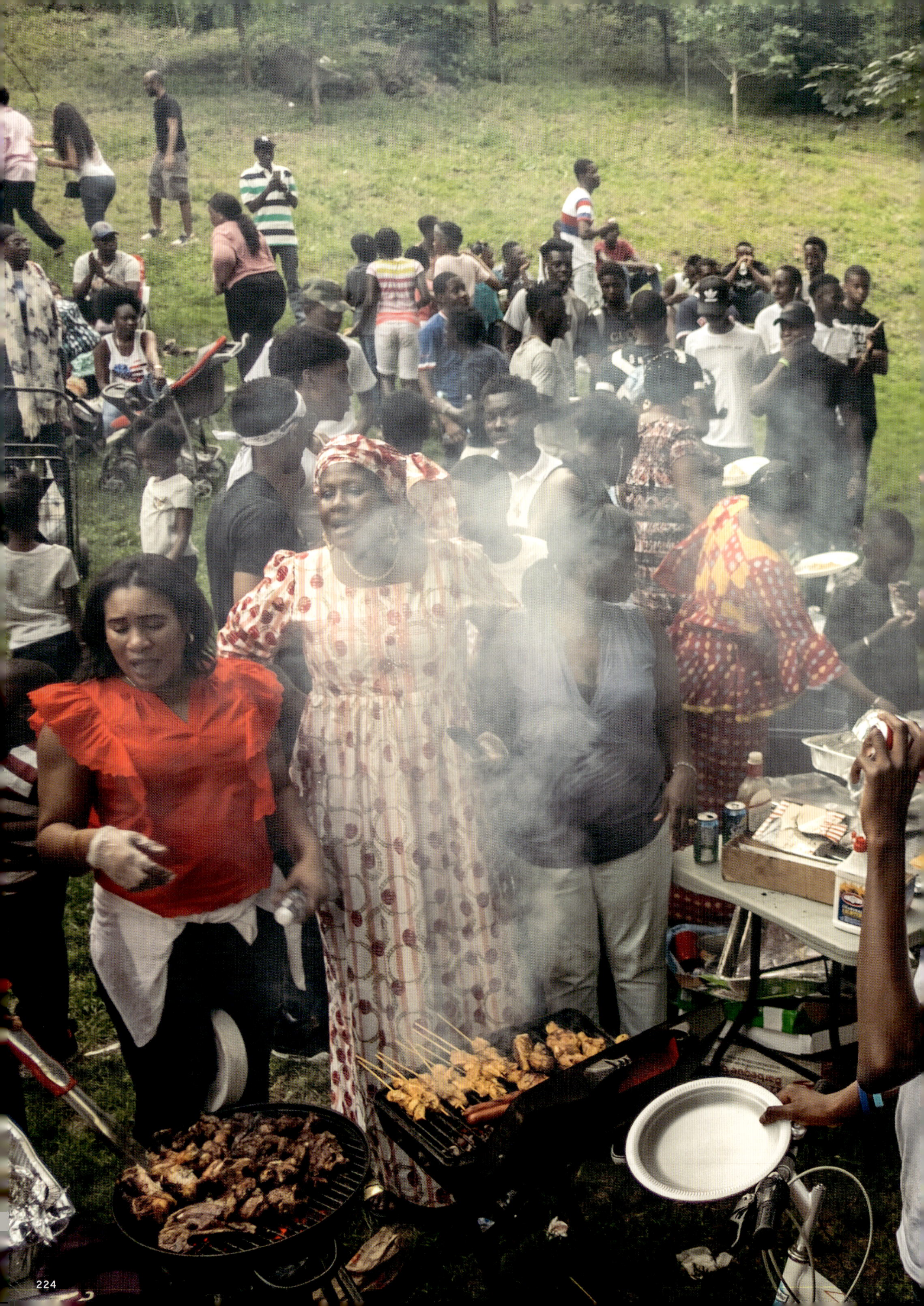

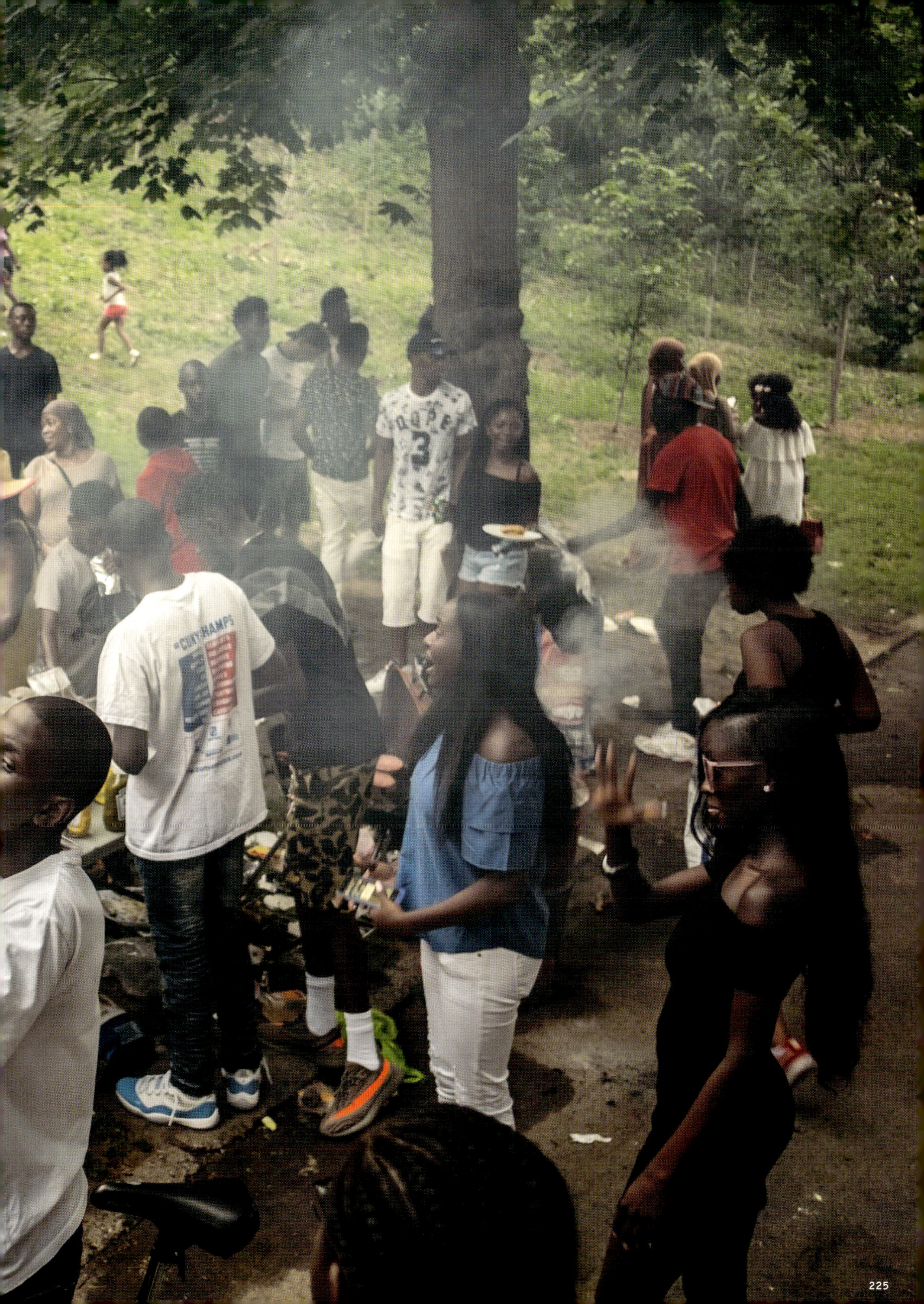

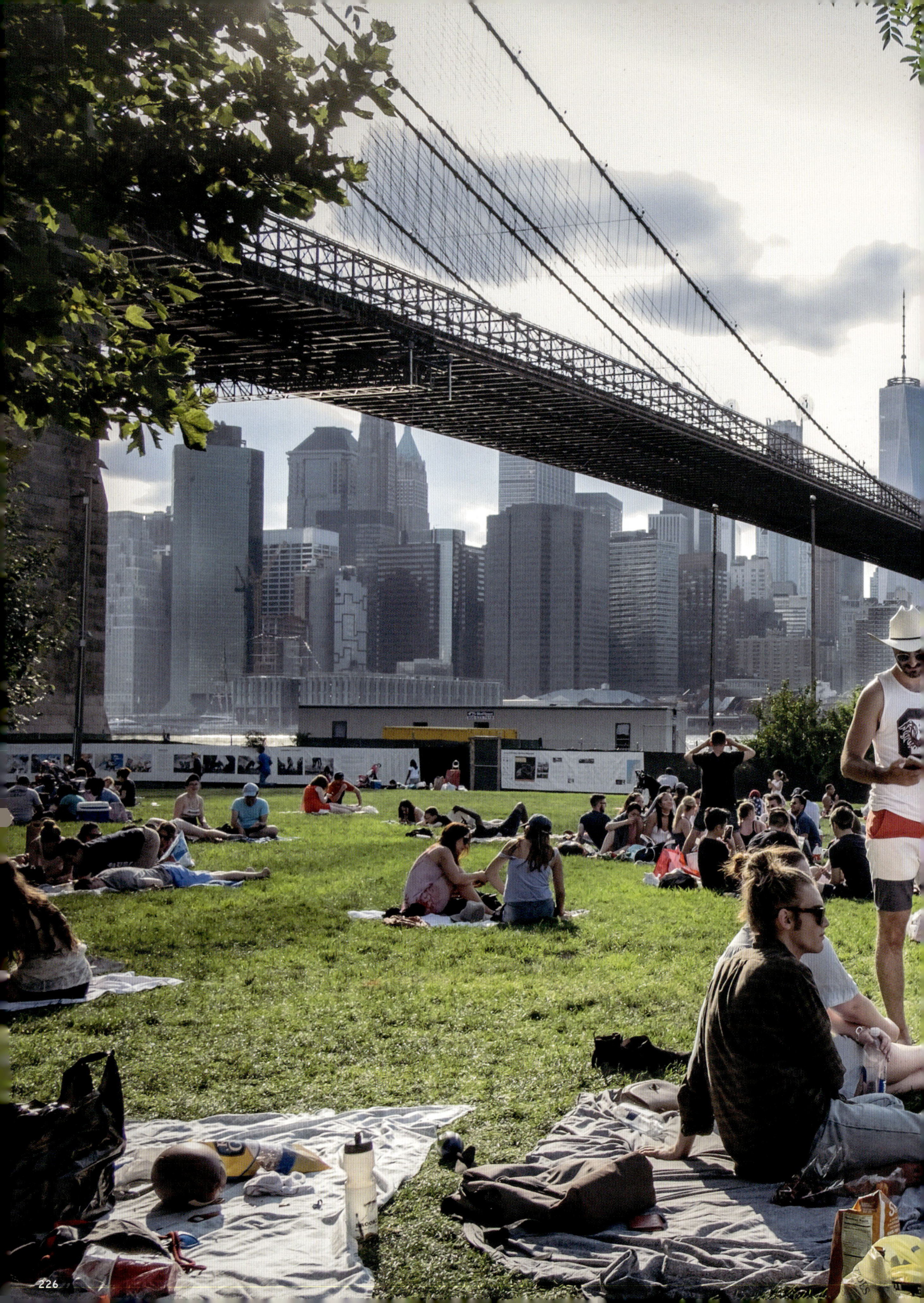

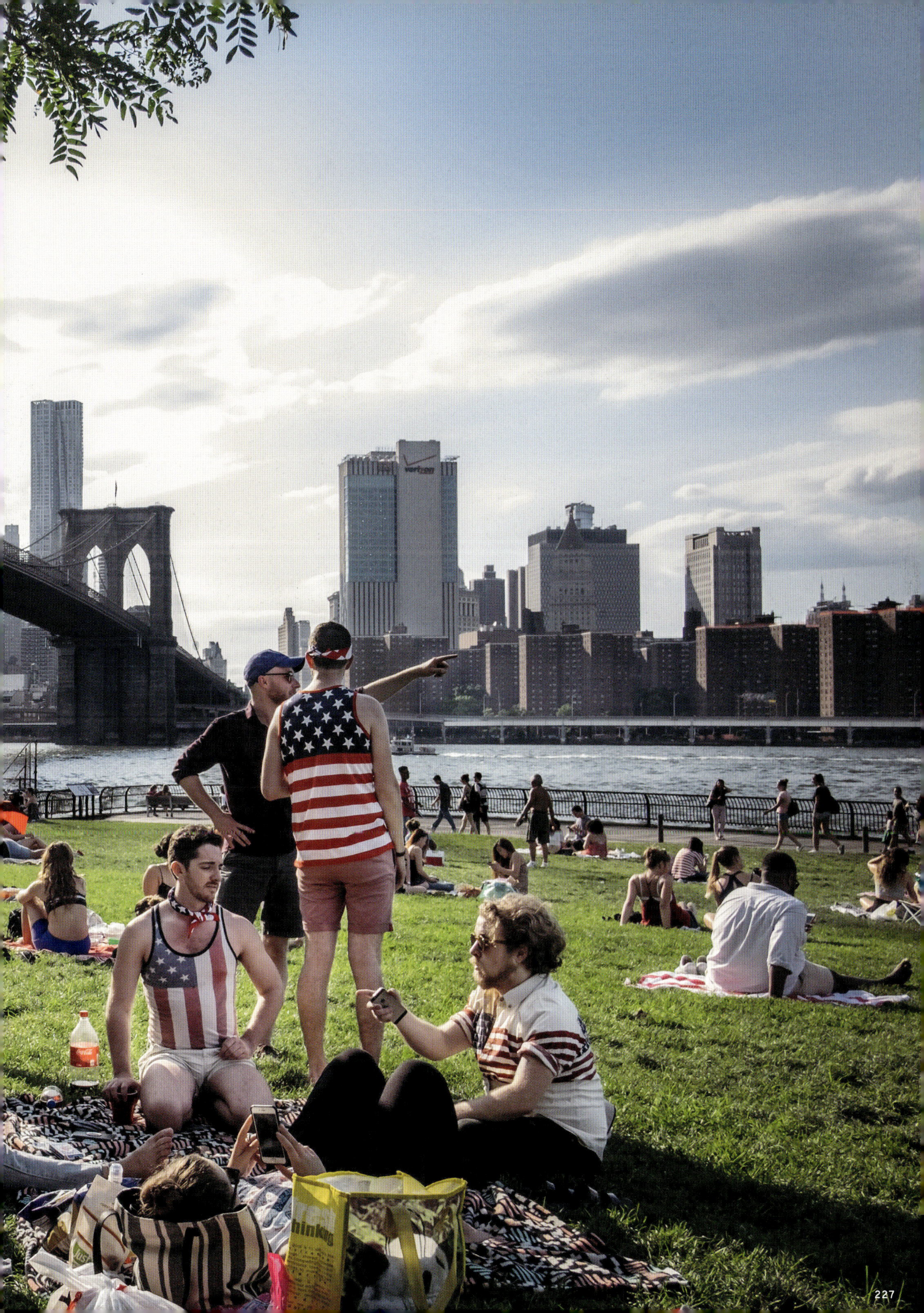

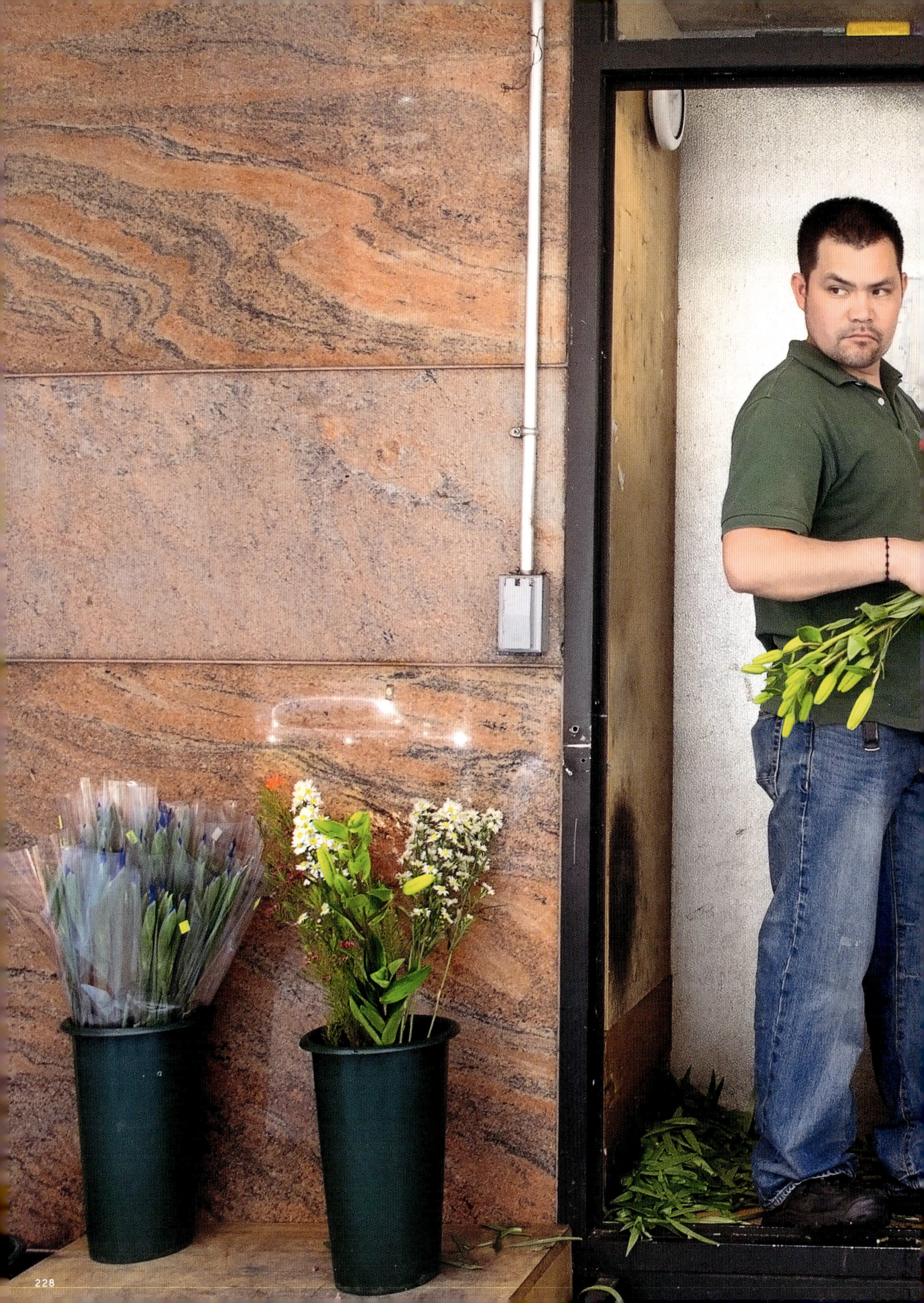

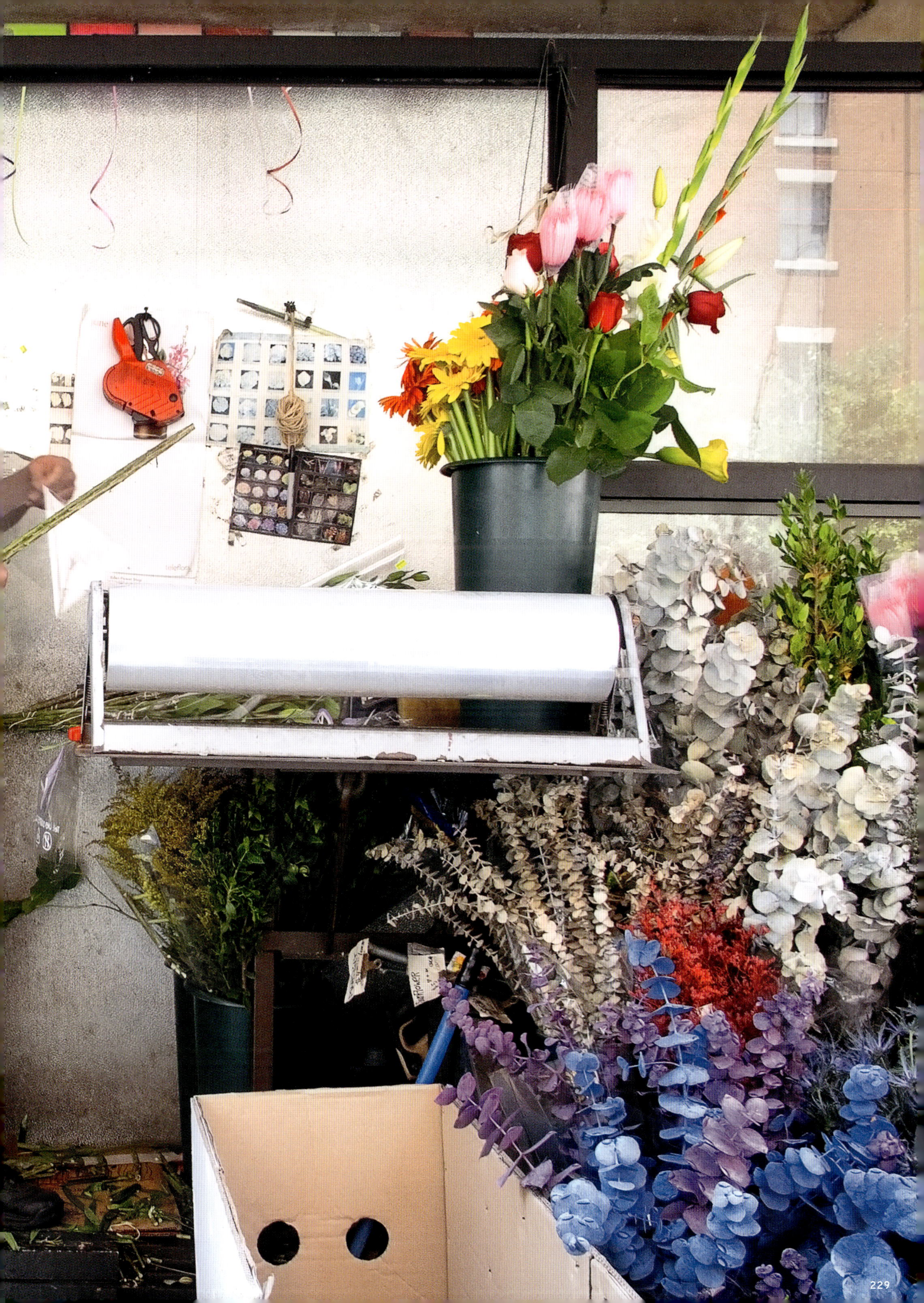

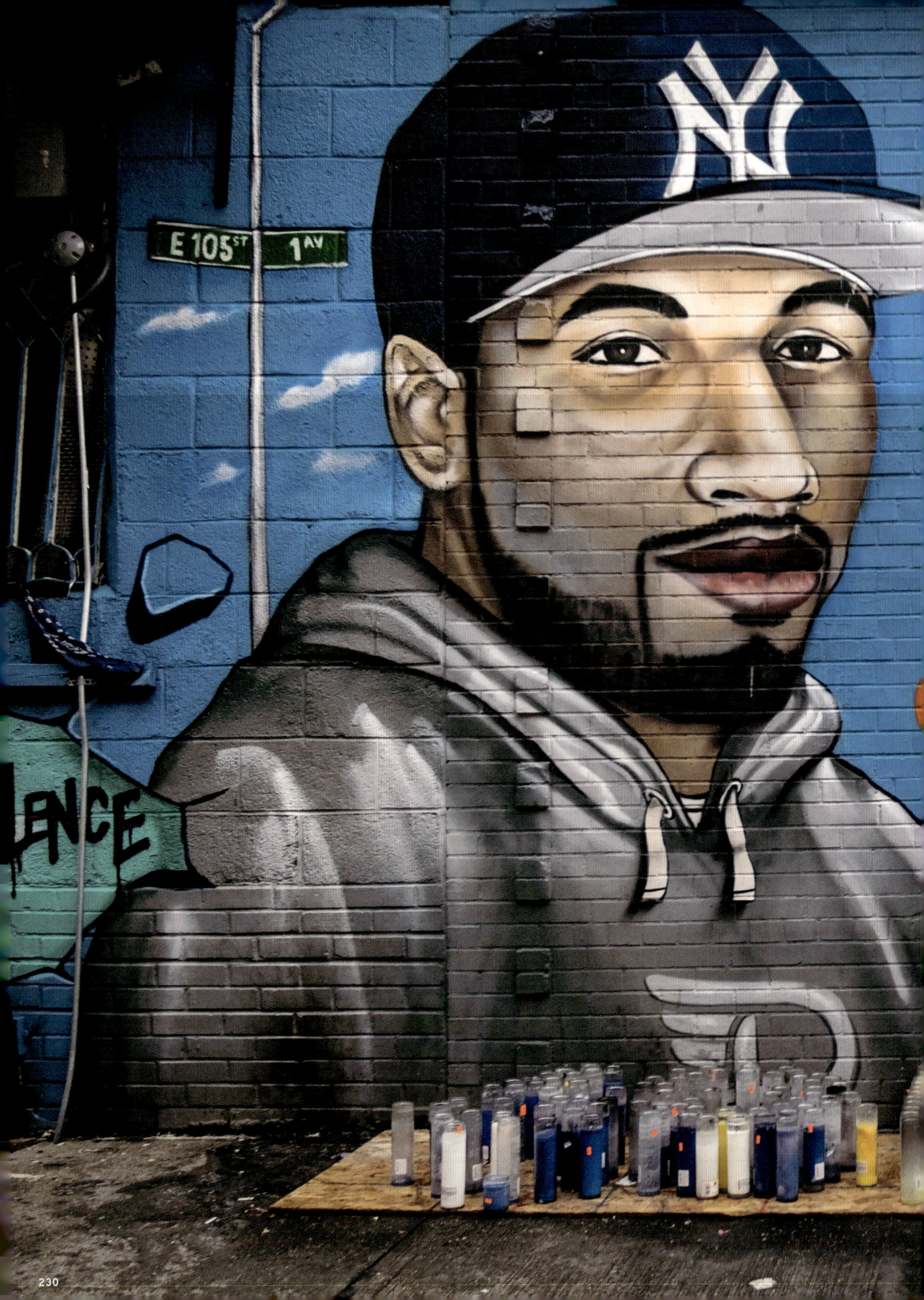

E 105 ST   1 AV
NY
LENCE

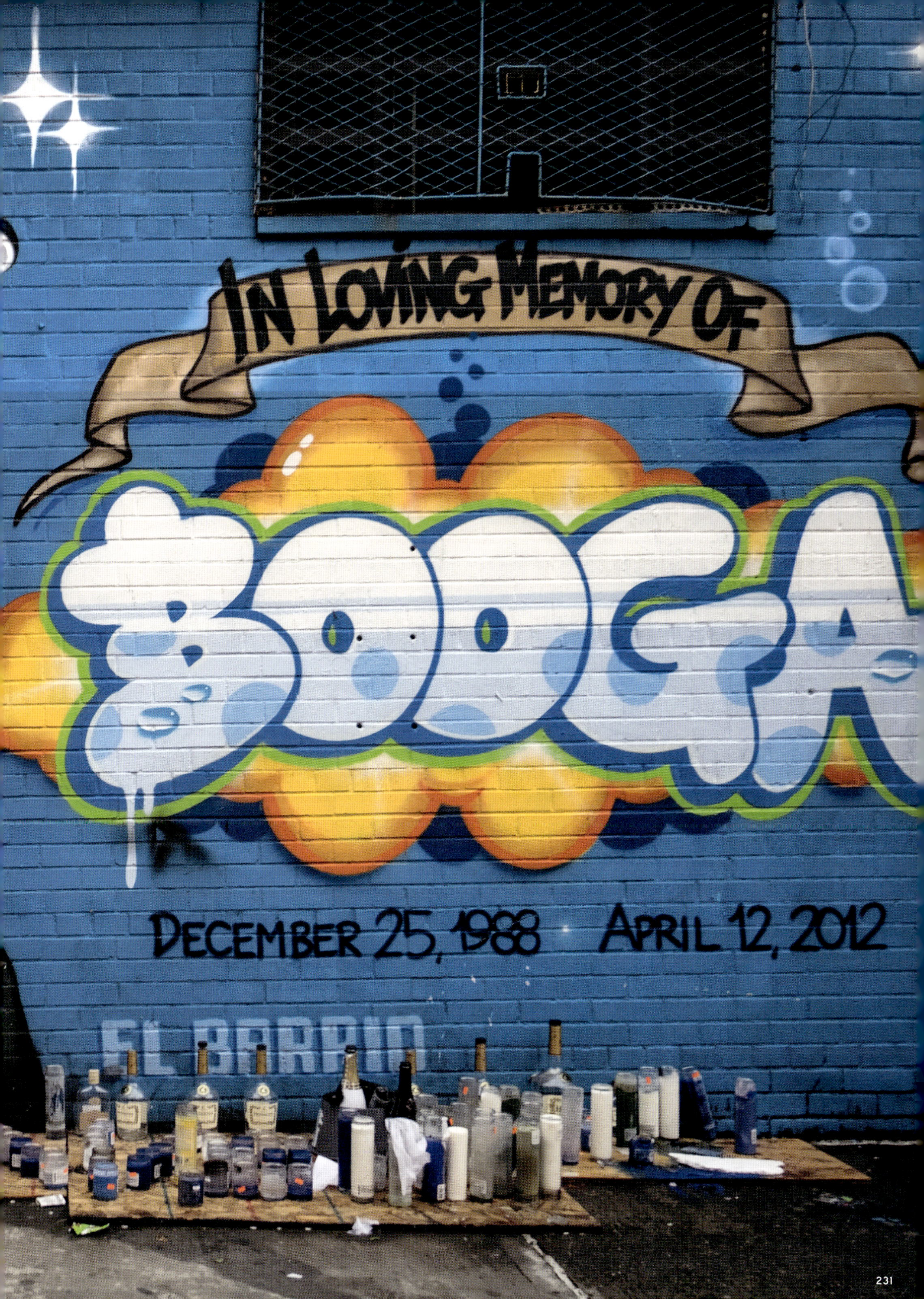
IN LOVING MEMORY OF
BOOGA
DECEMBER 25, 1988   APRIL 12, 2012
EL BARRIO

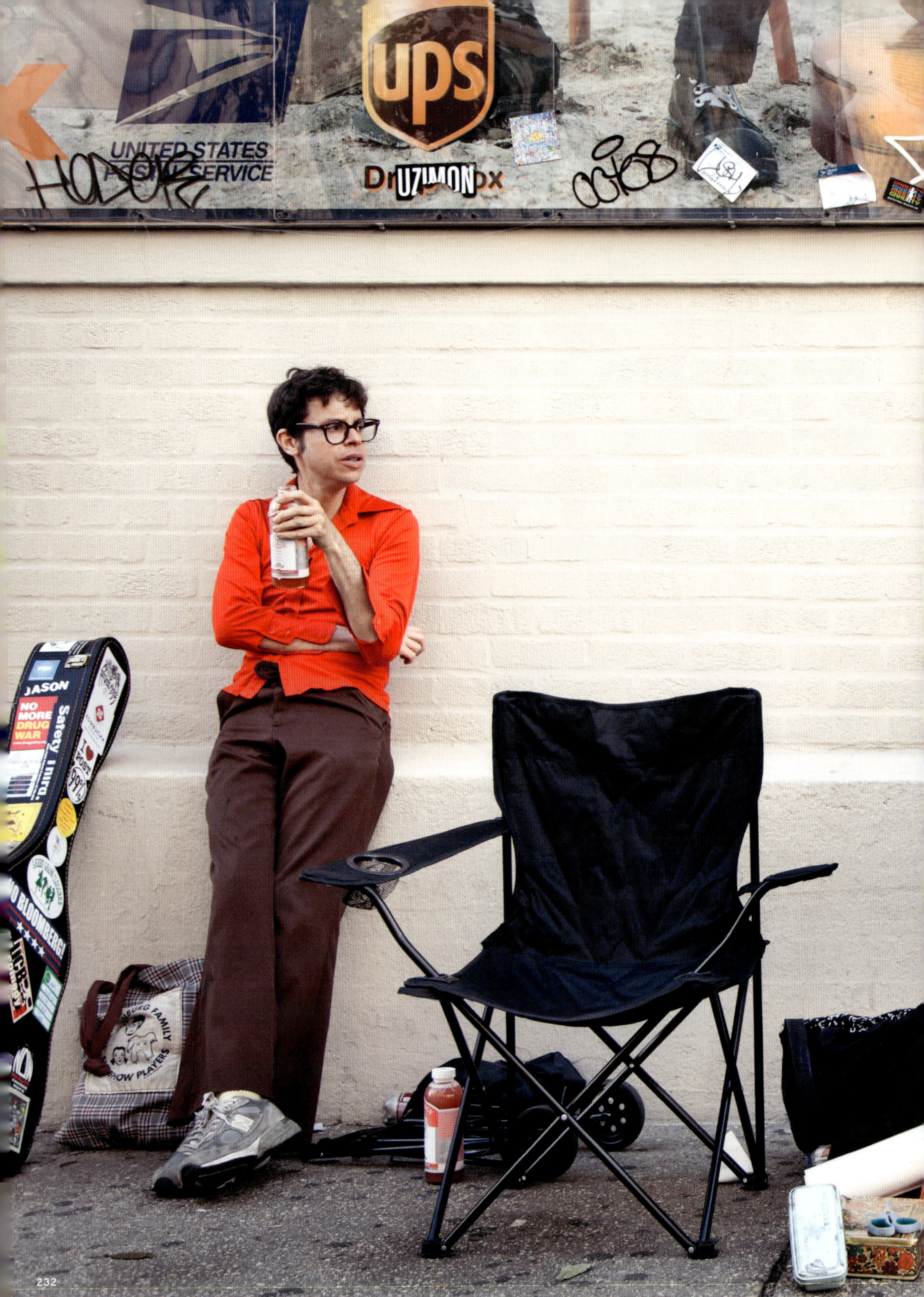

UPS
UNITED STATES POSTAL SERVICE
NO MORE DRUG WAR
JASON
Safety first.
BLOOMBERG

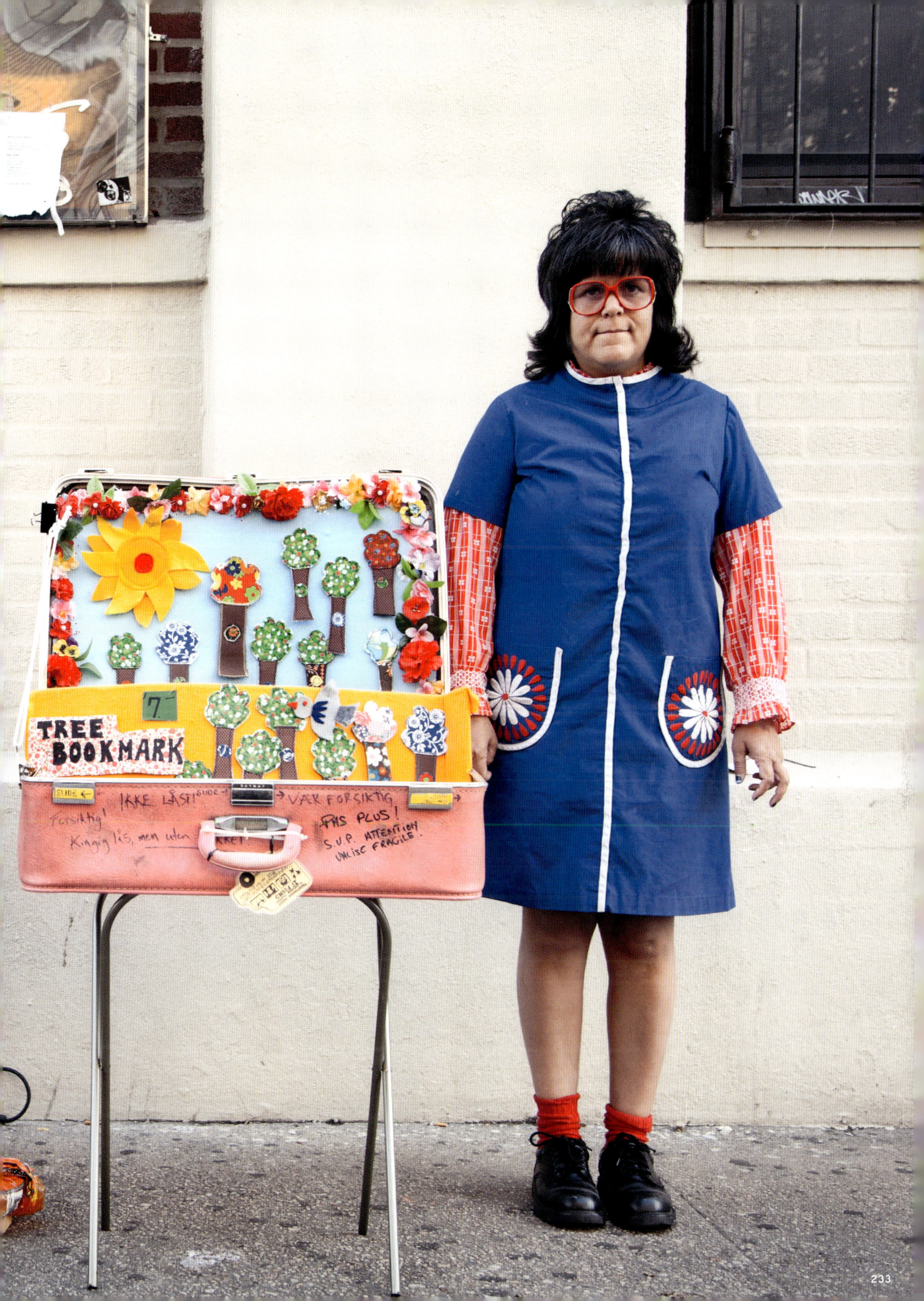

TREE
BOOKMARK
SLIDE ←
IKKE LÅST! SLIDE →
→ VÆR FORSIKTIG
Forsiktig!
Kingig lås, men uten
PAS PLUS!
S.U.P. ATTENTION
UNLISE FRAGILE.

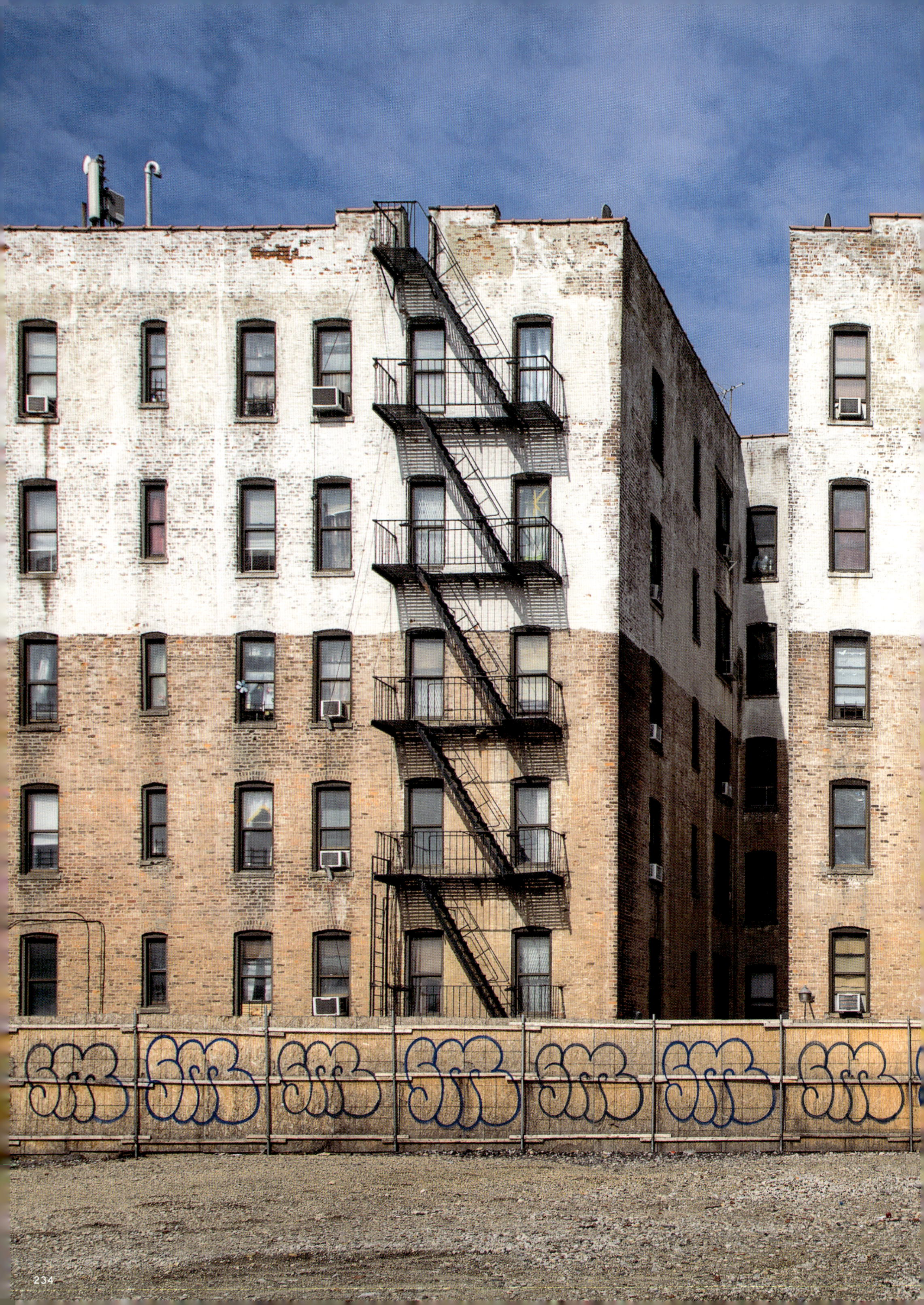

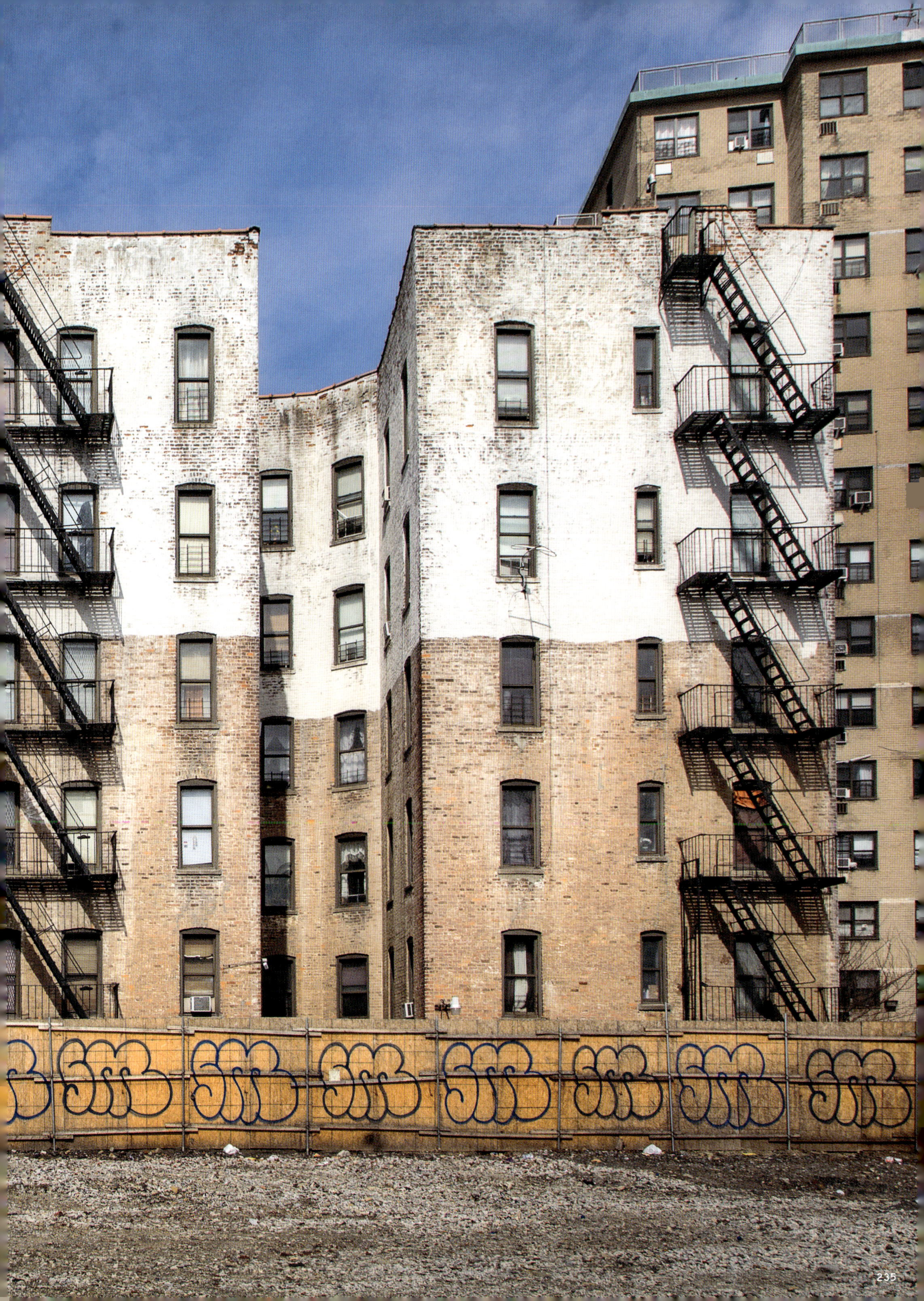

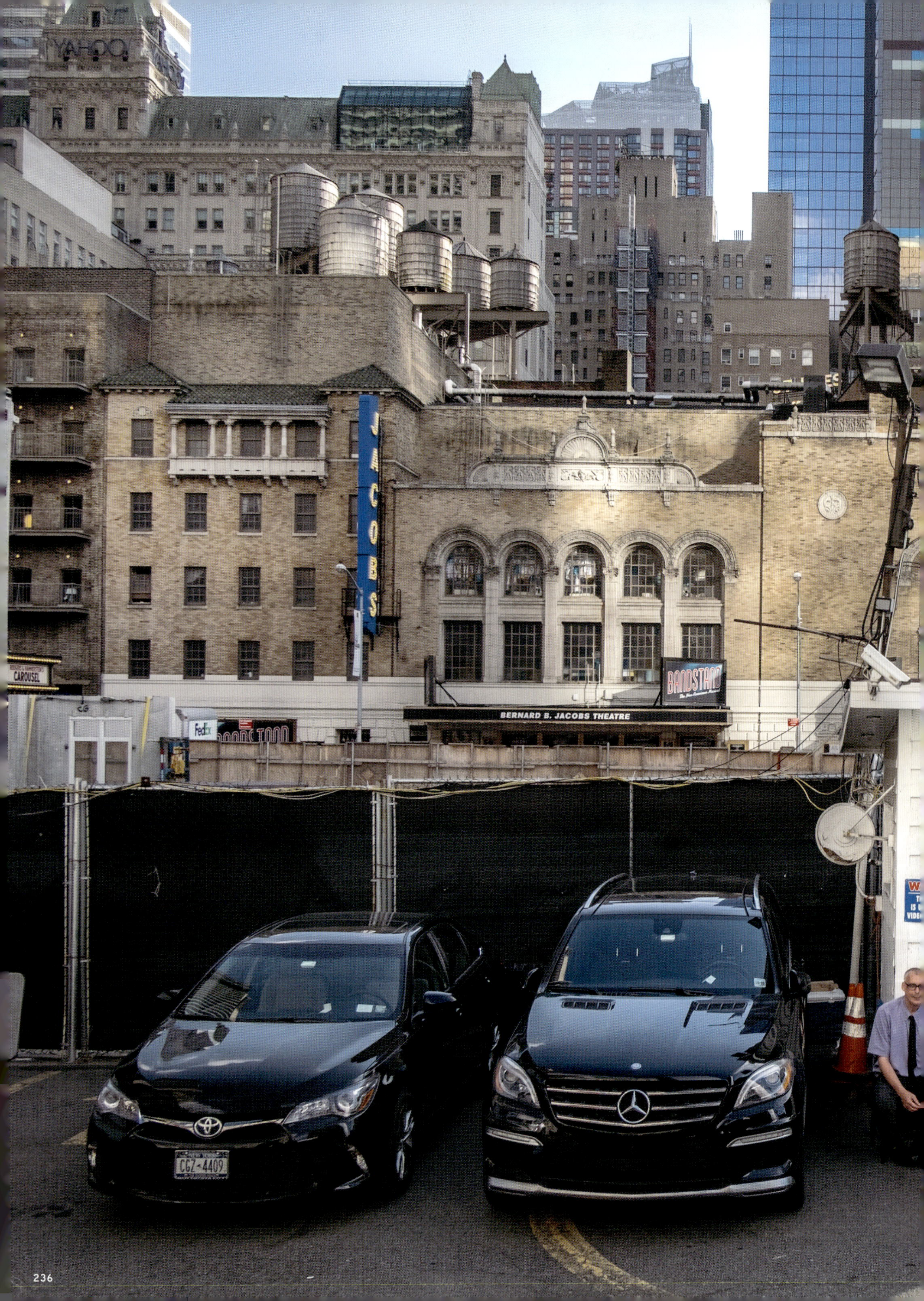

YAHOO!
JACOBS
CAROUSEL
BANDSTAND
BERNARD B. JACOBS THEATRE
FedEx

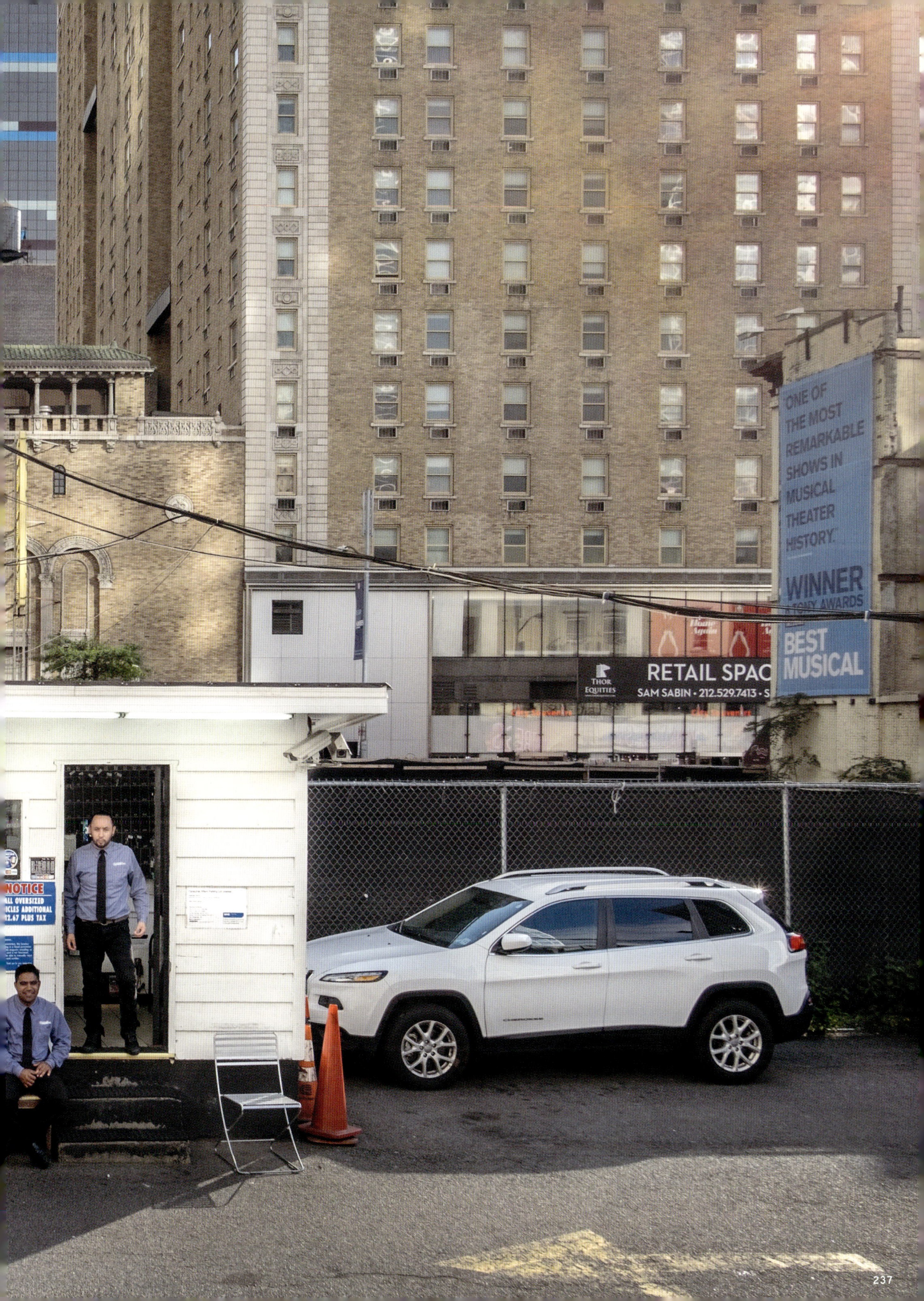
ONE OF
THE MOST
REMARKABLE
SHOWS IN
MUSICAL
THEATER
HISTORY."
WINNER
TONY AWARDS
BEST
MUSICAL
RETAIL SPAC
THOR
EQUITIES
SAM SABIN · 212.529.7413 · S
NOTICE
ALL OVERSIZED
CLES ADDITIONAL
2.67 PLUS TAX

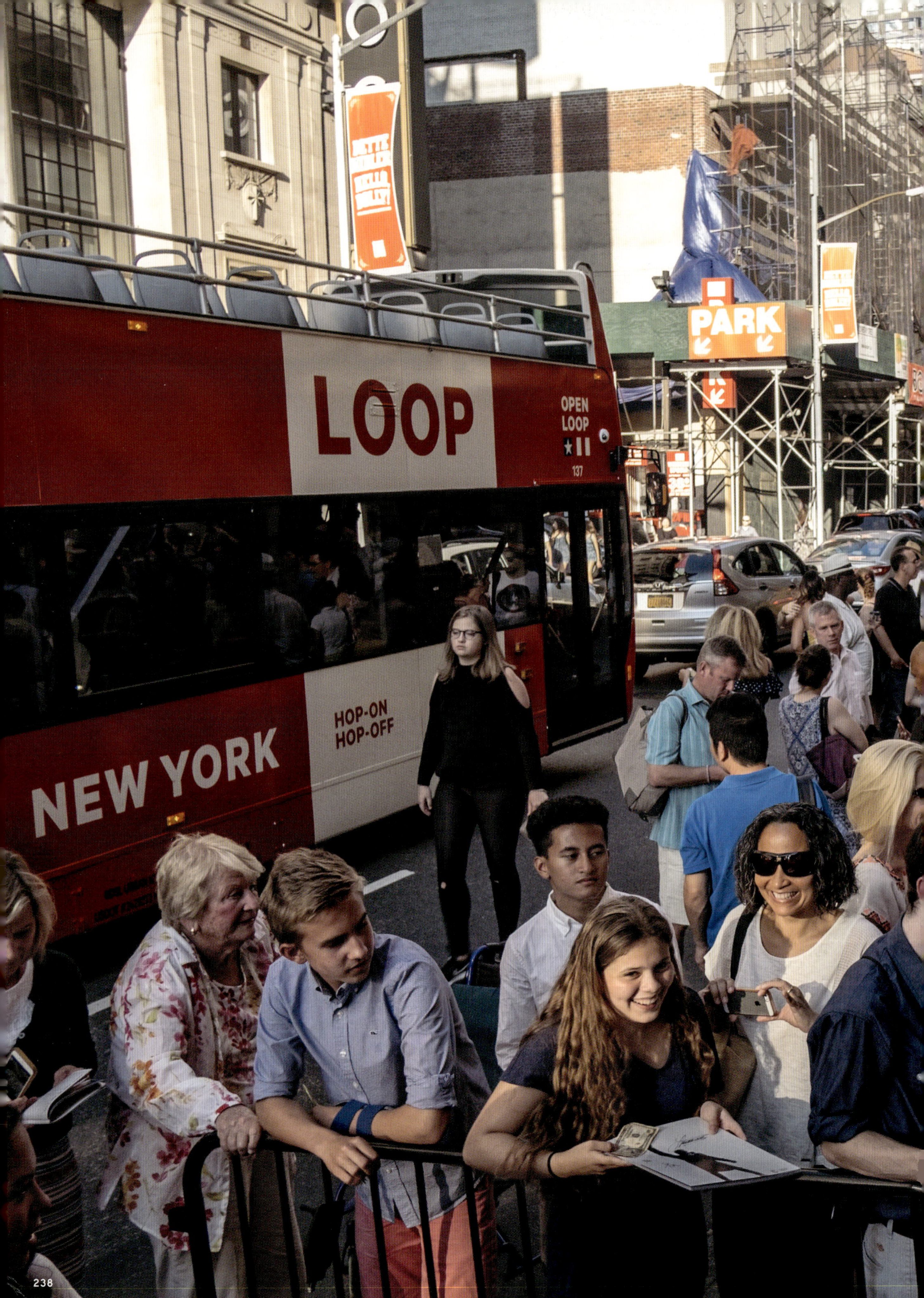

LOOP
OPEN LOOP
137
NEW YORK
HOP-ON HOP-OFF
PARK

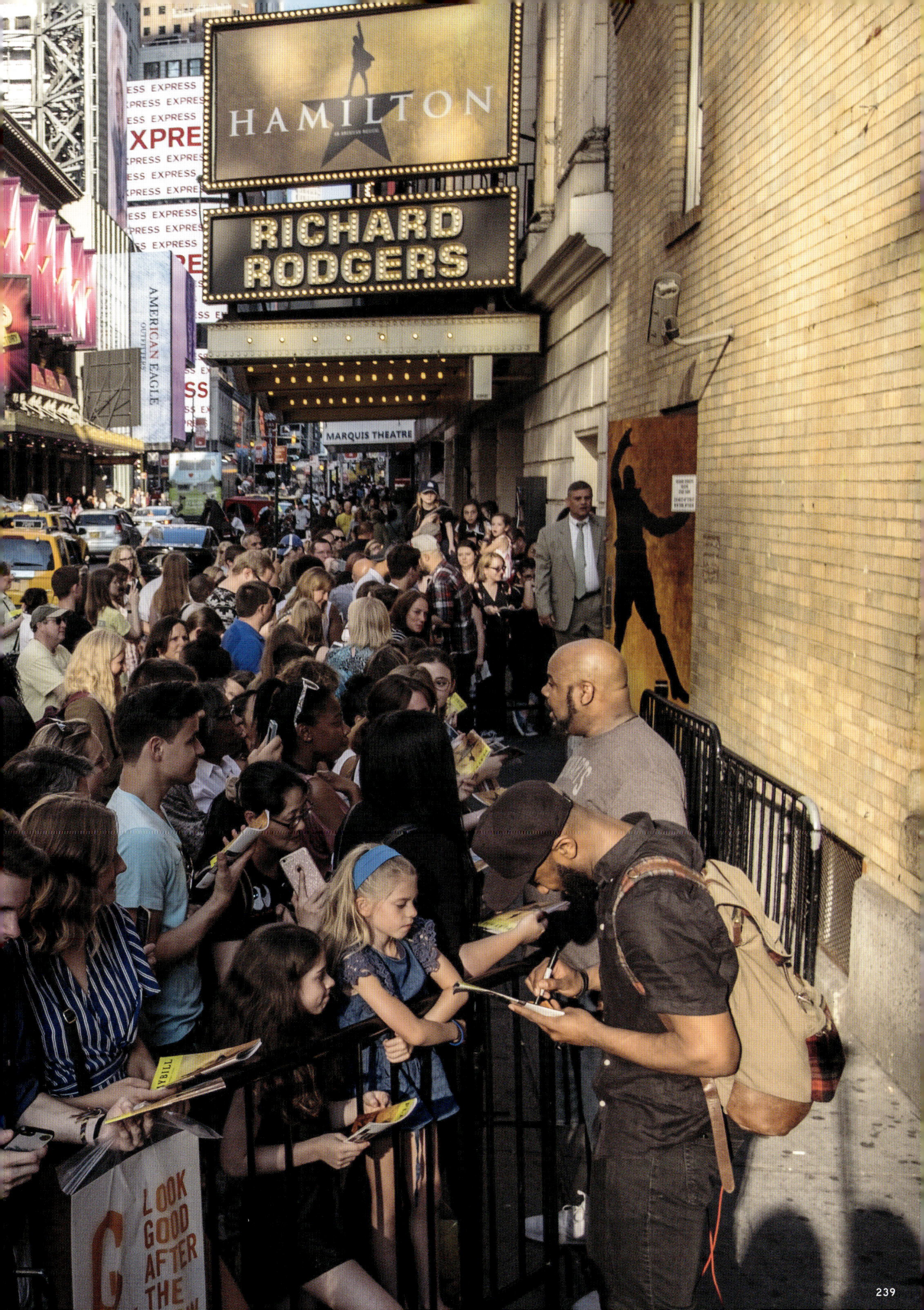
EXPRESS EXPRESS
XPRE EXPRESS
HAMILTON
AN AMERICAN MUSICAL
RICHARD RODGERS
AMERICAN EAGLE
OUTFITTERS
MARQUIS THEATRE
LOOK GOOD AFTER THE

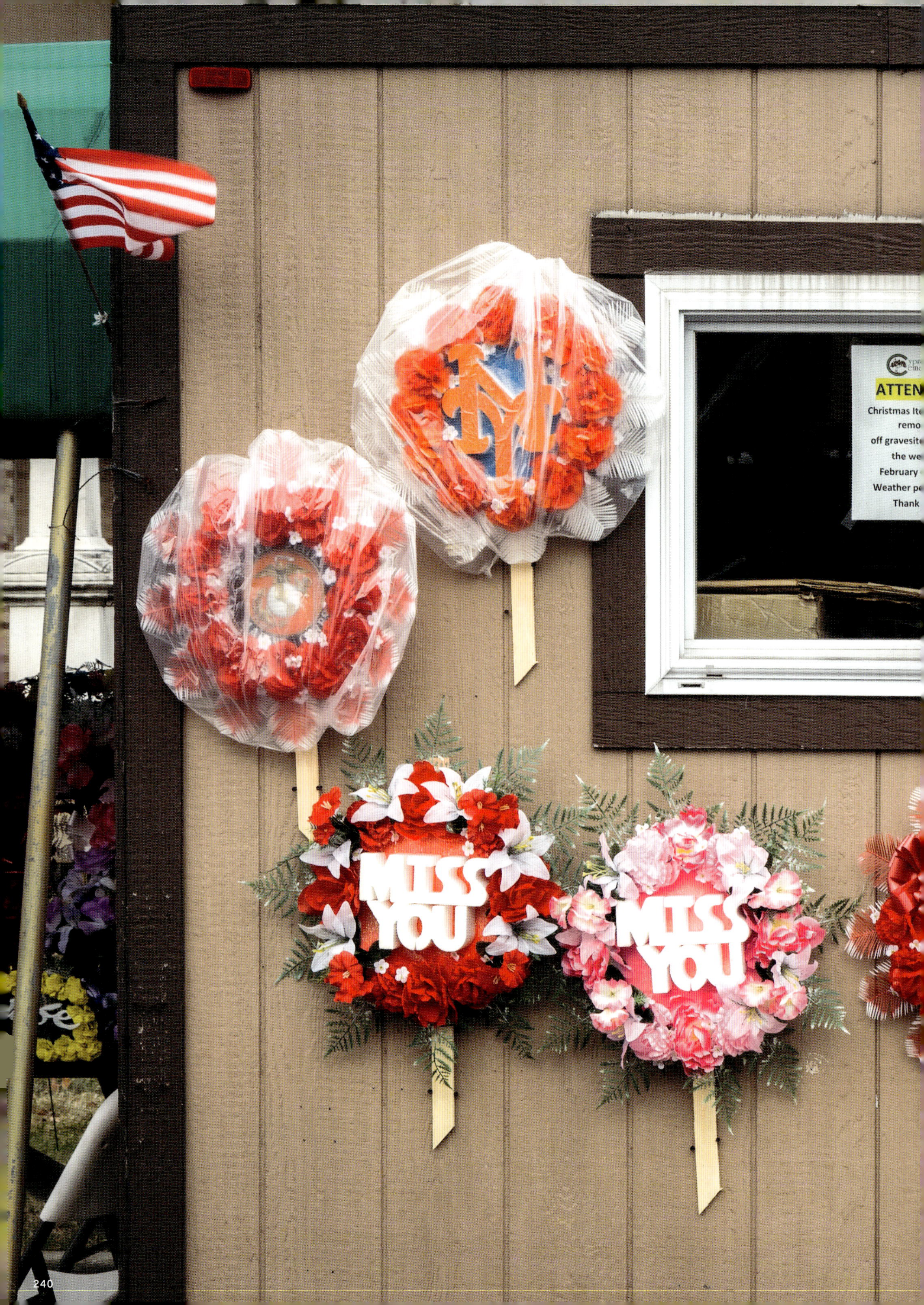
ATTEN
Christmas Ite
remo
off gravesite
the we
February
Weather pe
Thank
MISS
YOU
MISS
YOU

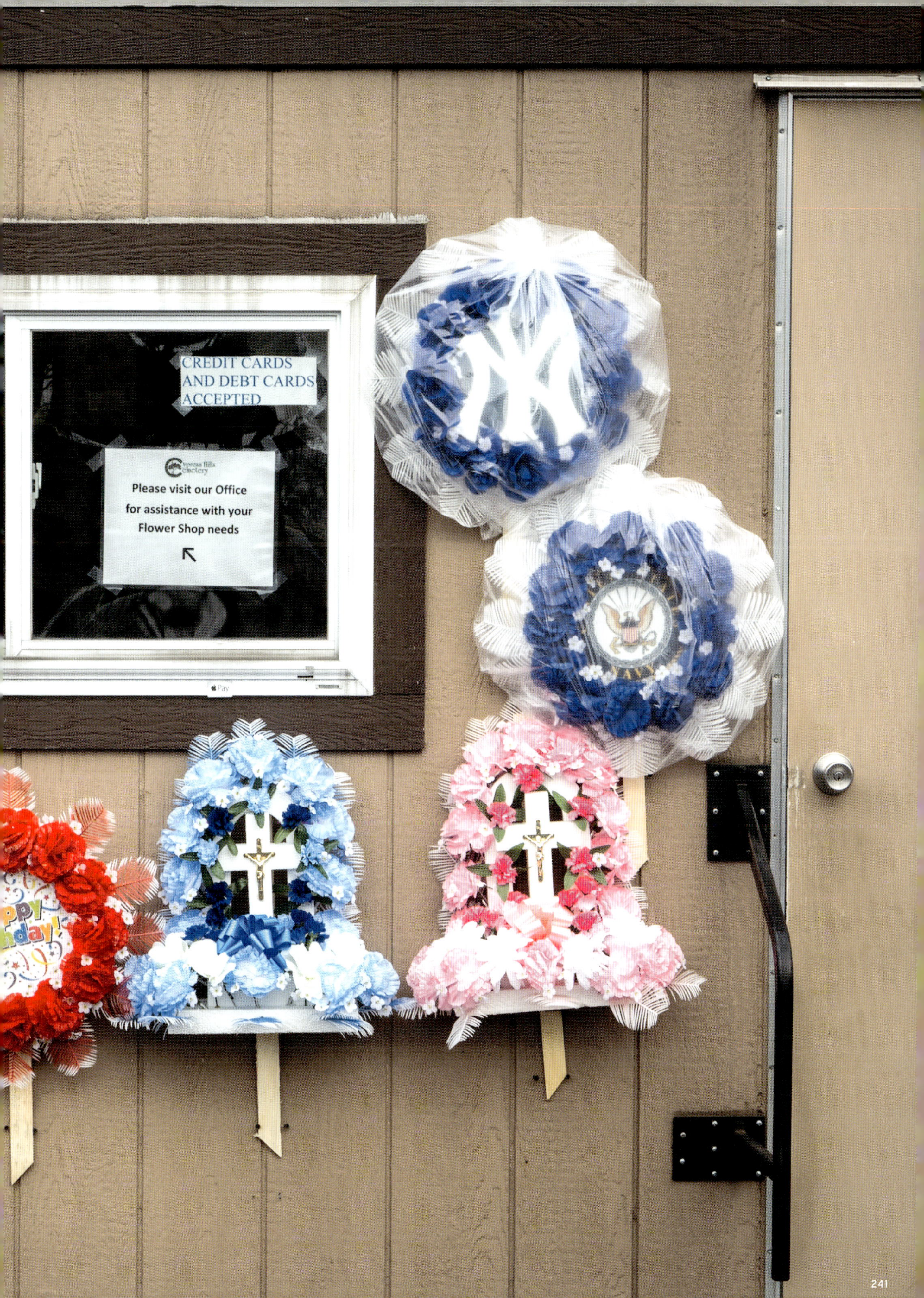

CREDIT CARDS
AND DEBT CARDS
ACCEPTED
Cypress Hills Cemetery
Please visit our Office
for assistance with your
Flower Shop needs
Pay

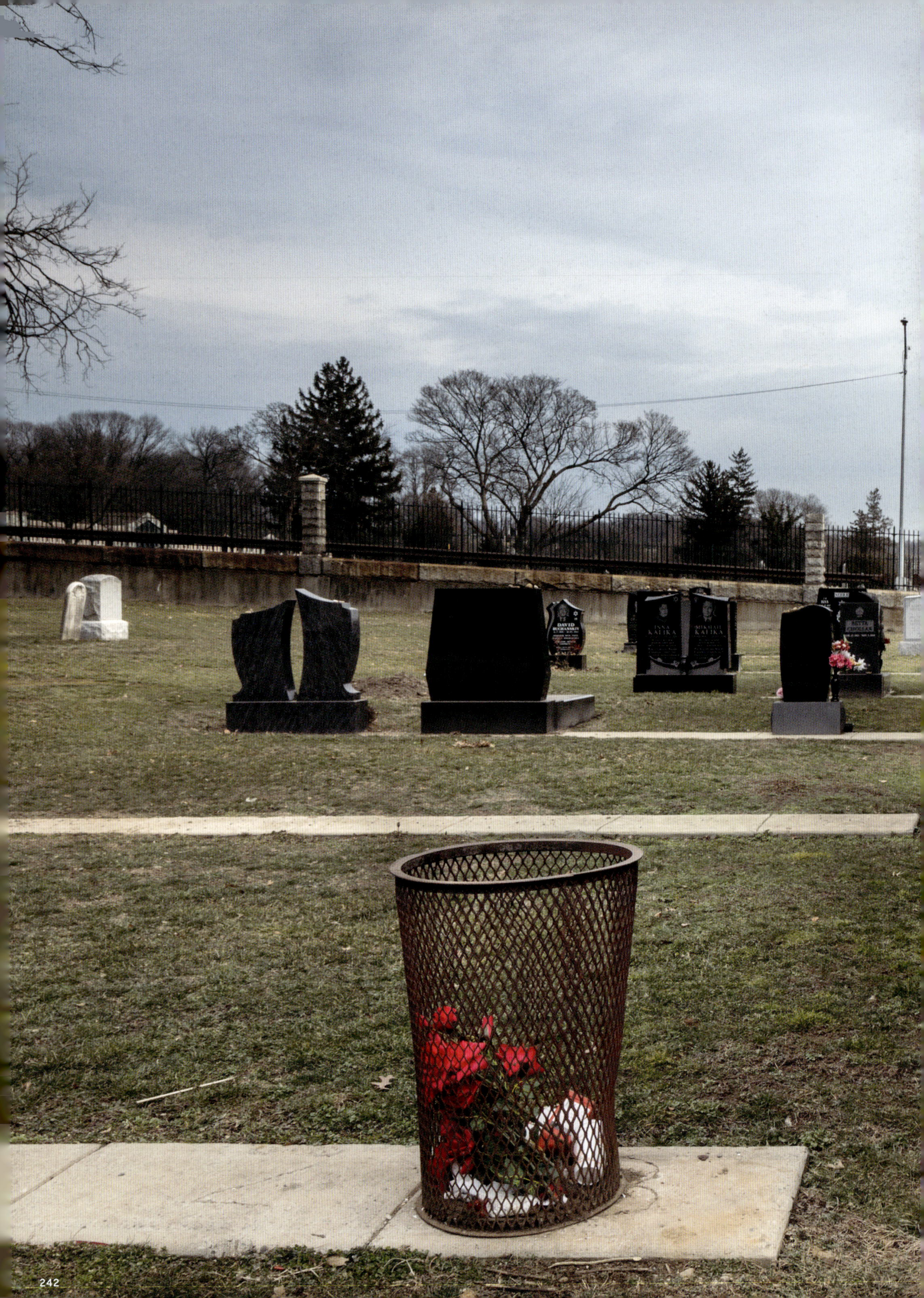

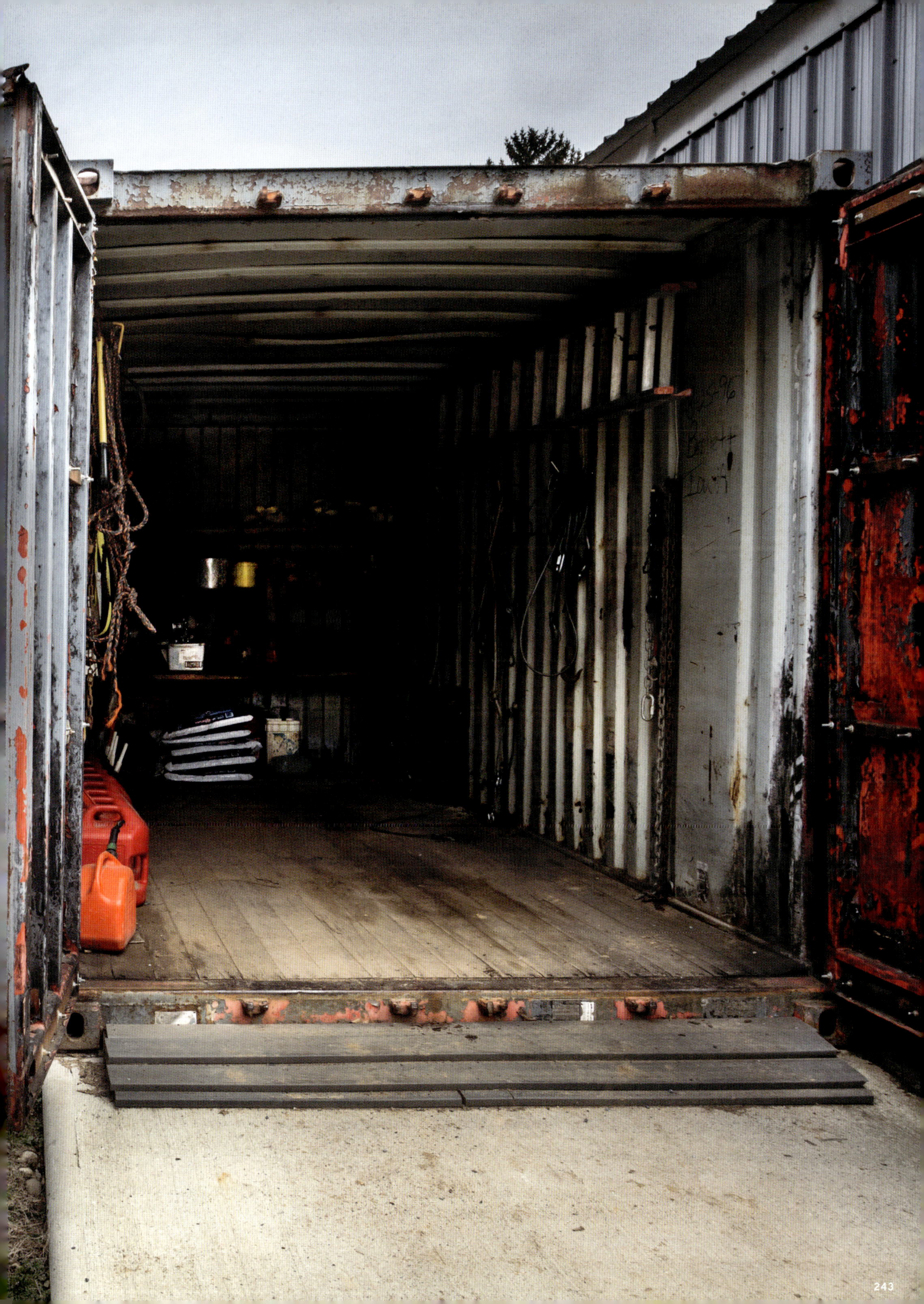

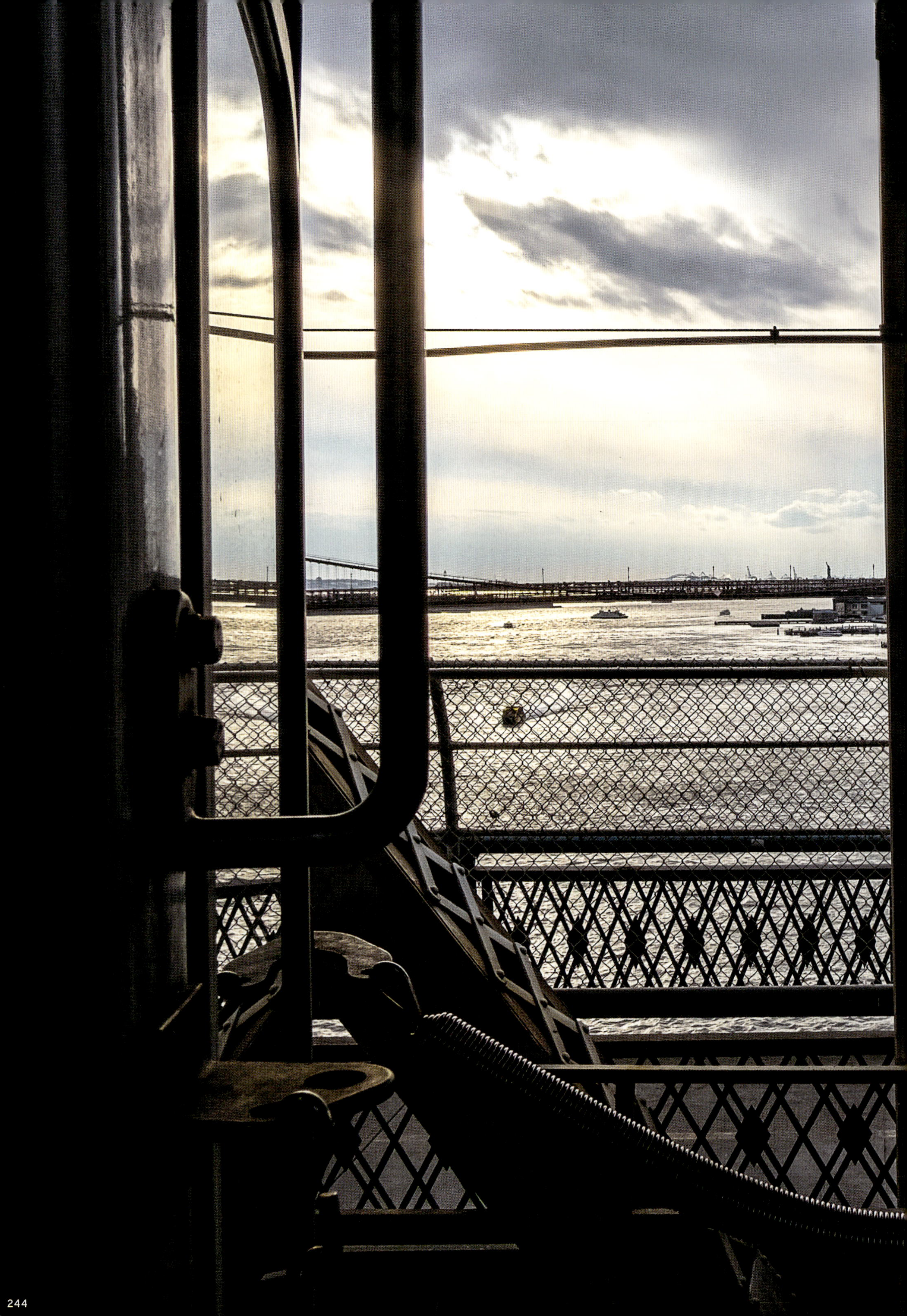

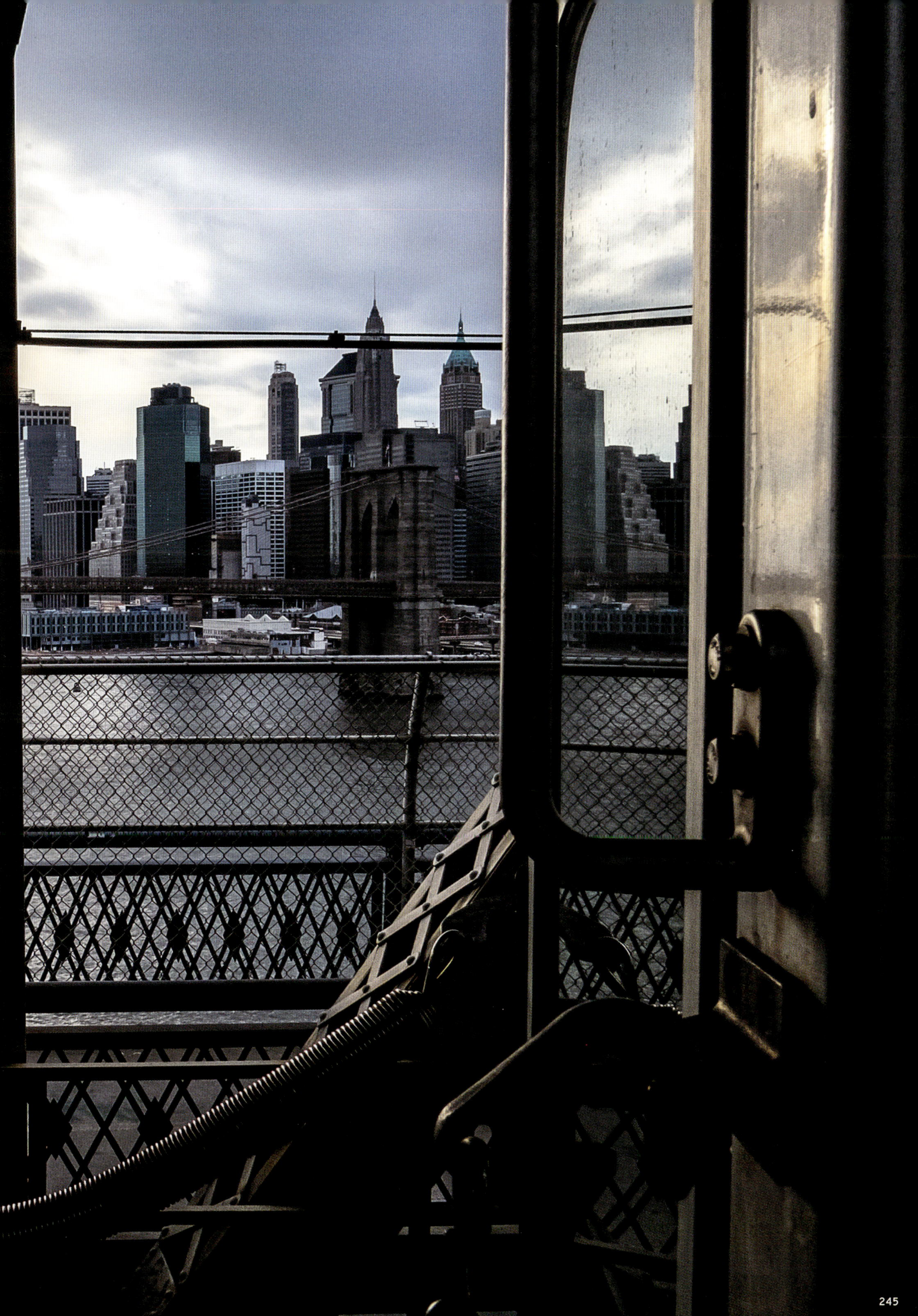

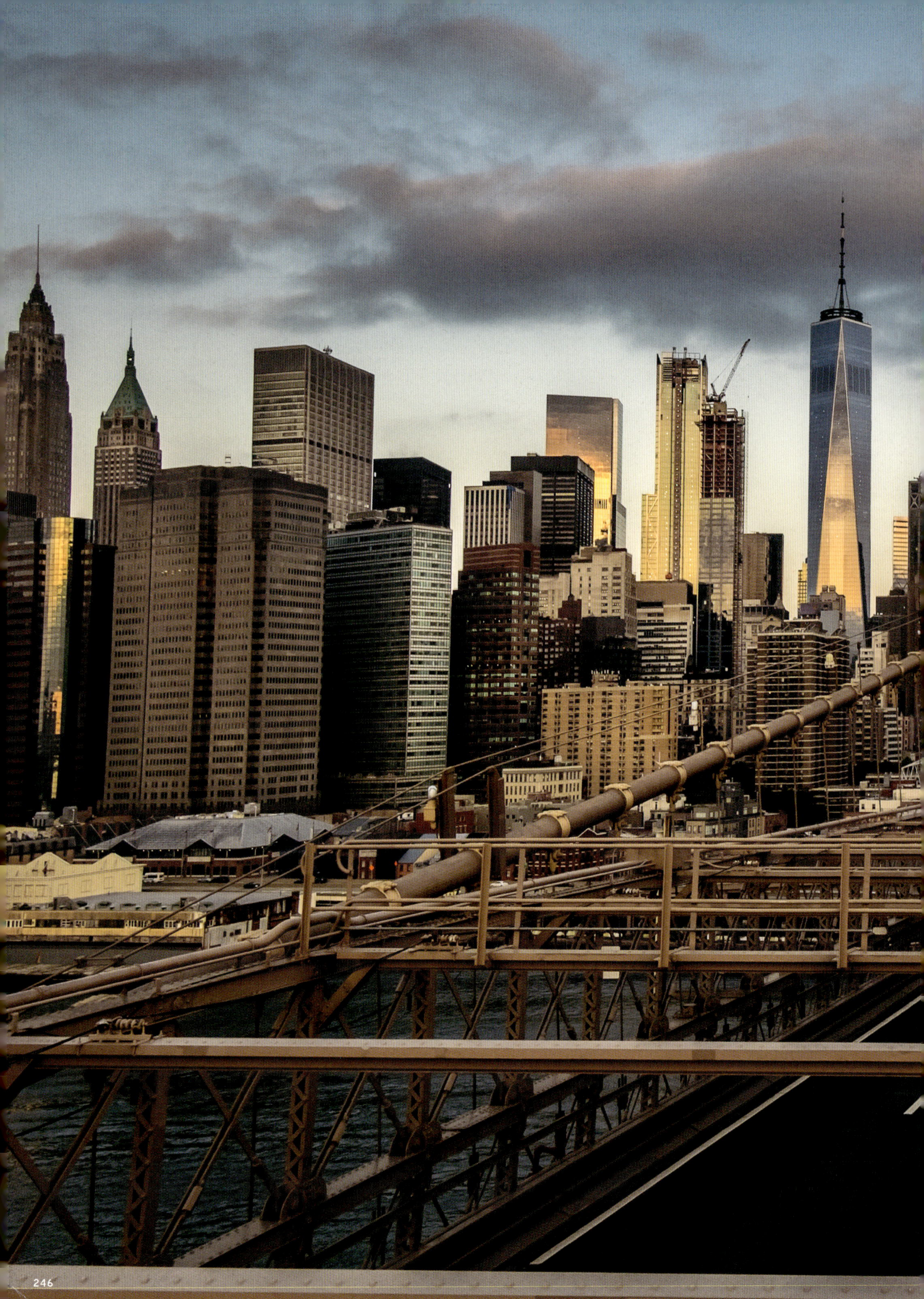

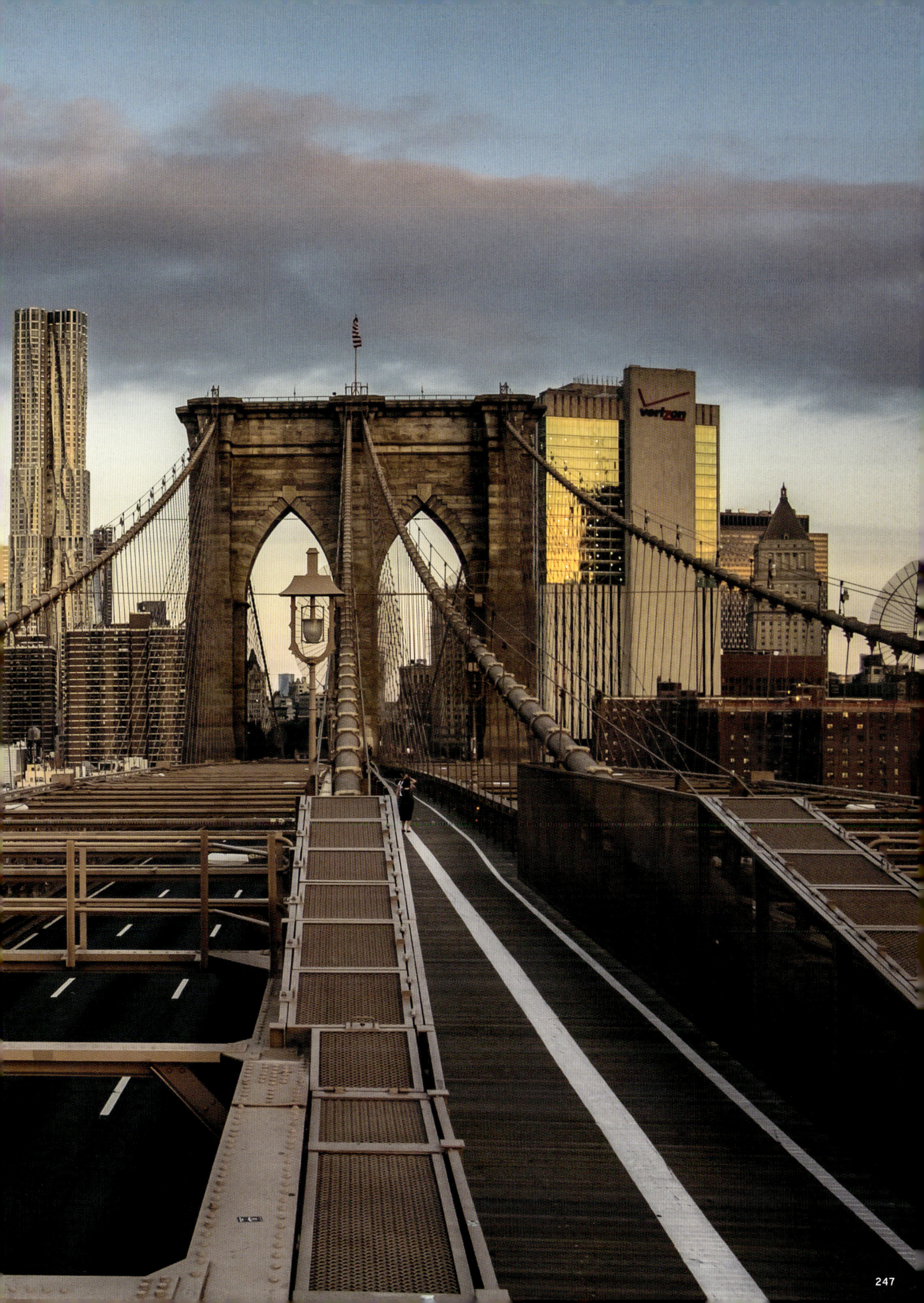

ABOUT THE PHOTOGRAPHER RICHARD KOEK

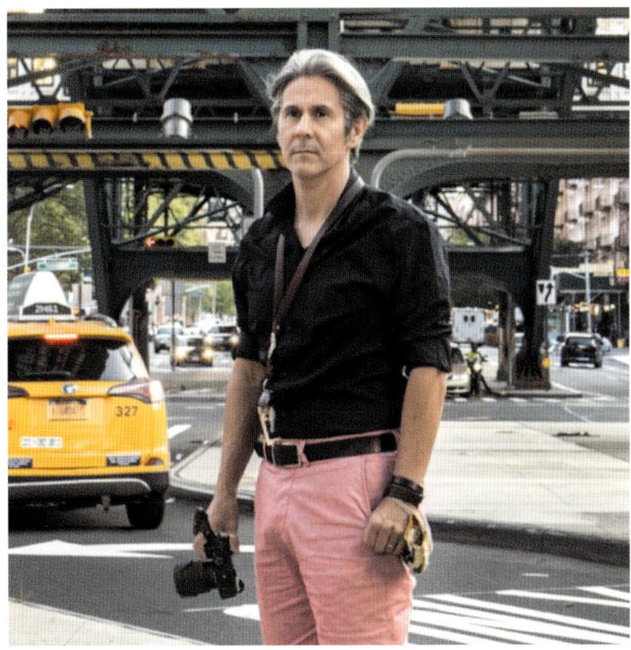

Dutch-American photographer Richard Koek is a visual storyteller. He shares his love of New York City and the people that live there by communicating with them through the lens. His sensibility for the complicated life in New York shows in his photographs, which are, rather than a decisive moment, an encouragement to viewers to form their own interpretation of his work. Every picture becomes a new narrative, unique to its beholder.

Born in the Netherlands and and raised by his Argentinean mother, Richard Koek (Amsterdam, 1965) decided to give up his profession as a tax lawyer to pursue his passion for photography in New York City. His work has featured in renowned titles including Interview Magazine, Stern, The New York Times, The New Yorker and The New York Review of Books. NEW YORK NEW YORK is his first monograph. Richard Koek lives in New York and Amsterdam, working for various publications, companies and non-profit organizations.

@richardkoek
richardkoek.com
info@richardkoek.com

INDEX

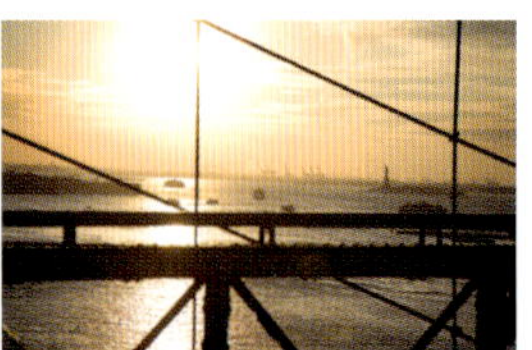

BROOKLYN BRIDGE
Page 1

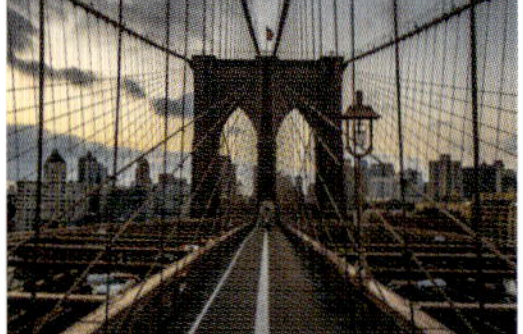

BROOKLYN BRIDGE
Page 2-3

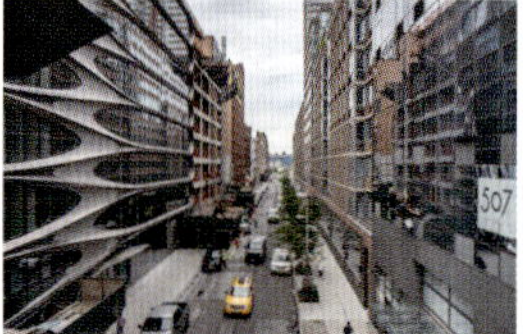

WEST 28TH STREET
Manhattan
Page 6-7

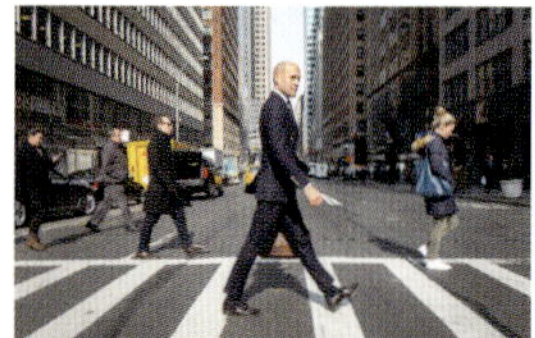

MADISON AVENUE
Manhattan
Page 8-9

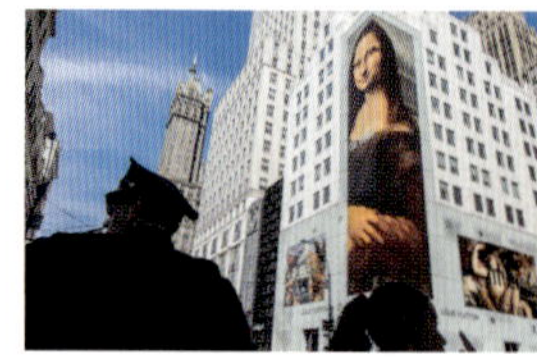

5TH AVENUE
Manhattan
Page 10-11

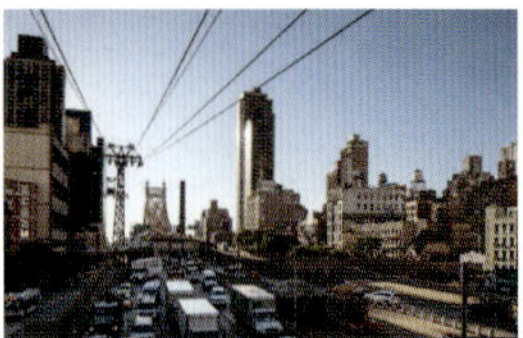

ED KOCH QUEENSBORO BRIDGE
EAST 60TH STREET
Manhattan
Page 12-13

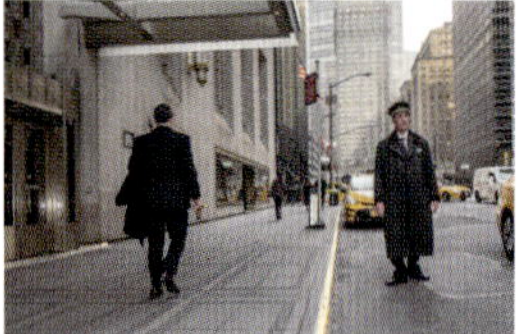

WALDORF ASTORIA
PARK AVENUE
Manhattan
Page 14-15

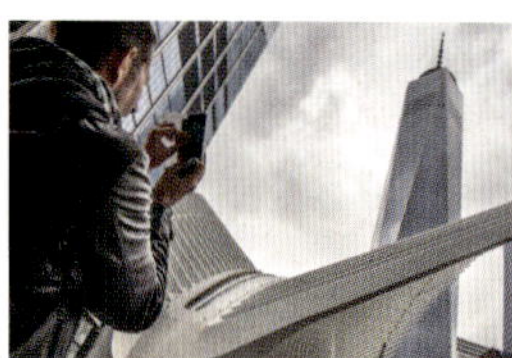

OCULUS, WORLD TRADE CENTER CHURCH
STREET
Manhattan
Page 16-17

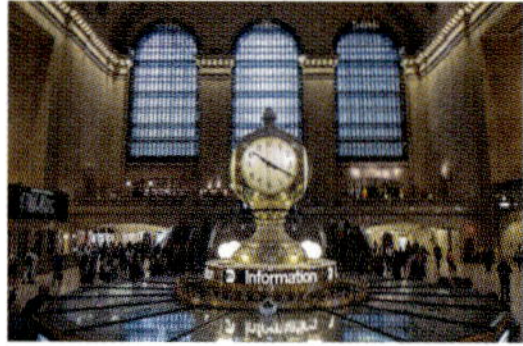

GRAND CENTRAL TERMINAL
Manhattan
Page 18-19

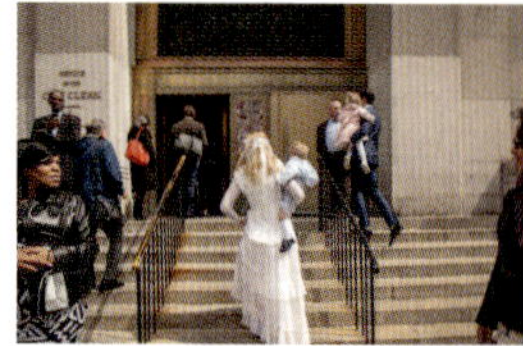

CITY CLERK'S OFFICE
WORTH STREET
Manhattan
Page 20-21

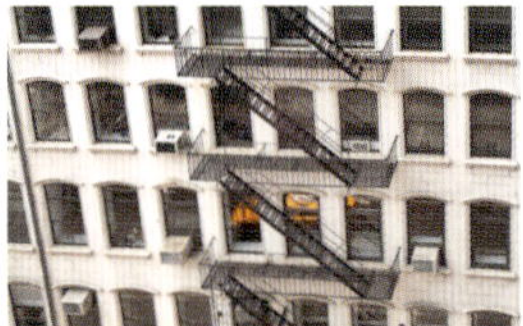

BROADWAY
Manhattan
Page 22-23

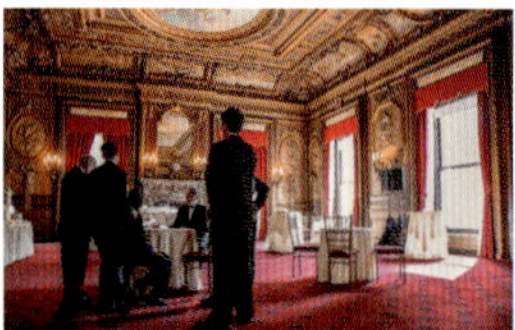

THE PIERRE
EAST 61TH STREET
Manhattan
Page 24-25

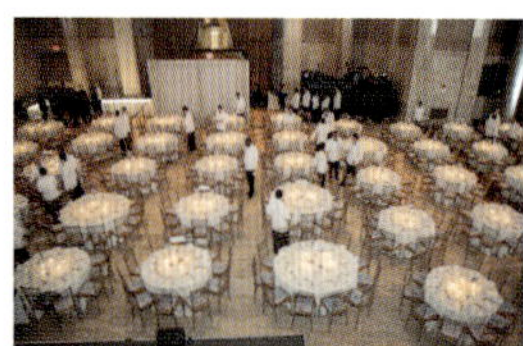

CIPRIANI
WALL STREET
Manhattan
Page 26-27

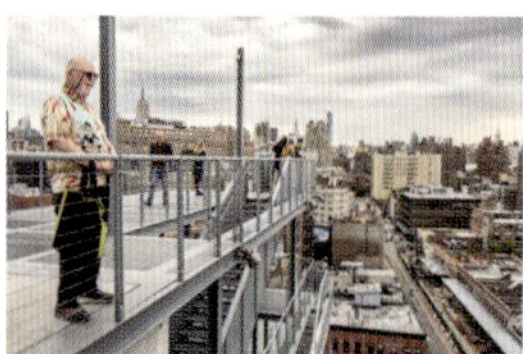

WHITNEY MUSEUM OF AMERICAN ART GANSE-
VOORT STREET
Manhattan
Page 28-29

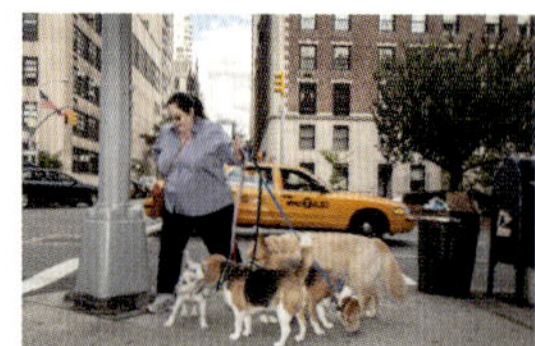

PARK AVENUE
Manhattan
Page 30-31

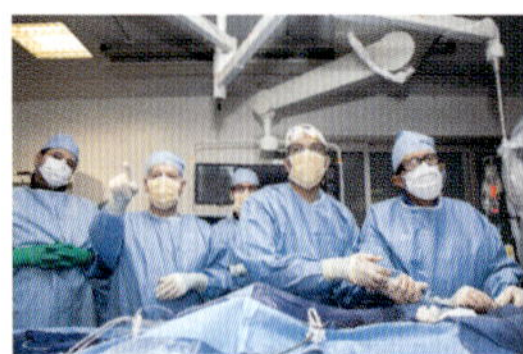

NEWYORK-PRESBYTERIAN/COLUMBIAUNI-
VERSITY MEDICAL CENTER
WEST 168TH STREET
Manhattan
Page 32-33

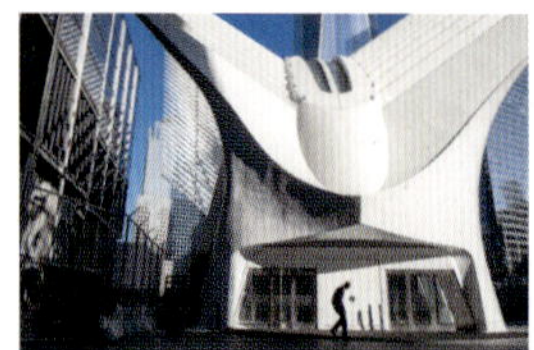

OCULUS, CHURCH STREET
Manhattan
Page 34-35

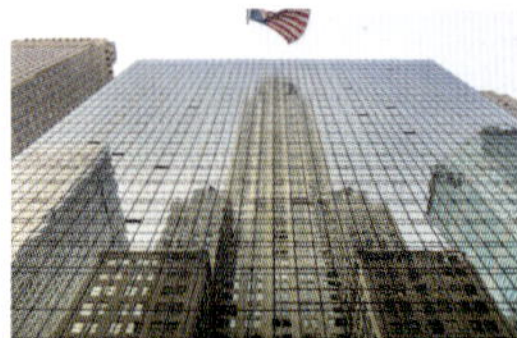

LEXINGTON AVENUE
Manhattan
Page 36-37

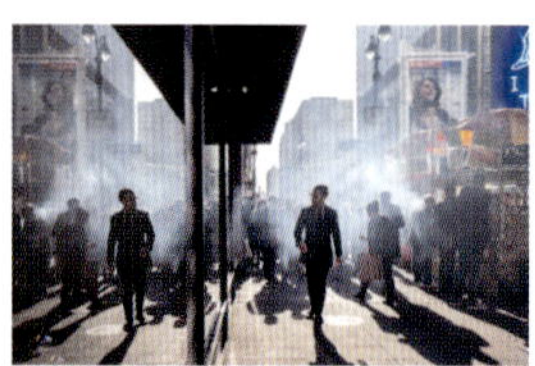

7TH AVENUE
Manhattan
Page 38-39

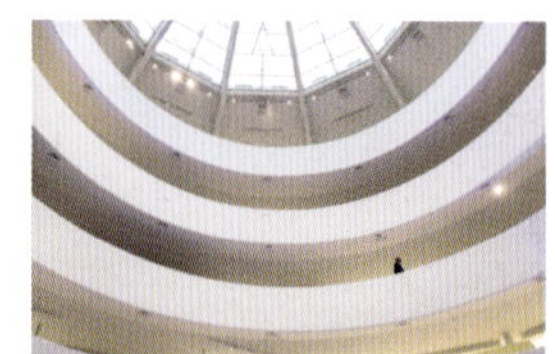

SOLOMON R. GUGGENHEIM MUSEUM
5TH AVENUE
Manhattan
Page 40-41

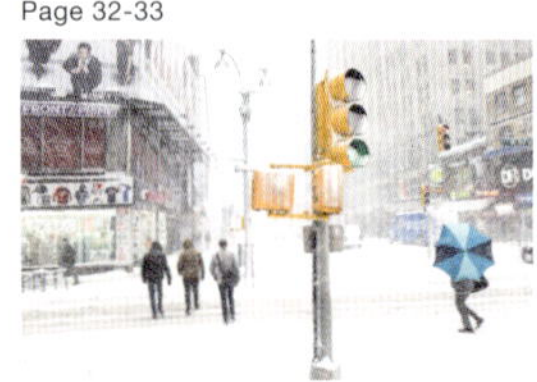

BROADWAY AND WEST 50TH STREET
Manhattan
Page 42-43

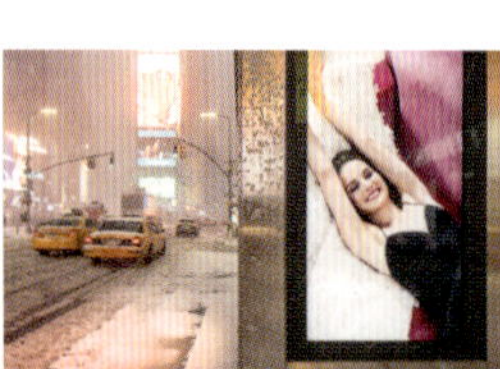

7TH AVENUE
Manhattan
Page 44-45

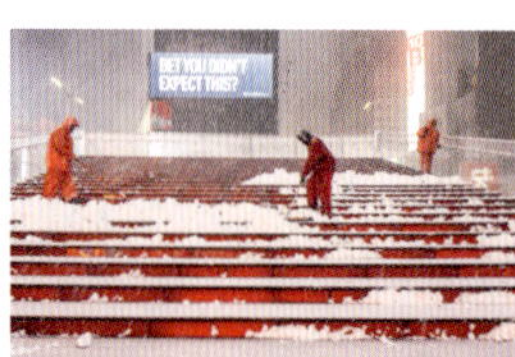

TIMES SQUARE
Manhattan
Page 46-47

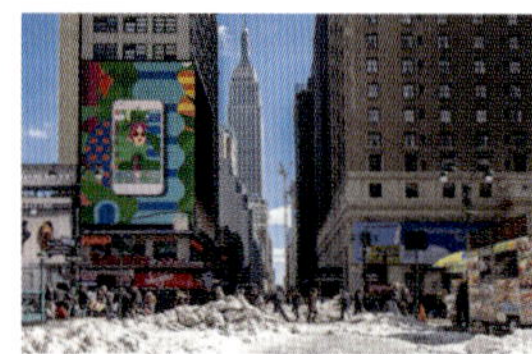

EMPIRE STATE BUILDING
WEST 33RD STREET
Manhattan
Page 48-49

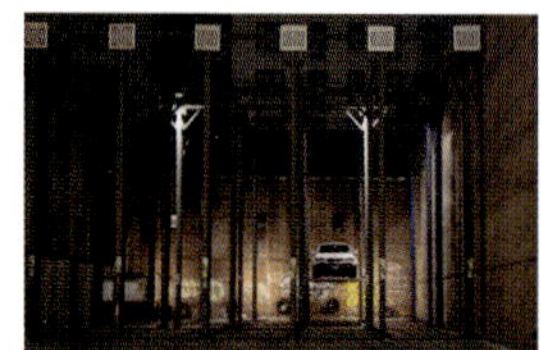

WEST 46TH STREET
Manhattan
Page 50-51

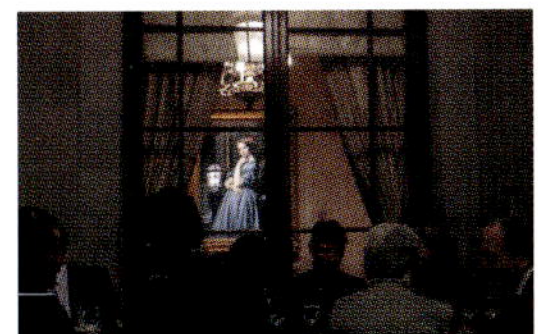

THE FRICK COLLECTION
EAST 70TH STREET
Manhattan
Page 52-53

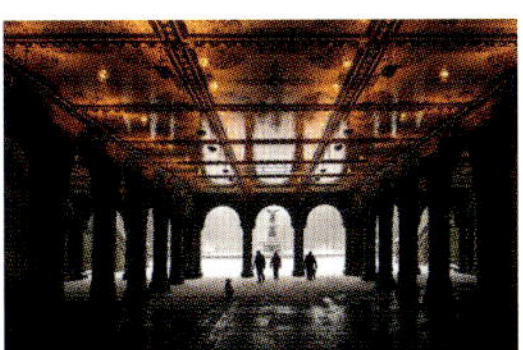

BETHESDA TERRACE ARCADE
CENTRAL PARK
Manhattan
Page 54-55

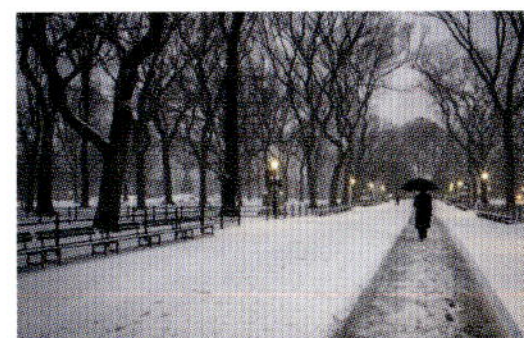

CENTRAL PARK
Manhattan
Page 56-57

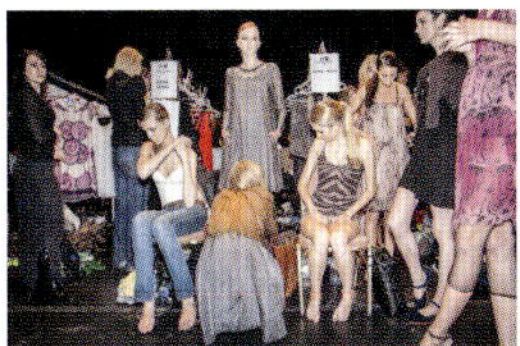

MANHATTAN CENTER
WEST 34TH STREET
Manhattan
Page 58-59

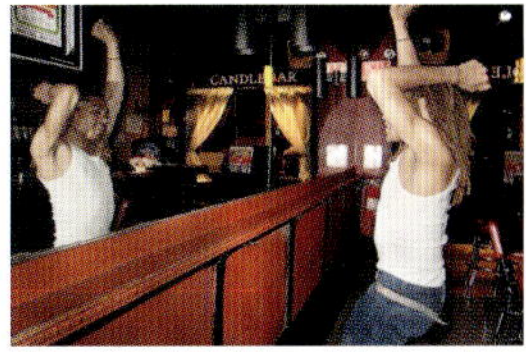

CANDLE BAR
AMSTERDAM AVENUE
Manhattan
Page 60-61

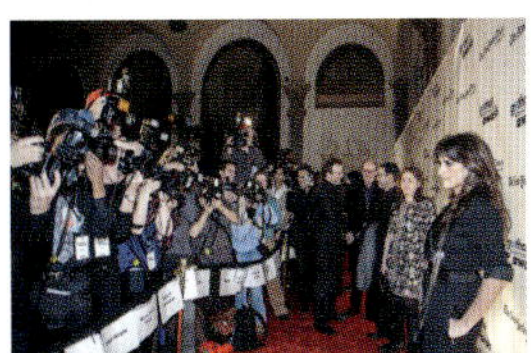

GOTHAM AWARDS. CIPRIANI
WALL STREET
Manhattan
Page 62-63

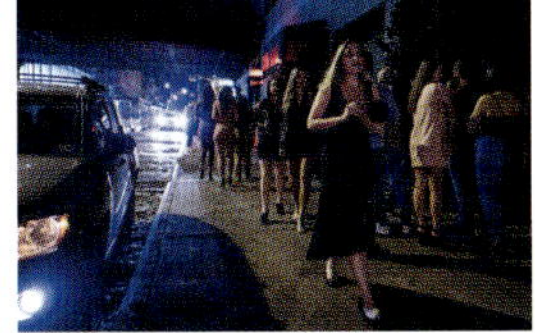

WEST 13TH STREET
Manhattan
Page 64-65

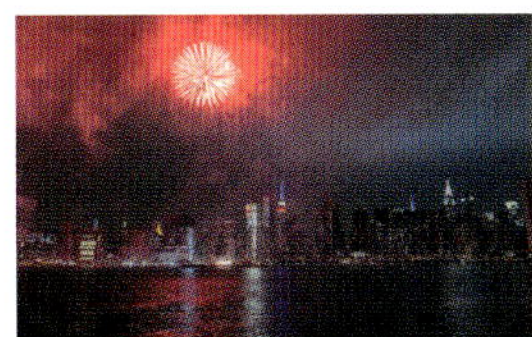

EAST RIVER
Page 66-67

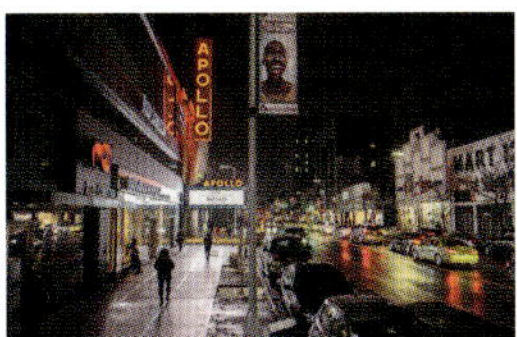

WEST 125TH STREET
Manhattan
Page 68-69

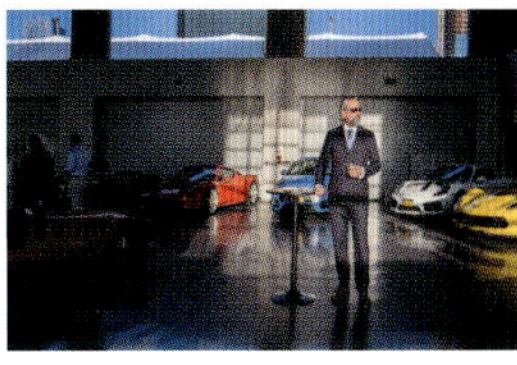

CLASSIC CAR CLUB MANHATTAN
PIER 76. 12TH AVENUE
Manhattan
Page 70-71

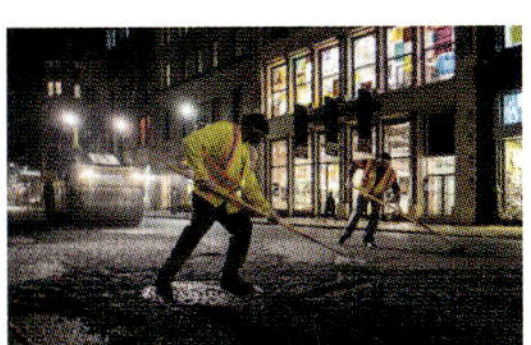

BROADWAY
Manhattan
Page 72-73

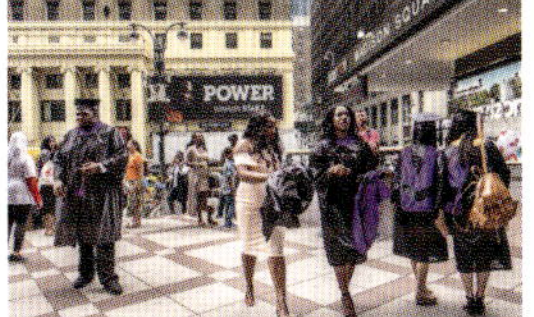

MADISON SQUARE GARDEN
7TH AVENUE
Manhattan
Page 74-75

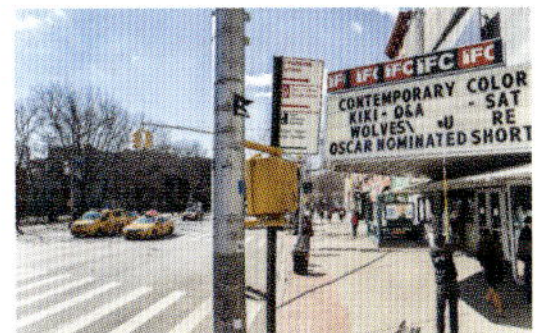

IFC CENTER. 6TH AVENUE
Manhattan
Page 76-77

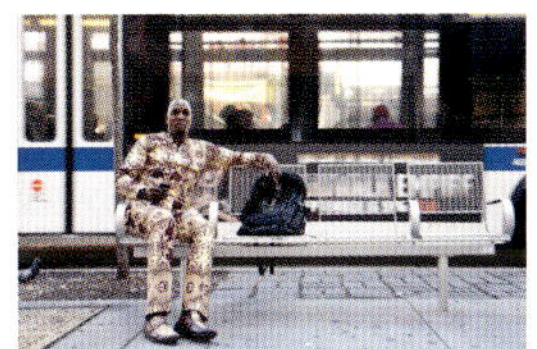

FULTON STREET
Brooklyn
Page78-79

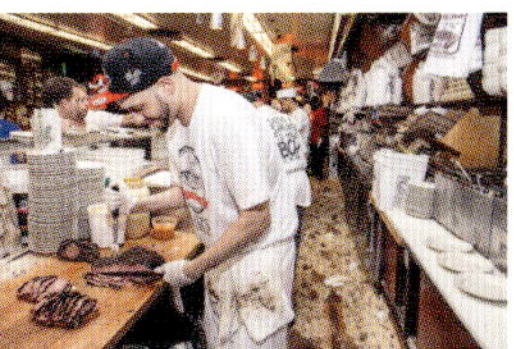

KATZ'S DELICATESSEN
EAST HOUSTON STREET
Manhattan
Page 80-81

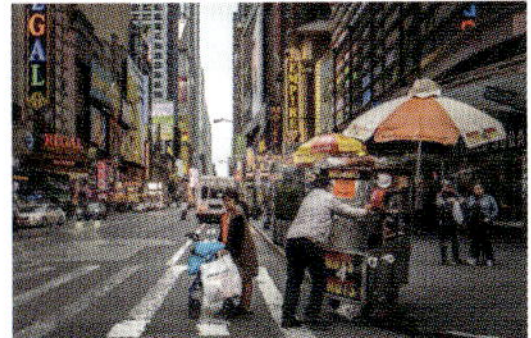

WEST 42ND STREET
Manhattan
Page 82-83

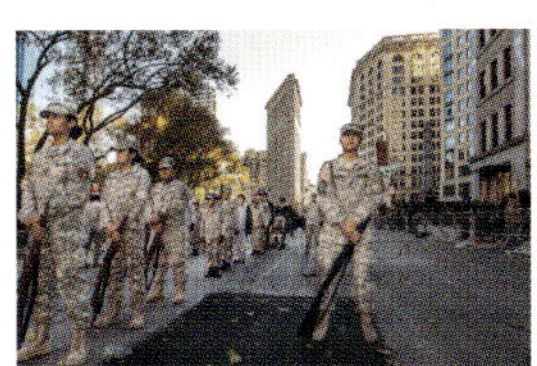

FLATIRON BUILDING
5TH AVENUE
Manhattan
Page 84-85

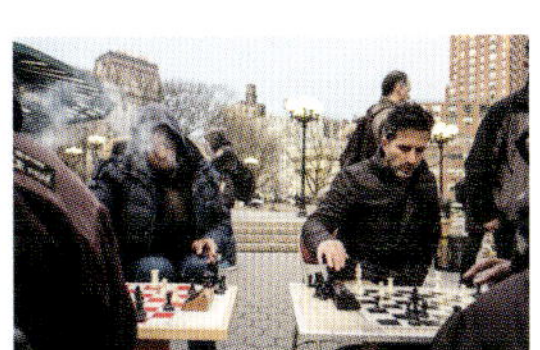

UNION SQUARE
Manhattan
Page 86-87

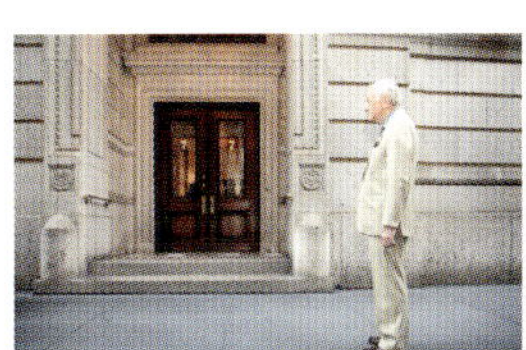

CENTURY ASSOCIATION CLUBHOUSE WEST
43RD STREET
Manhattan
Page 88-89

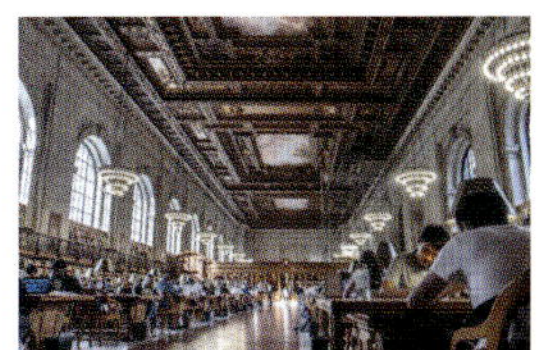

STEPHEN A. SCHWARZMAN BUILDING
NEW YORK PUBLIC LIBRARY, 5TH AVENUE
Manhattan
Page 90-91

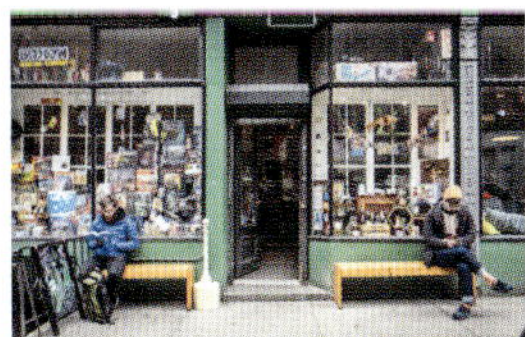

THE UNCOMMONS
THOMPSON STREET
Manhattan
Page 92-93

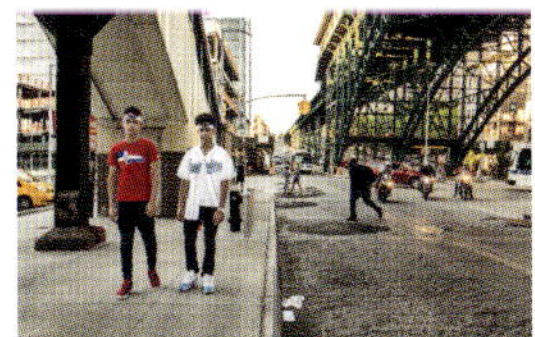

BROADWAY
Manhattan
Page 94-95

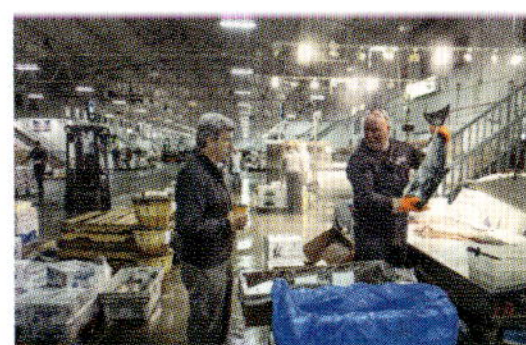

NEW FULTON FISH MARKET
FOOD CENTER DRIVE
Bronx
Page 96-97

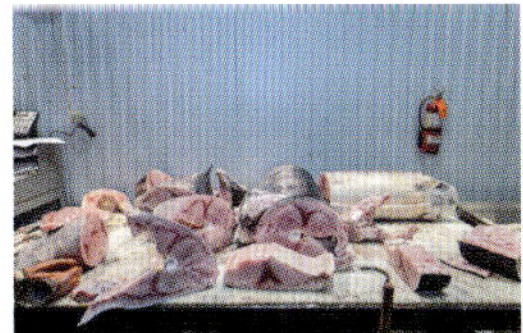

NEW FULTON FISH MARKET
FOOD CENTER DRIVE
Bronx
Page 98-99

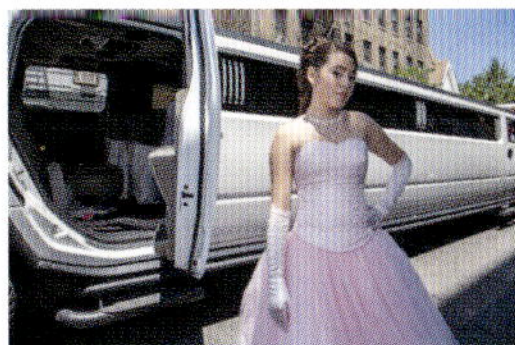

MARBLE HILL AVENUE
Bronx
Page 100-101

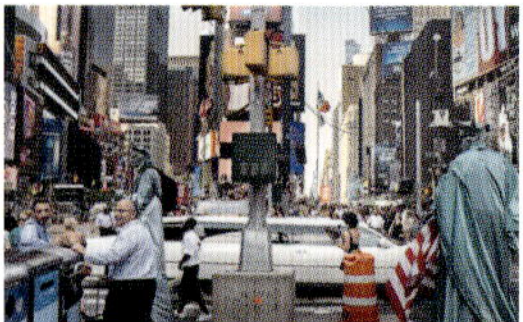

TIMES SQUARE
Manhattan
Page 102-103

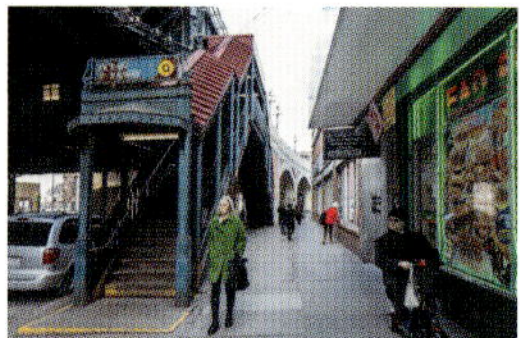

OCEAN PARKWAY
Brooklyn
Page 104-105

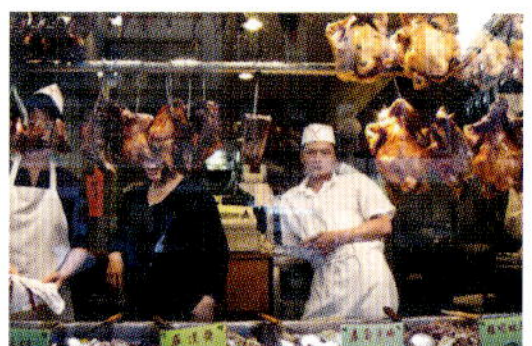

GRAND STREET
Manhattan
Page 106-107

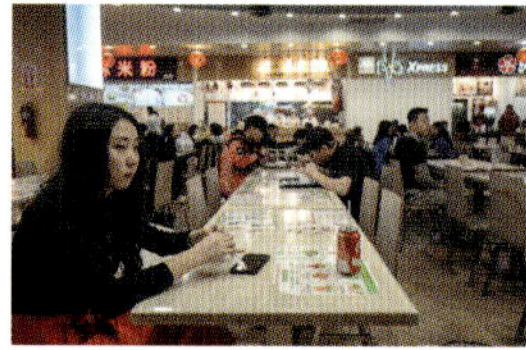

NEW WORLD MALL
ROOSEVELT AVENUE
Queens
Page 108-109

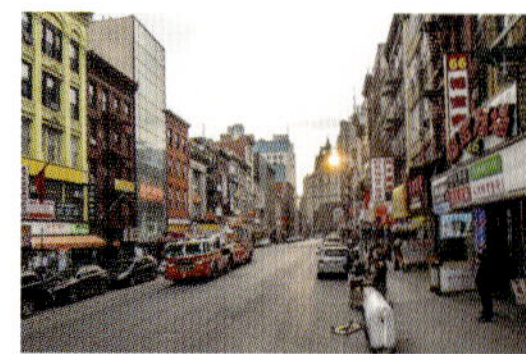

EAST BROADWAY
Manhattan
Page 110-111

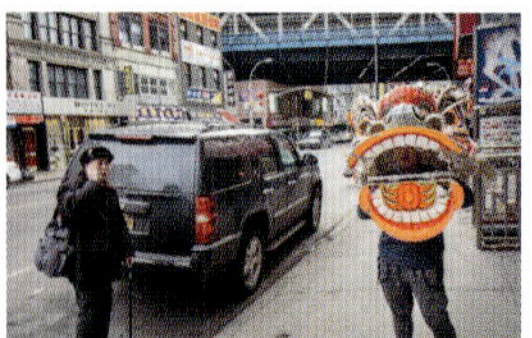

EAST BROADWAY
Manhattan
Page 112-113

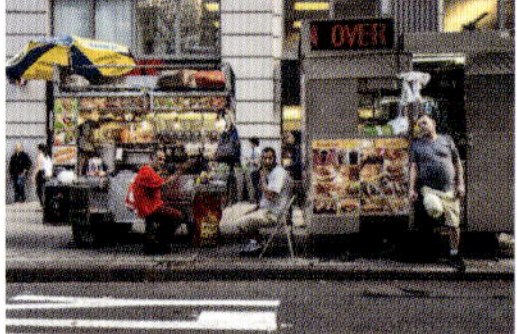

WEST 34TH STREET
Manhattan
Page 114-115

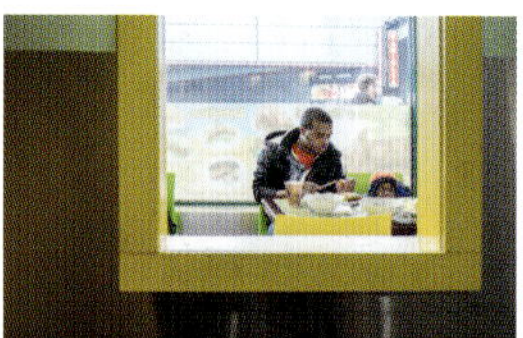

LA ABUNDANCIA
ROOSEVELT AVENUE
Queens
Page 116-117

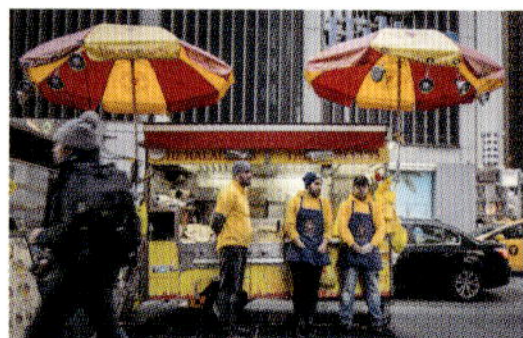

WEST 53RD STREET
Manhattan
Page 118-119

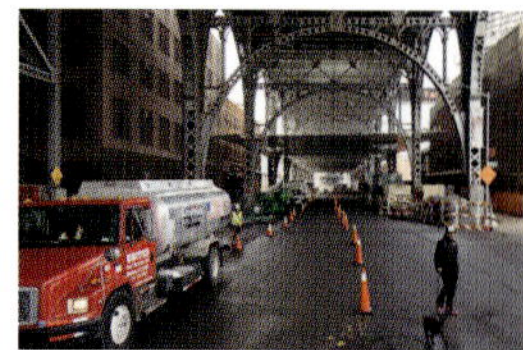

12TH AVENUE AND
WEST 134TH STREET
Manhattan
Page 120-121

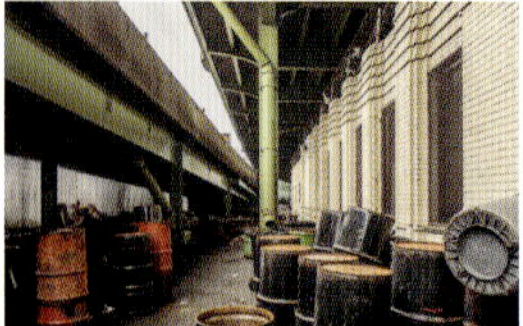

WEST 135TH STREET
Manhattan
Page 122-123

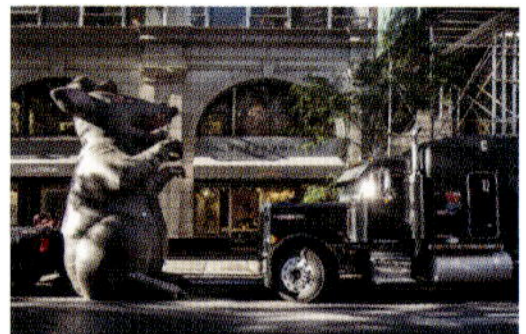

EAST 58TH STREET
Manhattan
Page 124-125

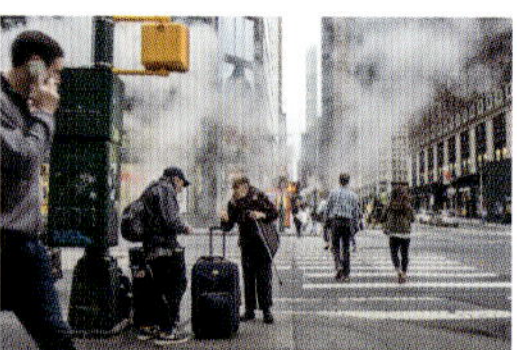

WEST 57TH STREET AND 8TH AVENUE
Manhatten
Page 126-127

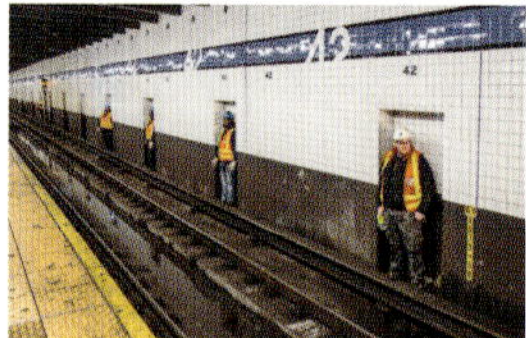

42ND STREET STATION, 8TH AVENUE
Manhatten
Page 128-129

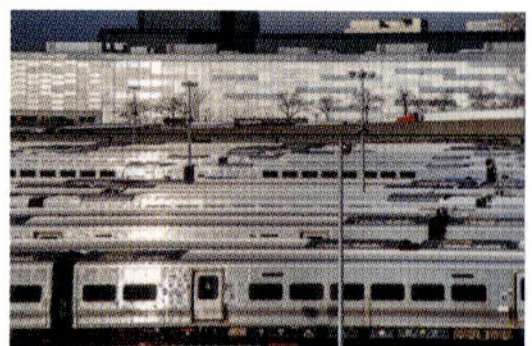

JACOB K. JAVITS CONVENTION CENTER WEST
30TH STREET
Manhattan
Page 130-131

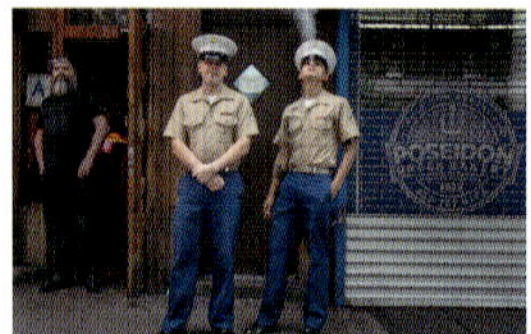

9TH AVENUE
Manhattan
Page 132-133

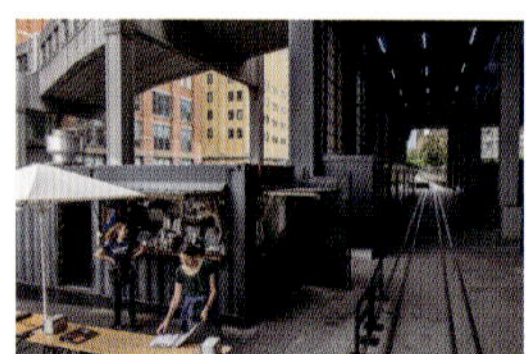

HIGH LINE
Manhattan
Page 134-135

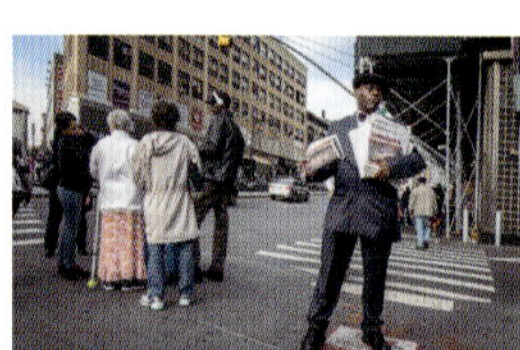

3RD AVENUE AND EAST 149TH STREET
Bronx
Page 136-137

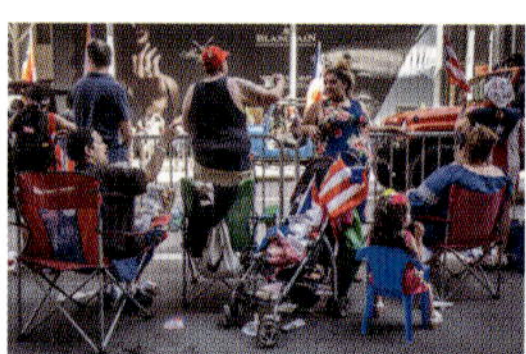

5TH AVENUE
Manhattan
Page 138-139

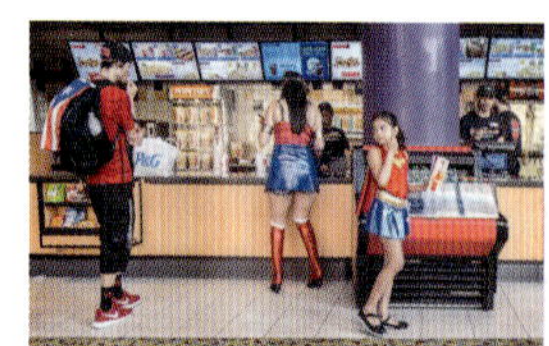

AMC EMPIRE 25
WEST 42ND STREET
Manhattan
Page 140-141

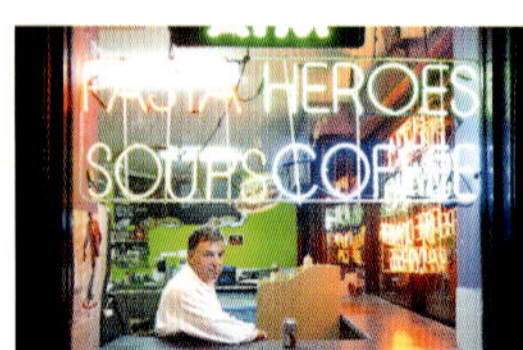

3RD AVENUE
Manhattan
Page 142-143

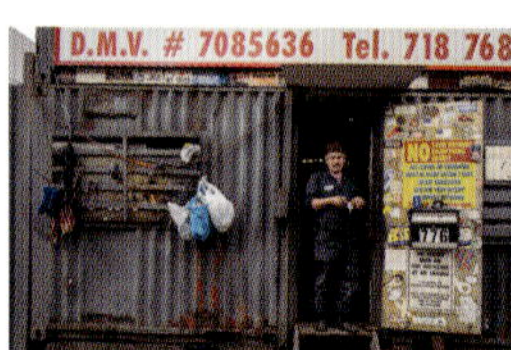

3RD AVENUE
Brooklyn
Page 144-145

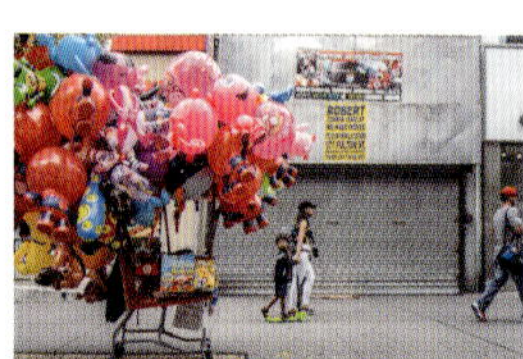

FULTON STREET
Brooklyn
Page 146-147

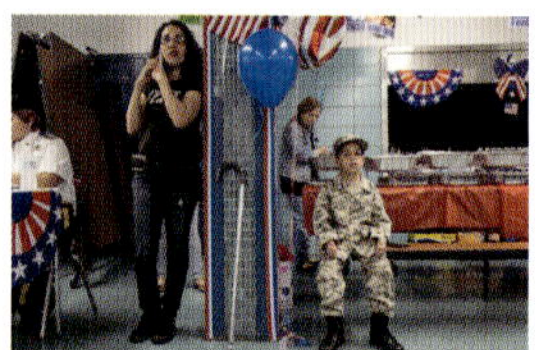

NEW YORK GRENADIERS CADET CORP
INTERMEDIATE SCHOOL 349
STARR STREET
Brooklyn
Page 148-149

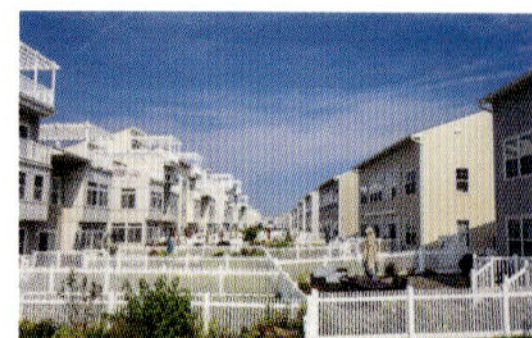

BEACH 67TH STREET
Queens
Page 150-151

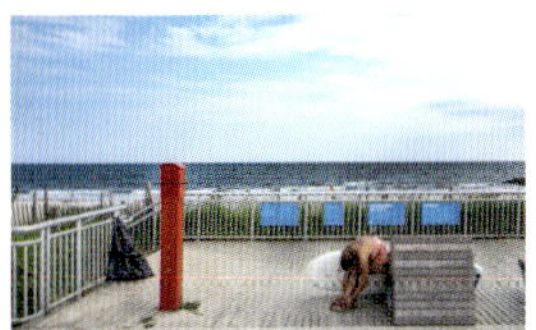

BOARDWALK
ROCKAWAY BEACH
Queens
Page 152-153

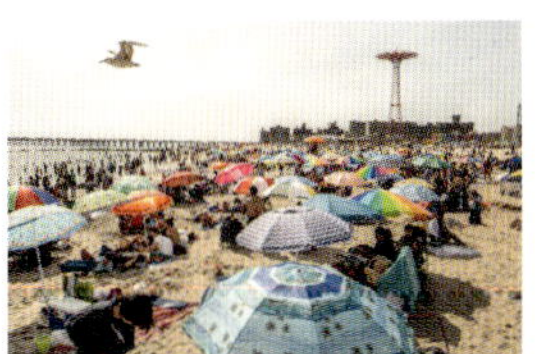

CONEY ISLAND BEACH
Brooklyn
Page 154-155

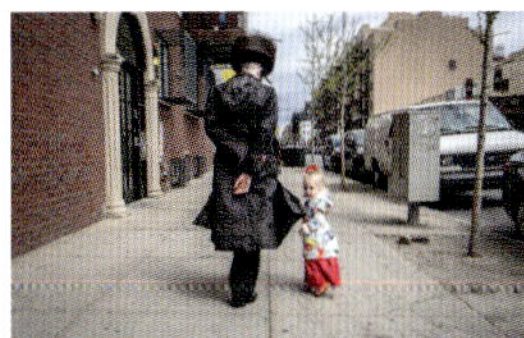

WALLABOUT STREET
Brooklyn
Page 156-157

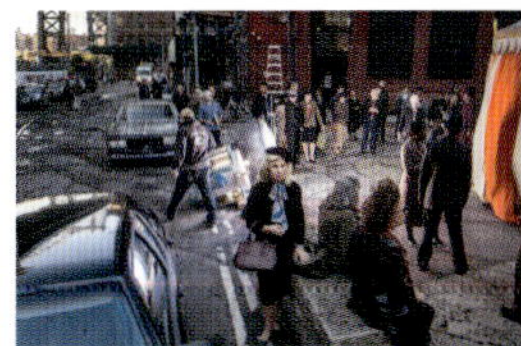

PEARL STREET, SET OF GOTHAM
Brooklyn
Page 158-159

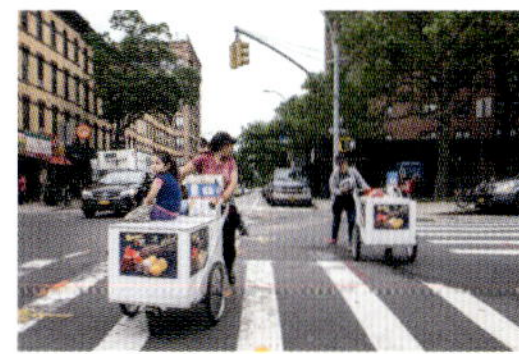

DEKALB AVENUE AND CLASSON AVENUE
Brooklyn
Page 160-161

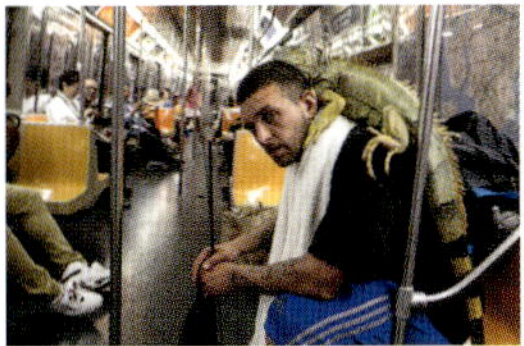

G TRAIN
Brooklyn
Page 162-163

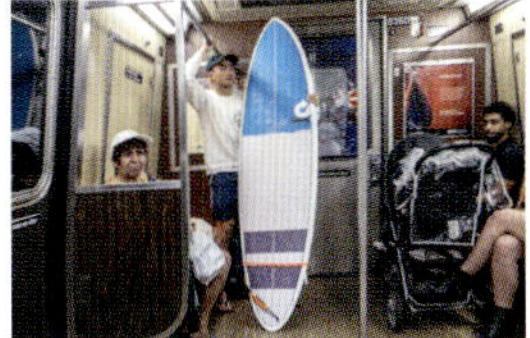

A TRAIN
Brooklyn
Page 164-65

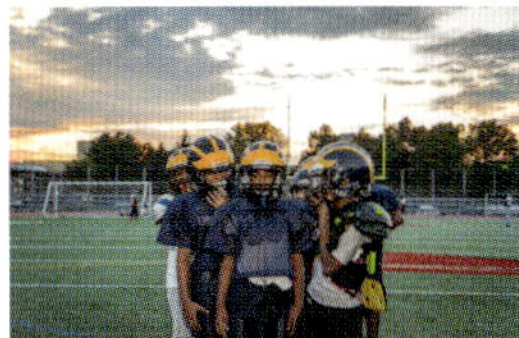

TITANS, BOYS AND GIRLS HIGH SCHOOL
FULTON STREET
Brooklyn
Page 166-167

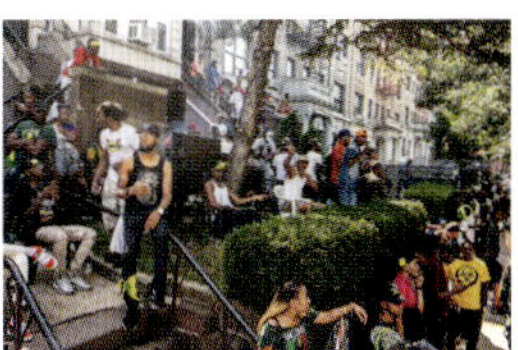

EASTERN PARKWAY
Brooklyn
Page 168-169

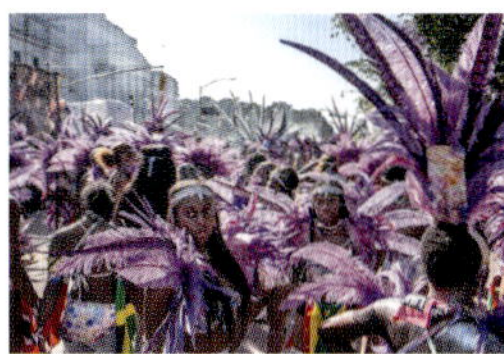

EASTERN PARKWAY
Brooklyn
Page 170-171

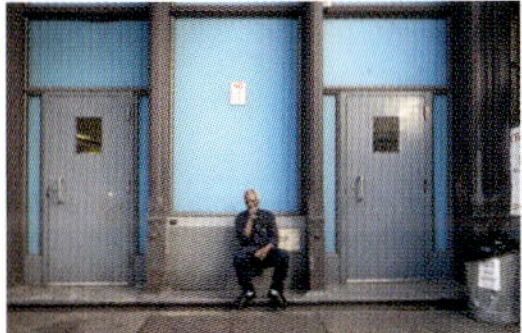

BOWERY
Manhattan
Page 172-173

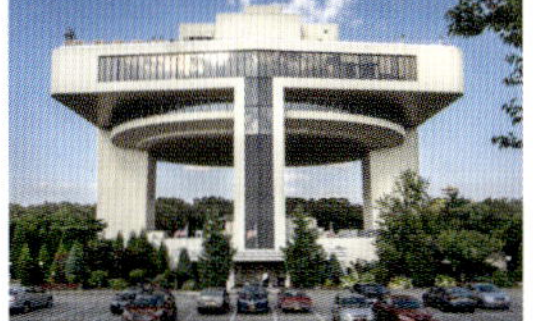

TERRACE ON THE PARK
Queens
Page 174-175

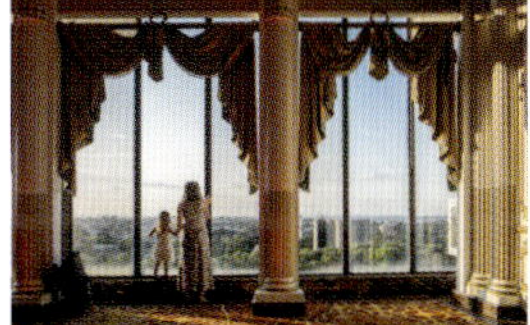

TERRACE ON THE PARK
Queens
Page 176-177

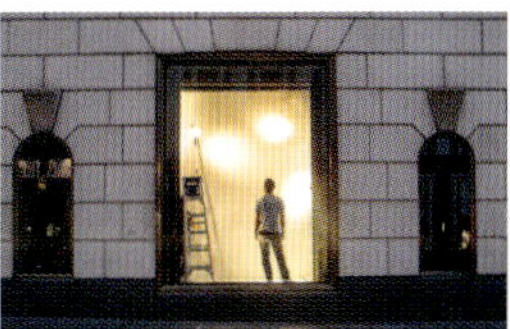

BERGDORF GOODMAN, 5TH AVENUE
Manhattan
Page 178-179

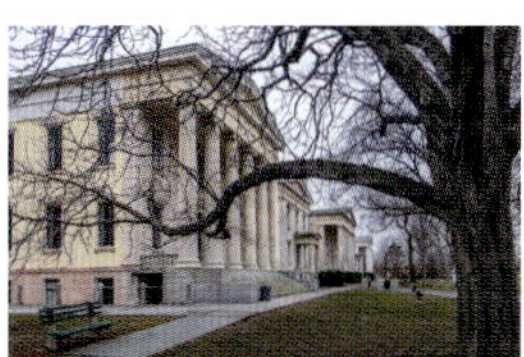

SNUG HARBOR CULTURAL CENTER &
BOTANICAL GARDEN, RICHMOND TERRACE
Staten Island
Page 180-181

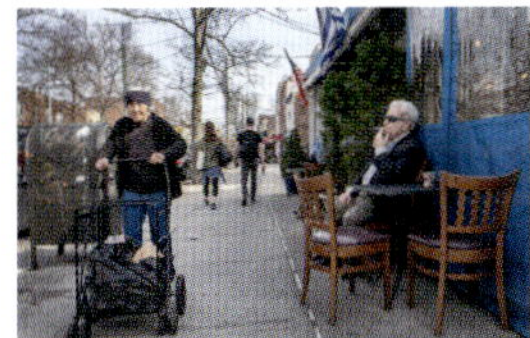

ASTORIA BOULEVARD
Queens
Page 182-183

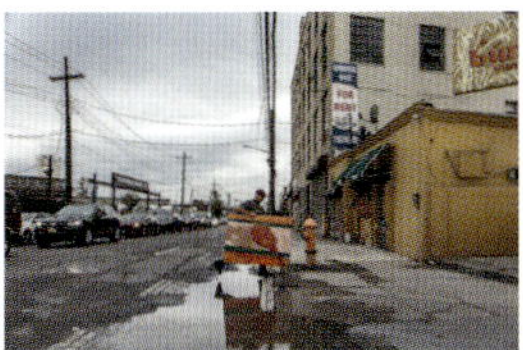

METROPOLITAN AVENUE
Queens
Page 184-185

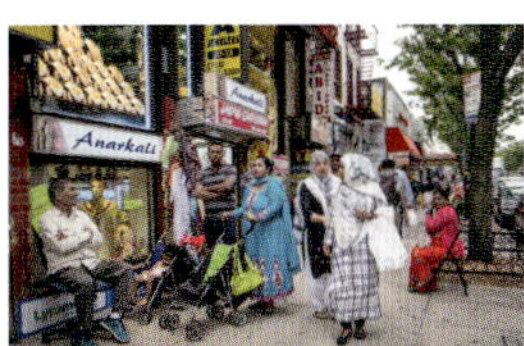

74TH STREET
Queens
Page 186-187

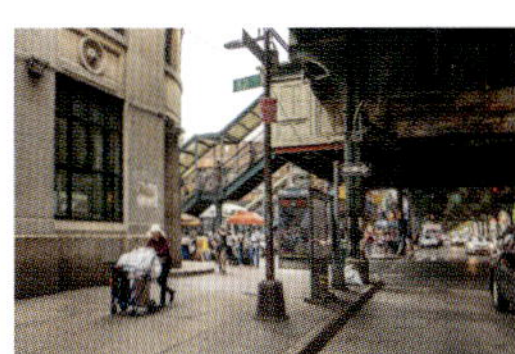

ROOSEVELT AVENUE AND 82ND STREET
Queens
Page 188-189

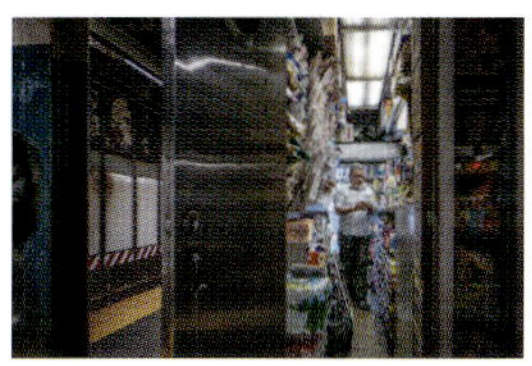

TIMES SQUARE
Manhattan
Page 190-191

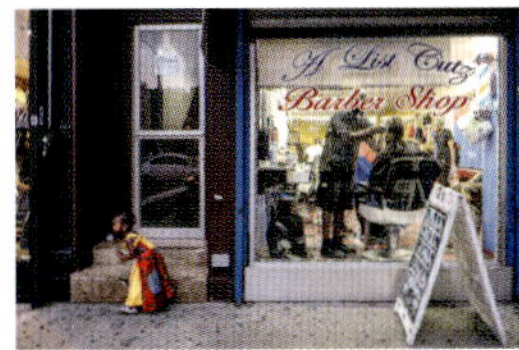

WEST 125TH STREET
Manhattan
Page 192-193

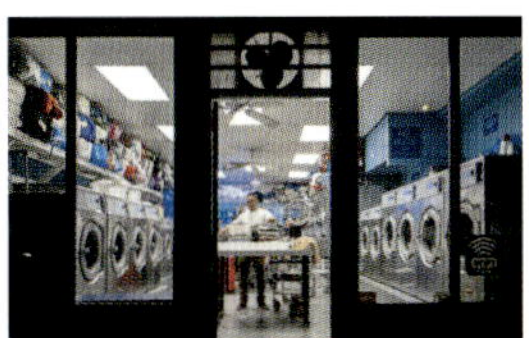

9TH AVENUE
Manhattan
Page 194-195

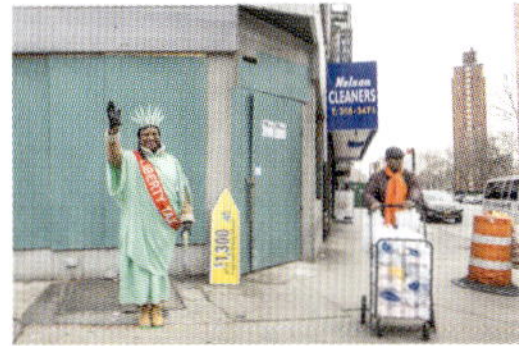

AMSTERDAM AVENUE AND
WEST 125TH STREET
Manhattan
Page 196-197

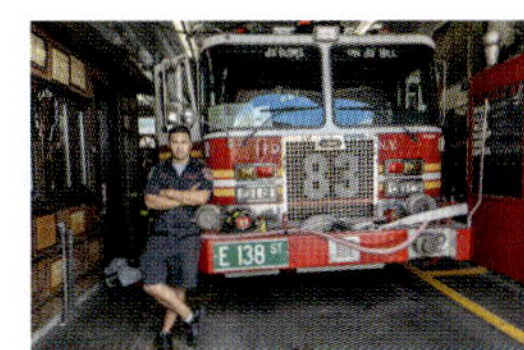

FDNY ENGINE 83, LADDER 29
EAST 138TH STREET
Bronx
Page 198-199

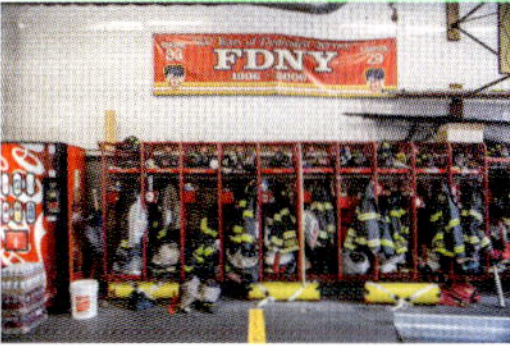

FDNY ENGINE 83, LADDER 29
EAST 138TH STREET
Bronx
Page 200-201

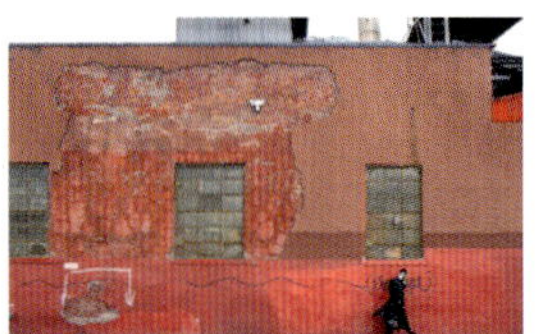

KENT AVENUE
Brooklyn
Page 202-203

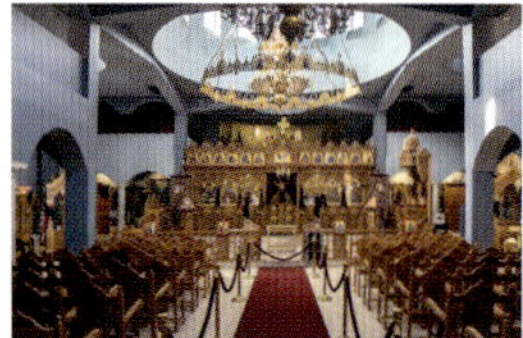

CATHEDRAL OF SAINT MARKELLA
26TH STREET
Queens
Page 204-205

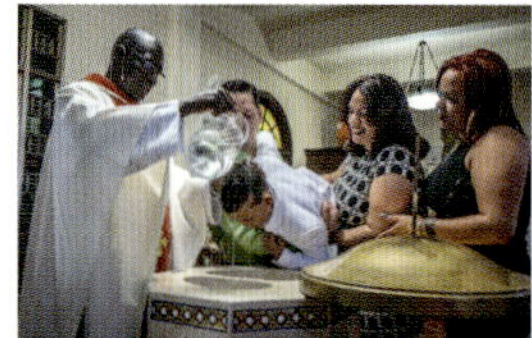

SAINT ANGELA MERICI CHURCH
MORRIS AVENUE
Bronx
Page 206-207

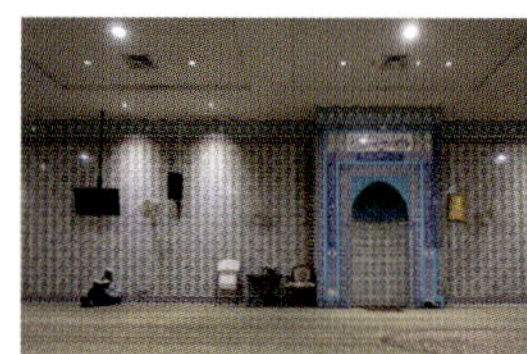

ISLAMIC CULTURAL CENTER
OF NEW YORK, 3RD AVENUE
Manhattan
Page 208-209

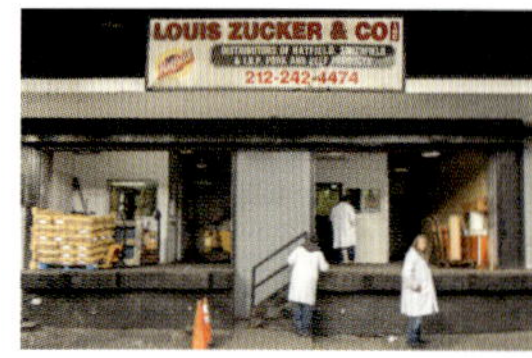

WASHINGTON STREET
Manhattan
Page 210-211

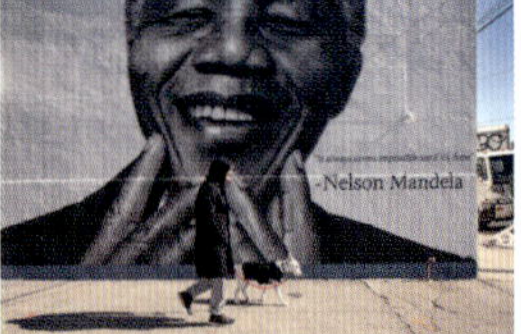

WYTHE AVENUE
Brooklyn
Page 212-213

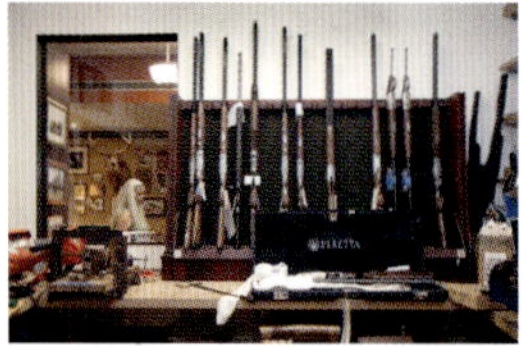

BERETTA, MADISON AVENUE
Manhattan
Page 214-215

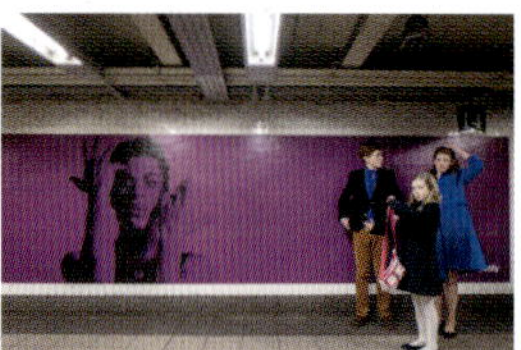

UNION SQUARE
Manhattan
Page 216-217

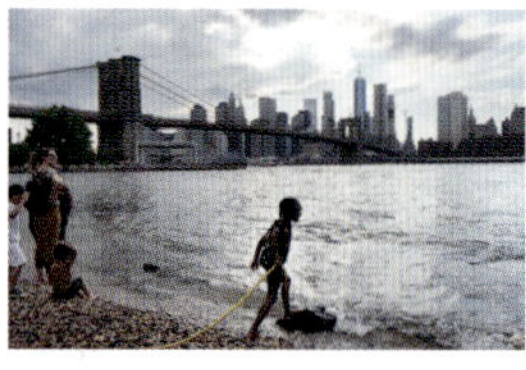

BROOKLYN BRIDGE PARK
Brooklyn
Page 218-219

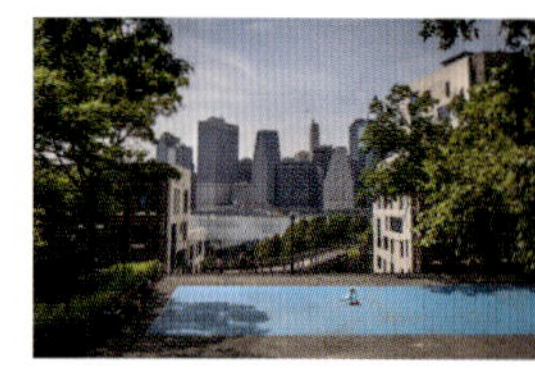

SQUIBB PARK
Brooklyn
Page 220-221

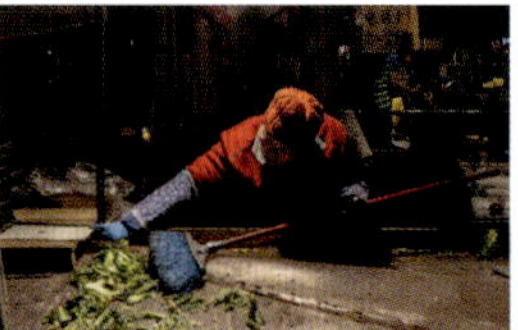

MOTT STREET
Manhatten
Page 222-223

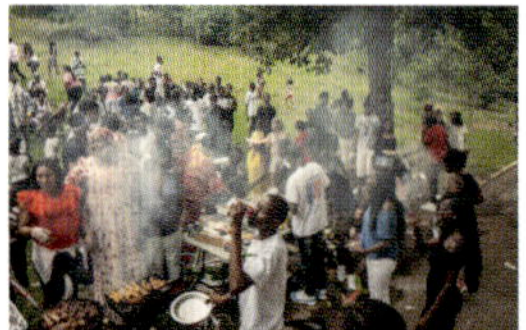

MORNINGSIDE PARK
MORNINGSIDE AVENUE
Manhattan
Page 224-225

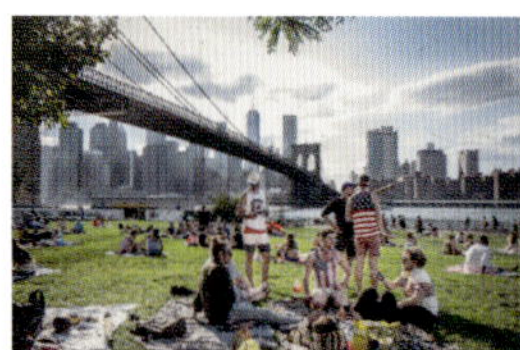

BROOKLYN BRIDGE PARK
Brooklyn
Page 226-227

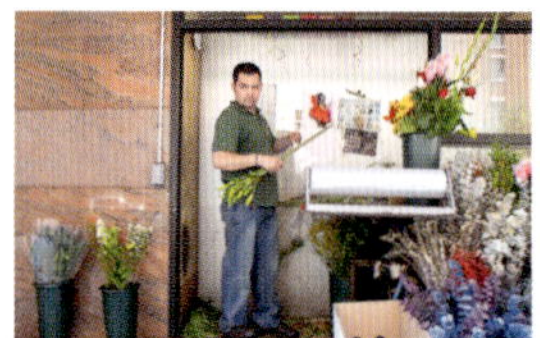

EAST 23RD STREET
Manhattan
Page 228-229

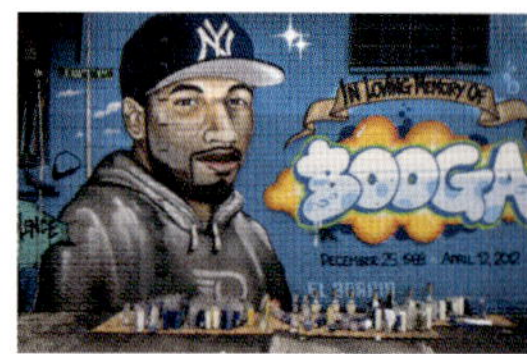

EAST 105TH STREET
Manhattan
Page 230-231

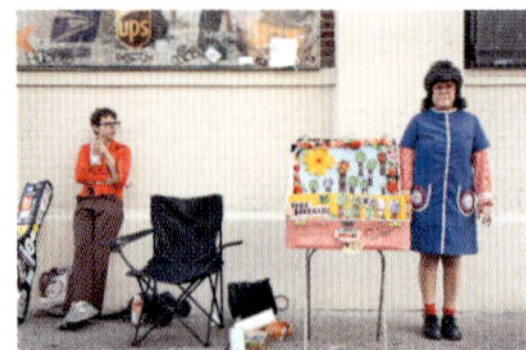

BOGART STREET
Brooklyn
Page 232-233

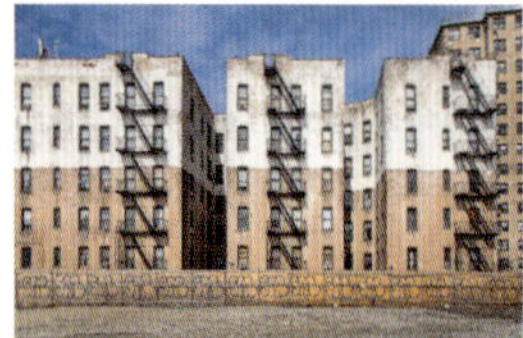

BROADWAY
Bronx
Page 234-235

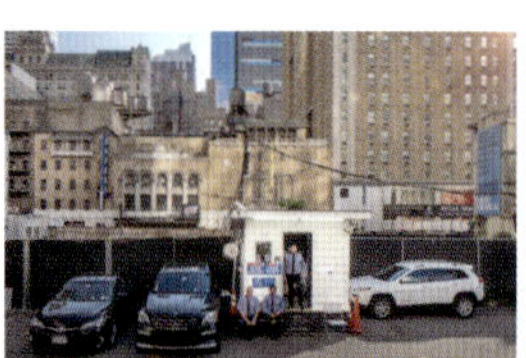

WEST 46TH STREET
Manhattan
Page 236-237

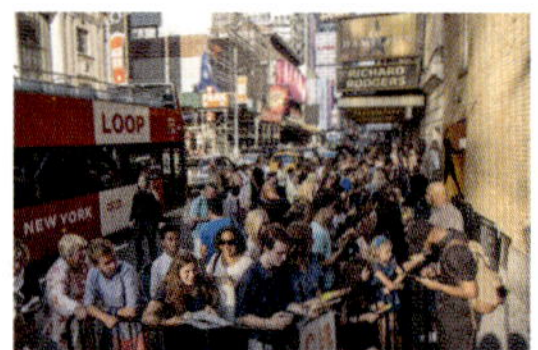

WEST 46TH STREET
Manhattan
Page 238-239

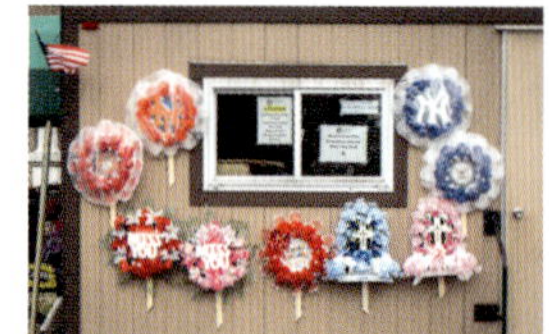

CYPRESS HILL CEMETERY
Brooklyn
Page 240-241

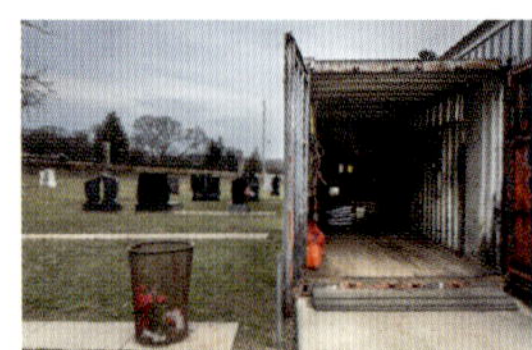

CYPRESS HILL CEMETERY
Brooklyn
Page 242-243

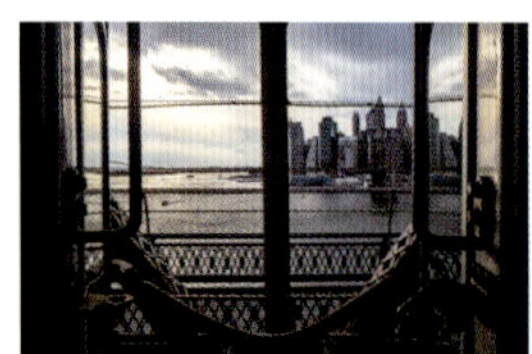

MANHATTAN BRIDGE
Page 244-245

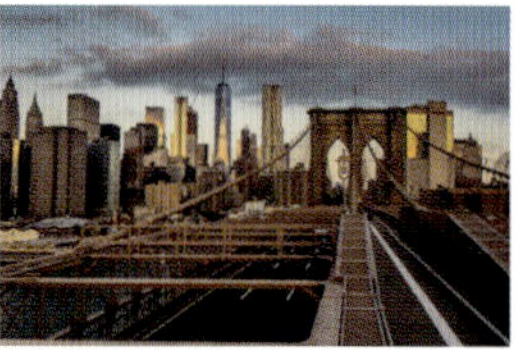

BROOKLYN BRIDGE
Page 246-247

"A SELF MADE MAN DOES NOT EXIST"
– Arnold Schwarzenegger

Thank you to all who carried me:
my HP, Ivy Koek, Vernon & Moeko Gabbert, Julia Gruen.
My PostcardsfromNYC Patreons:
Dedi Gunawan, Carl Van der Zandt, Margot Silvera, Dominic Gasparoly,
Amy Erwin and Lovely Dumlao, David Sena, Anne-Marie de Bruijne,
Reinald-Ykema Westerhuis D'angelo Thompson, Anneke Zuyderduin,
Fabienne Dohmen, Carlos Monino, Guillermo Burrowes, Emiko Tekada, Vera Kuipers,
Erica Enders, Raul van Loon, Rita Ormsby, Robert Kloos, Annebeth Rosenboom,
Richard van Maarseveen, Marilyn Antoine, Beth Dembitzer, Dorien van Boven,
Erik van Ginkel, Makeba Morgan Hill, Suzy Delvalle, Daniel Brooks, Laura Pedrick,
Annelies Sijmons, Sebastian van Heijnigen, Vinod Singh, Jildau Zwaagstra,
Ingrid Rieske, Jeroen Kuppens, Gerard Jongerius, Pieter Porte, Seán Hannan,
Thierry Valenbreder, Claudette Schoenmakers, Cindy Mantel, Christian Ouwens,
Peter Cohen, Marvin and Cindy Jonk, Ingrid Koelemeijer, Rodney Brouwer,
Edwin Zimmerman, Anousha Nzume, Danielle Shallcross, Erna Oosterveen,
Gerald l'Ecuyer, Diana Stok, Peter Mulder, Desiree Engelage, Dr. Jens Banach,
Ruth Gorissen, Daniel Däumler, Remko Schelbergen, Lena Medina, Marije Kramer,
Wendy Curtis, Jilian Brorby, Caronique Schreuder, Dienke Hondius, Albert Taylor
Hennings, Tessa Dikker, Espen Giljane, Sanjay Menon, Elizabeth Burke, Chau Trinh,
Leah Washington, Gil Vasquez, Familie Hendriksma, Paul Jansen, Lise Hughel,
Ide Ruijter, Loïc Devaux, Michael J. Burg, Jerome Joseph Gentes, Gabriella Sancisi,
Mary Jo Campbell, Scott Metzner, Charlotte Clay, Sandi Shannon Woods,
Cynthia van Elk, Erik Rikkelman, Marilyn Satin Kushner, Tom Brinkmann,
The New York Grenadiers Cadet Corp, The Cardiovascular Research Foundation,
Louis Begley, Marcus Jahmal, Rachel Foucher, Eric Joppy, Dean Sandler, Anita Storr,
Eddie Sanchez, Leslie and Godzilla, Jessica Ortiz, Brandon Rivera, Sharon Burke
and Rose Watson and all the beautiful people featured in this book.

COLOPHON

© Uitgeverij TERRA
Terra is part of Uitgeverij TerraLannoo bv
P.O. Box 97
3990 DB Houten
The Netherlands
info@terralannoo.nl
www.terra-publishing.com

Text and photography: Richard Koek
Graphic design cover and inside: Erik Rikkelman
Cover: Manhattan Bridge
Bracts: Manhatten and East River

First print, 2021

ISBN 978 90 8989 853 1
NUR 653

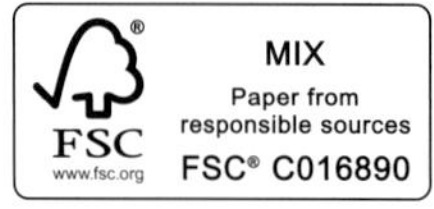

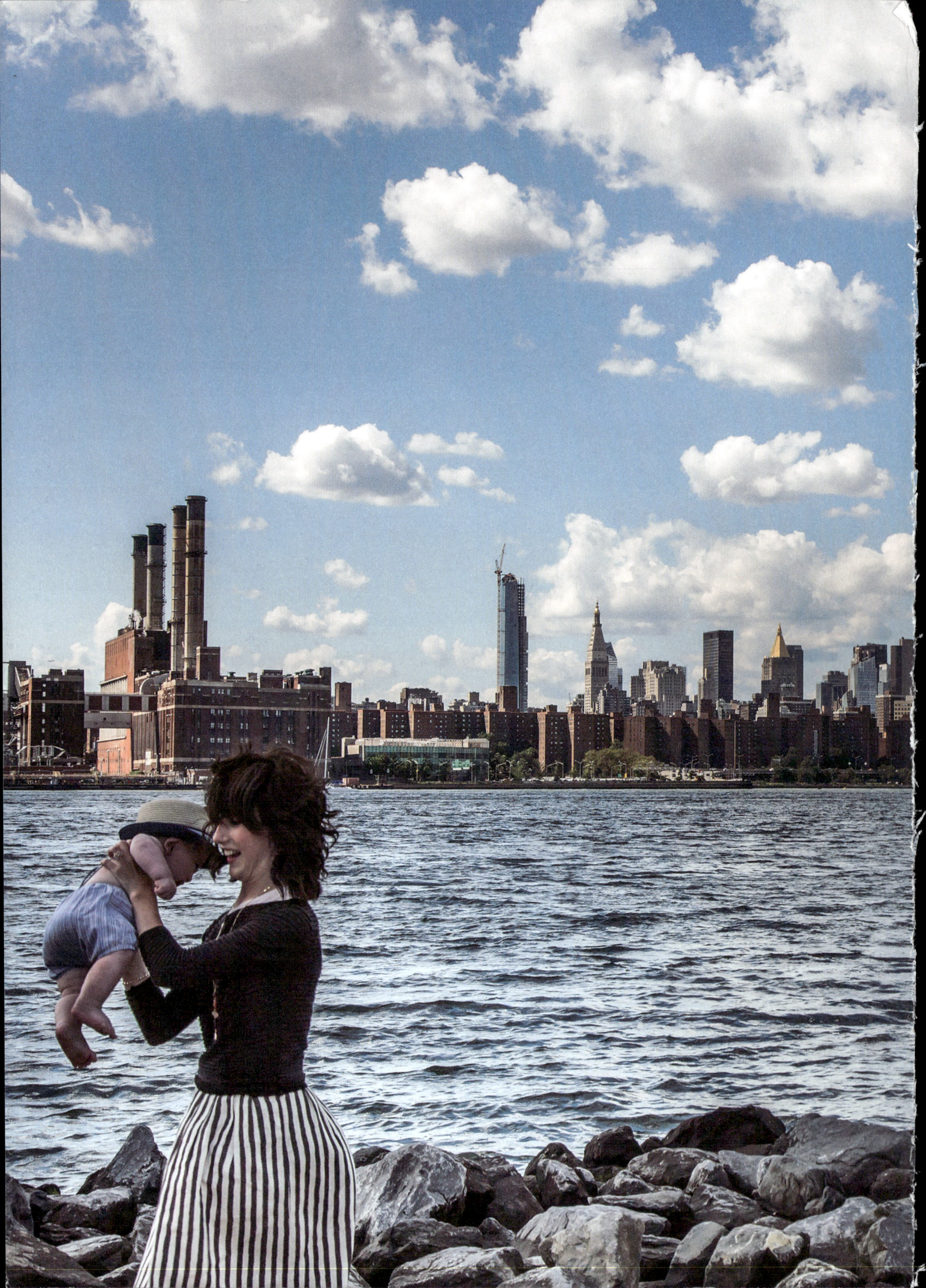